BARRON'S

SAT* SUBJECT TEST

WORLD HISTORY

5TH EDITION

Marilynn Hitchens, Ph.D.
and
Heidi Roupp, M.A.

BARRON'S

ABOUT THE AUTHORS

Marilynn Hitchens has taught AP World History at the high school level and is presently teaching world history at the University of Colorado Online. She is past president of the World History Association, which was instrumental in the development of the field of world history research and teaching. Dr. Hitchens has written extensively on both world history content and pedagogy as well as being a reviewer of textbooks.

Heidi Roupp taught world history at the high school level and served as president of the World History Association, where she organized professional development for AP teachers entering the field. Recognized as a teacher of teachers, she was first recipient of the prestigious American Historical Association Beveridge Family Teaching Prize and recently received the World History Association's Pioneer of World History award.

Photo credit, page 422: Turkey, Iznik, *Tankard (Hanap) with Tulips, Hyacinths, Roses, and Carnations*, late 16th century, Fritware with underglaze painting in blue, turquoise, red, and black, 19.6 × 15 × 10.5 cm (7¾ × 5⅞ × 4⅛ in.), Mary Jane Gunsaulus Collection, 1913.342, The Art Institute of Chicago. Photography © The Art Institute of Chicago.

All inquiries should be addressed to:
Barron's Educational Series, Inc.
250 Wireless Boulevard
Hauppauge, New York 11788
www.barronseduc.com

ISBN: 978-1-4380-0300-9

ISSN 2154–0365

Printed in the United States of America
9 8 7 6 5 4 3 2 1

10%
POST-CONSUMER
WASTE
Paper contains a minimum
of 10% post-consumer
waste (PCW). Paper used
in this book was derived
from certified, sustainable
forestlands.

Contents

**UNIT V
EMERGENCE OF A GLOBAL AGE
(ca. 1100 C.E.–1600 C.E.)**

**UNIT VI
FORCES THAT SHAPED THE
MODERN WORLD EXCHANGE
(ca. 1000 C.E.–1750 C.E.)**

World History in Perspective

Just as the history of the United States is more than the histories of each of the fifty states, world history is more than the study of individual civilizations. It is the study of human experience around the world through time. World history focuses on the big picture. What has impacted large numbers of people which has resulted in change? What has remained consistent in peoples' lives from one generation to another? Some of the changes world historians analyze are global migrations, demography, new technology, economic exchange, and alterations in the physical environment. World history develops a working knowledge of how the past has shaped the present.

World history is a macro history. In world history Columbus is more than an explorer's discovery of a "new world." Rather it is a larger story of the Columbian exchange that resulted from the discovery. The "Columbia exchange" involves human migrations, transatlantic trade, the exchange of plants, animals, diseases, and ideas among peoples on four continents. The resulting plantation system and slave trade continue to shape people's lives worldwide.

Much of this larger story depends on historical analysis of cross-cultural exchange. How is a new idea or a new thing accepted, ignored, or rejected by others? World historians use themes like industrialization to develop comparative studies of how specific societies industrialized. By considering carefully constructed comparisons, we can analyze how new ways of doing things have resulted in local and global change. World historians have used historical themes that impact more than one society. Global themes stretch understandings beyond local and national histories to gain a global perspective of the human experience.

Examples of these large-scale themes include

- The exchange and diffusion of products, ideas, and cultural traditions among societies.

- Changes due to technology and demography.

- Comparisons of political and social systems, their characteristics and the changes in these systems over time.

- Interactions among and within societies.

- Interaction between humans and the environment.

- Continuity and change across major historical periods.

WHY STUDY WORLD HISTORY?

You've probably heard the old saying that each generation writes its own history. The reason that old quote is still repeated is because problems change, which stimulates new questions about how the past led to the current issues. How does local change reflect global trends? Globalization is an old story that begins with the peopling of the earth.

World history is a relatively new field of historical study that was established in 1982. As a subject, it is expanding rapidly because world history can help us analyze foreign policy, the global market, and the developing global culture. By its very nature, world history requires consideration of multiple perspectives. Students, teachers, and research historians are all working together to construct a history that has never been told. It's like working on a 5000-piece jigsaw puzzle. Some corners of the puzzle are more complete. Other parts of the puzzle have big holes or are missing pieces. The missing pieces require more exploration, research, writing, critical review, and revisions by research historians.

When we started studying and teaching world history, we were interested in building a recognizable framework for pieces of the puzzle. Within the framework we wanted to leave space for specific world history scholarship, new sections of the puzzle. We felt that we could test our framework by reading the newspaper. New bits of news fit into the global story. As the story changes, as new sections get added to the old, new questions emerge. In the end, the whole project will be a success if we have provided a framework and a knowledge base that aids the understanding of current problems.

When we were in high school, we knew students we thought were very, very, very smart. They were just about perfect. They seemed to slide effortlessly from one difficult course to another, collecting A's as they moved along toward graduation.

When we became teachers, we learned a different side of the story. Students who do well work hard, but they also know how to work effectively. They set goals for themselves, and they know how to achieve them. So before you get started with Chapter 1, set goals, develop a study plan. Beyond a good score, what do you want to learn that might be useful information in the future? Think about people you know who are "lucky" because they enjoy the work they do and find their work important. The knowledge you accumulate now will shape the opportunities you have for future "luck."

STUDY STRATEGIES

Outline your goals on the inside cover of this book. Allow some space after each goal. After you're finished, look over the list. Devise a plan to achieve each goal. Record your plan in red ink under each goal. Look over this list tomorrow and frequently thereafter. Revise it. As new ideas and new goals develop, add them to the list. This is your study guide. This book is designed to help you become acquainted with the framework of world history and to help you learn the content.

This book is designed to help you study effectively to succeed on the SAT: World History test. The book contents are a synthesis of material presented in commonly used world history textbooks, with attention to test coverage and to world history

TIP

History is an important subject because it helps explain events and ideas in the past, which enable us to understand the present. And it helps develop critical thinking.

standards. The book also reflects the authors' perceptions of content and understandings that are essential and unique to world history. It anticipates future tests
that will continue to move away from Western civilization and an emphasis on the
twentieth century, and toward a more chronologically and geographically balanced
world history. As you prepare for this test, you have at least three ways to learn
world history—your teacher, your high school world history textbook, and this
book, which summarizes the content of world history textbooks in many high
school courses. Keep in mind that there is more than one way to tell a story. You
are introducing yourself to three stories. In the process you will learn what happened and develop skills to evaluate the histories.

How the Book Is Organized

The framework we have developed is divided into eight narrative units. Each unit
revolves around a major world history idea that dominates the chronological time
period. Facts important to this idea, such as people, places, and terms, are high-
lighted and defined within the text. At the end of each unit is a section called Cross-
Regional Developments. This section will help you see what is more universal about
the material and what developments important to human change over time
occurred within large areas. The second section, called Legacies, will help you
understand the continuity in history. Sometimes we like to think of these continu-
ities as trends that continue to the present. Each unit features visuals, maps, and
document excerpts. These will help you prepare for multiple-choice test questions
that appear on the exam in picture, map, chart, or quotation form. In the process
you will learn what happened and develop skills to evaluate the histories.

By presenting the material in a slightly different way from the text you are using,
you will be learning what happened and how to analyze historical interpretations of
what happened rather than just memorizing world history. This will help you prepare for the test. The SAT test questions will be phrased differently than the ones
in this book and those on tests in your world history class.

Document reading requires you to learn to analyze like a historian. In reading a
document, note the time period, authorship, place, and historical context of the
writing and then proceed to summarize the main points. Finally, reflect on style,
viewpoint, and cardinal characteristics. In tests, you are often asked to identify document excerpts. The documents appearing in each chapter have been chosen to help
you with this part of the test. They are of such importance in world history that students who claim world historical literacy should be able to recognize their origins,
identify the viewpoint, and discern the legacies of history in them.

The book ends with two sample multiple-choice tests. These questions are
designed to replicate the types of questions that might appear on the SAT test.
Check your answers and refer to the appropriate page numbers if you need more
review. It is important to learn information in context for understanding rather
than to memorize bits of "facts." There is a difference between passive memorization and active learning.

TIP

Pay attention to
the boldface words
used throughout
this book. They
frequently appear
on the SAT
Subject Test.

STUDY, STUDY, STUDY

By now you have an arsenal of study weapons and you have probably developed your own approach to study. The ideas we suggest may help you develop a new study weapon or help you improve what you already do.

As you begin a unit, glance through the sections to develop an overview of the content. Read the unit introduction. Then skip to the end of the unit and consider carefully the Cross-Regional Developments and Legacies. This information will help you develop an understanding of global patterns during the period as well as continuity and change within and among societies around the globe.

If you are forgetful, make flash cards on the computer, or you can make hardcopy flash cards; develop flash cards that can be part of the review later. As you print the word, say it out loud. Print the meaning and repeat that meaning too. If you follow this procedure, you will have involved your eyes, ears, and sense of touch in the learning process. If someone would just develop the key terms inscribed in white chocolate on a candy bar, we could involve the sense of taste and smell as well.

Read and review as though this information will appear on your driver's test.

Are you ready? Read the introduction to the unit. Review the cross regional developments and legacies. Develop an overview of the mateiral to be learned. What is the chapter about? Who is important to remember? What is the author comparing or analyzing? Read the content carefully. Note where events took place. It is good to have a world map available while you study. As you read about a place and learn its geographical characteristics, locate it on the map. After you have finished reading a section, you can write yourself notes in the margin, underline main ideas and evidence, outline the information, make a list of the ideas and details, or summarize the content. Design a timeline of key events and changes that impact large numbers of people. Carefully consider each map, illustration, and document. Review the key terms and your notes.

Once a week, review everything you have done. Periodically mix and match the content in your world history textbook with the material in this book. When you complete a unit, answer the unit questions. Check your answers. Highlight information that requires your attention. Study with a buddy. Occasionally review all of your notes. Star information you have forgotten. As you master the content, put the content to work, thinking historically.

Historical Literacy

Sources

Primary sources are written by those directly involved in an event. **Secondary sources** include information from primary sources and other secondary sources.

Historical literacy involves knowing content and historical analysis. Increasingly in history, students are being asked not only to have a basic knowledge of the subject matter, but to know how the historian is telling the story. What evidence is the historian using? How is the historian using evidence to construct the argument? Students must know, for instance, what constitutes evidence and how to evaluate it. This often involves evaluation of viewpoint, understanding of context, and the testing of conclusions.

This review book has dealt with historical methodology within the text itself, with explanations of causality, discussions of evidence, and representations of viewpoint. Visuals, documents, and maps are designed to engage you in historical thinking.

Listed below are some of the historical thinking skills that you should be acquiring in the study of world history. Following this discussion are a number of sample test questions with explanations that test your ability to deal with historical methodology.

1. **Chronological Thinking.** Historians attempt to pinpoint evidence in time and space. They then note change over time, trying to find patterns and discontinuities in this change, and what changes have been continuous and enduring, and which have not. In world history, similar changes have been continuous and enduring, and which have not. In world history, similar changes often occur at different times in different places across the globe. Sometimes change seems incidental to only one place or time period. World historians are apt to ask how and why this change occurred. This has made the question of cultural diffusion and of cross-regional exchange crucial for world historical interpretation. Testing for this type of understanding often involves questions that ask the student to put events in chronological order, pick which is not a logical explanation of change, state what cause-and-effect relationship occurred, and explain how this change occurred over time.

2. **Historical Comprehension.** Historians learn how to see the past through the eyes of those who lived it at the time. They know how to read various kinds of evidence, such as documents, pictures, data, and literature, with this in mind. For historians of world history, this means being sensitive to and knowledgeable about the cultural framework of different societies. Testing this often asks the student to come to conclusions about an author of a document, or the message of a visual, or the likely interpretation, given the time period and place.

3. **Historical Analysis and Interpretation.** For purposes of analysis, or the taking apart, of history, historians have tended to divide history into parts—political, economic, social, and cultural. For example, students must be able to identify the military as part of political history, class as part of social history, ideas as part of cultural history, and trade as part of economic history. With respect to interpretation, students should learn that there are often multiple causes, motives, interests, and records of experience that have shaped the past. In world history it is particularly important to be able to make valid comparisons between places and peoples, to see, for instance, that the same outcome (i.e., the agricultural revolution) may have occurred for different reasons in different parts of the world with different consequences. World history test questions will often involve the student's ability to make valid comparisons and to identify interpretations based on faulty analysis.

4. **Historical Research Capabilities.** Historical research capabilities involve the ability to determine time and context within an artifact, the ability to assess credibility of the artifact, and the ability to construct a sound argument or story from it. In world history this is a particularly important capability because not all societies have used Western ideas of evidence. Oral histories, myth histories, and art have become important artifacts where written evidence is lacking. A test question in this regard might ask you to come to some conclusion about a chart, graph, or written fragment.

5. Historical Issues—Analysis and Decision Making. Historians identify problems that confronted people in the past and come to some conclusions about the actions that were taken. In world history this is particularly challenging because societies differ. In evaluating evidence, historians must strive to be free from bias and educated in the traditions of many societies. On the exam, this skill is often tested with questions that deal with explanations about why certain decisions were made at a certain time and place.

The questions concerning historical analysis that appear on the SAT: World History exam are apt to test one or more of these skills in any one question.

ABOUT THE TEST

The SAT World History test is 60 minutes in length and consists of 95 to 100 multiple-choice questions. According to recent information from the Educational Testing Service, which produces the test, the subject matter is as follows:

Geographical		*Chronological*	
Global or comparative	25%	Prehistory to 500 C.E.	25%
Europe	25%	500–1500 C.E.	20%
Southwest Asia	10%	1500–1900 C.E.	25%
Africa	10%	Post–1900 C.E.	20%
East Asia	10%	Cross-chronological	10%
South and Southeast Asia	10%		
The Americas (excluding the U.S.)	10%		

All historical fields are covered—political, intellectual and cultural, social and economic, though, as in most texts, the emphasis is political. Some questions test historical methodology and habits of the mind, for example, concepts essential to historical analysis, such as "change and continuity," the ability to assess quotations from documents, and the capacity to interpret artistic materials. Some questions require understanding of commonly used terms like "civilization," and others test geographical knowledge. It will be helpful to you to obtain the *Official Guide to the SAT Subject Tests* prior to taking the test. You can do this by writing to the Educational Testing Service (Princeton, New Jersey 08541) or asking your school counselor.

TIP

Make flash cards of topics requiring more review. Carry them with you to study whenever you have time.

HOW TO PREPARE FOR THE TEST

The best way to prepare for the SAT World History test is to use this book as you proceed through your world history course. Remember, by learning the material in a slightly different way from the text you are using, you will be forced to understand, rather than just memorize, world history. This will also help in preparing for the test where questions are phrased differently from the ones in your text. If you do not purchase this book until you have finished your world history course, use it as a short text summary. The most important single technique in studying for the SAT test is to keep reviewing as you proceed with your course and with the chapters in this book. Review previous chapters to identify relationships between earlier material and the chapter under study.

Use the tests at the back of the book as practice. Allow 55 minutes, complete the test as if you were really taking it, and then analyze your score. If you missed questions pertaining to some particular era or place, review it in this book. Then try the second sample test.

HOW TO TAKE THE TEST

Review the following essentials of test taking.

1. Get a good night's sleep.
2. Locate your test ticket and review the location of the test. Give yourself adequate time to get there.
3. Bring several sharpened No. 2 pencils.
4. Budget your time. Do not linger over difficult questions. Finish the test and then go back to tackle the difficult questions.
5. Read the entire question. Choose the BEST answer. Words like "always," "never," and "only" are apt to be wrong. Think of chronology. Answers are often wrong because they refer to the wrong chronological era. In questions with EXCEPT or NOT, it sometimes helps to rephrase the question in the positive. Try to find similarities between two or three of the wrong choices in order to eliminate others.
6. Avoid wild guessing. Your score is based on the number right minus one-quarter point for every wrong answer.
7. Mark answers clearly and erase thoroughly.
8. If you finish early, review your answers.

Good luck!

Diagnostic Test

Before you begin using this book, we suggest that you take time to work through this Diagnostic Test. Although it is not a full-length SAT Subject Test in World History, it is representative of the difficulty level and types of questions you will be presented with on the actual exam. After you complete this test, review the answer explanations that follow so that you can get a sense of your strengths and weaknesses. You will then have a better idea as to what areas you need to pay more attention to as you progress through this book.

Immediately following the answer explanations is specific information about the content and length of the exam as well as some hints as to how to prepare for and take the actual exam.

1. Which of the following statements can be supported by the chart on the following page?

    (A) Cities are ranked from 1 to 42 according to their population by the year 2000.
    (B) All urban areas increased in size by the year 2000.
    (C) In 1992 more than 50 percent of the world's largest urban areas were in Third World countries.
    (D) The increase of the average annual growth rate (percent) of the majority of cities was greater between 1995–2000 than the years from 1992–1995.
    (E) New York City counted suburbs in its 1992 total, whereas Tokyo-Yokohama did not.

2. Which of the following statements would be the MOST difficult for the historian to prove?

    (A) The Pacific Ocean is three times as large as the Atlantic Ocean.
    (B) Although not generally recognized, William Gladstone was more effective as a prime minister than Benjamin Disraeli.
    (C) The Suez Canal increased trade between India and Britain after its completion.
    (D) The invention of the airplane changed the way people lived in the twentieth century.
    (E) There was little opposition in the United States to the dropping of the atomic bomb on Hiroshima.

Population, by World's Largest Cities: 1992 to 2000

City and Country	Rank	Midyear Population (1,000)			Average Annual Growth Rate (percent)	
		1992	1995	2000	1992–1995	1995–2000
Tokyo-Yokohama, Japan	1	27,540	26,447	29,971	1.1	1.0
Mexico City, Mexico	2	21,615	23,913	27,872	3.4	3.1
Sao Paulo, Brazil	3	19,373	21,539	25,364	3.5	3.3
Seoul, South Korea	4	17,334	19,065	21,976	3.2	2.6
New York, United States	5	14,629	14,638	14,646	(Z)	(Z)
Osaka-Kobe-Kyoto, Japan	6	13,919	14,060	14,267	0.3	0.3
Bombay, India	7	12,450	13,532	15,367	2.8	2.5
Calcutta, India	8	12,137	12,885	14,068	2.0	1.6
Rio de Janeiro, Brazil	9	12,009	12,786	14,169	2.1	2.1
Buenos Aires, Argentina	10	11,743	12,232	12,911	1.4	1.1
Manila, Philippines	11	10,554	11,342	12,846	2.4	2.5
Moscow, Russia	12	10,526	10,769	11,121	0.8	0.6
Cairo, Egypt	13	10,372	11,155	12,612	2.4	2.3
Jakarta, Indonesia	14	10,165	11,151	12,804	3.0	2.8
Tehran, Iran	15	10,102	11,661	14,251	4.6	4.0
Los Angeles, United States	16	10,072	10,414	10,714	1.1	0.6
Paris, France	19	8,589	8,764	8,803	0.7	0.1
Lagos, Nigeria	20	8,487	9,799	12,526	4.8	4.9
Karachi, Pakistan	21	8,174	9,350	11,299	4.5	3.6
Essen, Germany	22	7,506	7,364	7,239	−0.6	−0.3
Lima, Peru	23	7,026	7,653	9,241	3.7	3.3
Shanghai, China	24	7,000	7,194	7,540	0.9	0.9
Istanbul, Turkey	25	6,937	7,624	8,675	3.2	3.0
Taipei, Taiwan	26	6,924	7,477	8,516	2.6	2.6
Chicago, United States	27	6,483	6,541	6,568	0.2	0.1
Bogota, Colombia	28	6,176	6,601	7,935	3.2	3.1
Bangkok, Thailand	29	6,068	6,657	7,587	3.0	2.6
Madras, India	30	5,996	6,650	7,384	2.9	2.4
Beijing, China	31	5,791	5,865	5,993	0.4	0.4
Hong Kong, China	32	5,762	5,841	5,956	0.5	0.4
Santiago, Chile	33	5,464	5,812	6,294	1.9	1.6
Pusan, South Korea	34	5,161	5,748	6,700	3.6	3.1
Bangalore, India	35	5,060	5,644	6,764	3.5	3.6
Nagoya, Japan	36	4,909	5,017	5,303	0.7	1.1
Tianjin, China	37	4,857	5,041	5,288	1.2	1.0
Milan, Italy	38	4,718	4,795	4,839	0.5	0.2
St. Petersburg, Russia	39	4,645	4,694	4,738	0.4	0.2
Dhaka, Bangladesh	40	4,640	5,296	5,492	4.4	4.1
Madrid, Spain	41	4,577	4,772	5,104	1.4	1.4
Lahore, Pakistan	42	4,475	4,986	5,564	3.6	3.2

This chart relates to Question 1.

3. A preponderance of evidence about prehistoric life forms has come from East Africa because

   (A) the "Out of Africa" theory has proved that all humans originated in Africa.
   (B) archaeologists like the Leakeys have concentrated their efforts in East Africa.
   (C) when the continents were all united in Pangaea, Africa was at its heart.
   (D) the humid, tropical areas preserve human bone fossils better.
   (E) the Olduvai Gorge fault system reveals fossils easily.

4. Which conclusion based on the evidence included is correct?

   (A) The Indus valley civilization with its planned cities, piped water, and public drainage systems had a centralized political power.
   (B) Irrigation systems, bridges, road building, and large temple platforms indicate an increase in population in the altiplano region of what is now Peru.
   (C) Egyptian trade goods found in Crete and post and lintel construction similar to the system used at Karnak indicate that the Minoans and Egyptians traded and the Minoans copied aspects of Egyptian culture.
   (D) Montezuma's initial friendly attitude toward Cortes indicates the openness of Aztec society to strangers.
   (E) The continued Muslim use of the camel rather than wagons for transport on the overland trade routes of Eurasia indicates a resistance to change.

5. Estimates of the number who perished from the Black Death in Europe in the thirteenth century would LEAST likely be found in

   (A) church records.
   (B) personal diaries.
   (C) tax records.
   (D) newspapers.
   (E) shiplogs.

6. Given the rapid rise and spread of Buddhism during the reign of Ashoka, which of the following is the LEAST likely hypothesis about why this change occurred?

   (A) Buddhism was carried by merchants into new areas of India as they exchanged goods along the trade routes.
   (B) Buddhism appealed to the downtrodden.
   (C) A powerful secular leader converted to Buddhism and supported it.
   (D) Buddhism offered new forms of rich cultural expression.
   (E) Buddhism acquired many converts through the pilgrimages and sermons of Siddhartha Gautama.

Sample Test Questions 7 and 8 are based on this quotation. "The enemy advances, we retreat; the enemy halts, we harass; the enemy slackens, we attack; the enemy retreats, we pursue."

7. The strategies described in this passage can MOST closely be connected with

   (A) medieval warfare.
   (B) trench warfare.
   (C) mechanized warfare.
   (D) guerrilla warfare.
   (E) siege warfare.

8. The author of this passage would MOST likely have supported the strategy of which of the following military leaders?

   (A) Hitler
   (B) Philip II
   (C) Dwight D. Eisenhower
   (D) Napoleon
   (E) Ho Chi Minh

9. This statue is most closely associated with what culture?

(A) Incan
(B) Polynesian
(C) Chinese
(D) Indian
(E) Persian

10. The most important factor leading to an independent Pakistan was

(A) Great Britain's support for an independent Pakistan.
(B) the existence of Pakistani princely states.
(C) Gandhi's leadership in creating a sovereign Pakistan.
(D) the United Nations peace plan for the area.
(E) the existence of a Muslim majority in the area.

11. Which of the following statements concerning the wealth and independence of the Byzantine Empire would be most difficult to prove?

(A) a carefully designed defense system for Constantinople that included cisterns, walls, a chain across the harbor, and a small, well-trained army
(B) the skillful use of intelligence and diplomacy to establish a system of military alliances with Catholic popes and European kings
(C) Constantinople's development as a western entrepôt of the Silk Road
(D) the stimulation of the production of luxury products by master craftsmen.
(E) The Byzantine Empire inherited the grandeur of Rome

12. The two religions often in conflict in India since independence are

(A) Jainism and Hinduism.
(B) Hinduism and Buddhism.
(C) Buddhism and Islam.
(D) Islam and Christianity.
(E) Hinduism and Islam.

13. The Egyptian leader who agreed to recognize Israel in exchange for the Sinai was

(A) Anwar el-Sadat.
(B) Yasser Arafat.
(C) Gamal Abdel Nasser.
(D) Ussein Ibn Ali.
(E) none of the above

14. The Mongol invasion had all of the following consequences EXCEPT the

(A) reopening of the Silk Road.
(B) strengthening of maritime trade in the South China Sea.
(C) diffusion of gunpowder technology.
(D) demand for European products such as wool, porcelain, sugar, spices, and coffee.
(E) rise of the autocracy in Russia.

15. Which was NOT a significant factor in British industrialization in the eighteenth century?

    (A) increased agricultural production
    (B) rising population
    (C) river systems to provide a power source
    (D) a growing domestic and colonial market
    (E) the discovery of petroleum

16. The Alliance for Progress was

    (A) the United Nations' attempt to help less developed countries.
    (B) the agreement by Mexico and the United States to lower tariff barriers.
    (C) Teddy Roosevelt's policy of "Speak Softly and Carry a Big Stick."
    (D) The United States' program to use economic aid to prevent communism in Latin America.
    (E) Franklin Roosevelt's attempt to keep Latin America in the Western camp during World War II.

17. Which of the following is INCORRECTLY paired with a golden age of cultural achievement?

    (A) China—Sui, Tang, Song Dynasties
    (B) Rome—the reign of Julius Caesar
    (C) India—Gupta rule
    (D) Greece—Athens during the lives of Socrates, Plato, and Aristotle
    (E) Europe—Renaissance Italy

18. Which European treaty redrew European borders on the balance of power principle?

    (A) Berlin
    (B) Vienna
    (C) Versailles
    (D) Paris
    (E) Sevres

19. Rationalism and humanism were philosophical beliefs in

    (A) dualism, or life as a struggle between two opposing forces, good and evil.
    (B) the human intellect as the source of knowledge and artistic and physical potential for excellence.
    (C) ethical monotheism.
    (D) asceticism, or a mystical devotion to one's personal deity.
    (E) rule by religious leaders worshipped both as gods and kings.

20. The Byzantine Empire and its capital, Constantinople, were originally part of

    (A) Persia.
    (B) the Mauryan Empire.
    (C) Palestine.
    (D) Empire of Alexander the Great.
    (E) Rome.

21. Which was the first Asian country to industrialize?

    (A) India
    (B) China
    (C) Korea
    (D) Japan
    (E) Iran

22. Which of the newly industrializing countries became economic miracles after the 1970s?

    (A) Czechoslovakia and Poland
    (B) Taiwan and South Korea
    (C) India and Turkey
    (D) Vietnam and China
    (E) Brazil and Bolivia

23. The most likely explanation for the economic miracles of Question 22 is

    (A) loans from the World Bank.
    (B) education and industrialization.
    (C) democratic governments.
    (D) large amounts of raw materials.
    (E) adequate land.

24. Theories concerning the early stages of human development are constantly being revised for all the following reasons EXCEPT

    (A) there is little scientific agreement concerning fossil evidence.
    (B) analysis of fossils and artifacts discovered in situ provide information about the environment and how early humans lived.
    (C) scientists use new procedures such as accelerator mass spectrometry to acquire new information.
    (D) scientists use DNA codes to analyze similarities and differences between hominid fossils.
    (E) new physical evidence is being discovered.

25. Which anatomical change offers an explanation for the social development and environmental adaptation of *homo sapiens sapiens*?

    (A) vision
    (B) vocal cords
    (C) walking upright
    (D) hearing
    (E) muscular strength

26. Scientists who study the physical and cultural characteristics of both modern and ancient peoples are

    (A) paleontologists.
    (B) archaeologists.
    (C) anthropologists.
    (D) geologists.
    (E) sociologists.

27. Changes in the climate some two million years ago resulted in

    (A) tool making.
    (B) new artistic expression.
    (C) migrations.
    (D) longer life spans.
    (E) the disappearance of *homo sapiens sapiens*.

28. Evidence that the domestication of plants and animals occurred independently in different parts of the world is indicated by the location of early agricultural communities. Which of the following communities is incorrectly linked with its present day location?

    (A) Hallan Comi [Turkey]
    (B) Catal Huyuk [Guatemala]
    (C) Jarmo [Iraq]
    (D) Ban Po [China]
    (E) Tehuacan [Mexico]

29. Major growth in human populations has been the result of

    (A) expanding wealth.
    (B) permanent homes.
    (C) metal tools.
    (D) food and medicine.
    (E) growth of urban centers.

30. Peoples speaking Indo-European languages migrated from the Caucasuses to all of the following EXCEPT

    (A) Italy.
    (B) Greece.
    (C) Iran.
    (D) Egypt.
    (E) India.

31. Bantu migrations may have been initiated by desiccation of the

    (A) Deccan Plateau.
    (B) Ethiopian Highlands.
    (C) Central Asia.
    (D) Sahara.
    (E) Asia Minor.

32. Historians use the term gender to refer to

    (A) feminist politics of the 20th century.
    (B) categories of masculine and feminine history.
    (C) patriarchy.
    (D) matriarchy.
    (E) women's history.

33. Which of the following is not a consequence of the French Revolution?

    (A) European Liberal Revolutions
    (B) the Haitian Revolution
    (C) the American Revolution
    (D) Napoleonic Era
    (E) Revolutions of Latin America.

34. Which of the following choices best explains republicanism?

    (A) The individual is emancipated from governmental restraints.
    (B) All citizens possess equal political and legal rights.
    (C) Leaders assume the right to rule based on military and economic power.
    (D) The power to govern is granted by the people.
    (E) The power to govern is inherited by the leader.

35. All of the following were settled by Austronesian/Polynesian mariners EXCEPT

    (A) Madagascar.
    (B) Hawaii.
    (C) Easter Island.
    (D) Japan.
    (E) Indonesia.

36. Why did the Mongol conquests represent the last formidable nomadic challenge to sedentary peoples of Eurasia?

    (A) Settled peoples were increasingly able to defend themselves once they acquired gunpowder.
    (B) Nomads were unable to unite under a single leader.
    (C) Nomads were unable to defend their pastures from the incursions of settled peoples.
    (D) Religious conversions to Islam encouraged cultural changes from nomadic to settled life.
    (E) Nomads found caravan trade more profitable.

37. Neo-imperialism referred to

    (A) expansion of European states into neighboring European territories.
    (B) the formation of western alliances to expand trade and control resources.
    (C) acquisition of territory to exclude countries with competing interests.
    (D) acquisition of sparsely populated territory for immigration.
    (E) global expansion of military power.

38. One in three immigrants to the United States and one in two immigrants to Argentina returned to their homeland. What is the most likely reason that only one in 20 eastern European Jews returned to the land of their origin?

    (A) pogroms
    (B) famine
    (C) disease
    (D) discrimination
    (E) poor economic opportunities

ANSWERS EXPLAINED

1. **(C)** To answer this question, you need to look carefully at the information contained in the chart. Answer choice A is incorrect because the urban areas are ranked according to 1992 population figures. Answer choice B is incorrect because some cities will remain the same or decrease in size. One should also be wary of words like always, never, all, and one. Answer choice D is incorrect because the yearly percentage of population growth was less from 1995–2000 than 1992–1995. Answer choice E is incorrect because information concerning suburbs is not included in the chart.

2. **(B)** Choice B expresses an opinion. The other four statements can be proven or disproven using historical evidence.

3. **(E)** The other choices are informationally or logically incorrect. Choice A is incorrect because the "Out of Africa" model has not been proven. Choice B is incorrect because of faulty logic. The Leakeys concentrated their efforts in this area because of the possibility of finding such prehistoric fossils. Choice C is incorrect because of chronological inaccuracy; there was no human life until long after the continents were formed. Choice D is incorrect because tropical areas are one of the poorest places to find fossils, whereas dry or frozen sites or areas covered by volcanic ash are the best.

4. **(A)** Planned cities, piped water, and public drainage would have been impossible without some centralized mechanisms of organization. Choice B is incorrect because irrigation systems, bridges, roads, and temple platforms would not necessarily indicate increased population though they might indicate substantial population. Choice C is incorrect; while there is evidence of trade, there is no stated evidence to identify who copied from whom. Choice D is incorrect because the occasion is removed from its historical context. Montezuma welcomed Cortes in the belief that he might be the returning Aztec god Quetzalcoatl. Choice E is incorrect because this conclusion fails to consider that resistance to change is often for logical reasons. Camel transport was cheap and efficient while wagon wheels required extensive road building, so there was no reason to change.

5. **(D)** This question is asking you to identify the exception among the five options. Since the technology for printing newspapers was not available in Europe at the time of the plague, choice D is the exception. Questions asking for the exception, posed in the negative, make up one-quarter of the test. Negative questions may also be worded to indicate that all of the following are true—EXCEPT—or may be phrased to include the word NOT. Sometimes it helps in questions like this to read without EXCEPT, to determine which answer is different.

6. **(E)** Constructing a hypothesis based on historical data is one of the key skills of a historian. All of the choices are possible hypotheses that can be supported with evidence from the period except choice E. Siddhartha Gautama died in about 485 B.C.E., long before Ashoka ruled India in 250 B.C.E.

7. **(D)** This quote by Sun Zi in *The Art of War* provides basic strategies that the reader should infer to be most useful in guerrilla warfare.

8. **(E)** Knowledge of Sun Zi's strategies was used by guerrilla leaders like Mao Zedong (Mao Tse-tung) and Ho Chi Minh in the twentieth century.

9. **(D)** This Indian image is of Shiva, the Hindu symbol of destruction. Shiva is one of the Hindu trilogy of gods that also includes Brama, the Creator, and Vishnu, the Preserver of Life. The endless life cycle of creation, preservation, and destruction is fundamental to the cosmological and theological world view of Hindus.

10. **(E)** In 1947 following World War II, India gained independence and was partitioned into two countries, India and Pakistan. Since most Muslims lived in the eastern and western segments of northern India, these two areas became the new country of Pakistan. Later, in 1978, the Bengalis of East Pakistan revolted and established Bangladesh.

11. **(E)** The question is concerned with analysis of factors contributing to the wealth and independence of the Byzantine Empire. A carefully designed defense system, the skillful use of intelligence and diplomacy, the support of trade, and the production of luxury goods are all statements which can be evaluated through the use of additional factual evidence. Choice E is an opinion about the past.

12. **(E)** Hindu and Muslim hostility continues. Hostility, fueled by differences in religious beliefs, political aspirations and social customs, are intensified by rival claims to Kashmir dating from the independence and partition of South Asia into India and Pakistan.

13. **(A)** Through diplomacy during the Carter administration, Anwar el-Sadat and Menachem Begin reached a historic agreement known as the Camp David Accords. Egypt broke ranks with the Arab countries and recognized Israel in return for the Sinai.

14. **(D)** At the time of the Mongol invasions, Europe did not produce porcelain, sugar, spices or coffee. Mongol conquests resulted in trade and communication across Eurasia. Europeans were introduced to these products as well as gunpowder and printing. The other choices are accurate.

15. **(E)** Coal produced steam was the energy source which powered the steam engine developed by James Watt. Watt's steam engine was adapted by other industries such as flour mills, railroads, and sailing ships. The discovery of petroleum was not a significant factor as Britain industrialized in the late 18th and early 19th centuries.

16. **(D)** The Cold War kindled fears that other Latin American countries might follow the Cuban example. The United States pledged $10 billion in economic assistance in 1961 to Latin America through The Alliance for Progress.

17. **(B)** Rome is incorrectly paired with the reign of Julius Caesar as a golden age of cultural achievement. The Golden Age of the Roman Empire began with the reign of Augustus Caesar marked by a time of relative peace known as Pax Romana. The Golden Age, a period lasting for approximately 150 years, is remembered for the growth of cities and architectural accomplishments such as the Colosseum; artistic expression such as the literature of Virgil, Livy, and Horace; and the development of Roman law.

18. **(B)** The Congress of Vienna was based on the principle of balance of power to ensure a lasting peace. Negotiations led by Klemens von Metternich of Austria sought to establish an international equilibrium of political and military forces among the major powers. Following the settlement, participants agreed to meet periodically to settle international issues.

19. **(B)** Rationalism developed among Greeks who believed that beauty and order can be conceived in the human mind while humanism referred to the human potential.

20. **(E)** The Roman emperor Constantine (306–337 C.E.) built a new capital, Constantinople, on the site of the old Greek city of Byzantium. This site was easier to defend than Rome and promised to become a trading center for the profitable Eurasian trade. This marked the beginnings of the Byzantine Empire, which lasted until 1453 C.E.

21. **(D)** Japan was the first Asian country to industrialize. India, China, Iran, and Korea continued policies that failed to address Western expansion. In 1868 the Japanese ended the rule of the military shoguns, the Tokugawa, and restored the authority of the Emperor Meiji. The Meiji Restoration abolished feudalism and established policies leading to industrialization.

22. **(B)** Taiwan, South Korea, and Singapore became the economic miracles of the 1970s by integrating their own cultural traditions with aspects of both the communist and capitalist development models.

23. **(B)** Education is regarded as an important capital investment to ensure the success of development projects. Development depends on efforts of educated men and women to establish the infrastructure for successful development. South Korea's literacy rate of 99 percent is the highest in the world.

24. **(A)** Choices B, C, D, and E refer to ongoing scientific research among scientists investigating the early history of humanity. Answer A is questionable because the choice indicates little scientific agreement; when, in fact, there is considerable scientific agreement concerning the early stages of human development.

25. **(B)** While vision, walking upright, hearing and muscular strength accorded humans certain physical advantages, human vocal cords and the development of language led to social development.

26. **(C)** Anthropologists are scientists who study physical and cultural characteristics of people. Paleontologists study plant and animal fossils; archaeologists study the fossils and artifacts of ancient peoples; geologists, the physical characteristics of the earth; and sociologists, the institutions and functions of human groups.

27. **(C)** While tool making, new artistic expression, and longer life spans eventually occurred, the most immediate result of climate change was migration. E is incorrect because *Homo sapiens sapiens* are our present species.

28. **(B)** Catal Huyuk is incorrectly linked with Guatemala. The correct location is Turkey. While plant domestication occurred at Catal Huyuk, evidence at the Turkish site of Hallan Comi indicates the domestication of animals preceded farming. Evidence in Iraq at Jarmo, China at Ban Po, and Mexico at Tehuacan provides additional evidence that different plants were domesticated at these sites independently.

29. **(D)** Growth of human populations has been the direct result of food and medicine. Expanding wealth, permanent homes, metal tools, and the growth of urban centers came as a consequence of the agricultural revolution.

30. **(D)** Egypt was not a site of Indo-European migrations, however Italy, Greece, Iran and India were. Migrations of peoples have had lasting impacts in world history. The language spoken by Indo-Europeans developed into the modern languages spoken in Iran, India, and European countries such as Italy, Spain, France, and Greece.

31. **(D)** The Bantus expanded over much of the African continent south of the Sahara over a period of one thousand years. Some 90 percent of the languages in central and south Africa are of Bantu origin.

32. **(B)** Historians use gender as a term to relate to the roles that men and women have played in the societies in which they lived. Twentieth century women sought equality, advocating reforms such as the right to vote and equal pay for equal work. Patriarchy refers to societies where descent and succession are traced through the male line; matriarchy, through the female line. Women's history focuses just on women and women's roles through time.

33. **(C)** The American Revolution from 1776 to 1781 preceded the French Revolution from 1789 to 1799. The Napoleonic Era, the Haitian Revolution, the revolutions of Latin America countries and the European Liberal Revolutions followed and were consequences of the French Revolution.

34. **(D)** In a republican form of government, the power to govern is granted by the people. Citizens possessing equal political and legal rights live in a democratic society. In a monarchy, the power to govern is inherited by the leader. Individuals emancipated from government restraints would exist in a state of anarchy. A dictator is a leader assuming the right to rule based on military and economic power.

35. **(D)** Japan was settled by migrations of peoples from East Asia. Agricultural products and linguistic evidence of Austronesian/Polynesian settlers exists in Madagascar, Hawaii, Easter Island, and Indonesia.

36. **(A)** While each of the choices is plausible, guns and gunpowder were produced through the technology of settled peoples. Guns and gunpowder proved to be a formidable defense against nomadic attacks.

37. **(C)** Decolonialization after World War II led to the establishment of fragile nation-states that failed to last. Neo-imperialism followed. Neo-imperialism referred to the acquisition of territory by Western powers to exclude countries with competing interests. Neo-imperialism led to wars of national liberation.

38. **(A)** While all of the choices provide reasons why Jews did not return to eastern Europe, the correct answer is A, pogroms, which were organized persecutions or massacres beginning in the late 19th century.

The Beginnings of Human Society

(ca. 5 million B.C.E.–4000 B.C.E.)

THE MEANING OF SOCIETY

The very long period from 5 million B.C.E. to 4000 B.C.E. witnessed the evolutionary development of an animal species with unique qualities. Among the most important of these qualities is the social nature of humans. "Social" refers to the disposition to live with others and to form organized groups and communities for purposes of living and working.

In early human evolution anatomical changes centered on the development of vocal chords. Speech, language, and the social tendencies of the hominid (human) species increased communication among individuals and led to changes in the brain. The results of these anatomical changes were brain patterns that led to group planning, transmission of knowledge, and collective enterprise that helped the species survive, spread, and advance technologically.

People acting together are known as societies. **Societies** are organized groups of people who have identifiable languages and social structures that reflect values and meaning purposefully taught. The earliest identifiable form of society appears to have been the **hunter-gatherer** society, so-called because humans collectively hunted animals, gathered plant life, and lived in social groups comprising many villages or lineages, sharing a common ancestry, culture, and name. Although hunting and gathering appear to have been societal activities shared by all early peoples, groups differed in their strategies and customs. Hunter-gatherers on coasts fished, whereas those in the plains regions developed techniques for large-animal hunting. These differences led to the development of different cultures. **Culture** is the sum total of ways of life built up by a group of human beings and transmitted to the next generation.

One of the great leaps or changes in early human history occurred when the hunter-gatherer society evolved into a completely new kind of society based on **agriculture**. This shift seems to have intensified and made more complex the methods and structures of social interaction and communication. The story of why this happened and the outcomes of the transformation continue to fascinate historians and students alike. Suffice it to say, the social nature of the hominid species has distinguished it within the animal kingdom. Of all life on earth, humans can collectively change the environment rather than wait for the slow process of the environment to effect physical change. This is largely due to the collective effort of the species, an effort that has intensified as the technologies of communication have advanced.

The Emergence of Early Human Communities and the Peopling of the Earth

(ca. 5 million B.C.E.–10,000 B.C.E.)

TIMELINE	
14 billion years ago	Big Bang
5–6 billion B.C.E.	Solar system and Earth
6 million B.C.E.	Likely appearance of first human-like species
4.4 million B.C.E.	*Ardipithecus ramidus*, "Ardi," earliest known bipedal hominids
3.9 million B.C.E.	*Australopithecus afarensis*, "Lucy"
2.5 million B.C.E.	*Homo habilis*, the "toolmaker," and beginning of the Ice Ages
1.8 million B.C.E.	*Homo erectus* and migration out of Africa
400,000 B.C.E.	*Homo sapiens* and language
135,000 B.C.E.	*Homo sapiens sapiens* or modern humans
100,000 B.C.E.	*Homo sapiens sapiens* remains found over large areas

PREHISTORY

Earth's age is estimated to be between five and six billion years old. Scientists theorize that there was once one supercontinent called **Pangaea**, the center of which is present-day Africa. About 200 million years ago Pangaea broke into two large land masses called **Laurasia**, which formed the northern continents, and **Gondwanaland**, which formed the southern continents. Other pieces split off and began to drift toward their present locations. These splits are explained by the theory of **plate tectonics**. According to this theory, rigid plates form the outer layer of the earth's surface, but they float on a soft layer of magma or molten rock near the

TIP

Be sure you know the significance of all boldface words. They often appear on the SAT test.

earth's core. The molten rock pushes continents apart and drifting plates often collide, forming mountains like the Himalayas.

The first inhabitants on Earth left no written records. For this reason, this period is called **prehistory**—a time before written history. To understand this period, historians rely on the work of **paleontologists**, scientists who study the **fossils** of plants and animals; **archaeologists**, scientists who study the remains of ancient people (both fossils and **artifacts** or man-made objects); and **anthropologists**, scientists who study physical and cultural characteristics of people. Archaeologists use a method called **carbon 14 dating** to determine the age of various archaeological finds. This process measures the amount of radioactive carbon left in an object. Since all living things absorb radiocarbon from the air and lose it after death at a specific rate over time, the radioactive content can determine just how old a fossil is. The **accelerator mass spectrometry** separates smaller fossil samples, just one one-thousandth the size needed for carbon 14 dating, and counts carbon 14 atoms directly. Scientists also use genetics to trace the evolutionary patterns of human beings. In this instance, the **DNA** codes reveal similarities and differences between different **hominid** types.

Because history is the recounting of the human story through time, **chronology** is an important component in the discipline. Time is an artificial creation of the human mind to keep order. Different peoples in different places recorded time differently. In the Western world, where Christianity predominated, the system of B.C., meaning before the birth of Christ, and A.D., *anno Domini* or the year of the Lord, has been the standard measure of time since the Renaissance. In world history, however, increasingly the system of **B.C.E.**, meaning before the common era, and **C.E.**, meaning common era, are being used to reflect a common universal story. Likewise, from a geographical point of view, world historians prefer to use place names with a world perspective rather than a European one. Thus, the Middle East is often referred to in world history as Southwest Asia, the Far East as East Asia, Inner Asia as Central Asia, and India as South Asia.

Chronology	
B.C.	Before Christ
A.D.	*Anno Domini* (Year of the Lord)
B.C.E.	Before the Common Era
C.E.	Common Era

HOMINID DISCOVERIES

Noting that most of the early hominid fossils have been found in Africa, scientists are examining the possible links between environment and bipedal locomotion and between environment and the amount of fossil preservation. Africa 15 million years ago was a carpet of forest east to west with diversity of plants, animals, and primates. During the next few million years, however, the earth's crust began tearing itself apart in a line from the Red Sea through Ethiopia, Kenya, and Tanzania. As a result the land rose blister-like in Ethiopia and Kenya disrupting west to east airflow leaving East Africa in a moist air shadow. The tree cover there began to fragment into a mosaic of forest, woodland, and shrublands. About 12 million years ago a continuation of these tectonic forces led to the formation of a long spacious valley running north to south. This is known at the **Great Rift Valley** where most early fossils have been found. The Rift Valley posed an east to west barrier to movement of animal populations and a division between jungle and savannah environments. The Rift Valley might also be important in prehistory because of its ability to preserve fossils. Fossils are often found in volcanic ash, which is prevalent in the Rift Valley, and are easily evident because of revealed layers of earth.

Climate change like the **ice ages** may have influenced both preservation of fossils and changes in hominid development. The ice age denotes a geographic and climatic period of long-term reduction and increase in the temperature of the earth's surface and atmosphere resulting in the expansion and contraction of ice sheets. Scientists theorize that the earliest ice ages were around 2.7 billion to 2.3 billion years ago though the first documented ones are 1 billion years ago. Since then the history of the earth has been one of constant shifts between warming and cooling. Of interest to historians of human life is the effects these cycles may have had on human development and movements of hominids. The most current ice age started about 2.58 million years ago (the date coincides with the appearance of *Homo habilis*), and since then the earth has seen cycles of glaciation with ice sheets on 40,000- and 100,000-year time scales. Causes of ice ages include changes in Earth orbit; the motion of tectonic plates, which can affect wind and ocean currents; variations in solar output; the orbital dynamics of the earth and moon system; the impact of meteorites and volcanoes; and atmospheric composition (concentrations of carbon dioxide, methane, and so on).

EARLY HOMINIDS

Scientists consider walking upright (**bipedalism**) as the key distinguishing feature of **hominids** (humans). Walking upright left the hands free to hold, carry, and manipulate objects and to scan the horizon for predators and prey, and took less energy than walking on four limbs. Unlike Darwin, who tended to see a straight evolutionary pattern from one species to the next, scientists today note that multiple human species may have lived simultaneously. During the brief 200,000 year history of *Homo sapiens*, at least three other human species also existed.

To date the oldest hominid fossils are dated between 6 million and 7 million years ago, but their remains are too fragmentary at this point to be definitive. Beginning in 1994, **Tim White** and his team unearthed and analyzed the remains of about 37 individuals discovered in the Awash region of Ethiopia dated at 4.4 million years ago. The most complete skeleton found is of a woman of the species *Ardipithecus ramidus*, affectionately known as "**Ardi**." The fossils reveal a torso that allowed for upright walking, feet that lacked an arch but were capable of locomotion, a big toe that allowed for grasping objects and climbing, and flexible fingers. The teeth set lacked dagger-like upper canines typical in apes, but the skull and brain size were small. "Ardi" lived in woodlands and lived on a diet of plants, nuts, and small animals. The find is significant because it pushes the human story further into the past and into a different ecosystem that downplays the importance of open grassland to human development.

Australopithecus Afarensis

In 1974 **Donald Johanson** found skeletal remains of a different species, which came to be called *Australopithecus afarensis*. Found at **Hadar** about 4.5 miles from the Awash region in Ethiopia, the remains have been dated at 3.2 million years ago, though fossils of this type have been dated as far back as 3.9 million years ago. The most complete skeletal remains are of a woman the archeological team dubbed "**Lucy**." "Lucy" was about 3–4 feet tall and weighed about 110 pounds, smaller than *Ardipithecus ramidus* but capable of walking upright and with hands, feet, and teeth closer to more modern hominids than those of "Ardi." The brain size of the two species did not differ significantly; they were about the size of a present-day chimpanzee. The first evidence that confirmed that *Australopithecus afarensis* was not just capable of, but did walk upright, was found at **Laetoli**, Tanzania by Mary Leakey in 1974–1975. Dated at 3.5 million years ago, the footprints are of an adult and child.

Homo Habilis

In 1962–1964 **Mary and Louis Leakey** discovered a different species in the Olduvai Gorge in Tanzania that came to be called *Homo habilis*. This species lived between 2.5 million and 1.6 million years ago. It had disportionately long arms, a less protruding jaw than *Australopithecus*, and a cranial capacity less than half the size of humans but 50% larger than *Australopithecus*. *Homo habilis* is often referred to as the "**Handy Man**" because the remains are often accompanied by stone tools. Tool making was important because it allowed humans to live in many different habitats.

Homo Erectus

In 1969 **Kamoya Kimeu,** a member of **Richard Leakey's** team (son of Mary and Louis Leakey) made a spectacular find near **Lake Turkana** in northern Kenya near the Ethiopian border dated 1.6 million years ago. Dubbed the "Turkana Boy," the nearly complete skeleton reflected a species more similar to modern hominids than other types of earlier species. Named *Homo erectus*, the species had a cranial capacity larger than *Homo habilis* (910 cc—*Homo sapiens sapiens* is generally 1300 cc), a skeletal frame that was taller and narrower suggesting that *Homo erectus* was a hunter rather than a scavenger as *Homo habilis* was, and was losing body hair that was replaced by development of adaptive skin colors.

> **Did You Know?**
>
> Speech is considered crucial to the development of social and intellectual development.

Almost the entire span of *Homo erectus* falls within the most recent ice age. The adaptive quality of *Homo erectus* resulted in larger brains and human territorial expansion. Brain size increased about 25% between 1 and 2 million years ago, as southern Asia developed a warmer climate. Fossil finds suggest *Homo erectus* bands began migrating far and wide, ate a wide range of food, and used fire and hand axes. Scientists are looking for, but have yet to find, definitive evidence of speech in this earlier species. Speech is considered crucial to the development of social and intellectual development.

Homo Sapiens

Some 400,000 years ago yet another form of "homo" appeared. *Homo sapiens* ("consciously thinking human") was distinguished both by brain size and well-developed frontal regions where conscious and reflective thought takes place. This enabled *Homo sapiens* to understand the structure of the world around them, organize more efficient methods of exploiting resources, and communicate and cooperate in important tasks. From evidence at various sites, one group of *Homo sapiens*, or Neanderthal, honored and buried their dead, had a capacity for feeling and emotion, and possessed a sense of the afterlife.

Homo Sapiens Sapiens

Around 200,000 years ago our species, *Homo sapiens sapiens*, began to appear in the fossil record. Brain size was similar to that of *Homo sapiens* but body structure was less robust. *Homo sapiens sapiens* lived alongside *Homo sapiens* and perhaps even interbred with certain archaic *Homo sapiens* types, but gradually *Homo sapiens* became marginalized. One type of early *Homo sapiens sapiens* is **Cro-Magnon**. At Cro-Magnon sites like **Lascaux**, there is evidence of sculpture, painting, jewelry, and objects to exercise "sympathetic magic." One of the most noteworthy aspects of *Homo sapiens sapiens* has been its ability to move, discover, and adapt. *Homo sapiens sapiens* began moving out of Africa reaching the Middle East 70,000–50,000 years' ago, New Guinea and Australia 50,000 years ago, Europe and China 45,000–35,000 years ago, Northeast Asia and Alaska 20,000–15,000 years ago, South America 15,000–12,000 years ago, and Formosa and the Polynesian islands 3,500–2,500 years ago. How far and fast these movements were depended on climate, population pressures, and the invention of new technologies like long-range sailing vessels. These movements reflect the intangible human qualities of curiosity, imagination, and adaptability.

SURVIVAL TECHNIQUES

Theories of human development revolve around the idea that hominids developed unique survival techniques based on **culture** or learned behavior and social organization. Biological differences enable members of different species with specific characteristics to survive. Within this pattern becoming **bipedal** or walking upright was crucial in hominid development because two free hands with opposable thumbs enabled successful development and use of tools. Tools, in turn, created greater success in hunting and gathering. Human language, physically possible because of a larynx, enabled the development of strategy, group action, a sense of time, and remembered behavior. Mental activity related to increased brain size proved an advantage. Definitive fossil evidence for the development of speech is currently high on the list of paleoanthropological investigation.

DNA research has begun to shed light on theories of race. Some black-skinned peoples have been found to share closer DNA characteristics with people outside their race than within it. Skin color seems to have been an adaptation to environment. Dark skins protect humans from tropical ultraviolet rays, while pale skins are an adaptation to the scarcity of sunlight. Thus, different races with black skins live across the equatorial belt in Africa, India, and Australia.

The human need to explain the origins of the cosmos, Earth, and life has resulted in the development of different creation stories. Mesopotamians claimed that Earth and heaven were created as one primeval sea and then were separated by powerful human-like gods. These beliefs influenced the seven-day creation story in the Hebrew Book of Genesis. Hindus describe the creation of the universe out of nothingness and that a Big-Bang-like heat formed the cosmos and generated life. The Chinese myth says that the creator Pan Ku fashioned the sun, moon, and stars out of chaos and darkness, resulting in a unifying force in the universe known as *dao,* *"The way."* The Dogon people of West Africa speculated that life emerged from a world egg and expanded through the universe. Modern science now tells its own story, some of which is surprisingly like the origination stories of ancient peoples. Surprisingly these stories have many similarities with the story that science is now trying to tell.

MARY LEAKEY FINDS ZINJANTHROPUS

There was indeed plenty of material lying on the eroded surface, some no doubt as a result of the rains earlier that year. But one scrap of bone that caught and held my eye was not lying loose on the surface but projecting from beneath. It seemed to be part of a skull, including a mastoid process (the bony projection below the ear). It had a hominid look, but the bones seemed enormously thick—too thick, surely. I carefully brushed away a little of the deposit, and then I could see parts of two large teeth in place in the upper jaw. They were hominid. It was a hominid skull, apparently in situ, and there was a lot of it there. . . .

We devoted the rest of our time at Olduvai in 1959 to extracting it, recovering every fragment we could find by sieving and washing the soil, and to demonstrating that it was indeed *in situ* on what was clearly part of an extensive living floor with many stone artifacts and animal bones . . . I . . . devoted myself to the task of fitting the fragments of the skull back together.

This document was written by archaeologist Mary Leakey describing the moment she came upon one of the most important fossil finds in world history. It illustrates how important the Olduvai Gorge, Tanzania, has been in the search and discovery for prehistoric remains. The Leakeys called their find Zinjanthropus (from Arabic Zinj meaning "East Africa" and Greek anthropos meaning "human being"). Today, this fossil species is referred to as Australopithecus boisei *and is dated at between 1.75 and 1 million years ago. The document also emphasizes the importance of* **in situ** *("in its original place") discoveries. When found among tools and remains of animals, archaeologists can not only find remains, but discern how early man lived.*

The Development of Agricultural Societies

(ca. 10,000 B.C.E.–4000 B.C.E.)

TIMELINE	
2 million B.C.E.	Paleolithic
10,000 B.C.E.	Neolithic
8000 B.C.E.	Agricultural and pastoral revolutions
7000 B.C.E.–4000 B.C.E.	Agricultural communities in Jarmo (Iraq), Jericho (Jordan), Catal Huyuk (Turkey), Ban Po (China), Tehuacan Valley (Mexico)

HUNTER-GATHERER CULTURE

Historians have tended to divide the eras of hunter-gatherer culture into time periods based on the type of tools that hominids made. Thus, during the **Paleolithic** (*paleo* meaning old, and *lithic* meaning stone) or **Old Stone Age**, which lasted from two million years ago, with the appearance of *Homo habilis,* the tool maker, to 10,000 B.C.E., hominids fashioned tools from stone, wood, and bone by knocking and chipping them from a core. Carved bone spears, 90,000 years old, with barbed points were found at an ancient fishing site in eastern Zaire. They demonstrate a level of technology not achieved in Europe until 14,000 years ago. Evidence indicates that during the **Neolithic**, or **New Stone Age**, beginning about 8000 B.C.E., stone tools were made by chipping, grinding, and polishing, making them stronger and capable of cutting more deeply. Neolithic axes were used to cut down trees to clear fields. New tools seemed to be a response to the needs of the domestication of plants and animals, which coincided with the New Stone Age.

During the Paleolithic Era, groups of **hunter-gatherers** migrated widely, ultimately populating all but the most remote parts of the globe. Distances between land masses such as Siberia and Alaska were less during the last Ice Age because ocean levels were lower. This enabled groups of hunter-gatherers to begin crossing from Asia to North America 50,000 to 20,000 years ago. The earliest of these peoples were classified by anthropologists as **Amurians** and the most recent as **Mongoloids**. American Indians, or **Amerindians**, descended from these two groups.

The **culture**, or behavior patterns, arts, beliefs, and institutions of people like hunter-gatherers, has certain characteristics. Geographically, hunter-gatherers had well-defined territories and settled campsites. They learned to control fire. They knew the habits of animals and relied on plants as an essential part of their diet. They even knew how to plant the seeds of wild plants. Their tools evolved from a stone fist hatchet to harpoons and spears to bows and arrows. They wore sewn clothing. Women's life consisted of locating and gathering useful plants, tending campsites, and raising children. Men prepared for and joined in the hunt. Crucial to survival were communication skills, social and political organization, and actions based on reason, not instinct. Beliefs centered around nature and the afterlife. About 15,000 years ago, artists painted amazingly lifelike portraits of the animals they hunted and killed. Located deep within the earth in caves, they were painted either to appease the spirits of animals portrayed, or to persuade the "Earth Mother" to be bountiful.

The map referencing the peopling of the earth depicts a story of early and ongoing movement of humans in many directions and by many means. These stories are constantly being revised as archaeologists and other specialists acquire more data. For example, archaeologists and scholars are increasingly pointing to dates that the first human presence in the Americas preceded the end of the ice age, dating as far back as 30,000 B.C.E. Also being called into question is the theory that passage

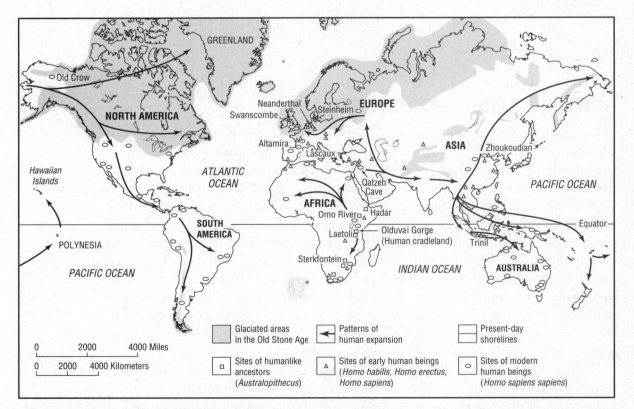

The Spread of Human Population About 10,000 B.C.E. Fire to keep warm, tools with which to make clothes and shelters, and the frozen land bridges created by the ice ages allowed humans to spread over vast territories. By 10,000 B.C.E., man's propensity to explore and seek out new homelands had enabled him to inhabit the globe.

south was made through a break in the ice sheets. Scholars are now looking at the likelihood that the first migrants hugged the coastline in skin-covered boats as they wound their way south along the western American coastline from Asia. This theory, in turn, has called into question that the Clovis were the first inhabitants of the Americas.

AGRICULTURAL AND PASTORAL REVOLUTIONS

Circa 10,000 to 8000 B.C.E., hunter-gatherer societies began to cultivate ground and plant crops. This was an activity that had probably been going on for some time, but then was intensified and extended. Women probably took the first important steps in this crucial change.

WOMEN AND THE AGRICULTURAL REVOLUTION
by Elise Boulding

Successful nomads have a much easier life than do farmers. Among the Kung bushmen today, the men hunt about four days a week and the women only need to work two-and-a-half days at gathering to feed their families. . .

What was it like once bands settled down? This was almost from the first start a woman's world. She would mark out the fields for planting, because she knew where the grain grew best. . . . The agriculture practiced by these first women farmers and their children producing enough food for subsistence only, must be distinguished from the agriculture which developed out of subsistence farming and which produced surpluses and fed nonfarming populations in towns. The first type is commonly called **horticulture** and is carried out with hand tools only. The second is agriculture proper and involves intensive cultivation with the use of plows and (where necessary) irrigation. . . .

Women also began to spend more time on making tools and containers. No longer needing to hold the family possessions down to what they could carry, women could luxuriate in being able to choose larger and heavier grinding stones that crushed grain more efficiently. . . .

The senior woman of the family and her daughters and sons formed the property-holding unit of the family.

This document was written by a twentieth-century scholar, Elise Boulding. According to her analysis, women probably played a crucial role in the agricultural revolution; they were the original seed breeders. It also illustrates the changes the agricultural revolution created in society. Division of labor between men and women increased, the place of women became more powerful especially as it became identified with fertility, and leisure time decreased.

Domestication of Plants

Agriculture, or seed selection and sowing of plants, seems to have developed independently in many parts of the world. It developed in Southwest Asia on the western slopes of the Zagros Mountains (Iran) and at sites like **Jarmo** (Iraq), rains supported sustained agriculture. The first successful type of agriculture was **slash-**

and-burn, a system that allowed farmers to grow grain in places where it did not grow naturally. **Girding** was a technique to cut the bark around trees to kill them, let in sunlight, and keep out weeds. After a few years, farmers burned the dead trees so the ashes could improve fertility. Meanwhile, farmers learned how to select types of seeds that did not fall easily off the stalks, produced abundant harvests, and were resistant to disease and weather. After five or six years, farmers usually had to move because of weeds or because of exhausted soil. This constant movement helped grain farming to be diffused far and wide. From Southwest Asia about 9000 to 10,000 years ago, it spread to the Nile Valley ca. 5000 B.C.E. Ancestors of the Chinese began farming millet ca. 7000 B.C.E. along the **Huang He (Yellow River)**. Recent discoveries suggest that people in the eastern Sahara were making pottery to store food and water, and between 8000 B.C.E. and 5000 B.C.E. people in the north central Nile region (Nubia), the Sahara region, and Ethiopia were cultivating crops like a nutritious grain and the banana-like *ensete*. In West Africa, crops were developed from local wild African plants like sorghum, millet, yams, and African rice. West African plants like sorghum and sesame were diffused to India and China about 2000 B.C.E. People in the Eastern Sahara had domesticated cotton perhaps as early as 5000 B.C.E. The first evidence of cultivated **maize** (corn) was in the Tehuacan Valley of Mexico about 4500 to 4700 years ago. Domestication of cotton, beans, squash, and guava is evident in the Supe Valley in Peru as early as 5000 B.C.E.

In other environments the domestication of plants took other forms. In tropical areas of Southeast Asia, root farming began by 5000 B.C.E. Very likely, where "hunter" fishermen frequented suitable harbors, women began to cultivate **root crops** like manioc, taro, cassava, and yams. Unlike farmers who sowed seed and harvested the plants, root farmers planted live shoots from parent plants and waited for the shoots to grow new roots. In cultivated patches, plants at various stages were grown together, indicating that the difference between summer and winter was slight. Another type of farming that had a more dramatic impact on society was **rice paddy farming**. Developed in the monsoon areas of the world, it very likely developed on the heels of planting methods already known. Rice grew in water-soaked fields or paddies. Soon farmers began planting rice seedlings in standing water. Later, methods of regulating water supply to the fields were developed. Historians are divided over the question of whether maize (corn) farming in the Americas developed independently or was carried from Asia. Regardless, its development seems to have followed that of grain farming in which selectively bred seeds are sown and harvested. By about 4000 B.C.E. the domestication of maize (corn) took place in central Mexico; by 2000 B.C.E. it was grown in Peru, and by 1000 B.C.E. in the southern United States.

Domestication of Animals

Pastoralism, or the domestication of animals, coincided with the development of agriculture. As populations settled down, hunters became pastoralists. This allowed a more reliable source of meat with less energy expended, and it led to the use of animals for carrying and pulling, and byproducts like milk and hides. In the plains regions of Asia, Africa, and the Americas, where it was too dry for agriculture, the pastoral cultures took shape. Moving with the flocks and engaging in subsistence agriculture, the nomadic life of the hunter-gatherers continued.

Did You Know?

The three main crops domesticated in the Americas were maize, potatoes, and manioc.

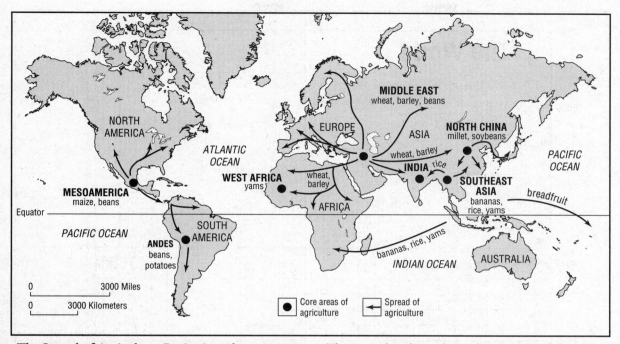

The Spread of Agriculture Beginning About 8000 B.C.E. The Agricultural Revolution began in Southwest Asia and northern China during the Neolithic period, roughly 8000–5000 B.C.E.

The dog was domesticated from the wolf about 12,000 years ago. New archaeological discoveries dating back 10,000 years in southeastern Turkey at **Hallan Cemi** indicate that the pig was the first animal to be domesticated for food. Domestication of animals preceded the transition to agriculture at this site. Taming sheep and cattle in western Asia followed. In the Americas, Amerindians domesticated dogs, turkeys, and guinea pigs. Early Peruvians tamed llamas and wool-bearing alpacas some 7000 years ago. Water buffalo and chickens originated in southern Asia. Domestication of the rabbit first began in the Roman era on the Iberian Peninsula. Amerindians appear to have had fewer large animals to domesticate.

Technology

Technological developments aided the development of agriculture. The soft chipped arrowhead, knives, and spears used for butchering meat in the Paleolithic period gave way to the polished hard stones of the Neolithic period. Attached to handles, they could be used to cut down trees to clear fields. Soon, animals pulled plows through the soil. More land was cleared for farming. The wheel was introduced in Egypt and Mesopotamia by 3000 B.C.E. Methods of controlling water supply, grinding grain, and storing it furthered the agricultural process. Boatbuilding and sailing enabled Neolithic peoples to develop long-distance trading networks using nearby rivers and coastal waters as avenues of transport.

The results of the Agricultural Revolution were dramatic. Population increased from two million in Paleolithic times to approximately 60 to 70 million in Neolithic times. While many people remained hunters and gatherers, the agricultural revolution bred two new cultures, agriculturalists and pastoralists, that were often at odds with each other over land. Specialization of the new cultures led to

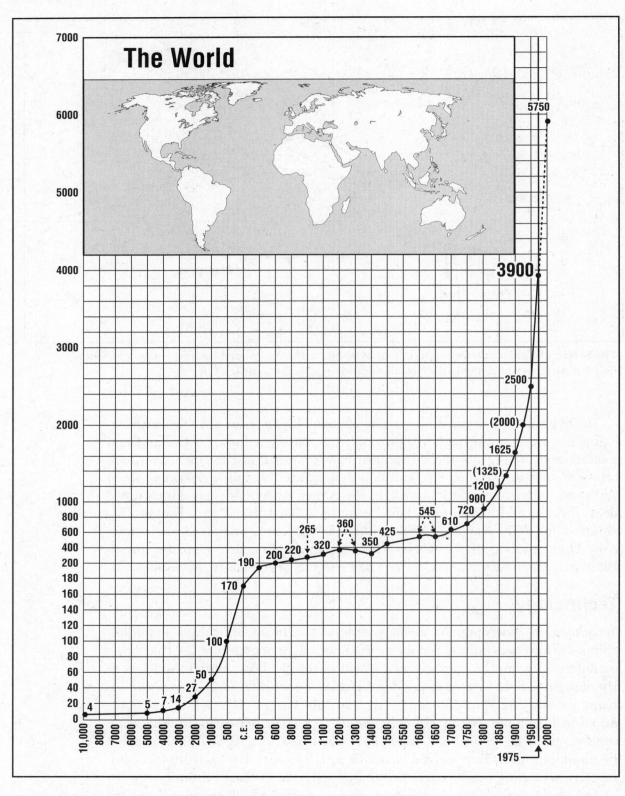

The Rise of World Population 10,000 B.C.E. to 2000. The human species had not only spread across the globe, but increased its numbers dramatically. Major growth in world population came on the heels of the agricultural and scientific revolutions. Food and medicine were major factors in population explosion.

increased trade and its mechanisms like carts and bridles, containers like jars and baskets, and mediums of exchange. It also led to settled communities.

AGRICULTURAL COMMUNITIES

In places where agriculture began to flourish, people began settling in communities. Such early communities have been found in **Jarmo** (Iraq), **Jericho** (Jordan), **Catal Huyuk** (Turkey), **Ban Po** (China), and **Tehuacan** (Mexico). Many of these communities reflect patterns of settlement found at Catal Huyuk.

As a result of the Agricultural Revolution, the early city of Catal Huyuk spread over 32 acres and at one time had 6000 inhabitants in the seventh millennium B.C.E. The houses formed a defense wall of sun-dried mud-brick. Residents climbed a ladder to a hole in the roof to enter their homes. They also used the rooftops to pass from house to house as there were no planned streets, though some random open spaces existed within the settlement.

There are architectural similarities among many of these early towns. They were often built of uniform mud-dried brick. Individual family dwellings were linked. Inhabitants built central squares for trade and ceremony and walls for defense. The society that emerged in these towns reflects growing specialization. Artisans made pottery for cooking vessels or to store grain, wine, and oil. Women skilled in weaving produced baskets or textiles. While some people were artisans, others engaged in trade, or in military, religious, or political endeavors, and still others in farming. New religions, based not on animal beliefs but on the sun and fertility, emerged. Keeping track of cycles and time for planting, and the transmission of such knowledge, became important. Growing wealth is reflected in the fine craftsmanship of jewelry, mirrors, and weapons. With these changes, the first civilizations were born.

Unit Review

Cross-Regional Developments

During the very long period in human history between 5 million B.C.E. and 8000 B.C.E., human beings developed physically, socially, technologically, and spiritually into a form we are familiar with today. This happened against a backdrop of geologic change including four ice ages.

- Physically, hominids became bipedal, increased their brain size, and developed the capability to speak.

- Socially, hominids began to live in extended groups that worked effectively together to improve hunting and survival.

- Technologically, humans fashioned tools to help them hunt and survive the cold weather of the ice ages.

- Spiritually and esthetically, early humans developed a sense of time and learned behavior, ritual religious patterns based on animal spirits, and methods of artistic expression.

Throughout this Paleolithic period, change was dominated by the slow process of adaptation to the environment.

During the Neolithic period in the transition from hunting and gathering to agriculture, humans began the process of changing the environment.

- The domestication of plants and animals revolutionized the lives of *Homo sapiens.*

- With the surplus of food, populations grew.

- Settled towns were established.

- Specialization of occupations began to appear.

- New technologies like the wheel, farm implements, irrigation procedures, building, timekeeping, and religions centered on the world of nature were developed.

This set the stage for the development of civilization and, with it, writing.

Legacies

The human past before the rise of civilizations left many legacies for the modern world. Anatomical changes led to speech, advances in tool making, and further adaptations to the environment. As humans adapted to the environment, they shaped the environment to meet their needs. These changes led to the first global legacy in human history, the peopling of the earth and the astounding story of human adaptation to a variety of contrasting environments in Africa, Eurasia, and the Americas based on a successful hunter-gatherer lifestyle. The second important legacy was the emergence of agriculture. Man's successful manipulation of the environment dramatically increased the tempo and nature of change in human history. It set the stage for the rise of complex urban societies.

Quiz

Matching:

Match the term in the left-hand column with its appropriate definition in the right-hand column.

1. Plate tectonics
2. Prehistory
3. Paleolithic
4. Girding
5. Horticulture

A. The first phase of the Agricultural Revolution
B. Old Stone Age
C. Before writing
D. Rigid plates of the earth floating on a soft layer of molten rock
E. Cutting bark around the tree trunk to kill the tree

Questions:

1. Human racial differences in skin color are due to

   (A) descent from different ancestral types.
   (B) differing DNA.
   (C) adaptation to the environment.
   (D) the "Out of Africa" model.
   (E) development of a multiple species.

2. The cave paintings at Lascaux illustrate

   (A) how *Homo erectus* lived.
   (B) how early agriculture developed.
   (C) the subjects related to early beliefs of Neolithic man.
   (D) the origins of the pastoral revolution.
   (E) early birth and death rituals of hunters and gatherers.

3. Scientists who study the remains of ancient peoples and their societies are

   (A) anthropologists.
   (B) paleontologists.
   (C) archaeologists.
   (D) historians.
   (E) all of the above.

4. All of the following are considered reasons for the survival of *Homo sapiens* and for successful adaptation to varied or contrasting environments EXCEPT

   (A) social organization.
   (B) language skills.
   (C) physical agility.
   (D) mental acumen.
   (E) learned behavior.

5. Neolithic stone tools can be distinguished from earlier tools because

   (A) they were made of bone, wood, and stone.
   (B) Paleolithic axes were shaped principally by chipping or pounding from a core rock.
   (C) they were often spears with barbed points of bone.
   (D) they were shaped by chipping, grinding, and polishing.
   (E) they were often spears with copper or tin points.

6. The type of agriculture requiring farmers to move every five to six years in search of new land was

   (A) root farming.
   (B) rice paddy farming.
   (C) maize (corn) agriculture.
   (D) slash-and-burn agriculture.
   (E) irrigated grain farming.

7. All the following were results of the domestication of plants and animals EXCEPT

   (A) population decrease.
   (B) development of towns and settled communities.
   (C) irrigation technologies.
   (D) diversity of occupations.
   (E) belief systems inspired by nature.

8. Societies are

   (A) sum totals of ways of life.
   (B) organized groups of people with identifiable languages and social structures that reflect common values
   (C) towns with communal gathering places.
   (D) groups of people who build common buildings and dwellings.
   (E) people with a common religion.

9. Methods used to date prehistoric artifacts and fossils include

   (A) analysis of other artifacts and fossils at the site.
   (B) carbon 14 dating.
   (C) accelerator mass spectrometry.
   (D) analysis of DNA.
   (E) all of the above.

10. Which of the following is arranged in correct chronological order?

    (A) Neolithic and Paleolithic
    (B) *Homo habilis, Homo sapiens,* and *Homo erectus*
    (C) Cro-Magnon, Neanderthal, and Java or Peking man
    (D) hunting and gathering, rice paddy farming, and slash-and-burn agriculture
    (E) None of these appear in the correct order.

11. Which of the following proved to be a physical advantage for humans living in groups?

    (A) bipedalism
    (B) hands
    (C) opposing thumb
    (D) brain capacity
    (E) speech

12. Early human migrations out of Africa may have been because of

    (A) climate change.
    (B) plagues.
    (C) changes in social organization.
    (D) improved technological development.
    (E) warfare between Cro-Magnon and Neanderthal.

13. The first cultivated crop in China was

    (A) maize.
    (B) millet.
    (C) wheat.
    (D) rice.
    (E) manioc.

14. The earliest forms of agriculture in Southwest Asia required

    (A) extensive irrigation.
    (B) the plow.
    (C) burning trees to fertilize the soil.
    (D) domesticated root crops.
    (E) permanent agricultural sites near a river.

15. *In situ* is an important concept in the work of archaeologists because

    (A) it helps identify places to find early humans.
    (B) it is the gorge where many fossils have been found.
    (C) it is a term developed by Mary Leakey to mean identification of *Zinjanthropus.*
    (D) it means a fossil discovery "in its original place," which can provide additional evidence about the environmental context of the fossil.
    (E) it can extend the area of investigation to surrounding areas.

16. Women were important contributors to the agricultural revolution because they were likely the gender who

    (A) made tools and containers.
    (B) performed essential agricultural tasks such as plowing and irrigation.
    (C) gathered edible plants and knew where grains grew.
    (D) found that farming required less work and less time.
    (E) traded grains for meat.

17. Nomadic pastoralists differed from hunter-gatherers because they herded domesticated animals in plains regions of Asia, Australia, Africa, and the Americas. Advantages of domesticated animals include which of the following?

    I. A reliable source of power and transport.
    II. A steady source of protein.
    III. A new degree of mobility.
    IV. The continuation of slash-and-burn agriculture.

    (A) I and II
    (B) I, II, and III
    (C) II, III, and IV
    (D) I, III, and IV
    (E) All of the above

18. Of the following foods, which was domesticated in the Eastern Hemisphere?

    (A) corn
    (B) potatoes
    (C) beans
    (D) wheat
    (E) squash

19. The Rift Valley is the result of

    (A) tectonic plate shifts.
    (B) the ice ages.
    (C) interrupted air flow from the Atlantic to Indian Ocean.
    (D) volcanic activity.
    (E) drying of an ancient river bed.

20. The most likely explanation for population increases in Neolithic times is

    (A) Migrations of hunting and gathering societies into new areas with an abundance of game and edible plants.
    (B) Improved tools such as harpoons, bows and arrows, fishing nets and boats.
    (C) Control and use of fire.
    (D) The transition from hunting and gathering to the domestication of plants and animals.
    (E) The development of successful practices and shared beliefs, passed from one generation to the next.

Answers

Matching:
1. **(D)**
2. **(C)**
3. **(B)**
4. **(E)**
5. **(A)**

Questions:

1. **(C)**	6. **(D)**	11. **(E)**	16. **(C)**
2. **(C)**	7. **(A)**	12. **(A)**	17. **(B)**
3. **(E)**	8. **(B)**	13. **(B)**	18. **(D)**
4. **(C)**	9. **(E)**	14. **(C)**	19. **(A)**
5. **(D)**	10. **(E)**	15. **(D)**	20. **(D)**

STUDY TIP

Make flash cards for more drill. The secret to success is practice, practice, practice!

The objective: to learn the story of the past well enough to tell it in all its details.

The goal: to understand how the past has shaped the present.

Early Civilizations

(to ca. 500 B.C.E.)

THE MEANING OF CIVILIZATION

About 4000 B.C.E., village culture gave way to **civilization**. The word "civilization" can be most closely connected to the word "city" and involves practices that are connected with urban life. Civilization is often defined as a state of human society in which a complex level of culture, science, government, and social life is reached. Among its distinguishing characteristics are

1. a degree of political order and power,
2. specialization of jobs and class differentiation,
3. city design and building projects that require complex systems to mobilize labor and technological skill,
4. establishment of religious centers,
5. writing systems, and
6. an agricultural surplus.

For historians, the notion of civilization has provided a framework for historical analysis. Such analysis breaks down human activity into components like political, social, economic, and cultural activities. "Political" refers to such aspects of life as rule (state, kingdom, empire, etc.), the military, and law. "Social" refers to such aspects as class, gender, and family. "Economic" refers to agriculture, commerce, industry, and money. "Culture" refers to human activities such as art, literature, and philosophy. By compartmentalizing the various activities of a group of people, a civilization can be more understandably described.

The earliest civilizations are closely connected with rivers and successful water management. They occurred in isolated areas worldwide though their chronological appearance on the Eurasian continent suggests some **cultural diffusion** in their development. The early civilizations are Mesopotamia, ca. 3000 B.C.E.; Egypt, ca. 3000 B.C.E.; Indus Valley, ca. 2900 B.C.E.; China, ca. 2200 B.C.E.; Mexican Olmec, ca. 1200 B.C.E.; and the Caral culture in Peru, ca. 2600 B.C.E. All successfully used water to create an agricultural surplus that freed numbers of people to engage in activities other than farming.

The early civilizations are often associated with the development of writing. Following the development of speech, the invention of writing during this period was the second great step in human communication, and it marks the boundary between prehistory and history. Writing first began with pictures or pictograms used to convey a message. Certain symbols, known as **ideograms**, were added to represent abstract ideas, such as a drawing of a heart to stand for the idea of love. Other symbols, **phonograms** (symbols based on sounds), could be arranged in various ways to represent sounds. With writing, people were no longer limited by time or distance in their efforts to communicate. As more people began to live in complex, urban societies, the need to keep accurate records of tax payments, religious rituals, commercial agreements, and laws created a new class of **scribes** who often served as an elite corps of recordkeepers in temples and courts. Writing enabled more people to learn what others knew and led to new discoveries.

Scholars of world history have begun to challenge the notion of "civilization." They have done so for a number of reasons. First, they note that human communities that generate economic surplus and develop complex societies involve only a tiny portion of the 2.5 million years of human history and only a small portion of the world's people. They further argue that the majority of the world's populations never lived within the bounds of the "grand societies" described in books. Second, they note that the idea of civilization is based on a biased concept. The notion that technology, writing, or culture is fundamental to civilization excludes many societies that were highly advanced but deficient in one or more of the fundamentals. The Maya, for instance, made remarkable discoveries in astronomy and math but were seemingly deficient in transport technology. Finally, world historians argue that in the contemporary world, the word "civilization" has tended to be equated with notions of superiority or advancement, leaving many peoples of the world to be unwittingly placed in the category of "backward." Therefore, world historians are increasingly looking for new terms, like "human community," instead of "civilization" to describe the capacity of many types of peoples to achieve specialization, town life, agricultural surplus, and distinguished cultures. This book will continue to use the word "civilization" because it is still used in many textbooks and on the SAT subject test, but the student should be aware that the word is increasingly being exchanged for terms that bear fewer value-laden connotations.

The Emergence of Civilization

(ca. 3000 B.C.E.–1500 B.C.E.)

TIMELINE	
3100 B.C.E.–1200 B.C.E.	Egyptian civilization
3100 B.C.E.– 2100 B.C.E.	Caral civilization
3000 B.C.E.–1600 B.C.E.	Mesopotamian civilization
2900 B.C.E.–1750 B.C.E.	Indus Valley civilization
2000 B.C.E.–500 B.C.E.	Mississippian culture (Adena and Hopewell)
1200 B.C.E.–500 B.C.E.	Olmec civilization
1200 B.C.E.–200 B.C.E.	Chavin civilization

COMPARATIVE DEVELOPMENT OF MESOPOTAMIA, EGYPT, INDUS VALLEY, MESOAMERICA, PERU, AND NORTH AMERICA

Mesopotamia

In Southwest Asia, stretching in a curve from **Mesopotamia** (the land between the **Tigris and Euphrates rivers**) in the east to Palestine in the west, lies an area of rich **alluvial** soil, or silt deposited by the Tigris and Euphrates rivers. By building dams and digging irrigation ditches, people in these valleys were able to grow crops on land that would otherwise have remained part of the desert. From present-day Iraq into Syria, Lebanon, and Israel, this agricultural area has been known in history as the **Fertile Crescent**.

By 3000 B.C.E. the towns in the valley of the Tigris and Euphrates rivers had grown into full-fledged cities of mud-brick buildings. The city and surrounding territory, or city-state, was governed by a ruler. The city was the residential center for the king, a thriving place of commerce, and a center of worship, as evidenced by the high, terraced pyramid, or **ziggurat**, topped with a temple.

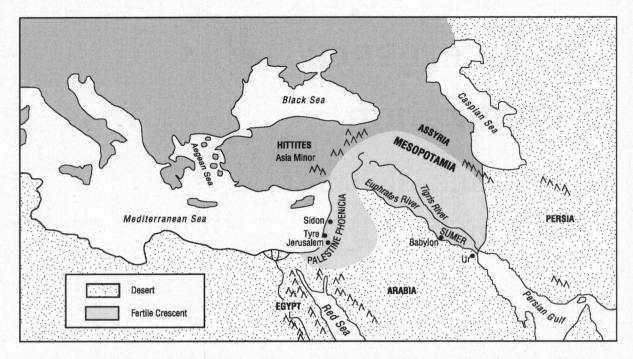

Better known as the Fertile Crescent, the area between the Tigris and Euphrates rivers has often been referred to as the Cradle of Civilization. The geography and climate of this area nourished the development of agriculture.

The **Sumerians** in the south laid the foundations for the civilization. Various invaders like the Akkadians came into the valley and adopted Sumerian ways. From time to time, groups of city-states formed alliances, and during the first 1000 years of Mesopotamian history, two empires were formed. In 2334 B.C.E. a great Akkadian warrior, **Sargon**, conquered Mesopotamia and established the first empire. The secret to Sargon's success was a large standing army that was a mixed blessing. Without a bureaucracy to collect taxes to pay soldiers and resupply the army, he could not sustain them in any one city for very long. He had to plan new military campaigns and was doomed to always be on the move. When Sargon died, his empire fell apart. In the five centuries after the fall of Sargon's empire, the Sumerian city of **Ur** dominated the others. In 1792 B.C.E., the Amorite king of Syria, **Hammurabi**, established a new Mesopotamian empire, **Babylonia**. It fell to the Hittites ca. 1600 B.C.E.

Politically, the history of Mesopotamia was a stormy one. The region not only suffered internal strife, but was a highway for invasion. It was, perhaps, out of the need for order among various peoples that laws were arranged systematically by topics for easy reference. **Hammurabi's Code** was based on the concept of an eye for an eye and of unequal punishment among classes, the lowest classes receiving harsher punishment than the upper ones. Nevertheless, it provided a notion of justice that was, for the first time, standardized and regularized.

> ## HAMMURABI'S CODE
>
> If a man has put out the eye of a free man, they shall put out his eye.
>
> If he breaks the bone of a free man, they shall break his bone.
>
> If he puts out the eye of a villain or breaks the bone of a villain, he shall pay 1 maneh of silver.
>
> If he puts out the eye of a free man's slave or breaks the bone of a free man's slave, he shall pay half his price.
>
> If anyone opens his ditches to water his crop, but is careless and the water floods his neighbors' field, he shall pay his neighbor corn for his losses.
>
> *Hammurabi's Code, probably written ca. 1760 B.C.E., was the first known attempt in world history to provide a code of law that was applicable to all and that would be the basis of justice. The principles of Hammurabi's Code were an "eye for an eye" and the idea that the higher up the accused was on the social scale, the lesser the punishment.*

Next to farming, the chief occupation of Mesopotamians was trade. A great part of the trade was carried on or dominated by the priests. Metal ingots were used for currency and the necessity for business records no doubt prompted the invention of a writing system called **cuneiform**. This was based on syllables. Words were written with a stylus on clay tablets and baked. To aid farmers, a system of time measurement or **calendar** based on lunar cycles was devised. A mathematical system based on scales of twelve was developed. The common problems of farming that ranged from clearing swamp land to creating irrigation systems were aided by development of a political order dominated by chiefs, kings, and priests. The needs of agriculture also produced great technological breakthroughs, among them the plow and use of oxen to pull it, the wheel and cart, and bronze, an alloy of copper and tin, to make sturdier tools.

Classes in Mesopotamia were rigid and fixed by law. They were nobles, freemen, and slaves. Women owned property and engaged in business. Slaves, usually either war captives or debtors, were common. They provided the labor force to build brick temples and irrigation systems.

The Mesopotamian gods were connected not with animals, as in hunter-gatherer societies, but with the forces of nature. While powerful, immortal, and invisible, the gods of this **polytheistic** religion tended to take on **anthropomorphic** forms, whereby they lived in hierarchies and oversaw human tasks. They were thought to be the architects of natural disasters. Since there were many such disasters, especially those associated with the flooding and rampages of the Tigris and Euphrates, the Mesopotamians tended to look on their gods as angry and wrathful. It is in this context that the narration of the flood that gave rise to the biblical story of Noah can be understood. The first great epic poem, the *Epic of Gilgamesh*, shows the Sumerians wrestling with the enduring questions of life, death, mankind and deity, and immortality.

> ### THE EPIC OF GILGAMESH
>
> The heroes, the wise men, like the new moon, have their waxing and waning. Men will say, "Who has ever ruled with might and with power like Gilgamesh?" As in the dark month, the month of shadows; so without him there is no light. O Gilgamesh, this was the meaning of your dream. You were given the kingship, such was your destiny; everlasting life was not your destiny. . . . Gilgamesh; who do you search? The life you seek you will never find. When the gods created the world, they made death a part of human fate.
>
> *About 2000 B.C.E. the Sumerians wrote down the world's oldest story, The Epic of Gilgamesh, which went back at least to 6000 B.C.E. in oral form. Gilgamesh was a literary hero based on a real person who had ruled a Sumerian city-state. Gilgamesh does great deeds but is unable to overcome the will of the gods or fate. The poem shows the Sumerians grappling with enduring questions of life and death, mankind and deity. There are many biblical parallels in the poem, including the stories of Adam, the Deluge, Noah's Ark, and the trials of Job.*

Egypt

Unlike the Tigris and Euphrates, which are subject to rain and torrents of flooding, the **Nile**, the world's longest river, flooded with annual regularity. With layers of silt to replenish the soil and water to nourish new crops, settled communities along the Nile prospered and united. While Mesopotamia lay open to invasion from all sides, Egypt was protected by the sea, desert, and river cataracts at its borders. Egypt was also nearly self-sufficient with enormous quantities of stone and abundant clay. Copper was obtained from Sinai and timber from Lebanon. Thus, Egyptian civilization emerged confident, tranquil, and insular.

Did You Know?

Early civilizations clustered around rivers.

Geographical unity gave rise to political unity under the authority of one king, a **pharaoh**. Pharaohs of the Egyptian **theocracy** were not only absolute rulers and owners of the country, but were also worshipped as gods.

Pyramid building required enormous social organization and architectural skills. The largest was built near Cairo at **Giza** by Pharaoh **Cheops** to shelter the body of the pharaoh through death and into the afterlife. The link between politics and religion can also be seen in the development of writing or **hieroglyphics**, priestly writings. Hieroglyphics were originally pictograms and later included ideograms and phonograms as well. In 1821 hieroglyphics were decoded by **Jean Champollion**, using the **Rosetta Stone**, a stone found in 1799 near Rosetta bearing parallel inscriptions in Greek, Egyptian, and the **vernacular** (common language), making it possible to decipher Egyptian hieroglyphics. The Egyptians also invented a paper-like material called **papyrus**.

The unified political history of Egypt began around 3100 B.C.E., when **King Menes** united **Lower Egypt**, situated in the north on the Nile Delta (where the Nile flows into the Mediterranean), with **Upper Egypt**, which extended along the Nile to the First Cataract at Aswan. He established the first of many dynasties, or successions of kings, who ruled Egypt for nearly 3000 years. The first period in

Egyptian history is known as the **Old Kingdom**. It lasted until 2200 B.C.E. This was followed by a period of civil wars and unrest until, in 2100 B.C.E., the prince of Thebes made himself ruler and established the **Middle Kingdom**. While the Old Kingdom was noted for its pyramids, the Middle Kingdom was remarkable for literature, art, and ideas. During the period of the Middle Kingdom, the Egyptians reclaimed land in the Nile delta in Lower Egypt through a massive drainage project. Beyond Upper Egypt they occupied Nubia. Trade expanded, linking Mesopotamia, Crete, and the Palestinian coast with Egypt. Like the Old Kingdom, the Middle Kingdom was torn apart by civil war and then by outside invaders, the **Hyksos**, in 1700 B.C.E.

About 1580 B.C.E. the Egyptians rebelled against the Hyksos and established the **New Kingdom**. During the New Kingdom, influences from outside were evident. Egyptians became efficient warriors and during the reign of **Thutmose III**, one of the greatest of the warrior pharaohs, Egypt extended its rule through Syria and Palestine and conquered Nubia to the south. Outside influences were evident under **Ikhnaton** (Akhenaton). The **monotheistic** idea of a single all-powerful god, the sun god **Aton**, permeated the nation's religion. **Howard Carter's** discovery in 1922 of Tutankhamen's tomb provided invaluable artifactual evidence of life during this period. Under **Ramses II**, the last of the great New Kingdom pharaohs, Egypt fought to retain its territory along the shores of the eastern Mediterranean, but by the tenth century B.C.E. Egypt had lost its empire and independence to foreign rule. During the imperial period, temples, rather than pyramids of the Old Kingdom, were the supreme architectural achievement. An outstanding example was at **Karnak**, a huge colonnaded temple complex built using the **post and lintel** construction, a style later employed by the Greeks.

NUMERICAL SYSTEM

Egyptian life centered around agriculture. The Egyptians planted, harvested, and developed a solar calendar of 365 days. Calculating boundaries of fields required a survey that prompted the development of geometry. Government officials collected taxes using a system of numbers and arithmetic based on the decimal. Egyptians, however, did not develop the concept of zero nor did they use money. They traded by **bartering** or swapping one item for another.

Trade moved easily up and down the Nile. The Nile current carried ships downstream in a northerly direction toward the Mediterranean. Seasonal **Etesian winds** worked against the current, propelling ships with sails south or upstream toward Luxor and beyond. Thus, two-way river traffic was accommodated.

EGYPTIAN SOCIETY

A stratified society offered individuals some freedom as well as constraints. Even though the majority of Egyptians were servants or laborers, slavery did not become widespread until the New Kingdom. The elite minority served the pharaoh as priests, nobles, and bureaucrats. Upper class women occupied an important place in Egyptian society as dynastic rights were **matriarchal** or traced through the woman's family. **Hatshepsut**, wife and half sister to two successive pharaohs, ruled for 40 years and was the only woman to serve as a pharaoh during this period. Occasionally, humble people, if talented, could rise to the upper classes. Most men and women were probably close to serfs as they could not easily leave their land and worked as laborers on the pharaoh's projects like the pyramids.

The Indus Valley

About 2900 B.C.E. a third civilization emerged in the **Indus River Valley**. Like the Tigris, Euphrates, and Nile rivers, the Indus River deposits a rich soil over a vast area. While not so isolated as the Nile, the Indus Valley is protected. In the north are the towering Himalaya Mountains, in the west, the Hindu Kush Mountains, and to the east, the Great Indian Desert.

In the Indus Valley, two great cities, **Harappa** and **Mohenjo-Daro**, as well as about 70 other ancient towns and villages, have been discovered. Far less is known about the Indus Valley than Mesopotamia or Egypt. Still, there is enough archaeological evidence to suggest that the Indus Valley possessed many of the hallmarks of early civilization. Harappa and Mohenjo-Daro were well-planned cities that included a walled central city where the rulers lived and where large granaries stored surplus crops as taxes. The rulers were very likely a strong priestly class. Although writing on seals has survived, it has yet to be deciphered. Inhabitants used a standard system of weights and measures. The residents enjoyed piped water, indoor bathrooms, public drainage systems, and ceremonial bathhouses. Upper classes were composed of rulers, priests, and wealthy merchants, while the lower classes lived in smaller dwellings inside and outside the city, primarily as farmers and artisans.

Like the other civilizations, the Indus Valley was supported by agriculture. Inhabitants traded with Mesopotamia, and they used resources that came from as far away as southern India and Tibet. About 1750 B.C.E. the Indus Valley went through some sort of crisis, either environmental or invasion, and was then abandoned.

Mesoamerica/Olmec

The process of change from hunter-gatherer society to agricultural is not well-known in **Mesoamerica**. Domestication of plants—beans, peppers, avocados, squash, and maize—probably began with the domestication of maize between 4700 and 4500 years ago. By 2000 B.C.E. villages and pottery of the **Archaic** period are evident. Around 1200 B.C.E. when Tutankhamen ruled in Egypt, the "mother civilization" of Mesoamerica, the **Olmec**, appeared (see map on page 49). Major sites are in the wet tropical forests of the gulf coast of eastern Mexico at **San Lorenzo** (1200–900 B.C.E.) and **La Venta** (900–500 B.C.E.). Maize cultivation along the rivers provided the basis for a state ruled by a hereditary elite in which religious ceremonies dominated much of life.

Olmec cities were probably ruled by powerful chiefs and reflect an amazing ability to organize resources and people in their building programs. Engineering genius is reflected in San Lorenzo, a city of about 2,500, which was built on an artificial dirt platform situated above fertile frequently flooded plains. Stones for the massive Olmec heads were brought from 60 miles away and some weighed more than 40 tons. Mobilization of labor was critical in the building programs which are comparable to the great pyramids in Egypt. The Olmec studied the starry skies in order to orient their cities and monuments. While the exact purpose of the huge stone heads in unknown, the artists created a distinct style that incorporated animals, especially jaguars and other supernatural beings. By about 650 B.C.E., the Olmec had created a simple hieroglyphic writing system that seems to have been developed more for records of kings, rituals, and the calendar than for commercial needs as in Mesopotamia. This system very likely influenced later Maya civilizations. Despite the nature and purpose of the writing system, commerce played a vital role in the rise and wealth of the Olmec. The Olmec traded with Mexico's west coast and Costa Rica especially, in search of basalt, obsidian, jade, and cocoa.

Peru

Along the central coastline of Peru (called **Norte Chico**) and up the valleys to the Andes mountains, a complex society with many of the features of those in Sumer, Egypt, Harappa, and China developed between 3100 and 1600 B.C.E. The Peruvian peoples worked metals like copper, gold, and silver to fashion tools and jewelry. The development of agriculture based on irrigation systems and cotton fishing nets freed many of the population to engage in building and religious activities. In the Supe

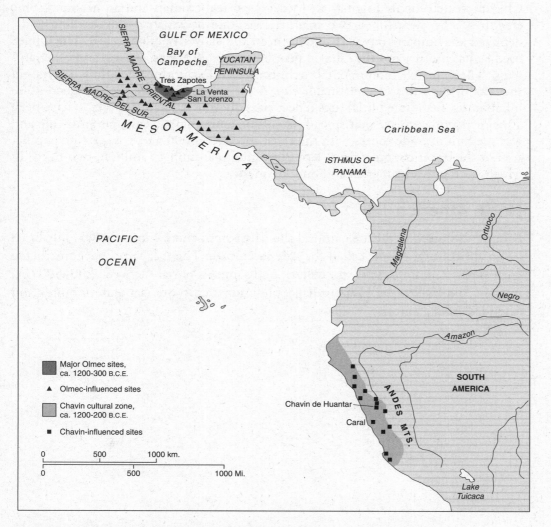

Olmec and Chavin Societies. The earliest known American states arose in Mesoamerica and the Andes. The Olmecs and Chavín both endured for a millennium.

Valley some nineteen pyramids are scattered over 35 square miles. The population is estimated at 20,000 in the valley and possibly 3000 at the central site, **Caral**, considered the Americas' first known city. Pyramids looked not unlike those in Sumer with staircases leading to an atrium-like platform. Caral seems to have been a thriving metropolis with dwellings, squares, and pyramids. The elite groups of priests, planners, and builders lived in large well-kept rooms atop the pyramid, the craftsmen lived in ground-level apartments, and the workers lived in outlying neighborhoods. Caral also became a major hub of trade routes both up and down the coast and into the Andes and Amazonian rainforest. No implements of warfare have been found. The Caral peoples developed a **quipu** (knotted textiles) system of recording, possibly to register tribute and business of state (later adopted by the Inca), musical instruments like flutes, and processes of mummification as in Egypt. About 2100 B.C.E. Caral seems to have been abandoned, possibly due to drought.

Did You Know?

The geography of South America produced two environments conducive to agriculture: 1) arid coastal valleys and 2) highlands or **altiplano** between the two major chains of the Andes.

In the altiplano, an urban society, the **Chavin**, emerged above 10,000 feet about the same time as the Olmecs, around 1200 B.C.E. and collapsed by 200 B.C.E. The Chavin created highly original art focusing on real animals and anthropomorphic creatures. They worshiped two main deities, one of which is the "smiling god," depicted as a human body with a feline head and clawed hands and feet. The Olmec used jaguar motifs, and the Chavin peoples venerated eagles, snakes, and other animals. They created monumental architecture and sculpture including a pyramid that sits in the ruins of their major city. At its height, the city probably had 3000 inhabitants. Elaborate burial sites reflect class division. Chavin appears to have been a major regional power that spread its culture and religious cults far and wide and was the hub of trade routes with the coast. Between 4000 and 1 B.C.E. the population of the Americas grew from 1 or 2 million to around 15 million, two-thirds of which were in Mesoamerica and South America.

North America

Around 2000 B.C.E. the area around the Mississippi and Ohio rivers was inhabited by an agricultural people called the **Adena culture**. The Adena people constructed great earthen mounds, some for defense and some for burial. Between 200–500 C.E. in the Ohio Valley, the **Hopewell** people built even more elaborate mounds and extended Adena culture.

Metallurgy and the Development of Early Civilization

(ca. 3000 B.C.E.–500 B.C.E.)

TIMELINE	
4000 B.C.E.	Bronze technology in Southwest Asia
2900 B.C.E.–1000 B.C.E.	Minoans, Mycenaeans, Dorians (Greece)
2500 B.C.E.–500 B.C.E.	Non Nok Tha and Dong Son peoples (Southeast Asia)
2000 B.C.E.–1122 B.C.E.	Xia and Shang Dynasties (China)
1600 B.C.E.	Iron Age Technology
1500 B.C.E.–200 B.C.E.	Vedic Age (India)
1400 B.C.E.–1200 B.C.E.	Hittites (Southwest Asia)

DEVELOPMENT OF CIVILIZATION IN THE MEDITERRANEAN BASIN, CHINA, AND SOUTHEAST ASIA

Metallurgy seems to have developed simultaneously both independently and as a result of technology diffusion in many parts of the globe. Early Mesoamerican and Peruvian civilizations used copper for tools; gold and silver were used for adornment. African populations worked iron. For agricultural civilizations, metallurgy's primary effect was on the development of agriculture. Metal hoes, plows, and other implements proved useful to both agricultural and nomadic societies. Pastoral societies, particularly in Eurasia, utilized metallurgy for weapons. This resulted in the conquest of earlier civilizations and then the development of new ones. This was particularly true as it affected history in the Mediterranean area, China, Southeast Asia, and India.

Around 4000 B.C.E. copper was mixed with tin to make **bronze**. This gave rise to a specialized group of artisans. Bronze production occurred around the Black Sea and in Southwest Asia. Use of metal allowed faster manufacture of a greater variety of tools than those of stone or bone. But sources of tin were scarce. Afghanistan was the source of tin for Mesopotamia. By the late Bronze Age, Afghanistan and probably Britain were the sources of tin traded in Egypt and Eastern Mediterranean societies. The scarcity of tin stimulated long-distance trade.

Mediterranean Basin

By 2900–2100 B.C.E. trade had become a motivation for extensive development of sea routes. Minoan society in particular was influenced by this development. The **Minoans** developed a civilized society on the island of **Crete** and traded widely with both Mesopotamia and Egypt. Copying art and architectural forms, math, and the alphabet, the Minoans developed important new artistic styles that are reflected in the colossal palace they built at the city of **Knossos**. Minoan navies carried their culture to Greece, giving rise to a new civilization called Mycenae.

The **Mycenaeans** were **Indo-European** invaders who spoke a language related to Greek. They entered Greece from the north about 1900 B.C.E and built fortress cities at Sparta, Thebes, Athens, and Tiryns. From these settlements on the mainland, early Greek chieftains advanced throughout the lands around the Aegean Sea. The most famous of these assaults was the siege of the city of **Troy**, probably around 1200 B.C.E., described in the great Greek epic poems *The Iliad* and *The Odyssey* by **Homer**. In *The Iliad*, the Mycenaean king Agamemnon kills the Trojan hero Hector, and in *The Odyssey*, Odysseus, a soldier who fought in the Trojan wars, makes an adventurous trip home to Greece. In both stories wisdom is the source of power and victory. In modern times these stories were regarded as myths until **Heinrich Schliemann** excavated ruins at Troy and Mycenae in the late 1800s.

About 1700 B.C.E. the civilized world, extending from the Aegean to the Indus, was overrun by nomadic conquerors. The success of these conquests was closely linked with an important advance in the technique of warfare, the **chariot**. The earliest known chariots were found in Central Asian burial mounds in what is now **Kazakhstan**. Mobility, firepower, and armor favored the charioteers. The weakness of charioteer warfare lay in the expense of the equipment. Bronze weapons and armor, horses, and the skilled leatherwork and carpentry required to construct a serviceable chariot were possible for only a few. The chariot age, therefore, was an age of military **aristocracy**, or rule by an elite upper class.

In Southwest Asia, the significance of chariot warriors was not so great as the civilizations were more firmly rooted. The invaders soon adopted the customs of the places they conquered. Some were absorbed into the civilization. For example, from the western end of the Fertile Crescent, the Hyksos invaded Egypt but were driven out by 1570 B.C.E. The Mycenaeans crossed from Central Asia into Greece and were absorbed into the Minoan culture. They, in turn, were overcome in 1200 B.C.E. and 1100 B.C.E. by the **Dorians**, nomadic peoples who became part of the Greek synthesis.

China

Although the **Xia (Hsia) Dynasty**, ca. 2000 to ca. 1600 B.C.E., may have used chariots and bronze, the charioteer invasion of the **Shang Dynasty** left a lasting and indelible record. The Shang, 1752 B.C.E. to 1122 B.C.E., the first Chinese dynasty that can be fully documented, began about the same time the Harappan Society was collapsing and Hammurabi ruled in Babylon. Like the Tigris and Euphrates, Nile and Indus Rivers, the Huang He or the Yellow River in northern China deposits a rich layer of **loess**, especially at the Ordos bulge, as it flows from its highland source in the Tibetan plateau to the sea. From ancient times, controlling the river by building and maintaining dikes and canals was a major preoccupation of leaders such as the semilegendary founder of China's first kingdom, **Yu** of the Xia (Hsia) Dynasty. By 1500 B.C.E. one of the tribes of the area, the Shang, predominated.

The Shang monarch was seen as the intermediary between the Supreme Being and ordinary mortals. His kingdom was viewed as the center of the world and he directed the affairs of state and bore ritual responsibility for abundant harvests and the well-being of his subjects. While he was served by a sizable **bureaucracy**, or government officials in the court, most of the peasant and artisan population of the kingdom was governed by **vassal** retainers.

In Shang society, peasants worked the land or were servants of aristocratic families. It is likely that slaves were artisans engaged in the manufacture of products that required a high degree of skill, such as weaving silk and casting bronze, both important inventions of this period. Peasants generally lived in modified **nuclear families** composed of husband, wife, children, and perhaps a grandmother or cousin, while the aristocrats lived in **extended families** consisting of several generations. The family **patriarch**, or the oldest male, ruled the family.

Shang artistic expression reached its peak in the ornately carved and expertly cast bronze vessels used to make offerings to ensure plentiful harvests. Concern for fruitful harvests led the Shang elite to put great stock in the predictions of the **shaman** priests whose prognostications were based on the **oracle bones**, or readings inscribed on bones and shells. Like Egyptian hieroglyphics, Chinese writing was **pictographic**. Over time, the number of characters increased substantially and united the diverse peoples of the region who spoke an array of languages, but understood the meaning of Chinese symbols within the content of their own language. Just as the symbol 5 refers to the word *cinco* in Spanish and five in English, Chinese pictographic symbols convey an idea to peoples with different languages and dialects.

> **Important Point**
>
> Wades-Giles spellings appear in this book in parentheses following the Pinyin version. Chinese words commonly used in English have one spelling.

The problem of transliterating Chinese characters into English has led to two systems—**Pinyin** and **Wade-Giles**. The newer Pinyin system, which was adopted by the People's Republic of China, is used in periodicals, newspapers, and books about modern China. The older Wade-Giles system is still used in Taiwan and in all English-language publications before 1979.

Southeast Asia

The Bronze Age reached Southeast Asia even before it reached China. By 2500 B.C.E. people in the **Non Nok Tha** culture in ancient Thailand were making bronze tools and implements. Bronze working reached its height around 500 B.C.E. in Vietnam when the **Dong Son** people created huge bronze drums decorated with beautiful designs.

IRON TECHNOLOGY AND THE DEVELOPMENT OF MILITARY EMPIRES

Iron was probably an accidental by-product of smelting copper or lead in the **Hittite** Empire in present Anatolia (Turkey). Its widespread use began about 1200 B.C.E., following the Hittite decline. The abundance of iron made it cheaper and more accessible, but the necessary technology made it more complex to produce. It had to be heated to higher temperatures and worked rather than poured.

The first major consequence of iron was that it set off another wave of barbarian invasions. The second consequence was economic. Sickles, plowshares, and other related agricultural tools were made with iron. This increased the efficiency of agriculture. The search for new sources of iron ore led to trade and exploration and, thus, spread civilization. It also led to large territorial states, or **empires** that incorporated conquered peoples. The **Assyrian** Empire and the **Persian** Empire are illustrative of the Iron Age. They built on and spread the legacies of the early civilizations, utilized metallurgy both in the military and civilian sectors, and created large imperial states that set the course of later civilizations in the area.

In Southwest Asia, the Hittites were the first people to work iron and spread the use of iron tools throughout the area. By about 1400 B.C.E. the Hittite kings, after many battles with Babylonians and others, extended their rule over a wide area between the Mediterranean and Black Seas. Yet they were weakened by conflict. About 1200 B.C.E. the Hittites were overwhelmed by barbarians. By 800 B.C.E., however, a line of energetic Assyrian kings brought all of Mesopotamia under their rule, creating a vast empire. From their capital at **Nineveh**, they ruled by force, relying on the military and terror to hold it together. In 612 B.C.E., the Assyrians were overthrown, and by 546 B.C.E. the Persians reconquered the area and created a new empire. The successful overthrow of the Assyrians was in part due to the **cavalry** revolution that occurred in the **steppes** (the plains of Eurasia) about this time. By mounting horses, bow in hand, whole tribes of nomads acquired mobility and striking power that hitherto had been reserved only for the aristocratic charioteers. The successful cavalry raids of the Cimmerians and Scythians encouraged revolt by rebellious Babylonians and other dissatisfied subjects for the final overthrow of the Assyrian state.

Vedic Age

Metallurgy and Aryan migrations gave definition to Indian society as well. Steppe nomads called Aryans, who spoke an Indo-European language called **Sanskrit**, used the **Khyber** and **Bolan Passes** through the **Hindu Kush** mountain range to migrate into India as early as 1500 B.C.E. The Aryans claimed the land that had been the Indus Valley civilization, where they began to settle down and practice agriculture. Some of the native **Dravidians** were conquered; others moved south. Knowledge of this aristocratic charioteer "heroic age" of Indian history can be found in the *Rig Veda*, the oldest religious writings in the world, and the *Mahabharata*, a vast epic poem describing heroic battles between horse-drawn charioteers. The other great epic poem of India is the *Ramayana*, a story of heroic Rama and his wife Sita.

BHAGAVAD GITA (MAHABHARATA)

The spirit that is in all being is immortal in them all: for the death of what cannot die, cease thou to sorrow.

Think thou also of thy duty and do not waver. There is no greater good for a warrior than to fight in righteous war.

There is a war that opens the doors of heaven, Arjuna! Happy the warrior whose fate is to fight such war.

But to forgo this fight for righteousness is to forgo thy duty and honor: is to fall into transgression.

The two greatest epics of Indian literature, the Mahabharata and the Ramayana, began to take form about 400 to 200 B.C.E. The Mahabharata is one of the longest epic poems in world literature. It describes an 18-day struggle between rival families for the throne of a kingdom in northern India. The most famous section is called the Bhagavad Gita. Its message is a religious one—that life is a never-ending journey toward perfection, a perfection that can be attained only by following the codes of conduct of one's caste. In this case, Arjuna is cautioned to fulfill the duties of the warrior caste.

By 900 B.C.E. the use of iron spread to South Asia. As in Southwest Asia, poor men protected themselves with iron weapons. New iron tools were used to clear the jungle, especially in the **Ganges River** Valley with its abundant **monsoons** (seasonal winds from the Indian Ocean that bring the summer rains essential to agriculture in South and East Asia). There, rice cultivation, with its higher yields and permanent fields, brought a full-fledged agricultural civilization into being.

Caste

Centralized monarchies supported by courtly centers, high artisan skills, and interregional trade between the Indus and Ganges Valley developed. The unique character of the emergent Indian civilization centered on **Jati** or **castes** (a Portuguese term). The origins of the caste system are obscure, but historians speculate that it was either a principle upon which the Indus civilization was built, or a way in which Aryans maintained control of those they conquered and ruled. Castes separated the society into groups and subgroups of families who shared the same occupation, inherited the same religious duties or **dharma**, and avoided social contacts with members of other castes. At first, caste practices were not strictly observed. Caste provided a means of bringing new groups into society. New groups became new subcastes. The fragile character of the Indian state and the strength of the local prince, or **raj**, resulted in large part from caste divisions. This was because the social, economic, and cultural bond of caste was stronger than the political ties to the state. Caste also helped maintain priest-led ancient magical rites. Habits of thought related to these ceremonies gave Indian religious tradition a **transcendental**, or an abstract, metaphysical, quality.

Vedas

Surviving records of the Aryans, written in Sanskrit, an Indo-European language, describe a pantheon of deities, among whom the principal war leader and strongest personality was **Indra**, the destroyer of cities and god of thunder and storm. The similarities between the Indian pantheon of gods and those of the Greeks suggest a common ancestor. The priesthood, which developed into the **Brahman** caste, accompanied the Aryans to invoke the gods and offer sacrifice. These rituals are found in the *Vedas*, four books of sacred knowledge originally composed and recited orally in Sanskrit. The oldest, the *Rig Veda,* is a collection of hymns to the gods believed to date from 1800 B.C.E. to 1300 B.C.E. By the late Vedic period, the third century B.C.E., the Hindu gods **Shiva** and **Vishnu** prevailed as examples or manifestations of **Brahma**, the universal, eternal force, present in all things. Like fire, Brahma was said to assume many shapes like the god of creation. The many forms or gods believers worshipped were all thought to represent specific aspects of Brahma. Shiva, the god portrayed as a cosmic dancer, was the aspect of Brahma that represented destruction. Another god, Vishnu, was the aspect of Brahma that maintained and preserved what had already been created. Thus, creation, preservation, and destruction, represented by these gods, symbolized the eternal, repeating cycle of life.

Much of Indian society, however, was unwilling to cede authority to the Brahman (or Brahmin) caste. A rival religious tradition based on **asceticism** developed. This largely oral tradition recorded in the *Upanishads* conceives the end of religious life as a quest for release from a cycle of rebirths, or **reincarnations**, by a process of self-annihilation in the All. The truly holy man did not need priests but could find this Truth in self-discipline, meditation, and asceticism. The merger of the Vedic and Upanishadic religious tradition marks the birth of **Hinduism** (a word derived from the word *Hindustan*, which means riverland).

Regional Interaction

(ca. 1000 B.C.E.–600 B.C.E.)

TIMELINE	
9000 B.C.E.–3000 B.C.E.	Dessication in the Sahara
6500 B.C.E.	Indo-European migrations
4300 B.C.E.	Domestication of the horse
3000 B.C.E.–1 B.C.E.	Hebrews
2000 B.C.E.–1000 B.C.E.	Phoenicians (Lebanon)
1000 B.C.E.–672 B.C.E.	Kush (Sudan)
900 B.C.E.–200 C.E.	Nok (Nigeria)
500 B.C.E.–1000 C.E	Bantu migrations (Africa)

COMMERCIAL INTERACTION

Kush

Largely due to expansion efforts of the early civilizations, new civilization centers grew up along the fringes of the early ones. These new civilizations used and improved on the innovations and cultural patterns of the early civilizations and often became conduits of interaction and exchange. To the south of Egypt, the kingdom of **Kush** (present-day Sudan) had become an independent state by 1000 B.C.E. In 715 B.C.E. the Kushites conquered Egypt, but their bronze weapons were no match for the Assyrian iron weapons, so they lost Egypt to the Assyrians in 672 B.C.E. Learning iron technology from the Assyrians, the Kushites established a new capital at **Meroe**, very likely because it was rich in iron deposits. The development of iron agricultural tools and weapons made Kush a powerful economic and military force. The people of Meroe also developed a phonetic alphabet and domesticated the elephant. Enterprising traders, the Kushites traded with East Africa, Arabia, and India from ports on the Red Sea.

The Phoenicians

The **Phoenicians** emerged around 2000 B.C.E. on the eastern Mediterranean coast of present-day Lebanon. They shared this coast with other peoples, including the **Lydians**, who migrated from Greece and are remembered in the West for developing the use of coined money. Tyre, Sidon, Byblos, and Beirut were all ancient Phoenician cities. Phoenicians acquired fame throughout the Mediterranean because of a vivid purple dye they produced from shellfish. The color, used in elegant clothing, came to symbolize royalty in Western civilizations. Phoenicians made their living as traders, shipbuilders, sailors, and colonizers. They gradually extended a network of markets across the Mediterranean Basin, along the Atlantic coast as far north as England, and south around the tip of Africa. The Phoenicians borrowed the Babylonian numbering system based on 60, which they introduced to others in the course of their trade. Their most famous colony, **Carthage**, would challenge Rome in the Punic Wars for control of the Mediterranean.

The most significant and lasting contribution of the Phoenicians to world history was their development of a phonetic alphabet. Because of their location, Phoenicians became acquainted with both Egyptian hieroglyphics and Sumerian cuneiform. By 1000 B.C.E. they had developed **phonograms**, a simplified method of writing using 22 consonants that symbolized sounds. Even today, Hebrew and Arabic languages use a writing system without vowels. Unlike the Egyptian system, the Phoenician symbols and the sounds they symbolized were fairly easy to learn and enabled more people to sound out words and understand the message. Thus, reading became less the exclusive activity of a few select scribes. The Greeks later added vowels to the Phoenician consonants that developed into the alphabet for all western European languages.

Southeast Asia

In Southeast Asia a lively seagoing trade developed. Using the monsoon winds and boats with sails, people easily traveled the waters between South Asia and the islands of Indonesia. During this period, mariners very likely reached Australia where they encountered the **Aborigines**, who had probably arrived during the Ice Age when the islands of Indonesia and Australia were connected. There the Aborigines developed a unique hunter-gatherer culture. Among their beliefs was **Dreamtime** when great ancestors walked the earth. The ancestors' spirit lived in all things and their life force continued to be passed on to new generations.

RELIGIOUS DIASPORA

Besides trade and war, religion was a vehicle of regional interaction. The **Hebrews** trace their origins to a nomadic herder named **Abraham** from the Sumerian city of Ur. According to the **Old Testament**, Abraham left Sumer at the command of his God, **Yahweh** (Jehovah), to found a new nation in **Canaan**, between the Jordan River and the Mediterranean Sea. **Jacob** led his descendants to Egypt during a famine. Later they were enslaved by the pharaohs. The book of **Exodus** in the Old Testament describes how **Moses** led the Hebrews out of Egypt about 1240 B.C.E. and traveled to **Mount Sinai** where he received the **Ten Commandments** from God. The Hebrews regarded the Ten Commandments as a **covenant,** or solemn promise, to worship Yahweh and to follow His religious and moral laws as His chosen people. The **Torah**, the first five books of the Old Testament, contains the Law of Moses that requires ethical conduct and belief in one God, **ethical monotheism**. By 1021 B.C.E. a leader named **Saul** united the Hebrew tribes under a single government and became the first king. His successor, **David**, built his capital at **Jerusalem**. David's son, **Solomon**, equipped with chariots, established trade networks, especially with the Phoenicians. Solomon built a huge blast furnace to smelt copper ore from the mines of the nearby Sinai. The copper provided him with a valuable export, but neither it nor the taxes levied on caravans were enough to cover expenses of his building programs, which included the temple in Jerusalem. To make up the difference, taxes and **corvee labor** were imposed. (Corvee labor is work required of those who could not pay their taxes in money or goods.) When Solomon died, the ten northern tribes revolted and became the kingdom of **Israel**. The two southern tribes united as the kingdom of **Judah**. By the 700s B.C.E., Assyria destroyed the ten tribes of Israel and Judah became a vassal state. When the new Babylonian Empire defeated Assyria, the Hebrews from Judah were led off into captivity. In Babylon, the Hebrew **prophets** reminded the captive people of the word of God and that a savior, or **Messiah**, would come. These religious wanderings illustrate an important aspect of cultural diffusion that took place at this time. The Hebrews absorbed and diffused metal technology and introduced the idea of monotheism far and wide.

THE TEN COMMANDMENTS

I am the Lord thy God. . . Thou shalt have no other gods before Me. . .
Thou shalt not make unto thee a graven image . . .
Thou shalt not take the name of the Lord thy God in vain. . .
Remember the Sabbath day, to keep it holy . . .
Honor thy father and thy mother. . .
Thou shalt not murder.
Thou shalt not commit adultery.
Thou shalt not steal.
Thou shalt not bear false witness. . .
Thou shalt not covet. . .

The Ten Commandments are important because they provide the ethical basis for both Judaism and Christianity. Their origins appear to be with the fundamental event in Hebrew history—Moses' leadership of the Hebrews from bondage in Egypt ca. thirteenth century B.C.E. The Hebrew god Yahweh ("he causes to be"), or Jehovah, appeared to Moses on Mount Sinai and made a "covenant," or formal contract, with the Hebrews to the effect that if the Hebrews followed the commandments, they would become the "Chosen People" of God. The Ten Commandments are more like Confucian thought than Hindu, Buddhist, and Daoist thought in the sense that the emphasis is on an ordering of human relationships rather than on mysticism, love, and Heaven. The first four commandments deal with the Hebrews' relationship with God, and the last six with their relationships with each other. As a Jew, Jesus embraced the Ten Commandments but added to them the idea of brotherly love, forgiveness, and the promise of a spiritual kingdom "not of this world." The Ten Commandments are commonly contained in the Book of Exodus, one of the Five Books of Moses that make up the Torah.

ECOLOGY, ENVIRONMENT, AND MIGRATION— AFRICA, EURASIA, AND LATIN AMERICA

The history of sub-Saharan Africa at this time demonstrates another aspect of regional interaction. Environmental change isolated the area from the crossroads of Southwest Asia and produced a situation in which all the changes of the period from agriculture to metallurgy were diffused into Africa from the outside at a later date. Beginning about 9000 B.C.E., the area of the Sahara Desert began to dry and by 3000 B.C.E. much of the area was desert. This **desiccation** caused populations to move either north toward the Mediterranean or south into the Sudanic region of Africa that is composed of dry **sahel** and grassy **savannas**.

The **Bantu migrations**, which took place ca. 500 B.C.E. to 1000 C.E., spread agriculture and iron making throughout Africa. These Bantu peoples probably originated in eastern Nigeria and moved first to central Sudan and then along the Congo into the forests of West and Central Africa, East Africa, and south along the Zambezi River into Zimbabwe and South Africa. About 90 percent of the languages south of a line from the Blight of Benin to Somalia are part of the Bantu family. The migration was probably set in motion by an increase in population due to farming and the desiccation of the Sahara. The early Bantu depended on agriculture and fishing and were village dwellers who organized their societies around kinship. Over a thousand years, the Bantu expanded over much of the continent, carrying with them agriculture, cattle raising, and iron technology.

Agriculture

Agriculture may have developed independently in Africa, but many scholars believe that the spread of agriculture and iron technology came from the centers of civilization in Mesopotamia. The first domesticated crops in Africa were millets and sorghums whose origins are in West Africa. Livestock also came from outside Africa. Horses were apparently introduced by the Hyksos and the camel from the Arabian peninsula, around the first century C.E.

Iron Technology

Iron technology probably entered either with the Phoenicians, who carried it to Carthage in North Africa and then along the coast, or by land across the Sahara into Nigeria, Ghana, and Mali, or by way of Ethopia where iron objects can be dated to 800 B.C.E. Iron represented power, and the blacksmith who made tools and weapons had an important place in society. One of the earliest iron-casting cultures of West Africa were the Nok people who thrived in the central part of Nigeria between 900 B.C.E. and 200 C.E. Nok artisans produced beautiful terra cotta (baked, unglazed pottery) sculptures of human and animal figures.

Pastoralism

Another aspect of ecology that significantly affected the movements of peoples especially in **Eurasia** was the nature of **pastoralism**. Nomadic societies lived together in small groups following their herds. Overpopulation or weather conditions unfavorable to grazing could unhinge the fragile balance between numbers of pastoralists and finite land areas.

Pastoral nomads that were concentrated mostly in the grasslands of Eurasia and the Sahara desert region, needed vast amounts of land for grazing. The balance between population and territory was a delicate one that could easily be upset by weather, infiltration of neighboring tribes, or a growing population. Pastoralists generally lived along the borders of settled societies and developed their own cultures centered around animals like horses (domesticated in Central Asia ca. 4300 B.C.E.),

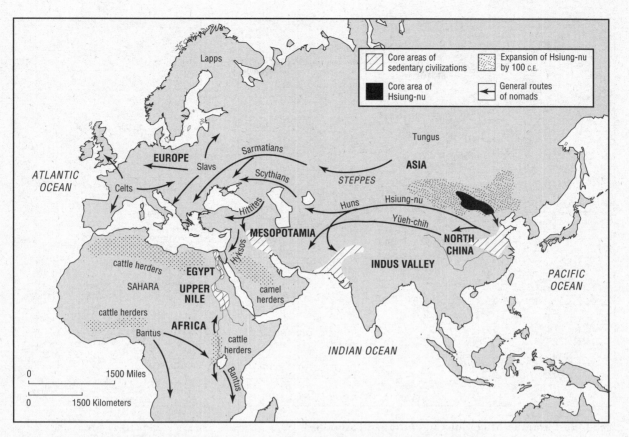

The Earliest Civilizations and the Migrations of Nomadic Peoples Beginning 2000 B.C.E. All of the earliest civilizations succumbed to the invasion of nomadic people. Nomadic people like the Hyksos had the advantage of mobility (the horse) and superior weaponry (bronze and iron technology) on their side. Nomadic people often destroyed existing societies but they also spread civilization.

camels (domesticated ca. 3000 or 2500 B.C.E. in Arabia), and dress and ceremony connected with a nomadic lifestyle. Among the pastoralists that had a great impact on world history at this time were the **Indo-Europeans**, a term derived from the common language of those peoples. Indo-Europeans originated most likely near the Caucasus mountains and expansion apparently occurred in several waves. Indo-Europeans may have moved into Europe ca. 6500 B.C.E. and possibly were the ancestors of the Celts and Greeks. Population increase, disease, drought, prolonged frost, or invasion may have precipitated another wave of movement ca. 3000 B.C.E. As the tribes dispersed driving their herds of cattle, sheep, goats, horses and camels, they encountered settled populations and often, as discussed, turned to conquest, which resulted in the dispersion of a family language group and a mixing of populations.

Large migrations of Eurasian pastoralists are particularly evident during three periods of history.

- The first began ca. 2000 B.C.E. when various Eurasian tribal movements resulted in the weakening of early civilizations like those in Mesopotamia, Egypt, the Indus Valley, Minoan Greece, and China.

- The second occurred ca. 400 C.E. to 800 C.E. when Asiatic tribes appear to have moved west out of the steppes pushing each other in a tidal wave that eventually overwhelmed the Roman Empire.

- The third and last wave was the Mongols ca. 1200 C.E. to 1400 C.E.

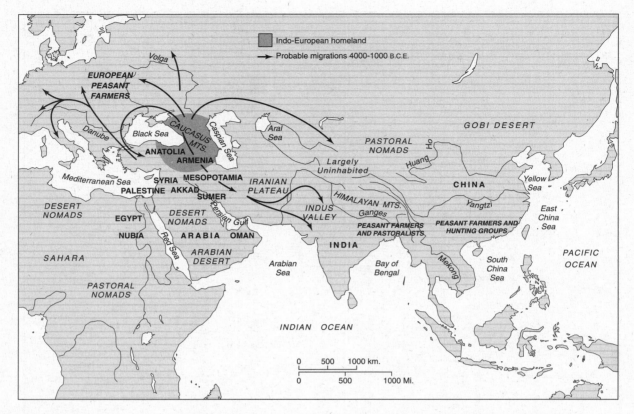

The Indo-European Migrations and Eurasian Pastoralism. Some societies, especially in parts of Africa and Asia, adapted to environmental contexts by developing a pastoral, or animal-herding, economy. One large pastoral group, the Indo-Europeans, eventually expanded from their home area into Europe, southwestern Asia, Central Asia, and India.

Environmental Factors

Early Andean and Southwestern U.S. societies seem also to have been vulnerable to environmental change. The Moche ca. 200 B.C.E. to 600 C.E. met environmental challenges that weakened their society. These included severe *El Ninos* (the periodic warm water currents in the Pacific that can bring higher temperatures, torrential rain, drought, and earthquakes). Moche leaders may have responded to resulting food shortages by increasing warfare and human sacrifice to appease the gods. The end result was the collapse of the Moche civilization and migrations of peoples elsewhere. A similar fate seems to have occurred to the Peruvian Aymara peoples at Tihuanaco. The Aymaras established an intricate irrigation system based on irrigation canals fed from the high Andes that were 400 percent more productive than the farming in the region today. Tihuanaco was abandoned by 1100 C.E. perhaps because of climate change that generated a drought so severe that rivers dried up. Along the Ohio River, the Hopewell culture rose ca. 200 B.C.E. to 50 B.C.E. The Hopewell constructed earthworks and engineering projects including a maze of 20-foot-wide canals that allowed them to reach both the Atlantic and Gulf coasts. The Hopewell practiced intensive agriculture, but between 300 and 600 C.E. they began to decline perhaps because of overpopulation that put stress on the land, a diminished maize crop due to a cooling climate, or the introduction of the bow and arrow into the region that stimulated warfare. The Anasazi seemed to have suffered a similar fate. When drought disturbed the fragile canyon maize-growing environment, the peoples dispersed. **Deforestation** is another part of the environmental story in world history. Europe was essentially extensive forest but between 500 and 1600 C.E. trees were cut to create agricultural land.

Unit Review

Cross-Regional Developments

Developments that occurred over wide regions of the globe during this period include

- the development of agricultural surpluses that created complex societies called civilizations;

- the invention of writing systems;

- metallurgy: first copper, then bronze, then iron;

- innovations in the military techniques of nomadic people like the chariot and cavalry that allowed them to attack the settled populations with impunity;

- the creation of larger states called empires with their bureaucracies and law codes;

- the diffusion of innovations by means of trade, migration, and invasion;

- the spread of Indo-Europeans across Europe and Asia;

- the origins of the Hindu and Jewish religions;

- the Bantu migrations from Nigeria into central and south Africa.

Legacies

The legacies of this period in world history are numerous:

- improvements in agriculture from irrigation to implements like plows and sickles appeared;

- the development of forms of political systems like kingdoms and empires occurred;

- specialization that led to greater artisanship and trade;

- writing systems that preserved records and knowledge;

- scientific and mathematical innovations that led to great building projects like temples, pyramids, and ziggurats, and walled cities with paved streets and sewers;

- metallurgy that progressed from copper to bronze to iron;

- new religious systems were developed that were more human oriented;

- military techniques and weapons were developed that brought the horse, chariot, and organized state armies to the fore;

- civilization spread.

The basis was set for the classical period.

Quiz

Unscramble:

Arrange the following in chronological order.

Phoenicia; Kush; Nok; Bronze Age; Iron Age; Aryan India; Shang Dynasty; New Kingdom Egypt

Matching:

E 1. Alluvial
G 2. Loess
F 3. Etesian winds
H 4. Altiplano
K 5. El Niños
I 6. Steppes
B 7. Monsoons
D 8. Desiccation
C 9. Prophets
L 10. Yahweh
A 11. Sahel
J 12. Savanna

A. Dry lands of Africa
B. Seasonal winds from the Indian Ocean that bring summer rains to India
C. Reminded Hebrews of the word of God
D. Land turning to desert
E. Soil or silt deposited after floods
F. Winds that pushed sailing ships upstream against the Nile
G. Rich, yellow brown soil deposits which give the Huang Ho (Yellow River) its name
H. Highlands of the Andes
I. Plains of Eurasia
J. Grasslands of Africa
K. Warm water currents in the Pacific that bring higher temperatures, torrential rains, and droughts
L. Jehovah

Questions:

1. Which technology ended chariot warfare?

   (A) bronze.
   (B) armor.
   (C) cavalry.
   (D) iron.
   (E) quipu.

2. Which is the great epic poem of Sumerian history?

   (A) *Bhagavad Gita*
   (B) *Mahabharata*
   (C) *Gilgamesh*
   (D) *The Iliad*
   (E) *Ramayana*

3. The development and widespread use of iron led to improved agricultural tools and weapons, giving a technological advantage to those societies that possessed the metal. The people responsible for the development of iron were the

   (A) Egyptians.
   (B) Babylonians.
   (C) Assyrians.
   (D) Hittites.
   (E) Phoenicians.

4. The archaeologist who provided evidence to prove that Troy was more than Homer's mythical tale was

    (A) Howard Carter.
    (B) Heinrich Schliemann.
    (C) Richard Leakey.
    (D) Donald Johanson.
    (E) Jean Champollion.

5. Indian religion shaped society through beliefs in the transcendental nature of life with its endless cycle of rebirths or reincarnations. The Hindu god that usually represents destruction is

    (A) Indra.
    (B) Brahma.
    (C) Shiva.
    (D) Vishnu.
    (E) Rama.

6. Which civilization was shaped socially by a belief in castes?

    (A) Minoan
    (B) Egyptian
    (C) Olmec
    (D) Indian
    (E) Chinese

7. Which leader was the first to establish an empire in world history?

    (A) Ramses II
    (B) Hammurabi
    (C) Yu
    (D) Saul
    (E) Sargon

8. Which text establishes the belief in ethical monotheism?

    (A) *Rig Veda*
    (B) *Torah*
    (C) *Gilgamesh*
    (D) *Mahabharata*
    (E) *Hammurabi's Code*

9. Which society possessed neither iron nor bronze?

    (A) Nok
    (B) Olmec
    (C) Kush
    (D) Aryan
    (E) Assyrian

10. Based on biblical accounts, which of the following combinations is in the correct chronological order?

    I. Solomon built the temple
    II. Abraham left Sumer for Canaan
    III. Jacob migrated to Egypt to avoid famine
    IV. Moses received the Ten Commandments on Mount Sinai
    V. The Hebrews were enslaved in Babylon where the Prophets reminded them of the promise of a Messiah.

    (A) II. III. IV. I. V.
    (B) II. V. I. III. IV.
    (C) V. II. I. III. IV.
    (D) II. IV. I. III. V.
    (E) III. IV. V. II. I.

11. Which early civilization is mismatched with its urban center?

    (A) Jerusalem—Hebrew
    (B) Meroe—Kush
    (C) Knossos—Shang
    (D) Caral—Norte Chico Peru
    (E) Ur—Sumer

12. Chariot warfare developed along with the development of

    (A) iron.
    (B) bows and arrows.
    (C) domestication of horses.
    (D) bronze.
    (E) peasant armies.

13. Which of the following statements about writing systems is FALSE?

    (A) Mesopotamian cuneiform began as pictures but changed into wedge-shaped symbols written with a stylus on a wet clay tablet.
    (B) Indus Valley writing was adapted from Mesopotamian cuneiform.
    (C) The Phoenician alphabet combined sound symbols to reproduce the spoken word.
    (D) Chinese hieroglyphics combined pictographs and ideograms into a system first carved into bone and later painted on silk.
    (E) Egyptian hieroglyphics originated as pictures but later included ideograms and phonetic symbols written on papyrus.

14. The first civilization to develop a legal code in which laws were arranged systematically by topic was

    (A) Egypt.
    (B) Mesopotamia.
    (C) Mesoamerica.
    (D) Peru.
    (E) the Indus Valley.

15. Terraced mud-brick temples in Mesopotamia that are thought to have served as warehouses for grain storage were

    (A) pyramids.
    (B) ziggurats.
    (C) mosques.
    (D) stupas.
    (E) basilicas.

16. Egyptian pharaohs of the Old Kingdom exercised unusual authority over their subjects because

    (A) they served as military commanders of a highly successful army.
    (B) they were respected for developing a lucrative trade with Mesopotamia, Crete, and Palestine.
    (C) they were worshipped as gods who ruled the society through an extensive theocracy.
    (D) they were recognized as the ruler by the royal family and nobility.
    (E) they inherited their position in the dynastic order through their father's family.

Bhagavad Gita

The spirit that is in all being is immortal in them all: for the death of what cannot die, cease thou to sorrow.

Think thou also of thy duty and do not waver. There is no greater good for a warrior than to fight in righteous war.

There is a war that opens the doors of heaven, Arjuna! Happy the warrior whose fate is to fight such war.

But to forgo this fight for righteousness is to forgo thy duty and honor: is to fall into transgression.

---

17. This excerpt from the *Bhagavad Gita*

    (A) reflects the Hindu belief that life is a journey toward perfection that can be attained by fulfilling the responsibilities of one's Dharma.
    (B) exemplifies the Shang Dynasty belief that there is no greater good for a warrior than a just fight.
    (C) portrays the history of Sargon's quest to establish the world's first empire in the fertile crescent.
    (D) is a segment of the first epic poem in world history.
    (E) describes the sacred duty of a warrior in the Egyptian rebellion against the Hyksos in 1580 B.C.E.

18. Which of the following societies developed a lasting concept of transcendentalism?

    (A) Hebrew
    (B) Egyptian
    (C) Non Nok Tha
    (D) Hindu
    (E) Chinese

19. Through the Ten Commandments, the Hebrews established their belief in

    (A) monotheism
    (B) polytheism
    (C) anthropomorphism
    (D) transcendentalism
    (E) brotherly love

20. What was a common physical characteristic of most earliest civilizations?

    (A) rivers that could provide water for agriculture
    (B) rainfall that encouraged the production of grain crops
    (C) a steady supply of alluvial soil
    (D) rivers that could be navigated easily
    (E) geographic barriers that provided protection from invasion

21. Empires rarely provided

    (A) specialization of jobs.
    (B) writing systems.
    (C) organized state armies.
    (D) gender equality.
    (E) systems of political order and power.

22. During the Bronze Age, military aristocracies dominated because

    (A) weapons and chariot warfare were available only to those who could afford the expensive equipment.
    (B) peasants were prohibited from owning bronze weapons.
    (C) most people were slaves.
    (D) only nobles were permitted to be warriors.
    (E) few people possessed the technological skills necessary for producing a chariot.

23. The major principle expressed in the segment of Hammurabi's Code was that

    (A) the laws were written to ensure justice.
    (B) the code ensured that the punishment fit the crime.
    (C) those who break the law will be fined.
    (D) laws are written in an organized code to establish a standard of behavior for all.
    (E) punishments are more severe for those who occupy higher positions in the class structure.

Answers

Unscramble:

Bronze Age; Phoenicia; New Kingdom Egypt; Aryan India; Shang Dynasty; Iron Age; Kush; Nok

Matching:

1. **(E)**	5. **(K)**	9. **(C)**
2. **(G)**	6. **(I)**	10. **(L)**
3. **(F)**	7. **(B)**	11. **(A)**
4. **(H)**	8. **(D)**	12. **(J)**

Questions:

1. **(D)**	7. **(E)**	13. **(B)**	19. **(A)**
2. **(C)**	8. **(B)**	14. **(B)**	20. **(A)**
3. **(D)**	9. **(B)**	15. **(B)**	21. **(D)**
4. **(B)**	10. **(A)**	16. **(C)**	22. **(A)**
5. **(C)**	11. **(C)**	17. **(A)**	23. **(B)**
6. **(D)**	12. **(D)**	18. **(D)**	

STUDY TIP

Chronology is to historians what concrete is to house construction. Chronology is the foundation. Knowing what happened first and what happened as a consequence is an essential skill to become a successful analyst. Check the timeline before reading the chapter.

Systems of Society and Culture: The Classical Age

(ca. 1000 B.C.E.–900 C.E.)

THE MEANING OF CLASSICISM

Between 1000 B.C.E. and 500 C.E., in many parts of the world, urban societies evolved to the point that they began to develop defining political, social, and cultural institutions and characteristics. Thus, for example, China began to develop patterns of thought and culture decidedly different from western Europe or India. In each case, these patterns were influenced by religious thought and traditions. Religious or philosophical thought legitimized governments, shaped class structure, and inspired the arts. These patterns became so significant that they influenced other societies and have remained important to this day in understanding cultural differences. The classical period ended between the third and sixth centuries C.E. due to internal political and economic weakness and a new surge of invasions, but classical institutions and ideas endured and have had broad influence.

Classicism, therefore, can be understood as defining and long-lasting civilizational patterns shaped by belief systems. Belief systems include both philosophies and religions. Philosophies reach truth by logic while religions seek truth by faith. Philosophies often dwell on secular concerns while religions tend toward concerns of the afterlife. Religions have priests and rituals. Both search for the meaning of life and are concerned with systems of ethics, that is, right and wrong. In some societies, like China, philosophies overshadowed religions; in others, like India, religions like Buddhism and Hinduism overshadowed philosophy. If there is a connection between the simultaneous rise of classical civilizations and the rise of the world's religions, it can probably be found in the idea that all the great religions of the world deal with patterns of ethics. Ethics tend to order human relationships. Successful ordering led to successful systems of human interaction and successful systems of society. The arts glorified beliefs in these systems. When classical civilizations reach a high point of cultural achievement, it is called a **Golden Age**.

Common to the classical experience were political systems that had institutionalized bureaucracies and armies often tied to religious hierarchies. Political leadership became systematized and legitimized by ideologies of power. Economic systems were expanding and complex, linking agriculture and commerce into large networks tied together by common coinage and rules of exchange. Wealth was created by surplus trade and expansionism. Social classes evolved into hierarchies of power, prestige, and wealth. Common also to the classical experience was a tremendous outpouring of art stimulated by increasing wealth, cultural exchange, and religious fervor. Large urban centers rose as did methods of transportation connecting them. The power and appeal of classical societies caused them to spread, often resulting in large, multinational empires.

Classical Greek and Persian Civilizations

(ca. 600 B.C.E.–200 B.C.E.)

TIMELINE	
ca. 1000 B.C.E.	Life of Zoroaster
612 B.C.E.–339 B.C.E.	Classical Hellenic Age
550 B.C.E.–331 B.C.E.	Classical Persia (Achaemenids)
499 B.C.E.–479 B.C.E.	Persian Wars (Greece and Persia)
431 B.C.E.–404 B.C.E.	Peloponnesian Wars (Athens and Sparta)
336 B.C.E.–323 B.C.E.	Alexander the Great
323 B.C.E.–30 B.C.E.	Classical Hellenistic Age

DEVELOPMENT OF THE GREEK STATE SYSTEM

One of the defining and long-lasting characteristics of Greek, or **Hellenic**, civilization was its political system. Elements of democracy (rule by the majority) reached sophisticated levels of development under the Greeks. This political system was tied to the Greek belief in rationalism. The origins of the Greek political system can be found in its early history.

Mycenae

When the Minoan civilization collapsed about 1400 B.C.E., political and commercial power in the Aegean passed to the mainland Greeks, who lived in small city-states grouped under the city of **Mycenae**. Each city-state had a king who was a military general, judge, and priest, but, unlike monarchs in Mesopotamia, his power was not absolute. He was advised by a council composed of heads of important Greek families and he lived a life not dissimilar to other Greeks, plowing his own fields and shearing his sheep.

Dorian Invasion

Shortly after 1200 B.C.E. the **Dorians**, Greek-speaking Indo-Europeans in the north, began moving south, overrunning most of Greece and overthrowing Mycenaean culture. Greece plunged into its Dark Age. The chaos and confusion led to further splintering and an exodus of Greeks to Crete and the Mediterranean coast of Southwest Asia (**Ionia**), where new communities, economically and politically independent of one another, were established.

Polis

Political decentralization, the mountainous Greek landscape, and a historical predisposition toward small states led to the most important political feature of classical Greece, the city-state, or **polis**. Not unlike today's nation-state, the polis was not just a place, but a culture around which a person's meaning and purpose revolved. The word **civic** comes closest to this meaning, that is, it formed the core of an individual's social and political meaning and responsibility. People identified themselves in terms of a community. Loyalty of individuals to their polis and the separation of the polis by geography would later deter Greek attempts to unify the city-states.

The typical city-state (polis) was composed of a city or town and the surrounding countryside of valleys and plains. **Athens**, for instance, included all the towns and villages of the peninsula of **Attica** in eastern Greece, and **Sparta** occupied the valley of a fairly large river. The men who owned the large farms, along with artisans and traders, usually lived in the city that was situated on fortified high ground for protection. Such a hill or citadel was called an **acropolis** or "highest city." The city-state was ruled by a king, who was advised by a council of elders. However, between 800 and 600 B.C.E., the kings lost most of their power to the nobility or large land-owning aristocrats. Since both officials and the council were elected by a few upper-class citizens, this kind of government was called an **oligarchy**, or rule by a few. Sometimes these oligarchs were referred to as **tyrants**, a word that denoted that a leader illegally seized power. Meanwhile, rising population and poor Greek land made Greeks, like the Minoans before them, increasingly turn to trade for a livelihood. The Greeks exported wine, olive oil, and woolen cloth and imported grain. To increase land and trade, the Greeks began founding new city-states that began to dot the Black Sea area, western Turkey, and southern Italy and France. Soon, the rising wealth of traders and the increasing impoverishment of the farmers and slaves who worked on the lands of the rich caused Athenian Greeks to challenge the power of the oligarchs. This challenge gave rise to one of the distinctive characteristics of Greek classical culture, **democracy**. In this system, government consisted of officials chosen by vote of the citizens and responsible to them.

Origins of Greek Democracy

The reasons for Athenian democracy, with its characteristics of equality and freedom of speech, seem to have originated in the economic and military nature of Greek life. In Mesopotamia, warfare was dominated by an aristocracy of charioteers, but in Greece, every citizen was also a soldier in the army or a rower in the navy. The army's strength lay in the **phalanx**, or a formation of eight ranks of infantry soldiers, in which all men marched together so closely that their large metal shields overlapped to form a wall. Here, rank and wealth mattered little. It was the free, farm-owning citizen-soldier with enough money to equip himself that provided the basis for Greek city-state security. The economic reason behind Athenian democracy was that farmers were simple townspeople who went to their fields each morning and returned in the evening. They were free men. Also, a civilization based on trade must have merchants, manufacturers, and craftsmen. Male citizens prospered and in their leisure time participated in the affairs of state alongside the aristocracy.

Hellenic Age

The **Hellenic Age** (612–339 B.C.E.) began with the process of democratization in Athens when an aristocrat, **Draco**, codified the laws for the Athenian polis and made them public. This code, though harsh, embodied the idea that the law belonged to all citizens. Then, in 594 B.C.E., the aristocrats elected **Solon** as chief magistrate or **archon**. His reforms included abolition of slavery for debt and limitations on land ownership. This served to empower the commoners, who were then given a place in the old aristocratic assembly.

Athenian Democracy

Athenian government was a **direct democracy**, meaning that all male citizens over 19 years of age were members of the **Assembly**, which voted on policy and taxes. The **Council of 500**, chosen by lot from the Assembly, served one year as a legislature. Besides this legislative branch, there were an executive and a judicial branch. **Juries** that tried all cases were made up of members of the Assembly chosen by lot. The executive branch was composed of a **commander-in-chief** and nine generals elected annually by the Assembly. Other officials were chosen by lot to serve for one year. By the process of **ostracism**, individuals considered dangerous to the state could be banished by the citizenry. The virtues of the Athenian democratic system were viewed by the Athenian leader **Pericles** in 431 B.C.E., in a funeral speech given in honor of those killed during the war with Sparta. He wrote, "Ours is an unrivaled constitution. So far from owing anything to our neighbors, it sets the standard for them. On account of its popular basis, it has come to be called *Democracy* or *Rule of the Masses*. But, in fact, we enjoy, as between man and man complete equality of legal status. In our public life individual talent is the one thing valued."

Though called a democracy, Athens was not a democracy as envisioned in the contemporary world. Women, slaves, and the foreign born could not vote. Those groups accounted for over half of the Athenian population. Nor were all Greek city-states democracies. Sparta, for instance, a state settled by Dorians in Laconia, a region of the southern Greek peninsula of **Peloponnesus**, conquered people in the region around their city-state and treated these peoples as slaves, or **helots**. About 25,000 Spartans ruled over 500,000 subjects. The powers of government rested in the hands of five selected officials called **ephors** who were aided by two kings and a council of elders. Rebellions against Spartan masters occurred; therefore, a great deal of Spartan life was directed toward creation of a strong army. When a boy was seven, he was taken away from his family and put in a military school. Spartans did not allow anyone to make a living in any other way but farming. Spartan girls had to undergo

TIP

The SAT Subject Test can include quotes and questions from secondary sources.

physical training to become healthy mothers. Sparta produced no writers or artists. When someone speaks of the "Spartan way of life," they are referring to a simple, vigorous military existence. The differences in values, lifestyles, and political systems between Greek city-states led to the end of the Greek classical age.

PERICLES' FUNERAL ORATION

Our form of government does not enter into rivalry with the institutions of others. We do not copy our neighbors, but are an example to them. It is true that we are called a democracy, for the administration is in the hands of the many not of the few. But while the law secures equal justice to all alike in their private disputes, the claim of excellence is also recognized; and when a citizen is in any way distinguished, he is preferred to the public service not as a matter of privilege, but as the reward of merit. Neither is poverty a bar, but a man may benefit his country whatever be the obscurity of his condition.

. . . For we are lovers of beauty, yet with economy, and we cultivate the mind without loss of manliness.

. . . To sum up: I say that Athens is the school of Hellas, and that the individual Athenian in his own person seems to have the power of adapting himself to the most varied forms of action and the upmost versatility and grace. . .

This speech can be compared to the Gettysburg Address in the sense that it was given while a great civil war was being waged among Greeks (the Peloponnesian Wars). It is the most eloquent statement of Athenian political and civic ideals. Pericles (ca. 494–429 B.C.E.) was the leading Athenian statesman when war broke out with Sparta in 431 B.C.E. His speech demonstrates the fundamental values and attitudes of Athenians—reverence for democracy, excellence, individualism, beauty, and love of Athens.

Persian Wars

The rise of Greece is connected with victory over the Persians. About 500 B.C.E. the Ionian Greek city-states on the eastern shores of the Mediterranean rose in revolt against their Persian master of Southwest Asia. Athens and other Greek city-states came to their defense. In revenge, the Persian king Darius decided to strike at Athens, the richest of the Greek cities, with a powerful fleet. In the **Battle of Marathon** (490 B.C.E.), which followed, the Persians landed an army on the Plain of Marathon in Greece but were defeated by the Athenians, who were led by a brilliant general, **Miltiades**. An Athenian ran the 26 miles from the Marathon plain to Athens to convey the good news, giving rise to the modern "marathon" of 26 miles. Ten years later the Persian king **Xerxes** sought revenge. At **Thermopylae**, a narrow mountain pass in Greece, the Persians massacred a Spartan army led by King Leonidas. The Persians conquered northern Greece and burned the city of Athens to the ground. They were finally stopped at the **Battle of Salamis Bay** when the Athenian fleet routed the Persian navy. Finally, Sparta and Athens joined forces to defeat the Persians at the **Battle of Plataea** in 479 B.C.E. Persian expansion into Europe halted.

Peloponnesian Wars

The battles with Persia confined Greek territory to northern Greece and the Peloponnesus. The Ionic Greek city-states on the eastern coast of the Mediterranean in Southwest Asia were lost. The continuing Persian threat resulted in a naval alliance of Greek city-states led by Athens called the **Delian League** (478 B.C.E.). In this confederation, each city-state contributed ships, men, and money. Soon, however, Athens began to demand tribute from other members of the league and to use league resources to advance its own trade, building programs, and security. As the leader of the Peloponnesian League, the Spartans became alarmed by the expansion of Athenian interests. This led to the **Peloponnesian Wars** (431–404 B.C.E.). The war pitted Athens and its allies against Sparta and its allies. Ultimately, Sparta triumphed.

Disunity among Greek city-states continued over the next 60 years. This gave **Philip of Macedon** the chance to invade. In 338 B.C.E. he destroyed a joint army of Thebes and Athens and became master of the Greek city-states. As recounted in the history of the Peloponnesian Wars by **Thucydides**, impassioned oratory by **Demosthenes** and **Isocrates** illustrated the inability of Greeks to unite successfully. Demosthenes pleaded for unity against the Macedonians, but Isocrates argued that outside rule would be preferable to continuing Greek squabbling.

CULTURAL ACHIEVEMENTS OF GREEK CIVILIZATION

Greek Polytheism

Greek **humanism** is the resounding cultural achievement of the Hellenic way of life. It permeated religion, politics, the arts, and intellectual life of Greece. Humanism refers to a system of thought and action that elevates human beings to the center of existence. Fundamental to this idea was **rationalism**, or the idea that order and beauty can be conceived, not by gods, but in the mind of man. The idea of humanism can be traced to Greek religion. The Greek gods were originally connected with nature. Thus, Poseidon was the god of the ocean and Apollo, of the sun. Gradually, they became **anthropomorphic**, that is, they took human form and characteristics. Apollo represented clarity and order, and Athena, wisdom. The many myths that surrounded the gods were stories of human struggles and lessons about life. This Greek religion was both individual and related to the polis. Individuals worshipped the gods, went to temples, and made sacrifices at altars on matters of personal concern. Gods also formed part of a social and civic life. Each polis tended to favor one deity around which festivals and celebrations revolved. Uniting all Greeks was the pantheon of major gods and the Panhellenic festivals that were held at **Olympia** in honor of Zeus and at **Delphi** in honor of Apollo. The festivities at Olympia included the athletic contests that have inspired the modern Olympic games.

Greek Drama

Greek drama had its origins in religious festivals. The plays were produced in large outdoor theaters. People listened as a method of instruction as well as entertainment. The tragedies were emotionally powerful plays built around the lives of legendary heroes and heroines. **Aeschylus** (524–456 B.C.E., *Oresteia* and *Prometheus Bound*), **Sophocles** (496–406 B.C.E., *Oedipus Rex*), and **Euripides** (ca. 480–406 B.C.E., *Trojan Women* and *Medea*), the three greatest Greek writers of tragedy, wrote dramas in which fate, frequently connected with a tragic character flaw, carried the hero from greatness to ruin. Greek comedies dealt in satire and they poked fun at political officials and prominent citizens. The most popular writer of comedies was **Aristophanes** (ca. 445–385 B.C.E.). His play *Knights* satirizes corrupt government officials, and *Clouds* ridicules philosophers. One of the greatest poets of the age was **Sappho** (b. ca. 612 B.C.E.). Her poetry, mostly about love, portrayed the complexity of the inner workings of human beings as clearly as Greek sculpture portrayed its outward contours.

Rationalism

The human quality of the popular religion of Greece is connected with the other belief system of the Greeks, especially the Athenians, that of rationalism. Rationalism is the belief that reason, or the intellect, is the true source of knowledge. Rationalist thought began with Greek observation and speculation about the natural world. The myths and epics of the Mesopotamians and Indians are ample evidence that speculation about the origin of the universe and mankind did not begin with the Greeks. The achievement of the Greeks is that they treated these questions in rational rather than mythological terms. Homer, in *The Iliad*, celebrates this faith in reason by suggesting that the Greek victory over the Trojans was due to superior brains rather than brawn. Early Greek thinkers did not distinguish between philosophy and science as their quest was for an understanding of the universe and an explanation of its principles. Thus, **Thales of Miletus** (ca. 585 B.C.E.), the so-called father of philosophy, described physical reality in terms of earth elements, thereby creating a school of philosophy called **materialist**. **Pythagoras**, a mathematician for whom a geometric theory is named (a theory previously known to the Babylonians), believed that numerical relationships formed the basic principle of the universe, giving rise to the idea of the "harmony of spheres." The distinction between philosophy and science began with **Hippocrates** (ca. 460–377 B.C.E.), the father of medicine. Hippocrates studied the human body and the effect climate and environment have on health. He separated natural science from philosophy, declaring that medicine was a separate craft. This separation was promoted also by the **Sophists**, who agreed that human beings were the proper subject of study. The Sophists traveled the Greek world teaching young men that nothing is absolute, that excellence can be taught, and that by logic and words even the laws of the polis could be questioned.

Philosophers

The Magnificent Three

Socrates
Plato
Aristotle

Socrates (ca. 470–399 B.C.E.) studied natural science but then became interested in human behavior and ethics. His fame rested on argument and the challenging of ideas through logically constructed questioning, the so-called "Socratic method." After Athens' defeat in the Peloponnesian Wars, Socrates became a scapegoat for the defeat because he had questioned the common opinions of the city's politicians. He was accused of corrupting the youth of Athens. At his trial, he was condemned to die by an Athenian jury after he refused to admit guilt. Although he could have escaped, he chose to drink the lethal dose of hemlock. He believed that as a citizen he could not defy his polis that had protected and sustained him all of his life. Although Socrates never wrote anything down, we know of his work through his pupil, Plato. **Plato** (427–347 B.C.E.) believed in the primacy of a world of immaterial forms that later provided the intellectual framework for Christian philosophy. In the book *The Republic*, Plato envisioned an ideal state ruled by philosopher-kings who were experts in the theory of forms and persons seasoned by practical experience.

Aristotle (384–322 B.C.E.), Plato's most distinguished pupil, advocated a life of moderation, or the "**Golden Mean**," to achieve personal happiness. In *Metaphysics*, he argued, contrary to Plato, that all matter was an inseparable unity of form and substance, and he sought to explain the concept of a single God. In *Poetics,* he analyzed the nature of poetry, and in *Organon,* he explored two means to acquire knowledge, the deductive and inductive. In *Politics*, he sought not a perfect state as Plato did, but a description of how government worked. He argued that the state should serve all citizens and when it was subjected to special interests, it became perverted. The concerns of philosophy and its methodology, which searched for truth through reason, supported the Greek political system. Citizens were encouraged to participate in the debate using rhetoric and logic, and the educational system supported these abilities. For Greeks, knowledge was virtue.

Arts

Reason and science also supported the Greek achievement in the arts. The concept of beauty involved balance and correct proportion. Temple architecture illustrated the two belief systems of the Greeks—gods and rationalism. After the Persians destroyed Athens, under the leadership of Pericles, the Athenians crowned the Acropolis with magnificent new temples. The most famous was the **Parthenon**. Dedicated to Athena, goddess of wisdom and patron of Athens, the temple is adorned with columns and appears balanced and proportioned from all angles. Columns of the **Doric** (plain), **Ionian** (scroll), and **Corinthian** (acanthus leaves) Greek style still grace buildings all over the Western world. In sculpture, humanism is reflected in the realistic and graceful representation of individuals. The greatest of the Greek sculptors, **Phidias**, created the equestrian procession on the Parthenon frieze. Reason also gave birth to the Western concept of history. **Herodotus**, the father of history, sought to write history in a new way. Rather than recounting myths, he gathered information for his *History of the Persian Wars*, pointing out to the reader events he could not verify. His successor, Thucydides, took the process a step further by using only facts he could verify and weighing and judging evidence in the *History of the Peloponnesian War*. This tremendous artistic and philosophical output is referred to as the **Golden Age of Greece** (last half of the fifth century B.C.E.) or the **Age of Pericles** (ca. 461–429 B.C.E.) because, during his leadership, Athens became a showplace for Greek achievement.

Greek Society

Alongside the richness of public life, the everyday life of Greeks was simple and stressed moderation. Most Greeks supported themselves by farming. Their possessions were few. Slavery was commonplace since most slaves were acquired by war. As in Mesopotamia, slaves received some protection under the law and could buy their freedom. Many served as teachers and household servants. Others worked in mines where treatment and conditions could be cruel. Women led a secluded life and were secondary in a basically patriarchal society. They were protected, however, by a dowry that remained their property throughout married life. Women were often idealized in the nature of Greek goddesses. Courtesans probably lived the freest of all Athenian women. The mistress of Pericles, Aspasia, was noted for her artistic and intellectual abilities as well as her beauty.

The Greek Way

Humanism, in both its rational and religious form, is the hallmark of the Greek classical period. Its emphasis on the human being, on intellect, and on artistic and physical potential for excellence influenced many other societies and continues to do so to this day. In the Greek ethical system, to know was to be virtuous. The polis, which institutionalized personal political participation, led to the idea of democracy. Philosophy, in its search for truth through logic, led to investigations into human nature and science. In the search for beauty in realism are architectural and sculptural monuments that are admired to this day. The Greek way of life that stressed excellence, "nothing in excess," and civic participation remains a classical ideal.

DEVELOPMENT OF CLASSICAL PERSIAN (ACHAEMENID) CIVILIZATION

The **Persians** and **Medes**, the two major groups of Iranian peoples, originated in Central Asia as part of a larger group of peoples known as the Aryans or Indo-Europeans. About 2000 B.C.E. these Iron Age charioteer Iranians moved south into the plateau between the Persian Gulf and the Caspian Sea. The geographical position of **Persia** (Iran) between India and East Asia to the east and Southwest Asia to the west has made it an Asian land bridge between cultures. These peoples, like the Hittites, fell under the spell of the more sophisticated cultures of Mesopotamia, but they went on to create one of the greatest empires of history, encompassing hundreds of peoples and cultures. In the process, they gave definition to their own culture.

In 550 B.C.E. **Cyrus II** (the Great), a Persian warrior, conquered the Medes and created a dynasty, the **Achaemenid**, which lasted until 331 B.C.E. Cyrus the Great organized a powerful army, and in 539 B.C.E. he conquered Mesopotamia, Syria, Palestine, and the Phoenician cities. In 540 B.C.E. he defeated the kingdom of Lydia and the Greek city-states of Southwest Asia. Cyrus's son Cambyses conquered Egypt. When **Darius** (521–486 B.C.E.) conquered the Indus Valley ca. 513 B.C.E., the Persians ruled Egypt, all of Southwest Asia, and western India, the largest empire the world had yet known.

In the classical tradition, Cyrus gave Persia an identity and asserted a God-given right to rule that survived repeated invasions. He also held an enlightened view of empire. Aware that many of the civilizations he conquered were more advanced than his own, he accorded all people respect, toleration, and protection. His subjects retained a large measure of local autonomy. They were free to continue their local customs and practice their religions. He freed the Jews and allowed them to return to Palestine. He broke down barriers between the different peoples he conquered like the insular Egyptians, religiously exclusive Hebrews, and aggressive Hittites. The greatest achievement of the Persians was establishing an effective government for diverse peoples and cultures.

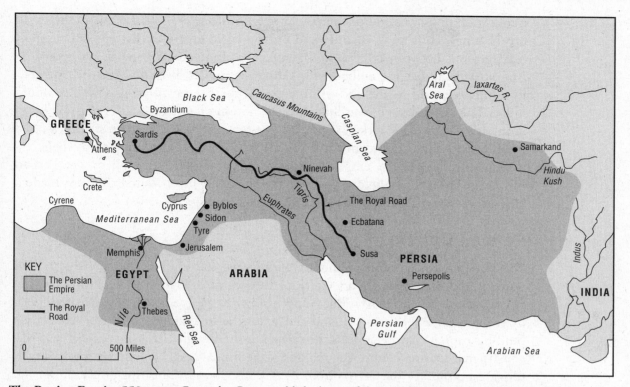

The Persian Empire 550 B.C.E. Cyrus the Great established one of the world's first empires. To rule such a large area effectively, he built roads, divided the empire into smaller areas called satraps, and pursued a policy of toleration toward differing peoples within the Empire.

Cyrus's successor, Darius, carried the art of statecraft to an even higher degree. He reorganized the empire into 20 tribute-paying satrapies, or provinces. To each he appointed a governor (**satrap**), a military commander, and separate inspectors who reported directly to him. In this way, he was able to keep a close watch on local government. He established a comprehensive code of laws, a stable currency, and an efficient postal system. The Persians did not engage in trade, which they considered a lowly occupation, but they did encourage it and facilitated it by building a network of roads. The most important was the **Royal Road**, which ran from Susa in Persia to Sardis in Anatolia (Turkey), a distance of more than 1500 miles and a journey of seven days. Stations were built every 14 miles to provide travelers with food, water, and horses. Rapid, long-distance communication was a cornerstone of Persian rule.

Zoroastrianism

The culture of Persia was dominated by an essentially ethnic religion, **Zoroastrianism**. Because it sought no converts, there was a policy of tolerance for Judaism and the Greek, Babylonian, and Egyptian forms of polytheism. Early Persian religion was polytheistic, though there was a chief god, **Ahuramazda**, the creator and benefactor of all living creatures. **Mithra**, the sun-god, whose cult would later spread through the Roman Empire, saw to justice and redemption. A priestly class, the **Magi**, developed among the Medes to officiate at sacrifices, chant prayers, and tend the sacred fires. Around 600 B.C.E., according to the *Zend Avesta*, a collection of hymns and poems, the prophet **Zoroaster**, or **Zarathustra**, began to preach a new concept of divinity and human life. He taught that life is a constant battleground between two opposing forces, a **dualism** of good as embodied in Ahuramazda and evil as embodied in **Ahriman**. It was the individual's responsibility to choose, and in the end, Ahuramazda, like the Egyptian god Osiris, would judge. The last judgment was linked to the notion of a divine and everlasting kingdom after death. The wicked would be condemned to eternal pain, darkness, and punishment. His ideas converted Darius, the royal family, and many believers throughout the Persian empire. Zoroastrianism survived the fall of the Persian Empire to influence religious thought in the age of Jesus. Zoroastrianism made a vital contribution to Manicheanism, a religion that spread across central Asia.

Persian Culture

Persian classicism combined the art of imperial statecraft of the ancient Iranian nomads, Zoroastrianism, and Greek artistic culture. Darius was defeated by the Greeks at the Battle of Marathon and his son Xerxes was similarly defeated, both by sea at Salamis (480 B.C.E.) and at Plataea the following year. But when Darius built his capital city, **Persepolis**, he turned to the Ionian Greeks for expertise. They constructed soaring columns and a great ceremonial hall, rivaling the Acropolis, to provide a center for the envoys from 23 nations who came bearing gifts each spring. In decorative reliefs and rock sculpture can be seen a blend of Zoroastrianism, the horse, and the balanced role of hierarchy and state executed in Greek humanist style. While Persia was soon to fall to Alexander (the Great) of Macedonia, and later to other invaders, the Persian culture and sense of identity established during the classical era remained and reemerged, reaching new heights during the Sassanian Empire and Abbasid Caliphate. As a result of the conquests of Alexander, a new synthesis of Greek, Persian, Indian, and Southwest Asian culture emerged.

THE HELLENISTIC SYNTHESIS

Did You Know?

Hellenism consists of Greek culture, thought, and way of life.

When the Greek cities were quarreling among themselves, an able and energetic ruler named Philip became king of **Macedonia** (northern Greece). In 338 B.C.E., he destroyed the joint army of Thebes and Athens and became master of Greece. King Philip was preparing for an invasion of the Persian Empire when he was murdered. His 20-year-old son, known as **Alexander the Great** (r. 336–323 B.C.E.), assumed the throne and began a campaign of conquest. By overthrowing the Persian Empire and by spreading **Hellenism**—Greek culture, thought, and way of life—from Egypt to India, Alexander created a new era of cultural synthesis called **Hellenistic**, an age that lasted from Alexander's death in 323 B.C.E. to 30 B.C.E.

Alexander of Macedonia

Philip had great admiration for Greek culture and had even brought Aristotle to Macedonia to tutor his son Alexander. Copying the great Greek heroes he had read about, Alexander began a campaign of conquest that over a period of 12 years created the largest empire up to that time. His empire covered about two million square miles. Vowing revenge for the Persian invasion of Greece in 492 and 490 B.C.E., Alexander led an army of Macedonians and Greeks into western Asia using the Persian network of roads to his advantage. In 330 B.C.E. he sacked and burned Persepolis. Next, he advanced on Syria, Palestine, and Egypt. At the Nile delta he founded the city of **Alexandria**. Then he pushed east into Afghanistan and Pakistan, crossing the Indus River. In 326 B.C.E., Alexander entered India. When his troops refused to go any further, he turned south to the Indian Ocean, and in 323 B.C.E. he died, just before his 33rd birthday.

Hellenistic Rule

Upon the death of Alexander, his mighty empire broke up among his warring generals. Antigonus became ruler of Macedonia and Greece, Seleucus became ruler of Syria, Palestine, Babylonia, and other Southwest Asian lands, and Ptolemy became the first of the Egyptian dynasty of **Ptolemies**. Over time, smaller independent states emerged like Pergamum and **Bactrian Greece**. The Bactrian Greek kings sent their cavalry probing toward the boundaries of the Chinese empire, and, in the middle of the second century B.C.E. Menander, the philosophic Greek king of the Punjab, fulfilled Alexander's ambition by leading an army of Greeks and Persians down the valley of the Ganges to capture Pataliputra, the capital of Hindustan (India). In rule, these new kings were more Eastern than Greek, but Greek culture blanketed the whole area and united it culturally, if not politically.

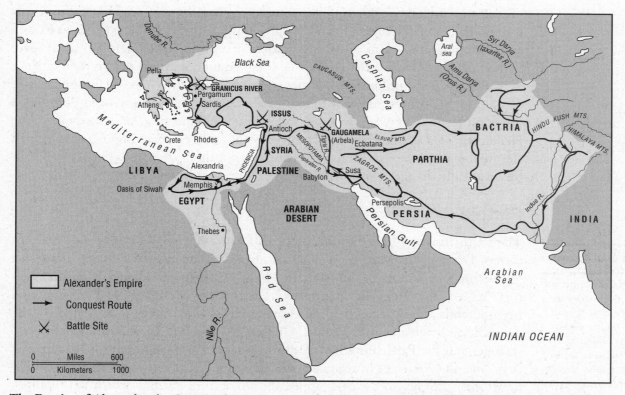

The Empire of Alexander the Great 336–323 B.C.E. In twelve short years, Alexander the Great created a huge empire, and in so doing, spread Greek culture far and wide.

Hellenistic Trade

The new political developments led to a diffusion of wealth and a great expansion of trade with East Africa, Arabia, India, and Central Asia, with some trade relayed as far east as China. To the west, trade went through the Straits of Gibraltar to Britain and Norway. Silver flowed from Spain, copper from Cyprus, iron from the Black Sea coasts, grains from Egypt, North Africa, and the Crimea, olive oil from Athens, dried fruit from Palestine, woolen goods from Anatolia, timber from Macedonia, marble from Greece, and linen, granite, and papyrus from Egypt. Alexander had found vast sums of gold, silver, and other treasure in Persia. This became the basis for the building programs of the Hellenistic kings. For this, slaves were needed, becoming a common item of trade except in Egypt where they would have competed with free labor. The caravan trade expanded. The Egyptian Ptolemies discovered how to use monsoon winds to establish direct contact with India. A common language emerged called **koine**, a dialect of Greek, which helped to facilitate trade and government.

Diffusion of Greek Culture

Trade transformed the Greek polis into a **cosmopolis** of differing peoples and activities. Cities became economic and cultural centers where people from all over the Mediterranean and Southwest Asia met. While the new kings gave their cities like Antioch, Pergamum, Pella, and, above all, Alexandria all the trappings of the polis like assemblies and councils, they could not afford to give them freedom. In a Hellenistic city, the Greeks represented an elite class of citizens because they were needed to run their kingdoms. This spurred many citizens to assimilate Greek culture in order to rise politically and socially. Opportunities for advancement as well as overpopulation led to an out-migration of Greeks, who then spread all over Southwest Asia. Because the Hellenistic kings could not afford to arm their citizens as in a Greek polis, professional armies emerged, using the Greco-Macedonian style of warfare that proved superior to that of the Southwest Asians. Greeks dominated other professions as well, such as architecture, engineering, and medicine. The Hellenistic idea of kingship that involved royal families, including women, helped elevate the position of women, especially those of the upper class. Thus, Greek culture was diffused and transformed by the Eastern traditions.

Parthia

Did You Know?

Parthia is important in world history as a force that spread Greek culture east and provided a safe highway along which goods and cultures from across Eurasia could flow.

The Parthians were Indo-European nomads who migrated from Central Asia into eastern Persia in the third century B.C.E. after the Achaemenid Persian Empire fell to the forces of Alexander the Great in 330 B.C.E. In the middle of the second century B.C.E., the Parthians conquered large parts of Persia, Afghanistan, and Mesopotamia. The Parthians adopted many Hellenistic traditions and made Greek the official language of the state. Gradually, however, Persian influences grew stronger and the Parthians adopted a form of Zoroastrianism and tried to replicate Achaemenid systems of bureaucracy like satrapies. Frequent wars with the expanding Roman Empire to the east sapped the strength of Parthia, which fell to a new Persian power, the Sassanians in 224 C.E.

Mystery Cults

Since Hellenistic cities lacked the emotional attachment of the polis, people searched for a sense of meaning and belonging in religion. To Hellenistic peoples, Greek cults and polytheistic traditions seemed sterile because of their attachment to ritual, festival, and particular places in the Greek homeland like Olympus. For this reason, Eastern religions, especially the **mystery cults** like Serapis and Isis, became popular. Serapis combined elements of the Egyptian god Osiris with aspects of Greek gods. All the mystery religions claimed to save their adherents from fate and promised life for the soul after death.

Hellenistic Philosophy

The cosmopolitan nature of Hellenistic life, its wealth, intermingling of cultural heritages, and its mobility, spawned an explosion in philosophy, science, and medicine. The Library at Alexandria became the repository for all the known knowledge of the ages. Philosophy, in particular, gave people in a changing world a sense of permanence and structure, and the intellectual outlet the polis had once offered. Three philosophies in particular became popular—**Cynicism**, led by **Diogenes** (ca. 412–323 B.C.E.), **Epicureanism**, advanced by **Epicures** (340–270 B.C.E.), and **Stoicism**, introduced by **Zeno** (335–262 B.C.E.). Cynics believed that happiness was possible only by living according to nature and foregoing luxuries. Social conventions contrary to nature were attacked, resulting in the present meaning of cynicism, a belief that all actions are for selfish motives. This philosophy was particularly appealing to the lower classes who saw its adherents go without warm clothing and sufficient food and housing. Epicureans believed that the principal good of human life was pleasure. Epicureans ignored politics and issues. Today, an epicurean is one who enjoys good food and drink. Stoics taught that people should participate in politics and world affairs but they ought not to try to change the order of things. Rather, they were to play the role assigned, for the question was not whether they achieved anything, but that they lived virtuous lives. Stoicism today refers to suffering without complaint. The Stoic concept of a universal state government by natural law was one of the great legacies of the Hellenistic world to Rome, as it became a valuable tool for the Romans to rationalize rule of an empire with many different peoples and laws. Duty of individuals to their fellows became a philosophical underpinning for the duties of Roman citizenship.

Hellenistic Science, Math, and Technology

Hellenistic culture's greatest achievement was in science. Mesopotamia, Persia, Egypt, and even India were intermingled with Greek thought. The cosmic observations of the Babylonians provided the raw material for the foundation of astronomy introduced by **Thales**. The most noble Hellenistic astronomer was **Aristarchus** (ca. 310–230 B.C.E.). He argued against Aristotle and **Ptolemy** (an Alexandrian mathematician and astronomer) that the earth was the center of the universe. He propounded, instead, the **heliocentric** theory that the earth and planets move around the sun, a theory that lay dormant until the Polish astronomer, **Nicolaus Copernicus** (1473–1543 C.E.) reinvestigated it. In geometry, Hellenistic thinkers discovered little new, but **Euclid** (ca. 300 B.C.E.) completed a valuable textbook of existing knowledge, *The Elements of Geometry*.

The greatest Hellenistic thinker was **Archimedes** (ca. 287–212 B.C.E.), an inventor and mathematician. Among his inventions were the Archimedean screw and the compound pulley. In his book *Plane Equilibrium*, he dealt for the first time with the principles of mechanics, including the lever. In *On Floating Bodies*, Archimedes founded the science of hydrostatics, advancing the theory that, whenever a solid floats in liquid, the weight of the solid is equal to the volume of liquid displaced. Using math, **Eratosthenes** (285–ca. 204 B.C.E.) calculated the circumference of the earth at 24,675 miles (it is actually 24,860 miles). He declared that a ship could sail from Spain either around Africa to India or directly west to India, a theory not really proven until the voyages of Vasco da Gama (1497–1499 C.E.) and Magellan (1519–1522 C.E.).

In medicine, **Herophilus** dissected corpses, leading to his conclusion that there were two types of nerves, motor and sensory, and that the brain was the center of intelligence. His dissections led to the invention of new surgical instruments and practices, while Heraclides dedicated himself to observation and the use of medicines. He noted how blood circulated through veins and arteries. One of the mysteries of Hellenistic science is that, although scientists of the period invented such machines as the steam engine, water organ, and air gun, they never used them as labor-saving devices, perhaps because slave labor was so abundant. Inventions were applied to the military, however, in the form of catapults and siege machines, advances that the Romans then used to gain supremacy over the very Hellenistic world that had developed them.

The Hellenistic Age

The Hellenistic Age spread Greek culture and incorporated the ideas and culture of Southwest Asia into it. The kingly traditions of the East merged with the Greek polis. Greek humanism and rationalism merged with religious traditions of Egypt and Mesopotamia. Hellenistic commerce flourished under the protection of competitive kingdoms, united by a common Greek language, coinage, and methods of exchange. Wealth brought building, especially of new cities, inventions, and social mobility. The polis became a cosmopolis embracing change and encouraging new ideas. The Hellenistic world later shaped Constantinople, the eastern Rome. To Southwest Asia, Alexander and his successors gave much of its art, especially the techniques of building and carving in stone. Hellenistic art became more realistic, often vividly portraying the lives of ordinary people. Bactrian Greeks developed a syncretic style that mixed the artistic traditions of Greece, India, Persia, and Egypt. Hellenistic rulers continued the concept of a united rule that Chandragupta adopted when he founded the Mauryan empire. When the Arabs finally destroyed the Greek cities of the East, they retained Hellenistic science, math, and medicine. While the kingdoms of the Hellenistic world were busy with their own squabbles, Rome emerged and gradually absorbed the Hellenistic world politically. Yet, as has been pointed out by historians, the "Romanization" of the Hellenistic world was slight while the Hellenization of the Latin world was conspicuous.

Classical Roman Civilization

(ca. 500 B.C.E.–500 C.E.)

TIMELINE	
753 B.C.E.	Founding of Rome
509 B.C.E.–44 B.C.E.	Roman Republic
264 B.C.E.–140 B.C.E.	Punic Wars (Rome and Carthage)
44 B.C.E.–476 C.E.	Roman Empire
7 B.C.E.–30 C.E.	Life of Jesus
27 C.E.–180 C.E.	*Pax Romana*
133 B.C.E.	Roman conquest of Greece
240 C.E.–651 C.E.	Sassanian Persian Empire
330 C.E.	Founding of Constantinople
395 C.E.	Division of Western and Eastern Roman Empire

DEVELOPMENT OF ROMAN CIVILIZATION

The Greek humanist tradition and the Roman concept of law and Judeo-Christian ethics are considered the hallmarks of Western civilization. From them emerge core values of the Western world—individualism, justice, and Christian love. It was in the classical age of Greece and Rome that these concepts emerged. The first of these, humanism, has been investigated in the previous section. The other two emerge during the classical age of Rome. In the first half of Roman history, during the republic, legal traditions developed and evolved to a sophisticated level, and during the second half, the Roman Empire, Christianity made its distinctive mark.

Founding of Rome

At about the same time (1000 B.C.E.) the Dorians moved south into Greece and plunged it into a Dark Age, the **Etruscans** moved down the Italian peninsula, settling north of the **Tiber River**. Several centuries later, escaping the Doric invasions of Greece, Greek colonists planted new settlements in Sicily and southern Italy. It was the Greeks who gave the name **Italy** to the peninsula. Between the Etruscans in the north and the Greeks in the south, around the Tiber River, lived a group of people called **Latins**. Their lands were protected by the Apennines, a mountain range extending the length of the Italian peninsula. According to ancient Roman tradition, the city of Rome was founded (753 B.C.E.) by two brothers, **Romulus** and **Remus**. Around 700 B.C.E. both Rome and Latium were subjugated by the Etruscans. Like Greece, the city-state of Rome was ruled by an Etruscan king, and in 509 B.C.E. large landowners rose in revolt, drove out the Etruscan king, and began to form a new government, a **republic** (power in the hands of the people, not the king). Unlike Greece, the republic was a unified state, instead of a series of independent city-states, able to withstand outside invasion and internal violence.

Roman Republic

The early republican form of government was based on the division of people into two classes:

1. The wealthy land-owning class called **patricians**, which made up about 10 percent of the population
2. The small farmers, artisans, and shopkeepers called **plebeians**.

At the head of the republic were two **consuls** who were elected from the patrician class. They commanded the army, presided over religious functions, and acted as judges who could veto one another. In times of emergency, the consuls could turn over their power to a dictator elected for a maximum of six months. The consuls were advised by a 300-member patrician **Senate**, which had been in existence even under the Etruscan king as an advisory body. Senators served for life, which provided continuity. The Senate decided questions of peace and war and proposed laws that were voted upon by the **Assembly of Centuries**, a body made up of all male citizens as organized for military purposes in units of 100, called centuries.

As in Greece, this form of government was gradually democratized. In 494 B.C.E., as a result of plebeian refusal to serve in the army against one of Rome's neighbors, plebeians were given the right to elect their own representatives called **tribunes**. The tribunes were elected by a special assembly of plebeians called the **Assembly of Tribes**. The Assembly of Tribes passed resolutions that tribunes then presented to the Senate for ratification. Gradually, the legal differences between patricians and plebeians disappeared altogether. By 376 B.C.E. a plebeian could serve as one of the consuls, and in 287 B.C.E. patricians were admitted to the Assembly of Tribes.

Roman Law

Democratization was also advanced by a law code, the **Twelve Tables** (450 B.C.E.). Soon it became customary for newly elected **praetors** (judges) to announce the laws they intended to enforce and those they considered out of date. In this way, the laws remained responsive to people's needs. These statutes, using precedents, customs, and procedures, became the basis of civil law, or *jus civile*. By the third century B.C.E., when trade had become more important, the Romans set up special courts to deal with the problem of differences between foreign and Roman laws. *Jus gentium* was the coalescing of Roman and foreign law.

The judge in charge made decisions that seemed fair, thus promoting the idea of justice over the laws of a particular country. This gave rise to the notion of *jus naturale*, or universal law. The sophistication, adaptability, and sturdiness of the Roman legal system included

- a common standard of justice creating a state of laws, not men

- judgments based on evidence

- an enumeration of rights including those of women, slaves, and property

- respect for law as reflected in the Roman symbol for justice

- the merging of Roman civil law with laws of foreigners

Roman Legions

The origins of the Roman system of jurisprudence, republicanism, and democracy can probably be found, as in Greece, in the military and in Roman values. Threatened by the Etruscans, every able-bodied Roman male was required to serve in the army. Roman farmers, used to outdoor work, made excellent soldiers. Originally, the Romans used the Greek phalanx system but it gradually was replaced by the **legion** system. Legions of from 3000 to 6000 men were made up of companies of about 120 men, loyal to each other and trained to fight by themselves, if necessary. Roman soldiers were equipped with helmets, shields, lances, swords, and later, iron-tipped javelins. They could attack the enemy from great distances. Superior arms, discipline, training, and steadfast loyalty soon made the Roman armies masters of the Mediterranean. They became more invincible than soldiers in the Greek phalanx.

Roman Religion

Values and religion also played a role. Early Romans regarded virtue and duty highly. They were careful to show gods the proper respect because they believed whatever happened to them was in the hands of the gods. Romans worshipped many gods, like those that protected home, family, and fields, but there were also, as in Greece, a pantheon of public and semi-anthropomorphic gods common to all Romans. Jupiter, god of the sky, sent rain and inspired magistrates. Mars protected armies. The chief priest, or **Pontifex Maximus**, prescribed prayers and sacrifices in the name of the Roman people. Before these gods, all were equal and all were dutiful.

From Republic to Empire

Conquests and the impact of new values from the Hellenistic world changed the Roman political system. The republic gave way to empire. Rome first conquered the Italian peninsula and then the Mediterranean. In the conquest of Italy, Rome fought numerous wars with its neighbors, and used diplomacy and alliances to gain control. Unlike the Greeks, the Romans extended citizenship to many of their allies, thereby spreading the Roman legal system, strengthening the state, and giving it additional wealth and manpower. Between 282 and 272 B.C.E., the Romans engaged in war with the Hellenistic king of Epirus, **Pyrrhus**, who had come across the Adriatic to the aid of Greek cities in southeastern Italy. With his defeat, Rome became master of all Italy.

The most important struggles were the **Punic Wars** (264–146 B.C.E.), which were fought between Rome and Carthage for control of Mediterranean power and wealth. The ancient Phoenician city of **Carthage** was the chief outlet for the lucrative trade of North Africa and the Carthaginian navy controlled the Mediterranean trade lanes of the Hellenistic world. In the First Punic War (264–241 B.C.E.), Rome won control of Sicily. When Rome went on to annex Sardinia and Corsica, Carthage sought revenge. This led to the Second Punic War (218–201 B.C.E.). The leader of the Carthaginian forces, **Hannibal**, daringly led his army, including elephants, through Spain and across the Alps into northern Italy. There he was thoroughly routed by the Romans. Rome then invaded Africa. At the **Battle of Zama** in 202 B.C.E., Hannibal was defeated by the Roman general **Scipio**. The result of the second war was that Carthage was forced to give up Spain. The Third Punic War (149 B.C.E.) led to the complete destruction of the city of Carthage. Because Macedonia had joined Hannibal during the Second Punic War, Rome conquered Macedonia and then Greece (133 B.C.E.) in order to gain control of this politically unstable and fragmented part of the Hellenistic world. By the second century B.C.E., Rome had become master of the whole Mediterranean world.

Consequences of the Punic Wars

The conquests completely changed the economic, social, cultural, and finally, political life of Rome. Economically, Roman soldiers came home to neglected farms that had been bought by wealthy landowners in their absence. These huge estates, or **latifundia**, were worked by slaves that had been imported from places of conquest. Former Roman soldiers out of work wandered to the cities where they became a class that was dependent on state handouts and entertainment. They fell prey to the politics of their generals who demanded allegiance to them and to the state. Meanwhile, grain was imported from abroad, from places conquered by the Romans. North Africa, particularly Egypt, became the breadbasket of the Romans. The wealth of conquest replaced taxation, and booty stunted the development of industry.

Did You Know?

As trade and empire increased, a new class of people arose, composed of merchants and bureaucrats.

More important, the basic Roman values of simplicity and morality were undermined by the influx of the more urbane and cosmopolitan Hellenistic ideas. Romans fell in love with Hellenistic culture. They were educated by Greek tutors, entertained by Greek plays, intrigued by Greek notions of government and philosophy, delighted by the luxury of the Greek cosmopolis, and tutored by Greeks in the art of moneymaking. Family life, the bulwark of old Rome, weakened. Political corruption became a science, luxury a goal. As the Roman satirical poet Juvenal wrote, "Luxury has fallen upon us—more terrible than the sword. The conquered East has avenged herself by the gift of her vices." Was Rome corrupted? The Roman state and the empire it ruled lasted for another six centuries. The Golden Age was yet to come. The high tide of prosperity lay in the future. The practical Romans simply took change in stride.

In 44 B.C.E., Rome became an empire despite almost a decade of reformers who attempted to stave off such a turn of events. In 133 B.C.E. **Tiberius Gracchus**, a tribune, attempted to return to the old ways by limiting the amount of land a person could own. In 123 B.C.E. his brother **Gaius** attempted to get the government to buy grain and sell it to the poor at low prices. Both attempts at economic reform failed due to opposition by wealthy senators. In the provinces, victorious generals used booty to pay off a political following.

The first general to successfully challenge the Senate was **Marius** (ca. 155–86 B.C.E.). He had created a professional army by opening the army to everyone and furnishing recruits with equipment. With a loyal force of soldiers behind him, he was able to override the Senate and have himself reelected consul four times. The Senate then threw its weight behind another general, **Sulla**, who, in 83 B.C.E., took over the government, executed Marius' followers, and restored the Senate to its old position of authority. In reality, he ruled as a dictator until 79 B.C.E., when he retired.

Julius Caesar

Rome was plunged into civil war. The major contest was between **Pompey** (106–48 B.C.E.) and **Julius Caesar** (ca. 102–44 B.C.E.). Pompey had earned his fame by conquests in the East, Julius Caesar by conquest in **Gaul** (France). Pompey was supported by the Senate, Caesar by the people. In 59 B.C.E. Caesar, Pompey, and a wealthy businessman, **Crassus**, agreed to share power and formed the **First Triumvirate**. Caesar left Rome and, while he was away, Crassus died. The Senate and Pompey became increasingly distrustful of the popular Caesar and forbade him to lead his army across the **Rubicon River**, the boundary between Gaul and Rome. Caesar defied the Senate and by this act brought the republic to an end. Pompey fled to Greece and then Egypt where he was killed. In 46 B.C.E. Caesar was appointed dictator, whereupon he launched a series of reforms including removing citizens from welfare rolls and sending them into the provinces. He restored agricultural self-sufficiency, and reformed the provincial administration. However, on March 15, the "**Ides of March**," 44 B.C.E., he was assassinated by a band of senatorial conspirators led by **Brutus**. Rome was once again at war. **Antony** (a former ally of Julius Caesar) and **Cleopatra** (the last of the Ptolemies) were defeated at **Actium**. In 30 B.C.E. Egypt became part of Rome. Order was restored in 27 B.C.E., when **Octavian**, a grandnephew of Caesar's, ended almost a century of chaos in which republican institutions had failed to function. He assumed the title of **Augustus**, instituted a **constitutional monarchy**, and inaugurated the empire, a period that lasted 500 years in the West and 1500 in the East.

Augustus Caesar

During the rule of Augustus and subsequently, the Senate became only an advisory body. Augustus was dictator, being, at the same time, chief military general, chief priest (pontifex maximus), and first citizen. The imperial system had all the strengths and weaknesses of any empire—good emperors who ruled wisely and gave the state a degree of solidarity and order unknown to republican governments and bad emperors, during whose reign corruption and disorder prevailed. During the reign of Augustus' descendants, the Julio-Claudian Dynasty, for instance, Tiberius and Claudius ruled with steady hands, but **Caligula** (r. 31–41 C.E.) was cruel and incompetent and ultimately was assassinated.

Pax Romana

In 69 C.E. Vespasian, the first emperor who was not a member of an aristocratic family, assumed power, and in 96 C.E. the Senate elected Nerva emperor. This illustrated the potential that existed in the Roman system for talented individuals to achieve upward mobility. Nerva's election initiated the rule of the Five Good Emperors—

Nerva, Trajan, Hadrian, Antoninus Pius, and **Marcus Aurelius**. Marcus Aurelius (r. 161–180 C.E.), known as the philosopher-emperor, wrote *Meditations*, a book of spiritual reflections in which he struggled with the paradox that as a man of peace, he spent most of his reign fighting Germans in Britain and on the Parthian (Persian/Iranian) frontier. His writings reflect a Stoic attitude of duty and acceptance. The period from Augustus through Marcus Aurelius (27 B.C.E.–180 C.E.) is often called the *Pax Romana* because it was a time of relative political peace when no major wars threatened the security of the empire. Peace encouraged trade and wealth.

After the death of Marcus Aurelius, a period of disorder ensued in which power passed into the hands of the military. Imperial leadership was up for bid.

CULTURAL ACHIEVEMENTS OF ROME

The Age of Augustus initiated 400 years of imperial rule that was celebrated both in literature and in stone. Rome was more notable as an imitator than an innovator. As with the rest of the Hellenistic world, Romans became Hellenized, copying Greek culture and then making their own special adaptations. In portraiture, Romans started with the Greek realistic style but by the later imperial period they moved toward idealized representations that celebrated Roman victory and achievement. The Romans were innovators, however, in **mosaic** decoration, an art form that reached its zenith in the eastern Roman Empire sometime later.

Roman Literature and Science

The Augustan peace inspired a Roman literary flowering, the "Golden Age" of Latin literature. The tone and ideal of Roman literature, like that of the Greeks, was humanistic and worldly. Though it frequently referred to the gods, it was in human terms. The three titans of the Roman literary world were **Virgil** (70–19 B.C.E.), **Livy** (59 B.C.E.–17 C.E.) and **Horace** (65–8 B.C.E.). Virgil's masterpiece is *The Aeneid*, an epic poem that is the Latin equivalent of *The Iliad* and *The Odyssey*. It recounts the founding of Rome through the exploits of the Roman hero, Aeneas, who escaped to Italy after the fall of Troy. Livy's history of Rome is the prose counterpart of the *The Aeneid*, while Horace is famous for his odes commemorating Augustus' victories. Together, these authors gave the Western world not just great literature, but **Latin**, the language of the Latin Christian church and the basis of the **romance languages** of Europe—Portuguese, Spanish, French, and Italian. Some important writing was in the field of science, a field in which Romans recapitulated Greek work rather than provide an innovative pure science. **Pliny** produced a multivolume encyclopedia entitled *Natural History*, in which he discussed a range of topics from biology to botany. Claudius **Ptolemy** produced many works on astronomy and geography. His theory that the earth was the center of the solar system, though wrong, dominated science for 1000 years. **Plutarch** (ca. 42–102 C.E.), whose interest in famous people was in their moral qualities, wrote a collection of biographical sketches of 65 Greeks and Romans.

Roman Architecture

The Romans learned from the Etruscans how to make rounded arches, but they devised a way to extend the arch into a **barrel vault** and to set two arches at right angles to one another to form a **cross vault**. Thus, the weight of a building was equally distributed and walls no longer needed to be as thick to hold up the roof as in the post and lintel system. The Romans also perfected the dome. Domes, vaults, and arches were used by the Romans to build palaces, theaters, coliseums, public baths, temples, public buildings, and aqueducts. Some of the most beautiful illustrations of Roman architecture are the **Pantheon** and the **Arch of Constantine** because they incorporate the Greek sense of balance and harmony and the Roman genius in building.

Growth of Cities

These building achievements are also notable because they can be found not only in the large urban centers, but also in towns. The Roman Empire, in contrast to the Hellenistic world, was marked by growth and development of cities besides those of the capitals, linked by a system of roads that facilitated trade and communication throughout the empire. There were 160 cities alone that lay beyond the Rhine far from Rome. Roman cities were self-governing. Emperors encouraged the growth of cities by passing special decrees. Trajan, for instance, made it possible for municipalities to receive bequests like libraries, temples, aqueducts, and charities. Cities also blossomed due to trade. However, they were vulnerable to outside invasion, plague, and insecure trade routes. In the third and fourth centuries C.E., when they were under attack, people abandoned the cities and fled to the countryside, but the legacy of independent towns was not forgotten.

Roman Society

Even relatively small urban centers were decked out with an impressive array of theaters, triumphal arches, baths, and fountains. Indeed, the provision of reliable drinking water and higher standards of hygiene are one of Rome's contributions to Western civilization. The Romans also improved the rural areas by introducing irrigation and drainage systems, as well as better agricultural tools. Tradesmen were organized into guilds (**collegia**) for social and religious purposes rather than for better wages and working conditions. While much has been written about the amusements of Romans, such as gladiator contests, chariot races, and the 159 public holidays that existed under Claudius, ordinary Romans dealt with everyday problems and enjoyed simple pleasures like most people through the ages. Taxes were collected from an imperial population of about 4.5 million, in order to finance public buildings. Taxation for the one million Roman citizens was abolished about 167 B.C.E. In the province of Africa, however, the standard tax for peasant farmers was one-third of their production plus six days' labor service. But they were protected by a powerful corpus of law that gradually offered protection for the poor, and even for slaves against wanton cruelty. Although not fully codified until the sixth century C.E., this body of law, known as **Justinian's Code**, is one of the greatest cultural and political achievements of Rome.

Imperial Law

Law rather than bureaucracies or the military was the Roman apparatus of imperial rule. Generally, the Romans gave a great deal of political autonomy to local governments and maintained small garrisons of soldiers scattered throughout the empire. While local laws continued to apply in many areas, Roman law provided a legal system accessible to citizens at any part of the empire and capable of facilitating commercial exchange. It was implemented by a bureaucracy accountable directly to the emperor. The *jus civile*, or civil law, which applied to Romans only and the *jus gentium*, or law of nations, formed the basis of general notions of law, the *jus naturale*. This law focused heavily on private property and family stability, objectivity and fairness, and evolution of the law to meet changing conditions. In this way, law rather than a common social structure, culture, or religion became the glue of the empire.

ROMAN DIFFUSION

Roman diffusion occurred by conquest and trade. After subduing the Italian peninsula and bringing Carthage to its knees (201 B.C.E.), Rome began an unremitting march to empire. First it turned on those who had helped Hannibal, the Macedonians, and the Celts in northern Italy. Caesar subdued Gaul (France), Augustus settled with **Parthia** (Persia/Iran) and then annexed Egypt, Galatia (Turkey), and Judea. Then he advanced over the Alps into the Danube and Rhine areas and conquered Spain. By the time of Hadrian (r. 117–138 C.E.) the empire had reached its limits, including Britain, Dacia (Romania), Mesopotamia, and Northwest Africa (Morocco). In the east, the ease of conquest can be explained by the fragmentation of the Hellenistic kingdoms. In the west, Romans moved into new territories in western Europe occupied by various tribes who had moved into the area north of the Alps during the late Bronze and early Iron Age. In the first millennium C.E. the Germanic tribes overran large parts of the area. The Germanic tribes eventually overran the western part of the Roman Empire, causing Constantinople, a new Rome in the east, to be built.

Roman Trade and the Silk Road

While Roman imperial expansion to the west was finite, geographically, expansion to the east opened up possibilities far across Eurasia. Roman military expansion to the east coincided with Chinese expansion to the west and the result was a period in history when two mighty classical civilizations came in touch with each other. The diffusion of Roman culture is tied intimately to the economics of empire and the trade system that sustained it. The vast amounts of building were funded through an imperial economic system that was self-sufficient in all essential commodities. Geographic factors like the Mediterranean and river systems flowing into it tied the system together. Since amber was in great demand and available in the Baltic area, the **Amber Road** developed, following the valleys of the Rhine, Danube, Vistula, and Elbe to Rome. Luxuries came from long-distance trade with India and China. Animals and grain came across the Mediterranean from North Africa. Stone for Roman building schemes and animals for the shows came from afar. The Roman Empire created a vast area with a single currency and low customs barriers. Commerce was protected from pirates by an elaborate network of roads and protected harbors. All areas used papyrus as a writing material. Armies stationed on the frontiers stimulated the economy in outlying areas.

Silk Road

In large part because of warfare, the Roman and Chinese empires came in contact with each other. Persia was the link between the two wealthiest and most commercially active realms in the classical world. An elaborate network of roads linked Parthia to China in the east, India in the south, and Rome in the west. The most important of the overland routes was the **Silk Road**. Rarely did a merchant travel the entire distance so this relay trade fostered the growth of cities and towns all along the route. Direct maritime trade was established in the second century C.E. Han Emperor Wudi (Wu Ti) took the momentous step of opening the Silk Road to Parthia and a later Han emperor sent an ambassador, **Kan Ying**, to the Roman Empire by sea (96–98 C.E.). In the province of Syria, Kan Ying left a fascinating firsthand look at the Greco-Roman world, noting that the commercial traffic between Parthia and India made tenfold profits. More than goods passed along these routes. Technology, ideas, religion, and art also spread. Buddist art based on Greek models portrayed the Buddha in the Greek style in central Asia. The West developed a taste for silk and spices, a taste that years later drove Europeans across the Atlantic. The trade routes also became the vehicle for diffusion of religious ideas.

Did You Know?

Wealth accumulated through war and taxation was concentrated in Rome.

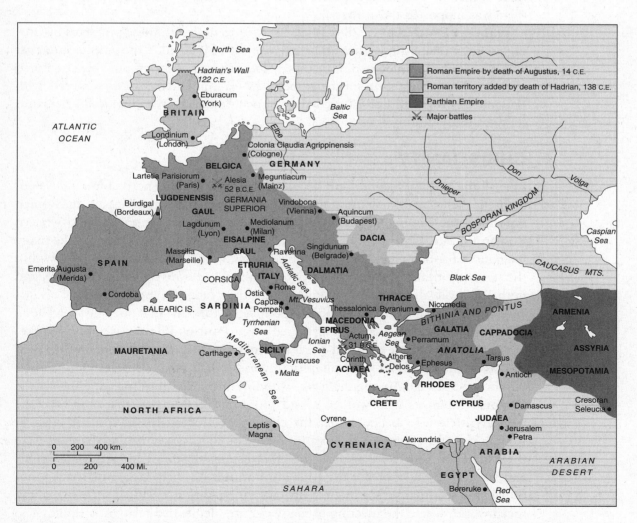

The Roman Empire, ca. 120 C.E. The Romans gradually expanded until, by 120 C.E., they controlled a huge empire stretching from Britain and Spain in the west through southern and central Europe and North Africa to Egypt, Anatolia, and the lands along the eastern Mediterranean coast.

Roman Economy

The fantastic outward wealth of the empire obscured some of its economic weaknesses. Rome depended on a system of agriculture that required the land to lie fallow in alternate years. Land transport was slow and expensive, depending on donkeys, mules, and oxen rather than horses. It was cheaper to ship grain across the Mediterranean than to cart it 70 miles. The commercial classes were weak both in capital and social esteem. The shop, not the factory, was the standard unit of production. Slaves were a very high proportion of the population in many areas. The wealth-consuming rather than wealth-creating nature of the empire, and the fact that it relied to such a high degree on trade, made it vulnerable.

Emperor Hadrian, who ruled from 117–138 C.E., withdrew eastern Roman troops to the Euphrates River and built a 73-mile wall across Britain near the border of modern Scotland to protect the empire from attack. From the time of Marcus Aurelius, the Romans were continually involved with repelling the Persians in the east and the Germans in the west. The constant threat of invasion or civil war made trade difficult. Decreasing trade made for decreasing tax revenue, and what little there was supported the army.

Emperor Diocletian (r. 284–305 C.E.) tried to deal with these problems by issuing an edict establishing price and wage controls. He divided the empire into East and West and appointed two more caesars for each half of the empire. He attempted to reestablish the authority of the emperor by claiming divine status complete with elaborate court ritual. This all needed a vast new bureaucracy, adding to the demands on the already diminishing treasury.

CHRISTIANITY

Like all the classical civilizations, belief systems heavily influenced cultural development. Hellenic and Hellenistic gods and rationalist beliefs enveloped the Roman state until the coming of Christianity. After that, both in the eastern and western Roman Empire, Christianity became an integral part of Roman culture. Like many religions, Christianity grew up in troubled times, both within the empire and within the state of Judea. It was the time when Rome moved from republic to empire, and in the civil wars that were fought in this transition, Judea suffered its share of ravages and military confiscations. Also, the political autonomy that the Jews had long enjoyed under the Romans was shattered when **Pontius Pilate** was appointed prefect. This meant Rome now had direct control over the area rather than indirect control, as occurred in the republican system. Besides war, there were also crop failures, famine, and plague. Among the Jews, two movements began to spread. One was the **Zealots**, extremists who worked to rid Judea of the Romans. The other was the **Apocalyptics**, who believed that the coming of a Messiah was near. A crisis in Roman paganism also played a part in the rise of Christianity. Essentially there were three kinds of Roman paganism—the official state religion of Rome, Roman cults, and the mystery religions of the Hellenistic world. All three lacked personal, emotional, and spiritual succor in a rapidly changing political world. In a cosmopolitan social world, where the meeting of many cultures demanded relativistic thinking to promote harmony, people lacked, but sought, moral anchors.

JUDAISM

The Christian religion has its roots in Judaism, the basis of which was the Ten Commandments and the belief in one god, Yahweh, often called Jehovah. Among the beliefs of Jews were the concept of sin and the original fall of man, accountability, the promise of redemption through a coming Messiah, the day of last judgment, and the idea that Jews were Yahweh's chosen people. These beliefs began to take shape in 539 B.C.E. when Cyrus the Great of Persia defeated the Babylonians, thereby ending the captivity of the Jews. Under Achaemenid Persian rule, the Jews were allowed to return to Palestine. There they recorded the core of Judaism, the Law, which can be found in the **Torah**. Acknowledged masters of the law, or **rabbis**, interpreted the law much as Roman praetors interpreted the Twelve Tables. These writings and interpretations were later collected and, along with other writings, formed the **Talmud**, the second great source of Judaism.

The Jews of the last century B.C.E. did not live exclusively in Palestine. Many of the **Diaspora** (dispersion of Jewish peoples outside of Palestine) remained in Persia. Others settled in Hellenistic cities like Alexandria or in the cities of North Africa,

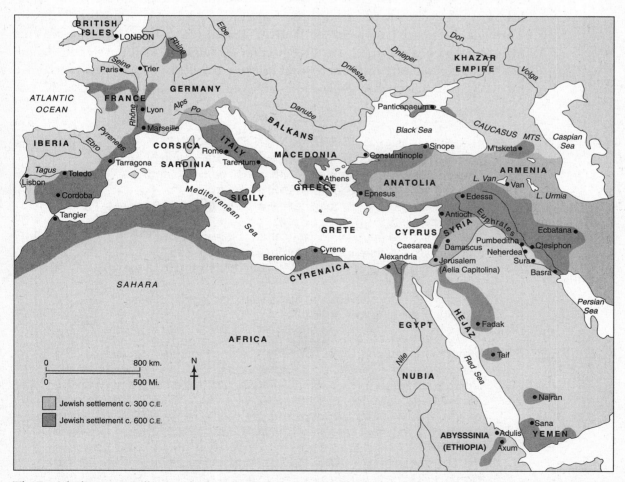

The Jewish diaspora. Following the Jewish Revolt in 66 C.E., the Roman destruction of the temple in Jerusalem in 70, and the defeat of the Bar-Cochba revolt in 135, the Roman government expelled the Jews from Judaea. These migrations spread Judaism north into Mesopotamia and Anatolia, followed trade routes throughout the Mediterranean and the Red Sea, and eventually resulted in Jewish communities being established as far afield as northwest Europe and Ethiopia.

Spain, and Gaul. A large community was established in Rome. Everywhere the Jews lived, they familiarized the non-Jews, or **Gentiles**, with their concept of monotheism, the moral principles of the Law, and the hopes for the coming of the Messiah.

Jesus of Nazareth

Jesus of Nazareth (ca. 5 B.C.E.–29 C.E.) was himself a Jew who followed the Judaic message, but he emphasized the importance of brotherly love, the love of God, and a kingdom in heaven, not on earth. He also insisted that he taught in his own name, not that of Yahweh. Twelve men, known as the Apostles, became his followers. Whereas Hammurabi's Code had taught an "eye for an eye," and the Judaic Law emphasized a set of rules of conduct, Jesus' message was one of forgiveness: "Bless your persecutors . . . Never repay injury with injury . . . Do not be conquered by evil but conquer evil with good." Jesus incited mistrust, not just among the Romans, but among the Jewish Zealots, who were disappointed that he refused to preach rebellion against Rome. The crucifixion of Jesus, while cruel, was not unusual for the time. Rumors of his resurrection, however, promised the faithful immortality. Soon, the rituals like **Baptism** and the **Eucharist** (communal celebration of the Lord's Supper) developed. The evangelical work carried on by the disciples and the establishment of a church turned a belief system into an institutionalized religion. Through the travels and work of **Paul of Tarsus** (ca. 5–57 C.E.), an essentially Hebrew religion was turned into a religion for all believers. Paul traveled the length and breadth of the eastern Roman world teaching that Jesus' message was proclaimed for all. St. Thomas reached India and established a church in Kerala in C.E. 52.

THE SERMON ON THE MOUNT

Blessed are the poor in spirit: for theirs is the kingdom of heaven.

Blessed are they that mourn: for they shall be comforted.

Blessed are the meek: for they shall inherit the earth.

Blessed are they which do hunger and thirst after righteousness: for they shall be filled.

Blessed are the merciful: for they shall obtain mercy.

Blessed are the pure in heart: for they shall see God.

Blessed are the peacemakers: for they shall be called the children of God.

Blessed are they which are persecuted for righteousness's sake: for theirs is the kingdom of heaven.

*The Sermon on the Mount is the essence of Jesus' teaching that stresses the importance of love, the avoidance of anger or violence, and the promise of a kingdom of Heaven especially for the downtrodden. Virtually all that is known about Jesus, his life and ideas, is contained in the **Gospels** (histories) of Matthew, Mark, Luke, and John. Near the age of 30, Jesus was baptized by a religious ascetic in the style of the earlier prophets. The virtual creator of Christian theology was Paul, who refined Christian doctrine in the face of Gnostic Christian refusal to acknowledge the Old Testament. Christian theology was further defined by the Nicene Creed (325 C.E.), which asserted that the Father and Son were fully equal, sharing one being and, together with the Holy Spirit, constituting the Trinity.*

The reasons for the popularity of Christianity are many:

- it embraced both men and women;

- it was less exclusive than the mystery religions;

- it appealed to common people and the poor in its communal celebrations;

- it gave a cause to many in an indifferent world of materialism and pleasure;

- its literature, like the **epistles** (Paul's letters to various Christian communities), the **gospels** (accounts of Jesus' life), and teaching inspired artistic expression.

Soon the religion also had a priesthood and ecclesiastical administration, including **priests** who met the local needs of parishioners, and **bishops** who headed communities of believers. By the fifth century, a successor to the Apostle Saint Peter, founder of the church in Rome, was designated the **Pope**. Using the framework of Roman law, the church began organizing its own body of law called **canon law**. All of this helped to ensure continuity within the church.

Christian Martyrs

Initially, the Roman government persecuted Christians because, with the establishment of the empire, Augustus incorporated the Eastern idea of god-kings to strengthen his rule. The refusal of Christians to offer sacrifices to the emperor opened them to charges of disloyalty and treason. As a result, Christianity was declared illegal, and for three centuries Christians were persecuted. Paradoxically, these persecutions and the **martyrdoms** they elicited made the religion even more popular.

Christian Roman Empire

By the fourth century there were Christians in every class and Christian communities scattered throughout the Hellenistic world and in Europe. This and the deteriorating situation on the frontiers caused Emperor **Constantine** to issue the **Edict of Milan** in 313 C.E. This edict made Christianity a legal religion throughout the empire. Constantine also encouraged the construction of churches and upheld the authority of Christian bishops in religious matters. He is most famous for building a new Roman capital, **Constantinople**, in the East. His desire to create a new Christian capital for the empire coincided with his belief that the new capital would be safer from Germanic invasions and would be at the center of trade that had shifted more to the east. In building his new city, he combined Hellenistic classicism with Christianity. The crowning building was the Church of the Holy Wisdom, better known as the **Cathedral of the Hagia Sophia**. Shortly before his death, Constantine converted to the new faith and every emperor afterward, with the exception of Julian, was a Christian. Christianity was made the official religion of the empire by edicts issued in 391 and 392. Worship of the old Roman gods was outlawed. Thus, Rome became the Christian Roman Empire, putting in place the third of the classical legacies to Europe.

Christian Sectarianism

In the early years of Christianity, local leaders were self-appointed or selected by their communities of faith. Different understanding of Christian beliefs developed.

One of the early doctrinal disputes was over the question of the divinity of Christ. **Gnostic Christians** who accepted many of the old Greek and Roman religious traditions sought salvation by escape from the material world. They believed in a divine Christ, not in Jesus as a person. Another group, the **Arian Christians** believed that because God by definition was uncreated and unchangeable, Christ could not have been a coequal. **Nestorian Christians** believed in the humanness of Jesus. Many of these beliefs were branded as **heresy** or denial of a doctrine of faith.

Roman Catholics

In 325 C.E. a church council was summoned that produced the **Nicene Creed**, determining that Christ was the "eternally begotten son of the Father." Emperor Constantine participated in the debate, paving the way for future emperors to claim they could do the same. The move of the Roman capital east to Constantinople and the fall of Rome to the Germans, however, made the pope, not the emperor, the supreme ruler of the land in the West. The emperor, however, was the ruler in the East.

Calling themselves **Catholic**, a word derived from the Greek meaning universal, Christians and their leadership claimed one world of belief united in the person of the pope. This set the stage for another dispute (besides that of secular religious rule) between the Christian church in the West and that in the East.

At first, Christians were against Greco-Roman culture, but gradually they assimilated it into their church organization and art. The blending of Christian and classical culture is evident in the work of **Saint Augustine** of Hippo (354–430 C.E.). His *Confessions* combines the Greco-Roman belief that knowledge and virtue are the same with the Christian idea that even knowledgeable people sin. According to Augustine, history is the account of God acting in time. Thus, as the Roman state in the West came under increasing attack by the barbarians, the church remained the repository of the Greco-Roman heritage.

Invasions

Beginning in the late fourth century C.E., large numbers of Germans moved into the Roman Empire in the West. German movements south have a variety of explanations—Germans were pushed by the **Huns** advancing from Central Asia, they were seeking warmer climates and new grazing lands, or they envied the wealth of Rome. For whatever reasons, one group, the **Visigoths**, rebelled against Roman rule in 378 C.E. and finally, in 410 C.E. their leader **Alaric** sacked Rome. In 476 C.E. a German general, **Odoacer**, seized power in Rome. The collapse of Rome did not end Roman history, for the empire that had already moved east to Constantinople continued on for another 1000 years. In Europe a new form of culture arose, shaping the Greco-Roman-Christian heritage in a new way.

Roman civilization began as an outpost of Hellenism. In the beginning it adopted its forms and values, but it added to it significant new contributions, principally Roman law and Christianity. Law was to Rome what Greek culture was to the Hellenistic world—the glue of classical civilization. Christianity in the West replaced Greek cultural glue when the Roman political structure fell to the Germans.

Classical Chinese Imperial Civilization

(ca. 500 B.C.E.–500 C.E.)

TIMELINE	
1027 B.C.E.–256 B.C.E.	Zhou (Chou) Dynasty
ca. 551 B.C.E.–479 B.C.E.	Confucius
402 B.C.E.–332 B.C.E.	Warring States Period
256 B.C.E.–206 B.C.E.	Qin (Ch'in) Period
207 B.C.E.–210 C.E.	Han Dynasty

CHINESE RELIGIOUS TRADITION—CONFUCIANISM, DAOISM, AND LEGALISM

As the Western world was being shaped by the classical ideas of humanism, law, and Christianity, China was developing its classical culture. The richness of Chinese belief systems has often been interpreted as a response to the complexity of humanity. Confucianism appealed to the mind, Daoism to the soul, Buddhism to the heart, and folk religions to the emotions.

Not unlike the West, where nature gods at first predominated, the origins of Chinese beliefs can be found in attitudes regarding man's relationship to nature. In earliest times the Chinese sought to appease the nature spirits. **Ancestors** were worshipped by the family because they provided the communication link to these gods. These rituals, embedded in folk religions, are still apparent in festivals and Chinese astrology. Whereas, in Western thought humans were regarded as the prime object of the natural order, and in Hindu thought the world of nature was regarded as transitory, the Chinese regarded the relationship between humans and nature as deep and reciprocal. To them, heaven, earth, and man constituted a single unity governed by the cosmic law or Dao. Within the Dao, two interacting forces were recognized—**Yin** and **Yang**. Each represented a constellation of qualities. Yin was negative, feminine, and passive; Yang was positive, masculine, and active. The essential difference between classical Chinese dualism and classical Western philosophy, the struggle between light and dark, hot and cold, was that the two forces were complementary rather than opposing. According to the Chinese, the aspiration of man was harmony rather than victory of one over the other. In a sense, the two major philosophies of China themselves reflected Chinese dualistic thought. **Daoism** sought harmony between man and nature while **Confucianism** sought harmony among men.

The emergence of formal philosophies—Confucianism, Daoism, and Legalism—occurred during the **Zhou (Chou) Dynasty** (ca. 1027–256 B.C.E.). The Zhou (Chou) period was a time of turmoil and transition. Not unlike the Greeks, who were struggling at the same time to achieve political harmony within the city-state system, the Chinese were being challenged to create a framework of thought and action for harmonious state rule.

Confucius

Confucius, or Kung Fu-tzu (ca. 551–479 B.C.E.), was born less than a century before Socrates and about the same time as Buddha. He was appointed court official by the prince of Lu and from that position reflected on the confused state of society. After he left that position, he became the center of a group of admiring disciples who wrote down his sayings and stories that later became a book, the *Analects*. The thoughts of Confucius centered on the duties and proper behavior of the individual within society. He taught that there was a universal natural law and that human beings should live according to this law. Within that law, he considered the family the basic unit of society. Proper family relationships should replicate those of society at large. In society at large, he identified five relationships that were to be ordered on the basis of **filial piety**, or respect for one's parents or elders:

- the ruler should be just and the ruled loyal;

- the father should be loving and the son respectful;

- the husband should be righteous and the wife obedient;

- the older brother should be genteel and the younger humble;

- the older friend should be considerate, the younger deferent.

Confucius also emphasized moderation and proper conduct, or *li*. A Confucian gentleman was a man of integrity, education and culture, and proper conduct. Because gentlemen were made, not born, a man of poor birth could become a gentleman without aristocratic birth.

Mengzi (Mencius)

Confucius, like Socrates, wrote nothing down. Confucius' most famous follower, **Mengzi** (372–289 B.C.E.), recorded Confucian thought and added to it. Mencius developed the idea of self-perfection and believed that through self-perfection society would be ordered. This idea first appeared in the *Record of Rites* (*Li Ji, Li Chi*):

. . .when the personal life is cultivated, the family will be regulated; when the family is regulated, the state will be in order; and when the state is in order, there will be peace throughout the world. From the Son of Heaven (Emperor) down to the common people, all must regard cultivation of the personal life as the root or foundation.

Mengzi taught that a moral leader must enjoy the respect and support of his subjects. A good ruler was thought to possess the **Mandate of Heaven** or a divine right to govern. If a ruler governed badly or was immoral, the people would rise up in revolt. The idea did not originate with Mengzi; rather, it was used by the Zhou (Chou) to justify overthrow of the Shang dynasty, but, in tying it to the wider philosophy of cosmic order, the idea of divine rule was legitimized. As a corollary to the Mandate of Heaven, the **Dynastic Cycle** was developed by later Chinese scholars as an interpretation of the past to predict the future. The theory asserted that Chinese dynasties repeat themselves, going through the stages of warring states, unification, barbarian invasions and conquest, absorption into the Chinese system, and finally, creation of a new dynasty based on the Mandate of Heaven. Because it lacks a priesthood, prescribed rituals, temples, and a concept of divinity, Confucianism is closer to a philosophy like humanism than a religion like Christianity. Yet, it is a creed that millions of East Asians follow as an ethical guide.

Daoism

Whereas Confucianism sought to order the proper relationships among men, Daoism sought order between man and nature. Though little is known for certain, the assumed founder of Daoism, **Laozi (Lao-Tzu)**, lived in the sixth century B.C.E. The book attributed to him, the ***Dao De Jing*** (*Book of the Way and Its Power*), was probably the work of several people and dates only from the fourth century B.C.E. According to Laozi (Lao-Tzu), the Dao, or way, was not a common code of social conduct, but a set of values that would allow a person to live in harmony with nature. This involved knowing the laws of nature and flowing with them rather than reordering them. Thus, the best ruler for a Daoist was the one who governed least. Daoist influence was greatest in the area of art and science due to the seclusion and observation of nature, which were preoccupations of its followers. A person could be both a Daoist and a Confucian—a Daoist when reflective and alone, and a Confucian when a member of the body politic.

Legalism

More pragmatic than Confucianism and less rooted in ancient Chinese thought was **Legalism**, a philosophy gained from many related schools of political thought that flourished during the late Zhou (Chou), primarily led by **Han Fei Zi (Han Fei-tzu** d. 233 B.C.E.) and **Li Si (Li Ssu** d. 208 B.C.E.). The ideal legalist state was authoritarian because human nature was evil. Laws should replace morality. The ruler must provide discipline to maintain order. Education was looked on as unnecessary and impractical as people must work and produce. Legalism as a political philosophy triumphed under the Qin (Ch'in) dynasty.

I Ching

Because of the philosophical nature of Confucianism, Daoism, and Legalism, Chinese people continued to cling to folk religions that provided an avenue for emotional and spiritual activities and thought. The *I Ching*, or *Book of Changes*, fulfilled some of the same purpose as the Shang oracle bones; that is, they were used to learn the will of the gods and predict the future. It is essentially a book of oracles, the contents of which are read by using randomly tossed coins. Chinese belief systems and philosophical thought emphasized the importance of nature as reflected in art and science, the high esteem in which peasants were held, the importance of the family and elders, filial piety that is reflected in the hierarchical nature of social and political relationships, and the theories of the Mandate of Heaven and Dynastic Cycle that legitimized government.

CLASSICAL CHINESE SCHOOLS OF THOUGHT

1. The master said, In serving his father and mother a man may gently remonstrate with them. But if he sees that he has failed to change their opinion, he should resume an attitude of deference and not thwart them; he may feel discouraged, but not resentful.

2. There is a thing confusedly formed,
   Born before heaven and earth.
   Silent and void
   It stands alone and does not change,
   Goes round and does not weary.
   It is capable of being the mother of the world.
   I know not its name
   So I style it "the way."

3. The nature of man is evil; his goodness is acquired.
   His nature being what it is, man is born, first, with a desire for gain.
   If this desire is followed, strife will result and courtesy will disappear.

4. There are two extremes which he who has given up the world ought to avoid.
   A life given to pleasures. . . and a life given to mortifications.
   By avoiding these two extremes, the seeker of Truth has gained the knowledge of the Middle Path which leads to insight, which leads to wisdom which conduces to calm, to knowledge, to enlightenment, to Nirvana.

Document 1 is Confucianist, 2 is Daoist, 3 is Legalist, and 4 is Buddhist. In Document 1 the emphasis is on the cardinal Confucian principles of proper conduct and filial piety. Document 2 reflects the Daoist emphasis on nature and discovering "the way" or Dao. Document 3 illustrates the cardinal principle of Legalism, which is that man is basically evil and, therefore, needs a dictatorial political system to order society. Document 4 illustrates the Buddhist emphasis on finding Heaven, or Nirvana, through enlightenment, self-knowledge, and a middle path. The Chinese found they could live with all these positions except Legalism because Confucianism appeals to the mind, Daoism to the soul, and Buddhism to the heart. Legalism rejects the basic proposition of Chinese thought, which is the harmony of the universe. Legalism is more Western in its view that man is basically evil and political systems must balance contending and opposing forces.

THE ZHOU (CHOU), QIN (CH'IN), AND HAN DYNASTIES

The **Zhou (Chou)** are believed to have been Turkic-speaking peoples from Central Asia. They referred to the subjugated Chinese as "black-haired people." When the Zhou (Chou) under **King Wu** overthrew the Shang, they adopted much of Shang culture but extended Chinese rule beyond the boundaries of the Shang. Confronted with the challenge of ruling a large territory of people unlike themselves, they built a second capital in the **Wei Valley** west of the Huang He (Yellow River). They gave huge tracts of land to members of the royal family and to others who had talent and were loyal. Not unlike feudalism in Europe, in formal ceremonies using written records the lord pledged loyalty to the king in return for grants of lands. On these grants of lands were enserfed peasants who lived in villages and tilled the land in the **well-field system**. In this system each of eight households cultivated one of eight plots that were arranged around a central plot and a well. The middle plot was tilled by all the families to provide the produce that would be given to the lord as tribute. In effect, the Zhou (Chou) king was political overlord of the land and supreme religious leader. The role of males as the head of the family, clan, and dynasty increased as the patriarch played the key role in the celebration of religious ceremonies designed to win the blessings of the ancestors or heaven. In the central core regions, Zhou (Chou) kings began to use regular, educated, salaried officials called **shi** to help them administer the kingdom. At first, the Zhou (Chou) kings were in strong control, but, because most of the lands given to lords were on the frontiers where expansion was possible, lords were able to become absolute rulers in their own right. China gradually became a land of independent kingdoms. During the period of the **Warring States** (402–332 B.C.E.) the entire political organization of the Zhou (Chou) collapsed.

In overthrowing the Shang, the Zhou (Chou) used the Mandate of Heaven to justify their rule. As the central administration of the Zhou (Chou) collapsed, the impoverished aristocrats gravitated to the border states, bringing their much needed talents to help nomadic warriors rule. This period saw the origins of a trained civil service based on talent. It also produced one of the most important martial classics of world history, one that has become the handbook for twentieth-century guerrilla warfare. *The Art of War* by **Sun Zi** (**Sun Tzu** ca. fourth century B.C.E.), who was very likely a contemporary of Confucius, is about how to win wars and battles with superior strategies and tactics rather than brute strength. Its central premise is that successful warfare is based on deception. Despite warfare, cities grew up around forts. Roads supplied the cities. Trade increased and was made easier with the invention of coined money. Iron technology blossomed during the Zhou (Chou). Chinese metalsmiths produced both wrought (shaped) and cast (poured) iron, an achievement not matched in Europe until the fourteenth century. Iron was used for weapons and for farming. Plows with iron shares broke the ground more easily. Continuing raids in the north drove the peasantry south and east so that by the end of the Zhou (Chou), the two great river systems of China, the Huang Ho (Yellow) and Yangtzi (Yangtse), had been settled. Rice growing in the southern parts began.

Qin Dynasty

In 256 B.C.E. the man who proclaimed himself **Shi Huangdi** (**Shi Huang-ti**), or First Emperor of the **Qin (Ch'in) Dynasty**, deposed the last Zhou (Chou) king. Although his rule lasted only 15 years, Shi Huangdi united China and from him

---

Did You Know?

The Zhou (Chou) period had a lasting impact on Chinese society. During this period, Confucian and Daoist philosophies were born.

the Western word **China** is derived. The Qin (Ch'in), of nomadic origin, were one of many rebel states in Zhou (Chou) China. The Qin (Ch'in) increased their power due to a number of factors. Gradually they conscripted peasants they had freed in battle into military service. Their superior bureaucracy ensured well-supplied and well-organized forces. They were receptive to military innovation. They were, for instance, one of the first states to use massed cavalry. Soon the Qin (Ch'in) had extended their power as far south as modern Hong Kong and they even invaded Vietnam.

The First Emperor of the Qin (Ch'in) considered a highly centralized state necessary for a united China. His prime minister Li Si (Li Ssu), a founder of Legalism, helped shape his centralization program. First, he crippled the nobility by ordering them to leave their lands and live at court. Then he took over their land and organized China into provinces subdivided into smaller units. Provinces were ruled by governors and officials who were appointed by the emperor and unable to claim hereditary rights to their positions. To harness the human population to facilitate tax collection, building projects, and military service, Emperor Qin (Ch'in) ordered a census. Then he centralized trade practices by standardizing the Chinese script, weights, measures, and axle lengths of carts. He furthered irrigation and land reclamation projects. He promoted the production of textiles, especially silk. To protect his empire from northern nomads, primarily the **Xiongnu (Hsiung-nu)**, he linked together existing walls and added sections to form one great wall, extending from the sea some 1400 miles west.

Among the other remarkable building projects of the First Emperor of the Qin (Ch'in) were a royal tomb and a terra cotta guardian army of 6000 life-size pottery men and horses. The royal tomb, called Mount Li, located near present-day Xian (Sian), was discovered in 1974 and has yet to be completely opened due to fears that exposure to the atmosphere will ruin the delicate artifacts. In a quest for immortality, the First Emperor of the Qin (Ch'in) ordered the building of the tomb in 208 B.C.E., two years before his death according to **Sima Qian (Ssu-ma Ch'ien**, ca. 145–90 B.C.E.), China's classical historian. Using over 700,000 conscripts, the tomb chamber is said to have reproduced in minute detail the universe over which he ruled. It included mechanically triggered crossbows set to shoot intruders and the various rivers of the empire were reproduced in quicksilver and made to flow mechanically. Heavenly constellations were depicted on the ceiling. The army of terra cotta figures surround the tomb. Their lifelike individualized demeanors suggest that actual soldiers and horses served as models. Portrayed in graceful, realistic style, complete with weapons and horse gear, the entombed army has left an authentic record of hairstyles, clothing, weapons, armor, and horsemanship of the period.

Despite his achievements the First Emperor of the Qin (Ch'in) was an unpopular ruler. As a Legalist, he distrusted Confucian scholars. They were purged and their literary heritage destroyed in a massive book burning. Heavy taxation and forced labor alienated the peasants. His death in 206 B.C.E. sparked massive revolts. Then **Liu Bang (Liu Pang**, 247–195 B.C.E.), a petty official of the Qin (Ch'in), defeated the Qin (Ch'in) successor and established the **Han Dynasty** (207 B.C.E.–210 C.E.). Liu Bang (Liu Pang) is one of only two commoners in Chinese history to establish a major dynasty. He is often referred to by his posthumous imperial title, **Han Gaozu (Kao-tsu)**. The Han dynasty, which lasted for over 400 years, saw the consolidation of Chinese civilization. Whereas the Zhou (Chou) gave

Did You Know?

The Great Wall is still regarded as one of the greatest structures of ancient times. It is the only human construction visible from space.

China its philosophy of statecraft, and the Qin (Ch'in) united China and gave it its name, the Han gave it its distinctly classical character by institutionalizing the largest, most effective, and enduring **civil service bureaucracy** in the preindustrial world. Chosen by examination, these scholar-bureaucrats, the **mandarins**, not only ran the state, but provided its creative genius and a reverence for education that endures to this day. Dynasties came and went, but the mandarins and their Confucian philosophy shaped the political, economic, social, and cultural framework of China. So closely do the Chinese identify themselves with this tradition that they refer to themselves as "**sons of Han**."

It appeared that China might return to a feudal order under Liu Bang (Liu Pang) because he rewarded his followers with grants of land. His successor, **Wudi (Wu Ti**, 140–87 B.C.E.), however, moved toward bureaucratic centralization by requiring that domains of vassals be divided among heirs and not passed on in perpetuity. This began an ongoing struggle in Chinese history between artistocrats and scholars. Liu Bang (Liu Pang) and Wudi (Wu Ti) also replaced Legalism with Confucianism. Some dedicated scholars had hidden their books or memorized them during the Qin (Ch'in) purges. In the Han Confucian revival, they elaborated the theories of the Mandate of Heaven and Dynastic Cycle. According to Han Confucianism, the emperor by mandate had divine powers and was responsible for protecting the empire from invasion and internal disruption. A thorough knowledge of Confucian teaching also became essential for employment and promotion in the Han administrative hierarchy. This was institutionalized in the establishment of an imperial university at the capital in **Changan (Ch'ang An)** in 124 B.C.E. At the end of the Han era, there were more than 30,000 students concentrating on memorization and interpretation of the Confucian classics. When formal examination for government positions began in the last century B.C.E., the first professional civil service was established. Theoretically, any Chinese citizen could take the exam, but because preparation required education, upper-class candidates had a decided advantage. Exams were scored strictly on merit, with the scores and the difficulty of the exam determining the scholar's rank at court.

Han Class System

The growing influence of the mandarins affected the class system. Gradually, in hierarchical style reflective of Confucian concepts of filial piety, the mandarin class ranked at the top of the social scale, below which were the peasants, who were revered for the vital connection they had with the land. Beneath them were the artisans, and lowest in rank were the merchants. Merchants were disdained because they produced nothing and merely made money by transferring produce. Outside the class system altogether were the military who, in Confucian thought, were symbolic of failure to maintain order.

> **Did You Know?**
>
> Mandarins gained position at the expense of aristocratic families.

Han Foreign Policies

The Han period was one of great imperial expansion despite nomads north of the Great Wall who were a repeated threat to the Chinese throughout their imperial history. The nomad could simply apply the skills he used daily, those of horsemanship and archery, to attack the Chinese frontier, while the Chinese peasant farmer had to interrupt his agricultural life and train as a soldier to defend the imperial boundary stretching some 1400 miles. From the Han to the Ching Dynasty, the Chinese generally followed one of two patterns of dealing with the nomads. One was to use military force against the nomads and defend the Great Wall as Qin (Ch'in) had done. The first Han Emperor Han Gaozu (Liu Bang, or Liu Pang) pursued a different policy. He presented the nomadic Xiongnu (Hsiung-nu) leaders with elaborate gifts, treated them as equals, and arranged marriages for them with imperial princesses. Later, the Emperor Wudi (Wu Ti) reversed this policy, using military force instead. Military colonies were established in strategic locations along the frontier from inner Mongolia to North Korea to prevent nomadic invasions from the north.

Arts, Sciences, and Technology

The wealth of the Han era led to classical achievements in the arts and sciences. Wealth was driven by improvements in agriculture and trade. During this period, the **ridge-and-furrow** system of planting was developed, with seeds planted in ridges along the furrows that collected water. To maintain fertility, manure and crushed bones were used. Excellent metallurgy led to more effective plows. New harnesses were developed that, instead of choking the animals, allowed them to pull heavier loads. Tea and sugar cane were still luxuries of the south, but silk was a large item of produce. **Porcelain**, a form of clay fired at very high temperatures, was invented. Unlike Rome, roads remained undeveloped and difficult to travel, but canals and dikes were extensive and facilitated trade. Merchants were encouraged because they brought in tax revenue, but were regulated. State monopolies also kept essential commodities under the control of the state as a lucrative source of income. City life reflected the splendid lifestyle of the rich as well as the poverty of the poor. Elements of Daoism developed into a popular religion. Entertainment for the rich included private musical troupes, while gambling and cockfighting entertained the poor.

Wealth and literacy combined to create lasting contributions to the sciences. Key to education, government, and the sciences was **Ts'ai Lun**'s (**Cai Lun**) invention of **paper** (105 C.E.), which was cheaper than silk. In the Han period, the study of history flourished. The Chinese, like the Greeks, began to conceive of history as a discipline where artifacts are examined and data analyzed. Sima Qian (Ssu-ma Ch'ien) wrote a classic study of Chinese history using eyewitnesses and written documents called *Records of the Grand Historian*. **Ban Qao** (**Pan Chao**), China's first woman historian and scholar, wrote poems and essays, notably *Lessons for Women*. In medicine, China produced its own Hippocrates, **Ching Chi** (**Ching Chih**), whose *Treatise on Fevers* became a standard work. The career of **Chang Heng** (**Ch'ang Heng,** 78–139 C.E.) was strikingly similar to that of Eratosthenes. Both concluded the earth was round and both built models to test their theories.

Much of China's intellectual life during the Han took place in the Han capital at Changan (Ch'ang An). Whereas Rome sprawled over seven hills, Changan was a picture of mathematically planned discipline, symbolic of the symmetry of the cosmos. The city itself was constructed in square blocks, each of which was walled and had only one gate with a watchtower that was closed at curfew. It resembled Rome in its massive public works—walls, roads, and canals. Most spectacular was not the Forum and Colosseum, but the Imperial Palace with its awe-inspiring audience halls, pavilions, granaries, arsenals, and artificial lakes. The city was also a hub of commerce and the eastern terminus of the Silk Road.

THE SILK ROAD

In 133 B.C.E. the Han drove the Xiongnu (Hsiung-nu) tribes north and then advanced into western Turkestan where they opened up direct relations with India. Chinese armies also conquered western Korea where they took over trade with Japan. They extended their rule to modern-day Hong Kong, and by 111 B.C.E. they had conquered northern Vietnam. The military conquests brought the Chinese into closer contact with distant peoples. This resulted in a dramatic increase in trade. Chinese merchants opened up a new route from southwestern China via the rivers of Vietnam and Myanmar (Burma) to ports on the Bay of Bengal. At first the Chinese left trade in the hands of foreigners, but later Chinese merchants gained control.

The origins of the Silk Road can be found in the continuous network of advanced societies stretched across the southern half of the continents of Europe and Asia. In the west was Rome, in the east was Han China; in between were the Kushan Empire of northern India and Afghanistan, and the Parthians who ruled Persia and Mesopotamia. The coexistence of these great empires meant that vast areas enjoyed internal peace and efficient government, conditions that made possible the growth of large-scale trade. The geography of Asia also made such a transEurasian route possible. There are no major seas or mountains to prohibit east-west movement, and the desert barriers can be circumvented.

Did You Know?

The Silk Road itself stretched 2500 miles across Central Asia.

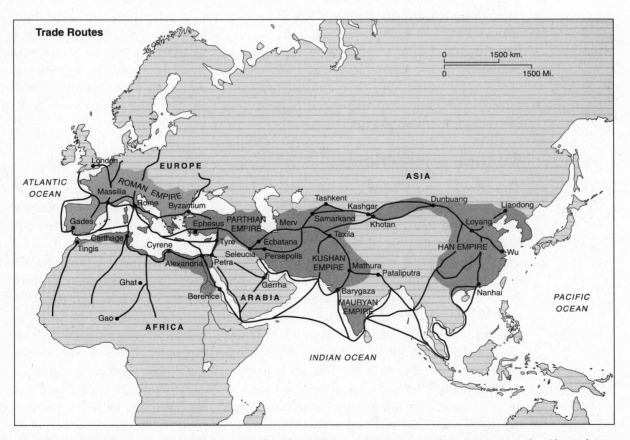

The Main African-Eurasian Trade Routes in the Classical Age ca. 200 B.C.E.–200 C.E. During the Classical Age of great empires, Europe, Asia, and Africa were linked on land and sea by vast trade networks. The Romans called the route linking China with the Roman world the Silk Road.

Long-distance trade between East and West Asia was also possible by sea because of the monsoon wind cycle. The broad expanse of warm ocean (Indian Ocean), the South Eurasian landmass, and a major mountain barrier (Himalayas) create unique climatological wind conditions. **Monsoon winds** are created by warming differentials between water and land. From June until September, the summer moisture-laden winds blow from the southwest until they hit the Himalayas, and from October to May they blow the other way, from the northeast. Ships could catch the winds going west in the winter and east on the return voyage in the summer. Long-distance trade was also spurred by product specialization and a demand for luxury goods that rich and stable empires could afford. By the second century C.E., trade routes covered Eurasia and sea routes ran from China to Africa.

From the Han capital at Changan, the Silk Road proceeded northwest to the frontier town of **Dunhuang (Tun-huang)**. A series of caravanseries dotted the arid deserts and windswept mountains until the convoys reached Merv in the Kushan Empire. From there, the Silk Road ran south of the Caspian Sea, through Parthia and the Roman Empire to the shores of the Mediterranean. As the name implies, Chinese silk, which probably comprised 90 percent of China's exports of the time, was much prized in Rome, where its manufacture was still unknown. The Romans became aware, even at this early date, that the educated Chinese were supremely confident of their civilization and had little need of the products of other cultures. Wrote Ammianus Marcellinus in 380 C.E., "There Seres (Chinese) . . . , study to pass their lives in peace . . . and so free are they from wants that, though ready to dispose of their own products, they purchase none from abroad." The sea route, while less known, was probably even more important and more durable. This was because land transport was more rudimentary and thus expensive (mules, camels, oxen), and because it was more vulnerable to political disruption. Instead of hugging the coast, merchant marine ships could sail rapidly and directly from India to Arabia and back in four months, some of them with the carrying capacity of 500 tons.

> **Did You Know?**
>
> China was famous for its silk, Southeast Asia for spices, India for textiles (calico, muslin, linen, and cotton), and Rome for glass, gold, and silver.

Cultural Interaction

The effects of such long-distance trade were not just commercial. Significant cultural interaction occurred as well. Thousands of people—sailors, camel drivers, merchants, monks, pilgrims, and porters mixed. One of the most important cultural interactions was religious. Zoroastrianism, Judaism, and Christianity were implanted in India and in Central Asia. Especially important for China was the spread of Buddhism, which penetrated China with the fall of the Han Empire. Peasant unrest due to heavy taxation and corvee labor culminated in a great revolutionary effort led by the Daoists in 184 C.E. After years of struggle, the last Han emperor was deposed in 220 C.E. and China was divided into three kingdoms. Like the Romans, the Chinese had incorporated nomadic peoples in their armies, but as government deteriorated, the nomads began to invade. During the period between the fall of the Han and rise of the Sui, called the Age of Disunity (220–589 C.E.), great commanders and warriors were transformed into legendary heroes. Their daring deeds were told over and over and finally written down in ***The Romance of the Three Kingdoms**, a novel not unlike the stories of King Arthur and his knights.

Buddhism

In the midst of this economic distress and political instability, Buddhism arrived from India, disseminated by silk merchants and missionaries. Not unlike Christianity, Buddhism offered spiritual solace and cultural cohesion in a time of political fragmentation. Chinese Buddhists blended practices from many Indian Buddhist sects and included some of their own values, like family lineage, in Buddhist teachings. Typically, second sons became Buddhist monks while the first sons maintained family responsibilities. Buddhism often competed with Daoism for the affection of the common people. Buddhism offered a clearer doctrine of personal salvation, but Daoist healing and connections with nature continued to win Chinese support. Confucianism, with its secular concerns, lost ground during this period but reappeared midway through the Tang Period.

Belief Systems and the State

The Chinese classical period established the major patterns of Chinese government, culture, and thought. Legitimization for rule, the Mandate of Heaven and Dynastic Cycle, begun in the Zhou (Chou) period, were formalized by Confucian scholars under the Han. This system of changing dynasties but continuous imperial rule lasted until 1911. The idea of a state run by Confucian scholar-bureaucrats, selected by merit, matured under the Han and is, perhaps, Chinese civilization's most important and enduring legacy. Dynasties came and went, but Confucian values of filial piety, proper conduct, and education gave hierarchical and civil order to the state. It was also the basis for literacy and scholarship. Legalism, at odds with the Chinese cosmic ideas of harmony, shaped the Qin (Ch'in) era of centralization, but it otherwise remained unpopular during the Han Dynasty. The long and stable rule of the Han stimulated trade that linked China with Eurasia along the Silk Road. Along that Road came foreign ideas, especially Buddhism.

CHAPTER 9

Classical Indian Civilization

(ca. 300 B.C.E.–500 C.E.)

TIMELINE	
ca. 563 B.C.E.–483 B.C.E.	Siddhartha Gautama (Buddha)
ca. 322 B.C.E.–232 B.C.E.	Mauryan Empire
320 C.E.–467 C.E.	Gupta Empire (Golden Age)

INDIAN RELIGIOUS TRADITION—HINDUISM, JAINISM, AND BUDDHISM

As in the West and China, Indian classicism was closely connected with the thought and belief systems of India. India's spiritual traditions blossomed in the sixth and fifth centuries B.C.E., about the same time as the Greek and Chinese religious and philosophical traditions. Indian religious thought gave the world three powerful moral and philosophical belief systems—Hinduism, Jainism, and Buddhism.

Hinduism

The most basic and enduring of the Indian religions is Hinduism, a religion that matured and triumphed during the classical age. The origins of Hinduism can be found in Aryan religious traditions, or **Brahmanism**, as revealed in the *Vedas* or hymns to the gods. Hinduism is both the oldest and most diverse of the world's religions, easily mutable and readily able to incorporate new ideas. The bedrock of Hindu belief is that there is a sacred division of society into castes, written in the *Code of Manu*, and that all Hindu gods are aspects of Brahma, the supreme, indefinable principle of life. The various deities are both aspects of Brahma and ritual vehicles to help reach Brahma, which is the goal of all Hindus.

The broad outlines of Hindu thought that had evolved during the Aryan period of Indian history matured during the classical era. The Brahman caste gradually worked out the basic outlines of their theology that encompassed both moral and spiritual ideas. According to the dogma, or religious teachings, to reach Brahma, people must follow a prescribed path. First, they must observe **dharma**, the moral duties of their caste. The degree to which dharma is observed determines one's **karma**, or the accumulation of good and bad deeds during life. Those who observed dharma could hope to be reincarnated in a higher caste in the next life. Those with bad karma would be reborn in a lower caste. The law outlines the proper human pursuits such as acquiring money honestly and pursuing pleasure and love for perpetuation of the family. When the moral law is observed, the endless cycle of birth, death, and reincarnation will end. **Moksha** is the release from the wheel of life and unity with Brahma, or the Universal All. In the long epic poem the *Mahabharata*, an ideal state based on dharma is personified in King Dharma's law.

THE LAWS OF MANU—THE STATUS OF WOMEN

Women must be honored and adorned by their father, brothers, husbands, and brothers-in-law, who desire their own welfare.

Where women are honored, there the gods are pleased; but where they are not honored, no sacred rite yields rewards. . . .

In that family, where the husband is pleased with his wife and the wife with her husband, happiness will assuredly be lasting.

Day and night women must be kept in dependence. . . .

Her father protects her in childhood, her husband protects her in youth, and her sons protect her in old age; a woman is never fit for independence. . .

The Laws of Manu are a collection of social codes based on early Indian customs from about 1000 B.C.E. Probably written by teachers of the Vedas (hymns and prayers to the Arian gods that, along with the Upanishads, or lessons of the nature of the universe, form the basis of Hinduism), the Laws of Manu reflect the Hindu idea that meaning in life can be found in fulfillment of one's caste duties. Women in Hindu society have a special and revered place because the pleasure of love is sanctified within the bonds of the family. Yet, women are subordinate. Large dowries that were to accompany women in marriage made girls a liability to their families in an essentially patriarchal society.

After the third century B.C.E. Hinduism began to emphasize the role of powerful gods like **Shiva**, the cosmic dancer who creates and destroys, and **Vishnu**, the preserver of creation, in reaching the ideal state of Brahma, or god-force. From the emphasis on a god-force of all life, not just human life, came the tradition of **nonviolence** toward all living creatures, which was lifted to new heights in Jainist beliefs. The ***Bhagavad Gita***, the best-loved hymn of Hindus and not unlike the Christian parables, is a spiritual guide to life's problems. In it, a warrior, **Arjuna**, struggles with the decision of whether to go to battle against his own kinsmen. **Krishna**, who is a manifestation of the god Vishnu, instructs him to carry out his duties as a warrior because "The eternal in man cannot kill; the Eternal in man cannot die." Thus, Hinduism emphasizes the everlasting nature of Brahma within each person even in death and the duty to one's caste (in this case the warrior caste).

CASTE

Religion justifies Jaiti or caste and the stability of the social system proves the validity of the religious teachings. And, not unlike Confucian thought, the hierarchical order established by religious thought, in this case caste, provided the framework for the orderly structure of the state. The Brahmans were the upper caste of priests and scholars. The ruling caste, the Kshatriya, were second. Beneath them were the peasants (Vaishya) and serfs (Shudra). Outside the caste were various groups of outcasts and slaves.

Caste hierarchy was reflected in the life of every village, which became a microcosm of the Hindu order and religious bond. Within the village each caste or subcaste was a community that shared religious duties, worked in similar occupations, and helped each other in times of calamity. In daily life, social functions as informal as sharing a meal or as formal as a wedding took place within the context of one's own caste. Hindu castes and religion were the glue of classical Indian civilization. As with Confucianism, the vast literature of Hinduism as preserved in **Sanskrit** (Hindu script) and other regional languages encouraged and elevated scholarship and united the peoples of India.

Did You Know?

Not unlike the yin and yang of Chinese cosmic thought, the caste system and the concept of Brahma are two sides of the same core of Hindu classical thought.

Jainism

Around the sixth century B.C.E. two reformers of Hinduism appeared. In part, this was a response to the pessimism of an endless cycle of death and reincarnation prior to reaching unity with Brahma. It was also a protest against Brahman ritual and the power and privilege of the Brahman caste. The founder and most influential thinker of **Jainism** was **Mahavira** (ca. 540–468 B.C.E.). Mahavira thought that the whole of the universe is composed of souls and matter. The only way for any soul to achieve the eternal oneness with Brahma was to rid itself of matter and rise to the top of the universe as a soul. Jains considered all life to be composed of souls so they believed that no life, either plant or animal, should be destroyed. Since this would logically lead to starvation and death, Jains devised a hierarchy of life, with human beings at the apex, followed by animals, plants, and inanimate objects. To do the least violence, therefore, one must be a vegetarian and shun material ways. In this way, nonviolence, which was already part of Hindu thought, became a cardinal principle of Jainism. It has influenced many from Emerson to Gandhi and Martin Luther King Jr. The extreme asceticism (self-denial) of the Jains, however, made it a fringe religion.

Buddhism

More influential was **Siddhartha Gautama** (ca. 563–483 B.C.E.), better known as **Buddha**, meaning **Enlightened One**. Both Buddha and Mahavira were Kshatriya, the class below the top and most likely to resent Brahman privilege. Buddha was also distressed by the pessimism of the endless cycle of life and the inability to change one's karma or place in this life until death. Saddened by this human suffering, he tried a life of asceticism and fasting but found it led nowhere. His contemplation then led him to the conclusion that happiness in this life could be found not in changing one's karma but in changing one's thoughts and attitudes. According to the **Four Noble Truths**,

1. life is suffering,
2. suffering is caused by desire,
3. one can be released from desire by following the **Eightfold Path**, after which
4. a state of grace when desire is extinguished (**Nirvana**) can be reached, releasing one from karma.

At the heart of the Eightfold Path (symbolized by a chariot wheel with eight spokes) was self-knowledge, a willingness to be free of suffering and desire, and a decision to adopt "right conduct" and "right speech." In this way of life, one practiced love and compassion, joy and serenity. Buddha also recognized that all things change with time, including death, at which time the combination of physical and mental parts becomes rearranged in a new form of life. In that way, there is life everlasting, not the extinguishing of life in oneness with Brahma.

The appeal of Buddhism, like Christianity, is that the Eightfold Path could be followed by anyone—noble or peasant, educated or ignorant. Anyone could attain enlightenment. Its emphasis on love, the life of the spirit, and an attainable Heaven was, like Christianity, equalizing and humanizing. It opposed the rigid hierarchy of Hinduism and released people from the endless cycle of life. Its success was also related to Buddhist proselytizing and institutionalization. A circle of disciples, the **Sangha**, systematized the faith and spread it far and wide, using the Asian trade routes. Temples, monasteries, statues of Buddha, and rituals made active participation possible.

Upon Buddha's death, Buddhism split into two sects—**Theravada** (Lesser Vehicle) and **Mahayana** (Larger Vehicle). The Theravada branch, which was popular in Southeast Asia, asserted that the tenets of Buddhism rested on the life and teachings of Buddha. It is called "lesser" because of its strict, conservative doctrines. The Mahayana branch, popular in China, Japan, Korea, and Vietnam, was more liberal, recognizing that beliefs could evolve and go beyond Buddhist scriptures. It emphasized compassion and was called the "larger" because it held that there were many ways to salvation. Mahayana Buddhism maintained that Buddha in his previous lives had been a **Bodhisattva**—a wise being, a buddha. Bodhisattvas had achieved enlightenment but had declined nirvana in order to help others. Around this sect grew a pantheon of heavenly buddhas and bodhissatvas to whom people could pray for enlightenment, becoming much like the saints of Christendom. The Buddha is usually represented as looking like the inhabitants of the country in which he is revered, although all the images hold certain features in common like the hand positions (**mudras**), which are used to show whether the Buddha is meditating, giving blessing, teaching, and so on. In India, Buddhism made a dramatic appearance under King Ashoka. Eventually, Buddha was worshipped as one of the many Hindu gods and Buddhism was folded into Hinduism. But it was from India that Buddhism spread over a wide area of Asia.

MAURYAN AND GUPTA CIVILIZATIONS

The strong village social fabric based on caste and the Aryan legacy of local princes or **rajas** made political centralization difficult and even irrelevant in India. However, during the classical period two great empires rose, the **Mauryan** (ca. 322–232 B.C.E.) and the **Gupta** (320–467 C.E.). Hindu and Buddhist thought and

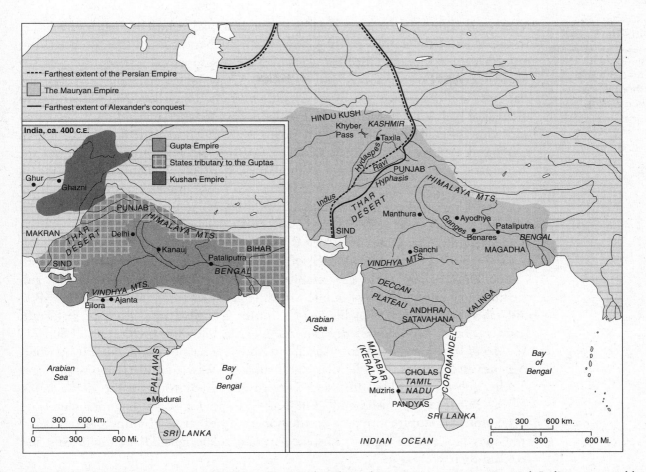

The Mauryan Empire, 322 B.C.E.–185 B.C.E. During the Classical Era major states arose in north India, most notably the Mauryan, Jushan, and Gupta Empires. The brief encounter with the Greek forces led by Alexander the Great, which reached the Indus River Valley in 326 B.C.E, may have stimulated the Mauryans to build India's first empire.

culture were interwoven through the contours of both empires, influencing art, scholarship, and architecture. Prior to the rise of the Maurya, India was in turmoil caused both by external invasion and internal unrest. Around 572 B.C.E. the Achaemenid Persians controlled the Indus Valley region. In the northeast around the Ganges Valley, a strong Aryan kingdom, **Magadha**, with the support of the Brahmans, ruled and formed alliances to rebuff the Persians. Unity was fragile, however, always susceptible to inter-Aryan rivalries and outside invasion. It was during this unsettled time, as in Zhou (Chou) China, that Buddha was born, setting off yet another conflict—between Buddhists and Hindus. This turmoil opened the door to yet another invasion, this time by Alexander the Great in 327 B.C.E. After Alexander's brief appearance in India, a number of Greek rulers controlled India's northwest territory, indirectly spreading Greek influence. Of particular importance was the flow into India of Greek astronomical and mathematical ideas and Greek artistic styles.

Mauryan Empire

The Greek invasion also left a political vacuum once Hellenistic kingdoms in the area weakened. The ruler of a small state in the Ganges Valley, **Chandragupta**

Did You Know?

Chandragupta
created the largest
empire yet seen in
Indian history.

Maurya defeated the Greek general Seleucus and made himself king in 322 B.C.E. In the heart of the empire in the Ganges Valley, Chandragupta then proceeded to build a capital city, **Pataliputra**, to which ambassadors came from all over the world. The city boasted a moat and walls with 570 watchtowers. Court style became elaborate and the palace rich in jewels and courtiers. The palace hall was similar to the palace hall at Persepolis. It was lined with carved sandstone columns decorated with vines of gold and buds of silver. Roads were built and trade flourished. Indian merchants exported elephants, silk, spices, cotton, and perfume to China and the Hellenistic cities. Chandragupta even requested of the Hellenistic kings that a sophist philosopher be sent. **Megasthenes**, a Greek ambassador to the imperial court of Chandragupta at Pataliputra in 302 B.C.E., found the splendor of India even greater than that of the Persian cities of the Seleucid Empire.

In statecraft, Chandragupta adopted the Persian style of administration by dividing the empire into provinces, each of which was governed by someone linked to Chandragupta's family. He also established a bureaucracy to oversee taxation and the financing and building of public works. He created a standing army of 500,000 and relied on the advice of his chief minister **Kautilya** in matters of statecraft. Kautilya's book the ***Arthashastra*** is not unlike Machiavelli's *The Prince* and Sun Zi's *The Art of War* in its advice to rulers about how to amass power and use it by whatever means as long as the ruler pleases his subjects. Wise administration of justice is another subject Kautilya addresses. "Government," according to the *Arthashastra,* "is the science of punishment." On Kautilya's advice, Chandragupta sent spies throughout his empire to report on the honesty of officials. Homing pigeons delivered messages to the capital. His secular-type rule alienated the Brahmans and reduced their power.

ASHOKA

The state reached even greater heights, however, under Chandragupta's grandson, **Ashoka**. In his reign (268–232 B.C.E.) India experienced unprecedented unity, peace, and prosperity. While Chandragupta's rule was **centralized despotism**, Ashoka's was **benevolent paternalism**. He continued the efficient and centralized rule of Chandragupta, but he is most famous for his embrace of Buddhism, an act that had important intellectual and religious consequences for India and for world history. Ashoka's conversion came in the wake of a bloody struggle for the throne in which Ashoka killed several of his brothers, and after a brutal battle for control of the eastern Indian state of **Kalinga**. Ashoka was filled with revulsion for his own responsibility in the wholesale slaughter of over 150,000 men. It is for this reason that he purportedly converted to Buddhism, as it emphasized compassion, nonviolence, and dharma that he viewed as a civic guide to behavior. He spread the religion throughout the empire and erected stone pillars along the roads with written edicts from Buddhist teachings. He built many beautiful **stupas**, or domelike structures that contained the remains of saintly monks. He encouraged pilgrimages to shrines, repairing roads and digging wells along the way to make the journey easier. He also sent missionaries to Ceylon (Sri Lanka), Pagan (Burma/Myanmar), and Southeast Asia, where Buddhism and the stupa design were adopted. He did not force conversion on his subjects. In fact, he honored India's other religions by building shrines for worshippers of Hinduism and Jainism. Because of this, Buddhism did not become an alien religion as Islam later did.

Did You Know?

Ceylon is now
called Sri Lanka.

Burma is now
called Myanmar.

The rule of Ashoka coincided with the expansion of the Roman Empire in the West and Han China in the East. Indian merchants, especially those exporting cotton that was much in demand throughout Eurasia, benefited from Ashoka's regime. Women also benefited because they could become Buddhist monks and thus engage in scholastic and artistic endeavors. Their place in the family was also strengthened under Buddhist law. Brahmans, however, resented their displacement as political advisers, as did warrior families who lost control of their small states under imperial centralization. Upon Ashoka's death, the empire was divided among rival family members and finally torn apart by internal warfare between local rulers. Shattered unity opened the door to outside invasion.

Kushan Invaders

Between 180 B.C.E. and 300 C.E. numerous invaders crossed into India, but most were ultimately absorbed into Indian society. Two foreign conquerors, however, did have an impact on India. One was the Hellenistic **Bactrian Greeks** who pushed deep into northwestern India in the second century B.C.E. Under **King Demetrius**, Indian and Greek culture blended. Demetrius transformed his capital at **Gandhara** into a Hellenistic city. Indian scholars studied Hellenistic medicine and astronomy. After that, a new wave of invaders, the **Kushan**, entered India ca. 100 B.C.E. Like the Bactrian Greeks before them, these invaders were gradually absorbed into Indian society and became the Kshatriya (warriors) caste. Although the Kushan were Buddhists, they were acquainted with Greek ideas and employed Hellenistic sculptors and artists. A new art, known as the Gandaran school, developed, using Greek styles to portray Buddhist subjects. Buddhist art, in turn, influenced the West. The use of halos, for instance, is reminiscent of earlier Buddhist work. Under the leadership of **Kanishka**, who converted to Buddhism, a great council of Buddhist monks, much like the Council of Nicaea, was held to regulate Buddhist teaching. Out of this convocation came Mahayana Buddhism, which was then carried along trade routes opened by the Kushan to China.

Gupta Empire

The Gupta Empire (320–467 C.E.) is considered the Golden Age of Indian culture because of its considerable output in literature, art, and science. In 320 C.E. **Chandra Gupta I** (unrelated to Chandragupta Maurya) came to power and, by alliance and conquest, created an empire in the Ganges Valley, making the capital again at Pataliputra (the ruins are under present-day Patna). Later Gupta rulers extended the empire as far west as Arabia, but it never attained the size of the Mauryan Empire because it did not include the Deccan Plateau. There, a strong state of **Dravidians** ruled. Dark-skinned and speaking **Tamil**, they grew rich and powerful by becoming the hub of the maritime trade route that stretched by sea from China, to Southeast Asia, India, Arabia, Africa, and Europe. Under Chandra Gupta I's rule, religious tolerance, economic prosperity, and intellectual achievement reached their zenith. Chinese Buddhist monk **Fa-hsien**, who came to India in search of Buddhist texts, wrote that he was never molested, in danger, or in need of a passport.

GUPTA ARTS, SCIENCES, AND TECHNOLOGY

The Gupta rulers were patrons of the arts and encouraged scholarship. Using the ancient Sanskrit language, the Indo-European tongue of the Vedic classics, the most famous of all India's poets and dramatists was **Kalidasa**. He wrote stories in complete contrast to the Greek tragedies in which humans wrestled with imperfection and fate. His works created an atmosphere of romance and tranquility in which happy endings abound. Advances in the sciences were encouraged by the founding of many universities. Perhaps the most important was a Buddhist monastery at **Nalanda** where over 5000 students were housed in small, austere cells. Indian scholarship of the period made important contributions to astronomy and math, among them quadratic equations and the use of the square root of two in algebra. **Indian numbers** (known in the West as Arabic numerals), decimals, and the concept of zero were developed as early as the third century B.C.E. and have since been adopted worldwide. Technology advanced, especially in the making of fine iron. One 23-foot column cast in the fifth century still stands rust-free despite monsoon rains. Using fine steel with sharpened edges, the scalpel was developed for surgery. Medicine made great strides. Hospital care was free, doctors knew how to set bones and developed plastic surgery, and **Caraka**, a great Indian doctor like Hippocrates, developed a code of ethics for doctors.

GUPTA ARCHITECTURE

Most of the buildings that have survived from the Gupta period were religious rather than secular because religious structures were usually built of stone rather than wood and brick, which disintegrated. Two forms of architecture dominated the period. The first was the stupa, which became more elaborate in decoration, often with scenes of the Buddha's life, and higher at the central pinnacle. The 56-foot-high stupa at **Sanchi** was surrounded by a walkway, around which worshippers followed the course of the sun through the heavens. The style reached its zenith in the great temples of Burma and Thailand. The second form was the **rock-cut temple**. Carved into a solid cliff of rock, the principal chamber was the **Chaitya**, rather like a Roman basilica. The two most impressive groups of rock-cut temples are at **Ajanta** (29 chambers) and **Ellora** (34 chambers). The temples were decorated with statues and **frescoes** (pictures painted on stucco), which brought to life the whole universe in which Hindus, Buddhists, and Jains believed they moved. By the end of the Gupta period, the free-standing temple emerged as an architectural form of great import. These temples reflect the reemergence of Hinduism between the sixth and fourteenth centuries and like the stupa form, reached their most sublime expression outside of India at **Borobudur**, Indonesia, and at Angkor Wat, Cambodia. Central to the temple was a small room housing the image of the god, like Shiva or Vishnu, to whom the temple was dedicated. This was joined to a hall for worshippers, which then led to a veranda. Above the shrine was an elaborately sculpted tower. Indian architecture, unlike Islamic and Christian, hugs the ground instead of soaring to the heavens. In part, this was due to limitations of architecture, but it also reflects the Hindu view that divinity is related to the earth and encompasses all of the earth's life forms. Indian architecture is also much more symbolic than realistic like the Greek. Statuary of Brahma symbolizes creation, Shiva destruction, **Lakshmi** fertility, and **Kali** death. Temple complexes were massive **mandalas** or cosmic designs.

Hindu Reform

The change in architecture reflects basic social change that occurred during the Gupta period. The Brahman class, which had been under attack for its excesses, gradually made a comeback. This was due to Buddhist weakness and Hindu reform. Gradually, Buddhist monks became concentrated in huge monasteries, obsessed with fine points of philosophy and isolated from urban and village life. The Hindu leaders, meanwhile, began to stress the importance of personal worship and participation, to build shrines and offer participation in cults to all castes and to women, and to otherwise bring Hinduism into the daily life of the people. Special gods were allotted to special occupations and to family rites of passage. As Hinduism's hold on the population strengthened, the Brahmans regained their role as **gurus**, or teachers, of local notables. Castes became more complex with additional subcastes formed. Buddhism was weakened when merchants who supported it faced financial losses as the Silk Road trade dwindled and Rome and Han China collapsed. Buddhism was then absorbed by Hinduism.

Hindu Society

Hinduism, in its reemergence, was in many ways more pervasive and soon more conservative than before. Life for the privileged could be luxurious, but it also emphasized a sequence of development infused with religious meaning. Men were to progress through four stages—student, family provider, hermit, and finally, holy man. Under Hindu law, women were legally minors subject to the protection of fathers, husbands, and brothers. The traditions of **sati (suttee)**, or the widow's self-emolation at her husband's funeral, developed. Despite these ritualized deaths of widows, in no society is love, and particularly that of a woman, so openly enjoyed. Lives of lower castes were harsher. Untouchables were restricted, divisions among the castes became more pronounced. Since India at this time was, perhaps, the most fertile and productive region in the world, the untouchables at times may have lived relatively well, with access to such foods as milk, eggs from domesticated chickens, rice, and sugar.

The rule of the Gupta ended with invasion by the **White Huns** of Asia, 480–500 C.E. They took control but were ultimately absorbed into Hindu society. Soon India fell into a patchwork of warring princes, or rajas. Not until the Moslem invasion and establishment of the Delhi Sultantate in the early thirteenth century did India reconstruct itself politically. This was of somewhat unimportant consequence since religion rather than politics was the basis of Indian identity.

Spread of the Indian Classical Tradition

The classical characteristics of India can more likely be found in the village than in the polis as in Greece, the bureaucracy as in China, the empire as in Rome, or provincial rule as in Persia. The social fabric of India, the caste, fundamental to Hinduism, served as a measure of both political and social order. The upper caste, or Brahmans, essentially provided the leadership through influence over the local lords. Hinduism's relationship to a broader universe made Indians connect themselves closely with the earth and life rather than with nature and the universe. Buddhism infused a needed measure of compassion into Hindu thought, and it inspired art and architecture, but it ultimately was absorbed by Hinduism. The rise of the two great empires, the Mauryan and Gupta, can be closely related to wealth built up by overland and sea trade with empires that flourished at the same time in Rome, Persia, and China. In the contest between trade that nourished Buddhism, and agriculture that nourished Hinduism, agriculture triumphed. Buddhism found a home elsewhere, primarily in Southeast Asia, Japan, and Korea, due to its diffusion from India. One of the great missionary religions, Buddhism reached Sri Lanka (Ceylon) and Myanmar (Burma) under the reign of Ashoka, China by the first and second centuries C.E., Korea in the fourth century, Vietnam and Cambodia in the fifth century, and Japan in the sixth century. It triumphed in places where it met weak indigenous cultures and was less successful in places like India and China where strong classical cultures existed. Where it triumphed, it created classical civilizations of its own, as in Cambodia and Japan.

Classical American and African Civilizations

(ca. 100 C.E.–900 C.E.)

TIMELINE	
800 B.C.E.–350 C.E.	Kush and Golden Age of Trade (Africa)
400 B.C.E.–100 C.E.	Aksum (Africa)
100 C.E.–700 C.E.	Bantu migrations to East and South Africa
100 C.E.–700 C.E.	Austronesian settlement of Madagascar
100 C.E.–900 C.E.	Teotihuacan (Mexico)
200 C.E.–700 C.E.	Moche (Peru)
300 C.E.–900 C.E.	Maya (Central America)

PEOPLES AND CULTURES OF THE AMERICAS

The peoples and cultures of the Americas remained isolated from Eurasia. The result was that invention and change were indigenous to the American continent. Farming, pottery, writing, timekeeping, and working of copper and gold developed independently. Iron and steel, gunpowder, glass, the plow, and practical applications of the wheel came later when the Old and New Worlds met. In the Americas there were fewer animals suitable for domestication than in Eurasia. Apart from the turkey, llama, alpaca, dog, and guinea pig, the early peoples of the Americas continued to rely on hunting and fishing for meat. Over the vast area of the Americas, hunting and gathering continued longer. In some areas, chiefdoms and farming peoples emerged and only in a few areas did civilized states arise. In the places where agriculture developed and could sustain large populations—the Teotihuacan Valley in Mexico, the Yucatan Peninsula, the Mound Builders in southern North America, and the Central Andes of Peru and Bolivia—brilliant classical civilizations arose whose splendor, achievements, and legacy make them worthy of the word classical. There is much more conjecture on the part of historians regarding these civilizations because of the complexities of a hieroglyphic language and because archaeological investigation is in its infant stage. New evidence is being uncovered and decoded daily.

Teotihuacan (Mexico) (100 C.E.–900 C.E.)

As the classical Greek civilization rested on the Minoans, Rome on the Etruscans, India on the Aryans, and China on the Shang, classical **Mesoamerican** (Middle America or Mexico and Central America) civilization rested on the agricultural **Olmec** who had preceded them (1200 B.C.E.–600 B.C.E.). About 150 B.C.E. the **Oaxaca Zapotecans** established a large urban center near modern Mexico City at **Teotihuacan**. Population estimates of the city, which covered nine square miles, reach as high as 200,000, making it greater than the cities of ancient Egypt or Mesopotamia and second to Rome. Prosperity rested on complex intensive agriculture that stimulated trade. Within the residential districts of the city, there is evidence of both a social and an ethnic mix of peoples.

Besides being a commercial center, Teotihuacan was also a religious and political center. Laid out in a grid pattern, streets paralleled two great avenues that intersected each other in the heart of the city. Pyramids to the sun and moon, 700 feet long and 200 feet high, dominated either end of the central avenue. The Pyramid of the Sun is about four times the size of the Great Pyramid of Cheops in Egypt. The many gods of Mesoamerica, the god of rain (feathered serpent), the goddess of corn, and the goddess of water, adorned palaces and temples. In fact, all art seems to have been religious in nature. These enormous pyramids, rivaling those in ancient Egypt, suggest a state apparatus able to plan such works and mobilize large numbers of workers. Priests and nobles seem to have been the upper class, and the lower classes were peasants and workers. The rich and powerful lived in large and lavish homes, while working people lived in apartment compounds or **barrios** at the edge of the city.

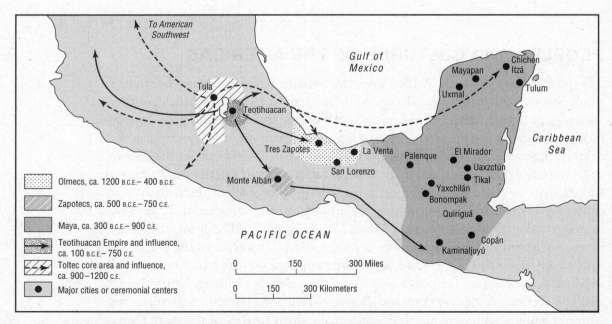

The Mesoamerican Classical States 1200 B.C.E.–1200 C.E. The classical Mesoamerican states were the Maya in the Yucatan and Central America and Teotihuacan in Mexico. Both owed their existence to earlier civilizations, the Olmec and Zapotec, and both succumbed to military invasion, first at the hands of the Toltec and then the Aztecs.

Teotihuacan's influence extended far south into Guatemala, causing some historians to look at Teotihuacan as a precursor or appendage of the **Maya**. Whether Teotihuacan was a separate political entity or a dominant cultural and ideological style that spread over much of Mexico is unclear. Teotihuacan probably exacted tribute from many regions as pottery and finely worked obsidian in Teotihuacan style are found in many areas. Regardless, Teotihuacan has many of the hallmarks of classical civilization—an enduring style, urban splendor, a culture with heavy religious overtones, and legacies for succeeding civilizations of Mexico like the Toltec and Aztec. It continued to flourish during the Maya period until about 700 C.E. Then it was burned by hordes from the southwest. A **Time of Troubles** followed (800–1000 C.E.), characterized by militarism and rule by priests in great cities and by warriors in small states. One of the states, the **Toltec** confederation, admired and absorbed Teotihuacan culture.

The Maya (300 C.E.–900 C.E.)

Contemporaries of the Tang Chinese, Charlemagne in Europe, and the Abbasids, the Maya of southern Mexico and Central America created a Golden Age of American classicism. The Maya world included a number of different languages and art styles, but it shared statecraft, a common written language, a calendar, and a mathematical system. Maya seems to have derived from the word **Zamna**, the early Maya culture god. Politically, it appears that families ruled the major Maya city-states and surrounding territories. These included Tikal, Copan, Quirigua, Palenque, and Chichen Itza. Inscriptions on monuments record constant warfare and the deeds of rulers such as **Pacal of Palenque** (d. 683 C.E.), who conquered nearby territory and was buried in a lavish tomb inside a pyramid at Palenque. The leaders had considerable civic and religious power. Elite scribes and priests helped administer the state. The rulers and scribes organized and participated in rituals of self-mutilation and human sacrifice. **Ritual ball games** in which players hit a rubber ball with their hips and elbows through a ring 20 feet in the air were forms of worship and sport.

AGRICULTURAL SYSTEMS AND URBAN CENTERS

Some Maya cities had populations of between 30,000 and 80,000, and the total Maya population was probably about five million. To support such a population, the Maya developed a number of innovative intensive agricultural systems. Besides irrigation and swamp drainage, they used a **ridged field system**. In this system, raised fields were built above low-lying, seasonally flooded lands bordering rivers. Another system, **milpa**, was particularly useful in areas with heavy rainfall and scorching sun. Farmers cut down patches of forest, burned the wood, and planted maize in the resulting ash. Besides maize, cotton was a crop in great demand. Rich Maya textiles appear all over Mesoamerica.

Cities had great noble palaces, pyramids where the elite were buried, **steles** (stone slab monuments), temples, altars, and ball courts. The pyramids were impressive, with sloping walls and flat platforms where temples were built using a **corbeled arch** (stone blocks placed like upside-down steps to span an opening). While evidence for trade and artisanship within the city is scant, the urban centers were very likely centers of exchange and there is considerable evidence that the Maya carried

Did You Know?

The Maya are often called the "Greeks of the New World" because they developed:
- a sophisticated political system
- a calendar accurate to within a second
- flourishing trade
- written language
- superior textiles
- elegant art
- the concept of zero and advanced mathematics

on extensive long-distance trade. Maya products are found over a large area. Wealth seems to have been concentrated in the hands of a few based on lineage that was traced both through the mother and father. Most other people were free workers, serfs, or slaves taken in battle.

MATHEMATICS AND THE SCIENCES

The religious elite were vital and powerful. It is from this class that the many cultural achievements of the Maya emerged. One was a system of hieroglyphic writing in which phonograms were added to a pictographic system. There were 850 hieroglyphic characters developed to record chronology, religion, astronomy, and dynastic lineage. Mayan hieroglyphs were written in **codices** (books) made of bark paper and deerskin or were inscribed on steles. One of the world's most exact methods of measuring and recording time was developed from systematic observations of the planet Venus. Using complex calculations, perseverance, and teamwork spanning several centuries, Mayan priest-astronomers developed a calendar with 365¼ days divided into 18 months of 20 days accurate to within seconds of our current calendar. The Maya also accurately predicted solar eclipses. They were advanced in mathematics, using a system (vigesimal) based on 20 and incorporating the concept of zero. Writing and timekeeping made the Maya recorders of history. While keen astronomical observers, they nevertheless viewed the universe as flat, with 13 levels of heaven above and 9 underworlds below. The Maya, like the Chinese, had a concept of dualism—male-female, good-bad—which emphasized the unity of all things rather than conflict and choices.

DECLINE OF THE MAYA

The collapse of the Maya is connected with the general cataclysmic decline in the whole Mesoamerican area between 700 and 900 C.E. During the eighth century the Maya stopped erecting commemorative steles and by 900 C.E. most major cities were deserted. Agricultural exhaustion is one of the explanations for Mayan collapse. The very success of intensive agriculture led to a population density around **Tikal** of over 300 people per square mile. Increasing population may have led to warfare among the Maya city-states and revolts among the peasantry in the face of increasing tax burdens. Another theory of decline suggests epidemic disease. Whatever the cause, the center of Maya culture began to move from the southern lowlands and highlands around Tikal to the **Yucatan** peninsula where Mexicanized families established themselves at **Chichen Itza**, carrying on Maya cultural tradition. By 1000 C.E. the militaristic Toltec overtook the Maya as well.

The Moche (200 C.E.–700 C.E.)

While the classical Mesoamerican cultures flourished, another American culture was being established in the Andean world. The Mochica state in the Moche valley developed along the Peruvian coast just north of the agricultural settlement of Chavin. The Moche appear to have expanded by means of conquest. Archaeological evidence reveals hilltop forts and military posts, and the artistic output is filled with representations of war, prisoners, and head taking. Warrior priests, buried with retainers, servants, and dogs, were covered with gold, silver, copper, and fine cloth. Some of the

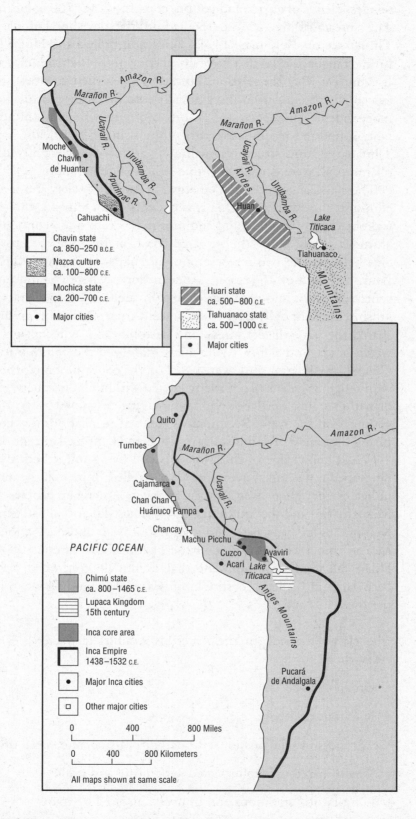

South American Classical States 850 B.C.E.–1532 C.E. The classical civilizations of South America, including Ecuador, Peru, and Chile, were situated on the western coast of the continent. The Chavin and Moche states along the northwestern coast were succeeded by the Inca of Peru.

textiles, blends of alpaca and cotton, combined over 100 colors into woven patterns. The spread of the Moche resulted in the development of two large cities at **Tihuanaco** on the shores of Lake Titicaca in Bolivia and **Huari** in southern Peru. In turn, Tihuanaco extended its political control through colonies as far away as Chile. It is unclear what the relationship was between the two cities, whether Huari began as a colony of Tihuanaco and gradually exercised wide control over other areas or was independent. Tihuanaco was an urban ceremonial center of about 40,000 inhabitants supported by intensive agriculture using raised fields, irrigation, and canals. Tihuanacan stone structures resembling great arches were carved out of single blocks of stone and were decorated with a structural feline motif.

The classical cultures that emerged in Andean society seemed to have had certain common characteristics. One is **verticality**, which means that the social and political objective of families and communities was to find economic niches at different altitudes. Thus, along the irrigated coast, maize could be grown, in the altiplano area between the two major mountain chains of the Andes, potatoes and grazing flourished, and on the eastern Andean slopes where tropical rain forests were concentrated, fruits and coca leaf were cultivated. Another characteristic is the idea of kinship units, or **ayllus**, based on descent from a common mythical ancestor. Ayllus shared the same dialect, dress, and customs. The ayllus assigned households land, water, herds, and rights. Ayllu chiefs mobilized the community for labor and war. Cooperative relationships were based on the concept of **reciprocity** that was infused with religious beliefs. Reciprocity existed within families, between men and women, or within states. For labor and tribute, citizens gained access to resources and irrigation from the state. Reciprocity extended to relationships between states, structuring diplomatic relationships much as the Chinese concept of tribute did.

While knowledge of the Moche is still being unearthed, they do seem to have developed a writing system and have excelled in metallurgy and textiles. Evidence indicates that there was contact between American peoples from the Andes to Mesoamerica and the southern United States. The ritual ball game, for instance, can be found as far away as the American Southwest and the Caribbean. The end of the Moche coincided with the collapse of the Maya. About 800 C.E. Tihuanaco and Huari fell to the **Chimu** state that eventually controlled over 600 miles of the Peruvian and Chilean coast. Chimu was still expanding when it was conquered by the Incas in 1465.

The classical period of the Americas exhibits characteristics of classical periods everywhere:

- Urban centers

- Religious creativity

- Advances in scholarship, arts, methods of rule, and social organizations

- Wealth based on sophisticated agriculture and trade

- Long-lasting traditions and imprints inspired by trade

AFRICAN CLASSICISM (1800 B.C.E.–400 C.E.)

Because African history for the most part lacks written sources, study of such civilizations has been arduously deciphered through archaeology, linguistics, and other fragmentary evidence. It is a history constantly being revised as new information surfaces.

Kush and Aksum in Northern Africa

Like other classical civilizations, important earlier societies preceded Kush and Aksum. One early state was **Nubia** (northern half of Sudan and southern Egypt). By 6000 B.C.E., villages in the area were producing and marketing pottery. An independent Nubian kingdom, **Kerma**, appeared between 1800 and 1600 B.C.E. Egyptian forces destroyed Kerma, but around 900 B.C.E. a new Nubian state, **Kush** (800 B.C.E. to 350 C.E.) emerged laying the foundations for a golden age of trade, culture, and metallurgy. During much of this time, Kush was a major iron producer for Southwest Asia. At its height, the capitol city of **Meroe** had a population of about 25,000 and contained sanitation facilities, public baths, and royal pyramids. The society was ordered by kings and queen-mothers, laws and traditions, military and elites, a rich musical and architectural tradition, and a written language based on the Meroitic cursive script that is only partially deciphered today. Overland caravan routes linked Kush with the Niger and Congo Basins and the Ethiopian highlands. Kush declined, in part, due to worldwide climate change, which also affected the Han Chinese and Roman Empires. Deforestation and overgrazing contributed to a drier climate. However, the legacy was kept alive in neighboring societies. Some peoples living a few hundred miles southwest of Meroe still show many signs of Kushite influence including recreational activities like wrestling, fashion, and body art. Several new kingdoms arose from the ashes of Kush, and contact with the Mediterranean world brought Christianity out of which grew a Nubian branch of the **Coptic** Christian Church based on the **monophysite** sect (a sect of Christianity that argued that Jesus had a single divine nature rather than being both divine and human). Many spectacular churches were built and sculpted from rock formations. Christian Kush faded with the Islamic conquest of Egypt in the seventh century C.E., but its churches and monasteries along with meroite pyramids remain a material legacy of Kush.

Another literate urban African state, **Aksum**, emerged in the rocky but fertile Ethiopian highlands beginning around 400 B.C.E. It benefited from proximity to the Red Sea that linked northern Ethiopia with Arabia and Southwest Asia. Aksum also maintained close ties with eastern Africa. It was already a center of agriculture, bronze, and ironworking and between 400 B.C.E. and 100 C.E. the export of ivory, gold, obsidian, emeralds, perfumes, and animals. Aksumites built temples and palaces of masonry, dams, reservoirs, irrigation, and terraces. They also developed an alphabet. Aksum benefited from cultural exchange with many societies. Aksum had a highly stratified social structure that was dominated by kings. Below royalty was an aristocracy that supplied top government officials, a merchant class that engaged in trade, peasants, and slaves. The capital city of Aksum had monumental architecture, was highly cosmopolitan and was also influenced by Christianity in the fourth century C.E. Aksum declined for a number of reasons; by 400 C.E. rainfall declined; the conquest of southern Arabia by Sassanian Persia in 575 diverted

Indian Ocean commerce from its ports; and political problems led to internal struggles. Unlike Kush, Ethiopian society persisted in recognizable form, demonstrating a continuity for almost 2000 years. Christianity became a deeply ingrained local religion producing a unique Ethiopian Christianity today. At the beginning of the Common Era, the African continent may have contained 15 million to 25 million people, much less than half of China. Almost half of this population lived in Egypt, Kush, and along the Mediterranean coast.

Sudanic and Bantu West Africa

People in Sudan (not present-day Sudan, rather the southern grasslands between the Sahara's southern fringe and the tropical Congo region) very early began developing towns, long-distance trade, and small kingdoms that were precedents for the later classical societies. In southern Sudan, now central Nigeria, the **Nok** peoples, mostly farmers and herders, were working iron by 5000 B.C.E. and creating an enduring artistic tradition. Meanwhile, the Mande and Ibo groups coalesced and formed complex religious traditions that included notions of cosmic order, their place in the universe, and a divine force or supreme being. By 6000–7000 years ago, the West Africans were, perhaps, early monotheists, a belief that existed alongside other gods and spirits. Also, the **Bantu** peoples were drawing in many differing languages based on their traditions of farming and metal working. They moved east and south from their homelands along the Niger River, occupying much of southern Africa.

While Kush and Aksum maintained close connections with Eurasia, complex urban societies like the **Mande** arose in the Sudan. The area was peopled by farmers who resided in small villages and city-dwellers. The farmers raised millet and sorghum and they grew cotton, which they made into richly colored cloth. In the Niger River delta, fishing became a major industry as well. Some Sudanese congregated in large towns and cities reaching populations of 30,000 to 40,000 of which **Jenne-Jenno** (in present-day Mali) was the major hub of a network of commercial centers along the Niger River. By the Common Era, trade across the Sahara linked Sudan to the wider world. The people worked copper, gold, and iron and exported grain, fish, and animal products in exchange for metals. The trans-Saharan trade that began well before the Common Era aided the growth of Sudanic societies. Salt moving south to the Sudan and gold moving north drove the trade. Sudanic cities also shipped north cotton cloth, leather goods, pepper, and slaves, but most important was gold, which the merchants of northern Africa then sold to Europe. The Sudanic peoples also traded meat animals to the forest societies on the west coast of Africa and they imported copper from the eastern region of the Niger. The Berber North African peoples dominated the caravan routes, and the salt trade was controlled by the **Garamante** (a tribal federation which inhabited the desert region). Large cities and states seem less common in sub-Saharan Africa than in other parts of the world, in part due to low population densities occasioned by soils that could not sustain the large settled populations leading to shifting agriculture.

Diverse **Mande** people (probably Soninke, Mandinka, Malinka, and Bambara) spoke closely related languages, shared many customs, and dominated the history of the western Niger River Basin. They also reflect what was typical of Sudanic classical societies. The Mande were the likely domesticators of African rice and lived in large walled villages, combining farming and fishing. As elsewhere in world history,

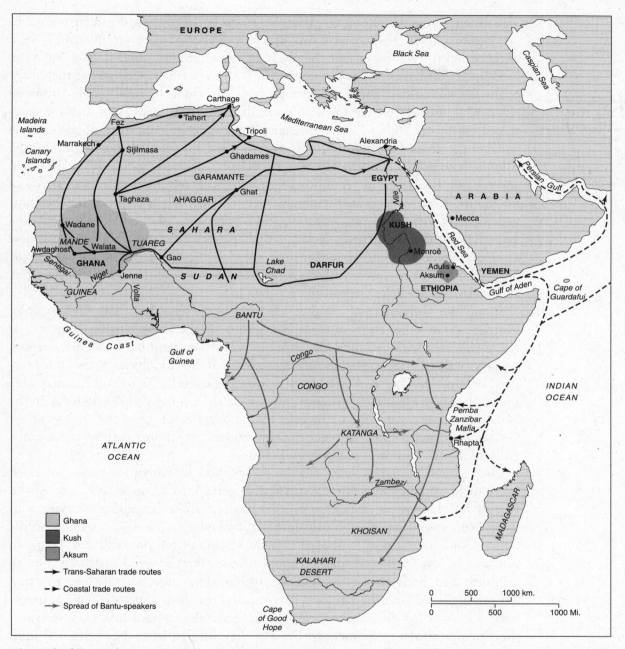

Classical Africa, 1500 B.C.E.–600 C.E. During this era, Kush, Aksum, and Jenne were major African centers of trade and government. Trade routes crossed the vast Sahara Desert and the Bantu-speaking peoples expanded into central, southern, and eastern Africa.

commerce stimulated states in the Sudan. The **Soninke** people of the mid-Niger formed, perhaps, the first major Sudanic state of **Ghana** perhaps as early as 500 C.E. Its probable stone constructed capital city is not far from Jenne-Jenno. Ghana flourished until the thirteenth century.

Mande of many classes probably enjoyed prosperity often from growing cotton or making elaborate and colorful cotton clothing. Early Mande political structures usually developed a theocracy in which chiefs and village heads combined religious and secular duties. One of the best known political and legal systems is called **chieftancy**.

Did You Know?

Kingdoms grew out of markets and from taxing the trade in gold and other goods.

The system in Ghana among the Akan was characterized by a dual-gender system; in every town and village there were two leaders, a chief and a queen-mother. They were not married to each other, but they were of the same royal family. They served as local leaders and assumed responsibility for both the women and men of the village or town. In addition, there was a group of advisors from the royal family known as elders who provided advice and direction. All of the clans apart from the one represented by the chief/queen were represented by a subchief, and they too advised the work of the chief. Chieftancy later became a powerful colonial tool of rule for the colonial powers of the nineteenth century. Britain used it to "indirectly" rule Ghana, and today it is adapted to yet another set of political conditions. With the arrival of kingdoms, more sophisticated structures were developed that included highly stratified societies with aristocratic, warrior, and commoner classes and a group of ritual and religious leaders. A respected class of oral historians and musicians known widely as **griots** memorized and recited history emphasizing the deeds of leaders. People believed in a distant creator god, drew no neat line between the living and the dead, and wanted to keep the favor of the good gods.

Along the **Guinea** coast another kind of society emerged. The Guinea coast stretches 2000 miles from modern Senegal to southeastern Nigeria. The area is mainly covered with swamp with few edible plants and animals for domestication. To survive there, people lived mostly in small self-sufficient villages where they practiced communal labor and developed rich social networks. Yams and bananas were the staple crops. Despite subsistence agriculture, the Guinea peoples traded with the Sudanic societies over land and by boat up the Niger River. Over time, many of the Guinea settlements came to practice some Sudanic traditions such as a theocratic political system and pronounced social classes.

Over several thousand years, iron-using speakers of **Bantu** languages migrated from their original homeland in eastern Nigeria into Central and East Africa. During the classical era, the Bantu peoples accelerated their expansion carrying with them many traditions of art, music, farming, and religion that had originated in the Sudan. Some Bantu peoples moved into the Congo region now called Katanga. In this area of less fertile soil, drought, and disease, they adopted the cultivation of sorghum and millet from the Sudanic region. They also migrated to the East African highlands and the Zambezi River and by the third century C.E. had entered what is now South Africa. As Bantu-speaking peoples entered new environments, they incorporated new influences. Because they worked iron, they possessed military and agricultural technologies more effective than many non-Bantus they encountered. In some instances, like the Mbuti Pygmies, their superiority in this regard allowed them to push groups into the thick rainforest of the Congo, while in southern Africa many of the Khoisan peoples were pushed into the desert regions. In many areas, however, the Bantu intermingled and assimilated. Sudanese cultural forms like the drums and percussion music, woodcarving, and ancestor-focused religions became widespread.

Eastern and Southern Africa

From 1000 B.C.E. to 400 C.E. the cultural, political and economic foundations of the stretch of land along the eastern side of Africa from Uganda to Natal were laid. Much of this was influenced by the Bantu especially in southern and eastern Africa.

For example, by the fourth century C.E., the Bantu Xhosa and Zulu peoples who lived along the southeastern coast of today's South Africa, mixed their languages and cultures with the local Khoisan cattle herders. The migrating Bantus also encountered the Nilotes in East Africa resulting in a mix of cultures. Bantus adopted pastoralism (cattle and goats) and mastered new agricultural techniques and diets. Austronesian mariners and migrants in outrigger canoes brought new Southeast Asian foods like bananas, coconuts, sugar cane, Asian yams, and chickens to East Africa early in the Common Era. These Indonesians introduced Austronesian housing styles and musical instruments. They established trading posts to barter pottery, beads, and utensils for ivory and animal products. Their influence reached the Congo River Basin and between 100 and 700 C.E., Austronesians settled the large island of Madagascar.

The east coast of Africa, where many Bantu speakers settled, developed a cosmopolitan society based on maritime trade. Wind reversal patterns in the Indian Ocean and along the coast from East Africa to Southwest Asia created seagoing trade even before the Common Era. East coast trade grew slowly during the classical era. An Alexandria-based Greek traveler who observed trade from Egypt's Red Sea ports sailing to East African ports like Rhapta in present-day Tanzania reported that local people made sown boats, used dugout canoes most likely of Bantu origin, and behaved "each in his own place like chiefs."

Societies like Kush and Aksum in northern Africa, Sudan and Bantu in western Africa, and mixtures of Bantu and Austronesian peoples in eastern and southern Africa between 1000 B.C.E. and 600 C.E. exhibited many of the hallmarks of classical societies that developed elsewhere in the world. They built substantial urban centers; sometimes created written scripts; developed institutions of law and rule that continued through the ages; participated in widespread trade networks that reached into Europe, Southwest Asia, and the Indian Ocean; developed sophisticated technology like iron; diffused their cultures far and wide; and developed religious systems that were both cosmic and Christian in nature.

MAJOR WORLD RELIGIONS AND BELIEF SYSTEMS

India

Hinduism. Hinduism is one of the oldest religions in the world and is indigenous to India. Hindus believe in one Supreme Being (Brahma as manifested in many gods and goddesses). To Hindus, humans are bound to ignorance and illusion but can escape through reincarnation (rebirth). Practices include yoga, devotions to god and goddesses like Shiva and Vishnu, pilgrimages to holy cities, and worship (puja). Important Hindu texts include the *Vedas* (scripture), *Upanishads* (poems), *Bhagavad Gita* (Hindu Bible) and the *Ramayana* (epic poem). As it spread, Hinduism blended and reincarnated itself in many forms like bhakti (devotional worship of a personal god). It also supported a social system based on caste or place in society, a doctrine that was outlined in the *Code of Manu.*

Buddhism. Buddhism was founded by Siddhartha Gautama (the Buddha) c. 520 B.C.E. in North India. According to Buddhism, the purpose of life is to avoid suffering and gain enlightenment through meditation and an "8-Fold Path" of living principles. Unlike Hindus, reincarnation occurs once enlightenment is achieved. Buddhism subsequently divided into two branches. Theravada emphasizes Buddha as a teacher, and Mahayana and its many sects tends to transform Buddha into a god. Major Buddhist texts include the Tripitaka and the Sutras. Buddhism spread from India to China, Tibet, and much of Southeast Asia.

Jainism. Jainism was founded by Mahavira c. 550 B.C.E. in northern India. According to Jains, the universe is eternal and all living things are classified in a hierarchy. The purpose of the belief system is to attain perfect divinity leading to liberation from the cycle of death and rebirth by avoiding all bad karma (destiny based on past life deeds). Chief among things to be avoided is harm to any living creature. The teachings of Mahavira are gathered into various collections that emphasize non-violence, truth, celibacy, and nonpossessiveness. This can be achieved by worship at home and in temples.

China

Folk Religion. As ancient as Hinduism, Chinese folk religion is centered on forces of nature particularly its dualistic nature (yin and yang), and on folk dieties. A good life and afterlife are attained through rituals and honoring of ancestors.

Confucianism. Confucianism was founded by Confucius or Kong Fuzi (551–497 B.C.E.). More a belief system like the Greek philosophies than a religion, Confucianism concentrates on defining and fulfilling one's role in society. Principles of conduct include propriety, and honor and loyalty to family and elders (filial piety). The major Confucian text is the *Analects,* a book of sayings collected by disciples, principally Mencius.

Daoism. Lao-Tzu 550 B.C.E. formalized earlier Chinese folk religion into a belief system that emphasized a synergistic life view in which the yin-yang opposites make unity or "Dao." The purpose is to achieve harmony, peace, and longevity, ultimately reverting back to non-being which is the other side of being. The belief system generated an attitude of detachment and non-struggle ("go with the flow" or Dao). Taichi, acupuncture, geomancy (*feng shui*), and alchemy are the principal ways to achieve the Dao. The major text of the belief system is the *Dao De Jing.*

Japan

Shintoism. Shintoism is the indigenous religion of Japan. It is a polytheistic belief system based on the *kami,* or ancient gods and spirits. According to Shintoism, humans are pure by nature and they can keep away evil by purification rituals and by calling on the gods at home or at shrines. Since death is bad, some humans become *kami* after death. Important texts are *Kojiki* or "Records of Ancient Matters" and *Nihongi* or "Chronicles of Japan." Shintoism remained an indigenous religion that sometimes intertwined with imported religious traditions like Confucianism and Buddhism. It is linked mostly to the codes and behaviors of the upper classes and the military.

Persia

Zoroastrianism. Zoroaster (Zarathustra) lived c. 6th century B.C.E., contemporaneous with Confucius, Socrates, Lao-Tzu, Mahavira, and Buddha. Zoroastrianism became the official religion of ancient Persia (Achaemenid) and is thought to have influenced other religions like Judaism. Zoroastrians believe in one supreme god, Ahura Mazda ("Wise Lord") who was opposed by a Satan-like figure, Mazda Ahura. Humans are free to do good or evil. Judgment led to Heaven or Hell. Heaven could be obtained by good deeds, charity, equality, and hard work. The major Zoroastrian text is the *Zend Avesta* (Commentaries).

Manichaeism. Founded by the Persian Mani (216–277 C.E), Manichaeism is a blend of Zoroastrianism, Buddhism, and Christianity that emphasizes a continuing struggle between powerful forces of dark and light. Manichaeism reflects the cross-cultural highway that Persia had become during the later Roman era. The religion was encouraged by the Sassanid Persian emperor Shapur I but soon was under attack by orthodox Zoroastrians in Persia. However, it spread both to China and to Europe.

The Middle East

Greek Religion. The early Greeks had a variety of religions but most believed in an Olympic pantheon of gods like Zeus. Greeks found that human life was subject to the whims of the gods and fate that could only be controlled by sacrifice, divination, festivals, games, plays, and secret initiations. There was some view of an afterlife of either paradise or the underworld. The epic poems of Homer and Hesiod reflect aspects of this early system.

Judaism. Judaism is the religion of the Hebrews (c.1300 B.C.E.). Adherents believe in one God, Yahweh, and are to obey God's commandments, live ethically and focus more on this life than the next. The sacred book is the *Talmud* or Old Testament of the Bible which chronicles the history of the Hebrews as well as the beliefs of its people.

Christianity. Founded by a Jew, Jesus Christ, c. 30 C.E. in Israel, Christians added to Hebrew beliefs. The basis of the message of Jesus was that all who have sinned can have salvation through faith in Christ, sacraments, good works, and love. In Christianity, the one god of the Hebrews became a trinity of Father, Son, and Holy Spirit. Christianity spread and developed by way of an institutionalized systems of churches, disciples, and common liturgies like those that can be found in the *Bible* particularly the *New Testament*.

Islam. Islam was founded by Muhammad 622 C.E. in Saudi Arabia. Islam sees Muhammed as the last in a long line of prophets in the Middle East including Christian prophets. Muslims believe in one God (Allah) and that humans must submit to the will of God to gain Paradise after death. In order to reach Paradise, believers must adhere to the Five Pillars of faith, prayer, alms, pilgrimage, and fasting. Believers worship in mosques (churches) led by prayer leaders. Islam has often become part of a theocratic system of church and state which in a century led to the development of two Islamic sects—Sunni and Shi'a. The Sunnis believe in the practices of the Prophet and the succession of caliphs (rulers). Shi'a believed that only religious leaders descended from Muhammad could rule. A variant of both Shi'a and Sunni Islam that gained many followers was Sufism that emphasized a mystical and personal approach to Islam. The major beliefs are in the *Qur'an (Koran)* or scripture and in the *Hadith* (traditions).

The Americas

Maya Religion. The Mayan civilization c. 250 C.E. in Central America developed a belief system that involved many gods. The Maya appeased and nourished the gods with festivals and sacrifices. Because the soul journeys through a dark and threatening underworld, sacrificial victims and women who die in childbirth go to Heaven. Elaborate burial for royalty ensured life continued for them in the life after much as the Egyptians believed. Worship was conducted by priests and royalty at stone pyramid temples. The *Popol Vuh* is the creation story of the Maya. The Dresden, Madrid, and Paris Codices have preserved Mayan oral and ritual traditions.

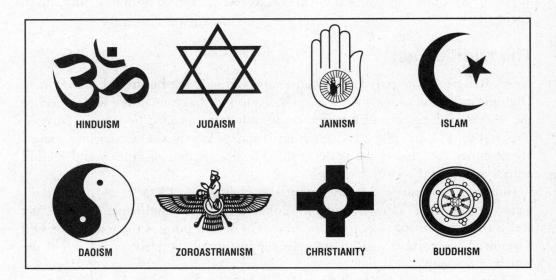

Religious Symbols. The religions of the world use symbolism to reflect and reinforce major ideas. The Hindu symbol represents all the sounds of the universe. The Hebrew 6-pointed star represents the six books of law, or the Torah. The Jainist open palm represents peace. The Islamic crescent and star reflect the divine light of Muhammad. The circle of dark and light represents the Daoist view that the cosmic forces are dualistic but complementary. The Zoroastrian symbol is the chief god Ahuramazda on wings in a boat representing the journey of good. The Christian cross symbolizes Christ's sacrifice in the name of human love and forgiveness. The Buddhist wheel represents the cycle of life, and the spokes the Eightfold Path to Enlightenment.

Unit Review

Cross-Regional Developments

The classical civilizations that rose in Greece, Rome, India, China, and the Americas touched people far beyond their borders largely due to long-distance trade and missionary activity. Among the important cross-regional developments of the classical period are

- the spread of Greek culture during the Hellenistic period;

- the spread of Roman culture to Western Europe;

- the expansion of Christianity beyond the Mediterranean to western Europe, eastern Europe, and Southwest Asia;

- the expansions of Buddhism to Central Asia, China, Southeast Asia, Korea, and Japan;

- the development of Eurasian trade along the Silk Road;

- the development of sea routes from East Asia to India, Arabia, and Africa; and

- the development of connections among Mesoamerican peoples and between Mesoamerica and the Andean area.

Legacies

The legacies of the classical period are important not just to the history of the West, Persia, India, China, and Mesoamerica, but to world history. During the preceding agricultural revolution, people began to live and work more closely together. The classical period ordered human relationships in a way that made greater civil order and cooperative action possible in these agricultural societies. The belief systems that were born during this period were often created in times of turmoil. In their emphasis on human relationships, they either transformed older systems into systems that were institutionalized in the political, social, and cultural lives of the civilization or created new belief systems that emphasized human ethics and meaning.

Among the legacies of the period are

- the rise of great states and empires like Greece, Rome, Achaemenid Persia, Mauryan and Gupta India, Kush and Aksum, Ch'in and Han China, and Teotihuacan, the Olmec, the Maya, and Moche;

- the rise of cities in both classically indigenous and cosmopolitan forms where human interaction elicited great thought and building;

- great literature of human joy, ethics, and fate;

- art using frescoes, mosaics, and statues;

- the architecture of palaces, temples, stupas, pyramids, and rock-cut temples with architectural features like columns, corbeled arches, and Roman arches and domes;

- the development of important technologies such as steel, paper, the compass, porcelain, and the ridged-field system, and infrastructures such as canals, sewers, irrigation systems, piped water, roads, postal systems, hospitals, and universities;

- systems of social order such as the Indian caste system, the Moche kinship associations, and the Chinese belief in filial piety; political order such as Roman law, Persian provincial system, Athenian democracy, Indian nonviolence, and the Chinese civil service; and economic change with the use of money, paper, printing, Arabic numerals, and the zero.

- the rise of the world's major religions and belief systems including humanism, Judaism, Christianity, Zoroastrianism, Hinduism, Buddhism, Confucianism, and Daoism.

Quiz

Unscramble:

Arrange the following in chronological order.

Gupta Empire; Alexander's Conquests; Roman Republic; Roman Empire; Han Dynasty; Golden Age of Greece; Punic Wars; Mauryan Empire; Maya; Buddhism; Christianity; Kush

Matching:

1. Buddhists
2. Ostracism
3. Sima Qian
4. Codices
5. Ancestor Worship
6. Mengzi (Mencius)
7. Pax Romana
8. Diaspora
9. Patricians
10. Karma
11. Gnostic Christians
12. Heresy
13. Mandarin
14. Ethics

A. The most famous follower of Confucius
B. Individuals considered dangerous to the state were expelled
C. Upper class of Roman society
D. Dispersion of people outside their homeland
E. Roman peace
F. Believe in "enlightenment" as a road to salvation
G. Scholar-bureaucrats earned positions in the government through an examination system in China
H. Tend to order human relationships
I. Believed Jesus had a single divine nature
J. Accumulation of good and bad deeds over a lifetime
K. A link between the gods and the living
L. Denial of the doctrine of faith
M. The Chinese Thucydides
N. Mayan books made of bark paper

Questions:

1. The single most important classical characteristic of the Greek polis that altered other societies and remains influential today is

   (A) literature.
   (B) art.
   (C) architecture.
   (D) political thought.
   (E) economic system.

2. Which circumstances would be least likely to lead to the development of democracy in Athens?

   (A) the unusual role of the king who farmed his own land and was advised by a council.
   (B) the success of traders, craftsmen, manufacturers, and farmers who challenged the power of the oligarchs.
   (C) the need for continued support of the common people to fill the ranks of the phalanx.
   (D) the demands by foreign-born residents of Athens to be made citizens and included in the political process.
   (E) the reforms by Solon that abolished debt slavery and limited the amount of land an individual could own.

3. Which of the following is incorrect?

   (A) Herodotus—*History of the Peloponnesian Wars*
   (B) Plato—*The Republic*
   (C) Aristophanes—*Clouds*
   (D) Sappho—*Love Poetry*
   (E) Sophocles—*Oedipus Rex*

4. As the world's largest empire, the powerful Achaemenid Dynasty did not

   (A) grant a large measure of local autonomy.
   (B) offer all subjects respect, toleration, and protection.
   (C) establish a comprehensive law code, stable currency, and an efficient postal system.
   (D) build a network of roads with stations offering food, water, and horses.
   (E) require all subjects to convert to Zoroastrianism.

5. Which of the following examples of Hellenistic beliefs advocated a universal state ordered by natural law where the citizen's duty was to strengthen society for others?

   (A) The Cult of Serapis
   (B) The Cult of Isis
   (C) Cynicism
   (D) Epicureanism
   (E) Stoicism

6. The birthplace of Christianity was in the

   (A) Roman Empire.
   (B) independent kingdom of Palestine.
   (C) Ptolemaic kingdom of Egypt.
   (D) Byzantine Empire.
   (E) Persian Empire.

7. Jesus was born

   (A) a Roman.
   (B) a Greek.
   (C) a Jew.
   (D) an Egyptian.
   (E) a Persian.

8. The first Bishop of Rome was

   (A) Saint Paul.
   (B) Saint Peter.
   (C) Saint Mark.
   (D) Saint Augustine.
   (E) Saint Jerome.

9. Diocletian tried to strengthen Roman rule by

   (A) dividing the empire between the East and West and appointing two Caesars to rule.
   (B) increasing taxes to pay for a larger army.
   (C) sending representatives to kingdoms along the Silk and Amber Roads to encourage trade.
   (D) building a series of forts and walls along the Roman borders.
   (E) issuing edicts to increase production of essential products with the promise of lucrative payments.

10. Which of the following was responsible for uniting China, linking existing frontier walls into the Great Wall, and standardizing Chinese script, weights, and measures?

    (A) Sun Zi (Sun Tzu)
    (B) Shi Huangdi (Shi Huang-ti)
    (C) Wu
    (D) Liu Bang (Liu Pang)
    (E) Wudi (Wu Ti)

11. The "Mandate of Heaven" was a belief held by Chinese that

    (A) ancestral worship was an essential element of religious ritual.
    (B) the ruler and nobles were selected to rule through the will of the gods.
    (C) a good ruler possessed a divine right to govern.
    (D) the ruler represented a divine presence on earth.
    (E) the ruler was recognized as a god.

12. According to believers, all Hindu gods are thought to be aspects of

    (A) Vishnu.
    (B) Krishna.
    (C) Shiva.
    (D) Brahma.
    (E) Lakshmi.

13. Buddha believed that a state of grace, or Nirvana, could be reached by

    (A) changing one's karma.
    (B) following the moral duties of one's caste.
    (C) being reincarnated as a Brahman.
    (D) following the Eightfold Path.
    (E) following a strict regimen of work and prayer

14. The Greek epic stories *The Iliad* and *The Odyssey* are similar to the

    (A) *Torah.*
    (B) *Ramayana.*
    (C) *Code of Manu.*
    (D) Codices.
    (E) *Meditations.*

15. Roman law changed as society changed because

    (A) all Romans were included in the law-making process.
    (B) a code of law known as the Twelve Tables was established and amended in the early days of the Republic.
    (C) an intricate code of civil law was devised to be applied equally to all.
    (D) special courts to deal with differences between Roman and foreign law in matters concerning trade were abolished.
    (E) newly elected judges announced laws they intended to enforce and those they considered out of date.

16. What system of Chinese thought saw the world as interacting opposites, Yin and Yang, which form the harmony of the whole?

    (A) Confucianism
    (B) Legalism
    (C) Daoism
    (D) *I Ching*
    (E) Buddhism

17. Which Roman leader is associated with the building of a new Roman capital in the East?

    (A) Julius Caesar
    (B) Caesar Augustus
    (C) Marcus Aurelius
    (D) Constantine
    (E) Justinian

18. The Mauryan ruler of India noted for renouncing war; advocating civic compassion, duty, and nonviolence; and respecting religions was

    (A) Kanishka.
    (B) Kautilya.
    (C) Chandragupta Mauryan.
    (D) Ashoka.
    (E) Chandra Gupta I.

19. Classical Chinese thought reflects all EXCEPT

    (A) the search for the "dao."
    (B) the search for truth by following a "middle path."
    (C) the need for social and political harmony.
    (D) the belief in God.
    (E) the necessity for strong government.

20. Siddhartha Gautama was designated by his followers as the Buddha, which means

    (A) King of Nepal.
    (B) Emperor of Buddhism.
    (C) the Great Teacher.
    (D) the Prophet.
    (E) the "Enlightened One."

21. The Sermon on the Mount reflects which fundamental aspect of Christianity?

    (A) Love your neighbor and hate your enemy.
    (B) Love your neighbor and your enemy.
    (C) Love God and follow the Ten Commandments.
    (D) Blessed are those who work and lead nations.
    (E) The kingdom of heaven belongs to those who are strong and successful.

22. The *Analects* sought to establish order among people by recognizing

    (A) the family as the basic unit of society.
    (B) that society could be ordered with all individuals exercising proper behavior and fulfilling their duties.
    (C) that families should establish proper relationships.
    (D) any man, either poor or privileged, could become a gentleman with proper conduct, or *Li*.
    (E) all of the above

23. Cyrus the Great's empire was conquered by

    (A) Justinian.
    (B) Augustus.
    (C) Pericles.
    (D) Alexander.
    (E) Miltiades.

24. Hindu asceticism refers to

    (A) conversion to Hinduism.
    (B) religious wedding rituals.
    (C) self-discipline and self-denial to reach a higher religious state.
    (D) the caste system.
    (E) belief in reincarnation in a cycle of birth, life, death, and rebirth.

25. Central to Hindu beliefs is the concept of dharma, which means

    (A) an endless cycle of death and rebirth.
    (B) release from the cycle of life.
    (C) nonviolence.
    (D) moral duties required of each caste and subcaste.
    (E) belief in many gods.

26. The most important commodity shipped out of Africa during the classical age was

    (A) salt.
    (B) gold.
    (C) cotton.
    (D) shells.
    (E) iron.

27. Whose teachings were the foundation of Buddhism?

    (A) Mahvera
    (B) Siddhartha Gautama
    (C) Chandragupta Mauryan
    (D) Ashoka
    (E) Kanishka

28. The most prominent group of peoples in classical Sudan were the

    (A) Mande.
    (B) Huari.
    (C) Nok.
    (D) Monophysites.
    (E) Austronesians.

29. The wheel inside a circle is the symbol of

    (A) Judaism.
    (B) Hinduism.
    (C) Buddhism.
    (D) Jainism.
    (E) Taoism.

30. The Punic Wars ended in the defeat of

    (A) the Romans.
    (B) the Etruscans.
    (C) the Celts.
    (D) the Greeks.
    (E) the Carthageans.

31. The two major geographical landscapes of Peruvian civilizations are

    (A) rivers and seacoasts.
    (B) coastal valleys and altiplano.
    (C) mountains and steppes.
    (D) deserts and oases.
    (E) valley floors and jungles.

32. The Maya are known as "The Greeks of the New World" for their

    (A) system of sports.
    (B) utilization of a city-state type of rule.
    (C) classical-style monuments.
    (D) diffusion of culture to southern Peru.
    (E) achievements in math and science.

33. Which of the following is incorrectly paired?

    (A) Hinduism – *Vedas*
    (B) Judaism – *New Testament*
    (C) Islam – *Qur'an (Koran)*
    (D) Confucianism – *Analects*
    (E) Buddhism – *Sutras*

34. Both China and the Greek city-states developed

    (A) the phalanx
    (B) tribute trade
    (C) coined money
    (D) democratic systems of government
    (E) a civil service system

35. Which of the following would be most difficult for a historian to prove?

    (A) Octavian (Augustus Caesar) esablished an empire that lasted 500 years in the West and 1500 years in the East.
    (B) Shi Huang Di (Shī Huang-Ti), the first emperor of the Qin (Ch'in) Dynasty, united China under one rule.
    (C) After Ashoka killed several of his brothers and fought to gain control of Eastern India, India experienced a period of unity, peace, and prosperity.
    (D) Miltiades led the Athenian army to defeat the Spartans on the Plains of Marathon.
    (E) In a 12-year campaign to establish an empire of two million square miles, Alexander of Macedonia became the greatest military commander of all time.

Answers

Unscramble:
Kush; Buddhism; Roman Republic; Golden Age of Greece; Alexander's Conquests; Mauryan Empire; Punic Wars; Han Dynasty; Roman Empire; Christianity; Maya; Gupta Empire

Matching:

1. **(F)**	3. **(M)**	5. **(K)**	7. **(E)**	9. **(C)**	11. **(I)**	13. **(G)**
2. **(B)**	4. **(N)**	6. **(A)**	8. **(D)**	10. **(J)**	12. **(L)**	14. **(H)**

Questions:

1. **(D)**	6. **(A)**	11. **(C)**	16. **(C)**	21. **(B)**	26. **(B)**	31. **(B)**
2. **(D)**	7. **(C)**	12. **(D)**	17. **(D)**	22. **(E)**	27. **(B)**	32. **(E)**
3. **(A)**	8. **(B)**	13. **(D)**	18. **(D)**	23. **(D)**	28. **(A)**	33. **(B)**
4. **(E)**	9. **(A)**	14. **(B)**	19. **(D)**	24. **(C)**	29. **(C)**	34. **(C)**
5. **(E)**	10. **(B)**	15. **(E)**	20. **(E)**	25. **(D)**	30. **(E)**	35. **(E)**

STUDY TIP
Become a visual learner. Careful observation is a lifelong skill. Recognizing religious symbols and understanding their meanings promotes understanding of the customs and beliefs of other peoples. Another kind of visual literacy comes from working with maps. Keep a map handy to become familiar with locations and geographical features. Places like Jerusalem have importance through many eras of world history.

Expanding Classical Systems of Society and Culture

(ca. 100 C.E.–1600 C.E.)

HISTORICAL PROCESSES: MIGRATIONS, DIFFUSION, INTERACTION, SYNTHESIS, AND SYSTEMS OF EXCHANGE

During the period 100 C.E. to 1600 C.E., ideas and institutions of the classical civilizations of the Mediterranean, India, China, and Mesoamerica spread far and wide. In so doing, they brought to many more parts of the globe the knowledge, ideas, and traditions of civilized society. The transfer of ideas did not always go one way, however. Often, when the classical civilizations came into contact with the indigenous peoples of outlying areas, the knowledge and traditions of the indigenous peoples mixed with, influenced, and transformed traditional classicism, producing a new **synthesis** (joining together of the two cultures) or distinctive new societies.

The Process of Classical Expansionism

The expansion of classical civilizations occurred as the result of a number of historical processes. One was **migration**. Often caused by ecological factors like climate changes and overpopulation, migrations caused peoples like the Polynesians to spread their culture over vast new areas of the globe. Another was the fall of classical civilizations. When classical civilizations like the Maya, Rome, Mauryan and Gupta India, and Han China weakened, outside peoples attacked, took over, and mixed with the classical civilizations. In doing so, they learned the ways of classicism. Another method of classical expansion was through **cultural diffusion** (spreading of culture). Through the spread of law, religion, and writing systems, western Europe and Japan were introduced to classicism. Another method of classical expansion was through trade. **Trade systems** (trade patterns that became complex, organized, and stable over broad areas), which arose in the South China, Indian, Arabian, and Mediterranean Seas, across the Sahara Desert, and along land and gulf routes in the southern United States and Mesoamerica, spread religion, culture, and technology across larger areas. The result was the expansion and alteration of classical culture.

Feudalism

The collapse of classical civilizations sometimes led to feudal interregna, or feudal breaks, in the patterns of classicism. **Feudalism** is characterized by decentralized political rule, and a political, economic, social, and cultural system oriented toward defense and warfare. In some places, as in Japan, medieval western Europe, and Russia, the feudal period left imprints on classical patterns as important as the classical patterns themselves. Sometimes, completely new civilizations emerged to fill the vacuums left by receding and collapsing classical civilizations. Such is the case with the rise of Islam, which emerged as a new "classical" civilization in Southwest Asia and North Africa.

Expansion of Society and Culture in East and Southeast Asia

(ca. 1500 B.C.E.–1200 C.E.)

TIMELINE	
1500 B.C.E.–900 C.E.	Polynesian Migrations
200 B.C.E.–700 C.E.	Yamato Japan
589 C.E.–618 C.E.	Sui China
618 C.E.–907 C.E.	Tang China, Golden Age
700 C.E.–1200 C.E.	Nara and Heian Japan
802 C.E.–1210 C.E.	Khmer Cambodia
960 C.E.–1279 C.E.	Song China

POLYNESIAN MIGRATIONS (1500 B.C.E.–900 C.E.)

One of the great migrations in history is the Polynesian maritime migrations across the 20,000-mile area of the Pacific Ocean from Southeast Asia to Easter Island and from Southeast Asia across the Indian Ocean to Madagascar. This was not a case of the spread from a great center of civilization to outlying areas. Instead, it was the spread of a culture and its adaptation to new challenges in relative isolation.

The **Polynesians** are a group of linguistically related peoples. Their language group, called **Austronesian**, can be found also in Madagascar, the Philippines, Indonesia, and Southeast Asia. However, they are not linguistically related to the peoples of New Guinea and Australia, where the land masses were linked during the last Ice Age and settled earlier, probably since 38,000 B.C.E. Polynesians were root farmers, not rice farmers. In many places their agriculture was complex and intensive, leading to highly stratified societies with powerful chiefdoms based on lineage. Through ritual and religion, these chiefs structured many aspects of life, from the ceremonial and public architecture to warfare. The commoners tilled taro and sweet potatoes, raised pigs and chickens, and fished. In Hawaii, for example, the high chiefs, or **ali'i**, rested claims on their ability to recite in great detail their genealogical lineages, while the commoners lived lives constrained by sets of **kapu**, or taboo.

Polynesians seem to have been Austronesian peoples from Taiwan who island hopped in a southeasterly direction beginning about 3,500 years ago. They reached New Guinea and the **Melanesian** Islands (a group of islands to the east of New Guinea and Australia extending from the Admiralties to Fiji, Togo, and Samoa). There they intermingled with the Papuan Melanesians. About 2,500 years ago, a group of these peoples, the **Lapita**, developed a new technology, the **outrigger** canoe, that enabled them to sail long distances. The long-distance double outrigger canoe was hollowed from two single tree trunks joined together by a platform that gave shelter to passengers, animals, and plants. It was driven by large triangular sails and guided by a steering paddle. The buoyant outriggers attached to the gunwales completed a sailing vessel that could travel over 124 miles a day and could sail against the winds and tides of the Pacific. Later known as **Polynesians**, these outrigger sailors mapped in their heads the locations of most Polynesian islands and settled the Pacific. Groups of them also settled New Zealand and Madagascar.

While it is unclear what initially drove the Polynesian migrations, once underway, there was no doubt that ecological fragility forced them onward. Upon reaching new islands, the Polynesians exploited the available resources and then they either had to develop new resources through their own ingenuity or emigrate, colonize, or begin anew on another island. Certain customs permeate the culture of the Melanesian and Polynesian peoples. One is the concept of "**kastom land**,"—a kind of "private" land that is held and supervised by a elected chief and his underling chiefs. They are charged with negotiating disputes regarding property lines, land utilization, and land encroachments. No change can be made in these boundaries unless commonly dis-

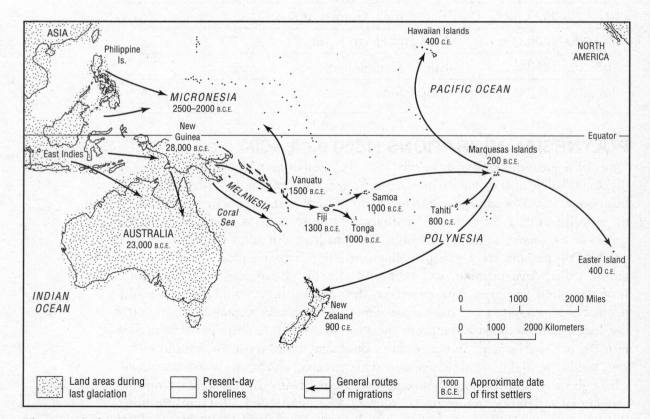

The Spread of Polynesian Culture 1500 B.C.E.–900 C.E. The greatest migration in world history was the Polynesian maritime migration, which took place across the vast distances of the Indian Ocean and the Pacific Ocean, one-third of the globe.

cussed by the whole land-owning group in "talking houses." This land-holding procedure led in the past to much tribal warfare and cannibalistic behavior. Today it faces a new challenge in terms of difficulty in modernizing countries by creating public use facilities like roads and industrial complexes on or through these lands.

Maori Culture

About the eighth century C.E. still another Polynesian group, probably from the **Society Islands**, sailed to New Zealand. There they established the **Maori** culture, which at its height in the late eighteenth century C.E. had the highest concentration of Polynesian people anywhere in the world. The Polynesians who immigrated to New Zealand faced a colder and harsher climate than their home islands. There were no native land mammals except bats and various kinds of **moa**, or large wingless birds. Overhunting led to their extinction. Polynesians introduced their staple crops supplemented with fish. A large and complex society of 200,000 people developed. Then, overpopulation and scarcity of resources created a society oriented toward war. Building fortresses, training males in the martial arts, and fierce combat in which the priest-leader, or **hapu**, could cut out the heart of the first enemy killed in battle illustrate the nature of Maori society in war. In woodworking and decoration they surpassed the Polynesian societies from which their ancestors came. They believed in a rich and complex spirit world in which gods and goddesses intervened in human affairs.

Easter Island

The history of **Easter Island** followed a somewhat similar pattern of settlement, exploitation of resources, scarcity, and depopulation. Probably no more than 20 or 30 Polynesian people from Tonga and Samoa reached Easter Island about 300 C.E. By 1550 there were 7000. A sophisticated culture had emerged in which large stone statues (commonly found throughout the islands in a less dramatic form) called **ahu** were built, but the ecological strain, particularly the deforestation of the island, led to war and the ultimate demise of this society's culture. The expanding Polynesians inhabited the Pacific. They spread their culture, foods, and technology to hitherto uninhabited areas of the globe.

Micronesia, Lelu, and Nan Madol

The **Micronesian** islands of the Pacific Ocean include the Caroline, Gilbert, Marianna, and Marshall Island groups. The most recent anthropological view is that the Micronesians have almost no genetic relationship to Melanesians but rather are descendants from migrating seafarers originating in Taiwan at least 3,500 years ago. Both the Polynesians and Micronesians seem to be a product of these seafaring peoples based on a similar Austronesian language. Ruins at **Lelu** (Kosrae) and **Nan Madol** (Pohnpei) suggest impressive imperial histories where kings conquered outlying islands, centralized rule, and embarked on vast building projects.

Kosraean society developed over 500 years ago. The empire was ruled by a king who owned all of the land, and high chiefs, who were given land by the king and who oversaw the commoners, who owned no land and who paid tribute to the king. The "city" contained over 100 walled compounds including dwellings, royal burial compounds, and six sacred compounds covering all of Lelu Island and adjacent

Did You Know?

The introduction of Buddhism is one of the few instances until modern times of the Chinese borrowing a major idea from abroad.

islets. A similar centralized state seems to have grown up on the island of Pohnpei under the Saudeleur dynasty. Construction most likely started there by the eighth or ninth century but the distinctive megalithic architecture was probably not begun until the twelfth or thirteenth century. The site includes dwellings for the king, ceremonial sites, tombs, and residence for the imperial family built of large megaliths that were chipped off the island mountains walls and carried to the compound. The beauty of the site today is that some of the buildings have been submerged, making the site an oceanic "Venice."

THE CHINESE GOLDEN AGE: SUI, TANG, AND SONG (SUNG) DYNASTIES

Chinese classicism did not end with the fall of the Han. Rather, it reached great heights under the Sui, Tang, and Song dynasties, inspired in part by Buddhism. The Golden Age with its cultural vibrance spilled over into neighboring societies.

Buddhism

With the fall of the Han Dynasty in 210 C.E. China became divided into many separate kingdoms. In a society troubled by disorder and disintegration, Buddhism appealed to the Chinese. Indian Buddhist monks came to China and Chinese pilgrims traveled west to India. Silk merchants also helped to diffuse this new tradition. The difficult process of translating Indian concepts like Nirvana into Chinese words, understandable as Buddhist terms, began about 200 C.E. Indian Buddhism was tempered by the imposition of Confucian values like the importance of the family and loyalty to the state. In the interim between the Han and Sui, many kingdoms like the Northern Wei supported Buddhism. The Wei built a number of cave temples with statues of Buddha in Chinese style and **pagodas**, structures reminiscent of the Han watchtowers. An important legacy of Buddhism for China was the increased use of paper and the development of **block printing**. Buddhist monks spread their message by use of the printed word, a tradition that the Tang later used to regularize the bureaucracy. It also led to the outpouring of literature during the Tang Dynasty.

The Sui and the Grand Canal

The period of disunity lasted until 589 C.E., when the **Sui Dynasty** welded the contending Chinese states together by conquest. Like the Ch'in, the center of Sui Dynasty power was in the **Wei Valley**, with the capital at Changan. Like the Ch'in, the Sui built roads and canals to connect the empire. The second Sui emperor, **Yangdi (Yang-ti**, r. 604–618 C.E.), began a campaign of expansion. He rebuilt the Great Wall, reconquered northern Vietnam and much of **Sinkiang** and Mongolia, but his campaign in Korea met with resistance. Following the model of the Chou and Han, he built a magnificent new capital at **Loyang**, but his most enduring achievement was the building of the **Grand Canal** from **Hangzhou (Hangchow)** in the south to **Beijing (Peking)** in the north. It cemented the unity of north and south China by bringing rice from the productive Yangzi (Yangtse) delta for troops and officials in the semiarid north. Heavy taxes and spending, corvee labor, and tyrannical officials caused rebellion, and in 618 C.E., after only 14 years on the throne, Yangdi (Yang-ti) was assassinated by a courtier.

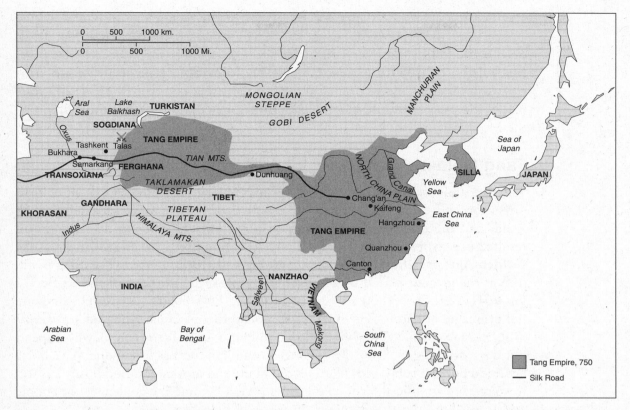

The Tang Empire, ca. 700 C.E. The Tang dynasty forged a large empire across Central Asia into Turkestan before their expansion was halted by Muslim armies at the Battle of Talas in 751. Control of Central Asia allowed the Tang to protect the Silk Road trade route. The Tang also controlled Vietnam and dominated Korea.

Tang Expansionism

Just as the Han benefited from the changes made by the Ch'in, so too did the new **Tang Dynasty** under the leadership of Emperor **Taizong (T'ai-Tsung)** profit from Sui initiatives. Under the Tang most of the Han-ruled territories were reclaimed by conquest. Chinese influence expanded along the Silk Road into Central Asia into what is today modern Afghanistan. The Chinese defeated the eastern and western Turks in Central Asia and extended their influence into North Vietnam, Tibet, and Manchuria. Korea became a protectorate. Members of the Tang Dynasty were to rule for 300 years.

The gradual immigration and **Sinification** (becoming part of Chinese culture) of the south below the Yangzi continued. China became the world's leading agricultural empire. Cotton and sugar, introduced from India, fostered new industries. By the late Tang, most of the imperial revenue came from the more productive south where double cropping in some areas became a common practice. In fact, the Tang Chinese found no other civilization that could rival the Celestial Empire. Rome was gone, and the Umayyad Caliphate was no match for Tang.

Diffusion of Printing

Territorial expansion reached its limit in 751 when a coalition of Arabs and western Turks repulsed the Chinese at the Battle of **Talas River** near Samarkand thus clearing the way for expansion of Islam into Central Asia. The battle is, perhaps, also significant because Chinese captives taught the technology of paper making and printing to the Arabs. Printing, which had begun ca. 600s C.E., was first developed by Buddhists using carved wooden blocks and ink to reproduce a whole page. Much later, by 1050 C.E., the Chinese had **moveable type** made of wood or clay. Koreans and Chinese produced the first moveable iron type by 1234, 200 years before the process was developed in Europe (or perhaps diffused into Europe by the Mongols).

Tang Golden Age

The recentralization of China under the Sui, growing prosperity as a result of Tang expansion and extension of agriculture, new trade via the Grand Canal and Silk Road, and the challenge and inspiration of an outside influence like Buddhism resulted in a resurgence of classical Chinese tradition under the Tang. Known as the **Golden Age**, or cultural high point, learning and arts flourished. The Tang is still seen as the greatest period of Chinese poetry especially in the works of **Li Bo (Li Po**, 701–762). Over 1800 samples of Li Bo (Li Po)'s poetry survive. His lines are full of images of nature. The mood is similar to that of Omar Khayyam's *Rubaiyat* in its passion for life. "Why should one toil away one's life?/ That is why I spend my days drinking . . ./Lustily singing, I wait for the bright moon." The horse became a popular subject for figurines full of life and movement. Buddhism was still in vogue and in official favor so the Tang period became the golden age of temple architecture and the artistic model for much of East Asia.

THE POETRY OF LI BO (LI PO)

A girl picking lotuses beside the stream—
At the sound of my oars she turns;
She vanishes giggling among the flowers,
And, all pretense, declines to come out.
Amid the flowers with a jug of wine
The world is like a great empty dream.
Why should one toil away one's life?
That is why I spend my days drinking. . . .
Lustily singing, I wait for the bright moon.

I drink alone with no one to share
Raising up my cup, I welcome the moon. . . .
We frolic in revels suited to the spring.

Li Bo (701–762 C.E.) was the titan of Chinese poetry during the Tang Golden Age. Some 1800 samples of his 20,000 poems survive. The legend regarding this excerpt, almost certainly untrue, is that Li Bo drunkenly leaned out of a boat to embrace the reflection of the moon and drowned, happy in his illusion. Tang poetry reflects Chinese love of nature, attention to form, meter, and rhythm, genuine emotion frequently sprinkled with light humor, and a songlike quality. It reflects an urbane, elegant, and brilliant culture at its height. The tone and essence of this poem remind the reader of the poems of Omar Khayyam (Rubaiyat) written during the Golden Age of Islam.

Porcelain, Silk, and Tea

Other achievements also mark the Tang Golden Age. Porcelain, which had appeared by the Tang period, was made into objects of exquisite beauty. According to legend, silk cocoons were smuggled out of China by two monks during Justinian's reign of the eastern Roman Empire. But in production and form, silk textiles had no rival outside of China. Tea, largely unknown in Han times, was introduced from southern Asia as a medicine. During the Tang Dynasty tea became the basic Chinese drink. Thus, the three great export items of China—porcelain, silk, and tea—gained stature during this period.

Cosmopolitan Changan

Changan symbolized the splendor of the Tang dynasty. Changan was the eastern terminus of the overland trade routes (the Silk Road) linking China with Central Asia. It covered some 30 square miles and included about one million people with another million living outside the walls. Laid out in a grid pattern, there were open spaces, theaters, vast supervised markets, and polo fields (a game imported from Persia, which originated in Central Asia). The palace faced south down a 500-foot-wide central thoroughfare to the south gate of the city. Exotic Zoroastrians, acrobats, horse traders, musicians, and story tellers from Central Asia mingled in the streets with artists and sculptors.

Crucial for restoration of Chinese unity were efforts undertaken by the Tang to rebuild and expand the imperial bureaucracy. To offset the power of the independent aristocracy, the Tang opened to all male Chinese subjects the Confucian-based examination system begun by the Han. Education was the prerequisite for an official career. While in theory merit and ambition were conditions for success, in practice established bureaucrats and the sons of prestigious families more often rose to upper levels. Still, a **meritocracy** (a system of bureaucratic advancement based on education rather than familial relations, wealth, or power) of sorts was established and lasted until the imperial system ended in 1912. The scholar bureaucrats, or **mandarins**, touched the lives of people at all levels, national, district, and local. They drafted decrees, monitored local affairs, and served as heads of departments. The **Bureau of Censors** kept track of officials at all levels and the Commission of Fiscal Census carried out a tax reform including taxes based on wealth.

The Demise of Buddhism in China

A Confucian-based mandarin revival threatened the old aristocracy and the Buddhists. Buddhism was also threatened by favoritism, which produced a backlash. The Tang **Empress Wu** (r. 690–705), for instance, gave vast sums to build and improve monasteries, and at one point she sought to make Buddhism a state religion. She commissioned large statues of Buddha, some two and three stories high, carved in stone or cast in bronze. By the middle of the ninth century there were nearly 50,000 monasteries in China. Monasteries acquired extensive land holdings and accumulated large gold reserves through donations and deposits for safekeeping. Monasteries served as banks, lending money and collecting interest. Buddhist success aroused animosity on the part of Daoists and Confucianists, and it was clear that the growing monastic orders were a major drain on the empire's resources. Measures to limit the monasteries became open persecution of Buddhism in the 840s from which Chinese Buddhism never recovered.

Rise of the Song (Sung)

The attack on Buddhism reflected a weakened Tang Dynasty. The demand for more taxes to pay for an extravagant court, an expanding army, a great drought in the north, and spreading dissatisfaction led to a series of rebellions beginning in 755, which eventually led to the dissolution of the Tang Dynasty in 907. The Vietnamese established independence in 939. In 960 a young general proclaimed a new dynasty, the **Song (Sung)**, which was to last more than three centuries. During the Song (Sung), economic growth and innovation continued. The Song (Sung) capital at **Kaifeng**, a city of over one million located near the great bend in the Huang He (Yellow River), became a huge commercial entrepot and center of manufacturing. There was a boom in iron and steel production and metal industries, using coal as fuel. Paper promissory notes and letters of credit followed by government issuance of **paper currency** served the growth of commerce. Government-distributed pamphlets printed in the **vernacular** (everyday language of the common people) promoted improved techniques in agriculture. A new class of educated elite, the **gentry**, established themselves at the local level. But the position of women declined. In wealthy households, women indicated the status of the family. To demonstrate to society that women were no longer needed for labor, their feet were bound until their arches broke and the foot was reduced by half, making it all but impossible for women to work outside the home.

The Tributary System

One of the reasons the Song (Sung) was a golden age of good government, prosperity, and creativity was Song (Sung) foreign policy. Instead of continuing the Han and Tang policy of holding on to outlying areas like Sinkiang, Tibet, Mongolia, Manchuria, Korea, Vietnam, and some fringes of northern China, the Song (Sung) policy was to defend the essential territory and appease neighboring barbarian groups in a complex **tributary system** based on money, bribes, and arranged marriages. As the planets revolved around the sun, so states revolved around China in orbits of descending order. States furthest away paid less tribute and made fewer **kowtows** (bowing before the emperor). States closest paid more obeisance but received gifts of greater value than the tribute to demonstrate the power and largesse of the Chinese emperor. Harmonious relationships between China and foreigners insured peace within the Chinese state since war required recruits and taxes that could upset the balance between the emperor and his people.

Did You Know?

The tribute system that began during the Han Dynasty matured into a sophisticated foreign policy with distaste for the warrior conflict.

The Southern Song

The policy failed, however, in 1122 when the Song (Sung) made an alliance with the Jurchen barbarians in Manchuria against another barbarian group. Following a successful military campaign, the Jurchen betrayed the dynasty and invaded northern China. Kaifeng was besieged, starved, and finally sacked. The Song (Sung) then moved south and established a new capital at Hangzhou (Hangchou). Cut off from the northern land routes, the Southern Song (Sung) turned in earnest to developing sea routes to Southeast Asia and India. This spurred a whole new commercial age and technological revolution. Chinese classical culture spread in Southeast Asia.

Maritime Trade

Permanent colonies of Chinese merchants expanded in Southeast Asia and along the southern China coast. These colonies included large numbers of foreign residents. Foreign accounts agree that these were the world's largest port cities at the time. Maritime trade provided a fifth of the imperial revenue. Advances in ship size and design created oceangoing ships, some of which could carry over 600 people plus cargo. The earlier Chinese invention of the compass, use of multiple masts, separate watertight compartments, and the stern-post rudder all predated the modern ships that carried Europeans to the Americas and beyond. Arabs carried Chinese goods to the Mediterranean. Domestically, trade flourished too, aided by an immense network of canals and navigable rivers. Both Ibn Battuta and Marco Polo visited Hangzhou (Hangchou) at different times. They marveled at its size, wealth, cosmopolitanism, and ethnic diversity.

Confucian Renaissance

Not unlike the European Renaissance, innovation and technological development also marked the Southern Song (Sung) period. The philosopher **Zhu Xi** (Chu Hsi) (1130–1200) founded **Neo-Confucianism**, a mixture of Confucian, Buddhist, and Daoist thought. Neo-Confucianism was a movement that emphasized self-perfection that supported state and society and provided a framework for understanding the world. Zhu Xi (Chu Hsi)'s "investigation of things" meant the study of moral conduct and the timeless lessons contained in the classics. Neo-Confucianism gained importance in Korea and Japan as well as China. Like Leonardo da Vinci, but three centuries earlier, Zhu Xi (Chu Hsi)'s journals recorded observations and theories like that of geomorphological uplift.

In addition to Neo-Confucianism, there were rapid developments in agriculture, manufacturing, and transport, such as tools and devices for cultivation and threshing, for water lifting (pumps), for carding, spinning, and weaving fibers; windlasses; inclined planes; and canal locks. Water clocks and water-powered mills were widespread. The earlier invention of gunpowder led to the development of explosives fired from bamboo or bronze tubes. In some ways, China resembled later eighteenth-century Europe undergoing early industrialization with its characteristics of commercialization, urbanization, and invention.

Expansion of Chinese Classicism

In 1234 North China was overrun by the Mongols and by 1239 the Mongols triumphed over the Southern Song (Sung). The vibrancy of the Chinese Golden Age under the Sui, Tang, and Song (Sung) was carried by the Mongols far beyond China's borders to Europe. Under the Sui, Tang, and Song (Sung) dynasties, arts and technology flourished, nourished by a strong economy and good rule. The Mandate of Heaven was solidified and strengthened by means of a liberalized civil service examination system that infused merit into its selection process. The introduction of Buddhism brought enhanced use of paper, and Buddhists developed block printing. Although Buddhism inspired the arts and architecture, Confucian tradition replaced Buddhism during this period. Chinese classicism expanded within China as the population moved south and it expanded outside of China with the rise of maritime trade, especially in Southeast Asia. By the tribute system Chinese diplomatic relations replaced the need to rule vast areas. Nowhere during the Golden Age did the Chinese classical system have more impact, though, than on Japan during the Nara and Heian periods.

NARA AND HEIAN JAPAN (700 C.E.–1200 C.E.)

Early Japanese history is cloudy, largely because written records do not begin until the eighth century C.E., after Japan adopted the Chinese art of writing from the Koreans. The Japanese spoken language, which is in the same linguistic group as Korean, indicates that the Japanese originally came from mainland Asia via Korea sometime between the second century B.C.E. and the second century C.E. Migrants slowly displaced the indigenous inhabitants. Earlier peoples migrated to Japan from China, Manchuria, Malaysia, and Indonesia, as well as Korea, to settle on the Japanese archipelago of four main islands, as well as thousands of smaller ones. Bronze tools and weapons from China entered via Korea about the first century C.E. and iron around 200 C.E.

The Yamato

By the third century C.E. the **Yamato clan** seized the narrow coastal plain south of Kyoto, near Osaka Bay. The clan, which traced its descent from the sun-goddess, subordinated other clans to create the Yamato state. Under the authority of their sun-goddess, the Yamato established a chief shrine giving rise to a religion known as **Shinto**, the way of the gods. Shinto was a unifying force. The chief deity of Shinto, the sun-goddess, became the nation's protector. According to the ancient teachings, the emperor descended from Shinto. Shinto also stressed the worship of ancestors and its rituals celebrated the beauty of nature rather than the wrath of gods. Those rituals emphasized cleanliness and respect for **kami**, the spirits of nature. During this period, Japanese and Korean contact was extensive, enriching Japan economically and culturally. According to tradition, the Korean King Song of the Paekche kingdom sent the Yamato court Buddhist images and scriptures in 552. Pro-Buddhists in the Yamato court used the religion to strengthen Yamato rule and to introduce Chinese political and bureaucratic concepts. The architect of this effort was **Prince Shotoku** (547–622), the author of the **Seventeen Article Constitution**. It was not really a constitution but a Buddhist blueprint that stressed the proper goals of government and ethical conduct.

Because Japan lacked trained personnel to build a bureaucracy of professional administrators, Prince Shotoku sent groups of Japanese to Tang China beginning in 607 to learn Chinese culture and Buddhism. The death of Shotoku in 622 resulted in political chaos, but finally, in 645, supporters of these policies overthrew the government and proclaimed the **Taika Reforms**, a bold effort to create a complete imperial and bureaucratic system like that of Tang China. The symbol of this new system was the establishment in 710 of Japan's first true capital and first city, modeled on the Tang capital, at **Nara** just north of modern Osaka. Reflecting Chinese influence, monasteries, pagodas, and Buddhist art flourished. The statue of the great Buddha, the focal point of Nara, was completed by a Buddhist monk from India at a ceremony in Nara in 752. Nara gave its name to the period that lasted from 710 to 794, an era characterized by the continuing importation of Chinese ideas, an imperial court, and Buddhism.

Fujiwara

Some aspects of Japanese culture as it evolved continued to be distinctly Japanese. Shintoism, the animistic, nature-centered, indigenous religion, continued in importance. Beautiful wood-carved Shinto shrines were built. Shintoism was practiced together with Buddhism. Unlike Mandarin China, but like Korea, feudal-style lords and hereditary nobles retained power. Despite the introduction of the Chinese examination system, hereditary aristocrats reserved most official positions for themselves. The Japanese emperor, unlike the Chinese emperor, was considered divine. After a Buddhist monk tried to usurp the throne, the emperor moved the capital from Nara to **Kyoto** (then called **Heian**), which was to remain the capital for 1000 years. Japanese study groups to China stopped after 838. Japanese leaders began to move even further away from the Chinese model as an expression of cultural independence. A phonetic system known as **Kana**, in which most of the symbols combine a consonant and a vowel, made it possible to transcribe spoken Japanese accurately. Kana replaced Chinese characters in popular writing. Art and architecture reflected the Japanese concern with texture and natural materials.

Rule by the **Fujiwara clan** (858–1086) ended the system of meritocracy. The Fujiwara increased their influence at court through intermarriage with the emperor's family. At court, aristocratic ladies and gentlemen devoted themselves to aesthetic endeavors. The best-known work of the Heian period is **Lady Murasaki**'s *Tale of Genji,* considered the world's first psychological novel with its insight into human behavior. The tale describes the refined and colorful life at court with its rivalries and intrigues. It is a romantic tale about the life of a prince and his many affairs, told with charm, candor, and attention to detail. It also reveals something about the life of women during the Heian period, suggesting that their lives were less conventional than those of men and that they were freer to express themselves.

The Fujiwara absorption with life at court blinded them to the rise of new families. The **Daimyo** (territorial rulers) expanded their estates and used their private armies to become *de facto* rulers over the lands they formerly had guarded for noble families. Peasants continued to work small plots of land but the Daimyo profited from their labor. As Japanese settlement spread slowly northeastward beyond the Yamato area after the ninth century, a new group of frontier warriors, or **samurai**, emerged as powerful factions that began to interfere with conflicts at court. In 1185 the Heian Era gave way to the Kamakura period, marked by the rise of feudalism in Japan.

Summary

During the Nara period, Chinese classical culture spread from Korea to Japan. The Japanese adopted and then adapted it. During the Heian period they developed a distinct Japanese classical style that was then spread to other areas of Japan. While the Chinese classical civilization dominated in East Asia, it was Indian classical civilization that began to dominate in Southeast Asia.

> ### THE TALE OF GENJI
>
> Though it seemed a shame to put so lovely a child into man's dress, he was now twelve years old and the time for his Initiation was come. The Emperor directed the preparations with tireless zeal and insisted upon a magnificence beyond what was prescribed. . . . The ceremony took place in the eastern wing of the Emperor's own apartments, and the Throne was placed facing toward the east, with the seats of the Initiate-to-be and his Sponsor in front.
>
> Genji arrived at the hour of the Monkey (3 PM). He looked very handsome with his long childish locks and the Sponsor, whose duty it had just been to bind them with the purple ribbon, was sorry to think that all this would soon be changed, and even the Clerk of the Treasury seemed reluctant to sever those lovely tresses with the ritual knife. . . .
>
> Duly crowned, Genji went to his chamber and changing into man's dress went down into the courtyard and performed the Dance of Homage, which he did with such grace that tears stood in every eye. . .
>
> *During the seventh and eighth centuries C.E., the Japanese court at Nara borrowed heavily from the Chinese. Later periods like the Heian (794–1185 C.E.) reaped the benefits. During the Heian period Chinese and Japanese ideas were blended. One family, the Fujiwara, acquired power, and they and their followers followed an elaborate court style. Many court women kept diaries and composed poetry written in Japanese (the men wrote in Chinese). The Tale of Genji was written by Lady Murasaki Shikibu and is not only a Japanese masterpiece, but one of the world's first novels. The novel, probably written about 1004 C.E., describes the many adventures of a legendary Prince Genji.*

KHMER CAMBODIA (800 C.E.–1200 C.E.)

Between 650 and 1250 Indian merchants and monks disseminated Indian classical culture along land and trade routes throughout Southeast Asia. The impact was so pervasive that historians often refer to this phenomenon as the **Indianization of Southeast Asia**, though in reality it was an intermarriage between Indian culture and the indigenous cultures of Southeast Asia. In Java, for instance, the indigenous peoples adopted the general narrative of the Indian epic, the *Ramayana,* but added to it native Javanese legends. Rulers tended to adopt a god-king (**devaraja**) pattern of rule rather than the Chinese view as intermediaries between humans and the cosmos.

The Indian Impact

When the Indians entered Southeast Asia, they encountered both indigenous peoples and newcomers. The newcomers were the Vietnamese, who established themselves on the eastern coast of the mainland and in 939 became independent of China; the **Thais**, who lived to the west in **Siam (Thailand)** and in the eighth century united in a confederacy and expanded northward against Tang China; and the **Burmese**, who migrated in the eighth century where they established **Pagan**, their capital, in the area of modern Myanmar (Burma). All three spoke languages that are distantly related to Chinese, but the Burmese and Thais wrote in Indian-derived script. The two indigenous peoples were the **Khmer** in **Cambodia** and the

Srivijaya on the island of **Sumatra**. Srivijaya, which originated as a city-state, became a maritime empire. Rulers created a strong navy to protect their seaborne trade and rule the waters around Sumatra, Java, and Borneo, but in 1025 Srivijaya suffered a stunning blow when a commercial rival in southern India launched a naval raid that succeeded in capturing the king and capital of the empire. In the wake of this defeat, Indian mythology took hold as did Indian architecture and sculpture. Sculptures often depicted **Bodhisattvas**, or saint-like beings who delayed their acceptance into Nirvana to help others seeking enlightenment. Exquisite Buddhist monuments like **Borobudur** (Indonesia) illustrate the influence of Indian Buddhist culture.

As Indian merchants and monks began to penetrate into Cambodia, the common people tended to adopt Buddhism because of its emphasis on compassion and equality, and the upper class, Hinduism because of its emphasis on social order. In the ninth century Khmer king Yasovarman started building a new capital and temple complex at **Angkor Thom**. He invited Brahmans from India to legitimize his claim to divine kingship and plan a city that reflected the structure of the world according to Hindu cosmology. Less than a mile to the south, Suryavarman II (r. 1113–1150) built another major temple complex known as **Angkor Wat** (*wat* meaning temple), which replicated the arrangement and style of the temples at Angkor Thom. At both sites Buddhist temples and sculp-

Did You Know?

Perhaps the greatest reflection of Indian influence can be seen in the 40-square-mile ruins of temples at Angkor Wat Cambodia.

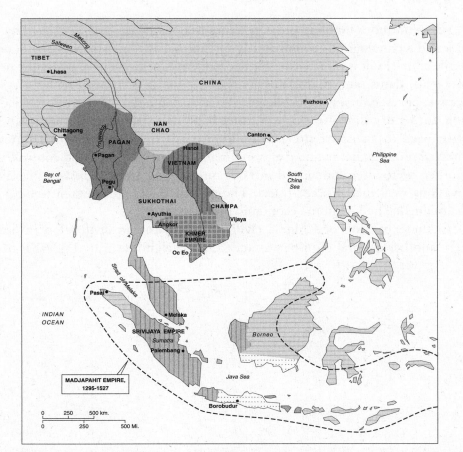

By 1200 the Khmer Empire (Angkor), which once covered much of mainland Southeast Asia, had declined. Sukhothai, Pagan, Srivijaya, Champa, and Vietnam were other major states.

tures, often of Bodhisattvas, were added beginning in the thirteenth century when Khmer rulers adopted Mahayana Buddhism.

Angkor Wat. The great artistic achievement of the Khmer Empire of Cambodia 802–1219 C.E. was the planning and building of Angkor Wat, the enormous and lavishly decorated temple complex that spreads over 40 square miles.

Such enormous building projects were sustained by the wealth created by a complex and technologically sophisticated agricultural system. The Mekong floodplain's fertile alluvial soil was made still more productive by a system of hydraulic networks of canals, dams, and dikes. The monsoon rains were controlled by a system of **barays**, or reservoirs, which collected water during heavy rains and provided irrigation during dry times. In this way, three harvests a year were possible. Canals were often used to transport stone to building sites. A highly organized bureaucracy directed projects that required enormous amounts of planning and controlled labor. Workers were often kidnapped in raids on outlying areas. Excessive spending and invasions weakened Khmer rulers. The extensive hydraulic systems could not be maintained. The kingdom's economic base declined.

To the expansion of Chinese civilization and Indian civilization in Southeast Asia, another cultural imprint was added in the eighth century C.E., that of Islam.

The Rise of Islamic Civilization

(ca. 600 C.E.–1200 C.E.)

TIMELINE	
570 C.E.–632 C.E.	Life of Muhammad
661 C.E.–750 C.E.	Umayyad Caliphate
750 C.E.–1258 C.E.	Abbasid Caliphate
900 C.E.–1100 C.E.	Kingdom of Ghana
1000 C.E.–1400 C.E.	Great Zimbabwe
1096 C.E.–1272 C.E.	Crusader States in the Middle East
1200 C.E.–1450 C.E.	Kingdom of Mali
1258 C.E.	The Mongols
1300 C.E.–1923 C.E.	Ottoman Empire

THE ISLAMIC CULTURAL SYNTHESIS

With the rise of **Islam**, Southwest Asia (Middle East), at the confluence of three continents, again became the focus of a rising civilization that expanded over large areas and was the precursor to the Global Age of Islam. In Islam can be found strains of earlier cultural heritages.

Bedouin Culture

Competition for water and pasture caused pastoral Arabs to divide into clans. Clans identified members as individuals descended from a common male ancestor, resulting in clan loyalties that crossed the division of interests between sedentary villagers and their nomadic cousins. For instance, the same Bedouin nomad clan that controlled trade of one village controlled the flocks around the village market. Some clans, like the **Umayyad**, dominated the politics and commercial economy of towns

> **Did You Know?**
>
> Islam is the wedding of two Arab cultures
> - the nomadic herder, the **Bedouins** and
> - the settled oasis dweller.

like **Mecca**. In a transcontinental trading system that stretched from the Mediterranean to Southeast Asia, Mecca was a vital center for trade and shipping goods. This city was also the site of the most revered religious shrine in pre-Islamic Arabia, the **Kaaba**. A truce suspending interclan feuds inside Mecca resulted in pilgrims, merchants, and Bedouin nomads flocking to the town to worship and trade in an atmosphere of peace. In the south of Arabia, a third indigenous Arab culture existed, that of the agriculturalist. The main focus of Bedouin cultural creativity in the pre-Islamic era was poetry, which was composed and recited orally. The poems were usually about heroics in war, lovers in passion and conflict, and great deeds of loyalty and generosity. Bedouin religion was a blend of animism and polytheism. Some tribes recognized a supreme God named Allah but ethics were founded in tribal codes of behavior rather than religion.

Islamic Culture and Beliefs

In the century before Muhammad, trade routes through Southwest Asia were seriously disrupted by the expanding conflict between Byzantium, which bridged Asia and Europe, and Sassanid Persia with its routes to East Asia. Unable to use the traditional land routes through Southwest Asia, merchants began traveling through the Arabian Peninsula. This contact acquainted the Arabs with all the cultural traditions of the area. Even earlier, the desert environment of the Arabian Peninsula led to a series of migrations to the north in the third millennium B.C.E., resulting in people as diverse as the Babylonians, Assyrians, Hebrews (Jews), and Arabs, all speaking **Semitic** languages. Successive cultural traditions came into Southwest Asia over time.

- The Egyptians under Ramses II;

- The Greeks during the Hellenistic Age;

- The Judeo-Christians under the Romans;

- The Persian, Zoroastrian, and Mithraian cultures of the Sassanid Empire.

Prior to the birth of Muhammad, the Arabs became acquainted with all of these traditions. In this way, the new religion and culture of Islam reflects a synthesis of Arab lifestyles, Semitic ethnicity, and the cultural traditions of Southwest Asia.

Muhammad

Muhammad was born about 570 C.E. into a branch of one of Mecca's leading families. A devout man, he described visions from the **Archangel Gabriel** in 610 C.E., who delivered the word of **Allah**, the Arabic word for God. The revelations Muhammad recited became the basis of Islam found in the verses of the Muslim holy book, the *Qur'an (Koran)*.

The most fundamental belief of Muhammad's new religion was the supremacy of Allah. **Islam** itself means submission to the will of Allah (God). As in Christianity, Muhammad believed in the resurrection of the physical body in the afterlife and an eventual Last Judgment. A **Muslim** is thus one who submits to the will of God and wins forgiveness by living by the **pillars of faith**, which are fivefold:

1. profession of the creed, "There is no God but Allah, Muhammad is His prophet."
2. prayer five times a day called by a **muezzin**, or reciter;
3. almsgiving, or **zakat**;
4. fasting during the holy month of **Ramadan**;
5. a pilgrimage to Mecca (**hajj**).

THE QUR'AN (KORAN)

Set no other god beside Allah . . .
Who hath ordered that you worship none but Him.
Show kindness to your parents, and to your kindred,
And to the poor, and to the wayfaring stranger.
Commit no adultery, for this is taboo and sinful.
Slay none whom Allah hath forbidden you to slay.
Rob not the orphan.
Keep your promises.
Cheat not when you sell.
Walk humbly on the earth.
Other than this is evil, a stench before the Lord.

Muslims believe the Qur'an (Koran) contains the words of Allah, or God, as spoken through Muhammad (570–632), the last of the great prophets. The central belief of Islam, meaning submission to God, is that Allah is worshipped as the only deity. Besides that, the faithful are called upon to live in accordance with the teachings of the Koran by performing mandatory observances called the "pillars of faith." Belief in the prophets, the Last Judgment, and that the good will enter paradise are key concepts of Islam, as of Christianity.

Islamic Beliefs

Another fundamental doctrine is that Allah has sent many prophets to preach and warn of the Last Judgment, including **Abraham**, of the Old Testament, who was the first to accept monotheism. Muslims accept Christians and Jews as people who worship the same God. Moses and Jesus are also recognized as Islamic prophets. Followers believe that these prophets, however, had possession of only part of God's message, but with Muhammad as the last prophet, the full and perfect religion was revealed. Devout followers believe the teachings and revelations preached by Muhammad are the sacred word of Allah recorded in the *Qur'an* (*Koran*). Islamic social teachings can be found in the *Hadith*, a collection of traditional sayings and acts of Muhammad. Both the *Hadith* and the *Qur'an* (*Koran*) are written in Arabic. They form the ethical basis of Islamic law, which is codified in the *Sharia*.

One of the appeals of Islam is its simplicity, instruction, and guidance in social affairs and its message of equality. Women are equal to men in the sight of Allah. Laws for dowries, divorce, and inheritance are given in detail. Women, for example, are entitled to half their dowry if they divorce and if they initiated divorce proceedings. They keep control of the property they bring to a marriage. Women are assured of rights, but, in continuance of Arab tradition, fathers and husbands have superior rights. Slavery is allowed but controlled by fair treatment. Fraud, slander, and perjury are condemned; gambling and money lending are forbidden, as is the consumption of alcohol or pork. Muslims believe that Islam will establish justice on earth. As Muslims they must lead a holy life and spread the Islamic faith (**Jihad**). Jihad is waged by four means: the heart, the tongue, the hand, and the sword. Through Jihad, defenders of the faith are assured of paradise. Because a Muslim was required to read and recite the *Qur'an* (*Koran*) in Arabic, the spread of Islam provided a unifying cultural element and language and an emphasis on literacy in all countries in which it was established.

In the eighth and ninth centuries a mystic Islamic movement known as **Sufism** developed in Baghdad. Like Christian monks, men and women wore a coarse wool robe called a *suf* from which the movement gets its name. Sufism, like the Christian monastic movement, taught that individuals could find salvation through fasting, prayer, and meditation outside the realm of daily life. Sufis played a considerable role in spreading the faith in Africa, India, and Southeast Asia where the practice of meditation was already part of religious custom.

THE SPREAD OF ISLAM

Islam spread rapidly and afar for a number of reasons besides the Sufi movement.

- The weakness of the Byzantine and Sassanian Empires in Southwest Asia made them vulnerable to outside attack.

- Islam as a religion was appealing because of its inspiring and clear message, daily responsibilities and rituals, and element of familiarity to people of the area.

- When united, the Arabs became a formidable military force that attracted others.

Arab Adoption of Islam

When Muhammad announced his revelations in Mecca, he found few supporters, especially among the Umayyad clan, who feared the new religion would cause pilgrimages to the Kaaba to decline, and with it, their income. In 622 Muhammad fled to Medina, a journey that is known as the **Hegira** (emigration) and this was soon recognized as the first year of the Muslim era. Between 622 and 628, when Muhammad returned to Mecca, he had won over 1000 converts. The appeal of Islam to the Arabs was twofold. Belief in one God provided a unifying element to the deeply divided and contentious clans, and it provided a social system that helped heal deep social rifts within Arabian society, as, for example, between clans. By the time of his death in 632, much of the Arabian peninsula had been unified under Muhammad who, in effect, had become both a political and religious leader.

Muslim Sectarianism

When loyal followers met to choose the new **caliph**, or successor to Muhammad, a division of opinion arose that was to have long-lasting effects. One choice was a relative of Muhammad, **Ali**, a cousin and son-in-law. The other was a political follower and close friend, **Abu Bakr**. The succession question led to the development of sects. The **Sunnis** believed that the caliphs should be selected by consensus (agree-

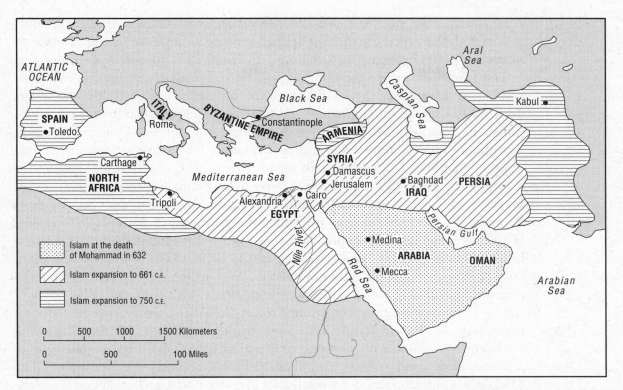

The Spread of Islam 632–750 C.E. In a little more than a century, Islam spread across North Africa and into Spain, throughout Southwest Asia, and as far east as China. Soon after, Islamic traders crossed the Sahara into Africa and controlled the Indian Ocean trade as far east as Indonesia.

ment) of the community of believers. The **Shi'ites** believed that the caliphs should be a relative of Muhammad. Sunnis believed that political and military power was the responsibility of the caliph. Religious policy, such as the interpretation of the *Qur'an* and the *Hadith*, was reached through study, discussion, and consensus of religious scholars known as the **Ulema**. Shi'ites believed that the successor of Muhammad, or **Imam**, is inspired by Allah (God). The Imam, therefore, is the political and religious leader of the community of believers.

> **Did You Know?**
>
> What began as a disagreement over succession resulted in religious divisions between Shi'ia and Sunni which continues to this day.

In the first phase of Islamic history, the Sunnis triumphed. Abu Bakr was elected successor. Shi'ites continued to support Ali, the cousin and son-in-law of Muhammad.

The passage of time sustained the division between Shi'ia and Sunni. Differences in beliefs, religious practices, and cultural traditions widened the sparation. Shi'ites became the majority in Persia (present-day Iran and southern Iraq) where Zoroastrians converted to Islam. Arabian cultural traditions shaped the Sunni sect, which is the majority of believers in the rest of the Muslim world.

The Umayyad Caliphate

The Umayyad unified the Bedouin forces and in rapid succession took Syria, western Iraq, Palestine, Egypt, and Libya. By the mid-640s the desert Bedouins were also putting together war fleets, making further inroads into the Byzantine Empire by way of the sea. An Arab advance in the west crossed North Africa into the Iberian peninsula and was finally halted in France by Charles Martel at the **Battle of Tours** in 732. In the last half of the seventh century Muslim armies broke into Central

Asia. Muslims did not force conversion on those they conquered, requiring only tribute and obedience. By the early eighth century an advance had been made to northwest India, inaugurating a contest with Hinduism that continues to this day.

The Umayyads moved the political capital to a more central point in their new empire, at **Damascus**, Syria. During the reign of the first caliph, **Muawiya** (661–680), a system of government and rule based on the Roman model was established. Regions were encouraged to develop agricultural and industrial projects, providing a solid base for prosperity and taxation. The Umayyads also pioneered important cultural developments. In the early years of Islam the faithful gathered in **mosques**, or places of worship, which were usually simple courtyards with roofed porticoes. Borrowing from the Byzantine dome design, the mosques became more elaborate. In 691 the Muslims built the **Dome of the Rock Mosque** in Jerusalem as a sacred shrine at the site where Muslims believe that Muhammad ascended into heaven. Because idolatry was forbidden in the Islamic faith, mosques were decorated with beautiful calligraphy and mosaics. As court life grew more elaborate, elegant poetry and song blended the old oral traditions with the new.

The Umayyads attempted to create a society in which a small Arab and Muslim aristocracy ruled over people who were neither Arab nor Muslim. Following Byzantine and Sassanian examples, Arab **emirs** were appointed as governors to maintain order and collect taxes. Local officials retained their positions. The Muslim warrior elite was concentrated in garrison towns and separated from the local population. It was hoped separation would prevent intermarriage and conversion and thus loss of taxable subjects. In reality, there was extensive interaction and conversion. The Umayyad elite, therefore, developed a policy in which converts continued to be taxed. Non-converts were allowed to live in their communities with their legal systems intact and to worship as they pleased. This policy made it easier to accept Arab rule since many had been previously oppressed, but it led to lasting fragmentation in Southwest Asia that bedevils unity to this day.

The other social aspect of Umayyad rule of import was the declining position of women. Historians of social history generally find that women had greater position in nomadic societies than in urban societies. This seems true in the case of Islamic history. Bedouin women had considerable freedom in terms of marriage partners, occupational choice, and clan decisions. This tradition was continued by Muhammad, who proclaimed the equality of men and women. However, under the Umayyads, seclusion and loss of rights occurred, especially among upper-class women. The harem and veil became twin symbols of the woman's status.

The Abbasid Caliphate

Social unrest between Arab Muslims and converts who were treated as second-class citizens, clan rivalries, and elaborate court spending brought down Umayyad rule. By the middle of the eighth century more than 50,000 warriors had settled in the eastern Iranian borderlands of the empire. They were angered by the fact that they were rarely given their share of booty. These opponents allied with another venerable family, the Abbasids, one of whose ancestors had been a cousin of Muhammad. The Abbasids defeated the Umayyads, and then slaughtered the remaining family members, except for the grandson of the former caliph, who fled to Spain and established the Caliphate of Cordoba.

The shift from Umayyad to Abbasid rule reflects a fundamental transformation in evolving Islamic civilization. One transformation was the growing regional identities and divisions. Umayyad rule was dominated by Arabs, the Abbasid rule increasingly by Persians. Another transformation was that the second-class converts became full members of the Islamic community, converting it into a cosmopolitan and universal faith embracing millions of converts as equals from Spain and Africa to China and the Philippines.

The rule of the Abbasids was firmly established in the reign of **Abdullah al-Mansur** (754–775). Al-Mansur moved the capital from Damascus to **Baghdad** where he built mosques and palaces within great walls. This further isolated the caliphs and engendered a fortress mentality among the rulers. He ruled from jewel-encrusted thrones like those of ancient Persian emperors. Once in a position of power, the Abbasids moved quickly to eliminate all dissenting groups, including the Shi'ites who had supported them in their takeover against the Umayyads. A vast bureaucracy was headed by a **vizier (wazir)**, or chief administrator. Sometimes the vizier (wazir) extended his own personal wealth and power through his position as chief administrator, even though the punishment for such corruption was death. The Abbasids became absolutists but stopped short of calling themselves divine, saying rather that they were the "shadow of God on earth."

The luxurious lifestyle of the Abbasid rulers reflected the tremendous growth in wealth and social status of the commercial and landlord class. This was linked to the expanding Afro-Eurasian trading network that was revived in East Asia under the Tang and Song (Sung) Empires. From the western Mediterranean to the Indian Ocean to the South China Sea, Arab **dhows**, or sailing vessels, with triangular or **lateen sails** carried goods from one civilization to another. Land routes were kept in good condition with stopping places along the way at **caravanserais**, a kind of camel motel. Long-distance trade was facilitated by the development of a banking system. Banks exchanged money, set exchange rates, issued letters of credit, and used checks three centuries before Europe did.

Besides commerce, artisan handicraft production increased. Much of the unskilled labor was left to slaves, many of whom were captured during slave raids in East Africa. In the countryside, a wealthy and entrenched landed elite emerged. Troops under the supervision of the emir were garrisoned in strategic towns. The majority of peasants did not own land and were tenant farmers, sharecroppers, or migrants. Agriculture thrived in part because of careful water management.

The Golden Age of Islam

The rule of Abassid caliph **Harun al-Rashid** was the Golden Age of Islam. Within the confines of the Islamic Abbasid Empire were centers of Hellenistic, Egyptian, Mesopotamian, Christian, Jewish, Persian, and Indian culture. The Arab tradition, by contrast, was meager. During the first phase of Abbasid rule (High Abbasid, 750–945), the main task was recovering and preserving the learning of ancient civilizations. Classics were preserved, translated into Arabic, and distributed throughout the empire. Indian numerals were learned by Muslim traders and carried to centers of Islamic civilization. Later they were known as Arabic numerals and transmitted to Europe. In the second phase (Late Abbasid, 945–1258), Muslim scholars and artists themselves made significant contributions to learning. Literary examples include the *Thousand and One Nights, a Series of Tales,* and *The Rubaiyat of **Omar***

Khayyam. Meanwhile, Muslim scientists absorbed and ultimately passed on the many inventions of the East like the magnetic compass, gunpowder, and paper. The use of glass lenses for magnification was an Arab discovery. Since Islam forbade the dissection of corpses, medical advances were made more in the area of infectious diseases. **Ibn Sina** (**Avicenna,** 980–1037) published the *Canon of Medicine,* in which he identified diseases and their causes. In the field of philosophy, the Spanish-born **Averroës** (**Ibn Rushd,** 1126–1198), who had studied the writings of Aristotle, taught that religious beliefs could not be reconciled with philosophy. Since education was highly valued in Islamic society, religious boarding schools known as madrasas began appearing and soon spread throughout the Muslim world.

The unity of the Islamic world was based on religion, the Arab language, and trade. The Abbasids failed to establish a united political empire. Spain never accepted Baghdad's rule and returned to Umayyad rule in 756. Egypt was taken in 969 by the **Fatamid** clan. Parts of Persia and territories east of the Oxus in Central Asia fell under control of the **Samanids.** By the eleventh century, the **Seljuk Turks**, originally from Asia, swept through Persia, Syria, Iraq, and most of western Asia. In 1055 they conquered Baghdad, and in 1071 they won a commanding victory over the Byzantines. Soon, however, other invaders appeared, first the Christian Crusaders in 1099 and then the Mongols in the early decades of the thirteenth century.

Islam in India and Southeast Asia

Islamic religion and culture spread to India and Southeast Asia. The first Muslim intrusion into India came during Umayyad and Abbasid rule by way of trade contacts and cultural exchanges. Traders brought Muslim culture to India and Hindu mathematicians and astronomers traveled to Baghdad. The Indian game of chess became a favorite in the Muslim world and some of the tales in the *Arabian Nights* are Indian stories. Arabs established trading colonies in coastal areas such as Malabar to the south and Bengal in the east.

Peaceful contacts, however, turned to military invasions during the eleventh century when Turkish Muslims led by **Mahmud of Ghazni** (971–1030) invaded northern India. Known as the "Sword of Islam," Mahmud mounted 17 plundering expeditions. Pillage and slaughter in the name of Allah did not make Islam popular among Indians, but the simplicity and promise of equality did. Islam replaced Hinduism and Buddhism in the Indus Valley (now Pakistan) and at the mouth of the Ganges (now Bangladesh). These incursions established Muslim rule in the Gangetic plain.

Muslim victories led to long-lasting enmity between Hindus and Muslims, especially in the Delhi area. Many Hindus were willing to take positions as administrators in the bureaucracies of Muslim overlords, or as soldiers, but they remained socially aloof. Often, Muslims were regarded by Hindus as just another caste, but at the top. In other regions of India, forced conversion was rare. Conversions that occurred were voluntary and mostly as the result of agricultural and commercial contacts or among low caste Hindus seeking equality. Sufis, the Islamic mystics, acquired recognition within villages or cities as holy men or individual saints in the tradition of Indian ascetics. For the most part, Indians maintained their caste identities and remained devoted Hindus. The spread of Islam into India set the stage for expansion to Southeast Asia.

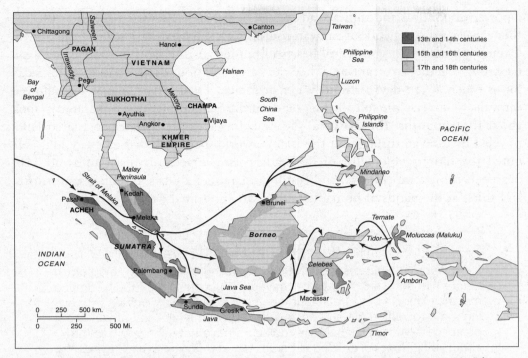

The Spread of Islam in Island Southeast Asia. Carried by merchants and missionaries, Islam spread from Arabia and India to island Southeast Asia, eventually becoming the major faith on many islands and in the Malay Peninsula.

The first areas to be won to Islam in the last decades of the thirteenth century were the small port centers on the northern coast of **Sumatra**. From these ports, the religion spread across the Straits of Malacca to Malaya, Thailand, Borneo, Java, and the Philippines. The island of **Bali**, where Hinduism had taken deep root at the popular level, remained largely impervious to Islam, as did the interior of the islands where Hindu-Buddhist dynasties remained strong. In Southeast Asia, local law and indigenous cultural staples endured. Javanese shadow plays, for instance, which were based on Indian epics, remained popular. Women retained their strong place in society as small-scale traders and matriarchal lineage patterns continued.

THE AFRICAN KINGDOMS AND CITY-STATES

Besides India and Southeast Asia, Islamic civilization penetrated sub-Saharan Africa, giving rise to important kingdoms and city-states in African history. Prior to this development, African societies were what scholars call **stateless societies**, that is, culturally and ethnically homogeneous societies without a central government. Ethnic and blood ties bound family members together and ordered political relationships. Some societies were small nomadic clans while others were large agricultural and herding kinship groups involving thousands of people. Between 800 and 1450 Islamic trade led to change and the rise of powerful African kingdoms.

The Camel Caravan

The **camel** had an impact on African trade comparable to that of the horse in Europe and Asia. Sometime before 200 C.E. the camel was introduced into North Africa and in the fifth century nomads fashioned a saddle for its use. This gave them

Did You Know?

The spread of Islam to Southeast Asia also occurred primarily at the hands of traders and sailors.

a powerful political and military advantage in the area. Between 700 and 900 C.E. they developed a network of caravan routes from the Mediterranean to the Sudan. Camels are efficient, economical beasts of burden. A thousand or more camels can be strung together in a caravan. They can carry 500 pounds as far as 25 miles a day for as much as ten days without water or forage. Their large, splayed feet allowed caravans to traverse the soft shifting sands of the Sahara. The transSaharan trip took about three months. **Ibn Battuta**, the Arab traveler often likened to Marco Polo, traveled by caravan throughout the Islamic world, perhaps as far east as China. He noted the indomitable spirit of the traders who traveled at night to avoid 110-degree daytime temperatures, and endured marauder attacks, blinding sandstorms, and thirst at the hands of nomadic raiders who poisoned wells.

THE TRAVELS OF IBN BATTUTA

So when he held a session at the beginning of Ramadan and I stood before him and said: "I have journeyed to the countries of the world and met their kings. I have been four months in your country without your giving me a reception gift and anything else. What shall I say of you in the presence of other sultans?" He replied: "I have not seen you nor known about you." The qadi and Ibn al-Faqih rose and replied to him saying: "He greeted you and you sent to him some food." Thereupon he ordered that a house be provided for me to stay in and an allowance to be allotted to me. Then, on the night of 27 Ramadan, he distributed among the qadi and the khatib and the faqihs a sum of money which they call zakah (alms distributed at the end of Ramadan) and gave to me with them 33 1/3 mithquals (standard weight of gold, about 4.72 grams). When I departed he bestowed on me 100 mithquals of gold. . . .

Ibn Battuta (1304–1369) was the Muslim world's Marco Polo (see Chapter 15). In 1325 he left his home in Tangier and for the next 30 years he covered 75,000 miles within the Dar al Islam ("the abode of Islam") where the sacred law of the Koran prevailed. He is a major source of our knowledge of African kingdoms of the time period, in this case, Mali. In this passage, Ibn Battuta meets Mansa Sulayman. The gold bestowed on Ibn Battuta is at the heart of the story as to why Islamic traders crossed the Sahara, why great African kingdoms arose at this time, and why they were Islamic.

Salt, Slaves, and Gold

Trade stimulated salt and gold mining and the search for slaves. Thick deposits of salt in the western Sahara were cut into slabs and strapped to camels for transport to the salt-scarce lands south of the Sahara where there was gold to trade. The rich gold veins were exploited by men hacking out the gold as women washed it, in a system not unlike American gold panning. North African Islamic states sought more gold to mint coins in the ninth and tenth centuries. Scholars estimate that by the eleventh century nine tons of gold were exported to Europe annually. Gold facilitated expanding trade in and between Christian Europe, North Africa, and Southwest Asia as the medium of exchange. Even with modern machinery from the same region, in 1937 only 21 tons were exported. West African gold was crucial to the **monetization** of

European commerce in the late Middle Ages and to the balance of payments in South Asia. Slaves, the second great export item, helped fill the armed forces of the Islamic regimes in Morocco and Egypt, and provided household workers for Muslim cities everywhere. Slaves in Muslim societies were not all black; in fact, the word slave comes from the word **Slavic** and refers to Caucasian Slavs from the area around the Black Sea. Demand for slaves remained high due to death by disease, **manumission** (freedom), or conversion of Africans to Islam. It is estimated that four million people were enslaved over an 850-year period, 650–1500 C.E.

TransSaharan trade caused settlements and cities like Jenne, Goa, and Timbuktu to grow. In the twelfth century, Kumbi had between 15,000 and 20,000 inhabitants, a size achieved by London and Paris only in the late thirteenth century. The most influential consequence of the transSaharan trade was the introduction of Islam. Islamic cultural and literary tradition, government, statecraft, architecture, science, and theology shaped the history of the great West African kingdoms of Ghana, Mali, and Songhay.

Ghana

Islamization began in 753 when Muslims first crossed the Sahara Desert into the **Sudan**. There they found a number of kingdoms, particularly the **Berbers**, who were indigenous Caucasoid nomads of Northwest Africa, originally Phoenician colonists. They also found a number of settled agricultural communities and remnants of a horse culture that had come from East Africa. (Horses cannot survive south of the Sudan due to the tsetse fly.) But it was the riches of **Ghana**, known as "the land of gold," that further enticed Muslim traders across the Sahara.

The nucleus of the territory that was to become the kingdom of Ghana was inhabited by the **Soninke** people by the fifth century C.E. The Soninke, who called their ruler Ghana, or war chief, had acquired iron technology and horses. The area they occupied was located north of the **Senegal** and **Niger Rivers**. (The kingdom of Ghana should not be confused with the location of the modern state of Ghana.) Its southern areas received enough rainfall so that, with skillful farming and efficient irrigation systems, crops supported a population of as many as 200,000. The rise of Ghana began in 992 when a Berber town situated on the trans-Saharan trade route was captured by the Ghanaians. This allowed Ghanaian leaders to reap the rewards of the trans-Saharan trade rather than the Berbers, and it led to the spread of Muslim culture into Ghana.

According to Muslim geographer **al-Bakri**, Ghana claimed 22 kings prior to the arrival of the Muslims. Ghana was a kingdom of such wealth that 20,000 gold coins could be traded in a single contract. Besides the royal monopoly in gold, wealth came from royal estates and tribute from subordinate chiefs to support an extravagant royal court. Rule passed from the king to his sister's son. Social classes consisted of the aristocracy at the top—king, court, and Muslim administrators—next the merchants, then the farmers and craftsmen, and, at the bottom, slaves. The army stood apart from these classes but, according to al-Bakri, "the king of Ghana can put 200,000 warriors on the field," perhaps an exaggeration though the force was likely formidable. The king of Ghana adopted the Muslim **diwan**, or agency, for recordkeeping. All justice derived from the king. Rulers held court and assigned judgment based on the supernatural, much like the European tradition of trial by ordeal. Ghanaian leaders did not officially convert to Islam but local merchants did. Rulers used Islamic traditions and culture to improve rule and embellish upper-class lifestyles.

Al-Bakri described how the religion of Ghana remained pagan and how foreign enclaves were built six miles from the capital. Ghana's independence ended in 1076–1077 when the **Almoravids**, Saharan tribesmen who had been converted to Islam, swept into Ghana and imposed a Muslim king on the Ghanaians. Overgrazing and the deterioration of agricultural lands may have hastened the kingdom's disintegration. Subsequent struggles between Ghanaians and Almoravids so disrupted trade that Ghana broke up into tribal units and power passed to Mali.

Mali

The collapse of Ghana caused many people to flee south. They found safety from Saharan marauders in more productive land with other **Mande**-speaking clans. This became the empire of **Mali**, which reigned as the most powerful West African state for 200 years (ca. 1250–ca. 1460 C.E.). The founder of the empire was **Sundiata** (ca. 1230–ca. 1255 C.E.), who put together a federal state of subservient governors, combining the southern half of Ghana, Mali, and parts of what is now Guinea. He thereby controlled a major gold-producing area and a communications network provided by the upper Niger River and its tributaries. The major sources of income were tribute and a tax on trade, although the economic basis of Mali was agriculture.

Sundiata claimed to be both tribal and Muslim, thus satisfying both Muslim merchants and non-Muslim rural populations. His son, **Uli**, however, was a pious Muslim. The wholesale conversion that followed had numerous benefits. It helped establish good trade relations with Arab states north of the Sahara and it helped politically. Rule of a large empire demanded an efficient, stable central administration with control over the governors. With the spread of Muslim education, scholars were educated who could serve as public servants. Gold and salt served as **mediums of exchange** though the government introduced cowrie shells as a medium of exchange in western Sudan to improve internal trade. A central currency system and systems of weights and measures added to the success of merchants and the growing prosperity of Mali. Mali's products were widely prized, including ivory, animal skins, slaves, and, especially, gold. The wealth allowed Mali leaders to purchase an army and arms from abroad.

Mali's zenith came under the rule of **Mansa Musa** (1312–1337). (In the Mandinke language, Mansa means emperor.) Mansa Musa extended Malian territory to a size roughly double that of Ghana, from Lake Chad to the Atlantic and from Morocco to southern Nigeria. Mali contained a population of eight million and controlled fabulous wealth. Mansa Musa further systematized government, appointing members of the royal family to be governors. He became a devout Muslim, leading to the most celebrated event of his reign, an event that was immortalized in a medieval European map. In 1324–1325 he embarked on a pilgrimage to Mecca during which he paid a state visit to the Egyptian **sultan** (a word Turks use for rulers rather than caliph, which is Arabic). On his entrance into Cairo, he was preceded by 500 slaves, each carrying a six-pound staff of gold, and he was followed by a host of retainers including 100 elephants, each bearing 100 pounds of gold. He lavished the wealth on the citizens of the city, leading an Egyptian official to record that Mansa Musa's gold brought terrible inflation throughout Egypt. Mansa Musa brought back with him the distinguished Muslim architect al-Saheli, whom he commissioned to build new mosques.

Timbuktu's 150 schools were devoted to the study of the *Qur'an* (*Koran*) and trade in books was the greatest in the world at that time. Muslim intellectuals and Arab traders married native women, resulting in a racially mixed and culturally diverse cosmopolitan population.

Songhay

Shortly after Ibn Battuta's visit in 1352–1353, the Mali empire began to crumble. Around 1375 **Songhay** fishermen refused to pay tribute and the Songhay leader, **Sonni Ali** (ca. 1464–1492) conquered Mali itself. Like Mali, Songhay was a Muslim kingdom that grew wealthy by control of the gold trade. The empire Sonni Ali assembled had its capital at **Gao** and was larger even than Mali. **Askia Muhammad**, who followed Sonni Ali as ruler, expanded Songhay territory with a professional army of slaves and prisoners of war until it became the largest kingdom in West African history. By 1591 Arab rulers in Morocco were strong enough to regain control over the West African gold trade and the whole area south of the Sahara fragmented into tribal kingdoms.

Islam and East Africa

The Islamic world trade system also had an impact on East Africa, leading to the rise of **Swahili** city-states. Even in Roman times, East Africa had strong commercial links with India and the Mediterranean. Greco-Roman ships traveled down the East African coast carrying manufactured goods and exchanged them for cinnamon, myrrh and frankincense, slaves, and ivory. Somewhere along the Horn of Africa, they caught the monsoon winds to India. After the death of Muhammad, a great emigration from Arabia accelerated Muslim penetration of the area. Although **Ethiopia (Abyssinia)** remained Coptic Christian, trading colonies were established along the coast and people converted. Beginning in the twelfth century, fresh waves of Arabs and Persians came down the coast and settled at **Mogadishu** and then pressed southward to **Kilwa**. Similarly, Indonesians crossed the Indian Ocean and settled in **Madagascar**.

The East African coastal culture emerged on the heels of Islamic trade. The culture was Swahili. Its poetry and vocabulary exhibit Arabic influence. Much of our knowledge of this area again rests on the account of Ibn Battuta, who observed the Muslim mosques at Mogadishu, the stone buildings in cities like Kilwa, and the life of the rich coastal, monopolistic, mercantile families. Leaders of these families took the Arabic title **sheik** (which by this time meant sultan) and ruled the small city-states. The Portuguese, who arrived in the late fifteenth century, were astounded by the wealth and prosperity of the area. Wealth rested on control of sought-after products and the import taxes that sometimes reached 80 percent of value. Slaves also were part of the trade complex, but their sale was never as valuable as ivory. Some slaves became soldiers in the armies of rulers in India. Others worked on docks and dhows.

Did You Know?

Timbuktu, the capital of Mali, which began as a campsite for desert nomads, became a thriving commercial entry port and great intellectual center with its famed mosque and university.

Great Zimbabwe

The Islamic trade complex seems also to have touched South Africa and was a component in creating an empire called **Great Zimbabwe** (ca. 1000–1400). While North, East, and West Africa had contacts with Arabia, Persia, and traders across the Indian Ocean, South Africa seemed far removed until the Islamic period. The earliest inhabitants were hunter-gatherers. In the eighth century, Bantu-speaking people reached Great Zimbabwe, bringing iron working and farming skills. Sometime before 1000, inhabitants of the area, the **Shona**, began panning the alluvial gold in the **Zambezi River** tributaries. Traders shipped the gold east to **Sofala** where it met up with the East African coastal trade complex. The wealth and power of Great Zimbabwe rested on this trade. Originally, the Shona panned gold, but by 1000 C.E. they were mining as far as 100 feet below the surface. They cracked the veins of ore using fire and water to heat the rock and rapidly cool it. Iron picks were used to split the ore from the surrounding rock and remove it. Skeletal remains of small females found at the bottom of these mining shafts indicate that mining accidents occurred as girls, working as miners, squeezed through the minuscule openings of these shafts to mine the ore.

Stone buildings without mortar were not all that unusual in southern Africa but a wall 32 feet high and 17 feet thick using 900,000 granite blocks to enclose 60 acres is. The wall encloses the ruins of two building complexes that appear to demonstrate the power and wealth of the ruler. Although the ruins were looted many times, evidence indicates extensive weaving of locally produced cotton but the wealthy appeared to favor Indian cotton imported from the coast. Birds carved of soapstone, fine gold jewelry and copper ornaments, a wide variety of iron tools, and Persian and Chinese ceramics indicate that Zimbabwe was a center of manufacture and trade.

Cultural and Commercial Empire

Great West, East, and South African states arose as a result of the growth and spread of Islamic trade and culture. The Africans supplied gold to the Islamic world, and from those profits built kingdoms and city-states of considerable wealth. With trade came a new culture, giving these kingdoms not just a new religion but Islamic literacy, trade, methods of statecraft, and artistic modes of expression. The history of Islamic civilizations is one of the first in history to illustrate what is a common modern phenomenon, that is, cultural and commercial hegemony that can wield power equal to that of political hegemony. In the case of Islam, a fragmented political state, whose cultural traditions and commercial networks ranged over large areas of the globe, touched and changed the lives of many across the Afro-Eurasian continent. Islam probably would have penetrated into Europe had it not been for the Christian outpost of Byzantium that provided a bulwark against the spread of Islam for 1000 years.

The Byzantine Empire, Kievan State, and Sassanian Persia

(ca. 500 C.E.–1453 C.E.)

TIMELINE	
240 C.E.–651 C.E.	Sassanian Empire
527 C.E.–1453 C.E.	Byzantine Empire
862 C.E.–1240 C.E.	Kievan Russian State
988 C.E.	Russian conversion to Christianity
1054 C.E.	Split between Roman Christian and Orthodox Christian Churches

THE BYZANTINE EMPIRE

The Roman Empire did not collapse completely in the late fifth century C.E. While the western part disintegrated into feudalism, the eastern part continued on for another thousand years. The **Eastern Roman Empire** was Greek in language, Roman in jurisprudence, and Christian in culture. Politically, it was distinguished by the twin rule of church and state, and culturally, it observed a form of Christianity called **Greek or Eastern Orthodoxy**. These traditions spread into southeastern Europe and Russia. Along with the Muslims, the Byzantines became preservers of the wisdom of the ancient world.

Origins

During the reign of Roman emperor Constantine (306–337 C.E.), Christianity was legalized. Constantine also took the bold step of building a new capital for the empire. **Constantinople**, the new Rome, was constructed on the **Bosporus** (the narrow straits between the **Black Sea** and the **Sea of Marmora**) because it was easier to defend from the devastating German raids than Rome. It was a commercial entrepot in the lucrative Eurasian trade and thus wealthy and urbane. Christianity was widespread there. When Rome fell to the Germanic invaders in the fifth century C.E., Constantinople effectively became politically independent.

Christian Church Split

One factor that separated the Eastern and Western churches was **monasticism**. Monasticism developed earlier in the East than in the West. No doubt influenced by ascetic aspects of Eastern religions, such as Buddhism, holy men and monks sought to follow Christ by fasting, celibacy, prayer, and separation from the world. In the West, the monastic movements had more to do with active missionary work than asceticism and denial.

In the 700s and 800s, yet another controversy emerged over **iconoclasm**, or prohibition of veneration of sacred pictures or images called **icons**. In 726 C.E. Byzantine emperor Leo III issued a decree that all images and paintings be removed from the churches. He was opposed by many in his own empire and by the pope in Rome. A church council at Nicaea in 787 C.E. declared iconoclasm a heresy. While Byzantine leaders finally agreed to this, the controversy intensified already strained relations. In 1054 the two churches finally split over the issue of the nature of the **Trinity**, or the concept of God the Father, God the Son, and God the Holy Ghost, which had been established in 325 by a church council in the **Nicene Creed**.

The final separation, or **schism**, between the Eastern and Western Roman Empires occurred in 1054 when the two churches split over theological issues that divided the Latin Christian or Roman Catholic church from the Eastern Orthodox church. One was the relationship of church and state. In the West, the **pope**, or head of the Catholic church based in Rome, had control over bishops, monks, and doctrine. By contrast, in the East, the leader of the church, the **patriarch**, had no such comparable authority. The Byzantine emperors recognized no papal directives from Rome and the emperors themselves regulated church structure. Thus, church and state ruled cooperatively in the East as was the tradition in Eastern countries like Persia.

Emperor Justinian

The Byzantine Empire reached its greatest height under Emperor **Justinian** (527–565 C.E.) and his wife **Theodora**. Theodora took an active part in the political life of the empire. She worked to improve the social standing of women by having Justinian issue a decree allowing a wife to own land. At one point, she helped save Justinian's throne by persuading him to stay and fight against rebels when they threatened the government. During the rule of Justinian, the Byzantine Empire reached its largest extent. Justinian helped to stave off the Sassanian Persians. He reconquered territory in North Africa, in southern Spain, and in Italy. He also was a great builder. He ordered construction of new roads, fortresses, aqueducts, monasteries, and churches, the most beautiful of which was the **Hagia Sophia**. Its enormous dome is anchored by four piers, making it seem to float overhead. Justinian's fame, however, rests mostly on the *Corpus Juris Civilis* or *Justinian's Code*. This monumental work preserved the Roman legal heritage and integrated the numerous and conflicting laws that had been observed in the Roman Empire. This body of civil law is the legal foundation for nearly every modern European country.

Under Attack

From the time of Justinian until Constantinople finally fell to the Ottoman Turks in 1453, the Byzantine Empire was under almost constant attack. Persians invaded Syria, Palestine, and Egypt and in 626 C.E. reached the walls of Constantinople.

From 674 to 678 C.E., the Arab Muslims lay siege to the capital and then gained former Byzantine territories in North Africa and southwest Italy and the Seljuk Turks defeated the Byzantines in the **Battle of Manzikert**, gaining control of Syria, Palestine, and Turkey. Then, in 1204 Christian crusaders attacked. By the late 1300s the empire consisted only of Constantinople and part of mainland Greece. It wasn't until 1453, when the Ottoman sultan, Mehmet II, lay siege to the city with cannons, that the capital finally surrendered. On May 29 **Mehmet II** entered the city, converted the Hagia Sophia into a mosque, and promised protection to the Greek Christians. The 1000-year-old Byzantine Empire passed into history.

Byzantine Defenses

That Constantinople survived so long under siege is probably due to its impregnable defenses. At the gateway to the **Golden Horn**, or waterway, on the northern side, a chain was hung in the water to prevent entrance of foreign ships. A system of cisterns freed the city from dependence on water pipelines that could be cut off in times of attack. Besides these physical attributes, the Byzantine military was small but well trained and equipped. Soldiering was hereditary. The officers were appointed by the emperor. The empire was divided into districts called **themes** where the district commander also acted as governor. The cavalry was equipped with **stirrups**, a Eurasian invention borrowed from the Persians but unknown to the Romans. This gave horsemen a steady seat while they used the bow and arrow, lance, and sword. The Byzantine navy was less efficient than the army but it possessed **Greek fire**, possibly a mixture of petroleum sulfur and pitch, which ignited when shot as a projectile onto another ship, turning it into a fiery inferno.

The other defense weapon the Byzantines possessed was intelligence. The Bureau of Barbarians may have been the first Central Intelligence Agency in world history. Spies fed information to the emperors, who then used sophisticated diplomacy to play one group of frontier people against another. The origins of much of today's diplomatic language and ranking comes from the Byzantines. As in the Chinese court, Byzantine emperors invested officials in silken robes and bestowed titles such as Excellency (used by ambassadors, governors, and Roman Catholic bishops today) and Magnificence (adopted by popes); England's monarch adopted the orb and scepter, protocol officers, and the order of precedence at imperial banquets. Ceremony and splendor shown to outside officials was meant to dazzle and thereby intimidate enemies into submission.

Byzantine Society

Byzantine society was highly regulated and hierarchical. Trades were organized in guilds that controlled prices, quality, output, and surplus. The emperor had monopolies in minting, armaments, and silk (an industry Justinian started with silkworm eggs smuggled from China.) Unlike in the West, money lending was legal but also regulated. There was an eight percent ceiling on interest. Idleness was a crime. Taverns closed at eight to prevent drunkenness. The church and government provided free medical and hospital care. Organizations took care of the poor, helpless, and blind. Women lived partly in seclusion in their own separate rooms, and when in public, they sometimes veiled their faces. The historian **Procopius** had to reserve his personal opinions for his *Secret History* in which he revealed the cruelty of an

---

Did You Know?

In essence, Constantinople is a fortress city, surrounded on three sides by water and on the fourth or landward side, by a series of walls and gates.

autocratic system where the emperor ruled by divine providence. Lacking an order of succession, usurpations and assassinations line the pages of Byzantine history. Of the 88 emperors from Constantine I to XI, 13 took to a monastery and 30 others died violently. The intricate court intrigue that characterized Byzantine imperial government comes to the English language in the word **byzantine**, which means extremely entangled and complicated politics.

The wealth and splendor of Byzantium was derived from trade and manufacturing. Constantinople's location gave it control of the trade routes between Russia and the Mediterranean, and between Europe, Asia, and Africa. Trade stimulated manufacturing. The Byzantines became master craftsmen. In the twelfth and thirteenth centuries craftsmen from all parts of Europe went to Constantinople to learn how to work with marble, enamel, precious metals, and gems; how to make chalices; how to decorate manuscripts; and how to make **mosaics** (pictures made by fitting small, flat pieces of stone or colored glass in mortar), an art form the Romans developed. For this reason, the decreasing size of the empire meant little to the survival of the empire, as agriculture was a small part of Byzantine economy. Boats and ships plied Byzantine ports and the city itself was a bustle of shops and markets. Feeding into this trade system were Russians, and it is in these links that one of Byzantium's most profound impacts can be found. From Byzantium, classical Roman culture spread to Russia.

THE KIEVAN STATE

The Russians are part of the Eastern **Slavic peoples** (Russians, Byelorussians, and Ukrainians) who migrated into the Baltic and Black Sea areas sometime during the Roman era. They lived in tribes and hunted, farmed, and fished. As Muslim power increased in the Mediterranean and Southwest Asia in the eighth century C.E., Byzantine Christians increasingly looked north into Southeast Europe and Russia for allies and trade routes to Europe. The **Dnieper River** formed the basis of an important trade network that went from Constantinople to the Baltic and then to Europe. Along this river road, the Russians traded honey, furs, and wax. The Scandinavians, or **Varangians**, provided boats in the summer and sleighs in the winter as well as protection up and down this route. As the *Russian Primary Chronicle* (first Russian history) relates, the 12 Russian tribes who were called **Rus** decided they needed a leader to unite them, so they called on the Varangians to send a prince. **Prince Rurik of Scandinavia** became the first Russian prince and the founder of the Russian state and dynasty in 862 C.E.

City-States

This first Russian state, called **Kievan Russia**, was really a confederation of about 300 city-states. Each city-state, like Suzdal, Pskov, and Novgorod, had a council, or **veche**, that hired a prince for protection but limited his powers. At the core of each city-state was a town, usually walled, with shops that sold manufactured goods and agricultural products from outlying areas. What united these city-states was the Grand Prince of Kiev, a law code, and Christianity. When Prince Sviatoslav, a descendant of Rurik's, won victories over Asiatic tribes to the east and west, Kiev became the strongest state in Eastern Europe. In 955 Olga, the first ruling princess, was converted to Orthodox Christianity by Byzantine missionaries. They had been sent to convert the Slavs in the wake of Muslim gains in Southwest Asia and increasing hostilities with Rome. After converting to Orthodox Christianity, the Russians adopted an alphabet known as the **Cyrillic alphabet**. This alphabet was named after **Saint Cyril**, a Byzantine missionary who had been sent to eastern Europe during the 800s C.E. to help convince the Slavs to turn to Christianity.

Adoption of Christianity

In 988 Olga's grandson, **Vladimir**, officially adopted the Orthodox faith for all Kiev. As the story goes, Vladimir sent ten men to observe Muslim Bulgarians, Catholic Germans, Jewish Khazars, and Orthodox Byzantines. It was the brilliance of the Byzantine court and church that persuaded them to adopt Orthodoxy. Inspired by the resplendent **liturgy** (Christian ceremony and rituals) in Hagia Sophia, the delegation "knew not whether we were in heaven or on earth. For on earth there is no such splendor . . ." Whereupon, Vladimir had his people, on pain of the sword, baptized in the Dneiper River. No doubt, in his decision, Vladimir considered economic and political relationships with Byzantium that were at the center of Kiev's prosperity. The adoption of Orthodox Christianity was the most important event in Russia's history. As in Byzantium, it made the church subservient to the state and thus set the pattern of political rule in which autocracy flourished for centuries to come. It influenced literature and art, especially the painting of icons in which Russian masters like Andrei Rublev excelled. During the rule of Yaroslav the Wise, 1019–1054, schools and libraries were founded and the first Russian code of laws was written. Yaroslav the Wise also had a copy of the cathedral of Hagia Sophia built in Kiev.

Fall of Kiev

The fall of Kiev coincided with the changing trade patterns of Byzantium. In the eleventh century, Venice offered serious competition to Byzantine trade in the eastern Mediterranean, making the "river road" to Europe no longer necessary. Then, in 1071, when the Seljuk Turks defeated a Byzantine army at Manzikert, the Byzantines lost the trade through Turkey to Asia. The Russians reacted by moving slowly to the northeast, founding new city-states like Moscow. In 1240 C.E. the Mongols invaded, sacked Kiev, and destroyed all but about 30 of the city-states of the Kievan Confederation.

   While Chinese classical systems of society and culture were spreading in East Asia, a new civilization based on earlier classical models was emerging in Southwest Asia. This Islamic civilization developed and then spread its culture throughout Southwest Asia, North Africa, Africa south of the Sahara, and by trade to East Africa and Southeast Asia. Along the way, this culture absorbed and preserved the classical heritage that had preceded it. Classical systems of Christian western Europe escaped Islamic conversion because of the Eastern Christian center at Byzantium, which became a bulwark against Islam for more than 1000 years. Byzantine culture, meanwhile, spread north into Russia, converting it to its own unique form of classical Western culture.

PARTHIAN AND SASSANIAN PERSIA
Parthia

The Parthians were Indo-European nomads who migrated from Central Asia into Eastern Persia in the third century B.C.E. after the Achaemenid Persian Empire fell to the forces of Alexander the Great in 330 B.C.E. In the middle of the second century B.C.E. the Parthians conquered large parts of Persia, Afghanistan and Mesopotamia. The Parthians adopted many Hellenistic traditions and made Greek the official language of the state. Gradually, however, Persian influences grew stronger and the Parthians adopted a form of Zoroastrianism and tried to replicate Achaemenid systems of bureaucracy like satrapies. Frequent wars with the expanding Roman Empire to the east sapped the strength of Parthia which fell to a new Persian power, the Sassanians in 224 C.E. Parthia is important in world history as a force that spread Greek culture east and because it provided a safe highway along which goods and cultures from across Eurasia could flow.

Sassanian Empire

In 227 C.E. a Persian noble, **Ardashir**, killed the Parthian king, seized the capital of Ctesiphon, and proclaimed the Sassanian Empire. The Sassanian rulers forged a large empire. To the east they fought the Afghanistan-based Kushans and to the west they expanded into the Caucasus region and Mesopotamia, creating long-standing conflict with Rome and later the Byzantine Empire. **Shapur II** (309–379 C.E.), Sassanian Persia's greatest monarch, made gains against the Romans. He extended Persian influence as far east as China. Sassanian Persia remained until the Arabs slew the last king in 651 C.E.

The empire that the Sassanians built was an important contact zone for international trade. Like the Parthians before them, Sassanian trade links stretched east as far as India, Central Asia, and China, and south as far as the Horn of Africa. Byzantine and Sassanian coins were used as currency in Silk Road cities. Persians produced some of the finest pottery, brocades, carpets, glassware, gems, incense, and perfume of the age. Along with trade went Manicheanism and Western religions as well as Sassanian culture.

The Sassanians considered themselves the successors to the Achaemenids 500 years before. At their height the Sassanian court, based in modern Iraq, provided a focus for a brilliant cultural mixing of Persian and Hellenistic influence. However, Sassanian kings wore traditional Persian dress, built great palaces in the classical Achaemenid style, and successfully allied the throne with Zoroastrianism. The priesthood, trained in judicial and administrative functions, and drawn from the ranks of the nobility, allied with the Sassanian monarch. As a state religion, the government imposed orthodoxy supporting the priesthood and sometimes persecuting other religions. By the fifth century, corruption and rigidity caused Zoroastrian followers to lose influence and allowed other faiths to emerge. Mithraism spread from the Roman Empire and Judaism and Christianity crept into the empire. One of the most important of the new religions was **Manicheanism**. Founded by the Persian, **Mani** (216–277 C.E.), the religion was a blend of Zoroastrianism, Buddhism and Christianity. It emphasized a continuing struggle between the forces of light and dark. The dualism influenced Islam and other Christian sects. The rise of new faiths led the Sassanian leadership to become more tolerant of diversity and it turned the capital city of Jundishapur into a cosmopolitan intellectual center. Sassanians collected scientific and literary books, translated Greek writings, and established noted hospitals and schools. The empire, its belief systems, and cosmopolitan culture were later swept away by the rise of the Islamic faith and its culture.

The Rise of Feudal States

(ca. 500 C.E.–1600 C.E.)

TIMELINE	
500 C.E.–1300 C.E.	Medieval Europe
768 C.E.–814 C.E.	Age of Charlemagne
936 C.E.	Unification of Germany
987 C.E.	Unification of France
1066 C.E.	Unification of England
1192 C.E.–1333 C.E.	Kamakura Shogunate
1240 C.E.–1462 C.E.	Appanage Russia
1338 C.E.–1573 C.E.	Ashikaga Shogunate
1600 C.E.–1867 C.E.	Tokugawa Shogunate

INTERPRETING FEUDAL INTERRUPTIONS

Change and continuity are the warp and weave of history. Historians, when examining the past, are always trying to detect what occurred, what changed, and what stayed the same. Greek, Chinese, Western, and Marxist historians have developed different ways of interpreting the past and, in particular, what legitimizes their view and interpretations of the past. The attempt to examine the past scientifically began with Thucydides (455–400 B.C.E.), the Athenian historian, who strove to write impartial history that separated fact from legend. Other civilizations have also tried to establish a framework for legitimate history. **Sima Qian** (Ssu-ma Ch'ien ca. 145–93 B.C.E.) established the tradition of Chinese history by writing the official history of the early dynasties. In his *Historical Records* he sought objectivity by extensively quoting original documents and by separating the narrative from his own editorial comments. He related change to the dynastic cycle and morality in the following observation that

. . . government of the Hsia dynasty was marked by good faith, which in time deteriorated until mean men had turned it into rusticity. Wherefore the men of Shang who succeeded to the Hsia reformed this defect through the virtue of piety. But piety degenerated . . . Therefore what was needed to reform this hollow show was a return to good faith, for the way of the Three Dynasties of old is like a cycle which, when it ends, must begin over again.

Islamic historian **Ibn Khaldun** (1332–1406) urged those who studied history to analyze the similarities and differences between the present and past, and to learn "the origins of dynasties and communities, the reasons for their coming into existence, the circumstances of the persons involved in them and their history." Some historians have gone to great lengths to try to create a **paradigm**, or model, that not only explains the past but is capable of predicting the future. This has been especially popular in modern history when the physical sciences discovered rules of the universe might be applied to the story of the human past as well. Historians, like **Edward Gibbon** (1737–1794), who wrote about the *Decline and Fall of the Roman Empire*, **Arnold Toynbee** (1889–1975), who described the vast diversity of civilizations that he believed rose and fell as a recurring pattern in his 26-volume *A Study of History*, and **Oswald Spengler** (1880–1936), who produced a cyclical theory of history in which he predicted the eclipse of Western civilization, have tried to rationalize the study of history. Marxist historians have also tried to make history scientific and thus predict the future on the basis of class struggle over materialism.

In examining the past, historians are fascinated by the reasons for collapse of civilizations. Throughout history, civilizations have risen and fallen, and besides describing these events, historians ask why they occurred.

In the view of some historians, all great classical civilizations collapsed. In the view of other historians, they merely evolved or changed. Views of the reasons for change or collapse vary, from outside attack to internal disorder, interaction with other peoples, ecological disasters, theological change, mass migrations, or the spread of infectious diseases. What happens in the interim between collapse and a new civilization is rarely the subject of historical investigation. Sometimes the interims are simply periods between dynasties, as in China or Egypt, so that with new leadership the collapsed civilization merely reappears with a few minor changes. Sometimes the interims are between the ancient period and the growth of classical civilization, as in the case of Zhou China. Sometimes the collapse is so total that the civilization never appears again, instead becoming a part of another's history, as is the case of Rome, which became subsumed into the history of the European world.

Feudalism

Somewhere in the middle are the feudal states, which carry remnants of the old but create new states that have considerable impact on succeeding history. Such are the cases with feudal Europe, Japan, and Russia. Feudalism as a system usually has the following characteristics:

- a decentralized political system oriented to defense;

- an agrarian economy;

- a hierarchical social system;

- a culture permeated by the military and a religious preoccupation with death.

MEDIEVAL WESTERN EUROPE

The word **medieval**, or between eras, portrays the interim nature of this period in western European history—after the collapse of classical Greece and Rome and before the modern period. Its culture was a combination of Judeo-Christian values, classical ideals and concepts, and Germanic traditions. The period has also been known in history as the **Dark Ages** because it was an age darkened by war and illiteracy, or the **Age of Faith** because Christianity was the most powerful unifying force of the time. It began with the nomadic invasions of the fifth century, invasions that struck again in the ninth century. Much of Europe and Asia was threatened by nomads, but the impact was perhaps greatest in the West because the nomads tended to migrate westward where land was more fertile and water plentiful, and because China and India were more capable of resistance both militarily and culturally.

Feudal System

The feudal system in part grew out of traditions of the Germanic tribes that attacked the Roman Empire. German tribes elected their chiefs, who led their warriors into battle. In return for military service, the warriors received weapons, subsistence, and a share of the spoils. As the feudal system evolved, the same kind of exchange, military service for land, became regularized and institutionalized. In concept, **lords** (chiefs) or nobles ruled districts with miniature governments of their own, dispensing justice, collecting fees, raising troops, and sometimes minting money. The **castle** was the seat of this political and military jurisdiction. Those needing land or seeking protection, the **vassals**, pledged personal loyalty, military service, and other duties to the lord in exchange for grants of land, or **fiefs** (**feudums**). The land grant was the means by which the vassal could outfit himself for battle.

On a fief could be one or many **manors**. A manor consisted of one or several peasant villages. Peasants farmed the land and made the implements of farming and war. Peasants entered into personal relationships with vassals, not unlike those between lords and vassals. In return for protection and use of mills, common pasture, and woodlands, the peasant gave the lord the product of his labor, usually one-third of the agricultural output. While the peasants who were **serfs** or **villeins** inherited their position and were bound to the land in exchange for protection, peasants who were free paid rent and could move, but they lacked any assurance of protection from the vassal. Serfs differed from slaves, who could be separated from the land they worked to be bought and sold.

Life for peasants revolved around their land, villages, and church. Strangely, many peasants were healthier than the nobility because their diet consisted of grains rather than meat. Much of the success of feudalism in Europe can be attributed to the peasant who cleared European land using the **open field system** (leaving half fallow) as a means of refertilization, and adoption of the breast-strap harness (which was developed in North Africa for camels between the second and fourth centuries C.E.) and collar harness (which had its origins in China ca. the third century C.E.), allowing use of the horse rather than oxen (horses were stronger and ate less) to till the fields.

Traditionally, historians emphasize the contractual nature of agreements between lords and vassals and vassals and peasants because they were often written down as well as endowed with the honor of one's word. Contractualism led to the carefully worked out systems of rights and responsibilities. Towns also entered into agreements with lords. The towns that existed were small, self-contained, and highly organized. Townsmen often received **charters**, or documents of self-government, from the lords. The townsmen regulated their affairs within the framework of **guilds**. These organizations regulated price, quality, and quantity of goods produced. Guilds also spawned the **university system** where students were taught by masters, hence "master of arts." Trade was generally dangerous due to wars between lords, pillaging nomads, and outside invaders. Therefore, roads, cities, luxury goods, and wealth were rare.

The Roman Catholic Christian Church

Surrounding this whole system was the Roman Catholic Christian Church headed by the pope in Rome. With the collapse of the Roman emperors, the popes, unlike the patriarchs in Constantinople, not only achieved independence from the state but claimed superiority over lords and monarchs. The Church remained a link with Roman tradition. The language of the Church was Latin. The papal bull **"Unam sanctam"** issued by Pope Boniface VIII in 1302 is the classic statement of the medieval Church's claim to spiritual and temporal supremacy. "Submission on the part of every man to a bishop or Rome is altogether necessary for his salvation." When **heresy**, or unorthodox views, appeared as they did in the thirteenth century by the Albigensians, the pope created the **Inquisition**, or interrogation, to convert, convict, and prevent the spread of these ideas. While the Church claimed superiority, in reality many kings and lords claimed the right to appoint local prelates (called **lay investiture**). This situation led to many conflicts and has never been completely settled even to this day, as the tradition of separation of church and state indicates.

> **Did You Know?**
>
> The Church provided the only extensive European organization in an otherwise unorganized time.

One vanguard of Roman Christian authority, power, and conversion was the monastic movements. Groups like the Cluniacs, Carthusians, Benedictines, Dominicans, and Franciscans cleared land, produced prayer books, ministered to the poor and sick, preserved learning, preached, and spread the faith. Another vanguard was the **Crusades**, or military campaigns of conversion. The most famous were the expeditions to free the Holy Land from the hands of the Muslim Turks. In 1095 **Pope Urban II** called the first of what turned out to be many Crusades. During the Fourth Crusade the Christian warriors even attacked fellow Christians in Byzantium. From time to time, crusader states were established, but by 1270 the area was once again in the hands of the Muslims. Crusades were also directed against Islamic infidels (**Moors**) in Spain and against pagans in northern Europe by the **Teutonic Knights** and **Knights Templars**.

Christian Culture

In an age of warfare and uncertainty, the Roman Catholic Christian Church provided a civilization and cultural basis for society. The Church was regulated by **canon**, or church, law, carrying forward the Roman legal traditions. Village life and holidays centered around the Church. The Church **sacraments**, or ceremonies, necessary to salvation, included baptism, confirmation, penance, the Holy Eucharist, extreme unction, matrimony, and the holy orders, which were observed under threat of **excommunication** (expulsion from the Church and thus condemnation to an afterlife in Hell). Nobility and warfare were regulated by the Church. "The Peace of God" declared that feudal warfare could not take place on Church property and the "Truce of God" forbade fighting from Wednesday evening until Monday morning, on holidays, and during the religious seasons.

The knightly code of behavior, called **chivalry**, was influenced by religion. The knight was expected to be courteous, treat prisoners well, be honorable and generous, and treat women as if they were the embodiment of the Virgin Mary. Much of the literature produced in this era, such as the King Arthur stories, revolved around religion, in this case the search for the Holy Grail, the cup from which Christ drank at the Last Supper.

The greatest architectural achievements of the age were churches. The **Romanesque** style was an adaptation of the Roman basilica and barrel arch form. It was characterized by heavy, thick walls and small windows. To add height and light, the **Gothic** style was developed in the late twelfth century in northern Europe. Gothic cathedrals had **flying buttresses** to brace high walls and exquisite stained glass windows. The most sublime example of this type is the cathedral at Chartres, France. Religion also dominated thought and learning. Monks studied and copied church manuscripts. The major philosophy of the period was **Scholasticism**, which was an attempt to wed religious beliefs to rational thought. The most famous of the scholastics, **Thomas Aquinas**, attempted to unify all knowledge and describe the nature and destiny of Christian man in his book *Summa Theologica*.

Charlemagne

Gradually in Europe certain lords became masters over large tracts of land and many vassals. This led to the formation of **monarchies** (a state headed by a hereditary king). Three monarchies began to take shape as early as the sixth century C.E.—the Frankish monarchy in France, the Anglo-Saxon monarchy in England, and the Holy Roman monarchy in Germany. The most famous of the early Frankish kings was **Charlemagne**. Charlemagne, who ruled from 768–814, conquered a large area in France, western Germany, and northern Italy, took steps to rule the territory efficiently, convert the heathen, and reunite the western territories of the Roman Empire. His efforts to reunite the Western Roman Empire failed, however, and in 843, by the **Treaty of Verdun**, the empire was divided among his three grandsons.

Western Europe Under Attack

Then, in the middle of the ninth century, a second wave of nomads, Magyars and Bulgars, swept across western Europe, plunging it back into feudalism. In the north another group of warriors, the **Vikings**, composed primarily of Swedes, Danes, and Norwegians, raided coastal villages and traveled by river far inland to loot and destroy poorly defended monasteries and isolated churches. Possible reasons for this sudden Viking expansion have been attributed to overpopulation, changes in climate, improved shipbuilding, or the desire for trade and booty. Viking ships, made of oak, weighed over 20 tons. They were designed with sails and oars for speed and maneuverability and could carry an attack force of 40 to 60 men and horses. One

---

Did You Know?

On Christmas Day, 800, Charlemagne was crowned by the pope as the Holy Roman Emperor, or Christain successor to the Roman emperors.

group of Vikings overran and later colonized northwestern France, which was known as **Norsemanland** (**Normandy**). Besides their trade in Russia, the **Varangians** (**Swedes**) crossed the Black Sea to Constantinople and farther east they made their way into the Caspian where they encountered the Persians. Another group of Vikings, the **Danes**, raided the coasts of Germany, France, and Spain, and were responsible for invasions of England. The **Norwegians** reached North America ca. 1000 and established lasting colonies—Greenland and Iceland. Later, in the eleventh and twelfth centuries, **Norman** invaders moved south into the Mediterranean to establish kingdoms in Italy and Sicily.

Unification of France

By the twelfth century, nomadic raids ended. In several parts of Europe strong fuedal lords began consolidating land and rule. Then they assumed the role of king and established their family's dynastic rule. Early in the twelfth century a line of **Capetian** monarchs (987–1328), centered around Paris, began to unite and extend their power. To strengthen their hands against the pope, Philip IV, "The Fair" (1285–1314) called a meeting of the **Estates General**, an assembly of the clergy, nobility, and common-ers, because he needed money above and beyond the feudal dues. Philip got his money and France held the first **parlement** in its history. Philip also began to hand-pick offi-cials whom he paid directly, to maintain a regular army, and to make the language of Paris the common tongue. Literature in the vernacular of the common people like *The Song of Roland* helped create a common literary heritage.

Unification of England

A strong king emerged in England in 1066 when, at the **Battle of Hastings**, Norman duke **William I** of France crossed the English Channel at the head of 5000 warriors and defeated the Saxon army under Harold. By means of an oath of loy-alty, the **"Salisbury Oath,"** a record of taxable property, the *Domesday Book*, and a Great Council, William began to centralize the English state. In 1166, by the "assize of Clarendon," **Henry II** brought the court system under royal control. Thereafter, English law became a **common law** for all Englishmen. Trial by a jury of 12 peers gradually replaced trial by sworn inquest or trial by ordeal. Then, in an attempt to bring the church under his control, he had his friend **Thomas à Becket** elected archbishop, but, once in office, à Becket refused to be a royal puppet. He was murdered sometime after in the Canterbury Cathedral, allegedly by Henry's knights. This episode has been somewhat immortalized in **Geoffrey Chaucer**'s *Canterbury Tales*, a literary masterpiece written in the vernacular in which pilgrims were going to worship at the shrine of Thomas à Becket at Canterbury. During this period, English nobles often held large tracts of land in France. Their absorption with properties in France and their long stays there led to one of the peculiarly English customs of law and government. In their absence from England, Englishmen began to limit the power of the monarchy and to establish a Parliament. This came under **King John**, who had irritated his vassals by losing English possessions in France, surrendering England as a fief to the pope, and mak-ing the vassals pay undue taxes. In 1215 these lords met King John on the meadow at Runnymede and made him sign a constitutional document called the **Magna Carta**. In it, John promised to respect the specific rights and privileges of the nobles, accept the principle of the rule of law, and promise that no tax shall be imposed except by the common council of the kingdom. Under successive kings Henry III and Edward I, the idea of **Parliament** as a permanent institution with powers of taxation came into being. Parliament was divided into two assemblies, the **House of Lords** and the **House of Commons**, which represented different constituencies.

Germany

Otto I (king 936–973) brought all of Germany under his control by allying with the Church in Rome. Later rulers like Henry III, however, weakened the monarchy when they tried to overstep their bounds and appoint the pope. This brought the question of lay investiture to a head, and in a compromise called the **Concordat of Worms** in 1122, Henry V surrendered his claim to invest bishops and the pope gave up his right to govern religious estates. In 1125, when the dynasty died out, Germany disintegrated into warring factions. In 1152, however, a new Holy Roman Emperor was chosen. Frederick Barbarossa, or **Frederick the Great** (emperor 1152–1190), reunited Germany and Italy, but by 1250 his line had died out and in 1278 another emperor, Rudolph of Habsburg, was elected. In 1356 the German princes in effect cemented the power of the lords over monarchs in the **Golden Bull**, which allowed seven "electors" authority over their own territories to choose the emperor. In this way, feudalism continued in Germany while in the rest of western Europe monarchs recentralized the state. Because of this, Germany and Italy were the last states in Europe to unite and did not do so until the nineteenth century. Portugal united under King John I (king 1385–1433) and Spain united under King Ferdinand and Queen Isabella in 1453.

Feudalism in Europe

The feudal period left a lasting imprint on the history of western Europe.

- Politically, it cemented the present-day divided Europe.

- It gave rise to long-lasting political traditions like parliaments, charters of rights, and constitutions.

- Culturally, it gave western Europe some of the greatest architectural monuments, cathedrals, castles, and walled towns.

- It endowed Europe with a concept of **chivalry**, or honor, attitudes toward women, and a Christian order of life.

The system itself helped western Europe survive repeated nomadic attacks, clear the land, and give rise to a new concept of nation-state, commerce, and social flexibility.

FEUDAL JAPAN

Origins

Internal conflicts rather than external invasion were important to the nature of feudalism in Japan. During the Heian period, emperors tried to centralize their authority while aristocrats sought to free themselves from it. The aristocrats won, leading to the rise of strong family groups like the Fujiwaras. It was the emperors' land laws that unwittingly contributed to the emperors' demise. The imperial government had tried to appropriate land and redistribute it among peasants to weaken powerful families. The opposite resulted because the government was too weak to enforce its policies. Provincial warriors, high government officials, and Buddhist monasteries became great landholders. In 1156 civil war erupted. It was during this period that the institutions of feudalism took shape.

In both Europe and Shogunate Japan, the military aristocracy held local power, a system of vassalage developed, and land was the source of wealth. To keep order on the **shoen**, or private domain, outside imperial control, feudal lords organized private armies of professional soldiers, the samurai. The shoen had its origins in the ninth century when local lords began escaping imperial taxes and control by giving their land to Buddhist monasteries that were exempt from taxes. The local lord then received his land back as a tenant who paid nominal fees, free of imperial taxes, and owned specific fields, or as dependent farmers, or both. In many cases the peasants were reduced to serfdom and treated as property of the lord. Artisans were also accorded little status and poorly paid. Peasants and artisans were separated by rigid class barriers from the warrior elite. They wore different styles of clothing, could not carry swords, or ride horseback. As in Europe, they turned to religion for salvation. Disorder within the society led to widespread belief that history had entered its final stage, **mappo**, or decline, in Buddha's law. A popular form of Buddhism called the **JoDo**, or **Pure Land**, sect offered the promise of bliss in heaven or the pure land for those who lived upright lives on earth. Central to this faith was belief in **Amida**, the Buddha of Infinite Light, who was thought to preside over the Western Paradise and was reminiscent of the Shinto sun-goddess.

Samurai Culture

The **samurai** originally only received **shiki rights**, or a certain portion of an estate's produce, but later they began receiving a grant of land for their service in a formal ceremony that included a religious element much like the knighting ceremony in Europe. The samurai had their own code of honor called **Bushido**, or **Way of the Warrior**, the bedrock of which was complete loyalty to the lord. The demands upon the warrior were harsh. A defeated warrior expected to be decapitated rather than held for ransom as was the European practice. To avoid dishonor, to demonstrate loyalty, or to display a protest, warriors committed **seppuku**, or ritual suicide by self-disembowelment. The code of conduct of the samurai emphasized self-discipline in order to face death, swordsmanship, respect for the faith, generosity to others, and sympathy for the weak and helpless. Physical hardship was routine; soft living, despised. The life of a samurai was symbolized in art by the cherry blossom that falls from the tree at the height of its beauty. Unlike the European warrior, Japanese samurai were expected to be graced in the arts. **Zen Buddhism** was the popular religion among the samurai because it emphasized meditation, giving the warrior the courage to face death. The tea ceremony and rock gardens ritualized methods of encouraging meditation. **Noh Theatre**, performed by two masked actors who were accompanied by music and chorus to create an aura of ritualized, poetic mystery, became the classical theater of Japan. Samurai went into battle in armor, often on horseback, wearing elaborate helmets that themselves became an art form. Castles were built as in Europe, the most famous being the **White Heron Castle**. In Europe, contractual and personal relationships were emphasized. In Japan, group values predominated.

The Kamakura Shogunate

During the feudal period, one family after another rose to power and at times united Japan. Unlike Europe, this did not lead to the end of feudalism largely because the Japanese **shoguns** were generals-in-chief rather than hereditary administrators or kings. Emperors retained their title but possessed little power beyond the court. The military class was more pervasive in Japan. While in Europe only two to three percent of the population belonged to the noble class, in Japan it was as high as ten percent. In 1192 civil wars and feuds abated when the **Minamoto** family and their leader **Yoritomo** (1147–1199) became shogun and began the **Kamakura Shogunate** (1192–1333). The Kyoto nobility and Buddhist institutions managed to retain a measure of their wealth and influence as Yoritomo built his **bakufu** (which, literally translated, means tent government). In an attempt to centralize rule, Yoritomo granted land rights but not the land to his vassals. He appointed military land stewards who collected taxes and military governors who maintained law and order. Before the end of the twelfth century, however, these officials had become hereditary officials and local officials in their own right. During the course of his rule, Yoritomo killed everyone within his own family who might challenge his rule. When he died in 1199 his wife's father became the de facto shogun. Rule passed to her family, who were known as the **Hojo** regents.

The Ashikaga Shogunate

In 1338 another military leader, **Ashikaga Takauji**, established the **Ashikaga Shogunate**, which lasted until 1573. This was a victory for the samurai, who took over civil authority throughout Japan but left Japan far from united. Rival heirs to the Ashikaga Shogunate battled with one another. More than 300 small states emerged, ruled by warlords, or daimyos. During this era, daimyos became virtual owners and rulers in their domain. For this reason, they began to try to build up the wealth of their areas by encouraging peasants to produce items such as silk, hemp, paper, dyes, and other marketable items. This growing commercial class began to resemble the medieval guild system in Europe.

The Tokugawa Shogunate

The pattern of recurring civil war was so entrenched in Japanese society that it took a succession of three remarkable military leaders and the use of gunpowder to restore order and unity. The Portuguese introduced gunpowder to Japan in 1543. Japanese children are taught that "Ieyasu ate the pie that Nobunaga made and Hideyoshi baked." **Oda Nobunaga**, the first of these leaders, defeated a powerful daimyo in 1560 and seized Kyoto eight years later. He then went on to subdue the rest of Japan and unite it by standardizing currency, eliminating customs barriers, and encouraging trade and industry. Where Nobunaga had subdued by force, **Toyotomi Hideyoshi** centralized institutions. He soothed the vanquished daimyos with lands and military positions but made them swear loyalty to him. His agents collected detailed information about taxable property much like the English *Domesday Book*. Finally, **Tokugawa Ieyasu**, who owned vast estates around Tokyo, followed by obtaining from the emperor the title of shogun and establishing the **Tokugawa Shogunate** (1600–1867). The Tokugawa isolated the emperor and nobility from the military class. The main aim of the Tokugawa was to establish control over (not abolish) the feudal lords. They did this by requiring all daimyo to reside in Edo in alternate years.

Gunpowder

In 1575, at the battle of **Nagashino**, 3000 foot soldiers equipped with muskets were stationed behind high wooden palisades under the command of Oda Nobunaga. As waves of mounted warriors attacked, Nobunaga's men fired continual volleys as they rotated their postions, firing and reloading. The resulting heavy losses demonstrated the significance of the new weapon and the strategy of continual fire. In 1584 Hideyoshi's victorious army included both a gun-carrying infantry and samurai with swords.

Once the Tokugawa Shogunate was firmly established, however, gunmaking was reserved as a government monopoly and the peasants were disarmed. Japanese Christians who rebelled against the shogun in 1637 (the Shimabara Rebellion) were the last in Japan to use guns until the arrival of the American warships in 1853. The gunpowder that had helped the Tokugawa come to power now became the privy possession of the Tokugawa, who built up a modern military under their control. Isolation was accompanied by anti-Christian decrees derived from the fear that Spain and Portugal were using Christianity to facilitate colonization of the country. Gunpowder also called into question the importance of individual bravery and the skillful swordsmanship of the samurai.

> **Did You Know?**
>
> The Tokugawa brought peace and prosperity to Japan and, more importantly, isolationism that protected Japan from European imperialism.

Prosperity and a subdued nobility with little to do led to a proliferation of spending by this increasingly superfluous class of samurai. The samurai spent heavily on **geishas**, or girls accomplished in the arts, and **Kabuki Theater**, which consisted of bawdy skits dealing with adventure, love, and romance. Katsushika Hokusai (1760–1849) was one of many artists who created Japanese woodblock prints or **Ukiyo-E**. These colorful scenes of daily lives of ordinary people were popular among merchants. Conspicuous consumption of the upper classes led to taxation and deterioration of peasant life. Peasant rebellions became a chronic problem. On the positive side, peace led to trade and commerce, the growth of urban life, and an expanding merchant class, as occurred in Europe during the Renaissance. Japan became centralized but feudal culture continued.

The Feudal Period in Japanese History

The feudal period in Japanese history left lasting imprints as it did in Europe.

- Politically, Japan was united under the leadership of a **shogun** or military dictator.

- The emperor was a figurehead.

- The samurai remained a powerful class as did daimyos.

- The samurai tradition left lasting cultural traditions like the tea ceremony, gardens, Zen and JoDo Buddhism, and attitudes toward honor, death, civil authority, and outsiders.

- Japan's gunpowder castles remain architectural monuments of the feudal period.

Origins of Russian Feudalism

Other societies also experienced the effects of collapse and exhibited one or more features of feudal orders. One was in Russia. The Kievan Russian state that had grown up on the fringes of the Byzantine Empire created a Russian consciousness and concept of Russian land. Its legacy was a uniform religion, a common language and literature, and a historical memory. But the twin terrors of Kievan Russia, internal division and invasion from abroad, caused the collapse of the Russian state and its division into **appanages**, or separate holdings by individual princes. The appanage period lasted from 1240 when the Mongols invaded to 1462 when Czar Ivan the Great declared Russia independent of Mongol rule.

The Mongols, or **Tartars** as they are cited in Russian sources, refer to mostly Turkic peoples who suddenly appeared in 1223 and again in 1237–1240. The inability of the Russian princes to unite in their own defense allowed the Mongols to attack with impunity. The princes on the frontiers tended to give in to the Mongols rather than fight, allowing the other city-states to be easily overcome. After conquest the Mongols settled down to rule indirectly through Russian princes. These princes became virtual autocrats in their domains responsible for delivering to the Mongols only taxes and recruits.

Appanages

There were three variations on the appanage theme: To the northwest were small city-states like **Novgorod** and **Pskov**; to the southwest were appanages like **Volynia** and **Galicia**; and to the northeast princely domains like Moscow and Iaroslavl. Pskov and Novgorod essentially escaped Mongol pillage. They became independent trading states. The towns were walled, formulated their municipal affairs in a way not unlike the European medieval town councils, and produced and sold under strong groups not unlike guilds. In the outlying areas, peasants farmed, bringing their produce to market in the towns. The greatest moment in Novgorodian history was the repulsion of the Swedes and Teutonic knights under **Prince Alexander Nevsky** in 1240 and 1242, respectively. These victories delimited the movement of Germans into Russia, which had already occurred in **Estonia**, **Lithuania**, and **Latvia**. It preserved Orthodoxy and halted a likely conversion to Catholicism.

By 1250 Galicia and Volynia, west of Kiev and at the foothills of the Carpathian Mountains, grew independent as the strength of Kiev waned. In this area, **boyars**, or aristocratic families, ruled. In 1197 Prince Roman united the two appanages and successfully defended them from incursions by the Poles, Hungarians, Lithuanians, and Polovtsy. Roman's son Daniel ruled the area that became an emporium of East-West trade. He even accepted the king's crown from the pope, thus delivering this area of Kievan Russia to the Catholic West. In 1253 the Mongols lay waste to the area, and by 1387 Galicia had been absorbed into the Polish state and Volynia into Lithuania. In the northeast appanages like **Rostov**, **Suzdal**, and **Moscow** began to gather strength against the Mongols. These states had suffered staggering blows by the Mongols, but their distance from the Mongol heartland allowed them to move toward independence more rapidly than in the Kievan heartland.

Whereas the evolution of Novgorod emphasized the role of the veche, and in Galicia and Volynia that of the boyars, in the northeast the prince predominated. One reason for this is that in the northeast there were many frontier lands into which the princes could expand. In so doing, they could pay off their warriors with land. Control of agriculture and the peasants became part of the Russian feudal system. By the rule of primogeniture, long lives, advantageous marriages, and the power of warfare, the Moscow princes were eventually able to free Russia from the Mongol yoke, claim independence from the Orthodox Church in Constantinople (because it had fallen to the Ottoman Turks in 1453), and reunite Russia much as the kings in Europe had been able to do.

Appanage Russia resembles other feudal periods under examination.

- A united state was shattered and decentralized.

- Small trade towns were apparent in some places; agrarian states, in others.

- Warriors and nobles predominated as the upper class.

- Religion played a role in preserving and identifying a cultural being.

In the end, the state was partially reunited with remnants of the warrior culture to influence the history to come.

Unit Review

Cross-Regional Developments

Classical civilizations underwent important changes from ca. 100 C.E. to ca. 1600 C.E. Significant among these changes were the decentralization of the state, collapse of empires, and interruption and mutation of classical values. For want of a better term, historians have often used the word "feudal" to indicate these patterns of society. Important cross-regional developments of this include

- the collapse of classical civilizations including Han China, Gupta India, Imperial Rome, and Teotihuacan and the Maya in Mesoamerica;

- the transformation of Roman and Chinese classical civilizations into the new states of Byzantium and Sui/Tang/Song (Sung) China;

- the Chinese migrations into South China;

- the spread of these new civilizations to other parts of the globe like Southeast Asia and Russia;

- the development of stylized decentralized states in western Europe and Japan;

- the rise of Islam and Muslim states and cultures;

- the rise of African kingdoms as a result of Muslim trade networks;

- the Austronesian migrations of peoples across the Indian and the Pacific Oceans.

Legacies

The legacies of this period are of great import to world history:

- the populating of the Pacific islands extended humankind over an area three times that of Eurasia;

- Chinese culture spread to Korea, Japan, and Southeast Asia and set the stage for its advance across Asia to Europe;

- the spread of classical Indian culture led to the rise of a brilliant society in Cambodia at Angkor Wat;

- Islam completely transformed the culture of Southwest Asia and spread to India, Southeast Asia, and Africa south of the Sahara;

- the Byzantine Empire created a bulwark against Islamic advance into Europe and formed the basis of the first Russian civilization at Kiev;

- Islam and Byzantium preserved the knowledge of the Western world;

- a decentralized feudal Europe united under the banner of Christendom, creating a new kind of culture bearing the seeds of and empowering a new western Europe;

- technological advances like the outrigger canoe, dhow, compass, cartography, gunpowder, horse collar, paper currency, and printing, to name a few, soon spread for all the world to use and possess;

- efficient transportation systems like the camel caravanserais and large ships led to long-distance trade networks other than those across central Asia;

- Golden Ages in China and Southwest Asia led to an outpouring of literature and art still enjoyed throughout the world.

Overall, expansion and interaction in world history has been a stimulating and creative force.

Quiz

Unscramble:

Arrange the following in chronological order.

Tokugawa Shogunate; Byzantine Empire; Polynesian Migrations; Tang Dynasty; Kingdom of Mali

Matching

1.	Sinification	A.	Everyday language of common people
2.	Vernacular	B.	Spirits of nature
3.	Kami	C.	Becoming part of Chinese culture
4.	Sufism	D.	Separation
5.	Charters	E.	Salvation through prayers, fasting, and meditation
6.	Sharia	F.	Documents permitting self-government
7.	Liturgy	G.	Samurai code of honor
8.	Bushido	H.	Islamic law that defines behavior
9.	Schism	I.	Ceremony and rituals
		J.	None of the above

Questions:

1. Which of the following choices is arranged in the correct chronological order?

    (A) Tang, Sui, Han
    (B) Sui, Han, Song (Sung), Tang
    (C) Shang, Han, Tang
    (D) Han, Tang, Sui
    (E) Han, Tang, Shang

2. On which of the following islands was the society destroyed through ecological degradation and war?

    (A) Easter
    (B) New Guinea
    (C) Fiji
    (D) Madagascar
    (E) Hawaii

3. Built to replicate the Tang imperial center, the site of Japan's first capital was

    (A) Changan
    (B) Nara
    (C) Kyoto
    (D) Angkor Wat
    (E) Loyang

4. Which of the following statements is FALSE?

    (A) Prince Shotoku stressed the proper goals of government and ethical conduct in the Seventeen Article Constitution.
    (B) Li Bo (Li Po) was the Chinese Buddhist monk who discovered gunpowder.
    (C) Empress Wu gave vast sums of money to support Buddhist monasteries.
    (D) Lady Murasaki wrote the world's first psychological novel, *The Tale of Genji*.
    (E) Emperor Taizong (T'ai-Tsung) defeated the eastern and western Turks to gain control of the Silk Road trade.

5. Who is recognized by Muslims as the last prophet?

   (A) Abraham
   (B) Ishmael
   (C) Abu Bakr
   (D) Muhammad
   (E) Moses

6. All of the following are pillars of the Islamic faith EXCEPT

   (A) belief in the creed that "There is no God but Allah, Muhammad is His prophet."
   (B) prayer five times a day.
   (C) almsgiving.
   (D) fasting during the holy month of Ramadan.
   (E) pilgrimage to Jerusalem.

7. Which Muslim nation is Shi'ite?

   (A) Syria.
   (B) Libya.
   (C) Egypt.
   (D) Iran.
   (E) Morocco.

8. Shi'ites recognize their leader, who fulfills both political and religious functions, as

   (A) Caliph.
   (B) Imam.
   (C) Emir.
   (D) Sheik.
   (E) Muezzin.

9. Within Jerusalem, there are holy sites sacred to

   I. Jews.
   II. Buddhists.
   III. Zoroastrians.
   IV. Christians.
   V. Muslims.

   (A) I, II, and III
   (B) II, III, and IV
   (C) III, IV, and V
   (D) I, III, and V
   (E) I, IV, and V

10. Like Christians, Muslims profess all of the following beliefs EXCEPT

    (A) monotheism.
    (B) resurrection.
    (C) the Last Judgment.
    (D) the teachings of Moses.
    (E) the Trinity.

11. The nomadic peoples indigenous to North Africa were the

    (A) Seljuk Turks.
    (B) Bedouins.
    (C) Berbers.
    (D) Mande.
    (E) Slavs.

12. Which was not a significant factor in the expansion of long-distance trade from 100 to 1600 C.E.?

    (A) dhows
    (B) domestication of the camel
    (C) monetization of trade and letters of credit
    (D) West African gold
    (E) manor system

13. The leader of Mali who, as a devout Muslim, embarked on an Islamic pilgrimage to Arabia was

    (A) Sundiata.
    (B) Mansa Musa.
    (C) Uli.
    (D) Sonni Ali.
    (E) Askia Mohammed.

14. Cultural characteristics of the Byzantine Empire included all EXCEPT

    (A) Greek.
    (B) Orthodox Christian.
    (C) Roman.
    (D) Muslim.
    (E) Persian.

15. The wealth and independence of the Byzantine Empire resulted from

    (A) a carefully designed defense system for Constantinople that included cisterns, walls, a chain across the harbor, and a small well-trained army.
    (B) the skillful use of intelligence and diplomacy to establish a system of military alliances with Catholic popes and European kings.
    (C) Constantinople developing as a western entrepot of the Silk Road.
    (D) stimulating the production of luxury products by master craftsmen.
    (E) all of the above.

16. Which happened last?

    (A) Empress Wu supported the construction of Buddhist pagodas.
    (B) Indian monks introduced Buddhism after the fall of the Han Dynasty.
    (C) Neo-Confucianism offered a return to Confucian traditions during the Southern Song (Sung) Dynasty.
    (D) Buddhism fell from favor in the Tang Court.
    (E) The Vietnamese established independence after the collapse of the Tang Dynasty.

17. The empires that were linked with one another through trade routes branching from the Silk Road ca. 100 C.E. were

    I. Rome
    II. Carthage
    III. Egypt
    IV. Mauryan India
    V. Han China

    (A) I and V
    (B) II and IV
    (C) I, II, and IV
    (D) I, II, and III
    (E) all of the above

18. The Chinese sought to lessen the threat of nomadic invasions from the north by employing all of the following EXCEPT

    (A) ending trade between the nomads and the court.
    (B) arranging marriages between nomadic leaders and imperial princesses.
    (C) locating military forts at strategic locations along the frontier.
    (D) constructing walls to defend the northern boundaries.
    (E) conquering the nomadic tribes of northern China.

19. Buddhism in China

    (A) stimulated the development of papermaking and printing.
    (B) resulted in the construction of many pagodas.
    (C) was introduced by Indian Buddhist monks during the disorder after the fall of the Han Dynasty.
    (D) fell out of favor during the Tang Dynasty.
    (E) all of the above.

20. Trans-Saharan trade in West Africa was linked to trade along the

    (A) Congo.
    (B) Amazon.
    (C) Nile.
    (D) Niger.
    (E) Zambezi.

21. Buddhists, Muslims, and Christians of different ethnic identities achieved cultural unity through

    (A) pilgrimages.
    (B) simple religious ritual.
    (C) conversions.
    (D) religious instruction.
    (E) all of the above

22. Which of the following is the least likely cause of cultural diffusion?

    (A) social structure.
    (B) migration.
    (C) trade.
    (D) military campaigns.
    (E) religious conversions.

23. Which statement regarding the Polynesians is FALSE?

    (A) Polynesian languages are part of the Austronesian language group.
    (B) Polynesians migrated mostly by outrigger canoe across a 20,000 mile area in the Pacific.
    (C) Polynesians were primarily root rather than rice farmers.
    (D) Polynesians settled an area from Australia to Easter Island.
    (E) Polynesians were led by high priests who could recite genealogical lineages.

24. Khmer Cambodia was primarily influenced by

    (A) Indian Buddhist and Hindu traditions.
    (B) Islamic mariners.
    (C) Chinese and Japanese Buddhism.
    (D) Greek classical architecture.
    (E) Austronesian migrants.

25. The major cultural influence on the rise of the Russian Kievan states came from

    (A) Mongols.
    (B) Christian Crusaders.
    (C) Byzantine Orthodox monks.
    (D) Islamic warriors.
    (E) Vikings from Scandinavia.

Answers

Unscramble:

Polynesian Migrations; Byzantine Empire; Tang Dynasty; Kingdom of Mali; Tokugawa Shogunate

Matching:

1. **(C)**		6. **(H)**	
2. **(A)**		7. **(I)**	
3. **(B)**		8. **(G)**	
4. **(E)**		9. **(D)**	
5. **(F)**			

Questions:

1. **(C)**	10. **(E)**	19. **(E)**
2. **(A)**	11. **(C)**	20. **(D)**
3. **(B)**	12. **(E)**	21. **(E)**
4. **(B)**	13. **(B)**	22. **(A)**
5. **(D)**	14. **(D)**	23. **(D)**
6. **(E)**	15. **(E)**	24. **(A)**
7. **(D)**	16. **(C)**	25. **(E)**
8. **(B)**	17. **(A)**	
9. **(E)**	18. **(A)**	

STUDY TIP

Identify the key events in each era that impact large numbers of people. What are the causes and consequences of these events?

Emergence of a Global Age

(ca. 1100 C.E.–1600 C.E.)

IMPORTANCE OF ENCOUNTER, EXCHANGE, AND DIFFUSION TO THE GLOBAL AGE

World history is more than the story of a progression of separate civilizations that can be compared in various ways. Contacts between different peoples and their responses are also part of the human story. This story is usually thought of in three ways: encounter, when different peoples for some reason come in contact for the first time; exchange, when people interact, learn, trade, or compete with each other; and diffusion, when ideas, cultures, and technology are transferred from one society to others.

From earliest times in the history of humans, people have moved, interacted, and exchanged ideas, technology, culture, disease, biota, and patterns of thought. The extent of this movement and interaction has been less apparent when the focus of study is on the individual civilization or nation-state. Because the focus of world history is on patterns of life over large areas and times, the importance of cultural interaction as an agent of change in history has become more apparent. In examining the exchanges that have taken place between groups of people, world historians have concluded that when one group of people encounters another group, exchange and diffusion of ideas, technology, biota, and the human genome occur. Often, what is foreign is adopted or adapted based on an assessment of its value to a society. World history is also interested in the "agents" of exchange. The agents appear, often as not, to be anonymous groups of people like merchants, missionaries, and mariners rather than identifiable kings, military leaders, or artists.

The increased tempo and volume of exchange across the Eurasian landmass and the seas that surround it during the period ca. 1100 C.E.–1600 C.E. is the prelude to the Columbian voyages and the advent of the Global Age. Merchants and missionaries were key agents in the transfer from China to Europe of technologies that were important to the Columbian voyages, like the compass, cartography, and long-distance ships. The growing exchange between the Italian states and Southwest Asia, and the Crusades, brought to Europe commercial mechanisms of exchange like letters of credit, insurance, and banking. These were already highly developed in the Islamic world.

Then, in 1453, the Byzantine Empire fell to the Ottoman Turks, Queen Isabella and King Ferdinand expelled the Muslim Moors from Spain, and the Inca ruler Pachacuti gained control over a vast empire along the west coast of South America. At the time, they appeared as discrete, unconnected events. Less than 50 years later, the three areas were connected in a web of international relationships. By 1500, for the first time in human history, the Pacific and Atlantic Oceans were corridors of, rather than barriers to, world exchange. The Global Age began.

One aspect of the Global Age was the development of a global trading system and exchange. Goods that once went back and forth across the Afro-Eurasian and the American continents now went around the globe. Silver mined in the Americas went across to Asia, and to Europe. Porcelain, spices, and silk flowed the other way. Letters of credit, insurance, and other institutions of exchange developed to finance and facilitate the long voyages, precious cargo, and growing demand. Another important aspect of the Global Age was the development of a world biota and genome pool. Plants, animals, diseases, and human beings crossed the world's oceans and established themselves in new lands. There, old and new mixed and produced new strains but less global variety.

The Global Age affected different peoples in different ways. Some tried to limit outside influence and others tried to adapt to new ways. The indigenous peoples of the Americas experienced turmoil and disease. Africans benefited from the introduction of nutritious food crops and new products, but they suffered from the developing slave trade. East Asians and Islamic peoples slowly lost dominance and wealth as patterns of global trade shifted in favor of Europe. Europeans largely benefited from contact with advanced civilizations and from flourishing trade they began to dominate. The Global Age slowly became identified with and was transformed by western Europe.

By systematically examining encounters between peoples of differing societies, cross-cultural interaction becomes clear as a process of change in world history. Encounter, exchange, and diffusion during this time period were historical processes that both caused the Global Age and intensified as a result of it.

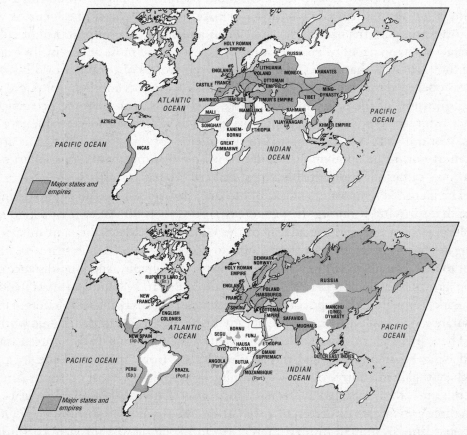

In 1453 world civilizations (settled peoples living in complex urban societies) were confined to middle Eurasia and small parts of the Americas and Africa. By 1700 civilization had pushed deep into Africa, across Russia, and into larger parts of the Americas. The spread of civilization took a great leap forward due to the ability of humans to traverse the oceans.

The Eurasian Highway

(ca. 1100 C.E.–1600 C.E.)

TIMELINE	
1071 C.E.–1270 C.E.	Crusades
1206 C.E.–1270 C.E.	Mongol Empire
1206 C.E.–1526 C.E.	Delhi Sultanate
1271 C.E.–1368 C.E.	Yuan Dynasty
1299 C.E.–1918 C.E.	Ottoman Empire
1348 C.E.–1350 C.E.	Peak of Black Plague
1501 C.E.–1736 C.E.	Safavid Persia
1526 C.E.–1858 C.E.	Mughal Empire

THE RISE OF THE MONGOLS

From 1200 to 1475 the world was on the threshold of a Global Age when all the continents would be linked. The Mongols played a vital part in setting the stage for this. As they swept across Asia, they reopened the highway along which passed to Europe Asian technology that was vital to the Atlantic voyages and that awakened in Europeans a taste for East Asian goods. The Mongols also preoccupied the states of Asia with their presence, leaving Europe free to transform itself in a way that prepared it for these new adventures, a way that became a precursor of the modern age.

Pastoral Nomadism

The Mongols were pastoral nomads whose lifestyles had evolved into well-defined forms. **Pastoral nomadism** probably originated when people with herds were driven from the fertile valleys of civilization. It was widely distributed across Eurasia about 800 B.C.E., displacing hunting-gathering. The pastoral lifestyle was nomadic because herdsmen followed their flocks. Indo-European and Turkic-speaking peoples dominated the Eurasian steppes as horse nomads, but some people followed reindeer herds, and others, as in Arabia, followed camels. In East and South Africa cattle were herded, and in the Andean Americas herders followed llama and alpaca. The land over which the pastoralists roamed was climatically harsh, marginally productive, and vulnerable to droughts and wind. The relationship between nomadic cultures and settled societies was mostly symbiotic, the nomads trading animals for goods produced in settled societies. When civilizations experienced disorder, so too did the nomads. Nomads often became the carriers of long-distance trade. However, with disruption in trade, nomads could become raiders. During times of population increase, nomads either retreated or settled down and became absorbed into civilization.

Competition for pasture land between nomadic societies bred a military culture where courage, physical strength, and the ability to forge a personal following led to leadership in societies that had no clearly established rules for succession. In the Asian steppes, rulers were often called **khans**. By the time of the Mongols, the Eurasian steppe people had adopted the horse stirrup, bow, and bridle. As horse archers, they were formidable cavalrymen and guerrilla fighters able to live off the land and cover vast distances. Social stratification was less complex and more egalitarian than among settled societies. The classes were usually divided between an aristocratic upper class and common people. Women acted as shamans (priests), settled questions of succession, and even became warriors. The tribe and clan were the basic social and political structures. Art was expressed in products that were carried or worn, as for example in bridles, saddles, tent tapestries, and ornate weaponry. The **Shamanist** religion, found in Central Asia, Siberia, Korea, and Japan, predominated among nomads in Central Asia. It is based on the belief that certain people (shamans) could serve as intermediaries between humans and deities. Since nomads were basically illiterate, their image has been shaped by writers in civilized societies who have tended to see them as "barbarian" (uncivilized) and cruel. This should not obscure the fact that in world history pastoral nomads have provided an essential role as herders, mercenaries, empire builders, long-distance traders, and agents of change.

The Mongols were one of many Eurasian steppe nomad groups who had attacked settled populations through the ages. So constant were the nomadic attacks on the northern Chinese frontiers that the Qin (Ch'in) Dynasty had constructed the Great Wall. Elsewhere, the Middle Egyptian kingdom had fallen to the Hyksos, Rome to Germanic tribes, and Gupta India to the Huns. The Mongol attacks became important in world history because of their breadth, the amount of change they elicited, and because they were the last of the great Eurasian steppe movements. From then on, the settled way of life became predominant and pastoralism was limited to small and isolated areas.

Genghiz Khan

Did You Know?

Genghiz Khan became known as the "Prince of all between the Oceans."

Periodically, a nomadic leader of unusual ability would be able to unite a number of tribes. Such was **Temujin** (1162–1227), who later became known as **Genghiz Khan**. Temujin was born around 1167 C.E. in **Mongolia**, north of China. He set out to settle frontier disputes with sedentary societies. Conquest followed. He began with China, which was vulnerable due to its division between the Ch'in with their capital at Beijing (Peking) in the north, and the Song (Sung) with their capital at Hangzhou in the south. In 1215 Beijing (Peking) fell, after which Genghiz turned west where he attacked the Islamic state of **Khwarizm** (between the Caspian Sea and Pamir Mountains). In 1220 he razed the city of Bukhara, slaughtering 30,000 of its defenders including women and children. In a sermon to the surviving population he said, "Oh people, know that you have committed great sins… If you ask me what proof I have… I say it is because I am the punishment of God." He returned from the western incursions and invaded China again in 1226 and died the next year.

Genghiz Khan ranks as one of the great empire builders of world history. In fact his was the largest empire in world history. In 20 years he extended rule from the Pacific Ocean to the Caspian Sea, and he died undefeated. Why was he so successful? Genghiz Khan forged the loyalty of members of different ethnic clans and tribes of steppe nomads such as the Turks into a well-led fighting force by disregarding family ties or social rank and promoting on the basis of ability and loyalty. The Mongol war machine was well organized. The army was made up of fighting units called **tumens** consisting of 10,000 cavalrymen. These were divided into 1000, 100, and 10 units with commanders at each level responsible for discipline and training. Commanders were personally chosen by Genghiz Khan and promoted based on their ability. Lightly equipped, fast moving, and agile, the army could cover 200 miles a day and hit an enemy from 400 yards. They intimidated many into surrender. Heads of their enemies were used to build columns as gruesome beacons to warn of further attacks. They were masters of deception, feigning attack in order to draw the enemy in closer and putting dummy soldiers on horseback to make the size of the army appear larger. As one chronicler wrote, "Detachment after detachment arrived, each like a billowing sea." After conquest, Genghiz Khan took keen interest in the arts and learning of the new subjects of his empire, but he continued to live in the steppes, establishing a new capital at **Karakorum**, south of Lake Baikal. He consulted Confucian scholars on how to rule China, Muslim engineers on how to improve trade, and he welcomed Muslim mullahs, Buddhist and Taoist monks, and Christian missionaries. All religions were tolerated, a script was devised for the Mongol language, and a law code put an end to tribal squabbles. In this way, cultural diffusion and exchange were encouraged.

The Mongol Empire

After Genghiz's death, his third son **Ogedei** was elected Great Khan. During his reign, the Mongol attack was extended against China, Persia, and Europe. In 1234 Ogedei overthrew the Northern Song (Sung) Dynasty of China and in 1237–1240, **Batu Khan**, a grandson of Genghiz's, launched the only successful winter attack on Russia, laying waste to the Kievan Confederation. Then Batu Khan proceeded into eastern Europe, nearly reaching Vienna and the Adriatic. Had the Mongols continued westward, the entire history of the European continent might have been different. As it was, disputes over succession after the death of Ogedei in 1241 caused Batu Khan to return to Mongolia. Eventually, Ogedei's nephew **Monke** was elected the Great Khan and he undertook a campaign against the Song (Sung) Empire in southern China. Meanwhile, Monke's younger brother, **Hulagu**, struck a decisive blow against the Islamic world by capturing Baghdad in 1253. Much of the world cultural heritage dating back to the Persian empire of Darius was thereby destroyed. Just as Ogedei's death in 1241 had saved Europe, Monke's death in 1259 saved the Muslim world. Rival claimants for succession caused Hulagu to withdraw, leaving a remnant force. The Muslims rallied under the leadership of the Egyptian Mamluks and in 1259, near Nazareth, defeated the Mongols. This defeat shattered the spell of Mongol invincibility and stopped the Mongol spread west. The death of Monke ended the unity of the Mongol Empire. From then on, the empire was divided into "**hordes**" and ruled independently. The younger brother of Monke, **Kublai Khan**, was proclaimed the fifth Great Khan, but had direct authority only over China, which fell under his control in the 1270s. Descendants of Hulagu ruled Persia, Batu Khan, Russia, and Chagatai, the Mongol heartland.

LONG-DISTANCE TRAVEL
THE TRAVELS OF MARCO POLO

The coinage of this paper money is authenticated with as much form and ceremony as if it were actually of pure gold or silver. To each note a number of officers, specially appointed, not only subscribe their names, but affix their seals also . . . When thus coined in large quantities, this paper currency is circulated in every part of the grand khan's dominions; no person, at the peril of his life, dares refuse to accept it in payment. All his subjects receive it without hestitation, because, wherever their business may call them, they can dispose of it again in the purchase of merchandise . . . such as pearls, jewels, gold, or silver. With it, in short, every article may be procured.

In 1272 a Venetian merchant, Marco Polo, set out for China. Polo served the great Kublai Khan for 17 years. On his return to Europe, he left a book detailing his travels and observations of the Tartars in Asia, lifestyle in India, and the fabulous life at the Chinese court. Marco Polo was awed by the luxury and advances of the Chinese, among them great cities, burning "black stones" (coal), paved roads, and paper money. Thus began the European enchantment with East Asia that ultimately led to great voyages of discovery and a world European empire.

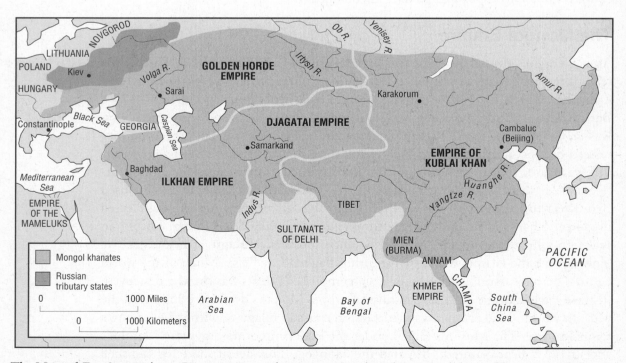

The Mongol Empire 1294 C.E. Between 1218 and 1227 C.E. Genghiz Khan created the world's greatest empire. At his death, as was Mongol custom, the empire was divided among his four sons.

Because the illiterate Mongols left no written record, Mongul rule is chronicled through the eyes of others. The Arab historian Abn al-Athir said he waited many years to record events too horrible to recall. The Great Chronicler of Europe Matthew Paris said, "Mongols are inhuman, beastly, rather monsters than men. . ." Papal legate Plano Carpini, who crossed into southern Russia in 1245–1246, wrote that "they besieged Kiev. . . barely two hundred houses stand there, and those people are held in the harshest slavery." By contrast, Marco Polo, a Venetian merchant who spent 17 years at the court of Kublai Khan, described the Mongol rule of China as brilliant, especially as reflected in the bustling trade and wealth of Hangzhou. The variation in viewpoint can be seen in the differences in impact left on each society.

Pax Mongolica

As a whole, the Mongols destroyed, but they also built new empires, reopened the land and maritime highways from east to west for trade, and established an imperial peace, the **Pax Mongolica**. As one Muslim historian wrote, the peoples of the khanate "enjoy such peace that a man might have journeyed from the land of sunrise to the land of sunset with a golden platter upon his head without suffering the least violence from anyone." This peace allowed the spread not just of goods, but of foodstuffs like sugar and citrus fruits, inventions like printing, gunpowder, windmills, and papermaking, as well as disease. The Europeans especially seemed to have benefited from Eurasian trade. From the 1240s on, European churchmen were allowed to travel eastward. The pope appointed a succession of archbishops to Beijing (Peking) to minister to the growing flock of believers. European merchants, chiefly from Genoa and Venice, also moved east in search of the goods they had formerly purchased in Southwest Asia (often called the **Levant** during this period). The total number of European merchants who traveled to Asia must have been substantial, for detailed guidebooks were prepared to help with the journey. The most comprehensive was written in 1340 by Francesco Balducchi Pegolotti, manager of a Cyprus branch of a large Italian banking firm. He gave merchants invaluable insights into routes and where in convoy they "would be as safe as if they were in their own home." Better known were the reports of Marco Polo (ca. 1254–1324), the Venetian merchant who left a detailed account of life at the court of Kublai Khan.

As a rule, the Mongols had less impact the more advanced the society they attacked. As for example in China and the Muslim world, they eventually became absorbed into the larger population.

Mongol conquests and empires represented the most formidable but last of the Asian nomadic challenges to the growing global dominance of the sedentary peoples of the civilized world. This was due to

- ever-diminishing amounts of land available to nomads;

- the Black Plague (see pages 217–219);

- the considerable numeric disadvantage of the nomadic peoples; and

- the increasing ability of settled populations to defend themselves once they acquired gunpowder.

THE COMPARATIVE MONGOL IMPACT ON CHINA (YUAN), KOREA, JAPAN, SOUTHEAST ASIA, RUSSIA (MUSCOVY), INDIA (DELHI AND MUGHAL), PERSIA (SAFAVID), AND TURKEY (OTTOMAN)

China (Yuan)

In 1279 Genghiz Khan's grandson, Kublai Khan (1216–1294), crushed the Southern Song (Sung), proclaimed himself emperor, and in the Chinese tradition founded the Yuan Dynasty (1271–1368). Heeding the words of Genghiz Khan's advisers that "the empire was won on horseback but it will not be governed on horseback," Kublai Khan set about finding a method of rule acceptable to the Chinese but keeping him in control. Distrusting the mandarin class, but needing their expertise and system, Kublai Khan assigned foreigners to the highest administrative posts, allowing Chinese scholars to serve in lower posts. He disarmed the Chinese and forbade them to assemble in large numbers. He divided society into four classes with varying rights and privileges. At the top were Mongols and their Asian allies, below them the north Chinese who were more compliant, then the ethnic Chinese, and finally minority peoples of the south. Some Mongol women made a considerable impact, as for example Kublai's wife, Chaki, who promoted the interests of Buddhists and pleaded for lenient treatment of prisoners, but the position of common Chinese women improved little. The capital was established at Beijing (Peking) nearer the Mongol homeland.

Despite efforts to remain aloof, the Mongols ultimately became absorbed into Chinese society. With 90 million Chinese armed with a venerable cultural tradition, and a few hundred thousand Mongols, this was inevitable. Kublai's capital was laid out in Chinese pattern and decorated with Chinese buildings. Kublai Khan gave his son a Confucian education and introduced others to the Chinese court and bureaucracy. He also patronized Muslim scholars. Persian astronomers corrected the Chinese calendar, made accurate maps, and ran hospitals. In this way, the richness of the Muslim world was spread across Asia. Despite Kublai's efforts at enlightened rule, dissatisfaction grew. Many Mongols were alienated because they wanted to preserve Mongol separateness. The Chinese scholar-gentry regarded the Mongols as uncouth barbarians and were threatened by the disappearance of the examination route to administrative office. The Chinese upper class was also threatened by the growing influence of the artisan and merchant classes that Kublai supported. To aid commerce, the Mongols expanded the money supply with paper money and, surprisingly for a landed people, built a war fleet that helped to cut down on privateering. Toward the end of his reign, Kublai Khan began to support overseas expeditions and explorations from southern China westward. The peasants also became dissatisfied. Though Kublai Khan restored the granary system for famine relief, reduced peasant taxes and labor demand, and formulated revolutionary plans for educating the peasantry, he also organized peasants into 50-unit cooperatives supervised by state officials that were unpopular.

In the last years of Kublai Kahn's long reign, his lifestyle became dissolute. This was followed by inflation and excesses by state officials and later rulers. By the 1350s, banditry and privateering escalated, famines hit, and secret societies dedicated to Mongol overthrow proliferated. In 1351 C.E. the rebels struck a decisive blow. The peasant monk **Hung Wu** and his followers drove the Mongols out of China and established the Ming Dynasty (1368–1644).

Korea

The Mongol attack shaped Korea, too. Korea, whose civilization grew up in the shadows of China and its tributary system, and had been particularly affected by Chinese Buddhism, was a land of aristocratic rule rather than bureaucratic administration as in China. Periodically, quarrels between Korean aristocratic households and protests by the common people broke out. Then, after a century of conflict triggered by the Mongol invasion in 1231, the Koryo regime (918–1392) collapsed and the Choson, or Yi, Dynasty was established on the Korean peninsula, ruling until 1910. In this way, a stronger centralized state was established, much as happened in Japan.

Japan

Even before establishing the Yuan Dynasty in China in 1271, Kublai Khan sent a message to Japanese leaders demanding submission. When Japan refused, Kublai Khan, with 15,000 soldiers and 900 ships, attacked Japan in 1274. After one day, storms overtook the fleet and the Mongols withdrew. To protect themselves, the Japanese built a wall around the harbor and prayed to the gods. They were not safe for long. On June 23, 1281, Kublai Khan launched another invasion, this time with 4400 ships, 142,000 disciplined men, and sophisticated weapons including arrows, gunpowder, and projectiles. On August 1, yet another typhoon, the **kamikaze**, or divine wind, hit, destroying all but 200 of the Mongol ships and saving Japan. In this way, the myth of the "divine wind" was born and subsequently revived during World War II when American invasion threatened. There were other indirect effects of the Mongol invasion on Japan as well. The attack weakened the Kamakura Shogunate because no booty was found among the wreckage of Mongol ships. This made it impossible to pay off impoverished samurai warriors who received less and less payment for their services at the same time their numbers were increasing. Soon the Kamakura were deposed, replaced by the Ashikaga Shogunate. Not until 1600 was a centralized state under the Tokugawa established. Isolationist attitudes toward the outside world also grew as a result of the Mongol experience.

SOUTHEAST ASIA

After conquering China, in 1288 the Mongols attacked **Pagan**, the capital of the great classical Burmese state, because it refused to bow to Mongol overlordship. In the wake of the attack, Burma was left fragmented and weakened. The Mongols also attempted a land and sea invasion of the temporarily unified Cham and Vietnamese state. The result was terrible devastation but the Vietnamese-Cham alliance ultimately repelled the Mongols. Meanwhile, the Mongols also mounted a naval attack on Java which also proved costly. But the attacks weakened the great classical states of Khmer Cambodia and Burma to the advantage of the Siamese (Thai) from southwest China who were spreading into the Cambodian and Burmese states.

Did You Know?

The Southeast Asians were among the few people that successfully resisted Mongol conquest and power.

Russia (Muscovy)

Compared to China, Russia was poorer, had fewer established traditions, and was more vulnerable to social and political destruction and change. For these reasons, the Mongol attack on Russia had a greater impact than it did on China. Out of the ashes of the Kievan city-state system destroyed by the Mongols grew the autocratic patterns of czarist Russia. The Mongols, **Tartars** as they are called in Russian sources (Tartar referred originally to the Mongol tribe, later to the Mongol-Turkic mix, many of whom had converted to Islam), suddenly came upon Russia. They appeared in 1223 in southeastern Russia, smashing the Russians and their rivals, the Polovtsy, and then disappearing into the steppe. They returned in 1237–1240 to impose their 200-year rule called the "Tartar Yoke." Many Russians fled north into the forest regions around Moscow, in this way settling new parts of Russia. Around Novgorod, the princes instituted a policy of cooperation with the Mongols because they were at the same time engaged with the Swedes and Germans. Once victory had been achieved, Batu Khan organized peasants into collectives of 100 for census and tax purposes. Then he withdrew from his domain called the **Golden Horde** and established his headquarters far to the south at **Sarai** on the lower Volga. From there, he ruled indirectly through the Russian princes. Most Russian upper classes submitted to Mongol rule as a way to protect their status. Even so, this class was decimated by battle and intermarriage with Mongols. Many Tartar names can be found within the Russian noble ranks from this point forward. The princes that served the Khan had to journey to the Mongol headquarters and pay humble obeisance, hand over the tribute they had collected from the Russian people on behalf of the Khan, and send military detachments on demand. Otherwise, the Mongols interfered little in Russian life.

The Independence of Russia and the Growth of Autocracy

The Russian princes who served as intermediaries of the Khan became virtual **autocrats** (rulers with unlimited authority) over the Russian people. Gradually, one prince, the prince of Moscow, became stronger than the other Russian princes. This was due to a number of factors, among them long life, the tradition of primogeniture that helped keep their holdings intact, and successful marriages and alliances allowing them to enlarge their territory and power. In 1328 Moscow prince Ivan I, or Kalita, meaning "Moneybags," received the position of Grand Prince, a commission that allowed him to gather tribute from the other princes for the Khan. As he collected taxes for the Mongols, he kept an increasing portion of the revenue for his own use. He used his increasing revenue to purchase more land. In 1328 he persuaded the Metropolitan of the Eastern Orthodox Church to move its headquarters from Kiev to Moscow, further strengthening the power of Moscow and its prince. The Mongols suffered their first defeat at the hands of Moscow in 1380 at the **Battle of Kulikovo** on the Don River. Under the leadership of Prince Dmitri "Donskoy," the Russians laid to rest the belief in Mongol invincibility. In 1395 Tamerlane invaded Russia and in 1408 the Golden Horde launched a major assault on Moscow to punish the prince for not paying tribute. In neither assault was Moscow captured, lending even more credence to the belief in the liberation powers of the Moscow princedom. From then on, the Mongols slowly lost power in

Russia and the Moscow princes to whom all Russians now looked for leadership assumed the position formerly held by the Khan as overlord. During the reign of **Ivan III, or Great** (1462–1505), Moscow declared Russian independence from the Mongols.

Two other events made the Moscow princes autocrats rather than rulers. The first was the creation of a state church. In 1453, when the Byzantine Empire fell to the Ottoman Turks, the Russian Church became independent of the Eastern Orthodox Church in Constantinople, creating the **Russian Orthodox Church** with its own patriarch or pope, independent of any power but that of the prince. Soon Moscow was considered the "**Third Rome.**" According to this doctrine, the first Rome in Italy was destroyed by the German tribes, and the second in Constantinople by the Turks. This left Russia as the true repository of the Christian faith. The second event was the reincorporation of the former Kievan territories into the new Moscow state. By claiming not just former territory but the former Russian heritage, Ivan III assumed the title of **czar**, or Caesar, Sovereign of all the Russias, and autocrat. Whereas autocrat originally referred to independence from the Mongols, it soon came to be synonymous with czar. To implement such authority, Ivan the Great promulgated a **Sudebnik**, or code of laws. Because all Moscow princes claimed descent from Rurik, the founder of the Russian line of princes, legitimacy for power rested not just on military power, achievement, and the church, but on bloodlines as well.

> **Did You Know?**
>
> **Autocracy** refers to power above and beyond political power, that is, power over the church and any other national institutions.

The Mongol Impact on Russia

The attack and subsequent indirect Mongol rule of Russia had a great impact on Russia's history. The destruction and heavy tribute set Russia back economically for centuries, keeping it isolated and preventing participation in the European Renaissance. It brought the Russian princes to power, and because they were essentially liberated khans, they had autocratic power over their Russian subjects. Yet, Russian autocracy cannot be entirely laid in the lap of the Mongols. It was the Russians themselves who made the church subservient to the state and institutionalized **serfdom** (the tying of the peasants to the land). Serfdom began during the reign of **Ivan IV, or Terrible** (1533–1584), when the independent land-owning class, the **boyars**, was purged and replaced by a dependent and politically loyal class of landed gentry. Then dynastic legitimacy was put in question when Ivan IV left no heir. He had killed his first son, his second died, and his third had disappeared mysteriously. This crisis led to civil war and Polish invasion. This period in Russian history is known as the **Time of Troubles** (1598–1613). During these years of turmoil, the population became refugees, the land was left barren. Starvation followed. This led to the passage of the so-called *forbidden years* laws forbidding peasants from leaving their land. These laws were never rescinded and so serfdom became institutionalized. In theory, the czar served God, the nobility served the czar, and the people served the nobility.

Thus, the Mongols absorbed little of Russian culture and contributed little of their own culture to Russia (unlike in Southwest Asia where Mongols converted to Islam). Through their destructive actions and their indirect rule of Russia, Mongols paved the way for serfdom and autocracy.

India (Delhi and Mughal)

When the Mongols invaded India, it was already a weakened and decentralized state. When they invaded Persia, however, the Golden Age of Islam under the Abbasid Caliphate was at its height. The great Mongol invasions of the early thirteenth century and Tamerlane's attack at the end of the fourteenth century made a shambles of the Muslim world. The result was threefold: first, the conversion of the Mongol nomads in Southeast Asia and their absorption into Islamic society; second, the growth in power of militant Turk nomads; and third, the creation of new Islamic empires like the Mughals, Safavids, and Ottomans, which possessed gunpowder and cannons.

At the end of the Indian classical age (480 C.E.), India experienced wave after wave of foreign invasions from Cental Asia. First came the Arab Muslims, then the Turkish Muslims, and finally the Mongol Muslims. The major result of these invasions was the importation of Islam, which, due to the ferocity of its entrance, left a history of religious division that has bloodied the pages of Indian history to this day. In 711 the first and least lasting Muslim intrusion came to India when the Arab Umayyad rulers invaded and later annexed territory in western India (Sind). Cultural interaction resulted and was particularly enriching to Islamic scholars, who learned **Indian math** (Arabic numerals), medicine, and astronomy. The second wave came in 1192 when Turkic Muslims from Afghanistan captured **Delhi** and extended control across northern India. Hindu and Buddhist statues, shrines, and temples were destroyed along the way. Many Buddhists took refuge in Tibet, establishing the fine Buddhist **lamaseries** (monasteries) that are so characteristic of that culture. In 1206 Qutb-ud-din established a Muslim kingdom in northern India, the **Delhi Sultanate** (1206–1526). Because the Muslims were a minority, Turks and Persians (Iranians) were recruited to run the government. Many of the recruits were themselves Muslim refugees fleeing Mongol devastation of Iran and Southwest Asia. Under the Sultanate, Persian influences deeply affected Hindu art and architecture, especially the introduction of the minaret, arch, and dome. The most stunning effect was the evolution of a new language, **Urdu**, which is a mixture of Persian, Arabic, and Hindi. It is the official language of Pakistan today. While Muslim and Hindu cultural exchange occurred, political, social, and religious separation caused tension. Most Indians looked at the invaders as a new ruling caste capable of taxing and ruling but otherwise irrelevant to their lives. A renaissance of pious Hinduism, or **Bhakti**, of the Gupta Brahmans, which emphasized reverence and devotion to a personal divinity, captured the religious lives of the people.

Tensions between Muslims and Hindus were based on such differences as the Muslim belief in one God, which conflicted with the Hindu belief in many gods. The Muslim subscription to the idea of social and religious equality ran counter to the Hindu belief in castes. The Muslim belief that the cow was just another source of food conflicted with the Hindu view that it was sacred. Belief in reincarnation by Hindus was opposed to belief in a day of final judgment and the promise of spiritual immortality by the Muslims. Finally, tensions grew between Muslim rulers and Hindu subjects. Unlike Buddhism, which was eventually folded into Hinduism, Islam remained aloof and connected in the Hindu mind with foreign invasion and rule.

TAMERLANE

The Mongol period of Indian history begins with the invasion by Tamerlane (Timur) in 1398. By this time the Mongols had intermarried with the Turkic steppe people, and many had become Muslim. **Tamerlane** claimed descent from the Mongol Jagatai (Genghiz Khan's second son), Lord of Central Asia, Iran, and Southwest Asia. From his capital in **Samarkand**, Tamerlane conquered Persia, the Fertile Crescent, and southern Russia. Then he invaded India for booty, and when he had finished his campaign of destruction, he retreated to Samarkand, leaving India again politically divided. In this way, Islam was once again swept into India, but in an even more hostile way than during the previous Delhi Sultanate.

THE MUGHAL EMPIRE

Almost a century later, in 1526, **Babur**, who claimed descent from Tamerlane and Genghiz Khan, invaded and established the Mughal Empire (1526–1858). Babur seems to have been driven by the fact that he had lost his original kingdom in Central Asia. Though he was outnumbered ten to one, Babur prevailed, among other reasons because he frightened hundreds of Indian war elephants that then trampled Indian warriors. Victory was also due to the use of guns and movable artillery, weapons that were to prove decisive in battle everywhere on the globe from 1450 to 1800. Those who had guns, like the Muscovite czars, Mughal Indians, Ottoman Turks, Ming Chinese, Tokugawa Japanese, Spanish, and Portuguese, created so-called "**gunpowder empires**." The Mongols were indirectly responsible for this turn of events, for it was along the reopened Silk Road that Chinese gunpowder technology moved to the West where the Byzantines, Europeans, and steppe people began to devise siege weapons and guns, bringing down castle defenses.

AKBAR

Babur was not just a conqueror, but a man of cultivated taste for the arts. He wrote one of the great histories of India, but he was an ineffective administrator and squandered his opportunity to create a politically cohesive Indian state. That was left to his grandson, **Akbar** (1556–1605), who may have been one of India's greatest rulers. Not only was Akbar an able military commander who assembled an empire including Afghanistan, Pakistan, Bangladesh, and all of present-day India north of the Godavari River, he also had a state vision. He staffed an administrative bureaucracy with Muslims and non-Muslims. He brought order to finances by creating a **diwan**, or bureau of finance, to mint money and create budgetary and tax procedures. He appointed 800 **mansabdars**, or imperial officials, who performed military, judicial, and financial functions at the local level. He left intact, however, life in the village communities. He is most famous for his policies of religious toleration, especially toward Hindus. He ended the pilgrimage tax, twice married Hindu princesses, and allowed Hindus to serve in the army and administration. However, the refusal of many Hindus to serve and learn Urdu hampered his efforts. Though Akbar considered himself a devout orthodox Muslim, he invited Jains, Nestorian Christians, Hindus, Jesuits, and Zoroastrians to join Muslim ulema in theological debates. The outcome was a **syncretic** religion (a religion that reconciles different views), called the Din-i-Ilahi, or "divine discipline."

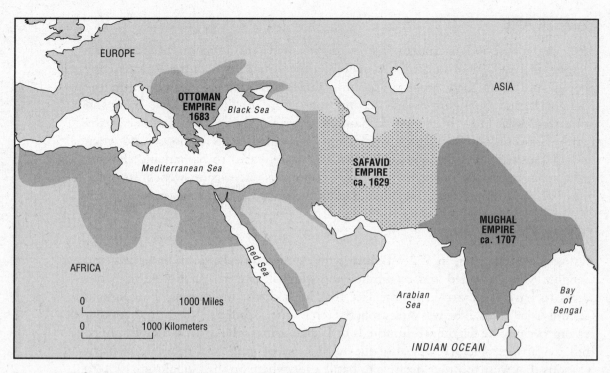

Ottoman, Safavid, and Mughal Empires ca. 1629–1707 C.E. At the same time that strong absolutist European states were emerging, strong empires stretched across Asia. The common element in the rise of these states was gunpowder, giving rise to the term gunpowder empires.

Historians are divided on whether Akbar's motives as a philosopher-king were theological or political. Regardless, the new religion of synthesis satisfied neither side and social divisions remain to this day. Akbar was also a patron of the arts, supporting painters of the Indo-Persian style and leaving a library of 24,000 books. The birth of his son, Jahangir, prompted the building of a new capital city (1569), Fatehpur-Sikri. The city included an imperial palace, a mosque, lavish gardens, thousands of houses for ordinary people, and a blend of Hindu architecture (flat stone beams and ornate decoration) and Muslim architecture (domes, arches, and courts.)

THE MUGHAL IMPACT

It was under the reign of Akbar's grandson, Shah Jahan (r. 1628–1658), that the legacy of the Mughals is most outwardly apparent. The Mongols who had swept Islam into India found the greatest expression of Hindu-Islamic synthesis in the artistic and architectural expression of Shah Jahan's reign. After subduing Muslim revolts and Portuguese resistance in Bengal, Shah Jahan reasserted Mughal control in the Deccan Plateau. He then proceeded to build a new capital city at Delhi, a city that became one of the great cities of the Muslim world, boasting fine boulevards and beautiful mosques. He built the **Red Fort**, named for its red sandstone walls, which housed the imperial palace, administrative treasury, and arsenal. The Hall of Public Audience was a room of restrained elegance to which only the most privileged came. Inscribed on the walls were the words, "If there is paradise on earth, It is here. It is here. It is here." Shah Jahan also ordered construction of the **Peacock Throne**, which was encrusted with emeralds, diamonds, pearls, and rubies. (In 1739 raiders carried it off to Persia.) But the most enduring monument was the **Taj Mahal**, a building of such sublime beauty it inspires world admiration. A garden tomb that employed 20,000 workers and took 18 years to build, it was built in memorial for his beloved wife, Mumtaz Mahal, who died giving birth to their fifteenth child. The tomb, of the purest white marble, sits on a vast platform of sandstone and marble overlooking the river Jumna. The Persian-style dome is actually a double dome similar to Italian Renaissance domes. The Taj Mahal, seen in a frame of four soaring minarets, seems to float, especially by moonlight when the white marble exudes a soft blue cast. Shah Jahan intended to build himself a companion tomb in black marble on the opposite bank, but one of his sons, **Aurangzeb**, executed his eldest brother and locked Shah Jahan away until his death.

Aurangzeb's reign was one of religious reaction. He enforced Muslim laws against gambling and drink, forbade Hindu practices like sati (suttee), reimposed the tax on non-Muslims, and ordered destruction of some Hindu temples. His expansionist exploits depleted the treasury and brought opposition not just from Hindus, but from other groups as well. From then on, India was again vulnerable, open to outside attack, as by the Persians in 1739 and later by the British. Hindu princes (rajas), Brahmans, and castes reasserted their interests. British and Portuguese merchants trickled in. The delicate Muslim-Hindu religious synthesis nurtured by early Mughal rulers unraveled, leaving religious tension, and political decentralization reemerged.

Persia (Safavids)

The conquest of the Islamic heartlands had begun under Genghiz Khan's grandson, Hulegu. In 1258 he destroyed Baghdad and murdered the Abbasid caliph and some 800,000 people who resisted. The Muslim world was left without central authority and its military strength was severely eroded. Throughout the fourteenth and fifteenth centuries, rival nomadic groups, infused with Turkic warriors, fought for control of the area. Amidst the chaos, two powerful families emerged, the **Ottomans** in **Anatolia** (Turkey) and the **Safavids** in Persia. The Safi al-Din family, which gave the Safavid Dynasty its name, gained power, launching a militant campaign to purify and reform Islam and to spread the religion among the Mongol-Turkic tribes of the area. As they began to preach Shi'ite doctrines, Sunni enemies battled back until 1501, when a Safavid commander, **Ismail**, won a string of victories and proclaimed himself **shah**, or emperor. Then, in 1514 at **Chaldiran** in northwest Persia, Sunni Ottomans and Shi'ite Safavids battled it out. Ismail's cavalry proved no match for Ottoman musketeers and cannons. The Safavids were defeated, limiting the spread of Shi'ite Islam westward. The Ottomans, however, could not follow up with an assault to end the Safavids. The result was the emergence of two empires and two sects of Islam in Southwest Asia.

The Safavid state (1501–1736) was strengthened by Ismail and by several factors: the loyalty of nomadic tribesmen who were granted grazing lands especially on the Ottoman frontier; the skill of Persian bureaucrats; and the vitality of Shi'ite Islam, which was proclaimed the official and compulsory religion of the new empire. Ismail's decision to make Shi'ite Islam the state religion when the majority of the people were Sunni proved crucial to the future of Persia (Iran) and Southwest Asia. It provided the ideological and institutional support for Safavid rulers. It melded

---

Did You Know?

The Taj Mahal took 18 years to build.

with a tradition of ethnic religious kings established during the Achaemenid and Sassanian Empires that had shaped the cultural and political identity of Persia. Safavid shahs claimed descent from one of the Shi'ite imams, or successors to Ali, the cousin and son-in-law to Muhammad. This gave rise to a **theocratic** (subject to religious authority) state that, even to this day, distinguishes Iran.

Safavid power reached its height under **Shah Abbas** (1587–1629). Shah Abbas built a strong national army and improved export trade by building up a cottage industry of carpet weaving and glazed building tiles. He endowed the arts, much of which appeared in the new capital city of his empire, **Isfahan**. The city boasted a bustling bazaar, 162 mosques, 48 seminaries where ulema studied Muslim science, 273 public baths, a vast imperial palace, wide boulevards, and public parks and pools.

Despite political and religious rivalries that emerged between the Ottomans and Safavids, their social systems had much in common. Both were dominated in the earlier phase by soldier-aristocrats who later retreated to landed estates and had resplendent lifestyles. Here, life was increasingly difficult for the peasants on whom they depended. As expansion slowed, land scarcity squeezed both peasant and aristocrat until banditry and uprisings became common, undermining dynastic power and legitimacy. Women faced legal and social disadvantages although the influx of more independent nomadic women during the Mongol assaults tempered this somewhat. Travelers to Isfahan often noted that women wore bright colors, made no effort to hide their faces, and were active in trade and money lending.

Inept rulers followed Shah Abbas. The monarchy weakened, Shi'ite theologians seized power, and in the eighteenth century Turks, Afghans, and Russians invaded and divided political power. Thus, the major impact of the Mongols on Persia was the rise of a new Islamic state dominated by the Shi'ite sect. The inability of either the Ottomans or the Safavids to reunite the Islamic world shattered by the Mongols continued the trend toward political fragmentation in Southwest Asia.

Turkey (Ottomans)

In the mid-tenth century, even before the Mongol attack on Southwest Asia, mobile and militant **Seljuk Turks**, nomads originating in Turkestan (central Asia), surged westward. They accepted Sunni Islam, swarmed over Persia learning Persian culture, and then pushed into the heart of the Abbasid Caliphate in Iraq and Syria. Baghdad fell to them in 1055 and the caliph became a puppet of the Turkish **sultan** (ruler, literally "he with authority"). The Turks did not control all of the Muslim world. By the middle of the eleventh century there were three Muslim centers of power—Cordoba in Spain, Cairo in Egypt, and Baghdad in Iraq. Into this politically divided but culturally united world in the early thirteenth century came the Mongols, crushing Baghdad (1258) and Damascus (1260). Mongol chief Hulagu tried to eradicate Muslim culture but a succession crisis made him return to Mongolia, leaving Egypt, North Africa, and Spain free of Mongol control. Hulagu's descendant, Ghazan, embraced Islam in 1295 and worked to revive Muslim culture in the area. Turks and Mongols intermingled with the cosmopolitan Muslim world of Arabs and Persians. While the Mongols became absorbed by Muslim culture, the disruptions they wrought facilitated the rise of other warrior nomadic groups who could fill the political vacuum.

THE OTTOMAN TURKS

Such a group was the Turkic warriors from western Anatolia (Turkey), the Ottomans, who began expansionist moves under their leader **Osman** (r. 1299–1326). Because the Ottomans lived in the borderlands between Islam and Byzantine Christendom, the leader considered himself "border chief" of the **gazis**, or frontier fighters, in the jihad, or holy war. The Islamic religious jihad principle in Ottoman hands turned into a political and economic weapon of expansionism. To use it effectively, they had to move against Christians rather than the fractured Muslim world.

First Osman wrestled northwestern Anatolia from the Byzantines and then crossed over the **Dardanelles** near **Gallipoli** in 1352 into the **Balkans**. Alarmed Christians under the Holy Roman Hapsburg emperor Charles V met the Ottoman force on the Danube in 1396 and on the Black Sea in 1444, only to have their forces wiped out. After centuries of attack, Constantinople was now surrounded. In 1453 Sultan **Mehmed II** (r. 1451–1481) in a six-week siege breached the walls of the Byzantine capital and put a final end to the venerable 2000-year history of Rome. Western technology proved decisive in the battle. Christian Hungarians working for the Ottomans cast a huge bronze cannon on the spot. The cannon shattered a city gate, allowing Mehmed's 100,000-man army to enter and rout the 10,000-man army that defended the circular walls and stone fortifications that had made the city impregnable for 1000 years. On May 28, 1453, Mehmed the Conqueror rode into the city on his white horse. Zealots of Islam removed the cross from atop Hagia Sophia and soon the muezzin's chant rang from minarets. In 1454 the first dated work from Gutenberg's printing press warned Christian Europe of the Muslim peril.

The warning soon became reality. This battle only initiated the expansionist phase of Ottoman history. The Ottomans took control of the Adriatic. In 1480 an Ottoman fleet lay plans for the conquest of the Italian city-states that, if completed as seemed likely because of the political instability of the city-state system, might have changed the history of Europe. As it was, Mehmed II died and his successor moved south instead into Syria, Palestine (1516), Egypt (1517), and North Africa. Under Suleiman (r. 1520–1566) the Ottomans reached their widest geographical limit. At the **Battle of Mohacs** (1526) he crushed the Hungarians, and three years later he besieged the Hapsburg capital of Vienna, where he was finally stopped. Each case of Ottoman victory was due to a lack of unity among European forces and superiority of Ottoman military organization and artillery. However, in 1571, at the **Battle of Lepanto**, the Ottomans lost their bid to control the Mediterranean when their fleet was driven off by a combined Spanish, Venetian, and Hapsburg force led by Charles V.

OTTOMAN RULE

Not only did Ottoman expansionism reach its zenith during Suleiman's rule, but the classic form of the Ottoman social and administrative system was established. This was heavily influenced by military organization. According to Ottoman historian **Mustafa Naima**, Ottoman society was divided into producers of wealth, Muslim and non-Muslim, and the military. The state responsibility was to supply the justice necessary to produce wealth needed to support the military. The ruling class was all Muslim and mostly descendants of Turkish families related to the Ottomans. In return for bureaucratic service,

> **Did You Know?**
>
> The reign of **Suleiman the Magnificent** (r. 1520–1566) brought the Ottoman Empire to its height.

this class received **trimars**, or landed estates, but only for their lifetime as the sultan owned all the land and it reverted back to him upon death. For civil and military service, the sultan's agents rounded up Christian boys between the ages of 12 and 20 from poor villages of the empire in a system known as **devshirme**. All were taken as slaves and converted to Islam, and the brightest 10 percent were trained to read and write Arabic, Ottoman Turkish, and Persian in preparation for civil service jobs. Others known as **janissaries** (Turkish for *recruits*) were prepared for military service. The system allowed social mobility for non-Turkish peoples and many Slavs, Greeks, and Armenians rose to high position in the state. It also ensured a talented pool of state servants who were loyal to the sultan for their jobs, their promotions, their income, and even their lives. All authority rested with the sultan and designated state servants like generals and provincial governors, or **pashas**. The sultan's closest advisers, or **vizirs**, met together in a diwan, or council, to make important decisions. The Grand Vizir acted as a prime minister.

Under Suleiman I, the Ottoman state witnessed the height of cultural achievement. Suleiman was known in history as *the Lawgiver* because of his influence on civil law. His image can be found in the United States Supreme Court along with other great lawgivers like Solon, Moses, and Thomas Jefferson. The law regulated penalties for criminal acts, reformed administration and legal procedures in order to root out corruption, and introduced the idea of a balanced budget. Europeans called Suleiman *the Magnificent* because of the lavishness of his court and his presumptions of power. He began a letter to the European monarchs with "I who am sultan of sultans, the sovereign of sovereigns, the dispenser of crowns to the monarchs of the earth…" He adorned the capital of Istanbul (the Ottoman name given to Constantinople) with palaces and mosques, among the most famous the Topkapi Palace and the Suleimanye Mosque. A contemporary of Michelangelo, **Pasha Sinan** (1491–1588), a Christian rounded up in the devshirme, designed 312 public buildings. Poetry dominated literary expression. Written in Turkish, it followed classic Islamic (Arabic) forms and rules. Perhaps the best known Ottoman art form was the beautiful glazed pottery of Iznik, which was influenced by Ming blue and white and Persian craft styles. Books on history and astronomy were written. Of special interest was the *Book of the Sea* (1521) by Piri Reis, which contained 129 chapters, each with a map incorporating Islamic and Western knowledge of the seas. Medical scholarship and research advanced in the fields of surgery and disease. The large number of public hospitals in Istanbul attests to Suleiman's interest. Istanbul's great bazaars were filled with merchants and travelers going from England to Malaya. Coffeehouses became popular places for men to gather, debate politics, do business, and play chess. Most businesses were organized into guilds highly regulated by the government.

DECLINE OF THE OTTOMANS

By the seventeenth and eighteenth centuries, weaknesses in the Ottoman system became apparent and irreparable. One was the necessity for military conquest to support the army and bureaucracy. When that stopped, the empire lacked the influx of new manpower that kept the system fluid and merit based. The system also relied heavily on the sultan's ability to rule. Some sultans became lavish and decadent. With no tradition of succession, usurpations of the throne were common. Rival claimants were often confined to the palace and "**harem**" (the place in a Muslim house assigned to women), leading to the exaggerated stories of concubinage and debauchery. Expanding population led to inflation, famine, and revolts. The result was that, during the sixteenth century, the Ottomans made no advances in Europe and, as has already been noted, in 1514 they were unable to follow up on the defeat they inflicted on the Safavids at Chaldiran.

THE MONGOL IMPACT

Nowhere the Mongols touched remained the same after they swept across Eurasia, but the impacts and legacies differed. Though the Mongols never successfully invaded Japan, the attack itself had repercussions. The Mongol attack gave rise to the myth of the kamikaze (divine wind); it promoted a psychology of isolation toward the outside world, and it paved the way for the eventual unification of Japan under the Tokugawa. In China the Mongols defeated the Song (Sung) and established a new dynasty, the Yuan. Ironically, this changed the Mongols more than the Chinese. Kublai Khan became another Chinese emperor. The mandarin bureaucracy remained and Chinese values remained intact. The Mongols were instrumental in reopening the Silk Road and strengthening maritime trade in the South China Sea. This whetted the European appetite for Asian goods, diffused technology necessary for the Atlantic voyages, and gave European mariners crucial practice for long-distance open sea voyages. As a result of the Mongols, the use of Chinese gunpowder was spread, initiating an age of gunpowder empires.

Russia too was overcome by the Mongols, but, unlike China, the attack wiped out the political and social systems of Kievan Russia. The 200-year Tartar yoke gave rise to autocracy because the Mongols left Russian princes with supreme authority in Russian lands. The Russian princes then turned the free peasants into serfs. In the fight to liberate Russia from the Mongols, Christian Orthodoxy under state control created legitimization for divine rule of the Grand Prince of Moscow. In India descendants of the Mongols brought with them the Islamic faith. The militancy with which Islam was introduced into India made Islam unpopular among Hindus despite the efforts of the Delhi Sultanate and Mughal rulers to integrate the two religions. The Mongols did what India had been unable to do except on rare occasions, which was to unite Indian kingdoms politically. The result was that, during the Delhi and Mughal Empires, roads, trade, and building reached new heights stimulated by contact with China and Persia.

In Southwest Asia, the ailing Abbasid Caliphate was still the symbol of unity and authority for the majority of Muslims. In 1258, however, when the Mongols sacked Baghdad, a united single, universal Islamic authority never again reasserted itself. Instead, Egypt, North Africa, and Spain became independent and in the Islamic heartland, militant Turkic tribes asserted their authority over the other parts of the Islamic world. After their defeat at Ain Jalut in 1260 the Mongols withdrew to Persia, leaving a power vacuum in Anatolia. Earlier, Byzantium would have taken advantage of it, but the sack of Constantinople by the Crusaders in 1204 weakened Byzantine power. Into this no-man's land came the Ottoman Turks. The Ottomans failed to march east, however, in some measure because Tamerlane, who claimed descent from Genghiz Khan, defeated and captured the Ottoman sultan, Bayezid, in 1402. After the demise of Tamerlane, a group of Turkic warriors, the Safavids, rose in Persia, creating a militarily and ideologically (Shi'ite Muslim) state hostile to the Ottomans. While the Ottomans inflicted a crushing defeat at Chaldiran in 1514, largely because they possessed big guns, they turned their attention against the Mameluks of Egypt, regaining the holy places of Islam—Mecca, Medina, and Jerusalem—in 1517. This gave the Safavids rule of Persia and cemented for posterity the ethnic, territorial, and ideological split between Arab and Persian, Sunni and Shi'ite Islam. Meanwhile, the Ottomans built a strong state and finally overcame Byzantium in 1453, giving Islam a pathway into Europe. This set off a titanic struggle between Islam and Christianity, stimulating support for the European voyages for trade, conquest, and conversion. By 1500 **Dar al Islam** (the community of Islam) monopolized Eurasian trade.

A Legacy of Leadership

In this titanic struggle between the Islamic world led by the Ottomans and the European Christian coalition, there was a star-studded cast of great personalities of world history. In addition to the Great Suleiman there were

1. **Charles V, Hapsburg** monarch of imperial Spain and the Holy Roman Empire

2. **Francis I**, the Christian king of France

3. **Martin Luther**, the reformer who unintentionally shattered the Christian coalition and diverted Christian resources from the struggle with the Ottomans

4. **Henry VIII** of England, enemy of Catholics

5. **Ivan the Terrible**, who stamped autocracy on succeeding pages of Russian history.

At the same time, around the world other great personalities emerged—Babur, who lay the basis for the Mughal Dynasty, Ismail, who founded the Safavid Dynasty, Hideyoshi, ruler of Japan, and Montezuma and Atahualpa, who led great civilizations in the Americas. That such forceful political personalities could converge at this point in world history, at the doorstep of the Global Age, is only partially explainable, and otherwise as mysterious as the rise of great religious leaders 2000 years earlier. In Eurasia, these great leaders stepped in to fill the vacuum left by the Mongols and with new gunpowder technology were able to dominate large areas.

THE CRUSADES

Origins of the Crusades

Besides the Mongols, other forces were at work that markedly changed the course of events. The Crusades and the Black Plague significantly affected large areas of the world at this time and particularly Europe. The Crusades reshaped Europe, signaling the end of medieval times. The **Battle of Manzikert** in 1071 was the event that initiated the Crusades. Some time prior to this, the Seljuk Turks established leadership of the Muslim world by sacking Baghdad in 1055. Seljuk Turks initiated a remarkably successful partnership between "men of the sword," mainly of Turkic origin, and "men of the law," mainly of Arab and Persian origin. At Manzikert, the Seljuk Turks defeated the Byzantines and drove the Christians out of most of Southwest Asia. Byzantine emperor Alexius I, in despair, sent messengers to **Pope Urban II**, regretting past differences between Constantinople and Rome, and pleading for help to save the empire and to preserve Christianity in the East. Pope Urban II, convinced of the need for reuniting the Roman and Orthodox Churches, hoped to extend his authority over all Christendom and to make Rome once again the capital of the world. He called for a Crusade. In doing so, Urban II demanded revenge against the infidel, "an accursed race wholly alienated from God" who had "depopulated them by pillage and fire." He also promised Crusaders that they would find Jerusalem "a paradise of delights" and would be "assured of the reward of imperishable glory in the kingdom of heaven." The remission of sin for those who crusaded or gave money was known as an "**indulgence**." He also declared a three-year truce among nobles and promised to protect the families and property of Crusaders.

Western Christians flocked to join the movement. Pilgrimages to the Holy Land, which had been made since earliest Christian times, were now in jeopardy. Also, the medieval warrior world was in search of a mission since no new outside barbarian threat had appeared since the tenth century. Trade between northern Italian merchants and the Byzantines was now put in danger as well, so the merchant class lent money to Crusaders. When the warriors died in battle, money lenders acquired their land as repayment. Ordinary people went too, for adventure. Younger sons of nobility joined for a chance to carve out a feudal fief. Kings were anxious to be rid of these troublesome nobles and therefore supported the Crusades. Between 1096 and 1270 many papally approved expeditions made their way to the Holy Land.

The First Crusade

Priests and monks preached the Crusade all over Europe. Forty thousand people responded. Ten thousand of them were peasants like Walter the Penniless and Peter the Hermit who lived off the land as they marched, quarreled among themselves, and destroyed Byzantine Christian property. Most were massacred by the Turks. About 20,000 to 25,000 were knights who successfully moved against Jerusalem, recapturing it in 1099. Emperor Alexius regained control of parts of Anatolia. Crusaders set up states in a strip of land that extended all the way from the upper Tigris River valley to the boundary of Egypt. The **Crusader states** resembled feudal states of Europe, complete with castles and courts. Italian merchants set up trading posts in their ports. A steady stream of pilgrims, soldiers, settlers, and merchants flowed back and forth between Southwest Asia and western Europe. However, there were differences. While Catholicism was the official religion, Orthodox Christians, Jews, and Muslims were ruled tolerantly. Many Europeans adopted customs of the land they conquered, wearing turbans and flowing robes, taking baths, visiting Arab physicians, intermarrying with local women, and teaching the Quran in their schools.

Soon both secular and religious disputes divided the Crusaders, divisions that the Muslims learned to play upon. Led by Bernard of Clairvaux, leader of a branch of the Benedictine monks, the Cistercians, kings like Louis VII of France took up the cross. Distrusting each other, French and Germans traveled separately and both looted Byzantine cities on their way. The Byzantines retaliated by mixing chalk with their flour and rushing the Crusaders, still divided, into the arms of the Turks.

A quarter of a century later, the Turks found an able leader in **Saladin** (1138–1193). He reunited the Muslim world from Egypt to Mesopotamia, surrounding the Crusader states on three sides. He refrained from attacking the Crusader states until a petty Christian lord attacked a caravan in which his sister was traveling. Then, in 1187 he destroyed a Christian army and seized Jerusalem, conquering all of the Crusader states except Tyre. Three of Europe's greatest kings led the Third Crusade to recapture the Holy Land: Frederick Barbarossa, the Holy Roman Emperor, Richard the Lion-Hearted of England, and Philip Augustus of France. They captured the city of Acre in 1191 after a siege of a year and a half. When Frederick Barbarossa was drowned and Philip returned to France, Richard and Saladin carried on a religious war that became part of legend. In 1192 Richard and Saladin signed a truce that left the Crusaders with a foothold in the Holy Land and little else.

Later Crusades

Later Crusades deteriorated into campaigns of greed, gore, glory, and loot. In 1198, Pope Innocent III called the Fourth Crusade. The Crusaders assembled in Venice but lacked the money to pay for their journey. The Venetians persuaded them to attack Zara, their rival on the Adriatic Sea, to pay for the trip, and then convinced the Crusaders to join in an attack on Constantinople. In Easter week of 1204 they tore apart the altar of the Hagia Sophia for its gold and jewels, ransacked the libraries, seized many of the greatest Byzantine art treasures, and ousted the Byzantine ruler. They then established a "Latin Empire of Byzantium," which lasted half a century. In 1261 the native Byzantines recaptured Constantinople and restored Orthodox Christianity. The Fourth Crusade discredited the crusading movement and so intensified the hatred between Catholic and Orthodox Christians that the two groups never again joined to fight the Muslims. The winners were the Muslims and northern Italian cities who gained commercial concessions from the Byzantines. These Crusades left a lasting memory of Christian/Islamic conflict in the Middle East.

More successful from the European Christian point of view were the Crusades against the **Moors** (Muslims) on the Iberian peninsula that had been part of Islam since the Umayyads established themselves as rulers in the eighth century. By 1034 the old Caliphate of Cordoba had broken up into quarreling kingdoms. Taking advantage of this, the Christian knights by 1055 had occupied Toledo and central Spain, but Berber warriors from North Africa came to the aid of their Muslim neighbors. During this struggle, one of the great heroes of Spanish history, immortalized by Cervantes, was "**el Cid**" ("Master") who fought first for his native Castile, then for the Moors, and finally for himself as ruler of Valencia. Gradually, during the twelfth and thirteenth centuries, the effort to oust the Moors was successful. Sargossa, key to eastern Spain, fell in 1118. The king of Portugal conquered Lisbon in 1147, and in 1212 the combined armies of the Christian states drove the Moors from all but the southern coast and city of Granada. Other successful Crusades occurred in northeast Europe where **Teutonic Knights** conquered and controlled lands on the southern coast of the Baltic, now Estonia, Latvia, and Lithuania, and converted the inhabitants to Latin Christendom. A number of other Crusades were called by popes mainly against "**heretics**" (persons who believe other than the official doctrine), but because the Holy War was against fellow Christians, the attempt at creating a political weapon out of the crusading spirit only succeeded in discrediting the Church.

Effects of the Crusades on Europe

While the Crusades failed to accomplish their stated mission against the Muslims, they had dramatic effects nonetheless. One effect was the increasing power of royal authority at the expense of the popes. Papal taxes that were imposed to pay for Crusades were later misused and led to increasing secularization and the Reformation. Royal authority grew because many powerful lords died in the Crusades, because kings used the Crusades as an excuse to impose new taxes, and because the increased cost of living hurt nobles on limited cash incomes, forcing them to sell feudal rights to peasants and towns who wanted to increase their rights. The Crusades revolutionized warfare, introducing Europeans to new weapons like the crossbow and techniques of building fortifications. Merchants and townsmen copied Muslim weavers, gold- and silversmiths, and architecture. Returning Crusaders introduced Arabic numerals, algebra, Greek philosophy, and Arab medicine to Europe.

Trade with the East grew. Silks, spices, and sugar, when first brought back, were upper-class luxuries and later necessities. Even common Europeans were introduced to dates, yogurt, and coffee. Trade in these and other products led to new trade routes and commercial towns all over Europe. A few went eastward to Persia and some all the way to China. The journals of **Marco Polo** and the fictional adventures of Sir John de Mandeville were widely read, stimulating interest in travel and geography. When the Portuguese started down the western coast of Africa, they hoped, among other things, that they were starting a Crusade to attack the western flank of Islam. The date of the fall of the last Crusader stronghold at Acre in 1291 is as good a date as any to mark the beginning of the change in Europe from medieval to modern times.

> **Did You Know?**
>
> The greatness of Venice can be traced directly to the Crusades. The Crusades helped Europeans learn about Asia.

Effects of the Crusades on the Muslims

While in the chronicles compiled by Muslims the Crusades are scarcely mentioned, they had an effect on them, too. The Crusades weakened the Byzantine Empire and thereby empowered the Turks in their impending successful assault against Byzantium in 1453. Bitterness between Christians and Muslims grew while trade between Muslims and Europeans strengthened. Pockets of Christians like the Maronites remained in Southwest Asia, increasing the religious fragmentation of the Middle East. On the whole, however, the "exchange" was largely a one-way process. While Muslims imported weapons and horses from Christian Italy and Byzantium, and beeswax, slaves, and timber from Russia, Muslim people were only marginally affected politically and militarily, and culturally, even less.

THE BLACK PLAGUE

Like the Crusades, the Black Plague (1348–1350), while affecting many parts of Asia, seems to have had an unusual effect on Europe. The plague is thought to have originated in the 1320s in China thereafter sweeping back and forth across Eurasia along land and maritime routes. The Black Plague was really a form of bubonic plague that was spread by deadly parasites carried in the stomach of a flea that was attracted to house rats and to humans. Another form was the pneumonic variety that was spread by coughing and was usually fatal. The best defense was to kill the rats. Instead, people killed dogs and cats, believing they were the source of infection, and the rats multiplied even more. The Black Plague was never known as such during its time, but the name was given, some argue, because "blackness" became a metaphor for the magnitude of the epidemic, one utterly without hope or light. It might also have become known as such because the disease causes black nodules to form on the skin. Still other explanations describe the endless days of funeral processions and black-robed gravediggers. The mortality rate was probably high wherever it struck and there is some evidence of plagues in China at this time, which helped bring down the Ming, and of its presence among the Mongols, decimating their ranks. The plague weakened Mamluk rule in Egypt, but records from Europe are better known and suggest losses of close to 40 to 45 percent there. Rural areas were hit as hard as cities but the rich who could flee to the safety of hills survived somewhat better. Otherwise, death was indiscriminate—merchants, one-third of the College of Cardinals, and three archbishops of Canterbury within a year.

The plague's passage replicates the paths of "international trade." The plague spread faster by sea and river than by land. Thus, London, which exported great quantities of wool to Italian ports, was affected before Paris, and remote inland areas of Europe were not affected until 1350. Its origins are still obscure, but a group of Genoese who returned to the West after the seizure of the fortress at Kaffa in the Crimea reported that Mongol besiegers began to die of a strange disease that gave the victims "black swellings that oozed blood." In desperation, the Mongols hurled the rotting corpses over the city walls by catapult, so when the Genoese survivors escaped from Kaffa, they carried the plague with them. Most died when they reached Sicily. Having traveled remorselessly across Asia, the Black Plague arrived in Europe first at Pisa and Genoa, and then Marseilles. In 1348 it moved north into France and east into Spain and the rest of the continent. Only a handful of places escaped—central Poland, Silesia, and Milan.

The Plague's Effects

What were the effects of the plague in Europe? One was a long period of economic recession as death ate into the labor force for harvesting and production. On the other hand, the shortage of labor pushed wages up and caused many peasants to assert their rights, move to wage labor, and acquire land from dying nobles. The power of the Church declined, not just because many high officials died, but because many of the best priests went out to minister to the sick, only to then meet their own death. People also lost faith in spiritual powers as they observed that the pious died along with the heathen.

The plague crept into literature and art. One of the greatest literary works was the *Decameron* by Giovanni Boccaccio. In it, seven young women and three young men escape the sights and smells of the plague in the hills around Florence. There each day one of the young people tells ten stories. Another literary master, Francesco Petrarch, left 366 love poems to Laura, who died of the plague in 1348, 21 years to the day after he met her. One of the most vivid pictorial images is the

"Dance of Death," a series of 24 sketches in which men and women of all stations of life are shown. Each had recently died and each was forced to dance around the graveyard with moldering corpses. In popular culture, perhaps, there was a children's game, "Ring Around the Rosie," the "rosie" being the place where the flea bit.

Thus, while the Crusades introduced Europeans to the culture, technology, and learning of the East, the Black Plague changed the internal complexion of Europe and other societies. Both signaled the end of medieval times and set the stage for a European awakening that led to the Global Age.

THE DANCE OF DEATH

Pope: I was, while alive, called holy.
         I feared no one.
         Now I am led wretchedly to death:
         in vain do I resist.

Corpse: Lord Pope, pay attention to the piper's tune!
         You have got to hop to it!
         Dispensations do not help
         When Death wishes to dance with you!

         Ring around the rosies
         Pocket full of posies
         Ashes, ashes
         We all fall down.

The legend of the Dance of Death, which came to the fore during the Black Plague, tells of an encounter between three living and three dead men in which the corpses speak. From this legend were drawn a series of 24 pictures in which men and women from all stations in life who had recently died were forced to dance around a graveyard of moldering corpses. The series begins and ends with a caution that life is brief, that death may come at any moment, and that sin is to be avoided. In this reading, even the pope must abide by the Dance of Death. In the posie rhyme, the ring around the rosies describes the red rash that followed the plague victim's jawline, and the posies tell how people put flowers in their pockets to fend off the disease. Ashes to ashes is when they die and fall down.

Expanding Maritime Trade Routes

(ca. 1100 C.E.–1600 C.E.)

TIMELINE	
1120 C.E.–1475 C.E.	Italian maritime trade in the Levant
1200 C.E.–1450 C.E.	Islamic and Indian trade domination of the Indian Ocean
1294 C.E.	Hanseatic League
ca. 1300 C.E.	Flanders Fleet
1368 C.E.–1644 C.E.	Ming Dynasty
1405 C.E.–1433 C.E.	Voyages of Zheng He
1420 C.E.	Beginning of Portuguese voyages

OCEANIC TRADE ROUTES

The increased tempo, breadth, and sophistication of maritime trade paved the way for the Atlantic voyages. Maritime trade gave seamen increasing experience in sailing the open oceans, spawned new technologies necessary for long-distance voyages, and introduced Europeans to the products and cultures of the East. Three trade routes in particular gained status during this time period: those in the Indian Ocean carried on by the Ming and Muslim traders, the Mediterranean and African routes of the Italian and Portuguese traders, and the Nordic routes in Europe.

The Ming

The spread of Chinese civilization south during the Song (Sung) and then encouragement of both overland and sea trade during the Yuan set the stage for the spectacular sea voyages of the Ming. There had been many coups and countercoups as rival claimants for the Chinese throne tried to overthrow Mongol rule. During the 1340s and 1350s, when Europe was convulsed by the Black Plague, China was afflicted by floods, droughts, and epidemics. This touched off uprisings, the most powerful of which was led by Zhu Yuan-chang (Chu Yuan-chang), a southern rebel who in 1368 proclaimed a new dynasty, the **Ming** (1368–1644). After Zhu's death in 1398 his fourth son, **Yongle** (**Yung-lo**, 1405–1433), assumed the throne. He moved the capital back to the former Mongol capital of Beijing (Peking), employed 200,000 workmen, and built the famous "**Forbidden City**" in the center. The city was designed like a series of Chinese boxes, one walled city inside another. At the core was the Imperial Palace, or Forbidden City, surrounded by a red brick wall and moat. Around it was the Imperial City, itself surrounded by a wall 14 miles long. After passing through the Meridian Gate, visitors crossed a river, and went through an imperial gate into the largest courtyard of the palace, where great drama was achieved by the play of roof lines of golden tiles and upswinging eaves decorated with golden dragons that symbolized the power and wisdom of the emperor. Dominating the view was the marble platform and red-columned Hall of Supreme Harmony in which the emperor held audience.

Reinvigorating its strong maritime history stretching back to the eleventh century, China became the greatest maritime power in the world, but the purpose was more political and military than commercial. Yung-lo had two motives in launching expeditions. First, he sent them in search of Chien Wen, a serious contender for the throne, who, it was rumored, had escaped to Southeast Asia. Second, he sent them to explore, expand trade, and provide the imperial court with luxury objects. Led by Muslim admiral **Zheng He** (**Cheng Ho**), the expeditions crossed the Indian Ocean to Ceylon, the Persian coast, and the east coast of Africa. Navigating by compass, the first expedition carried 27,800 men, and involved 62 major ships. The voyages greatly extended the prestige of the Ming in Asia. Trade, however, was in

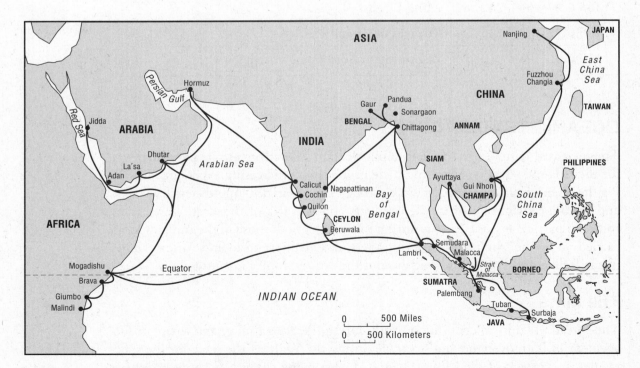

The Voyages of Zheng He (Cheng Ho) 1405–1433. At the same time the Chinese were exploring the South China Sea and the Indian Ocean as far west as Africa, Prince Henry of Portugal was inching down the west coast of Africa. Both set the stage and amassed some of the necessary technological knowledge and experience for the voyages of Columbus.

the form of tribute rather than exchange. Nineteen states, including Java, Sumatra, Malacca, and the west coast of India, participated. Just before Zheng He (Cheng Ho) left on his seventh and final voyage, he carved the following inscription into stone: "The Imperial Ming Dynasty, in unifying seas and continents. . . The countries beyond the horizon at the ends of the earth have all become subjects. . . the barbarians beyond the sea. . . have come. . . bearing precious objects and presents."

THE VOYAGES OF ZHENG HE (CHENG HO)

The country of Ku-li (Calicut) (a city on India's southwest coast) is the great country of the Western Ocean.

In the fifth year of the Yung-lo (period) the court ordered the principal envoy, the grand eunuch Zheng He (Cheng Ho), and others to deliver an imperial mandate to the king of this country and to bestow on him a patent conferring a title of honor, and the grant of a silver seal, (also) to promote all the chiefs and award them hats and girdles of various grades.

So Zheng He (Cheng Ho) went there in command of a large fleet of treasure-ships, and he erected a tablet with a pavilion over it and set up a stone which said "Though the journey from this country to the Central Country is more than a hundred thousand li (one-third of a mile), yet the people are very similar, happy and prosperous, with identical customs. We have here engraved a stone, a perpetual declaration for ten thousand ages."

The king of the country is a Nan-k'un (upper class) man; he is a firm believer in the Buddhist (probably Hindu) religion; (and) he venerates the elephant and the ox.

Under the reign of Ming emperor Yung-lo (1402–1424), six great fleets were sent through the waters of Southeast Asia and the Indian Ocean as far as Arabia under the command of China's most famous admiral, a Muslim eunuch of Mongolian ancestry named Zheng He (1371–1435). These ships were commissioned to accept the "submission" of various "barbarian" rulers and to stimulate Chinese trade as a result of the severing of the Silk Road by Tamerlane. The expeditions were huge. On the first voyage (1405–1407) there were probably 317 vessels, including 62 massive "treasure ships." The expeditions were stopped after Yung-lo because their cost was too high and traditional Chinese contempt for trade and foreigners reasserted itself. China never dominated the Indian Ocean trade and isolationism set in. The record of these voyages was made by Ma Huan (ca. 1380), a Chinese Muslim who joined the expeditions as an Arab translator. The reading illustrates China's view of itself and others.

The voyages led to publication of geographical works such as the *Treatise on the Barbarian Kingdoms on the Western Oceans* (1434), putting China considerably ahead of Portugal, whose seafaring began a half-century later. The expeditions also led to Chinese emigration to Southeast Asia and parts of southern India. The voyages were suddenly terminated in 1435 due to the pressures from Confucian court intellectuals who found the new wealth and knowledge of the merchants a threat, and because the voyages were primarily political rather than economic and became a drain on the treasury. There is no doubt world history would have been different if the Chinese government-sponsored voyages had continued, for the European expeditions making their way down the west coast of Africa were no match for the Chinese in military and merchant organization. After these voyages, financial pressures from supporting an elaborate court style and nomadic incursions on the northern frontier weakened the Ming. Coastal raids attributed to Japanese pirates were common. Vietnam liberated itself from China in 1427, and the mass refusals to pay taxes weakened the Chinese government and army.

Dar al-Islam and Islamic Trade Routes

While the Chinese maritime activity was primarily political, Muslim activity followed commerce. Arab merchants generally sailed in **dhows**, vessels with two or three masts and triangular, or **lateen**, sails, and built in India of teakwood. They were less sturdy than Chinese **junks**, which were large (some able to carry 1500 tons), and used a square sail. The Indian Ocean trade was driven by monsoon wind patterns well described in Arab sea manuals like those of **Ibn Majid** written toward the end of the fifteenth century. He described one complex that circulated between West India, Arabia, and the east coast of Africa, and another that circulated from East India through the Bay of Bengal and the Straits of Malacca and back. Ibn Majid's manual also described in detail sailing directions going down the east coast of Africa, rounding the **Cape of Good Hope**, and sailing up the west coast of Africa

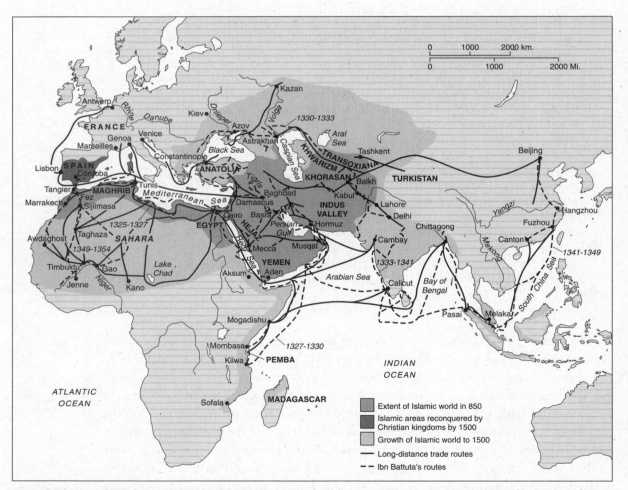

Dar al-Islam and Trade routes, ca. 1500 C.E. By 1500 the Islamic world stretched into West Africa, East Africa, and Southeast Asia. Trade routes connected the Islamic lands and allowed Muslim traders to extend their networks to China, Russia, and Europe.

to the Mediterranean, the reverse of the route Vasco da Gama was later to take. Majid's account does not include any notations of Arabs sailing to China, which they had done earlier. Following the voyages of Zheng He (Cheng Ho), Chinese ports were closed and Chinese fleets had withdrawn from the Persian Gulf, leaving an enormous vacuum for the Portuguese to fill 70 years later.

The web of trade relationships was even larger in the Islamic world as a whole. **Dar al-Islam** ("Abode of Islam") refers to the Islamic world stretching from Morocco to Indonesia that was joined by both a common faith and trade. After the destruction of Abbasid Caliphate in 1258, Arab political power in the Islamic world diminished, but Islam grew rapidly across Africa, through the Indian Ocean, and into the Southeast Asian archipelago. This hemispheric system was built not just on a common faith, but on a shared understanding of the world, common legal systems, networks of scholars and saints, and most of all economic exchange facilitated by these commonalities. Using Arabic advanced shipbuilding and navigation, an increasingly integrated trading system emerged that linked the eastern Mediterranean, Middle East, East African coast, Persia, India, and East and Southeast Asia. Over the sea routes traveled the spices of Indonesia and East Africa, the gold and tin of Malaya, the textiles of India, the gold of southern Africa and the silks, porcelain and tea of China to distant markets. Mechanisms and communication methods to facilitate profitable business expanded.

Arab merchants came to know that Persian saffron fetched a high price in China while Chinese porcelain was in demand in Greece, Greek brocade in India, Indian iron in Syria and Syrian glass in Yemen. Between 1000 C.E. and 1500 C.E. the Straits of Melaka in Southeast Asia and Hormuz at the Persian Gulf were the endpoints of a key maritime trade system.

Indian Traders

The geography of the Indian peninsula naturally divided Indian Ocean trade between west and east India. In the west, a major area of trade grew up on the **Gujarat** peninsula. Horses were especially important because the Indian military used horses but needed to import them from Arabia and Persia where they could be bred and raised. Other items of trade included foodstuffs like grain and sugar, weapons, cotton, silk, and spices. The presence of Gujaratis in East Africa was typical, cotton cloth being a major item of export. By the thirteenth century, expansion in Mediterranean trade fed into Indian Ocean trade, and in 1303–1304, when Gujarat was absorbed into the Delhi Sultanate, trade vitality in the area increased even more to meet the conspicuous consumption of the Delhi elite. Ibn Battuta described **Cambay**, the major port of Gujarat, as "one of the most beautiful cities . . . the majority of its inhabitants are foreign merchants." Further down the west Indian coast was another area of trade centered at **Malaba** and **Calicut**. On the east coast, Indian **Tamil** traders, organized into commercial corporations supported by the **Chola** state, dominated the trade. In this area, wealthy merchants controlled supply by "putting out" raw material into the homes of spinners and weavers. Indian textile technology at this time included the vertical loom, block printing, and the spinning wheel, which was introduced into India from Turkey in the fourteenth century. (It was not introduced into Europe until the sixteenth century.) In the twelfth century the Tamils lost ground as Muslim merchants from the west took over these roles.

Did You Know?

By intermarrying with local women and practicing their faith, Muslim merchants in this trade diaspora grew prosperous and converted others to Islam.

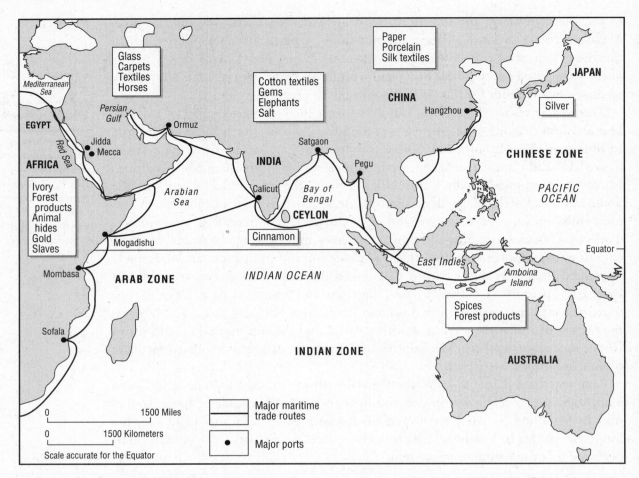

Before the arrival of the Europeans, Indian Ocean trade was extensive and largely in the hands of the Indian and Muslim traders. These traders used the monsoon winds to travel back and forth across the ocean rather than hugging the coastlines. Once the Portuguese appeared, the Muslim traders could no longer compete because the Portuguese mounted guns on their ships.

While the Arabs dominated the Indian Ocean trade, Persian, Indian, Malaysian, and Chinese ships (the latter until the 1430s) all participated, mostly peacefully. Merchants did not depend, as did the Italians, on state armed convoys to guard passage. Ships tended to travel together for mutual assistance due to the limited sailing times of the monsoon winds. This multiethnic, laissez-faire system was unprepared for the armed Portuguese, especially when the Chinese withdrew.

ITALIAN AND PORTUGUESE TRADERS

Feeding into the growing Indian Ocean and South China Sea trade between 1120 and 1475 were the Italian mariners. In 1368, when the overland Silk Road was closed by the Ming, trade swung back to older sea routes. Venice and her rival Genoa developed good relations with the Muslims and, as a result, began to exploit the opportunities of Southwest Asia, or the Levant. They exported to the West caviar from Russia, sugar from east Mediterranean islands, and wine from Greece. The most competitive and callous item of trade that neither the popes nor the Venetian senate could stop was slaves from the shores of the Black Sea. Men were sent to serve in the armies of the sultans of Egypt and girls, especially the blond

Circassians, were sold into domestic servitude and prostitution in both Muslim and Christian cities.

In some measure, growth in Italian trade was the result also of changing conditions in Europe. At first, Italian and Flemish (**Flanders**—where the North Sea meets the English Channel) traders had little contact with each other, for ships were too primitive to brave the Atlantic and robbers and barons subjected overland trade to attack and tolls. In the twelfth century, however, lords in central France established fairs where Flemish and Italian merchants met. The riverine systems that crisscross Europe also helped promote trade as they were easier to navigate than roads. The principal European route began in the **Levant** (the eastern shore of the Mediterranean), where Italian ships took on cargoes of luxury goods from the Islamic-dominated Eastern trade and delivered them to the ports of Venice, Pisa, and Genoa. Here, merchants shipped them either by sea to the harbors of southern France up the river valleys or overland. Early in the fourteenth century the first "**Flanders Fleets**" made the 2500-mile voyage from their home port of Venice around southern Italy and the coast of Spain to the Atlantic ports, carrying cargoes of sugar, wine, spices, and armor in exchange for leather, hides, and primary wool cloth. As in India, merchants near wool-growing regions in England and Germany developed a "putting out" system in which raw wool was put out to workers who made it into cloth for set fees. In the Flanders Fleets were great galleys, sometimes as long as 150 feet, manned by crews of 200 sailors who could transport large amounts of bulky goods relatively inexpensively.

Italian Commercial Cities

A few Italian cities dominated the sea lanes of the Mediterranean and the overland routes to Europe. Milan became a center of silk, wool, and armor. Venice controlled most of the trade with the Mediterranean. Florence was the richest of all because its merchants sailed to all parts of the world. It was home to some 80 banking houses. Venice, as a maritime community overwhelmingly dependent on trade in spices and exotic goods from the East, tried to maintain a neutral policy between Christendom and the Islamic world. For a time, the precarious policy worked but the Turkish advance continued and eventually overwhelmed Venetian trade. Venice's traditional rival with the Orient, Genoa, reacted completely differently to the rise of Ottoman power. Its merchants shifted wealth into opportunities presented by Spain and Portugal. They lent money to kings, ran lucrative monopolies, and, most important, backed voyages of exploration.

Portuguese Voyages

The Portuguese discovery of a sea route from Europe to India began with a Crusade rather than a voyage of exploration. In 1415 the king of Portugal led an army to conquer the Moorish pirate base at Ceuta, just across the Straits of Gibraltar. Among those present at the successful capture was one of the king's sons, **Henry the Navigator**. As the younger son, Henry was excluded from politics and chronically short of money. Nevertheless, within a few years of the capture of Ceuta, seamen in his service began to sail along the Atlantic coast of Africa. To aid in these endeavors, he established a school for navigators in Portugal where the best mapmakers, sailors, and seamen exchanged information about the winds, currents, reefs, and harbors.

The Portuguese discovered the uninhabited Madeira, Azores, and Cape Verde islands ca. 1420. They were soon populated, and brought under cultivation with the help of Genoese capital, becoming profitable producers of sugar. Other islands that were populated required greater effort to claim.

As Henry inched down the African coast, gold and slaves in Guinea promised new wealth. The pace and scale of Portugal's endeavors then increased and by the 1460s Henry's captains had traveled 2000 miles down the West African coast. Now the motive was no longer religious or exploratory but commercial. In 1445 the first great slave auction for Europe to involve West Africans was held at Lagos. In the words of the chronicler Azurara, "Some held their heads low with their faces bathed in tears . . . They parted husbands from wives, fathers from sons, brothers from brothers . . . It was a terrible scene of misery and disorder. . . ." Yet slavery was a universal fact of life in the fifteenth century. There were European slaves in Southwest Asia, Moorish slaves in Europe, and a well-established system in Africa where servitude was the normal punishment for crime.

The profits from this activity were so substantial that the voyages continued even after the death of Prince Henry in 1460. Patronized by the Portuguese government, the explorers discovered the "Gold Coast," "Ivory Coast," and "Slave Coast," whose names reflect their primary products. In 1488 **Bartholomew Dias** rounded the Cape of Good Hope, named because the Portuguese hoped now to find the water route to India. In Europe, the Dias' voyage had finally proved wrong Ptolemy's theory of an extended African continent. In 1490 cartographer Henricus Martellus accurately depicted the sea route, prompting the Portuguese to outfit a new fleet in

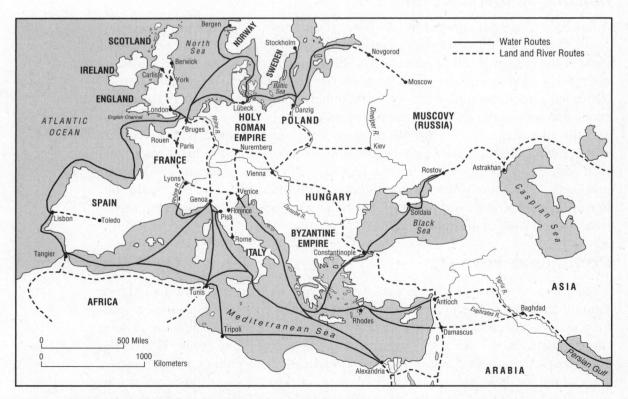

European Trade Routes in the Fifteenth and Sixteenth Centuries. Increasing trade within Europe by land and sea ended medieval times and created the commercial capital and mentality necessary for launching long-distance trade voyages.

1497 commanded by **Vasco da Gama**. He rounded the Cape of Good Hope and then arrived at the port of Mozambique where the crew was amazed at the sight of Muslim dhows loaded with cloves, pepper, coconuts, gold, silver, and pearls.

From Mozambique, da Gama sailed to Mombasa, where the king provided him with experienced Muslim pilots for the trip across the Indian Ocean. In 1498 da Gama and his crew reached Calicut. When he returned to Portugal in 1499, his cargo of pepper and cinnamon was worth 60 times the cost of the voyage. The Portuguese were among the first to use knowledge and experience of Muslim and Chinese sailors to sail the seas and innovations developed by the Venetians to construct stronger hulls. In 1500 they mounted heavy cannons on their ships, giving them a tremendous military advantage by being able to destroy ships at a distance rather than by ramming. The Portuguese understood that the Indian Ocean trade was firmly in control of the Muslims, and so the contest for wealth also became a religious contest to divert wealth into Christian hands. Therefore, in 1500 a fleet of 14 vessels under **Pedro Alvares Cabral**, having accidentally discovered Brazil on the way, entered the Indian Ocean to destroy the Muslim seaborne commerce.

The Portuguese misunderstood much of what they saw along the way, taking, for instance, the Hindus for errant Christians. In the 1480s along the west coast of Africa, they came in contact with a remarkable African people who lived in the forest of central Nigeria, probably descendants of the ancient Nok (500 B.C.E.–200 C.E.), who practiced agriculture, used iron tools, and produced Nok sculpture.

Around 1000 C.E. another group of people, the **Yoruba**, whose major city was **Ile-Ife**, produced some of the greatest achievements of African art in wood and ivory. The Yoruba were organized in a small number of city-states under the authority of regional kings who were considered divine. Much of the art is centered around the kings. A pattern similar to the Yoruba city-states could be found among the Edo people to the east. A large state called **Benin** was formed sometime in the fourteenth century under Ewuare the Great (1440–1473). Benin City was described by early Europeans as a city of great population and broad avenues. The **Oba**, or ruler, lived in a large royal compound surrounded by a sizable entourage. His authority was the theme of the magnificent artistic output in ivory and cast bronze. Soon the bronzes and ivories began to include representations of Portuguese soldiers and themes reflected contact with outsiders.

NORDIC ROUTES

Besides growing maritime activity in the Indian Ocean, around Europe and Africa, the **Nordic** (North European) countries began active trade and exploration. Towns developed, many with circuits of walls to protect against Viking raids. **Lubeck**, on the Baltic, was rebuilt and fortified in 1143 by the local count, who sent messengers to every country inviting anyone desiring land to come and settle. The multitudes of peoples who responded provided the economic base for prosperity of towns of the area.

Wealth was also due to a series of treaties reducing conflict and facilitating access to each others' markets. In time, these alliances grew into the **Hanseatic League** under Lubeck's leadership (1294), linking over 200 towns and cities from London to Novgorod, and from Bergen to Cologne. Hanseatic counting houses held ready stocks of metals, fish, textiles, and Russian furs. Across regular, well-defined trade routes along the Baltic and North Seas, the ships of league cities carried goods that were exchanged for finished products like cloth. Hanseatic merchants established foreign trading centers called "factories." The most famous of these was the London Steelyard, a walled community with warehouses, offices, a church, and residential quarters for company representatives. Their meetings in Flanders joined two huge zones of commercial activity, the Nordic and Mediterranean, which, in turn, fed into the Indian Ocean trade.

Both the Eurasian highway and the maritime trade complexes formed the background for the emergence of the Global Age. The Eurasian highway introduced Europeans to the goods of the East, and the maritime trade complexes gave mariners considerable experience in open sea sailing. Compared to overland travel, sea trade was fast, efficient, and cheap. Unlike the camel caravans, there were few political barriers to surmount, and wind was a cheap if not a free source of fuel. The Portuguese were the first to explore the route to India and East Asia. The unexpected discovery of America by the Spanish introduced Europeans to yet other sources of wealth and prospects for conversion. Had the Americas been poor, it is unlikely this new continent would have transformed the history of the world as it did.

The Americas
(ca. 800 C.E.–1600 C.E.)

TIMELINE	
700 C.E.–1400 C.E.	The Pueblo peoples
800 C.E.–1475 C.E.	Chimu (Peru)
900 C.E.–1168 C.E.	Toltecs (Mexico)
1224 C.E.–1520 C.E.	Aztec Empire
1439 C.E.–1525 C.E.	Inca Empire

THE TOLTECS AND CHIMU

In the Americas, as classical civilizations like the Olmecs (Mexico), Zapotecs (Mexico), Maya (Yucatan), and Chavin (Peru) declined, others rose to take their place and carry on their traditions in a new way. In Mexico, the Toltecs moved into Mexico's central valley and created an empire that lasted from 900–1168. The Toltec Empire appears to have been a loose military alliance involving peoples from the northern desert area. The Toltecs adopted the former cult of the feathered serpent Quetzalcoatl. The Toltecs built their capital city at **Tula** and filled it with rich ceremonial architecture. The city was home to between 30,000 to 60,000 people and became a center for obsidian mining and processing and copper tools. The Toltecs maintained large trade networks that included parts of the southern United States and peoples in the Andes. The empire, which reached into some areas of the classical Maya territory in the Yucatan, collapsed in the twelfth century due to drought, famine, war, and disrupted trade routes. Several centuries of political fragmentation followed.

Beginning in 800 C.E., a powerful **Chimu** state emerged in the old Moche region on the Peruvian coast. By 1200 the Chimu ruling class were descendents of the former Moche and controlled a sizeable empire stretching 600 miles to the south. The capital city, **Chan Chan**, housed a population of about 25,000 to 50,000 and was filled with adobe walled compounds and three story high secluded palaces for the Chimu lords. Deceased leaders had elaborate funerals that included human sacrifice. The Chimu were great builders and constructed hundreds of miles of terraces, vast irrigation projects, and 25-foot-wide roads. The irrigation system captured water from five separate Andean river valleys and channeled it into reservoirs to irrigate fields of maize, beans, cotton, peanuts, and fruits. By the fourteenth century the Chimu were in decline possibly because of overpopulation and climate change from El Nino. By 1475 they were conquered by the Incas.

THE AZTECS

The rise of the Aztecs coincides with the Crusades in Europe, the Mongol movements across Eurasia, and the rise of African kingdoms due to intensified Islamic trans-Saharan trade.

In the several centuries before Columbus, the Americas continued to display significant diversity in cultural systems, but there were significant changes also, particularly in the increasingly extensive organization of agriculture and in the ability to form larger political units. Two of these states dazzled the Europeans on their arrival—the Aztec in Mexico and the Inca in Peru.

The **Aztec** (1224–1520) Empire grew up on the heels of the Toltec state, which collapsed in 1224 when the Chichimec captured Tula. The last of the Chichimec to arrive in central Mexico were the Aztec, who spoke the same Nahuatl language as the Toltec. They absorbed the cultural achievements of predecessors of the area including the Olmec, Maya, Teotihuacan, and Toltec. One of these traditions was the legend of **Quetzalcoatl**. The legend describes a powerful struggle between the Toltec tribal god Tezcatlipoca, who required human sacrifice, and Quetzalcoatl, who gave his people bumper crops and fostered learning and the arts. Tezcatlipoca won the battle, continuing the tradition of human sacrifice, and Quetzalcoatl was driven into exile, promising to return. By a remarkable coincidence, the year Quetzalcoatl had promised to return happened to be the year the Spaniard Hernando Cortes landed in Mexico.

The Aztecs settled on a few swampy islands in Lake Texcoco where they founded the city of **Tenochtitlan** (Mexico City) in 1325. In 1428 they embarked on a policy of territorial expansion. **Moctezuma I** (r. 1440–1469) conquered the area around the central plateau and by the time of **Moctezuma II** (r. 1502–1520) all of central Mexico from the Gulf to the Pacific and south to Guatemala had been conquered.

Thirty-eight subordinate provinces paid tribute to the Aztec state. Aztec strategy was to ally with neighboring states, defeat common enemies, and then turn on their allies. The professional army was maintained by the food produced in the fertile gardens called **chinampas** and by the heavy tribute paid to the Aztecs from all conquered people. The *Codex Mendoza*, one of the few surviving manuscripts concerning pre-Columbian America, contains a copy of the register of tribute paid annually to the Aztec emperors. Meticulously noted were clothes, armor, maize, and even a live eagle. There was another more important form of tribute too, that is, captives who could be sacrificed to the bloodthirsty gods of the tribe. Tens of thousands of victims were sacrificed each year by having their hearts ripped out of their bodies. During certain occasions, like the consecration of the great new temple at Tenochtitlan in 1487, 20,000 men and women were ritually murdered. The rationale for such human destruction can only partially be understood in terms of a pessimistic theology that believed that sacrifices, however numerous, were not enough to avert ultimate destruction. Population pressures as indicated by frequent famines and revolts might also have played a part. Or, ritual human sacrifice could have been an instrument of state terror to crush dissent.

Aztec Society

Early Aztec society lacked sharp social distinctions, but soon it became complex, stratified, and ordered. At the top of the social and political pyramid was the emperor, who ruled by right as well as by inheritance and election. The monarchy passed from the emperor to the ablest son, chosen by a small oligarchy of chief priests, warriors, and state officials. The emperor was chief warrior but also chief benefactor and judge. Records show Aztec emperors were serious public servants. The emperor Moctezuma I distributed 20,000 loads of grain when a flood hit the city. Below the emperor were the temple priests. Aztecs looked to priests for divination, omens, and signs of upcoming events. Because the emperor and wealthy gave generously, the temples possessed enormous wealth. Along with the priests, the upper class was composed of high military officials and governors. The upper class had its origins in the heads of the original clans, or **calpulli**, plus those who rose to the top through service or great deeds. In local affairs the calpulli still regulated social and political life. The great lords lived grandly and luxuriously in palaces and only they could wear jewelry and embroidered cloaks.

Beneath the upper class were the warriors. All freemen could become warriors if they passed through a grueling military training that included capture of prisoners for ritual sacrifice and skill with the use of a **macana**, a paddle-shaped wooden club edged with bits of obsidian. This weapon was so ferocious it could slash the head off a horse in one blow. If a young man failed to become a warrior, he joined the plebeian, or working class. These people performed all sorts of agricultural, military, and domestic services. Unlike nobles, priests, orphans, and slaves, this class paid taxes, but they also had rights and could own land and share in tribute. Beneath the worker class were the landless workers who were bound to the soil like serfs. Slaves were the lowest class, usually prisoners of war or criminals. Female slaves often became concubines. However, unlike European slaves, they could possess goods, save money, buy land and houses, and even have slaves in their service and buy freedom. Much of what is known about Aztec life comes from **Bernardino de Sahagun**, a Spanish missionary priest who in the sixteenth century prepared an extraordinary encyclopedia called *The General History of Things of New Spain*. Among the aspects of Aztec culture he noted was the position of women, who could own and inherit property but were subordinate in political and social life. The technology of the Americas to some extent limited social development. Women in Mesoamerica spent six hours a day grinding corn by hand on stone slabs, or **metates**, whereas in Egypt, grist (grinding) mills were powered by animals and water wheels.

Tenochtitlan

Among the outstanding features of Aztec society were its cities and sophisticated agricultural and trade systems. When the Spanish entered Tenochtitlan in 1519, they could not believe their eyes. This island city, often compared to Venice, was approached by four great highways that connected it with the mainland. Wide, straight streets and canals crisscrossed the city, and boats and canoes plied the canals. Thousands of one-story stucco houses lined the roads and a large sophisticated aqueduct carried pure water from distant springs to parks and marketplaces. Crowning the central square was the great temple of **Huitzilopochtli**, the Aztec war god. Built as a pyramid and approached by three flights of 120 steps each, the 100-foot-high temple dominated the skyline.

THE GENERAL HISTORY OF THINGS OF NEW SPAIN

Montezuma came later. In front of the messengers, the captives were killed—their hearts torn out, their blood sprinkled over the messengers; for they had gone into great danger; they had looked into the very faces of the gods; they had even spoken to them.

After this they reported to Montezuma all the wonder they had seen, and they showed him samples of the food the Spaniards ate.

Montezuma was shocked, terrified by what he heard. He was much puzzled by their food, but what made him almost faint away was the telling of how the great lombard gun, at the Spaniards' command, expelled the shot which thundered as it went off. The noise weakened one, dizzied one. . . .

As to their gear, it was all iron. They were iron. Their head pieces were of iron. . . .

Their animals they rode—they looked like deer—were as high as roof tops.

They were very white. Their eyes were like chalk. . . .

Their dogs were huge. . . .

When Montezuma was told all this, he was terror-struck. He felt faint. His heart failed him.

Most of the Aztec written sources were destroyed by the Spanish when they arrived in Mexico in the early sixteenth century. One surviving manuscript, the Codex Mendoza, which is written in pictographic script, has yet to be translated. As a result, we have few sources for Amerindian culture before the arrival of the Europeans. One exception is The General History of the Things of New Spain *by Bernardino de Sahagun (ca. 1499–1590). A Franciscan missionary who arrived in New Spain in 1529, he possessed a thorough knowledge of the Aztec language and a scientific curiosity. Relying on the tales of the people and narratives of elderly storytellers, as well as observations, he produced a 12-volume ethnographic work on Amerindian society. This remains today the principal source for the study of Mexican culture at the time of the Spanish conquest. In his own day, Sahagun's work was confiscated by royal decree (1578) because it was seen as an effort to preserve native culture and block transformation of society into a Spanish Christian state. It was only rediscovered in the nineteenth century.*

Tlatelolco

Tenochtitlan's sister city was **Tlatelolco**, the site of a market offering a profusion of products as well as order and efficiency. Fixed places in the market sold certain items from gold, silver, and precious stones to feathers, mantles, and embroidered goods, tobacco, cloves, pottery, amatle (bark) paper, and axes of copper, brass, and tin. The variety of goods illustrates the long-distance trade networks that sent the hereditary class of pochteca (merchants) as far north as the pueblos and as far south as Central America. Most trade was barter but cocoa beans and gold dust were sometimes used as currency. Pochteca became wealthy and some of the trade was state supported and had political overtones whereby merchants served as spies, ambassadors, and government agents. The other remarkable aspect of Aztec economic life was its sophisticated agricultural system. Vast quantities of maize, beans, and other food were brought into

Tenochtitlan. In and around the lake the Aztecs developed chinampas, or garden islands. The yield from these was high, as many as four corn crops a year.

The Aztec Empire was in many ways never really integrated, as local rulers often acted as surrogates and tribute collectors. Because of this, the century of Aztec expansion left local areas relatively unchanged. In the long run, this and the system of terror tribute weakened the empire and led to its collapse at the hands of the Spanish.

THE INCA

The Inca Empire existed for less than a century and played only a minor role in Andean history, but it was spectacular in its political and social organization and sophisticated building. Inca was originally the name of a governing family of Amerindian people who settled in the basin of Cuzco. In 1438 **Pachacuti** Inca came to the throne. He and his successors in a period of 40 years extended Inca control for 2000 miles along the Andes, including Lake Titicaca, Peru, Ecuador, much of present-day Chile, and parts of Argentina. Some authorities rank Pachacuti and Topa Inca, his son, with Alexander the Great and Napoleon. By 1532, 16 million people owed allegiance to the Inca ruler. This astounding growth was due to the emperor's rigid control by means of a highly trained bureaucracy, a state religion, a powerful conscripted army, and, most remarkably, an advanced communication network. An elaborate system of roads linked every part of the empire. Professional architects, engineers, and administrators supervised a work force and materials needed to build these paved roads, bridges, and tunnels that linked **Cuzco**, the capital, with the distant fringes of the empire. The reason for the empire seems to be found not just in economic gain, but in religion. The Inca believed that all a ruler's wealth should go to his male descendants to be used to support the cult of the dead Inca's mummy for eternity. Thus, each new emperor had to carve out new lands and tribute to support him in his afterlife.

Whereas the Aztecs controlled people by terror, Inca civilization was consolidated by imperial policies like the imposition of a common language on the various Amerindian cultures of the Andes valley. Pachacuti made **Quechua** the official language of his people and administration, sending colonists to subject regions and forcing them to adopt the language. The Incas also imposed their pantheon of gods—the sun-god, divine ancestor of the royal family, his wife, the moon-god, and the god of rain. The Incas held the sun to be the highest deity and the magnificent Temple of the Sun in Cuzco was the center of the state religion. Within it, all the mummies of past Incas resided. Other magnificent temples are scattered throughout the empire. One of the most beautiful is the citadel at **Machu Picchu**, which clings to a crag on the mountain surrounded by clouds. Priests led prayers and, on special occasions or disaster, human beings were sacrificed. Imperial unity was also achieved by forced participation of local chieftains in the bureaucracy and by transfers of inhabitants to other parts of the empire. Sometimes emperors gave newly acquired lands to victorious generals and distinguished civil servants.

Inca Society

Just as in medieval Europe, Inca peasants worked several days each week on their lord's lands, state lands, or construction projects. The state required everyone to marry and sometimes decided when and to whom. As is common in states where

Did You Know?

The rise of the Inca coincides with the voyages of Zheng He during the Ming Dynasty, Portuguese voyages down the coast of West Africa and into the Indian Ocean, and the rise of the Islamic state of Melaka.

there are high male death rates, polygamy was practiced. One of the outstanding features of Inca society was its socialistic approach to paternalism. Common people were denied choice and were regimented, but the Incas took care of the poor and aged, distributed grain in periods of shortage, and assisted in natural disasters. On the other hand, the security did not mean equality. The nobles were called "Big Ears" because they pierced their ears and distended the lobes with heavy jewelry. Nobles were exempt from agricultural work and other kinds of public service. The

South America and Mesoamerica, 900 C.E. to 1500 C.E. The Mayas and Aztecs in Mesoamerica and the Incas in the Andes forged the most densely populated societies, the most productive farming, and the best organized governments. The Incas built one of the world's largest empires. Other urban societies also flourished in Mexico and South America.

economy of the Inca was essentially based on agriculture, wherein complex irrigation systems permitted the farming of steep hillsides. Llamas were used as beasts of burden and alpacas were raised for their long fine wool.

Inca Culture

Inca cultural achievements include the making of beautiful pottery and cloth, and objects made of gold, silver, and copper. The Inca had no system of writing but they did make use of a system of knotted strings, or **quipu**, which functioned something like an abacus. Inca stone cutting was remarkably accurate. The best buildings were constructed with stones fitted so perfectly that they did not require mortar. Large irrigation projects, agricultural terraces, and systems of roads display a technical ability unsurpassed in the Americas.

The history of the world would have been quite different had the Spanish explorers found nothing in the Americas comparable to the riches of India, or no subjects for conversion, for they would very likely have passed over it and moved on. Instead, they found a brilliant and wealthy culture that rivaled India and the East. And so it was that this newly discovered hemisphere became part of the world system.

THE PUEBLO AND MISSISSIPPIANS

Only a few North American societies formed cultures and built large cities like the Aztecs and Incas. The Pueblo and Mississippians, however, founded impressive towns that spread over large areas. Their rise was earlier than the Inca and their societies were largely dispersed by the time of Columbus. There is evidence that major North American societies 600 C.E. to 1500 C.E. traded with Mexican, Mayan, and Indian communities on both the coasts of North America.

The Pueblo

The **Pueblo** (from the Spanish word for permanent town) faced a challenging environment in the American Southwest. It was too dry to raise maize, but the Pueblo learned how to farm the dry land by selecting the right seeds, building around riverbeds, and constructing man-made reservoirs, terraces, and small dams. Though their agricultural existence was fragile, they mined turquoise, fashioned it into ornaments, and traded it over long distances with societies in Mexico and on the Pacific coast. Due to this economic exchange, the Pueblo incorporated Mexican cultural traditions like the feathered serpent and ball court.

Several distinct cultures emerged within Pueblo society, including the **Hohokum**, **Mogollon**, and **Anasazi** ca. 700 C.E. The Hohokum built large buildings like at **Casa Grande** (presently Arizona). Casa Grande is dominated by a large structure made of thick adobe three stories high atop a platform mound. The surrounding town probably housed 2200 people. The Hohokum also developed masonry technology for house building. About 1300 C.E. both the Hohokum and Mogollon settlements were abandoned due to drought. The Anasazi flourished between 700 C.E. and 1400 C.E. They used huge sandstone blocks to construct masonry homes over large sections of the American Southwest including major centers at **Mesa Verde** and **Chaco Canyon**. Mesa Verde probably housed 2500 people with 30,000 living in surrounding areas. In Chaco, adobe towns sat on the rim of the canyon and contained multistoried houses built around central plazas. The Anasazi are noted for their beautiful ceramic work and kivas, circular pits that were used for religious purposes. An intricate road network connected the Anasazi and Chaco towns. The total Anasazi population probably numbered 100,000 but was dispersed over a large area. Like most Pueblo societies, the Anasazi lived in egalitarian communities and practiced matrilineal kinship and matrilocal residences (husbands moved into the wives' residences). Women owned the homes, crops, and fields, but men dominated the administration of the towns and the council of elders that made the major political decisions. From 1200 C.E. to 1400 C.E. the area sustained a severe drought, though deforestation, soil erosion, disease, and invasions by outsiders might also have played a part in their demise and dispersal ca. 1400 C.E.

The Mississipians

The **Mississipian** culture existed in the vast Mississippi and Ohio River Basins and was contemporary to the Pueblo. A series of these Mississippian mound-building peoples existed for centuries, and based their lives on cultivation and trade. The main

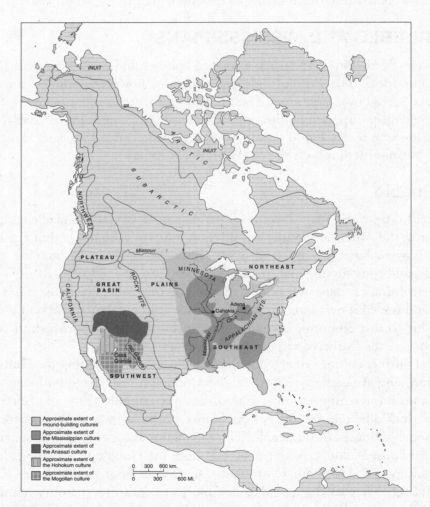

Major North American Societies, 600 C.E. to 1500 C.E. Farming societies were common in North America. The Pueblo peoples such as the Anasazi in the southwestern desert and the Mound Builders in the eastern half of the continent lived in towns. The city of Cahokia was the center of the widespread Mississippian culture and a vast trade network.

Mississippian center, **Cahokia**, was strategically located near the junction of the Mississippi and Missouri Rivers (St. Louis today). At its peak, Cahokia was a city including surrounding areas of about 30,000 to 60,000 people. The downtown covered 200 acres while the surrounding areas of thatched houses covered probably 2000 acres. Cahokia was a major trade entrepot for the midsection of North America. Trade networks reached the Great Lakes, the Gulf of Mexico, and the eastern woodlands. Cahokians made baskets, beads, copper ornaments, wooden utensils, and stone tools. Cahokia reflects Mesoamerican influences like central plazas, platform mounds topped with temples and elite houses, and markets that surround the settlement. Cahokia's priest rulers presided over rituals atop the pyramids and worshipped the sun. Cahokian society was matrilineal and divided into classes. The common people were often called upon to provide sacrificial individuals to accompany the ruler into the voyage to the hereafter when he died. Cahokia culture reached far and wide and spawned smaller versions of itself as at Moundville in Alabama. By the time the Europeans arrived, the culture had collapsed probably due to soil depletion, overpopulation, epidemics (including what seems to be the first appearance of tuberculosis), and class tensions. The last remnants of the Mound Builders were at Natchez in the lower Mississippi Valley, which was wiped out by the French in 1731. After the Europeans arrived, guns and horses changed the lifestyle of the North American populations giving enhanced power to the pastoral plains Indians.

Unit Review

Cross-Regional Developments

In the period 1100–1600 the expanding classical systems were fundamentally overwhelmed and changed by large overarching forces.

- The Mongols destroyed old systems, and in the process ended up creating new and larger states, among them Yuan China, Muscovite Russia, Mughal India, Safavid Persia, and Ottoman Turkey.

- Both by land and sea, Mongols facilitated large Eurasian exchange systems through which goods, technologies, and learning fundamental to the Global Age passed.

- The Eurasian exchange brought gunpowder from Asia to Europe, which transformed the military, destroyed medieval structures, and created "gunpowder empires."

- The Mongols continued the spread of Islam, which particularly affected India.

- Ottoman Turks in Southwest Asia overcame Byzantium, placing pressure on Christian Europe.

- Maritime trade complexes in the Indian Ocean, Atlantic Ocean, and North Sea gained strength, gave mariners experience in long-distance sailing, and illustrated their superiority in terms of speed and cost of sea trade.

- Within the Americas, large and sophisticated states in Mexico and Peru emerged at the same time Europeans began looking for a passage east.

Legacies

Among the legacies of this period are

- the rise of great new empires and states like Tokugawa Japan, Yuan and Ming China, Delhi and Mughal India, Muscovy Russia, Safavid Persia, Ottoman Turkey, Aztec Mexico, and Inca Peru;

- the cementing of the national and religious divisions between Shi'ite Persia and Sunni Ottoman;

- the end of European medievalism by means of the Crusades and the Black Plague;

- increased maritime trade;

- emergence of gunpowder empires;

- the end of the Byzantine Empire and the consequent march of Islam into Europe;

- the rise of great American civilizations—the Aztec and Inca;

- monuments of architecture like the Forbidden City, Taj Mahal, Tenochtitlan, and Machu Picchu.

Quiz

Unscramble:

Arrange the following in chronological order.

Black Plague; End of Ottoman Empire; Mongol Empire; Conquest of the Incas; Conquest of the Aztecs

Matching

1. Kamikaze		A.	Rulers with unlimited power
2. Autocrat		B.	A type of religion that reconciles different beliefs
3. Syncretic		C.	Divine wind
4. Tamil		D.	Ruler of an African city-state
5. Lateen		E.	Ethnic traders living on the southeast coast of India
6. Oba		F.	Triangular sail
7. Quipu		G.	Stone used for grinding corn
8. Metate		H.	Knotted strings for counting

Questions:

1. Which of the following was the original faith of the Mongols?

   (A) Islam
   (B) Shamanism
   (C) Buddhism
   (D) Christianity
   (E) Sufism

2. Which of the following societies continued into the twentieth century?

   (A) Muscovy
   (B) Ottoman Empire
   (C) Delhi Sultanate
   (D) Mughal Empire
   (E) Safavid Persia

3. The Mongol leader of the Yuan Dynasty who was responsible for the unsuccessful attack on Japan was

   (A) Temujin (Genghiz Khan).
   (B) Ogedei.
   (C) Batu Khan.
   (D) Hulagu.
   (E) Kublai Khan.

4. Which leader encouraged a syncretic Indian religion, organized a diwan, and appointed mansabdars to represent the government at the local level?

   (A) Tamerlane
   (B) Akbar
   (C) Babur
   (D) Aurangzeb
   (E) Shah Jahan

5. Of the following, which language emerged as a new language of trade and became the official language of Pakistan?

   (A) Persian
   (B) Arabic
   (C) Hindi
   (D) Turkic
   (E) Urdu

6. Iran developed a separate identity from other Islamic states of Southwest Asia because

   I. the Ottoman Turks who conquered Iran were Shi'ite.
   II. the Safavid leaders claimed to be successors to Ali, cousin and son-in-law of Muhammad.
   III. the ruler of Iran, Shah Abbas, built a strong, independent national army with the assistance of Sir Anthony Sherley.
   IV. the Safavid leaders established a theocracy.

   (A) I, II, and III
   (B) I, II, and IV
   (C) I, III, and IV
   (D) II, III, and IV
   (E) all of the above

7. The Ottoman Turk who conquered Constantinople was

   (A) Shah Abbas.
   (B) Osman.
   (C) Mehmed II.
   (D) Suleiman.
   (E) Saladin.

8. The janissaries served as

   (A) ambassadors.
   (B) managers of landed estates.
   (C) the sultan's closest advisers.
   (D) provincial governors.
   (E) None of these

9. Among the causes that inspired volunteers to participate in the Crusades was

   (A) the arrival of the Seljuk Turks in Baghdad.
   (B) the promise of Pope Urban II to defeat the Moors.
   (C) the promise of indulgences.
   (D) the desire of Richard the Lion-Hearted to capture Jerusalem.
   (E) the hope of reuniting the Roman and Orthodox Churches.

10. Effects of the plague included

    (A) population losses in Europe of 40 to 45 percent.
    (B) decline of the power of the Church.
    (C) increase in wages.
    (D) economic recession.
    (E) all of the above

11. Which of the following choices appears in the correct chronological order?

    (A) Inca, Aztec, Olmec, Maya
    (B) Aztec, Maya, Inca, Olmec
    (C) Maya, Inca, Olmec, Aztec
    (D) Maya, Olmec, Inca, Aztec
    (E) Olmec, Maya, Aztec, Inca

12. The first maritime power to navigate the Indian Ocean in order to extend political and military power, as well as trade in luxury products, was

    (A) Portugal
    (B) Spain
    (C) England
    (D) France
    (E) China

13. Which of the following peoples built Ile-Ife, a city noted for its art in wood and ivory?

    (A) Nok
    (B) Yoruba
    (C) Edo
    (D) Soninke
    (E) Abyssinian

14. What advantages did sea trade offer?

    (A) few political barriers
    (B) wind was a free source of fuel
    (C) shipping was more efficient
    (D) new sources of wealth
    (E) all of the above

15. All of the following cities were Muslim centers of Islamic culture and education in the period from 1200 to 1600 C.E. EXCEPT

    (A) Delhi.
    (B) Timbuktu.
    (C) Cairo.
    (D) Cordoba.
    (E) Kiev.

16. The Portuguese explorer who accidentally discovered Brazil was

    (A) Bartholomew Dias.
    (B) Vasco da Gama.
    (C) Pedro Alvares Cabral.
    (D) Ferdinand Magellan.
    (E) Christopher Columbus.

17. The first Christian capital of the Roman Empire was

    (A) Rome.
    (B) Constantinople.
    (C) Alexandria.
    (D) Jerusalem.
    (E) Milan.

18. Which of the possible consequences of the Mongol invasions was least likely?

    (A) opening of the Eurasian landmass to trade.
    (B) diffusion of technology such as gunpowder to the West.
    (C) creation of new, larger states with armies and central administration.
    (D) five hundred years of peace and prosperity for Mongol-administered lands.
    (E) the spread of the Black Plague along trade routes into Southwest Asia, the Mediterranean Basin, and Europe.

19. Which of the states listed below stopped a Mongol invasion?

    (A) Yuan China.
    (B) Muscovite Russia.
    (C) Mamluk Egypt.
    (D) Safavid Persia.
    (E) Ottoman Turkey.

The Voyages of Zheng He (Cheng Ho)

The country of Ku-li (Calicut) (a city on India's southwest coast) is the great country of the Western Ocean.

In the fifth year of the Yung-lo (period) the court ordered the principal envoy, the grand eunuch Zheng He (Cheng Ho), and others to deliver an imperial mandate to the king of this country and to bestow on him a patent conferring a title of honor, and the grant of a silver seal, (also) to promote all the chiefs and award them hats and girdles of various grades.

So Zheng He (Cheng Ho) went there in command of a large fleet of treasure-ships, and he erected a tablet with a pavilion over it and set up a stone which said "Though the journey from this country to the Central Country is more than a hundred thousand li (one-third of a mile), yet the people are very similar, happy and prosperous, with identical customs. We have here engraved a stone, a perpetual declaration for ten thousand ages."

---

20. According to the Zheng He (Cheng Ho) document above, the Chinese method of recording time was based on

    (A) significant events such as the delivery of an imperial mandate to the king of Calicut.
    (B) recording events within the context of ten thousand ages.
    (C) recording events in accord with the year of the emperor's rule.
    (D) numbering years according to the Buddhist calendar.
    (E) numbering years from the birth of Confucius.

21. According to this document, the purpose of the government-sanctioned voyages to Ku-li (Calicut) was

    (A) to collect tribute from the ruler of Ku-li (Calicut).
    (B) to promote trade and return to China with Indian products.
    (C) to stimulate new economic ties.
    (D) to explore and map the Western Ocean (Indian Ocean).
    (E) to establish ties with the ruler of Ku-li (Calicut) and his court.

22. Cultural change occurs as the result of

    (A) encounter when different peoples came in contact with each other.
    (B) exchange when people interact and learn from each other.
    (C) diffusion when ideas and technologies are spread from one society to another.
    (D) traveling agents like merchants, missionaries, and mariners coming in contact with different peoples as part of their work.
    (E) all of the above.

23. Who united the Inca Empire?

    (A) Montezuma I
    (B) Montezuma II
    (C) Quetzalcoatl
    (D) Bernardeno de Sahagun
    (E) Pachacuti

24. According to the *General History of Things of New Spain*, Montezuma was terror-struck by Spanish

    (A) guns.
    (B) head pieces of iron.
    (C) horses.
    (D) huge dogs.
    (E) all of the above.

25. Which statement regarding Indian Ocean trade is INCORRECT?

    (A) Arab merchants sailed in dhows powered by lateen sails.
    (B) Chinese mariners sailed in great fleets with large ships called junks.
    (C) Major trade areas in India grew up along the west coast at Cambay and Calicut, and on the east coast in the Chola state.
    (D) Portuguese merchants preceded Arab merchants in the development of trade.
    (E) Monsoon winds annually reversed directions allowing winds facilitating open ocean sailing back and forth across the Indian Ocean.

26. Which event precedes the others?

    (A) Portuguese voyages down the west coast of Africa begin.
    (B) Zheng He's (Cheng Ho) Indian ocean voyages commence.
    (C) Safavid Persia is established.
    (D) Charlemagne is crowned emperor of the Holy Roman Empire.
    (E) India is unified under Mughal rule.

Answers

Unscramble:
Mongol Empire; Black Plague; Conquest of the Aztecs; Conquest of the Incas; End of Ottoman Empire

Matching:
1. (C)   5. (F)
2. (A)   6. (D)
3. (B)   7. (H)
4. (E)   8. (G)

Questions:
1. (B)   10. (E)   19. (C)
2. (B)   11. (E)   20. (C)
3. (E)   12. (E)   21. (E)
4. (B)   13. (B)   22. (E)
5. (E)   14. (E)   23. (E)
6. (D)   15. (E)   24. (E)
7. (C)   16. (C)   25. (D)
8. (E)   17. (B)   26. (D)
9. (C)   18. (D)

STUDY TIP
Review, review, review those flash cards. Identify topics that need attention. Reread the topic in its historical context. Add the page numbers to the flash cards in case the historical information related to the topic is needed for further review. Remember: The goal is learning, not memorizing.

Forces That Shaped the Modern World Exchange

(ca. 1000 c.e.–1750 c.e.)

THE MEANING OF MODERN

The word "modern" has been used by historians to define the set of values and cultural characteristics that form the basis of the contemporary world. "Modernity" is usually associated with the culture of western Europe and its diffusion later to other parts of the world. In the twentieth century, concepts and artifacts of modernity were increasingly internationalized, adopted, and adapted by various cultures around the world.

The modern world is characterized by global exchange and by notions of government, society, and culture that differ markedly from those of the classical and post-classical world. The notions include secularism, liberalism, nationalism, and industrialism. All emerged in the period when Europe was transformed and then launched the maritime voyages that finally linked the separate continents of the world.

Secularism refers to the idea that political and social life should pertain to the temporal world and not to religion or to the Church. Secularism emphasizes the importance of science, technology, and progress as defined by the material world rather than the spiritual world. In political systems, secularism denotes the separation of church and state.

Liberalism is generally understood as a political viewpoint that originated in western Europe during the eighteenth and nineteenth centuries. It stresses limited state interference in individual life and representation of people in government, and it urges the importance of constitutional rule and parliaments. Liberty and political (not economic) equality are its hallmarks. When democratic, liberalism means rule by the majority. Classical liberalism often refers to the stress on laissez-faire economics, or noninterference of the state in the economy (almost the opposite of what liberal means today). Liberalism became the philosophical basis for the nation-state structure.

Nationalism is a belief that the political institutions of governance should be based in the "nation." The "nation" is defined as a body of people who are united by territory, language, ethnicity, and choice, rather than by religion, conquest, or dynastic affiliation. Nationalism emphasizes the will of the majority and common people rather than the elite and powerful. Most of the world's population today lives within the political institutional framework of the nation-state.

Industrialism refers to the use of machines rather than human power as the source of production. Attendant to an industrial society are laborers rather than peasants, entrepreneurs rather than landlords, and cities rather than villages and towns. Industrialism implies new means of communication and transportation like steamships, cars, airplanes, telephones, computers, and the Internet. Mostly it promises greater prosperity as a result of increased production and decreased cost of goods. It implies a more powerful state because of a mechanized military. Increasingly, it has also meant pollution and environmental dislocation and damage.

Modernity has been an aspiration for many due to its promise of freedom and prosperity. Its problems, like pollution, megalopolises, and hedonism, have caused many to not just adopt, but adapt the notions of modernity or to particularize it in a way that the old and familiar values can remain alongside the new. Modernity has been rejected by some, altered by others, and is a continually evolving concept. Modernity today probably means cell phones, computers, space exploration, weapons of mass destruction, and global interaction.

The Transformation of Europe

(ca. 1000 C.E.–1750 C.E.)

TIMELINE	
987 C.E.–1428 C.E.	Formation of the French nation-state
1066 C.E.–1300 C.E.	Formation of the English nation-state
1300 C.E.–1500 C.E.	European Renaissance
1337 C.E.–1453 C.E.	Hundred Years' War
1492 C.E.	Unification of Spain
1500 C.E.–1795 C.E.	Age of Absolutism
1517 C.E.	Martin Luther and Protestant Movement
1618 C.E.–1648 C.E.	Thirty Years War
1642 C.E.–1649 C.E.	English Civil War
1701 C.E.–1713 C.E.	War of the Spanish Succession

THE RISE OF THE NATION-STATE

The transformation of Europe from a decentralized, agricultural, and religious state to one ordered by a new culture of nation-states and of secular values acted as a prelude to the Global Age. The transformation seems to have had a powerful effect on the ability and desire of west Europeans to launch the voyages of discovery.

Until this period in history, there had been no such political entity as a nation-state. Up to this point, **states**, defined as sovereign entities, had been based on conquest and control (empires), dynastic heritage and lineage (kingdoms), cultural and religious bonds (tribes, theocracies), or civic cohesion (polis or city-state). **Nations** imply another bond—that of people who share a common language, geography, history, and culture. The strength of the nation-state is that it is a sovereignty of people rather than leadership. **Niccolo Machiavelli** (1469–1527), author of *The Prince*, is recognized as one of the first writers to note this new relationship in which the prince must be cognizant of the people.

> ## MACHIAVELLI'S *THE PRINCE*
>
> . . . One ought to be both feared and loved, but as it is difficult for the two to go together, it is much safer to be feared than loved, if one of the two has to be wanting. For it may be said of men in general that they are ungrateful, voluble, dissemblers, anxious to avoid danger, and covetous of gain; as long as you benefit them, they are entirely yours, they offer you their blood, their goods, their life, and their children as I have before said, when the necessity is remote; but when it approaches, they revolt. And the prince who has relied solely on their words, without making other preparations, is ruined; for the friendship which is gained by purchase and not through grandeur and nobility of spirit is bought but not secured, and at a pinch is not to be expended in your service.
>
> *Niccolo Machiavelli was a diplomat for the republican Florentine government until the Medicis returned to power in Florence and sent him into exile. In his isolation, he reflected on the political problems of Italy.* The Prince *is dedicated to Lorenzo de' Medici, who reflects the primary theme of the book, which is how to acquire and keep power. Machiavelli ransacked classical history and used his own observations to argue that a successful prince must recognize that power, not virtue, is the cardinal principle of princely conduct. The realism of his analysis is often heralded as the beginning of the modern age of politics.*

The nation-state became a unique European political entity growing out of the struggles of kings to diminish the power of the nobility and Church by allying with the power of the people. In putting together a nation-state, all kings did certain things in common: they regularized a common language, claimed a geographically separate territory, passed laws common to all, developed institutions like parliaments where people other than nobility could have a voice, and raised and paid for standing armies through a commercial money economy. Some even used religion as a bond. Many nations became conglomerates, joining and homogenizing different ethnic groups. In some cases, certain ethnic groups remained isolated within the dominant nation as minorities.

Secular Education

At the same time that nation-states began to form in the thirteenth century, secular **universities** appeared. This was in response to the needs of the new bureaucratic states and the increasingly political churches. During medieval times, schools were overwhelmingly connected with churches or monasteries. By the eleventh century, wealthy businessmen in Italian cities like Bologna established municipal schools. By the twelfth century cathedral schools in France and schools in Italy developed into universities. University faculties grouped themselves into schools of law, medicine, arts, and theology. The teachers were known as "**scholastics**" who, in lectures, tried to use faith and reason to arrive at truth. They explored Roman law and Greek and Arabic medical texts. Examinations were oral and difficult. Passage testified to competence in a given subject and was technically a license to teach. One of the most inspirational teachers of the day was **Peter Abelard** (1079–1142) because he did not merely repeat what was orthodox philosophy, but challenged accepted dogma by systematic questioning. **Saint Thomas Aquinas** (1225–1274), meanwhile, devoted his time to collecting and organizing knowledge on all topics. These collections were published as summa, or reference books, the most famous of which was *Summa Theologica*, which dealt with a vast number of theological questions.

Formation of the English Nation-State

England, France, Germany, and Spain provide classic studies of how nation-states were formed, some more successfully than others. English nation-state building began with **William I "Conqueror"** (r. 1066–1087). After he defeated the Saxons in 1066 he set about creating a cohesive state. First, he created a Great Council of lords to help him rule and required that every feudal lord take the **Salisbury Oath** recognizing him as supreme ruler. At the same time, to make sure everyone paid his full taxes, he compiled the *Domesday Book*, a record of taxable property. He also attempted to tame the Church by appointing the Archbishop of Canterbury as the highest ranking church official. In 1166 Henry II brought the courts under royal control when he issued the **Assize of Clarendon**. Among other things, this created a system of grand and petit juries, the processes of indictment, and English law as the **common law** of the land. To maintain control over the Church, Henry II appointed his friend **Thomas à Becket** archbishop. When Becket insisted that the Church be free of temporal control, Henry's knights assassinated him. Institutionalization of **rights** came in 1215 when English king John found himself needing money to pay for wars. Meeting the barons on the field of Runnymede, John received his money in return for signing the **Magna Carta** (Great Charter), wherein he gave basic liberties to the Church, nobles, and city of London, and promised each freeman protection from imprisonment except by "legal judgment of his peers." In addition, taxes could not be imposed except by common council of the kingdom. Besides the principles of laws and rights, the English nation-state established the principle of **parliament**, or lawmaking, in the hands of the people. During the reign of Edward I (r. 1272–1307), an assembly of four powerful groups of the realm was called—bishops, barons, knights, and towns. This served as a model for later parliaments.

The development of a common language and culture also played a part in nation building. For three centuries after the Norman conquest, the ruling classes of England retained their French Norman customs and language while the Anglo-Saxons spoke German dialects. Gradually, however, the two races and languages merged. Some writers like **Geoffrey Chaucer** (ca. 1340–1400) were writing their stories (*Canterbury Tales*) in the **vernacular**, or everyday language. By the sixteenth century, **William Shakespeare** (1564–1616) was writing plays not only in the national language, but with national themes such as stories about English kings.

THE MAGNA CARTA

John, by the grace of God king of England, Lord of Ireland, duke of Normandy and Aquitaine, count of Anjou: to the archbishops, bishops, abbots, earls, barons, justices, foresters, sheriffs, provosts, serving men, and to all his bailiffs and faithful subjects, greeting . . .

1. First of all . . . the English church shall be free and shall have its rights intact and its liberties uninfringed upon . . .

8. No widow shall be forced to marry when she prefers to live without a husband . . .

12. No scutage or aid shall be imposed in our realm unless by the common counsel of our realm. . .

14. And, in order to have the common counsel of the realm in the matter of assessing an aid . . . we shall cause, under seal through our letters, the archbishops, bishops, abbots, earls and greate barons to be summoned for a fixed day—for a term, namely, at least forty days distant,—and for a fixed place. . .

39. No freeman shall be taken, or imprisoned, or disseized, or outlawed, or exiled, or in any way harmed—nor will we go upon or send upon him—save by the lawful judgment of his peers or by the law of the land . . .

. . . Given through our hand, in the plain called Runnimede, between Windsor and Stanes, on the fifteenth day of June, in the seventeenth year of our reign.

King John of England was in disfavor among his lords in 1215 for two reasons: first, he had lost some of England's sovereignty by becoming a vassal to the pope, and second, he had used extreme measures to raise money for his wars in France. The barons objected and made him accept a charter—the Magna Carta—affirming their rights. The document became the basis for limiting power of the monarchs, giving rights to the people, securing due process and the right of representation for those being taxed.

Formation of the French Nation-State

The French, meanwhile, were building their new nation-state. Under the **Capetian** kings (987–1328) in the Ile de France, a well organized centralized government took shape. During the reign of **Louis IX**, a uniform coinage, standard system of law, a **parlement**, or high court of trained lawyers, nobles, and clergymen, developed. A money tax was introduced and a court of commoners so that appeals could be made over the heads of nobles. Having brought the nobility under control, **Philip IV the Fair**, challenged the power of the Church and called the first **Estates General** (the three estates were the clergy, nobility, and commoners from the towns) to strengthen his hand against the pope. The result was the **Babylonian Captivity** (1305–1377), transferring the papacy from Rome to Avignon, France. Before he died, Philip governed most of France and the language of the Ile de France supplanted many local dialects. Then, a vernacular literature in the form of **fabliaux** (little songs about animals) and **chansons de geste**, or heroic tales, became popular, giving Frenchmen a common literary heritage.

The Hundred Years' War

The **Hundred Years' War** (1337–1453) between England and France added the last element to the nation-state building process, for it finally delimited the French and English territory and forced inhabitants to identify themselves as either English or French. Up to this time, many nobles owned parcels of land in both countries. In the first phase of the war (1337–1360), the English won battles both on land and sea, probably due to the use of artillery for the first time. In the second phase of the war, France received most of the French lands lost to the English previously, only to lose them again in the third phase. The final phase of the war (1429–1453) began with a miracle when a French peasant girl, **Joan of Arc**, claimed to hear mysterious voices directing her to lead an army to free France of the English. She led French troops to victory and finally drove the English from most of France. For her pains, she was burned at the stake. By the war's end, the kings with their standing armies, financed by a growing commercial class, had been strengthened at the expense of the nobles. The loyalty of the middle class had been gained, the rights of the popes to appoint bishops and abbots and hear local appeals had been challenged, and the peasants, in some measure because of the Black Plague, had agitated for higher pay and greater freedom.

Failure of the German Nation-State Building

The German effort at nation-state building failed and localism triumphed. The reason, perhaps, lay in the goal of its leader, which was to create a **Holy Roman Empire** rather than a German state. The continued reliance on and ties with the Church, and imperial acquisition rather than state consolidation, caused power to remain in the hands of the local princes in Germany. The close relationship with the Church, however, led to the **Investiture Controversy**. At issue was who had power to appoint bishops and abbots—the Church or state. By the Concordat of Worms (1122) the German emperors surrendered their claim to invest bishops, and the popes gave up their demand to govern religious estates.

When the House of Hapsburg won control of Germany in 1278, the princes were powerful enough to enact the **Golden Bull** (1356), which granted them the right to choose the emperor. After 1438 the head of the Hapsburgs was always elected emperor, but only by promising not to interfere with the sovereignty of 300 independent governments. National feeling led some Germans to want to restore a central government. This, Hapsburg emperor **Maximilian I** (r. 1493–1519) tried to do, but he succeeded not in tying Germany together, but in creating a multinational empire when he added the Netherlands and then, by marriage, Spain to his domain. German emperors from time to time claimed territory in Italy too, especially because of the close relationship with popes.

Failure of the Italian Nation-State Building

Italy was divided into a number of governments. In the north, towns became independent, fighting each other bitterly with hired soldiers, or **condottieri**, and in the south, Italy was divided between the kingdoms of Naples and Sicily. Thus, in Germany and Italy, no nation-states were formed until the nineteenth century because both Church and nobility maintained control.

Formation of the Portuguese and Spanish Nation-States

On the **Iberian peninsula**, the nation-state of Spain took shape. One of the peculiarities of this process was that Catholicism rather than secularism became a cardinal principle of national identity. For centuries the crusading against the Islamic Spanish Moors had failed to unite the Iberian peninsula. Portugal achieved independence under John I (1385–1433), who was elected king by the Parliament, or **Cortes**. In alliance with England, he drove the Spanish and Arabs from his boundaries. During this period, the rest of the Iberian peninsula was divided also among the Christian kingdoms of **Castile** and **Aragon**, and the Moorish state of **Granada**. In 1469 **Ferdinand**, heir to the throne of Aragon, married **Isabella**, heiress to Castile. This paved the way for a single Spanish monarchy. Ferdinand and Isabella reorganized the central government, codified laws, sent royal officials to every part of the country to perform tasks once performed by the nobles, and supported the middle class. They depended on the Church, however, to help drive out the Moors from Spain. Granada fell in 1492. After winning control of Spain, they turned their attentions to sponsoring the voyages to the East.

Nobles and the Church lost power as the king and the moneyed middle class consolidated power in the new nation-state. In exchange for winning the hearts and pocketbooks of the growing commercial class, institutions like Estates Generals and Cortes were established, giving more people a voice in the government. England, France, Portugal, and Spain succeeded in this process while Germany and Italy did not. This had longlasting consequences for the history of Europe.

THE RENAISSANCE

Another aspect of the transformation of Europe besides nation-state building was the transformation in culture from one based in religion to one infused with the scientific and secular spirit. The European Crusaders brought back more than goods from their forays in Southwest Asia. They also became acquainted with the world's scientific and scholarly heritage that had been preserved by Muslim and Byzantine institutions of learning. In 1453, when Byzantium fell to the Ottoman Turks, many Byzantine artists fled to Italy, where they passed on their knowledge of paint, color, and technique to Renaissance painters and artists. The worldliness of the Church and popes who engaged extensively in wars and politics secularized much of the Christian mission. In addition, increased commercialization brought the wealth necessary to finance a flourishing of the arts. Finally, the competitive nature of the Italian city-states ruled by despots, or oligarchs, created an atmosphere conducive to change and innovation.

Did You Know?

The **Renaissance** (fourteenth to sixteenth centuries) was first and foremost a cultural movement that began in Florence, Italy, and then moved into northern Europe where commerce also flourished.

Italian Renaissance Characteristics

The word "renaissance" technically means "rebirth," referring to the rebirth of classical Greek and Roman civilization that had stressed science and secularism. The scientific part of the equation led to experimentation and exploration. The intellectual hallmarks of the Renaissance include individualism, humanism, and secularism. **Individualism** stressed uniqueness, creativity, genius, and personality. Typical of the spirit was Leon Battista Alberti, architect, artist, mathematician, educator, musician, and poet, who remarked, "Men can do all things if they will."

The second hallmark of the Renaissance was **humanism** derived ultimately from the Latin *humanitas* meaning the literary culture needed by anyone who would be considered educated and civilized. It stressed the relearning of antiquity and the classics and copied the classical authors' concern with man's problems and possibilities on this earth rather than remote issues of God. Humanism also stressed the classical interest in science. **Leonardo da Vinci**, who is remembered for his artistic masterpieces the *Mona Lisa* and *The Last Supper*, tinkered with inventions ranging from a flying machine to a water pump.

The third hallmark of the Renaissance was **secularism**. Secularism is a basic concern with the material world instead of with eternal and spiritual considerations. The economic changes and rising prosperity of the Italian cities worked to shift people's thoughts toward money and what it could buy. Church leaders did little to combat this new spirit because they participated in it as well. Pope **Julius II** (r. 1503–1513) patronized artists like **Michelangelo Buonarroti**, who endowed the Church with the Sistine Chapel, the Dome for St. Peter's Basilica, and the "Moses" part of the tomb for Julius II.

Renaissance Art

The artistic output of Rome and Florence is the most distinguishing legacy of the Renaissance. While the subject matter of the early Renaissance was overwhelmingly religious, the techniques were classical, illustrating balance, harmony, and restraint. Painter, sculptor, and architect, Michelangelo Buonarroti's statues of *David, Moses,* and the *Pietà*, and frescoes of scenes from the Bible covering the ceiling of the Sistine Chapel remain monuments to his mastery of the human form.

Artists during the Renaissance were revered as free intellectual workers who, because of their genius, were sometimes considered divine. Increasingly, art symbolized power. Wealthy merchants and oligarchs commissioned artists to glorify themselves and their families in the form of frescoes, religious panels, and tombs. Steadily, the art became more secular in content and realistic in style, reflective of the culture of a small mercantile elite.

The Northern Renaissance

The Renaissance in the north was oriented more toward writing than visual arts, but it also occurred in a milieu of commercial activity around Flanders. The literary emphasis may have been due to European development of movable type by **Johann Gutenberg** around 1450. Paper had been invented by the Chinese in the second century; the Muslims learned the technology in the eighth century and began exporting it to France and England around 1300. Just as the Koreans had done previously, Gutenberg used interchangeable blocks of metal, each with an engraved letter, to form pages of words that could be printed using a printing press. Presses began to appear in Italy and northern Europe. Where a medieval copier could only produce two books a year, the publisher Froben printed 24,000 copies of a book by Erasmus.

The Northern Humanists had a profound faith in the power of the human intellect. According to the **Scholastic** Renaissance philosophy, classical ideals of broadmindedness and stoic patience were joined with Christian virtues of love, faith, and hope. Probably the most famous of the Scholastics was **Desiderius Erasmus**. In his book *In Praise of Folly* (1511), he launched a humorous attack on the problems of the Catholic Church. Another northern humanist, **Thomas More** (1478–1535), explored the idea of an ideal socialistic community in *Utopia* (which literally means "nowhere"). The fine arts in the north were more influenced by medieval traditions, using engraving and religious themes, for example. But they adopted the Italian style of depicting the world realistically and accurately. Painters like Pieter Bruegel, Jan van Eyck, and **Albrecht Dürer**, the "Leonardo of Germany," painted everyday subjects as well as religious subjects with attention to perspective and proportion.

THE REFORMATION

The Renaissance spirit of individualism and reason met head on with growing secularism and corruption in the Church, producing a serious challenge, not just to its power, which had already been under attack by the kings, but to its theology. Christian humanists like Erasmus were already satirizing Church corruption, which took several forms—immorality and illiteracy of priests, pluralism, and absenteeism (clerics holding many benefices and collecting taxes but never visiting the parishes), ostentatious wealth, military involvement of popes, and **indulgences** (payment for the remission of sin). Not unaware of the situation, Pope Julius II called a **Lateran Council** to Rome from 1512 to 1517 to discuss the issues. Before reform could be instituted, **Martin Luther** in 1517 forced the issue when he attached to the door of the Wittenburg church the **Ninety-Five Theses**, or propositions, on indulgences. At the heart of Luther's attack was the question of where authority in Christianity lay—with the church or the individual. Luther argued that salvation could be attained by faith alone, that religious authority resided in the individual conscience, that the church was the entire Christian community, not just the clergy, and that all vocations were of equal merit. **Charles V** of the Holy Roman Empire reacted by declaring Luther an outlaw in the **Edict of Worms**. In 1529 German princes met to "protest," lending the name **Protestant** to a movement that was formally defined in the **Confessions of Augsburg** in 1530.

THE NINETY-FIVE THESES

6. The Pope has no power to remit any guilt, except by declaring and warranting it to have been remitted by God. . .

21. Thus those preachers of indulgences are in error who say that by the indulgences of the Pope a man is freed and saved from all punishment.

28. It is certain that, when the money rattles in the chest, avarice and gain may be increased, but the effect of the intercession of the Church depends on the will of God alone . . .

37. Every true Christian, whether living or dead, has a share in all the benefits of Christ and the Church, given him by God, even without letters of pardon. . .

On October 31, 1517, Martin Luther, an Augustinian monk, as was the medieval custom, pinned on the church door of Wittenburg his 95 principles with regard to the misuse of indulgences. In effect, the theses challenged the pope in matters of faith. Thus began the Protestant Revolt, which split the Christian church, the Christian faith, and the political and social landscape of Europe. It also played a part in the voyages of discovery, the commercial revolution, and the growing spirit of individualism.

The Triumph of Lutheranism

Luther ignited not just religious but political and social unrest as well. Townspeople were attracted because they resented the fact that ecclesiastics were exempt from taxes and civic responsibilities. Peasants were attracted because, in his treatise **On Christian Liberty,** Luther wrote, "A Christian man is the most free lord of all and subject to none." This the peasants interpreted as license to rebel against the local lords, which they did in 1525, even though Luther disassociated himself from it. As Lutheran theology developed, it exalted the state and subordinated the church to the state, positions crucial to the development of nation-states. Charles V's preoccupation with his territories in Flanders, Spain, Italy, and the Americas, and the Muslim seige of Vienna by the Ottoman Turks in 1529 prevented him from taking strong measures against the Protestants. The result was that Germany was torn apart politically. Between 1521 and 1555 the Hapsburg-Valois wars between Germany and France advanced the cause of Protestantism. In this contest the ironic situation occurred where Catholic French kings were supporting Protestant German nobles. Finally, in 1555 Charles V agreed to the **Peace of Augsburg**, accepting the status quo and officially recognizing Lutheranism.

Catholic Counter-Reformation

The Catholic Church soon set about reform and hopes of a Counter-Reformation. Between 1545 and 1563 the **Council of Trent** met to work on reconciliation and reform. Reconciliation became impossible when Lutherans and Calvinists who had been invited insisted that the sole basis for discussion was the Scriptures, but the Council corrected many of the abuses that had previously plagued the Catholic Church. New religious orders played powerful reform roles. The **Society of Jesus**, or Jesuits, founded by **Ignatius of Loyola** (1491–1556), was one of them. Jesuits played a powerful role in converting Asians, Latin American Indians, and others to Catholicism and in spreading Christian education. Another instrument of the Counter-Reformation was the **Inquisition**, which ferreted out heretics and punished them.

Religious Wars

Despite these efforts, religious wars erupted. In most cases they were intertwined with nation-state and colonial rivalries. France was the scene of bitter battles between French Protestants, or **Huguenots**, and Catholics, as well as new rebellions by landed nobles against royal authority. These ended only with the granting of tolerance to Protestants in the **Edict of Nantes** in 1598. In 1618 the **Thirty Years' War** raged in Germany. German Protestants and their allies, such as Lutheran Sweden, were pitted against the Holy Roman Emperor backed by Spain. It was ended by the **Treaty of Westphalia** in 1648, in which princely states and cities chose one religion or another. This treaty reduced Spanish power in favor of France. Religious wars broke out in England, too. These were often intertwined with questions of royal power. During the sixteenth century Elizabeth I and Catholic Mary Queen of Scots quarreled, and in the 1640s civil war broke out, resulting in limited religious toleration in 1688.

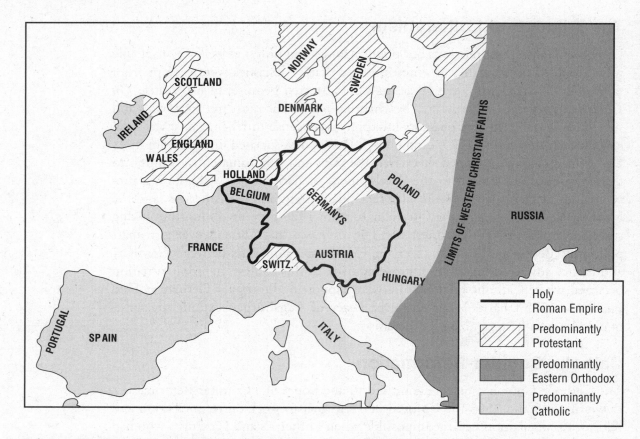

Religious Divisions in Europe 1600 C.E. The Protestant Revolt divided Europe. Germany was most affected by the division, a factor in the inability of Germany to become a nation-state until the late nineteenth century.

The wars promoted growing literacy, concentration on family life, and secularism as people became disillusioned with the power of religion to maintain peace. Martin Luther's anxieties about salvation illustrated that the religious convulsions had one foot in past medieval times. But they also opened the door to the modern secular world. The Renaissance humanist spirit favored individual salvation over church dictate. The political complexion of Europe changed as well. Part of the religious conflict was intertwined, not only with the creation of nation-states, but with commercial rivalries and changes in class structure.

THE COMMERCIAL REVOLUTION—THE CAPITALIST SYSTEM AND MIDDLE-CLASS CULTURE

The **Commercial Revolution** can be compared to the Agricultural Revolution in importance in world history. It affected political, social, and cultural institutions and was the impetus for the Industrial Revolution. Like the Agricultural Revolution, the Commercial Revolution did not occur overnight. Muslim commercial practices such as banking and plantation agriculture were adopted by Europeans, setting the stage for the European commercial revolution. Trade and barter had been a fact of life for as long as there was a surplus. What changed and made it a so-called "revolution" was the amount of people engaged in trade, the distances and range of items that were included in trade, the change in society and culture that took place, particularly the growth of the middle class, and the capitalist system. Aspects of the Commercial Revolution have already been noted in the rise of maritime trade complexes, the nation-state, and the scientific and secular spirit. While only 10 percent of the population engaged in trade in the sixteenth century, merchants exerted influence far beyond their numbers.

The origins of the Commercial Revolution were in the late Middle Ages when there was a great increase in trade in luxury items from the East and staple items like wool in Flanders. Some merchants operated between the countryside and the towns, while others operated on an international scale. For example, merchants might buy raw wool in the sheep-grazing countries of Spain and England. They would then sell it to cloth manufacturers in the Netherlands and Italy in a "**putting out**" or "**domestic**" **system**. In this system, the merchants would distribute or "put out" wool to individual cottage weavers and then collect the finished cloth product to sell in the marketplace. This system greatly undermined the medieval guild system and was a prelude to the factory.

Capitalism

The capitalist system under which commerce was practiced greatly aided its development. Under **capitalism**, ownership of private property gave traders the impetus to take great risks in return for great profits. This profit or "capital" they often reinvested in their own businesses or held in banks to lend to others. Out of this free exchange pattern came a free market where supply and demand regulated price and became a way of reckoning cost and profit. Private ownership, profit or capital reinvestment, and a free market are the hallmarks of the capitalist system.

Reasons for Commercialization

Greater commercialization occurred for three reasons:

1. In the sixteenth century massive imports of gold and silver from Spain's colonies in Latin America both provided specie for an expanding economy and forced prices up. New wealth, in turn, heightened demand. Inflation, in turn, hurt landlords with fixed rent and encouraged merchants to take new risks, for borrowing was cheap when money was losing value.
2. The world population grew 20 percent between 1500 and 1650, causing an increase in demand, production, and exchange in items from cloth and pewter tableware to feather beds.
3. Colonial markets increased trade and stimulated manufacturing.

The hopes for high profits lured many merchants into overseas ventures that were risky due to the cost of outfitting ships, the dangers in the voyage, and the uncertainty of market price. Merchants who were willing to take great risks were called **entrepreneurs**. Entrepreneurs developed new ways of doing business to reduce the financial risks. They developed a system of **insurance** and formed **partnerships** or **joint stock companies**. To protect markets and create monopolies, they formed trading leagues like the Hanseatic League, or in partnership with government were granted regional monopolies as, for instance, the English East India Company, the Dutch East India Company, and so on, which increasingly pushed out Arab and Indian traders in East Asia and the Indian Ocean.

Banking

Aspects of the modern banking system like loans have existed for a long time. The historical record often emphasizes not the merits of a loan but the results of defaulting. In Mesopotamia around 4000 B.C.E., debtors who defaulted on loans of items like food became indentured servants to creditors until the loan was paid off. Creditors in ancient India and Nepal would fast on the debtor's doorway in order to humiliate the debtor until the debt was paid. Around 1000 B.C.E. in some North African tribes, failure to pay a creditor was viewed as a sign of dishonesty that affected the whole tribe in such a way that the debtor was removed from the tribe. Moslem and Christian doctrine looked at loans as sinning if the profits of loans were excessive or harmful. In Europe, loaning money for a price (**usury**) was considered "unchristian." So in European history before the modern era, loaning money for a fee was often the economic activity of the Jewish bankers.

However, as commercial capitalism got under way, loans in the secular world began to take on the notion of "investment" or partial ownership rather than debt. Not only did merchants need to reduce risk, they needed vast amounts of capital. This gave rise to the **modern banking system**. The Muslim inventions of banking, letters of credit, and checks were copied by Italian merchants. At first, banks were private firms. The Medici bank in Florence made loans to both entrepreneurs and monarchs, who were also generally cash poor. **Johann Fugger** founded another influential bank in Germany in the late 1300s. Since monarchs felt no obligation to repay a predecessor's debt, many private banks either went bankrupt or charged exorbitantly high interest rates. States backed public banks like Banco di San Giorgio in Genoa (1584) and the Bank of England (1694). Government revenues from taxes and tariffs as well as deposits by individuals and other countries were the assets of national banks. To increase state wealth, governments began instituting a policy of **mercantilism**. This policy attempted to create a favorable balance of trade by increasing exports over imports by means of tariffs, trade monopolies, and increased foreign trade. European monarchs saw the advantages of increased trade and production, for they could tax the wealth of merchants and of imports. They often used military hardware and overseas empire to create even more wealth.

The Rise of the Middle Class

The rise of the merchant class completely reshaped the culture of the period and laid the basis for the middle class. Dietary habits changed as tastes became more sophisticated. Contact with the Eastern civilizations introduced Europeans to eating with forks and knives and using napkins. Many serfs improved their social position by moving from the countryside. One historian estimates that by 1600 the average Western peasant or artisan owned five times as many "things" as his southeastern European counterpart. Better furnishings prompted people to stay at home. Women became regulators of the domestic social routine. The changes in values and destruction of old ways contributed to the new tensions in the family and the role of women, resentments against the poor by communities unwilling to accept their poverty, and uncertainties about religion. The rich merchants, meanwhile, spent conspicuously and attempted to move into the aristocracy by buying up land and becoming landed gentry. The idea of "upward mobility" began with the Commercial Revolution.

The Commercial Revolution in Holland

A classic study of the Commercial Revolution as it occurred in **Holland** is instructive. By the Peace of Westphalia (1648), the seven northern provinces of the Netherlands (Holland being one and the most important) became independent of Spain. Within each province, an oligarchy of wealthy merchants called "regents" held power and a federal assembly met at The Hague to handle foreign affairs. Holland, because of its navy and wealth, dominated the republic. The merchants and financiers who controlled the government were not aristocratic but middle class, emphasizing the value of thrift, hard work, and moderation. They also divorced the state and religion, welcoming people of all faiths. This, in turn, attracted foreign capital and investment and made Holland a financial clearinghouse. The fishing industry gave Holland its start. Profits from herring stimulated the largest merchant marine, estimated at 16,000 ships, and the lowest shipping rates in Europe. Because all the wood for ships had to be imported, Holland bought whole forests from Norway. They controlled the Baltic grain trade, and, because they dealt in bulk, they could not be undersold. Soon they became known for precision lenses (for the newly invented telescope for muskets) and diamonds. In 1602 a group of regents formed the **Dutch East India Company** as a joint stock company. Within half a century, the Dutch were competing with the Portuguese, seizing the Cape of Good Hope, Ceylon, and Malacca, and giving stockholders a 30 percent annual return on investment. The Dutch West India Company, founded in 1621, traded with Latin America and Africa. Trade and commerce brought tremendous wealth and the highest standard of living in Europe. Wealth, however, also brought war in the 1670s with England and France and the long war of the Spanish Succession.

> **Did You Know?**
>
> Western Europe became the seat of new wealth that completely changed the world economy.

Summary

Views on why the Commercial Revolution occurred in western Europe vary. Some historians believe the rise of the nation-state with the political alliance of king and merchants was the reason. Others find a link between capitalism and Protestantism. The Protestant work ethic and frugality contributed to the accumulation of capital. Still others find the answer in Europe's maritime adventures, which brought spectacular wealth and specie to fund commerce. Yet others see the spirit of the Renaissance, of secularism, science, and adventure as the reason.

ABSOLUTISM

The rise in power of kings as heads of nation-states, the secular spirit, and commercialism gave European heads of state unprecedented power. This was especially so because a money economy combined with taxing abilities gave kings the means to build and maintain large state military and bureaucratic systems. This led to war. In fact, there were only five years of complete peace in Europe during the sixteenth century.

Absolutism means the unlimited power to govern. The absolutist state is one in which sovereignty is embodied in the person of the ruler as exemplified in Louis XIV's statement, "L'etat c'est moi!" (I am the state). Absolutist kings often claimed to rule by "divine right," that is, they were responsible to God alone. They tried to control all important institutions of state including the church, the bureaucracy, and the military, and they often set court style. Instead of being dependent on the nobility and church as medieval kings were, absolutist monarchs freed themselves from this by gaining financial support from the nobility in return for freedom from taxation, by the creation of bureaucracies that, in some countries like France, utilized the middle class and in others an aristocratic elite, and by the right to maintain permanent standing armies. Underpinning absolutist power was the power to raise revenue by forcing taxes higher, devising alternative methods of raising revenue or gaining empire.

Absolutism in Spain and France

Spanish absolutism preceded that of the French and had a more international flavor to it. As with all absolutist states, the Spanish in the sixteenth century developed a permanent bureaucracy, a standing army, and national taxes. Spain also had monarchs whose claims to divine right were connected with Roman Catholicism. They ruled as defenders of the faith. Spanish gold, silver, and armies dominated Europe and much of the world in the sixteenth century. Unlike France, Spanish wealth was based on specie from the New World rather than commerce and the middle class, largely as a result of expulsion of the Jews and Moors. As in France, wars became an artifice of absolutism and empire. **Philip II** believed England under the rule of Elizabeth I was the major factor in his inability to regain control of the Netherlands and restore Catholicism. From behind the walls of the beautiful **Escorial** palace, the Versailles of Spain, he plotted his holy war. Pouring millions of Spanish ducats into a vast fleet, the **Spanish Armada** sailed for England in 1588 only to be decisively defeated by the British. From then on, Spain went into decline.

The best example of an absolute monarchy of this period is France under **Louis XIV**. **Cardinal Richelieu**, as first minister of state, set in place the cornerstone of French absolutism by subordinating all groups and institutions to the monarchy. He leveled castles to crush the nobility, and never called a session of the Estates General. He introduced agents of the central government called **intendants** into the provinces, regulated economic activity, collected taxes, recruited for the army, and put down a Huguenot revolt. The strength of the government, however, was in some measure related to the government's ability to tax, but this was limited by hereditary exemptions of the wealthy and rights of provincial assemblies. Building a magnificent palace at **Versailles** became a symbol of order and the king's power. It is decorated in a style called **baroque** that is characterized by religious emotionalism, drama, and lavish decoration and frescoes.

Under foreign minister **Jean-Baptiste Colbert** (1619–1683), France followed a rigorous mercantilist policy. The state supported new and old industries in order to make France self-sufficient and avoid imports. Colbert also built a formidable merchant marine. The commercial classes prospered from 1660 to 1700 as a result, but the brunt of taxes still fell on the poor French peasants, many of whom emigrated. To unify the state religiously, Louis XIV revoked the Edict of Nantes in 1598, causing many skilled craftsmen to flee.

The Military

As with all absolute monarchies, the military consumed a great amount of time and money. The growing power of the state coincided with great changes in warfare. The crucial development, both for land and sea, was the use of artillery. Cannons became larger and more powerful. Starting with the Portuguese, ships were designed with side-mounted guns that destroyed by gunfire rather than ramming. This technique was used in European naval warfare until the twentieth century. The key to land warfare of the period was the **bastion** with its low walls, vast moats, and outworks, with defensive cannons to protect it from artillery. Blockades became the major offense to counteract this, causing sieges to be the most common form of warfare. During the Spanish struggle to suppress the Dutch revolt, the siege of Haarlem (1572–1573) lasted seven months; that of Ostend, three years. This led to the great "military revolution" of the age—the **field army**. In the early sixteenth century the field army consisted of about 10,000 lancers and archers. From the late sixteenth century, most of the infantry was armed with muskets. In the 1590s, starting with the Dutch, field training and firing drills were developed. Army size grew. The major battles of Louis XIV's war in the 1700s involved as many as 100,000 per army. The cost meant that small countries could only go to war in alliance with large countries.

France led the way in changing the character of warfare. Minister of War Le Tellier created a professional army, employing soldiers rather than nobles, standardizing weapons, and utilizing training, discipline, drill, promotions, and so on. Empowered, Louis XIV prepared for the **War of the Spanish Succession** (1701–1713). Provoked by dynastic and territorial questions, the Dutch and English countered the French acquisition of the Spanish Netherlands and rich trade with Spanish colonies. The wars ended with the **Treaty of Utrecht** in 1713 where balance of power and partition principles prevailed. Louis XIV's grandson Philip remained the first **Bourbon** (French) king of Spain but France surrendered Newfoundland, Nova Scotia, and the Hudson Bay territory to England. England acquired Gibraltar, Minorca, and control of the Spanish African slave trade. The very concentration of French power caused enemies to attack at the periphery and, to some extent, the conflicts of European powers were "world wars" that were fought as much for overseas empire as for territory in Europe. These rivalries, in their way, led to the West's domination of the world.

Russian Absolutism

Peter the Great (r. 1682–1725) of Russia was yet another example of an absolutist monarch. He completely revamped the Russian government, dividing the state into provinces and appointing governors, creating a senate, making the church a state agency, and creating a merit-based, military-civilian bureaucracy in which nobles and non-nobles alike had to work their way up the ranks. Instead of building a palace like Versailles or the Escorial, he built a new city, **St. Petersburg**, from which to rule. He set European styles for Russia, including the cutting of beards. Like other absolutist monarchs, he waged war incessantly from 1700 to 1721 against Sweden in the **Great Northern War**, giving Russia much of Estonia and Latvia. He established a regular service army, infantry, and special forces of Cossacks (frontier horsemen).

Other absolutist states were created in Austria under the **Hapsburgs** and in Prussia under the **Hohenzollerns**. In neither of these states were the nobility and serfdom sufficiently extinguished and the forces of nationalism sufficiently inspired to create absolutist nation-states.

The Failure of Absolutism in England

In England limited monarchical power and constitutionalism (or limitation of government by law) emerged. In 1588 **Elizabeth I** exercised great personal power, manipulating, as her father Henry VIII had done, the House of Commons to pass legislation. But debt during the reign of Elizabeth I, the last of the Tudor royal family, and James I, the first of the Stuart royal family, soon became an issue, as did religion. Many in England wanted to inject middle-class values and ethics into the Church of England and "purify" it (**Puritanism**). When Scotland revolted, Charles I was compelled to call Parliament. The **Long Parliament** as it was called (1640–1660), to his dismay, enacted legislation limiting the power of the monarch. Soon **Civil War** broke out (1642–1649) between Parliament and its supporters, the Roundheads, and the king and his supporters, the Cavaliers. When parliamentary forces prevailed, Charles I was beheaded (1649) and kingship abolished. A **commonwealth**, or republican form of government, was formed. However, **Oliver Cromwell** (1599–1658), who had controlled the parliamentary army, controlled the government. He instituted a Puritan military dictatorship of sorts, which collapsed on his death. In 1660 the Stuart monarchy and Parliament were reestablished, but distrust between king and Parliament grew during the reigns of Charles II and James II. James II suspended the Parliament at will, reviving the absolutism of his father, Charles I. This caused the **Glorious Revolution** (1688–1689), in which, without bloodshed, William and Mary accepted the English throne from Parliament, recognizing Parliament's supremacy once and for all.

The internal transformation of Europe, including the growth of the nation-state, the rise of secularism and science, the Commercial Revolution, and absolutism, produced the spectacular changes that led Europeans to launch the Atlantic voyages and introduced the Global Age. The nation-state was the political framework necessary to launch the voyages, science gave them the means, the Commercial Revolution the reason, and absolutism the military wherewithal to dominate the seas and lands touched by the adventurers.

The World Exchange

(ca. 1450 C.E.–1750 C.E.)

TIMELINE	
1394 C.E.–1500 C.E.	Portuguese exploration of coast of West Africa
1450 C.E.–1650 C.E.	Spanish conquest of Central and South America
1494 C.E.	Treaty of Tordesillas
1500 C.E.–1850 C.E.	Columbian Exchange
1500 C.E.–1800 C.E.	Atlantic Slave Trade
1500 C.E.–1850 C.E.	Russian Exploration and Settlement of Siberia
1540 C.E.–1700 C.E.	Spanish, French, Dutch, English, and Russian colonization of North America
ca. 1571 C.E.–1800 C.E.	Manila Galleon trade

THE VOYAGES OF DISCOVERY AND CONQUEST OF THE AMERICAS

The transformation of Europe and global politics prompted the voyages of discovery. An Atlantic exchange among Africa, America, and Europe soon became worldwide. Nation-states became the vehicle of spectacular voyages west. The discoveries, conversely, enriched the nation-states of Europe and their monarchs, fueling even more competitive adventures and commercial enterprise. The Americas, Africa, and Europe were changed in the process.

Portuguese Exploration

The period from 1450 to 1650, when Europeans discovered, explored, and then migrated to the Americas, launched a Global Age in world history. Much of the sailing and map knowledge of European sailors had come from Chinese and Arab traders engaged in the Indian Ocean trade complex during the preceding centuries, knowledge that was welcomed by an increasingly secular and worldly Europe. Also, the growing power of the Ottoman Turks in the Middle East gradually closed trade routes east prompting Europeans to look for a route down the coast of Africa. In this sailing experience, Europeans gained knowledge of trade that could possibly carry them across the Atlantic Ocean. The Portuguese started the process when, in 1415, they took Ceuta (a Muslim city in northern Morocco) in search of gold, an overseas route to the spice markets of India, the Christian conversion of the Muslims, and a search for **Prester John,** the mythical Christian ruler of Ethiopia. Navigators at **Prince Henry**'s School of Navigation explored the coast of West Africa ca. 1394–1460. Between 1481 and 1495, the Portuguese established trading posts on the Guinea coast where gold from Timbuktu was brought back to Lisbon. In 1487 **Bartholomew Dias** rounded the Cape of Good Hope and between 1497 and 1499, **Vasco da Gama** reached India. He returned with Indian wares, prompting King Manuel to dispatch 13 ships under **Pedro Alvares Cabral** to set up trading posts in India. On April 22, 1500, during the voyage, the coast of South America was sighted and claimed for Portugal. Returning from India, half of Cabral's fleet was lost, but the six spice-laden ships that did return more than paid for the whole expedition. Thereafter, regular expeditions were sent, pitting Muslims against Christians for control of the Indian Ocean trade. From 1509 to 1515 **Alfonso de Albuquerque** destroyed the Muslim coastal forts with cannons at Calicut, Ormuz, Goa, and Malacca, the vital centers that controlled South Asian trade.

Spanish Exploration

Spanish exploration began with the fall of Granada in 1492, signaling the end of Muslim kingdoms in Spain. Then Isabella ordered the Jews to convert or leave the country (200,000 may have left), severely disrupting some aspects of the economy. With religious unification established, Isabella and Ferdinand financed the Genoese merchant **Christopher Columbus**' (1451–1507) project to reach the Indies by going west. On August 3, 1492, Columbus, with three small vessels—the *Santa Maria, Nina,* and *Pinta*—sailed from Palos, Spain, landing in the Bahamas in October. Reconnoitering around Cuba and Haiti, Columbus found some gold and some unfamiliar plants, but no grand Asian civilization with spices, silks, or pearls. Columbus returned to Spain in January 1493, having left a crew in **Hispaniola** (Haiti). Between 1492 and 1502 Columbus made three more voyages, discovering San Salvador, Puerto Rico, Jamaica, Cuba, Trinidad, and Honduras.

Columbus' voyages fueled rivalry between Spain and Portugal. To keep peace between his two Christian nations, the pope negotiated the **Treaty of Tordesillas** in 1494. The Treaty drew a **Line of Demarcation** that ran 1100 miles north and south of the **Azore Islands** in the Atlantic around the globe. This gave Portugal trading rights in India, China, the East Indies and eastern Brazil, and the Spanish in the Americas. The search for precious metals not found in the Caribbean caused Charles V of Spain in 1519 to commission **Ferdinand Magellan** (1480–1521) to find a direct route to Southeast Asia. He found his way around **Cape Horn** to the Pacific, sailing to the **Malay Archipelago**. Though Magellan was killed, the expedition returned to Spain by way of the Indian Ocean and the Atlantic, proving the earth was round and bigger than once thought.

Spanish Conquest

Soon after the initial voyages, the conquest began. Spanish adventurer **Hernando Cortes** (1485–1547) crossed from Hispaniola to Mexico in 1519. With 600 men, 17 horses, and 10 cannons, he subdued the Aztec Empire and took the Aztec emperor **Montezuma** captive. This feat was due to help received by Cortes along the way from disgruntled Aztec subjects, who believed that Cortes might be the fabled **Quetzalcoatl**, who was supposed to return that very year. European disease (against which the Aztecs had no resistance), horses, and superior European weaponry aided the conquest. Between 1531 and 1550 the Spanish gained control of rich silver veins in northern Mexico. The story of Mexican conquest was repeated in Peru. **Francisco Pizarro** (1470–1541), another **conquistador** (explorer, conqueror), crushed the Inca Empire in Peru when he imprisoned and then killed Inca leader **Atahualpa**. As in Mexico, disease greatly aided Spanish conquest. Pizarro opened the richest silver mine in the New World at **Potosi** in the Peruvian highlands. Once the Spanish found bullion in the New World, they lost interest in the spice trade.

Reasons for Discovery and Conquest

Reasons for exploration and conquest vary. Some historians stress technology, noting the Portuguese development of the **caravel**, a light, three-masted sailing ship that, though slower than a galley, could hold more cargo. When fitted with cannons and powered by the wind, it gave Europeans navigational and military superiority. Another reason was spices. Europeans used Asian spices like nutmeg, mace, ginger, cinnamon, and pepper. When the Ming expelled foreigners and the Ottomans captured the eastern Mediterranean trade, Europeans were forced to find a new route to the spice market. Yet another reason for exploration was, no doubt, the Renaissance spirit of curiosity. Government sponsorship and national rivalries also stimulated explorations. Until the likelihood of riches seemed possible, investors had been reluctant to expend the massive sums necessary for the expeditions. Social conditions in Spain and Portugal were also a cause. After the **Reconquista** (reconquest of Spain from the Muslims), young upper-class Spanish found economic and political opportunities limited, as the aristocracy controlled the land and administrative positions. Spanish law forbade noble participation in economic ventures. Ambitious young men sought their fortunes in the New World as a result. Religion also played a part. The desire to convert others was real and of deep conviction. There is no greater testament to this than the 70,000 churches and 20,000 missions

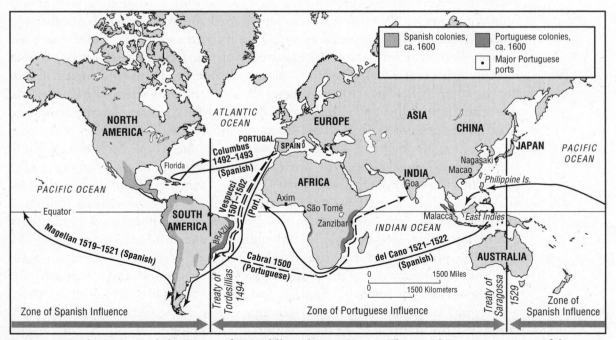

European Explorations and the Treaty of Torsedillas 1492–1529 C.E. The initial European voyages of discovery were led by the Spanish and Portuguese. In the early sixteenth century, the two countries virtually divided the world into two spheres of oceanic influence.

that the Spanish built in the New World. The final reason for exploration and conquest was wealth. As Cortes announced on his conquest of Mexico, "I have come to win gold, not plow the fields like a peasant." Indeed, between 1503 and 1650, 16 million kilograms of silver and 185,000 kilograms of gold from mines at Zacatecas and Guanajuato in Mexico and Potosi in Peru entered Seville's port.

THE COLUMBIAN EXCHANGE

Between 1500 and 1850 perhaps 10 to 15 million Africans and 5 million Europeans crossed the Atlantic. In terms of disease, Amerindians, long isolated, suffered more than the Europeans. Measles and smallpox devastated Indian populations. The Indian population of the Caribbean was almost totally wiped out, and in Mexico there were 25 million Indians in 1519 and 1 million in 1605.

In Peru the population is estimated to have fallen from 1.3 million in 1570 to 600,000 in 1620. Disease went the other way, too, as syphilis seems to have had American and European origins. In terms of animals, the Spanish introduced horses, cattle, sheep, chickens, goats, and pigs. The arrival of horses gave the plains Indians like the Apaches the mobility to hold off the Europeans for 300 years and cattle soon replaced Indians in Mexico. In 1587, 100 head of cattle were abandoned in the Rio de la Plata. So receptive was the American environment to cattle that 20 years later their numbers had swelled to 100,000. Parrots and other exotic animals went to Europe from the Americas. In terms of foodstuffs, Europeans brought wheat, melons, olives, and most important, sugar cane, which became the basis of plantation economies. Subsequently, bananas, coffee, and coconuts were introduced from other parts of the world encountered by Europeans. From the Americas went corn, potatoes, tomatoes, tobacco, and chocolate. The potato became a staple of Russia and Ireland, and manioc (tapioca) and casava spread to tropical regions in Asia and Africa.

Cultural exchange occurred alongside biological exchange. The sixteenth- and seventeenth-century Spanish came to the New World with a religious as well as economic imperative. They had just concluded a religious war against Islam that had lasted 700 years. The conquistadors easily appropriated an attitude of missionary zeal to bring Catholic Christianity to the native peoples, an especially important religious mission as Islam was making gains in eastern Europe and Protestantism was spreading elsewhere. Following the conquistadors came the **missionaries**—the Franciscans, then the Dominicans and other orders like the Mercedarians, Augustinians, and Jesuits. One missionary method for attracting and holding the attention of the people was to appropriate the native power places like the temple locations. Some of Latin America's most impressive Christian churches were built directly on top of such places, like the Cathedral of Mexico City and the Cathedral of Cuzco. The missionaries also used art as a vehicle of information. In their artistic renderings, European artists were both instructed and learned from the native population producing a hybrid form that integrated local and indigenous patterns. For instance, in the Andes, the people found it easy to identify the Virgin Mary of the Christian tradition with *Pachamama*, the earth mother, and numerous paintings, especially the mountain shaped, triangular-skirted Virgin Mary paintings like the "Our Lady of the Victory of Malaga" invite this kind of interpretation. There were other artistic adaptations like the insertion of the native musicians, local flora, and dark-skinned angels. Yet another kind of fused art is reflected in the "**Santeria**" or "Worship of Saints," which blended the African pantheon with the iconography of Catholic saints.

THE EMERGING "ATLANTIC WORLD"—THE AFRICAN DIASPORA AND THE PLANTATION SYSTEM

Spanish Rule in the Americas

The Caribbean experience laid the framework for Spanish economic and political control in the Americas. The Portuguese model of African-European relationships based on forts, trade in gold and slaves, and private investment by royal contract proved unworkable in the Caribbean, where there was no gold. Therefore, more extensive colonization started. The **encomienda** system, or grants of Indians to the Spanish, grew. The Spanish began to build towns according to a grand plan, with

Colonial Empires of the New World 1776 C.E. The Spanish and Portuguese were the major imperial powers in Latin America, while the English and French dominated the North American continent. Both Spain and Portugal created New World administrations based on the concept of viceroyalties, or secondary royal states.

the town hall, major church, and governor's palace in the central plaza. In 1570 Spain issued a basic set of instructions for setting up towns. Administrative institutions were created.

The Spanish king ruled through the **Council of the Indies**, which made policy and appointed governors, or **viceroys**, and oversaw the treasury office and the royal court of appeals, or **audiencia**. Spanish legal tradition transferred, as did the Catholic Church, represented by contingents of missionaries such as the Dominicans, Franciscans, and Jesuits. Holders of ecclesiastical powers were nominated by the Spanish crown. The Catholic Church profoundly influenced the intellectual and cultural life of the Americas. Construction of baroque cathedrals, publication of religious books, and education was dominated by the Catholic clergy, creating an ideological as well as political and cultural framework for society.

Indians continued to die in large numbers because of disease, dislocation, and the rigors of mine work. In 1542, Spanish legislation called the **New Laws** prohibited exploitation and enslavement of Indians. In Mexico the decree was ignored and in Peru there was revolt. This led to a public debate about how the colonies should be run. Bishop **Bartolome de las Casas** argued that Indians were like children who needed protection and care. Others argued they were slaves. Eventually, the government retreated from the New Laws. On ranches, in mines, and on private estates like Cortes' estates, which had 23,000 Indian vassals, forced labor was permitted, although some government agents and missionaries tried to improve local conditions and temper the worst of the abuses. To address the shortage of labor and prevent the growth of a new nobility, the Crown moved to end the encomienda system in the 1540s. Thereafter, colonists and descendants increasingly sought grants of land creating rural estates, or haciendas, that produced agricultural products mostly for the local market.

LAS CASAS AND THE BLACK LEGEND

This infinite multitude of people (the Indians) was . . . without fraud, without subtlety or malice. . . toward the Spaniards whom they serve, patient, meek and peaceful. . .

To these quiet Lambs . . . came the Spaniards like most cruel Tygres, Wolves and Lions, enrag'd with a sharp and tedious hunger; for these forty years past, minding nothing else but the slaughter of these unfortunate wretches, whom with divers kinds of torments neither seen nor heard of before, they have so cruelly and inhumanely butchered, that three millions of people which Hispaniola itself did contain, there are left remaining alive scarce three hundred persons. . .

Bartolome de las Casas took part in the Spanish conquest of Cuba in 1513. He was shocked by the Spanish treatment of the American Indians and argued aggressively with the king of Spain that such treatment was not worthy of a Christian monarch. The Spanish king, Charles V, tried to implement las Casas' ideas, but resistance from Spanish settlers meant they only partly succeeded. The ideas of las Casas, which can be found in his General History of the Indies, *led to the so-called "black legend," which theorized that American Indians had souls and that Amerindian genocide was due to the Spanish killing them. In fact, disease was a greater factor in Amerindian deaths than mass murder, though warfare, enslavement, and work on plantations and in mines made many more vulnerable to foreign illnesses and death.*

The African Diaspora

By the mid 1500s so many Indians had died that an alternative source of labor was necessary. The African slave **diaspora** (dispersion of peoples) began. The Portuguese had engaged in slaving to help pay for their voyages. In 1455 a papal bull recognized the "right" to enslave any non-Christian in the course of exploration. From the 1540s the Spanish Crown began to sell licenses to the Portuguese slave traders so that by the 1650s there were some 40,000 Africans in Mexico and perhaps 30,000 in Peru. In Brazil and the Caribbean, the figures were much higher. In the 1550s the Portuguese began to settle Brazil's coastal plains and cultivate sugar in large amounts. This labor-intensive industry between 1550 and 1800 brought, perhaps, 2.5 million black slaves to Brazil. The picture was repeated in the Caribbean where sugar production brought about two million from Africa. Historians still debate the total number of Africans involved in the Atlantic slave trade. Probably some 25 million to 30 million left Africa, perhaps one-third to a half survived, and probably 9 million to 12 million landed in the Americas, a third of whom were women.

The Plantation System

Based on a single crop like sugar produced by slave labor, Brazil was the first great plantation colony and a model for others. The hierarchy of the plantation became the hierarchy of society, with the white planter family as the aristocracy controlling local social and political life. Below them were the bureaucrats, officials, and merchants often linked to the plantation owner by marriage. At the bottom were slaves distinguished by their color. The scarcity of European women led to a mixing of the three major ethnic groups—Indian, European, and African, and the creation of a multiracial society, one in which distinctions of race and place of birth were crucial. From the three original groups, many combinations of ethnic and racial categories grew—**mestizo** (European-Indian), **mulatto** (African-European), **zambo** (Indian-African), **castizo** (Mestizo-European), etc. The people of mixed origin, called **castas** (a Portuguese word meaning race or lineage. **Caste**, the Western term for a Hindu social class, is derived from castas) were an increasingly large population relegated to secondary status. Over time, even whites were categorized between **peninsulares**, or those born in Spain, and **Creoles**, those born in the New World. Like the old Roman family, women were in a subordinate position as the father had legal authority over children, though women could inherit property. The intermingling of racial groups, cultures, and trade patterns among Africa, the Americas, and Europe created an "Atlantic World."

North America

European settlement soon spread to North America but with less success. The first French settlement in Florida was destroyed in 1565 by the Spanish, who established a settlement at St. Augustine. The first English attempt at **Roanoke** (1587) was abandoned. Sustained colonization began only in the seventeenth century at Santa Fe (1605) by the Spanish, at **Jamestown** (1607) by the English, and on the **St. Lawrence** in Quebec (1608) by the French. Gradually, by supplying tribes with weapons and then aiding allies against the less well-armed people west, the Europeans colonized—the Pilgrim Fathers in Massachusetts, the Puritans in

Massachusetts, Connecticut, and Rhode Island, and the Catholics and Protestants in Maryland. Soon there were one-crop plantations in Virginia, first tobacco and then cotton, and the importation of Africans reached there as well. The movement and mix of peoples, cultures, crops, and bullion between Africa, the New World, and Europe created an Atlantic World and the African diaspora in the Americas.

AFRICA AND THE SLAVE TRADE

Slavery is a very old story in human history. Practically every civilization and society has practiced some form of it. Slave relationships range from legalized human ownership as was practiced in the American colonies to **enserfment** as was practiced in Russia (bondage to land of an estate), **peonage** (servitude because of debt or penal obligation), conquest slavery, indentured servitude, caste, and concubinage. In some societies, it was a state of being that was highly regulated by laws and social norms and in which slaves could win or buy their freedoms, or even move up in the society in which they were enslaved. For instance, in the Ottoman Empire, Christian youths were "enslaved" as "janissaries" but became elite soldiers and bureaucrats within the Islamic Ottoman state. Slavery was sometimes a political situation, and at other times a social position. Prior to 1500, African slavery was closely connected to tribal conflicts in which prisoners of war became slaves. Slavery as we study it, ca. 1500 and beyond, was very much an economic situation and became increasingly encumbered with racial overtones. It is within this context that the Atlantic slave trade existed, notwithstanding the fact that slave emigration out of Africa was not confined to the Atlantic. While mostly male slaves were moving from West Africa to the Americas, mostly female slaves were moving out of East Africa to serve as domestic servants or concubines in the empires of Asia. And within Africa, African kings increasingly saw slavery as a marketable item used to enrich their own states.

The Demand for Slaves

The demand for African slaves arose from two conditions. First, American agricultural enterprise, particularly sugar, required new sources of labor. Second, indigenous American populations lacked the immunities to European diseases and so died out in large numbers, necessitating again a new source of labor. New population might have been drawn from Europe, and it was to some extent. Europeans, however, lacked acquired immunity to tropical diseases like yellow fever and malaria. Newly arrived settlers from Europe died in such numbers that a European population in the Caribbean could be sustained only with a continuous stream of immigration. African populations had some immunity from tropical diseases and were the most desirable possible immigrants, whether slave or free.

Just as the demand for slaves owed something to the shifting ecology of disease in the Atlantic basin, the supply of slaves from Africa owed something to the African environment. African soil is generally poor and variable rainfall means that crop failure and famine can result. When rains failed, people either had to flee or die. Those who fled were easy victims for the slave trade. Some sold themselves or family members in order to survive. Others had to take refuge with alien societies, which they entered as kinless people with no rights. As such, they too were easily passed on into the slave trade. Between 1746 and 1754 Songhay experienced a series of bad harvests, which brought measurable increases in slave exports during a period

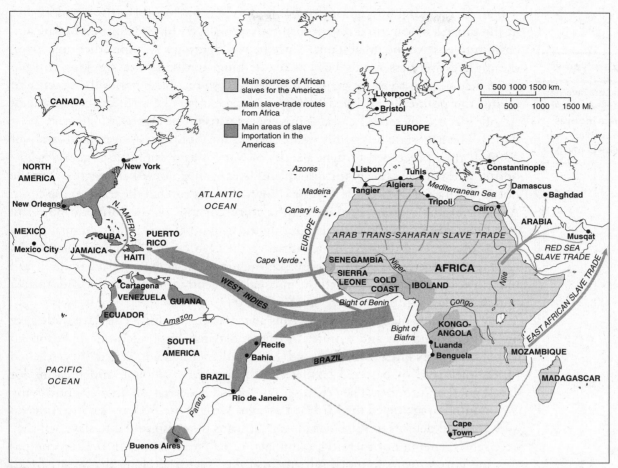

Transatlantic Slave Trade, 1526–1870. The heavily shaded arrows indicate that, during the period 1526–1870, a larger number of Africans were transported across the Atlantic than to North Africa and Western Asia. The majority of slaves in the Atlantic trade came from what is today Angola, Congo, and Nigeria and ended up in Brazil and the West Indies.

that slave exports were generally falling. In the 1790s when a severe famine struck in Angola, slave exports jumped to twice the level of the 1770s.

Economic Considerations

Another underlying economic condition of the development of the slave trade was the low cost of slaves in Africa. Buying a slave from Africa rather than bringing a slave child up from existing populations implied that African slave dealers could sell slaves for less than it cost to bring up a child to working age. The economic situation at the mouth of the Gambia River in the 1680s illustrates part of the underlying condition. At that time, a young male slave ready for shipment sold for an assortment of goods that cost £5.50 in Europe. Five pounds of sterling would have bought 17 trade muskets or 200 liters of brandy or 349 kilograms of wrought iron. £5.50 was roughly the cost of food to support a slave for six years. The slave was bought from African dealers for only £3.40. Thus, it was more profitable for both African and European slave traders to buy slaves rather than support indigenous slave population growth.

If an African king was fighting one of his brothers for control of the kingdom and in the process he captured one of his brother's villages, he was entitled by law and custom to enslave the inhabitants. Since he was fighting a war for other objectives, the captives were essentially costless to the king, but costly for the king to keep since they needed constant guard, to be fed and so on. Thus began the practice of selling the politically enslaved to foreign merchants. The political expansion of Asante was one of several cases of imperial expansion in eighteenth-century West Africa. The new state was firmly established in the Gold Coast hinterland in about 1700. It then proceeded to fight a series of wars of aggression, first against neighboring states of the same ethnic group and later against non-Akan neighbors in the north. With each outbreak of war, new flows of slaves entered the trade to the coast. Another example was the nineteenth-century collapse of the formerly powerful Oyo Empire in southwest Nigeria. During the height of Oyo's power, comparatively few Yoruba entered the slave trade but when the Oyo Empire collapsed, the Yoruba became the largest single ethnic group in the nineteenth-century slave trade. Brazil and Cuba in particular received an unusual concentration of Yoruba and Yoruba culture overlays culture in those areas to this day.

The slave trade made many Europeans and Africans wealthy. The slave trade gave rise to new kingdoms and empires in Africa. Slaving ships sailed out of European ports, such as Nantes in France and Liverpool in England. When they reached Africa, they sold or bartered textiles, beads, iron bars, alcohol, and firearms for slaves, gold, and timber. They then set sail for the Americas on an often horrifying two-month voyage called the **Middle Passage**. Most of the Africans sent to America were enslaved debtors or prisoners of war. Africans were also sold into slavery if they were rebels, enemies of the king, criminals, or refugees. European trading companies and governments founded settlements called **factories** along the West African coast to collect slaves. Europeans did not travel into the interior where they lacked resistance to African diseases. African kingdoms and merchant groups controlled the interior slave trade and used military power, if necessary, to prevent Europeans from interfering in the trade business.

New African States

One of the kingdoms that profited from the slave trade was **Ashanti** located in the Gold Coast (present-day Ghana). Its first great political leader was **Osei Tutu** (d. 1717), who built a powerful army using guns purchased from Europeans. With these weapons he conquered weaker neighbors and sold prisoners into slavery. This "guns-for-slave" exchange was repeated all over Africa. In the 1720s, under king **Agaja** (1708–1740), **Dahomey**, inland from the **Bight of Benin** (present-day Lagos, Benin, and Togo) increasingly turned to this exchange that was controlled by the royal court, whose armies (including a regiment of women) were used to raid for more captives. Over 1.8 million slaves were exported from the Bight of Benin between 1640 and 1890.

Slaves also played a role in the rise of **Songhay**, **Kanem-Borneo**, and **Hausaland** in the Niger region of western and central Sudan, though, as Muslim states, the slave trade was somewhat reduced because the Koran forbade Muslims to enslave fellow Muslims. Under the reign of Muhammed Toure (1492–1528), the expansionist consolidation of Songhay greatly increased the number of slaves on royal lands. Slaves were also sold at the large market in Goa where traders from North Africa bought them for sale in Cairo, Istanbul, Lisbon, and Naples, and for sugar plantations in Sicily and domestic servitude in Portugal and northern Italy.

The slave trade also affected the east coast of Africa. Slaves from the interior along the Zambezi River were shipped to Arabia and Southwest Asia, while on islands like **Mauritius** (in the Indian Ocean) and **Zanzibar**, Swahili, Indian, and Arabian merchants followed the European model and set up plantations producing cloves and other items, using African slave labor. In 1652 the Dutch East India Company established a colony on the Cape of Good Hope. Large farms developed that depended on slave labor from Asia and Africa. The labor needs of the expanding colony led to a series of wars with the San and Hottentot populations who, as a result, were pushed further north and west across the Orange River in 1760 by Dutch (**Boer**) farmers. Around 1800 the Cape colony had 17,000 settlers and 26,000 slaves.

Changes in African Society

The arrival of the Europeans caused basic social changes in West African societies. One was **chattel slavery** (slaves considered as legal property). Slaves were used as craftsmen, sailors, and farm workers, uses unknown until the Europeans came. Another was a new class of **metis**, or mulattos, resulting from intermarriage of Africans and Europeans, primarily French. This class adopted the French language and Catholic religion, and gained economic and political power. The political consequences varied. In the Congo, the perpetual search for slaves undermined the monarchy and destroyed political unity. In Dahomey, however, the slave trade became a royal monopoly, profiting the state. The king of Dahomey, for instance, made a gross income of 250,000 pounds (English) from the export of slaves. A portion of this income was used to improve the living standard of the people. The European introduction of corn, pineapple, cassava, and sweet potato to West Africa improved the African diet to the degree that population increased. The new African societies that arose were often influenced by European culture—French in Senegambia, English in the Gold Coast, and Portuguese in Angola. European influence did not penetrate the interior, despite the export of 12 million slaves—3 percent from 1450 to 1600, 16 percent from 1601 to 1700, 52 percent from 1701 to 1800, and 28 percent from 1801 to 1900. When nineteenth-century European empire builders arrived, the interior of Africa was still a mystery.

Some researchers argue that slavery was good for Africa because it removed excess population that might have died anyway of starvation and famine, and because it brought Africans in contact with Western civilization and particularly with immigration to the Americas. Others trace "African Backwardness" more to the influence of the slave trade than to African isolation. More recently historians have come to other conclusions. One is that the slave trade affected different parts of Africa in different ways. Some small societies were barely affected; others were completely destroyed. Some, like Benin, refused to participate. Another conclusion is that while the slave trade generally lasted about 200 years, from the mid-seventeenth to mid-nineteenth centuries, the slave trade rarely lasted so long in any one region, leaving the possibility of recovery. Historians also note that the number of dead in the act of capture must have been several times the number shipped from the coast, though

Did You Know?

An important debate about the slave trade in Africa centers on the problem of assessing its damage to African societies.

deaths occurred also in enormous numbers in transit. While the slave trade was a terrible human disaster, it is not considered "genocide" as there was no effort to wipe out a race or ethnic group. On the other hand, in the 20 million Africans taken across the Atlantic and the millions of others who died before or on the way between the fifteenth and nineteenth centuries, it can be compared to Stalinist destruction of the peasantry, epidemiological disasters, and other imperial policies across the tapestry of human history.

EUROPEAN TRADE IN INDIA AND EAST ASIA

India

Although the Portuguese were the first Europeans to establish trade with India, Muslim traders continued to transport goods in the Indian Ocean basin. In 1510 the Portuguese established the port of **Goa** on the Arabian Sea. Then, early in the seventeenth century, with a charter signed by Queen Elizabeth, 80 London merchants organized the **British East India Company** to compete with the Portuguese for control of the Indian spice and cotton trade. In 1619 Mughal emperor Jahangir granted the company important commercial concessions at the port of Surat on the west coast. Subsequent British gifts, bribes, and medical supplies enabled the British to set up 27 other trading ports, or "factories," along the coasts. The lynchpins of British trade were at three centers—**Madras**, **Bombay** (acquired by marriage from the Portuguese), and **Calcutta** (present-day Chennai, Mumbai, and Calicut, respectively). The "factories" themselves were walled compounds containing warehouses, residences, gardens, and offices of the British East India Company. The company president had political authority over all residents. The British East India Company sold silver, copper, zinc, lead, and fabrics to the Indians and bought cotton goods, silks, pepper and other spices, sugar, and opium. Substantial profits were made by both Indian and English merchants. Since profit was the main motive of the company, interference in Indian politics and missionary activities was discouraged.

Disorder and violence, which wracked the Indian countryside in the early eighteenth century, forced company officials to man their small trade garrison with native troops, **sepoys**, and to gain some political control in the surrounding areas. Indian political weakness also encouraged the French to form the French East Indian Company in Bengal and elsewhere. Both the French and English employed sepoys. From 1740 to 1763 Britain and France competed around the world to define their respective spheres. India became one of the battlegrounds. The French won many land battles but English seapower decided the contest when French reinforcements were prevented from entering India. In the **Treaty of Paris**, 1763, France recognized British control in India. In this way the British government became involved in Indian politics and under the **India Act** of 1784, the governors were to be picked from outside the company. From then on, the British increased their holdings through puppet Indian princes, sepoys, and an effective British-trained administrator working with the British East India Company.

Commerce and Conversion

Everywhere European traders went, Christian missionaries were soon to go. In India, from the 1540s on, **Francis Xavier** and his Jesuit order converted thousands of low-caste fisherfolk and outcastes through their care of the poor. In the early 1600s Italian Jesuit **Robert di Nobili** tried a new approach by attempting to convert the elite class, a strategy the Jesuits tried elsewhere in Asia but without much success. Most often, it was the lower classes who were converted, as in the Philippines where, after conquistadors had established control, administration was turned over to the friars and priests. In 1582 Jesuit **Matteo Ricci** (1552–1610) settled in Macao (present-day China) on the mouth of the Canton River. Ricci sought first to convert the emperor and elite groups. This he did by presenting Christianity on Chinese terms (emphasizing education) and by presents of Western technology like clocks and astronomical equipment. But the Chinese ultimately rejected Christianity because it ran counter to Chinese traditions of ancestor worship and public order (Jesus was executed as a criminal). The Chinese story of merchant and missionary was repeated in Japan.

In 1542 Portuguese traders arrived in Japan. The Dutch and English quickly followed suit. In 1547 Francis Xavier landed in Japan and won many converts. The Japanese feared a repeat of the wholesale conversion and control of the Philippines, and so, in 1635, the Japanese expelled the Spanish and Portuguese. The shogun Tokugawa Ieyasu suppressed a revolt by Christian peasants known as the **Shimabara Rebellion** in 1637–1638. Thereafter, the Japanese banned all Western books on science and religion and limited contact with Europeans to one Dutch ship a year.

MATTEO RICCI

The Chinese are the most industrious people, and most of the mechanical arts flourish among them. They have all sorts of raw material and they are endowed by nature with a talent for trading, both of which are potent factors in bringing about a high development of the mechanical arts… Their skill in the manufacture of fireworks is really extraordinary and there is scarcely anything which they cannot cleverly imitate with them…. Their method of making printing books is quite ingenious…. The simplicity of Chinese printing is what accounts for the exceedingly large number of books in circulation here and the ridiculously low prices at which they are sold. Such facts as these would scarcely be believed by anyone who has not witnessed them.

Matteo Ricci was the first Jesuit to enter China (1582). The document illustrates the continuing admiration Westerners had for the Chinese, who seemed more advanced in every way. Though Gutenberg had already invented moveable type, to Ricci China was still far ahead of the West. To win over and convert the Chinese, Ricci developed a phenomenal memory, a talent the Chinese admired because it helped them pass the civil service examination. Ricci also brought Western trinkets and mechanical devices like watches, which intrigued the Chinese. His efforts at conversion were negligible, largely because the pope refused to permit a softening of Catholic doctrine or the acceptance of Confucian rites. Ricci is a reflection of his times both as a Jesuit of the Catholic Reformation spirit, and as a Western traveler to East Asia.

China

After Ming cessation of the long-distance Indian Ocean voyages, trade did not cease in China. The Ming merchant marine transported products to the Philippines and brought back sweet potatoes, tobacco, firearms, and silver from the Spanish fleet at Manila. The Dutch meanwhile transported tea in boatloads to the Europeans. Southern China enjoyed considerable prosperity in the late sixteenth and early seventeenth centuries because Japanese, Portuguese, and Dutch merchants paid in silver for Chinese silks and ceramics. The steady flow of specie into China devalued Chinese paper currency and the Ming emperor had to recognize the triumph of silver as a medium of exchange. The blue and white porcelain so typical of the Ming was imitated by Muslim craftsmen in Baghdad and Isfahan, and soon copied by Westerners, such as the Wedgwoods in England. The word "china," meaning porcelain, entered the English language in 1579.

As in Europe, Chinese merchants began to invest large amounts of capital in commercial and craft industries like silk making, cotton weaving, porcelain manufacture, printing, and steel production. As a result, there were great technological advances from looms to new machines for working the soil, sowing seed, and irrigation. The population increased from 70 million in 1368 to 130 million in 1600, making China the world's most populated country. This and other problems, like ostentatious living by the imperial court, a large, expensive army to protect against the **Manchus** in the north (Manchuria), a recalcitrant bureaucracy, and famine, brought down the Ming dynasty in 1644. The Manchus invaded from the north and established a new dynasty, the **Qing**. The Qing purged the old bureaucracy and replaced it with new officials. In its heyday in the eighteenth century, the empire covered much of Asia—China Proper, Manchuria, Mongolia, Tibet, and Sinking—with tribute trade from Myanmar (Burma), Nepal, Laos, Siam, Annam, and Korea. Imperial factories produced porcelain masterpieces that were shipped worldwide.

THE MANILA GALLEONS

European overseas exploration and conquest stimulated the formation of successive commercial empires—the Portuguese, Spanish, Dutch, and English. The Spanish dominated in the Americas, the Portuguese, Dutch, and English in Asia. The **Manila galleons** tied the whole system together.

Portuguese Trade

In the sixteenth century the Portuguese were the predominant sea power, establishing control over Asian and then world commerce. From Africa to Lisbon went gold and ivory, and from India to Lisbon went textiles that were exchanged for Asian spices.

Dutch Trade

In the latter half of the seventeenth century, the Dutch replaced the Portuguese. In 1599 a Dutch fleet returned to Holland with spices and a 100 percent profit return, prompting the establishment of the Dutch East India Company in 1602. Its stated aim was to wrest the spice trade from the Portuguese. By sailing directly to Indonesia, thereby avoiding India, and by helping local princes against the Portuguese, the Dutch won rich commercial concessions and, ultimately, control of the Indonesian archipelago. Trading armor, firearms, and linens, the Dutch gained a monopoly over the spice trade. Dutch profits whetted the appetite of the English, who went on to establish the British East India Company and dominate trade in India.

The Galleons

The Spanish, meanwhile, took the **Philippines**, and, with their **galleons** (trade warships with three or four decks at the stern and one or more at the bow), created a world exchange. Galleons were a synthesis of Europe and the Orient. Designed in Spain, they were built in the Philippines of durable tropical wood cut by laborers on outlying islands. Anchor lines and rigging were of Manila hemp and ship hardware, such as fasteners, handles, and metal plating, were forged by Spanish, Chinese, or Malay smiths. The galleons carried Spanish terra cotta and Chinese porcelain. Magellan had made contact with the Philippines on his voyage, and in 1565 a fleet sent from America under **Miguel Lopez de Legazpi** claimed the islands already occupied by Chinese traders for Philip II of Spain, hence the name "Philippines." In 1572, the Spanish claimed Manila, with the best natural harbor in Asia. The city grew to 80,000 in 1640.

The galleon system evolved out of the need to protect Spanish ships sailing for Spain full of precious metals. To discourage pirates and foreign ships, the Spanish developed a convoy system. Spanish galleons crossed the Pacific from Acapulco to Manila loaded with American silver. Galleons returned to Acapulco loaded with Chinese silks, porcelain, and lacquer. These were then transshipped on the convoy to Spain along with American silver. From Spain, ships went to India, Malaya, and China, where they were loaded with Eastern treasure. In Manila, the world entrepôt, Eastern goods met American silver. The trips in overloaded galleons often became epics of suffering and endurance that took as long as a year to complete. On more than 40 occasions between 1565 and 1815 ships did not arrive, either wrecked or lost at sea.

Transfer Specie

This trade and American precious metals should have made Spain rich. Instead, as Sancho de Moncada wrote in 1619, "The poverty of Spain resulted from the discovery of the Indies." Between 1500 and 1650, 181 tons of gold and 17,000 tons of silver went to Europe. Some stayed in the Americas to build and decorate an estimated 70,000 churches and 20,000 missions. Other bullion paid for Spanish debt and wars. American treasure also led to European inflation during the sixteenth century, eating up more wealth. Nor did the windfall stay in Europe. Most silver ended up as coins in China, India, and Southeast Asia. Before the Industrial Revolution, few products produced in Europe could be sold at a profit in the East. Thus, imports had to be paid for with silver. In this way, the silver of America paid for the riches of Asia. Scholars estimate that over half went to China, though recent scholarship suggests that silver went to China not as payment for European goods but because the demand for silver was great due to Chinese conversion to a silver standard during the Ming rule, following an inflationary spiral stimulated by paper money during Mongol rule.

COLONIZATION AND THE END OF THE FRONTIER

After the European explorers, traders, and missionaries came the colonists. In some places in the world, colonization was sparse. In Africa, for instance, the forbidding interior, wracked with malaria and difficult travel, prevented European settlement until the nineteenth century. In other areas that were heavily populated like India and China, opportunities for colonization were limited. In Australia, New Zealand, the Americas, and Russia, however, land emptied by diseases beckoned Europeans. Slowly, around the world, frontiers were settled.

Did You Know?

European colonization of the Americas was tied to European maritime expertise, missionary impulses, access to resources, and dissatisfied social and religious groups.

Mercantilism (a policy used by governments that built a nation's wealth by encouraging exports over imports resulting in reserves of precious metal) generally tied colonies to the mother country, which saw partial political control as a way to ensure access to cheap supplies of precious metals, cash crops, timber, and new markets. Not only the Spanish colonized in South America for those reasons. In 1530 the king of Portugal offered large land grants to nobles who would set up colonies in Brazil. By about 1550 the Portuguese controlled 15 towns up and down the Brazilian coast. Then came the Dutch, establishing themselves in Guiana north of the Amazon and on the eastern tip, northeast of the Brazilian highlands.

Spanish Colonization in North America

In North America, the Spanish, French, and English carved out colonies. The Spanish settled as far east as the Mississippi and as far north as New Mexico and southern California. **Francisco de Coronado** in the 1540s moved across Texas to Kansas in search of gold, while **Hernando de Soto**, with a like vision, advanced into Florida. The Catholic Church, however, was the primary force in colonizing New Spain north of the Rio Grande. Missionaries spread the gospel among the Indians, and in 1769 the Spanish began to consolidate their holdings by building the first of several **presidios** (military garrisons) in San Diego. Simultaneously, **Junipero Serra** and other Franciscan monks established a series of **missions** (religious outposts). Indians were either persuaded or sometimes coerced into living and working at the missions in a Spanish effort to create permanent agricultural communities.

French Colonization in North America

France also sent explorers and missionaries to claim vast tracts and they staked out territory on the St. Lawrence in an effort to find a **Northwest Passage** to Asia. In 1608 **Samuel de Champlain** founded the royal colony of Quebec, and in 1627 the king chartered the **Company of New France** to encourage emigration. This proved a failure, however, for several reasons. First, population pressures were not as great in France as in England and French peasants were discouraged by reports of cold weather. Also, the French government refused to let French Huguenots (Protestants) emigrate for fear of political revolt. Instead, French Canada became a fur trading enterprise and fertile ground for Jesuit Catholic conversion. **Jacques Marquette**, a French Jesuit priest, and **Louis Joliet**, a fur trader, reached the Mississippi, and in 1681 the French claimed sovereignty over the whole Mississippi River system in the name of Louis XIV (Louisiana).

Dutch Colonization in North America

Meanwhile, the Dutch had little interest in conversion or territory. They sought commerce. **Henry Hudson** of the Dutch East India Company named the Hudson River and established fur trading posts on Manhattan Island. In 1621 the Dutch government gave a trade monopoly to the **Dutch West India Company** in America. Soon thereafter, the company "purchased" Manhattan Island from the Indians and founded **New Amsterdam** as the capital of its New Netherlands colony. The growing threat of New England and New France caused the Dutch government to encourage migration by granting huge estates along the Hudson River to wealthy Dutchmen, but the lure of profitable slave trade and plantations in Brazil outweighed the appeal of North America. After a series of Anglo-Dutch wars, New Amsterdam became a British colony.

English Colonization in North America

Like New Netherlands, the first English settlement in North America was a **corporate colony**, an enterprise started by ambitious merchants. In 1606 the merchant stockholders of the **Virginia Company** of London received a charter from James I giving them the right to exploit the riches of North America and to "propagate the Christian religion." The Jamestown Colony barely survived its first winter, but once it was clear tobacco would grow in the area, the plantation system was underway. The colony also attracted settlers without grants of land. Maryland was settled as a proprietary colony and as a refuge for Catholics. Both Virginia and Maryland used contracts called indentures to attract settlers. **Indentures** bound migrants as laborers for a period from four to seven years in exchange for passage. Plymouth, meanwhile, was settled by **Pilgrims** in 1620. Sailing on the *Mayflower*

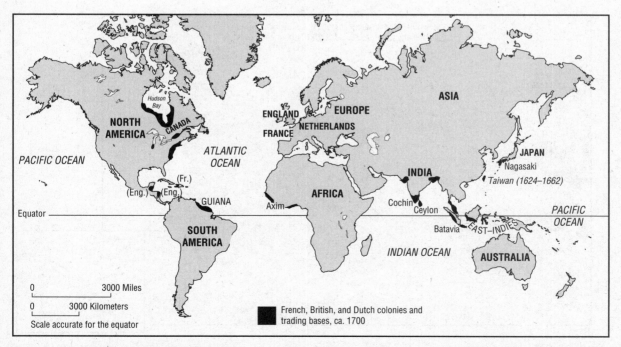

French, British, and Dutch World Holdings in 1700 C.E. After exploration came conquest, trade, and settlement. The Spanish and Portuguese were gradually eclipsed by the French, British, and Dutch, especially in the lucrative trade areas of the world in East Asia.

and lacking a charter from James I, they created their own constitution, the **Mayflower Compact**. **Puritans** followed to the Massachusetts Bay Colony in the 1630s. Everywhere Europeans pushed the frontier, Amerindian societies fought, were destroyed, or were forced to fashion a new life.

Russian Colonization

In the sixteenth century, when Europeans were making their way across the vast oceans, Russians were moving into the regions east of the Ural Mountains. Many were runaway serfs. Others were **Old Believers**, religious traditionalists like the Puritans fleeing in order to continue forbidden rituals. The most fearless pioneers were the fur traders and trappers. One such trader was **Anika Stroganov**, whose agents in the early 1500s crossed the Urals in search of furs that they exchanged for liquor. In the course of the forays, the Stroganovs mapped much of **Siberia**. By 1594 they had a monopoly of the region's fur trade. Then, in 1581 **Yermak**, a Cossack (horseman) chieftain in the czar's employ, swept across Siberia in search of gold, claiming territory for Russia as he went. Subsequently, fortresses were built in such places as Tobolsk, Sunger, and Yakutsk on the **Lena River**. In 1639 a small band of Cossacks reached the Pacific coast at **Okhotsk**. Later in the century the Russians explored **Kamchatka**, the **Kuriles** (1711), and eventually crossed the Bering Strait into Alaska, establishing the **Russian American Company** and founding permanent settlements. By 1812 the Russians had established a trading post at Fort Ross, just a few miles from San Francisco. Also during the seventeenth century, the Russians moved into the Amur Valley on the Chinese border. The Sino-Russian border was established by the **Treaty of Nerchinsk**. Subsequently, Siberia became not just a haven for free farmers, but also a place of exile.

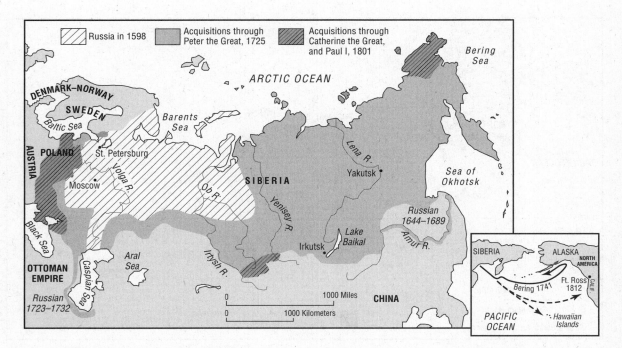

End of the Frontier, Russia 1598–1801 C.E. The European explorations marked the last chapter in the human story of the peopling of the globe. Pristine frontiers vanished, especially in Russia and the United States, where sparsely populated areas were soon occupied by sedentary civilizations.

The Portuguese, Dutch, and English dominated the Indian Ocean exchange, but they met up with the Spanish and Chinese in Manila, creating a world market. From the East went luxury goods paid for with American silver extracted by Indian and African slaves. From the plantations went tobacco and sugar. Merchants, missionaries, and then colonists followed to all parts of the globe. In places with sparse population, as in the Americas and Russia, the end of the world's frontier was in sight.

Unit Review

Cross-Regional Developments

There were important cross-regional developments between 1000 and 1750 that helped shape the modern world. These include

- the development of a new type of political unit, the nation-state;

- growing European exploration;

- conquest of the Americas and Russian conquest of Siberia;

- an African exodus that created an Atlantic diaspora;

- a world exchange of peoples, specie, plants, and animals;

- transformation of the military due to artillery;

- conquest of the oceans by means of ships like the caravel and galleon

- plantation economies; and

- a world exchange based on American bullion.

Legacies

This period brought the world into modern times. Thus, many of its legacies are apparent in the contemporary world.

- Political legacies include the rise of the nation-state and, as a consequence, a divided Europe reinforced by religious separations;

- parliaments, constitutions, national literature and national identities emerged;

- the tremendous artistic, literary, and scientific output of the European Renaissance, some of the world's greatest contributors being Michelangelo, Erasmus, and Newton;

- a secular spirit, mechanisms of exchange, the capitalist system, and a middle class;

- standing armies and navies and drills developed, as did warfare based on artillery;

- absolutist states grew strong because of this state military;

- in the Americas are the legacies of vanished Indian populations, multiracial societies, and states of differing national character based on language and cultural traditions;

- institutions of global exchange including long-distance trade; and

- global diffusion of foods like tomatoes, tea, and sugar.

Quiz

Unscramble:

Arrange the following in chronological order.

Reformation; Commercial Revolution; Discovery of America; European Renaissance; Columbian Exchange

Matching:

1. Common law
2. Inquisition
3. Mercantilism
4. Baroque
5. Puritans
6. Commonwealth
7. Reconquesta
8. Indentures
9. Mulatto

A. Republican form of government
B. A dramatic, emotional style of art characterized by lavish decorations and frescos
C. A search for heretics during the Counter-Reformation
D. Government policy to create a favorable balance of trade by increasing exports over imports
E. Wanted to purify the Church of England
F. English law developed from "common" practices
G. Reconquest of Spain from the Muslims
H. African-European
I. Bound migrants to labor from four to seven years in exchange for passage to the Americas

Questions:

1. Which of the following occurred first?

   (A) the Renaissance
   (B) the Commercial Revolution
   (C) the Magna Carta
   (D) the Crusades
   (E) the Reformation

2. Who was the author of *The Prince*, an analysis of how the prince should gain, maintain, and increase power?

   (A) Peter Abelard
   (B) Thomas Aquinas
   (C) Francesco Petrarch
   (D) Niccolo Machiavelli
   (E) Thomas More

3. All of the following were hallmarks of the Renaissance EXCEPT

   (A) secular experimentation in the sciences.
   (B) rebirth of Greek and Roman classics.
   (C) individualism.
   (D) humanism.
   (E) scholasticism.

4. Which of the following artists was responsible for the frescoes of the Sistine Chapel?

   (A) Michelangelo
   (B) Raphael
   (C) Albrecht Dürer
   (D) Leonardo da Vinci
   (E) Hieronymus Bosch

5. Who was responsible for uniting Spain?

   (A) Baldassare Castiglione
   (B) Ignatius of Loyola
   (C) Maximilian I
   (D) Capetian kings
   (E) Ferdinand and Isabella

6. Who was responsible for uniting the French in successful resistance to the English during the Hundred Years' War?

   (A) Capetian kings
   (B) Louis IX
   (C) Charles V
   (D) Huguenots
   (E) Joan of Arc

7. Who initiated the Reformation?

   (A) Ignatius of Loyola
   (B) Martin Luther
   (C) Thomas More
   (D) Thomas Aquinas
   (E) Desiderius Erasmus

8. Which of the following scientists, in *On the Revolution of Heavenly Bodies*, reasserted the Greek and Chinese theories that the universe was heliocentric?

   (A) Nicolaus Copernicus
   (B) Johannes Kepler
   (C) Galileo Galilei
   (D) René Descartes
   (E) Isaac Newton

9. A major social change connected with the emergence the "modern world" is

   (A) capitalism.
   (B) slavery.
   (C) rise of the middle class.
   (D) the development of the nation-state.
   (E) liberalism.

10. A Counter-Reformation of Catholics in the sixteenth century led to

   (A) the Peace of Augsburg.
   (B) the formation of new religious orders like the Jesuits.
   (C) reconciliation between Catholics and Protestants.
   (D) religious toleration of Protestants.
   (E) the Treaty of Westphalia.

11. Greater commercialization occurred in the sixteenth century because of

   (A) a larger population engaged in trade.
   (B) the introduction of new products.
   (C) expanding markets.
   (D) "cheap" money.
   (E) all of the above

12. Joint stock companies proved to be popular because they

   (A) monopolized trade within a specific market.
   (B) utilized letters of credit and checks for trading purposes.
   (C) encouraged "putting out" or the "domestic system" for textiles in Italy and the Netherlands.
   (D) gained access to an expanding system of credit.
   (E) reduced financial risks for the investor.

13. Which of the following occasions permanently established constitutionalism and the supremacy of the English Parliament over the monarchy?

   (A) the Glorious Revolution
   (B) the Long Parliament
   (C) Oliver Cromwell's Puritan commonwealth
   (D) signing the Magna Carta
   (E) expansion of legislative power during the reign of Elizabeth I

14. The site of the first encomienda system in the New World was in

   (A) Mexico.
   (B) Virginia.
   (C) Brazil.
   (D) Peru.
   (E) the Caribbean.

15. Which Jesuit priest sought to convert the Ming court through Western education and presents of Western technology?

   (A) Francis Xavier
   (B) Robert de Nobili
   (C) Matteo Ricci
   (D) Junipero Serra
   (E) Jacques Marquette

16. A dividing line drawn by the pope to separate Portuguese and Spanish claims was established through the

   (A) Treaty of Tordesillas.
   (B) Treaty of Westphalia.
   (C) Edict of Nantes.
   (D) Treaty of Paris.
   (E) Council of Trent.

17. Which was not a signfiicant factor in the improverishment of Spain following the discovery of America?

   (A) Much of the gold stayed in the Americas to build churches and missions.
   (B) Bullion was used to pay for Spanish debt and wars.
   (C) American silver was used to pay for Asian products.
   (D) The importation of so much American gold and silver led to inflation within the Spanish economy.
   (E) The establishment of the encomienda system.

18. Why did the Chinese demand for Spanish silver from its American colonies increase in the 16th century?

   (A) In the Americas the Spanish increased their purchases of Chinese goods in silver.
   (B) Silver was coveted by Chinese jewelers who supplied a global demand for Chinese jewelery.
   (C) Chinese paper money had become worthless during the late Mongol period causing the Ming to establish silver as the major currency.
   (D) The price of silver in China was lower than in the rest of the world.
   (E) The Manila Galleons made travel from the Americas to China possible.

19. The only product not traded along the transcontinental routes from China to Europe and Africa in premodern times was

    (A) silk.
    (B) calico.
    (C) tobacco.
    (D) glass.
    (E) cotton.

20. Gold for minting coins that ended a barter economy in Europe in the premodern period came from

    (A) Scandinavia.
    (B) sub-Saharan Africa.
    (C) Southeast Asia.
    (D) Central Asia.
    (E) Arabian Peninsula.

The Ninety-Five Theses

6. The Pope has no power to remit any guilt, except by declaring and warranting it to have been remitted by God. . .

21. Thus those preachers of indulgences are in error who say that by the indulgences of the Pope a man is freed and saved from all punishment.

28. It is certain that, when the money rattles in the chest, avarice and gain may be increased, but the effect of the intercession of the Church depends on the will of God alone . . .

37. Every true Christian, whether living or dead, has a share in all the benefits of Christ and the Church, given him by God, even without letters of pardon. . .

---

21. Individuals who read Martin Luther's Ninety-Five Theses above might conclude all of the following EXCEPT

    (A) Luther was disloyal to the Church.
    (B) Church officials selling pardons had no power to pardon sinners.
    (C) money from the sale of indulgences was a source of Church income.
    (D) every true Christian should share the benefits of the Church without paying indulgences.
    (E) true Christians should start their own church.

22. A social reason for Spanish exploration and conquest was

    (A) the development of the caravel.
    (B) a demand for spices like nutmeg, mace, ginger, cinnamon, and pepper.
    (C) competition and rivalries between the Spanish and other Europeans.
    (D) the opportunity for disinherited Spanish nobles to advance.
    (E) the desire to convert pagans to the Roman Catholic faith.

23. Which is NOT true of the Atlantic slave trade?

    (A) Demand for slaves in the Americas arose from the lack of indigenous Indian laborers and plantation agriculture.
    (B) Africans were enslaved as "janissaries" who could become elite soldiers and bureaucrats.
    (C) Africans often became slaves due to poor economic conditions and internal African warfare.
    (D) The Atlantic slave trade affected different parts of African in different ways and some not at all.
    (E) Some African kings grew rich from the slave trade.

24. Which is mismatched?

    (A) Spain—colonization of the southwestern United States and Florida
    (B) Russia—colonization of Siberia and the northwestern coast of North America
    (C) France—colonization of the St. Lawrence River
    (D) England—colonization of the eastern coast of the United States
    (E) Holland—colonization of Jamestown

25. European absolutist kings became increasingly powerful due to their ability to

    (A) tax in a money economy dominated by a wealthy commercial class.
    (B) maintain large bureaucracies.
    (C) raise and maintain large state militaries.
    (D) colonize and imperialize worldwide.
    (E) all of the above.

26. Which of the choices below arranges the architectural monuments in the correct chronological order?

    I. the Colosseum at Rome
    II. the Taj Mahal of India
    III. the Dome of the Rock Mosque of Jerusalem
    IV. the Forbidden City of Beijing
    V. the Pyramids of Egypt
    VI. the Parthenon of Athens

    (A) V, II, VI, I
    (B) V, VI, III, IV
    (C) IV, I, VI, II
    (D) IV, I, III, II
    (E) I, VI, III, II

Answers

Unscramble:
Commercial Revolution; European Renaissance; Discovery of America; Reformation; Columbian Exchange

Matching:

1. **(F)**	6. **(A)**
2. **(C)**	7. **(G)**
3. **(D)**	8. **(I)**
4. **(B)**	9. **(H)**
5. **(E)**	

Questions:

1. **(D)**	10. **(B)**	19. **(C)**
2. **(D)**	11. **(E)**	20. **(B)**
3. **(E)**	12. **(E)**	21. **(E)**
4. **(A)**	13. **(A)**	22. **(D)**
5. **(E)**	14. **(E)**	23. **(B)**
6. **(E)**	15. **(C)**	24. **(E)**
7. **(B)**	16. **(A)**	25. **(E)**
8. **(A)**	17. **(E)**	26. **(B)**
9. **(C)**	18. **(C)**	

STUDY TIP

What is the difference between primary and secondary sources? Each day for a week, review a document from a different unit of the book. Cover the explanation and answer the following questions:

- Is the source primary or secondary?
- What is the time period?
- Who wrote the piece?
- What are the main ideas?
- What is the author's viewpoint?
- Does the document offer lasting ideas?

Check your answers with the explanations.

Patterns of Modernity in the Nineteenth Century

UNIT **VII**

(ca. 1750 C.E.–1914 C.E.)

GENDER IN WORLD HISTORY

By definition, **gender** refers to categories of masculine and feminine. In history, it relates to the roles that men and women have played in the societies in which they lived. In approaching an analysis of gender in world history, historians have tried to describe gender roles in three types of human societies: hunter and gatherer (the earliest lifestyle), agricultural and pastoral (beginning ten thousand years ago), and urban (beginning five thousand years ago). In each type of society, the way humans earned their living and their lifestyles changed. With each change, class differences became more distinct, leading to the question of whether the differences in the roles that men and women played increased also.

One theory of history proposes that as human lifestyles passed through the three stages, **patriarchy** increased. Patriarchy refers to a system of social organization in which descent and succession are traced thought the male line (in contrast to **matriarchy**, which refers to social organizations in which descent and succession are traced through the female line). Implicit in this analysis are questions of equality and power, the assumption being that in matriarchal societies, power is held in the hands of women (making men less powerful and equal) and in patriarchal societies, in the hands of men (making women less powerful and equal). Many historians are now proposing that in hunter-gatherer societies neither patriarchy nor matriarchy predominated. In these early societies men and women played different roles, but neither role superceded the other. Men hunted and women gathered. Both were equally important to survival. According to historical analysis, in the next stage of human life—agricultural societies—matriarchy predominated. In these societies fertility of soil was linked to human fertility. Consequently, women were esteemed for their procreative powers and descent was traced through the female line. In agricultural societies, men and women equally tended to fields and animals. In urban society, as the theory goes, patriarchy has been the norm. In urban societies men have tended to dominate in politics and economics, and descent has normally been traced through the male line. Why this has happened is unclear, but one of its reflections has been that the history of urban societies has generally been written by men, about men. Although women make up about half the world's population and always have, until the modern age, male historians have focused on the lives of men and the areas in which men have predominated.

Scholars of world history are trying to redress this historical bias by researching and writing about the roles of women and about the areas of history in which women played important roles. Such areas include family, sexuality, popular culture, domesticity, and work. Gender history, therefore, has often been equated with "women's history," though technically it is a study of the roles of both sexes.

Much of contemporary gender history revolves around the examination of the changing role of women in the modern world. This examination has identified this changing role as a major pattern of the modern world. The period 1750 to 1914 witnessed a number of changes in the role of women. One was increased political rights. Another was the movement of women out of the home and into the workplace. Industrialization was a key factor in this shift. Finally, women have been able through modern medicine and cultural attitudes to control their sexuality and the timing and number of pregnancies. This has freed women to participate in a wider range of human activity. These changes have made historians question whether history may be moving into a new stage of history in which the inequalities of the classical urban lifestyle are giving way to a new era of equal and more complex gender participation.

Liberal Democratic Movements

(ca. 1450 C.E.–1850 C.E.)

TIMELINE	
1600 C.E.–1800 C.E.	Development of Enlightenment Thought
1775 C.E.–1783 C.E.	American Revolution
1789 C.E.–1799 C.E.	French Revolution
1799 C.E.–1815 C.E.	Age of Napoleon
1800 C.E.–1850 C.E.	Romanticism
1804 C.E.	Haitian Revolution
1810 C.E.–1825 C.E.	Latin American Revolutions
1848 C.E.	European Liberal Revolutions

SCIENCE AND POLITICS—THE ENLIGHTENMENT

Enlightenment Science

Liberalism is an ideology based on Enlightenment ideas that favored emancipating the individual from restraints, especially governmental, economic, and religious. It came to be equated with freedoms during this period. **Democracy** refers to a system of government in which all citizens (however defined) have equal political and legal rights, privileges, and practices. **Republicanism** refers to a political system in which the power to govern is granted by the "people" (however defined) rather than inherited or assumed by force.

The origins of **liberal democratic** thought can be traced to the science and politics of the Enlightenment. The scientific view that the natural world is regulated by laws of nature that maintain order and harmony in the universe influenced politics. The **Scientific Revolution**, stimulated by Islamic science, began during the sixteenth century in Europe. Renaissance science used the scientific method to discover the **laws of nature**. It was born in the medieval university system when science began to develop as a distinct branch of philosophy. Using rationalism, the scientific method involved experimentation and observation, reason to interpret the results, and math to prove and predict. The giants of the revolution included **Nicolaus Copernicus** (1473–1543), **Tycho Brahe** (1546–1601), **Johannes Kepler** (1571–1630), **Galileo Galilei** (1564–1642), **Francis Bacon** (1561–1626), **René Descartes** (1596–1642), and **Isaac Newton** (1642–1727). The two giants of methodology were Bacon and Descartes. Bacon formalized the empirical, or **inductive, method**, which called for observations, measurement, experiment, hypothesis, and verification, while Descartes championed the **deductive method**, a mathematical approach that began with simple, self-evident truths and advanced to more complex truths. Copernicus, using astronomy and observation, in a startling publication, *On the Revolution of Heavenly Bodies*, postulated the axial theory of the universe, that is, that the planets revolve around the sun. Brahe went on to build one of the most sophisticated observatories of the day and to amass volumes of data that helped Kepler formulate the laws of planetary motion.

Where Copernicus had speculated, Johannes Kepler proved his theories mathematically. While Kepler was unraveling the secrets of planetary motion, Galileo, using experimentation, showed that a uniform force like gravity produces a uniform acceleration, and formulated the law of inertia—an object continues in motion forever unless stopped by some external force. The accomplishments of Kepler, Galileo, and others put the old astronomy and physics in ruins, but it was left to Isaac Newton to create a new synthesis of theory and observation. His contribution was in proving mathematically the basic laws of physics. In his immortal *Principia* he outlined the universal laws of gravitation—that every body in the universe attracts every other body in a precise mathematical relationship. From Kepler's elliptical orbits and Galileo's objects in motion, Newton unified the whole universe in one constant system.

Various reasons have been given for the Scientific Revolution, among them

1. The Renaissance, which stimulated investigation into classical and Muslim science
2. The development of new instruments like the telescope, barometer, thermometer, pendulum clock, microscope, and air pump
3. New methods of thought
4. Protestantism, which made scientific inquiry a question of individual conscience and not of religious doctrine.

Enlightenment Thought

The impact of the Scientific Revolution was more on how people thought than on changes in technology, which did not occur until the nineteenth century. It was the most important fact in the eighteenth-century **Enlightenment**. The Enlightenment was the intellectual movement centered in France that advocated using scientific methods to study human society. Rational laws could describe social behavior. The Enlightenment had a profound impact on the politics and culture of the urban middle class and upper classes. Basically, it believed that, as there are scientific **laws of nature**, so are there **laws of society**. The Enlightenment introduced the idea of progress, or the belief that the discovery of the laws of nature and man could produce a steadily improved human condition. The Enlightenment tried to find new truths in a period of chaos and confusion. Religious truths were being challenged by the new science, and the rapidly growing travel literature on non-European lands and cultures served to challenge the *status quo*. Absolute morality and truth were challenged by new thinking. Much of the new thinking was developed by a group of intellectuals in France called the ***philosophes***.

Natural Rights

Essentially the "laws of society" supported the view that all men have **natural rights** including life, liberty, and property, that government is a contract between ruler and ruled and, if violated by the ruler, there is a license to rebel, and that, properly aligned, government is a balance of power. **Thomas Hobbes** (1588–1679) was the first English philosopher to apply natural laws to those of society. After observing the chaos and conflict of the English Civil War, he observed in his book *Leviathan* that a state without laws is brutish. To avoid such a state of affairs, people must enter into a contract with the ruler in which they give up some of their freedom and thereby forfeit their right to rebel. **John Locke** (1632–1704) went a step further, writing that all people have natural rights to life, liberty, and property, which the government is responsible for protecting. Because the purpose of government is to establish order, the ruler, to stay in power, must have the consent of the governed. If the ruler acts as a tyrant and has broken the contract, the people have the right to rebel. In France, **Charles, Baron de Montesquieu** (1689–1755), focused on the question of how to promote liberty and prevent tyranny. He argued that despotism could be avoided if the power of the state were divided so that neither one person nor one governing body had unlimited power. Montesquieu envisioned **separation of power** with distinct branches of government (legislative, judicial, executive) responsible for specific functions of government, each with power to check the other branches.

The most famous, perhaps most representative, philosophe was François Marie Arouet, known by his pen name **Voltaire** (1694–1778). Unlike Montesquieu, he concluded that since human beings "are very rarely worthy to govern themselves," the best government was one with a good monarch. He also disputed the idea of equality between the classes, but he did advocate equality before the law. He expanded the idea of rights to include **civil rights**, especially the choice of religion and cultural expansion. He wrote, "I do not agree with a word you say, but I will defend to the death your right to say it." His view of a deistic God, a great clockmaker who built an orderly universe and then stepped aside and let it run, embodies the core of the philosophe spirit.

The last of the great philosophes was **Jean-Jacques Rousseau** (1712–1778). Passionately committed to individual freedom, Rousseau argued in *The Social Contract* (1762) that sovereign power is vested in the people, not the monarch, and that the "general will" (democracy), reflecting the common interests of the people, is sacred and absolute. Influenced by Chinese political thought, Rousseau believed that if the ruler ignored the will of the people, the social contract was broken and the people had the right to revolt. The concept of the "general will" has been used by dictators (Hitler) and democrats (Jefferson) alike. (Dictators espouse the belief that they represent and embody the true interest of the sovereign masses.) Rousseau, while a typical Enlightenment thinker, also had one foot in the oncoming romantic period, as he did not agree that rationalism and civilization were liberating. Rather, he believed feeling should complement intellect. He argued in *Emile* that education in the form of natural, unspoiled development could avoid the corrupting influences of civilization.

ROUSSEAU AND THE SOCIAL CONTRACT

Man is born free but is everywhere in chains. One thinks himself master of others, but is himself the greater slave. How did this change take place? I do not know. What can render it legitimate? I believe I can answer this question. . . .

If, therefore, we take from the social compact everything that is not essential to it, we shall find it reduced to the following terms: "We, the contracting parties, do jointly and severally submit our persons and abilities, to the supreme direction of the general will of all, and, in a collective body, receive each member into that body, as an indivisible part of the whole."

Jean-Jacques Rousseau was the most radical of the philosophes. While John Locke emphasized natural rights and representative government, Voltaire constitutionalism and the rule of law, and Montesquieu a balance of power, Rousseau advocated democracy and social equality. In Rousseau's view, true liberty can only be obtained when men retain all rights except those given to the general will or majority of the people. To him, liberal government was a social compact as well as a political contract, one in which social as well as legal relationships are based on equality and rule of the majority. Rousseau's ideas were important for shaping liberal ideas in the nineteenth century, but they were used also in the twentieth century by dictators like Hitler who saw themselves, not as chosen by the "general will," but as the embodiment of the "general will."

Enlightenment thought was used to justify the bourgeois revolution (Hobbes, Locke), blueprint future governments in terms of natural rights (Locke), civil rights (Voltaire), separation of power (Montesquieu), and the social contract (Rousseau), and to create a path of human progress along which all human beings should travel. It especially provided the intellectual framework for the bourgeois revolutions in France and the Americas.

LIBERATION

The American Revolution of 1776, the French Revolution of 1789, and the revolutions in Latin America during the first part of the nineteenth century were, to varying degrees, wars of liberation from colonial masters, social revolutions, and political revolutions. In a social sense they can be bulked together under the term **"bourgeois"** (middle class) because they reflect the growing power and culture of the middle class, whose money economy gave them the motivation to seek political power and social status in the name of liberty and equality.

THE AMERICAN REVOLUTION

The **American Revolution** (1775–1783) has been regarded as both a conservative war of independence and a radical political revolution. In a conservative sense it was only asserting traditional liberties of English citizens, but in a radical sense it achieved goals that went way beyond those of independence. Both views are probably correct, as in the American context, liberal ideas took a much more democratic flavor.

The immediate issue in the revolution was taxes. The expenses of the Seven Years' War caused Britain to try to raise money in the colonies by means of a Stamp Act in 1765 (on documents, newspapers, cards, etc.). The Americans protested, in part because they regarded themselves as Englishmen who could not be taxed without representation. They also protested because they were used to greater religious and political freedom as the colonial assemblies made most of the important laws. They considered themselves distinct because of their greater social and economic equality. Most were independent farmers, not landed gentry, indentured servants, or slaves. By September 1774, colonial assemblies began to meet to protest other perceived abuses including the Coercive Acts, which curtailed local elections and town meetings. In April 1775, fighting began in Lexington and Concord, and on July 4, 1776, the Second Continental Congress adopted **Thomas Jefferson**'s draft of the **Declaration of Independence**, which listed tyrannical acts and then proclaimed rights for all humanity, not just Americans: "All men are created equal. . .they are endowed by their Creator with certain inalienable rights. . . ."

In America the conflict often took the form of civil war pitting loyalists, who were politically conservative, wealthy, and loyal to Britain, against liberals like Benjamin Franklin, John and Samuel Adams, and Patrick Henry, often wealthy too but infected with Enlightenment thought and self-rule. As the war progressed, with George Washington leading the rebel troops, liberalism advanced, causing state governments to extend the right to vote to many people.

The war also became internationalized. France sent volunteers in 1779 and 1780. The Spanish and Dutch declared war on Britain, and Catherine the Great of Russia helped organize a League of Armed Neutrality. Faced with an imperial war and with reverses at Yorktown, in India, and in the West Indies, Britain offered independence and territory between the Appalachians and Mississippi to Americans, mostly to keep them out of French and Spanish hands (Treaty of Paris, 1783). Many Americans who remained loyal to Britain immigrated to Canada.

Gathering in Philadelphia in the summer of 1787, delegates to the Constitutional Convention framed a government based on liberal principles of constitution, rights, and a national republic. Equality, as it existed in the document, meant before the law, not equality of political participation or economic well-being. The Revolution ignited the world's imagination in terms of progress, liberalism, and changing international conflicts. Soon liberal principles spilled over into France.

THE FRENCH REVOLUTION

Taxes were also at the heart of the French Revolution. Expenditures in the American war caused the French government to look for new sources of taxes. In general, the **first and second estates** (clergy and nobility) had been exempt from taxes, but, facing bankruptcy in 1788, **Louis XVI** imposed a general tax on all landed property by decree. The decree met such resistance that he was forced to call the Estates General (Legislature) into session. Included in the 1200 delegates who arrived in May 1789 were members of the growing **third estate**, or middle class, mostly lawyers and government officials, not merchants or delegates from the laboring poor. When the first and second estates refused to meet with the third estate, the third estate renamed itself the **National Assembly** and withdrew to a large indoor tennis court. There they swore in the famous **Tennis Court Oath** not to disband until a constitution was written. Meanwhile, the lower classes, or **sans culottes**, who had suffered inflation and food shortages, took to the streets. On July 14, 1789, they stormed the **Bastille**, a medieval fortress where prisoners were held; the sans culottes carried banners for "**liberty, equality, and fraternity**." In the countryside peasants revolted, causing the so-called Great Fear (fear of vagabonds and outlaws). The result was that on August 4 all feudal dues paid by peasants were ended, and on August 27 the National Assembly issued the **Declaration of the Rights of Man**. This document closely followed the American Declaration of Independence, and guaranteed liberal ideas like equality before the law, representative government for a sovereign people, and individual freedom based on the idea of natural rights. During the next two years, in the spirit of the Enlightenment, a constitutional monarchy was established, wherein all lawmaking power was placed in the hands of the National Assembly, the nobility as a legal order was abolished, and the property of the church was nationalized.

THE DECLARATION OF THE RIGHTS OF MAN

1. The aim of society is the common welfare. Government is established to guarantee to man the enjoyment of his natural and inalienable rights.

2. These rights are equality, liberty, security, and property.

3. All men are equal by nature and before law.

4. Law is the free and solemn expression of the general will. . . .

5. All citizens are equally eligible for public office. . . .

9. The law must protect both public and individual liberty against the oppression of those who govern.

13. All men are presumed innocent until proved guilty . . .

16. The right of property is the right which belongs to every citizen to enjoy, and at will to dispose of, his goods, his revenues, and the fruit of his labor and industry.

The Declaration of the Rights of Man was issued August 27, 1789 by the French National Assembly, which had taken control after the Bastille Revolution on July 14. This French liberal document had an American flavor to it. In fact, American Ambassador Thomas Jefferson helped in its drafting. It became the French revolutionary credo. Only two pages long, it was propagandized throughout France, Europe, and around the world. The results of the French Revolution did not enshrine its values completely. Instead, the Napoleonic Code became the legal basis for much of twentieth-century French and European law.

Domestic and International Aspects of the French Revolution

Changes brought debate on both sides. Edmund Burke (1729–1797) wrote the classic conservative view in *Reflections on the Revolution in France*, arguing for inherited privilege and against the chaos and tyranny revolution inspired. Mary Wollstonecraft (1757–1797) wrote a blistering rebuttal, *A Vindication of the Rights of Woman* (1790), in which she argued for the elimination of economic and sexual inequality. Amidst this debate, the kings and nobility of Europe felt threatened, as did Louis XVI and Marie Antoinette, his unpopular Austrian wife. The French royal family was caught as they tried to escape to Austria. Meanwhile, the Legislative Assembly, elected in 1791, was decidedly more liberal than the National Assembly. The majority, loosely allied as **Jacobins** and led by **Maximilien Robespierre** (1758–1794), enlarged the republican crusade outside Europe. France declared war on Austria and Prussia in order to "incite a war of people against kings . . ." Rumors of treason and threats from outside French borders led to the fall of the monarchy and rapid radicalization of the revolution.

The French Republic

In September 1792, the National Convention, elected under expanded franchise by universal male suffrage, proclaimed a republic and sentenced Louis XVI to death. The National Convention then declared war against Britain, Holland, and Spain. In an atmosphere of French defeats, food shortages, and inflation, Robespierre created the Committee of Public Safety, which carried out a campaign of terror. For the first time in history the French conducted a total war effort with a planned economy, revolutionary terror, and modern nationalism. Rationing, nationalized workshops, requisitioning, weapons manufacture, and imprisonment and execution of political enemies under the **Reign of Terror (1793–1794)** seemed to many to pervert the ideals of the revolution. But French national feeling, the sense of a life and death struggle against outside enemies and those hostile to the revolution, and a forced draft of French young men for the army made French armies victorious in 1794. At this point, the National Convention on 9 Thermidor (July 27, 1794) led the "Thermidorian Reaction" against the excesses of the National Convention. Robespierre was executed, and yet another constitution was written, this time with a five-man executive, the **Directory**. In 1799 **Napoleon Bonaparte**, who had gained fame defeating Italian armies in Austria, ended the Directory in a coup d'etat and substituted a strong dictatorship, thus ending the revolution.

Napoleonic Era

During the **Napoleonic Era (1799–1815)** France created an empire and then lost it, enshrined many of the revolutionary ideals, both at home and in other countries it occupied, and in the end returned to a semimonarchy. Napoleon's greatest civil achievement was the **Civil Code (1804)** based on Roman law in which two fundamental principles of the revolution were reasserted—equality of all citizens before the law, and security of wealth and private property. But the Code, as in Roman law, recognized men as the head of the family and made women dependent. Because France was at war during most of Napoleon's reign, basic political freedoms like freedom of the press and security from political imprisonment were violated. In 1802 Napoleon controlled Holland, the Austrian Netherlands, and most of Italy. When he made plans to invade England, he was soundly defeated by **Lord Nelson** at the **Battle of Trafalgar**. Napoleon then turned his attention to the East, decisively beating a combination Austrian/Russian force at the Battle of **Austerlitz** in 1805. He moved into Prussia and, when defeat was certain, Russia sued for peace at **Tilsit** in 1807.

The Grand Empire considerably impacted the people of Europe by abolishing serfdom, but Napoleon's conquest and heavy taxation turned many against him and the revolution. France itself began to experience shortages due to the British counter-blockade to France's Continental System, which was designed to keep British goods from Europe. When Russia resumed trade with Britain, Napoleon invaded on June 6, 1812. This was a fatal mistake. By late fall the French had advanced to Moscow. When Alexander I of Russia ordered the evacuation of Moscow, Napoleon occupied a burned-out city. As winter came, retreat began. Only 30,000 men out of an army of 600,000 returned to France. In April 1814, Napoleon abdicated his throne and the Bourbon dynasty was restored. The new monarch, Louis XVIII (r. 1814–1824) restored rights. He accepted a constitutional monarchy. At this point, Napoleon staged a comeback but was decisively defeated at **Waterloo** in 1815.

The Role of Women

Women played an important role in the French Revolution. They were a public revolutionary force in the first months of 1789. Seven thousand women seeking cheaper bread marched to Versailles in October 1798. Women's success in organizing demonstrations gained them political influence that some of their leaders used to further legal reforms in education, marriage, divorce, and widows' rights. In 1791, **Olympe de Gouges** attempted to extend the revolution's Declaration of the

Europe in 1815 C.E. After the French Revolution and defeat of Napoleon, the map of Europe was significantly altered. A balance of power principle was established at the Congress of Vienna in the hope of maintaining European peace. Germany and Italy remained divided and the Europeans' attention toward expansion turned abroad.

Rights of Man by publishing a pamphlet entitled ***Declaration of the Rights of Woman and of the Female Citizen***. In 1792, **Mary Wollstonecraft** published ***A Vindication of the Rights of Women*** in which she advocated feminist ideas later taken up in the twentieth century, like educational opportunity and professional achievement. In 1793, reform legislation was introduced that reduced the interference of the Roman Catholic Church, allowed divorce, and allowed for inheritance by illegitimate children. However, these gains were rolled back in the Napoleonic Code of 1804. For women the Code represented the conservative reaction of the Napoleonic era against the revolution.

Congress of Vienna

At the **Congress of Vienna**, led by **Klemens von Metternich** of Austria, and composed of representatives of Russia, Prussia, Austria, and Great Britain, construction of a peace settlement based on balance of power principles was undertaken. To do this, France was returned to its pre-war size, territories were balanced elsewhere, and there was agreement that the members would meet periodically to settle international crises, a system called the "**Congress System**." This lasted well into the nineteenth century and kept the peace in Europe.

Views on the French Revolution differ. Some historians emphasize the importance of the conflict between the growing middle class, or bourgeoisie, which made up 8 percent of France's population, and the upper classes. Revisionist historians see the middle class and upper classes as much more fluid and disunited, and thus not so important to the conflict as the outdated medieval bureaucratic monarchy. Other debates have to do with whether or not the French Revolution was really a liberal democratic and bourgeois revolution since it returned to a dictatorship with Napoleon and a partial monarchy with Louis XVIII and a social and economic system that was little changed. Most historians agree that France and Europe were forever changed and that liberal ideas made a considerable impact on France and Europe as a result of the French Revolution.

LATIN AMERICAN REVOLUTIONS

The revolutions in Latin America were closely connected with those in America and France. From the American Revolution came the ideas. Particularly appealing to **Creole** (American-born Spanish) leaders was the Declaration of Independence, which served as a reason for their own revolution. The slogan of the French Revolution, "liberty, equality, and fraternity," appealed to other sectors of the population, but as the French Revolution became more radical, it was rejected by the Creole elite. As an extension of the French Revolution, the revolt in **Haiti**, France's great island sugar colony in the Caribbean, was a prelude to the Latin American revolutions. Slaves, under the leadership of **Toussaint L'Ouverture**, seized the moment and staged a rebellion that resulted in the proclamation of the independent republic of Haiti in 1804. To the Creole elite of Latin America, such a lower-class revolt was to be avoided, but to the lower classes, it was a symbol of hope. Independence, when it did come, lacked social transformation. The Haitian revolt is the only successful slave revolt in world history.

What sparked the Latin American revolts was the war in Europe. Portugal was invaded by France in 1807, and in 1808 Napoleon's brother Joseph sought to

Did You Know?

Balance of power meant an international equilibrium of political interests and military forces that would preserve the freedom and independence of the great powers.

Did You Know?

The Haitian revolt is the only successful slave revolt in history.

replace Ferdinand VII and rule Spain. Since everything in Spanish America was done in the name of the king, the Creoles argued that the removal of the legitimate king shifted sovereignty to the people. In the colonies, in places like Caracas, Bogota, and Mexico, Creoles set up **juntas** (groups of people controlling the government after a revolution) to rule in place of Ferdinand VII. Independence movements followed. In Mexico, Creoles led by **Father Miguel de Hidalgo** won a number of early victories in 1810, but when Hidalgo called for Indian and **mestizo** (mix of Indian and white ancestry) help, he lost the support of the Creoles, who feared social rebellion. He was executed, but in 1820, **Augustin de Iturbide**, a Creole officer, linked up with insurgents and the combined forces occupied Mexico City. Iturbide was named emperor and briefly included Central America in the Mexican Empire. However, the Central American states established their own independence and Mexico became a republic in 1838.

In northern Latin America (present-day Venezuela), a movement for independence, centered in Caracas, began in 1810 under the leadership of a wealthy Creole officer, **Simon Bolivar**. In 1822 his victories in Venezuela, Colombia, and Ecuador led to a new nation called Grand Colombia. However, political and regional differences led to its breakup. Bolivar rejected all efforts to crown him king and in 1830 he left Colombia republican and independent.

In South America (present-day Brazil), another movement coalesced under **Jose de San Martin** around Buenos Aires. A booming commercial center, its residents resented Spanish trade restrictions. Jose de San Martin's forces ranged across the Andes to Chile and Peru. Brazil's quest for independence occurred without upheaval. When Napoleon's troops entered Portugal, the royal family fled to Brazil. Under popular pressure, Brazil declared independence in 1822.

By 1825 all of Spanish Latin America had gained political independence and, despite plans to create some form of monarchy in the 18 new states, all emerged as independent republics with representative governments, fullfilling Enlightenment ideas. In none, though, was there a radical redistribution of property or reconstruction of society.

Results

The Latin American revolutions produced political fragmentation and independence, but not revolutionary change. Political stability proved elusive as Creole leaders, who led the revolutions, had no experience in government. In practice, generals, or **caudillos**, ruled. Independence brought economic problems with the destruction of land and mines and dislocation of the colonial market system. The three-tiered socioracial structure composed of whites, mixed, and blacks persisted. Immigrations of Europeans and Asians in the second half of the nineteenth century complicated the picture. Immigrants were usually at the bottom of the social ladder though they could move up more quickly than blacks. The Roman Catholic Church remained strong, but was continually vulnerable to liberal reformers who wanted to secularize the state. In terms of culture, the dominant role of the Creoles tended to Europeanize life in Latin America. During the romantic era of the 1830s, however, local customs became idealized. The appearance of secular education created some opportunities for women, though for the upper class, women's lives changed little. Lower-class women, however, often controlled the local market.

Born of Enlightenment liberalism, many questions related to government and society remained unresolved by independence and appear similar to those in the twentieth century in the experience of emerging nations. The colonial heritage left little tradition of participatory government, and the highly centralized colonial state created dependence and resentment of government. Class and regional differences divided the new nations and wealth was unequally distributed. The rise of industrial capitalism then placed the new nations in an economically dependent position.

The middle-class or bourgeois revolutions based on Enlightenment thought produced varying degrees of social and political change. In North America the most complete revolution took place, establishing independence, a republican government, and some social leveling. In France, the revolution resulted in significant political change, but social change was minimal. In Latin America, independence was achieved without significant political and social change. In all places, nationalism based on liberalism played a significant role in the political process.

The Enlightenment, with its ideals of liberty, equality, and fraternity, contrasted with slavery. The French philosophes called for an end to slavery, but English Protestants, such as the Quakers, Baptists, and Anglicans, began the political campaign to abolish slavery. In 1795 the Dutch ended their shipments of slaves, followed by most other countries by the end of the Napoleonic Wars. Africans freed in the Americas or freed by the British navy en route to slave markets were returned to settlements in Sierra Leone, Liberia, and the Gold Coast. In 1833 slavery was declared illegal in the British Empire. Gradually, slavery was abolished in one country after another as it became less profitable. In the United States, however, slaves were not freed until the conclusion of the American Civil War. In the 1880s, Cuba and Brazil were the last major countries to abolish slavery in the western hemisphere.

NEW NATIONALISM IN EUROPE

Besides the Americas, Latin America, and France, liberal movements occurred in other parts of Europe particularly in Greece, Italy, Germany, and the Ottoman Empire. Infused into these movements was a heightened spirit of **nationalism** (a feeling of allegiance to a national group rather than to monarchy) that combined ideas of national liberation, nation-state building, and republicanism.

Since the fifteenth century, Greece was ruled by the Ottoman Turks. In 1812, **Alexander Ypsilanti** led the Greeks to revolt. The Great Powers, who had pledged to preserve the balance of power status quo at the Congress of Vienna, were against such revolution, but Americans, Europeans, and Russians responded enthusiastically, especially after Ottoman Turkish atrocities fanned outrage. In 1827 a combined British, French, and Russian fleet destroyed the Turkish fleet at Navarino, resulting in a Russian protectorate over Romania. Greece declared its independence (1830).

Meanwhile, in France, the 1789 liberal revolution experienced setbacks during the reigns of Louis XVIII and Charles X. When Charles X stripped much of the middle class of its voting rights and censored the press, the streets of Paris once again erupted in 1830. The French Revolution is immortalized by the great romantic painter **Eugène Delacroix** in *Liberty Leading the People,* in which Liberty unites the worker, bourgeois, and street child in a righteous crusade against privilege and oppression. This revolution produced a new leader, **Louis Philippe** (r. 1830–1848), but republicans, democrats, social reformers, and the poor of Paris were bitterly disappointed as the elite actually tightened its control.

Revolutions of 1848

The potato famine in Ireland had echoes on the continent in 1846 when poor harvests led to higher food prices. Workers were introduced to the ideas of socialism.

Once again revolution started in Paris when the government refused to consider electoral reform (only the rich could vote for deputies and many were docile bureaucrats). The people were enraged and called for the abdication of Louis Philippe and the drafting of a constitution for France's Second Republic. Yet there were profound differences in the revolutionary coalition in Paris. One group, representing the workers, wanted a republican socialist government, while another, representing the middle class and owners of land (the bulk of the peasantry), were frightened by the socialists. In an attempt to pacify the workers, "national workshops," or public works programs, were established, but when the workers invaded the newly elected Constituent Assembly, the workshops were suspended. Barricades went up on the streets of Paris and three days of class war ensued, the so-called "**June Days**," in which 10,000 were killed. The Republican army triumphed. France returned to a constitution with a strong executive led by Louis Napoleon, a nephew of Napoleon Bonaparte.

News of the upheaval in France led to demands all over Europe for written constitutions, representative government, and greater civil liberties. In the beginning, urban workers united with middle-class liberals, peasants, and nationalists. In the Austrian Empire, for instance, Hungarian nationalists led by **Louis Kossuth** demanded national autonomy, civil liberties, and universal suffrage. Students, workers, and peasants joined the protests. The coalition fell apart, however. When the monarchy abolished serfdom, the peasants lost interest in other social and political questions. Then national questions superseded social and political ones. When Hungarian nationalists tried to recreate the ancient Hungary of Saint Stephen out of a mosaic of nationalities, the minorities went over to the monarchy. In Prague, Czech nationalists came in conflict with German nationalists. The middle class withdrew when the urban poor presented their own demands for suffrage and socialist workshops. The result was that the conservative aristocratic forces reasserted their strength and crushed the revolution.

A similar course of events happened in Germany with the additional problem that the 38 states of the German Confederation were still not unified. The middle-class Prussian liberals wanted to establish a liberal constitutional monarchy that would then merge with the other German states. Following the fall of Louis Philippe in France, the workers and artisans joined the middle class in revolt on the streets of Berlin. On March 21, 1848, King Frederick William IV gave in to demands to grant Prussia a liberal constitution merging the other German states into it. Immediately, two problems emerged. One was that the workers wanted a more radical program of universal voting rights, a minimum wage, and a 10-hour workday. The other was that the German states called for a national constituent assembly to write a federal constitution instead of a Prussian constitution to which others would accede. As the Constituent Assembly debated, it got bogged down in a battle with Denmark over control of Schleswig and Holstein. By 1849 the stalemate enabled Frederick William to reassert his royal authority and grant a conservative constitution, but this too failed when Austria refused to join. Germany returned to a confederation, having failed to unite first in a liberal national state and then a conservative German Empire.

ROMANTICISM

The artistic and cultural movement that accompanied liberalism in the first half of the nineteenth century was **romanticism**. It was kindled in part by the spirit of the French Revolution that believed radical reconstruction was possible in all segments of society. Romanticism was a reaction to the enforced rules of classicism and of the Enlightenment. It stressed emotionalism, imagination, and yearning for the unattainable. In its quest for the new, it put emphasis on the role of the individual. Thus, the solitary inventor like Edison, the great political figure like Napoleon, the starving artist, the misunderstood, and the man ready to die in a duel were its heroes. What emerged was a confidence in the collective destiny of Western culture. Most romantics saw the growth of modern industry as ugly. Thus, much of the artistic and literary works had subjects rooted in nature.

Among the greatest of the romantics was German poet and dramatist **Johann Wolfgang von Goethe** (1749–1832). Goethe began with one foot in Enlightenment thought, as he was a keen observer of nature and a scientist. His conception of nature was highly romantic, though, because he saw the cosmos as the ultimate living organism composed of innumerable individual elements, a notion that was easy to apply to the relationship of the individual to the state. The notion of the state as a living organism influenced German nationalism thereafter, infusing it with a special sense of uniqueness and destiny. The leading English romanticist was **William Wordsworth** (1775–1850), whose works are filled with fantasies of the glory of the English countryside. In France, Victor Hugo's (1802–1885) famous *Les Misérables* depicted the hero, Jean Valjean, as a romantic hero of goodness and justice. The most famous English artists, **J. M. W. Turner** (1775–1857) and **John Constable** (1776–1837), painted wild storms, sinking ships, and the unspoiled English countryside in emotional terms. Hector Berlioz (1803–1869) exemplified the romantic tradition in music with the rich orchestral coloration of *Symphonie fantastique*. One of the earliest romantic composers, **Ludwig von Beethoven** (1770–1827), wrote symphonies that inspired not just emotional heroics but patriotic sentiment as well. In Russia, the romantic movement was reflected in the Slavophile movement, which idealized the Russian land and agrarianism, and in the music of composers like **Pyotr Tchaikovsky**. Women in romantic attire came to stand allegorically for revolution itself as Delacroix's famous painting *Liberty Leading the People* illustrates.

Another aspect of the romantic era was its interest in questions regarding the nature of women and the nature of love. In the romantic era, women assumed new importance, though the image of women created by men during the era remained conservative and often contradictory. For instance, aristocratic and upper-middle-class women played influential roles in the intellectual circles of the Enlightenment. At the same time, Rousseau wrote that the "education of women should always be relative to men." In art, women were portrayed as both liberated and autonomous, but also domestic and subservient. Romantic women novelists like the Brontë sisters and Mary Ann Evans ("George Eliot") in England and Aurore-Lucile Dupin ("George Sand") in France published, but under fictitious male names.

With the Industrial Revolution and its problems, the optimism of liberals and romantics changed to social comment and realistic portrayals of society's ills, but with the strong Western liberal belief that utopian solutions could be found to solve even the most difficult problems.

Industrial Revolutions and European Imperialism

(ca. 1750 C.E.–1914 C.E.)

TIMELINE	
1750 C.E.–1800s C.E.	Enclosure Acts England
1765 C.E.–1825 C.E.	Spinning jenny, water frame, steam engine, and locomotive
1776 C.E.	*Wealth of Nations* by Adam Smith
1848 C.E.	*Communist Manifesto*
1850 C.E.–1870 C.E.	Unification of Germany and Italy
1850 C.E.–1900 C.E.	Realism
1869 C.E.	Suez Canal
1885 C.E.	Berlin Conference
1891 C.E.	Trans-Siberian Railway

THE INDUSTRIAL REVOLUTION

The coming of industry transformed western Europe and then world society, in part of a process that historians call **modernization**. Modernization is considered a process of political, military, economic, social, and cultural change along the lines of Western societies. The hallmarks are republican and democratic political systems, a free market, economies and military establishments based on technology and industry, secularism, and consumerism. The Industrial Revolution began at about the same time as the political revolutions in France and America, but its impact was more profound, second only, perhaps, to the agricultural revolution. Although it may have seemed to happen in a more evolutionary manner, in terms of world history, it was sudden and abrupt, occurring in the course of only 100 years.

The **Industrial Revolution** (a transformation of the economy, environment, and living conditions due to the replacement of human labor and energy with mechanized processes, energy sources, and technologies that spurred innovation particularly in production, transportation, and communication) began in England due to a number of factors. Among them:

- a stable government that had avoided the liberal political revolutions of the period;

- an experienced business class;

- a central bank;

- a class of wage-earning peasants;

- a large domestic market due to cheap goods made possible by navigable rivers; and

- an agricultural revolution that produced enough surplus to free agricultural laborers for industry.

These agricultural changes started in the Low Countries (Belgium and Holland) and were adopted by the British. They revolved around intensive agriculture associated with innovations like **enclosed fields** (common grazing lands were put into private cultivation), continual crop rotation, heavy manuring, a wide variety of new crops, and sowing seeds with a drill rather than scattering them by hand. The enclosure movement changed farming into a capitalist market venture in which all sorts of improvements were made to increase profits. Even before the Parliament passed the hundreds of enclosure acts of the eighteenth century, peasants had fenced off fields for sheep grazing, producing for the lucrative wool market. By 1870 the English farmer produced 300 percent more food than he had produced in 1700. Other reasons for English industrial pioneering are related to the increased demand for goods and English control of commercial networks supplying them. Between 1700 and 1774 England's North American colonies absorbed 2.2 million surplus population from England, Scotland, and Northern Ireland. This population, through agricultural and resource development of vast lands in the Americas, achieved a standard of living high enough to create increased demand for goods. Meanwhile, England, in its competition with France, in effect became master of the seas after the War of the Spanish Succession. By this war, Britain obtained territory in North America and gained control of the West African slave trade. Then, after the Seven Years' War (1756–1763) and the Treaty of Paris (1763), France lost all its mainland possessions in North America and in India. Britain's colonial empire became a stimulus for many branches of English manufacturing.

Industrial Technology

The pressure to produce more cotton textiles in England created the world's first large factories. Before the Industrial Revolution, India dominated the world market in cotton textile production. Before machines, four or five spinners were necessary to keep one weaver steadily employed. Thus, there was great impetus to find ways of improving spinning. In 1765 **James Hargreaves** invented his cotton spinning jenny (a wheel turned by hand supplied the power) and **Richard Arkwright** invented the water frame, in which water supplied the power. By 1790 the machines produced ten times as much cotton yarn as in 1770. The Arkwright invention used water to power several hundred spindles and thus required large specialized **factories** (buildings with power-driven machines used to produce goods) that employed hundreds of people. By 1831 the cotton textile industry was largely mechanized and factories dotted the riverbanks of England.

The next breakthrough came in the age-old problem of energy and power. In fact, the energy revolution replaced human, then animal and wind, power with other energy sources. This was a monumental transformation in world history that powered the factory system and fueled transport. Coal, which had been used to heat homes in Europe since the 1640s, was first employed by **James Watt** (1736–1819) to power a **steam engine**. The steam engine was adapted to work in many industries. It was used to power steam-driven bellows in the iron industry, to power flour, malt, and sugar mills, and to pump water out of coal mines. The steam engine was applied to sailing ships and then overland transportation. In 1825 **George Stephenson** built an effective locomotive. The railroad companies in England had to get permission to build and had to pay for rights of way, but otherwise were free to build railroads all over England.

In 1860 Britain produced about 20 percent of the world's output of industrial goods. This, in turn, increased wealth and population, which grew from 9 million in 1780 to 21 million in 1851, and average consumption per person increased by 75 percent between 1780 and 1851. Another aspect of industrialism was that science was used not only to improve technology, but to develop new products like dyes (Perkins), batteries (Volta), generators (Faraday), and photography (Daguerre).

European Industrialization

The new technologies that developed in England soon spread to the continent where they developed in a somewhat different way and made advances of their own. National governments throughout Europe believed industrial power equaled international power so industrialization took place with full government backing. The instability of the French Revolution set the continent back, necessitating more government action to catch up. In some cases, English technology arrived on the continent surreptitiously. Until 1825 it was illegal for artisans and skilled mechanics to leave Britain, and until 1843 to export textile machinery and other equipment. Many talented and ambitious workers slipped out, however, like William and John Cockerill of Lancaster, who built a factory that produced steam engines, machinery, and locomotives in France. One way the German government played a much larger role in industry was by setting high external tariffs and creating an internal customs union among the German states, the **Zollverein** (1834). The Zollverein, not unlike the contemporary European Union, lowered tariffs, customs, and taxes on goods traveling between various German states. Also, big stockholder or industrial banks supported industrial development. The most famous was the **Crédit Mobilier of France**, founded in 1852 by two young Jewish journalists, Isaac and Emile Pereire. The result was that all European states as well as the United States, Canada, Russia, and Japan raised industrial levels in the nineteenth century, and by 1913, the United States had passed Britain, and Germany was rapidly closing in. This was in contrast to the non-Western countries, where cottage industry decreased because of competition from Western mechanical industrialization that flooded the world markets.

Did You Know?

The significance of the railroad was tremendous because it reduced the cost of shipping overland and integrated internal local markets and world markets.

URBANIZATION

Industrialization led to urbanization. By 1914 a mere 10 percent of England's population was rural. A similar, if not so dramatic, shift occurred in Germany and the United States between 1870 and 1914. An example of abrupt and large-scale urbanization occurred in Germany when **Alfred Krupp** set up his armaments works in the Ruhr in the 1840s, which transformed the whole valley into a European industrial powerhouse. City life bred new classes of urban workers (**proletariat**), an entrepreneurial middle class (**bourgeoisie**), and a whole new urban culture. Education became more important as the demand for a literate workforce and trained bureaucracy increased. In most countries, compulsory education for young children was introduced by law (Britain, 1870, France, 1882). Methods of work and play changed too. At first, destitute people and orphans filled the ranks of factory workers, but the outlawing of pauper apprentices in 1802, and the use of steam power rather than water power, attracted whole families to the cities to work. Although much has been written about poor working and living conditions in the cities, for the first time, the standard of living improved to the point that people could feed themselves adequately and still have enough money left for amusements. This can be seen through the popularity of daily newspapers, bicycles, the rise of the popular theater and revues, and movies (1890). Industrial and urban growth ushered in the age of mass consumption and culture.

Industrial Cities

At first, cities grew willy-nilly. This created more problems in old medieval towns than in new cities. There, the typical city was a "walking city" without public transport. Parks and open space were nonexistent. The hasty erection of small, closely packed houses in already congested areas led to slum conditions, while the incursions of new roads and railways added to pollution. Infectious disease spread rapidly and filth lay underfoot everywhere due to lack of plumbing and sewage facilities. The question was, who was responsible for the plight of the city? Soon it became a matter of public concern and responsibility. The philosopher **Jeremy Bentham** taught that public problems could be solved on a rational basis according to the dictum the "greatest good for the greatest number," and **Edwin Chadwick** advocated a public health movement that included clean, piped water, public parks, and transportation. Under the leadership of **Georges Haussmann**, Paris was completely transformed with broad boulevards and parks and streetcars. Meanwhile, **Louis Pasteur**'s (1822–1895) germ theory replaced the miasmatic theory (that bad odors cause disease). Pasteur's work allowed identification of organisms that caused disease and vaccines to protect against them. **Joseph Lister**'s (1827–1912) "antiseptic principle" led to the use of disinfectants and improved the surgical and public hospital environment. Gradually, cities became modern complexes using the machines and science that had bred industrialism to solve the problems of industrialism. Industrialization and urbanization also spawned some new ways of thinking about the world.

Architecture

The architecture of the 1800s exhibited both liberalism and industrialism. When European architects set out to design important public buildings, they harkened back to two traditions—the Greco-Roman, as embodied in the Paris Opera (1861–1875), and the Gothic, as embodied in the British Houses of Parliament, completed in 1857. These structures architecturally reflect the pride Europeans felt in their culture and the political advances in a time of liberalism and national self-confidence. New industrial-age materials like **iron girders** and **glass** also found their way into the period's architectural construction. Joseph Paxton explored these new principles and materials in the construction of the **Crystal Palace**, which housed the great **Exhibition of 1851** in London's Hyde Park. The steel frame allowed construction of large windows to let in light, but in exterior decoration, the older ideas of architectural grandeur remained. The technical possibilities of steel frame construction allowed American architects in the late 1800s to build sky-scrapers like the Wainwright Building in St. Louis (1891) and the Woolworth Building in New York (1913). In decoration, however, traditional conceptions of magnificence remained. The skyscraper reflects the genius of the modern metropolis where people, by means of elaborate transportation systems and offices piled one on top of another, created the structure of modern civilization, a whole artificial landscape.

IDEOLOGIES—SOCIALISM AND REALISM

The Origins of Socialism

With industrialization, the Enlightenment ideas of scientific order that so transformed politics changed to the romantic belief in progress in the human condition. **Socialism** resulted from a romantic and utopian view of how this would be achieved for workers. Socialism had its roots in the classical liberalism that seemed to favor the middle class over the worker. The principal ideas of liberalism—equality and liberty—continued to be important during the early nineteenth century. But **laissez-faire**, or opposition to government interference (a form of liberalism that is often called **classical liberalism**), left a gap in the social and economic needs of the industrial age. The idea of a free economy was outlined by **Adam Smith** (1723–1790), whose *Inquiry into the Nature and Causes of the Wealth of Nations* (1776) founded modern economics. In this treatise, Smith argued against mercantilism on the basis that free trade creates wealth through specialization. He outlined the characteristics of a **free capitalist economy**—private property, profit, and a free market whose "invisible hand" guides and regulates supply and demand. The classical liberal idea that government should not interfere often became a doctrine used by businessmen to outlaw labor unions (as it restricted free labor competition) and other government interference in the workplace. Other thinkers added to Smith's view that government should not interfere in the economy. **Thomas Malthus** (1766–1834) argued that population always tends to rise faster than the food supply. If the government were to interfere with emergency welfare, it would make matters worse as the population would rise even further, whereas a hands-off policy would return population to equilibrium levels. **David Ricardo** (1772–1823) in his *Iron Law of Wages* postulated that population could be controlled by wage rates. If wages rose, population would rise, as families would have more children, whereas if wages were just high enough to keep workers from starving, population growth would equal the supply of food.

THE WEALTH OF NATIONS

The annual revenue of every society is always precisely equal to the exchangeable value of the whole annual produce of its industry, or rather is precisely the same thing with that exchangeable value. As every individual, therefore, endeavours as much as he can both to employ his capital in the support of domestic industry, and so to direct that industry that its produce may be of the greatest value; every individual necessarily labours to render the annual revenue of the society as great as he can. He generally, indeed, neither intends to promote the public interest, nor knows how much he is promoting it. By preferring the support of domestic to that of foreign industry, he intends only his own security; and by directing that industry in such a manner as its produce may be of the greatest value, he intends only his own gain, and he is in this, as in many other cases, led by an invisible hand to promote an end which was no part of his intention. Nor is it always the worse for the society that it was no part of it. By pursuing his own interest he frequently promotes that of society more effectually than when he really intends to promote it. I have never known much good done by those who affected to trade for the public good.

Adam Smith became the "father of economics" by brilliantly analyzing how the capitalist free market works. His discoveries include the law of supply and demand, the law of competition, and the law of self-interest. In his famous book The Wealth of Nations, *he tried to explain that trade brings wealth and, therefore, the policy of mercantilism should be abandoned in favor of free trade. As a classical economist, he argued that the economy would prosper if it was left alone, a policy that became known as laissez-faire. His ideas again found favor in the latter part of the twentieth century as socialist systems failed to create wealth. In this excerpt he explains that the individual profit motive leads to the good of all when guided by the invisible hand of the free market.*

French Utopian Socialists

It was against a backdrop of these classical liberal ideas, which seemed to represent the interests of the middle-class capitalist factory owners, that socialism developed. To socialists, the liberal practices in politics and economics appeared selfish, individualistic, and lacking in community spirit. Socialist thought, which originated in France, began to challenge classical liberal ideas. Socialists argued that government should rationally organize the economy and not depend on competition, that the poor should be protected, that wealth should be more equally distributed between rich and poor, and that private property should be abolished in favor of state ownership. There were four giants of French utopian socialist thought:

1. One of the earliest socialist thinkers was **Count Henri de Saint-Simon** (1760–1825). He believed that the "doers" in society—the scientists, engineers, and industrialists—should plan the economy, create public works projects, and create national banks.
2. **Charles Fourier** (1772–1837) envisioned a social utopia in which self-sufficient communities lived communally, and in which women were totally emancipated.

3. **Louis Blanc** (1811–1882) advocated universal voting rights and government-backed workshops and factories guaranteeing full employment.
4. **Pierre Joseph Proudhon** (1809–1865), in a pamphlet *What Is Property?* wrote that property was theft as it was profit stolen from the worker, but Proudhon also feared the state as a solution to the problem.

English Utopian Socialists

In England other utopian thinkers were addressing the plight of the workers. There, however, the result was that socialist thought found its way into legislation and government action that significantly improved the lot of the worker. **Robert Owen** (1771–1858), a successful Scottish cotton manufacturer, testified before a parliamentary committee about the poor working conditions in factories, especially for women and children. He suggested that, if people were healthy, they would be better producers. He advocated that the fruits of labor should be shared by philanthropy, and that owners should follow a paternalistic attitude by setting up ideal communities in which the focus was not the factory but the community. **Jeremy Bentham** (1748–1832) taught that the government should follow a policy of the "greatest good for the greatest number and, therefore, should be actively involved in solving problems like urban blight and the right to vote, unionization, and education." **John Stuart Mill** (1806–1873) in his famous *Essay on Liberty* argued that, to protect the rights of individuals and minorities, voting rights should be extended. These voices on behalf of the working man resulted in a series of legislative acts on behalf of workers that altered the classical liberal laissez-faire position. In 1833, the **Factory Act** limited the workday for children and required that factories establish schools for children under nine. Reformers published a shocking picture of children in mines leading to the Mines Act of 1842, prohibiting work for all women as well as boys younger than 10 underground. In 1884, in the Third Reform Bill, the right to vote was given to almost every adult male. By 1900 the Labour Party had formed, advocating redistribution of wealth by means of an income tax. In this way, the utopian socialist program was fulfilled in England by means of a democratic system.

Marxian Socialists

In Germany, a new kind of socialism, scientific or Marxian socialism, developed. Marxian socialism had its origins in the scientific rationality of the Enlightenment and in **George Hegel**'s (1770–1831) theory of change (dialectics). Dialectics described a process of being, or "thesis," that produced non-being, or "antithesis," resulting in a state of becoming, or "synthesis." In the *Communist Manifesto,* **Karl Marx** (1818–1883) and **Friedrich Engels** (1820–1895) applied Hegel's theory to economic relationships between classes. According to the *Manifesto,* "the history of all previously existing societies is the history of class struggle" and a state of conflict between the bourgeoisie, or capitalist factory owners, and the workers, or proletariat, over material things, hence, **dialectical materialism**. Based on history, Marx predicted that, just as the bourgeoisie had triumphed over feudal aristocracy, the proletariat would conquer the bourgeoisie in revolution. This revolution would produce **communism**, a utopia in which the state would wither away, there would be freedom from want, and the world would be united in a world of international workers, a world without national boundaries. The book concludes with the line, "Working Men of All Countries, Unite." Marxian socialism failed in its bid to influence world history during the revolution of 1848, the year the *Manifesto* was published, but it steadily gained converts in Germany and Russia during the last half of the nineteenth century and became a dominant force in the twentieth century, ironically in the nonindustrialized countries.

COMMUNIST MANIFESTO

The history of all hitherto existing societies is the history of class struggles. . . .

In short, the Communists everywhere support every revolutionary movement against the existing social and political order of things.

In all these movements they bring to the front, as the leading question in each, the property question, no matter what its degree of development at the time.

Finally, they labor everywhere for the union and agreement of the democratic parties of all countries.

The Communists disdain to conceal their views and aims. They openly declare that their ends can be attained only by the forcible overthrow of all existing social conditions. Let the ruling classes tremble at a Communist revolution. The proletarians have nothing to lose but their chains. They have a world to win.

WORKING MEN OF ALL COUNTRIES, UNITE!

The Manifesto *was published in 1848 as the platform of the "Communist League," a workingmen's underground association in Europe. Marx and Engels were commissioned to prepare for publication a complete theoretical and practical program. When the 1848 revolution failed, the document lingered until Russian theorists picked it up to use as a guide for their revolution. In most industrialized countries in Europe, legislation had improved the lot of the worker to the point that the* Communist Manifesto *seemed irrelevant. In countries like Russia, however, where neither social nor political revolution had taken place, and industrialization was on the march, the theories of Marx and Engels became a bible for political and social change. The* Communist Manifesto *advocates not just socialist programs like nationalization of industry, but revolution to overthrow existing states.*

Realism

In the second half of the nineteenth century, as industrialism and the worker class gained strength, the artistic and cultural movements moved from a romantic view of liberty and progress to social comment and a realistic depiction of life experiences. This included an application of science to society and its problems. **Realism** reflected life as it was, recorded and observed and used scientific objectivity rather than emotional intuition. **Emile Zola** (1840–1902) was the literary giant of the realistic movement. Zola wrote carefully researched stories about urban slums, coal strikes, and the stock exchange. He sympathized with socialism and his concern was inequality. In England, Mary Ann Evans (1819–1880), who wrote under the pen name **George Eliot**, in her great novel *Middlemarch* examined the way people are shaped by their society. In the visual arts, painters like **Edgar Degas** in *Women Ironing* captured the hard work of the laboring classes.

Determinists

The realists were also **determinists**. Unlike the romantics who glorified individual freedom, the realists believed human beings were governed by unalterable natural laws of heredity and environment. In particular, science was used to study society, giving rise to "social science." One of the most famous determinists was **Charles Darwin** (1809–1882), who concluded in *On the Origin of Species by Means of Natural Selection* (1859) that life had evolved or changed on the basis of a struggle for survival. Darwin's theory was applied to society by **Herbert Spencer** (1820–1903), a **Social Darwinist**, who argued that social progress occurred as a result of human survival of the fittest. Meanwhile, scientists began delving into the mind. **Sigmund Freud** (1856–1939), founder of psychoanalysis, theorized that much of human behavior was motivated by unconscious emotional needs. The exploration of the mind was reflected in literature too, especially in the works of Russian author **Feodor Dostoevsky**, whose works are filled with elements of conscience, guilt, and resentment. Realism reflected both the problems of urban industrial society and the faith in science to expose, understand, and correct the weaknesses in the social and economic fabric of late nineteenth-century Western society.

The New Ideologies and Women

During the nineteenth century, both liberals and socialists began to advocate change in the status of women. Middle-class women began to fight against the Napoleonic Code that enshrined the principle of female subordination. **Feminists** campaigned for equal legal rights for women as well as access to higher education. Later in the nineteenth century, middle-class women scored significant victories, such as the 1882 law giving English married women full property rights. In the years before 1914 middle-class feminists (advocates of political, economic, and social rights equal to those of men) increasingly shifted their attention to attaining for women the right to vote. Women were also inspired by utopian and Marxian socialism. Often at odds with middle-class feminists, socialist women leaders argued that liberation of (working-class) women would come only with the liberation of the entire working class through revolution. They championed the cause of working women and won some practical improvements, especially in Germany, where Bismarck pioneered social welfare legislation including better working conditions and security for working women.

Liberals and Socialists on Rights for Women
Declaration of the Rights of Woman
and of the Female Citizen, 1791

Olympe de Gouges

Woman, wake up; the tocsin of reason is being heard throughout the whole universe; discover your rights. The powerful empire of nature is no longer surrounded by prejudice, fanaticism, superstition and lies. . . . Oh women, women! When will you cease to be blind? What advantage have you received from the Revolution?. . . unite yourselves under the standard of philosophy; deploy all the energy of your character, and you will soon see these haughty men, not groveling at your feet as servile adorers, but proud to share with you the treasures of the Supreme Being. Regardless of what barriers confront you, it is in your power to free yourselves; you have only to want to . . .

Form for a Social Contract Between Man and Woman

We, _____ and _____, moved by our own will, unite ourselves for the duration of our lives, and for the duration of our mutual inclinations under the following conditions: We intend and wish to make our wealth communal, meanwhile reserving to ourselves the right to divide it in favor of our children and of those toward whom we might have a particular inclination. . .

I offer a foolproof way to elevate the soul of women; it is to join them to all the activities of men. . .

* * * * * * * * * * * * * * * * *

The Communist Manifesto, 1848

Karl Marx and Friedrich Engels

The bourgeois sees in his wife a mere instrument of production. He hears that the instruments of production are to be exploited in common, and, naturally, can come to no other conclusion, than that the lot of being common to all will likewise fall to the women.

He has not even a suspicion that the real point aimed at is to do away with the status of women as mere instruments of production.

For the rest, nothing is more ridiculous than the virtuous indignation of our bourgeoisie at the community of women, which, they pretend, is to be openly and officially established by the Communists. The Communists have no need to introduce community of women; it has existed almost from time immemorial. . . .

Nevertheless, in the most advanced countries the following will be pretty generally applicable:

10. Free education for all children in public schools. Abolition of children's factory labor in its present form. Combination of education with industrial production, etc., etc.

These two readings demonstrate that women's rights, including education, were important in both the liberal and socialist movements of the 19th century. Alarmed that the liberal democratic French Constitution of 1791 did not contain or even consider women's suffrage and rights, Olympe de Gouges protested and then proposed the equality of men and women in politics and marriage. A half century later, Marx and Engels argued that the bourgeois capitalist societies in England, France, and the United States treated women as cogs in a productive system oriented to profit. Also advocating for women and education, communists referred to the superior nature of communist society because it had always advocated a "community of women" and education for children.

EMPIRE

The European race for world empire, which occurred in the second half of the nineteenth century, was the industrial counterpart to the European search for markets during the Commercial Revolution. In 1800 the Europeans and North Americans dominated 35 percent of the world's land surface; by 1914 they controlled 84 percent. During the period, European money, migrants, and manufactured goods streamed particularly into Africa, Asia, and South America, resulting in tensions between European powers and putting millions of black and brown peoples under the control of whites. Intensification of European empire building was influenced by the unification of Germany and Italy.

Unification of Germany and Italy

Attempts to unify Italy and Germany finally succeeded in the second half of the nineteenth century. Italy and Germany became nation-states. This served to step up the competition for empire among the European states, adding two new contestants. Unification of Italy took place between 1858 and 1870. Two leaders instrumental in unification were **Count Camillo Cavour**, who united Sardinia and the Piedmont (northwest Italy), and **Giuseppe Garibaldi**, who rallied the people of Sicily. The two then supported King Victor Emmanuel II in his election bid in 1861. The Parliament proclaimed him king of Italy "by grace of God and will of the nation."

German unification, meanwhile, came at the hands of **Otto von Bismarck**. In his position as prime minister of Prussia, Bismarck hoped to unite Germany "not with speeches. . .but with blood and iron." Bismarck's plan, supported by Wilhelm I, was to unite the German states under Prussia. To do this, he fought three wars. In the war with Denmark, he obtained Schleswig Holstein. In the war with Austria, the Seven Weeks' War (1866), Austria approved the dissolution of the confederation of German states, and in 1867 the northern states were joined with Prussia. In 1870, Prussia fought France (the **Franco-Prussian War**), which ended in German victory and French cession of Alsace-Lorraine. In 1871 delegates wrote a constitution for a new German Empire made up of all the German states except Austria. The Germans called their empire the **Second Reich** (*reich* meaning empire, the First Reich being the Holy Roman Empire).

Once united, Germany rapidly industrialized and began to challenge Britain's industrial supremacy. Germany was able to do this for several reasons:

1. Germany imported technology;
2. Britain's traditional power sources—water and coal—were soon eclipsed by a German internal combustion engine that ran on petroleum and could drive machines, automobiles, and ships;
3. tariffs were introduced to protect infant industry.

Germany was not the only area where industrial output advanced. Industrial output doubled between 1870 and 1914 in Britain, in Germany it quadrupled, in the United States it trebled, and in Russia it increased ninefold. Thus began the scramble for raw materials and commodities overseas and a race to control and monopolize the areas from which supplies came. The scramble occurred mostly in Africa and Asia, areas rich in mineral and human resources and in shipping lanes, strategically located islands, and coaling bases. Indigenous peoples were unable to defend against European military might.

Causes of Imperialism

There were other reasons for empire. One was demographic. In the nineteenth century, Europe's population soared from 190 million to 423 million. Thus, empire became a place for excess population and a full 40 million people emigrated. Another was the transportation revolution. Large ocean-going steamships allowed fast transport across the world's seas. Likewise, on land the railroad allowed penetration of central Africa. The **Trans-Siberian Railroad**, begun in 1891 and completed in 1905, linked Europe and Asia. Railroads and irrigation allowed development of unpromising terrain in Kenya and Nigeria, where land was transformed into plantation colonies that grew tea, coffee, cotton, tobacco, and cocoa at great profit. Motor cars and airplanes completed the transportation revolution. Empire in Africa was also made possible by the mass production of quinine in 1830, providing Europeans defense against the tropical disease, malaria. Another cause of imperialism was the fact that the national borders in Europe had essentially been frozen by the Congress of Vienna in 1815. Thus, European nations seeking expansion and resources had to look beyond the borders of Europe or face the prospect of a war within Europe. This competition abroad often led to acquisition of territory, not for its own sake but to keep other European countries from doing so. This type of imperialism is often known as **neo-imperialism**. Finally, empire became a focus of national adventure and missionary zeal. **Cecil John Rhodes** (1853–1902) discovered diamonds, made a fortune, and then became prime minister of the Cape Colony. Missionaries like **John Livingston** spread Christianity. Europeans justified their intrusion in terms of bringing enlightenment and civilization to native peoples. Indeed, schools, hospitals,

Did You Know?

The opening of the Suez Canal in 1869 cut the sea journey from Europe to India by almost half, while the Panama Canal, completed in 1914, shortened the sailing time between New York and San Francisco.

"THE WHITE MAN'S BURDEN"

Take up the White Man's burden—
 Send forth the best ye breed—
Go bind your sons to exile
 To serve your captives' need;
To wait in heavy harness,
 On fluttered folk and wild—
Your new-caught, sullen peoples,
 Half-devil and half-child.

Take up the White Man's burden—
 In patience to abide,
To veil the threat of terror
 And check the show of pride;
By open speech and simple,
 An hundred times made plain,
To seek another's profit,
 And work another's gain.

This poem by Rudyard Kipling, written in the latter half of the nineteenth century, expresses a typical rationale for European imperialism in Africa. Kipling believed that Europeans had a duty to spread their civilization throughout the world in order to bring progress to native peoples. It was the beginning of racial overtones because many of the areas of the earth imperialized by Europeans had populations with dark skins.

and churches were established and roads built. The notion of white racial superiority was rarely questioned. Nowhere is the sentiment more clearly delineated than in **Rudyard Kipling**'s poem "The White Man's Burden." Imperialism had its critics too, like economist **J. A. Hobson** (1858–1940), whose work *Imperialism* influenced Lenin and others. He contended that imperialism was an outgrowth of capitalism's need for labor, raw materials, and markets. **Joseph Conrad** (1857–1924) also castigated Europeans for pure selfishness in "civilizing" Africa.

Imperialism in Africa

In 1880 European nations controlled about 10 percent of Africa, but by 1914 they had gobbled up almost the entire continent. Only Ethiopia in northeast Africa and Liberia on the West African coast remained independent. Before 1880 the French had conquered Algeria and the British had taken over the Dutch possessions in Cape Town. This had caused the Dutch settlers (**Afrikaners or Boers**) to make their

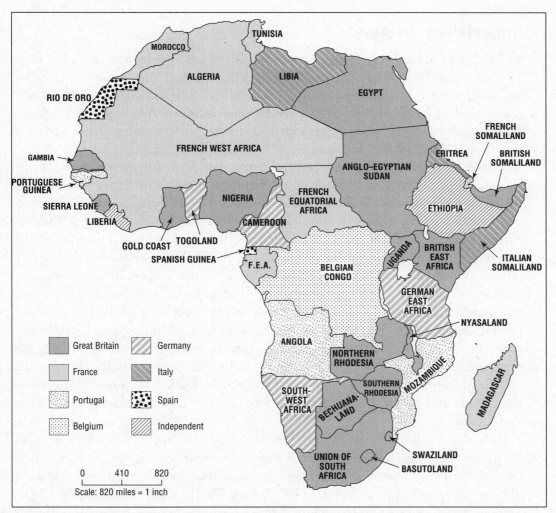

European Imperialism in Africa 1914 C.E. Unlike in China, where the European powers claimed only spheres of influence, European powers carved up the African continent. Only Liberia and Ethiopia remained independent. The imperialization of Africa was often more costly than productive, but raw materials, the Western predisposition to civilize, and, most of all, the desire to keep African territory out of rival European hands resulted in the partition of Africa.

Great Trek into the interior (1835) where they fought the **Zulu** people. In 1853 the Dutch proclaimed their independence, creating the Afrikaner states, the Orange Free State and the Transvaal. Between 1880 and 1900, however, Britain, France, Germany, and Italy created empires in Africa. Even the Afrikaner states were conquered by the British in the **Boer War** (1899–1902). In 1884 Leopold II of Belgium took over the entire Congo Basin, which he ruled directly and exploited mercilessly. Leopold's foray into Africa caused Bismarck of Germany to arrange an international conference establishing principles for European claims in Africa. The **Berlin Conference** (1884–1885) declared "effective occupation" the determining factor in laying claim. This set off another relentless push to the interior. Shortly thereafter, Germany claimed Togoland, the Cameroons, Southwest Africa, and East Africa. France extended its control over much of West and North Africa. Then, Britain claimed Zanzibar and thrust southward from Egypt into Sudan. On the Upper Nile, Britain came in conflict with France, a contest that ended with France capitulating. This illustrated the explosive nature of European competition. This relentless quest for African empire became known as the **Scramble for Africa**.

Imperialism in Asia

In Asia, the imperialist competition was no less fierce. Czarist Russia began in the 1820s to push against the steppe Muslim Khanates and one by one they fell—Tashkent in 1865, Samarkand and Bukhara in 1868, Merv in 1884—and finally, to the borders of India, where they met the British, who had expanded by war and the **doctrine of lapse** (native states without a clear successor fell under British rule) into the Punjab, Afghanistan, and Burma.

The British, meanwhile, acquired India, the "jewel" in the crown of the British Empire. This occurred as a result of the **Sepoy Rebellion** in 1857. This mutiny, which began among native regiments of the British army in India, involved princes and landowners as well as peasants. It resulted in the transfer of India from the British East India Company to the crown. A British viceroy was responsible for enacting the government policy in India. The British began educating Indians for jobs in the Indian civil service and building railroads to open Indian markets to British goods. The British encouraged the production of cotton rather than food crops and discouraged local industries that might compete with British factories. During the 1880s famines led to the deaths of millions of Indians and fostered sporadic revolts by poorly armed peasants. British telegraph lines, new railroads, and the Suez Canal increased communication and trade between India and Europe. British-educated middle-class Indians organized the **Indian National Congress** in 1885. This new political party demanded an end to British rule by the early twentieth century.

In China in the early nineteenth century the Europeans were confined to the coast. By then they had persuaded Chinese merchants to accept Indian opium instead of silver for purchases. In 1839 the imperial court decided to use force to halt the trade, but were defeated (**The Opium War**). In the Treaty of Nanking in 1842, China was forced to cede Hong Kong to Britain, to open five cities to foreign trade, and to accept low tariffs. The economic dislocation caused by the loss of silver resulted in widespread discontent and brought on the **Taiping Rebellion** in 1853. Leaders of the revolt capitalized on ancient Chinese traditions and ideas taken from Christian missionaries. They favored a redistribution of land, equality

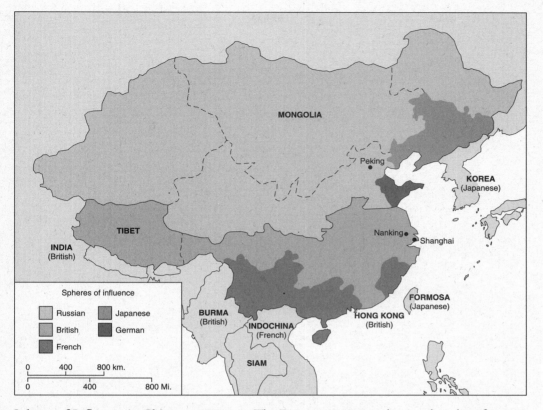

Spheres of Influence in China ca. 1910 C.E. The Europeans were another in a long list of outsiders in world history who penetrated China. Russia, Britain, France, Japan, and Germany all sought trade privileges, and to secure them, they carved out spheres. In an ironic way, this competition saved China from conquest by any one of them, but it led to the end of Chinese Imperial rule.

between men and women, and a reduction in taxes. The rebellion took 14 years to suppress and cost 20 million lives, further weakening Ch'ing rule and leading to another round of European incursions and trading concessions.

In response to Chinese weakness, the Russians occupied the Amur basin and Vladivostock. Britain acquired Burma; France, Indochina; and Japan, Korea. This string of defeats led to the **Boxer Rebellion** (1900), aimed at ousting foreigners. The Ch'ing, in desperation, had to call in the Western powers to restore order. In return, China was divided into spheres of influence by the Western powers. Meanwhile, the Dutch extended their rule from Java throughout the East Indian archipelago (Indonesia). The United States, as a result of the **Spanish American War** (1898), gained Cuba and the Philippines.

Results

The people of Africa and Asia initially tried to drive out the unwelcome foreigners, but, overpowered by superior weaponry, they responded in various ways. Some **modernizers** tried to adapt, while **traditionalists** tried to maintain the old ways. For some, on both ends of the spectrum, social and economic advancement was the result. Inevitably there were **anti-imperialists** as well, who resented foreign domination. Learning about liberalism and nationalism from their masters, eventually they used such theories to overthrow the Europeans in twentieth-century wars of liberation.

CHAPTER 22

The Spread of Modernization and the Transformation of Society

(ca. 1800 C.E.–1914 C.E.)

TIMELINE	
1839 C.E.–1876 C.E.	Tanzimat Reforms
1853 C.E.	Crimean War
1861 C.E.	Emancipation of serfs in Russia
1863 C.E.	Emancipation of slaves in America
1868 C.E.	Meiji Restoration
1904 C.E.	Russo-Japanese War
1905 C.E.	Revolution in Russia
1908 C.E.	Young Turk coup-d'etat

MEIJI JAPAN (1868)

In the areas of the world that were not overcome by European imperialism, governments took note of the power Europeans had assumed as a result of modernization. They began to copy industrialism and tinker with their political systems to accommodate economic change. In most cases, liberalism was introduced only in a limited way, industrialism came from the top down, and nationalism became a potent rationale for change. Japan, the Ottoman Empire, and Russia all attempted to modernize with varying results.

Japan's ability to change in the face of the Western challenge contrasted sharply with Chinese impotence. Perhaps change was possible for Japan because Japan had a history of imitation and fewer goods that the West wanted. At first, however, it seemed that Japan would be laid open for Western exploitation like China, India, and Africa. In 1853 American **Commodore Matthew Perry** arrived with a fleet in Edo Bay near Tokyo to threaten bombardment if Americans were not allowed to trade. The Japanese were forced into concessions. In 1858 other European nations followed suit. Then Japan changed course. Unlike China and India, which were ruled by foreign dynasties, Japanese political authority was exercised by a dynasty of military autocrats, the **Tokugawa shoguns**. Their failure to stand up to the Westerners caused unrest so serious that in 1868 **Emperor Meiji** threw out the shogun system and reclaimed the right of the emperor to rule in the **Meiji Restoration**. Immediately, both political and economic restructuring started.

Meiji Restoration

Ironically, the Tokugawa period, which had created a centralized Japanese state, also set in place much of the framework for Meiji modernization plans. By requiring all daimyo to reside in Edo and Osaka on alternating years, these cities exploded in population. Edo had a population of over one million in the eighteenth century, making it a leading world city. Demands for providers of goods and services grew. The position of the samurai, or privileged ruling class, which made up 5 percent of the population, shifted. Samurai became educated and moved into the bureaucracy. Removing the samurai from agriculture also had the effect of creating an agricultural sector that began producing for the market. The Tokugawa also built roads, a political infrastructure, and ports, and fleets.

The new Meiji government abolished feudalism, replacing the domains of the daimyos with a system of nationally appointed prefects. From this centralized base, Emperor Meiji and his **genro** (advisers) were able to effect change. They sent samurai officials abroad to study economic and political institutions and technology. A national education system and a conscript army financed by a new tax system were established in 1872. The army introduced peasants to the discipline of the military and educated them to be both a modern workforce and the foundation of a modern army. The feudal fighting tradition was put aside in favor of formal officer training and upgraded armaments. Stipends to the samurai class were abolished, impoverishing many, but this became the impetus for samurai to support reform in politics and business.

The bureaucracy was reorganized and opened to talent on the basis of civil service examinations. The bureaucracy grew from 29,000 officials in 1890 to 72,000 in 1908. A constitution based on the German model gave the emperor control over the military and the ability to appoint ministers. The parliament, or **Diet**, passed laws and approved the budget. Only about 5 percent of the adult male population could vote, however, due to high property qualifications. Political parties arose but they had limited power and the most liberal of them was suppressed. To avoid becoming a colony, Japan sought to exploit rivalries of the colonial powers abroad. The structure that evolved was highly centralized and gave power to the genro, an oligarchy of wealthy businessmen and former nobles.

Japanese Industrialization

The Meiji government industrialized. Problems like scarce capital, unfamiliarity with new technology, and fear of foreigners resulted in government control. The Ministry of Industry, created in 1870, oversaw economic policy and operation.

State banks were created to fund trade and provide industrial capital. State-built railroads spread across the country. Rapid steamers connected the islands. Guilds and internal tariffs were abolished to create a national market. Land reform gave individual ownership to farmers, raised agricultural output by the introduction of fertilizers and mechanized equipment. Private enterprise expanded. Older merchant families and some newcomers established factories producing textiles, chemicals, and food products. By the 1890s, large new industrial combines, called **zaibatsus**, emerged as a result of accumulations of capital and far-flung merchant and industrial operations. Japan, unlike other industrializing countries, depended on exports and had no prior capital built on foreign trade to rely on. Thus, the burden of production and the money for investment fell on poorly paid workers at home and in sweatshops, who turned out silk destined for foreign markets. A few big corporations provided benefits and social organizations, but maintained low wage policies and prohibited labor organizations.

Social Change in Japan

Many social changes resulted from industrialization. One was demographic. Population grew from 35 million in 1873 to 55 million in 1918. This strained resources and maintained low wages. Japanese education stressed science and technical subjects. They copied Western fashions, learned Western standards of hygiene, and adopted the Western calendar and metric system, but they did not adopt Christianity and retained many of their traditional emphases, especially the inferior position of women. Industrialization affected the family as men moved to the cities, leaving women behind. In 1900 Japan had the highest divorce rate in the world. **Shintoism** appealed to the new nationalist concerns with Japan's distinctive mission and the religious functions of the emperor. Modernization also caused many tensions in Japanese life—tensions between generations, between old and new, and between the traditional and foreign. The government urged national loyalty and devotion to the government.

As Japanese industrial power grew, in imitation of the West and in self-defense, Japan joined the ranks of the imperialist powers. Japan also needed markets and raw materials. In 1879 Japan annexed the Ryukus, and in 1895, after war with China, it acquired **Taiwan**. In 1904 conflicts over Russian influence in Manchuria and Japanese influence in Korea led to the **Russo-Japanese War**. Japan won handily. In 1910 Japan annexed Korea. This war is often seen as a turning point in world history because it marked the first major defeat of an industrial European empire by a non-Western power, setting in motion a process of decolonialization that was to dominate twentieth-century history. It also illustrated an alternative route to modernization from that followed by the West. Meiji modernization was unusual in that it avoided the revolutionary pressures that afflicted Russia and China, while maintaining rule from above.

OTTOMAN REFORM

Ottoman attempts at modernization and reform were less successful than those of the Japanese in safeguarding the Ottoman state from Western imperialism. Yet they did have a profound impact on the course Turkey would take in modern times. In the seventeenth and eighteenth centuries, the Ottoman Empire appeared to be in decline. Questions of dynastic succession, a series of incompetent rulers, rising population, increased taxes, corruption, foreign competition that deprived artisans of their livelihood, and an impoverished peasantry, all served to weaken the Ottoman state. Both the Austrian Hapsburgs and the Russians expanded at Ottoman expense. In 1683, in an Ottoman attack on Vienna, a strong allied Christian force and Hapsburg heavy artillery gave the Europeans victory. The peace treaty signed at **Karlowitz** (1699) proved a turning point as the Ottomans lost to Austria the vast, wealthy provinces of Hungary and Transylvania.

Meanwhile, after Russian Westernization under Peter the Great, the Russians advanced across the steppes, taking the Caucasus and Crimean areas. In 1804 a Christian uprising in **Serbia** was ended at great cost. In 1830 Greece gained independence; in 1867, Serbia. In addition, the Ottomans signed a series of agreements with the Europeans called **capitulations**. Not unlike the treaty ports given by China to the Western powers, the capitulations allowed French, English, and Hapsburg merchants to travel, buy, and sell throughout Ottoman dominions, pay low customs duties, and be exempt from Ottoman law. At the beginning of the nineteenth century, loss of territory, pressures of European imperialism, and unresolved internal problems caused the Ottoman Empire to be called "**the sick man of Europe**."

Modernization of Ottoman Turkey

Ottoman survival rested on European inaction due to fears among themselves that others would gain more from dismemberment, and on Ottoman reform. But internal reform was dangerous business because of vested interests among strong groups like the *ulama* (Muslim religious scholars, primary interpreters of Islamic law, and the core of Muslim societies). There were deep divisions among the ruling elite as to how reform could be achieved. Some argued for far-reaching change based on the European model. Others backed reforms based on precedents. It was in the interests of some to forestall any change at all. A first series of reforms were carried out under Sultan Selim (1789–1807). These were aimed at improving administration and building a new army and navy. The Janissary corps was so threatened by this that they revolted and killed him in 1807. A more skillful sultan, Mahmud II, in 1826 secretly built a small professional army with European help, and then subdued the Janissaries, threatened provincial nobles into submission, and launched a series of reforms based on Western models, despite protestations by the religious experts. He established a diplomatic corps and an army and navy on Western models. In succeeding decades, particularly during the **Tanzimat reforms**, (1839–1876), a state-run postal and telegraph service was introduced; universal education emphasized science and technology; and legal reforms, newspapers, and a constitution were developed. The reforms helped religious minorities, but did little to improve the role of women or artisans. The reforms did not settle the tensions between conservative elites and the Western-educated bureaucrats who favored ending the sultantate. In 1908, in resistance against the despotism reintroduced by Sultan Abdul Hamid (r. 1878– 1908), the Westernized officers and civilians united in an organization called the **Young Turks** and staged a bloodless coup in 1908. This led to the rise of Mustafa Kemal or **Ataturk** (1881–1938) after World War I and the emergence of a Westernized Turkey.

Modernization of Egypt

An even more astounding modernization program was undertaken by **Muhammad Ali** (1769–1849) in Egypt. In 1798 French armies under Napoleon invaded the Egyptian part of the Ottoman Empire. When they left, the Albanian-born Ottoman general Muhammad Ali stepped in to fill the vacuum. He immediately set about building a new state and military based on Western lines. His policies of modernization attracted large numbers of European fortune seekers, including engineers, doctors, policemen, financiers, shippers, and high government officials. One of the most important changes Muhammad Ali made, and one that was duplicated in many modernizing countries, was the development of commercial agriculture geared to the European market. Peasants had been poor but self-sufficient, growing food for their own use on state-allotted lands. But to pay for a modern army, high ranking officials and members of Ali's family began carving out large private holdings to grow crops like cotton for export. Peasant tenants provided the labor. Landlords often borrowed heavily from abroad, but still made personal fortunes. Modernization and accumulation of capital came on the backs of the peasants.

The modernization trend was continued under Muhammad Ali's grandson, **Khedive** (prince) **Ismail** (r. 1863– 1879). He promoted a large irrigation network that furthered estate building. He borrowed large sums to install modern communications, and with his support the **Suez Canal** was completed by a French company in 1869. In addition, young Egyptians were educated in Europe; Arabic instead of Turkish became the official language; and Cairo acquired modern boulevards and hospitals. The cost of modernization had another detrimental effect typical of many modernizing countries. Incurring colossal debt to European countries, Egypt could not pay interest on the debt. This caused the governments of France and England to intervene financially and politically to avoid Egyptian bankruptcy. When violent nationalist reaction occurred, a British expeditionary force occupied Egypt. British rule resulted in somewhat better conditions for peasants, as well as the tax reforms necessary to ensure that revenues repaid foreign bondholders. The British did not encourage education in fear of inciting political unrest. The Egyptian experience provided a new model for European expansion based on military and political domination, justified by civil stability and consistent administration. It was a model repeated in many places, as in the Caribbean by Theodore Roosevelt, and in China by the European powers under the guise of the Ch'ing Rule.

RUSSIA

Unlike Egypt and like Japan, Russia maintained its independence and became a substantial industrial power. In the nineteenth century Russia was a large multinational empire. Liberalism and nationalism were considered dangerous and subversive ideologies that the czarist leadership tried to repress, especially after they were introduced into Russia during Napoleon's invasion. In fact, much of the great outpouring of literature of nineteenth-century Russia had as its backdrop the struggles for liberal reform. When the Russians lost the **Crimean War** in 1853 to England and France because they lacked a modern military, the urgency for reform was apparent to all. In the 1850s almost 90 percent of Russia's population lived on the land, bound to their lords in hered-

Did You Know?

The modernization of Russia had many of the hallmarks of the Egyptian experience—heavy financial and technological borrowing from abroad and capital formation on the backs of the peasants.

itary serfdom and working the land with old-fashioned techniques. The Crimean War caused hardship on them, too, and raised the specter of revolt. To avoid this and to free the peasantry to provide a labor force for industry, the **Emancipation of Serfs** was proclaimed in 1861. Along with emancipation were other reforms. **Zemstvos**, or institutions of local government, marked a first though limited step toward popular participation in government. Political modernization was scant next to economic modernization, however.

Russian Industrialization

With the peasantry freed from bondage to the land and available as an industrial labor force, Russia embarked on a program of industrialization. The first step came with the creation of an extensive railroad network in the 1870s. The government encouraged and subsidized this effort. By the 1880s the railroad lines had almost quintupled since 1860. This had the effect of stimulating Russia's coal and iron sectors and linking Russia with the Pacific (**Trans-Siberian Railroad**). It also stimulated the grain export market to Europe, which helped pay for Western machinery and technology. In this way, the peasantry in Russia, too, underwrote industrial capitalization. Under **Sergei Witte**, Minister of Finance from 1892 to 1903, the government enacted high tariffs to protect Russian industry, improved the banking system, and encouraged Western investors to build great factories with advanced technology. By 1900 half of Russian industry was owned by foreigners. On the positive side, this did not lead to foreign political influence and Russia surged to fourth place in world steel production and second to the United States in petroleum production. On the negative side, Russia did not create a class of entrepreneurs nor was the agricultural sector modernized.

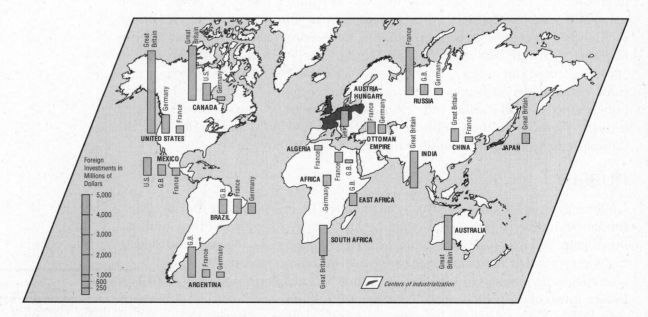

Industrial Development and Foreign Investment about 1900 C.E. World industrial development in 1900 was confined to a few places on the globe, primarily western Europe and the northeast coast of the United States. However, European countries made substantial investments in many places around the globe, primarily in infrastructure projects like railroads and resource development like mines and agriculture.

The Revolution of 1905

Russia's defeat in the Russo-Japanese War led to an explosion of grievances by the peasants, factory workers, and ethnic minorities, which made up 55 percent of the population in 1900. On **Bloody Sunday**, January 9, 1905, a peaceful demonstration of factory workers marched to the Winter Palace in St. Petersburg, carrying icons and singing "God Save the Czar." Suddenly, troops opened fire, killing and wounding workers in the crowd. During the summer, there were more protests across the country, including the sailors on the battleship *Potemkin* in the Black Sea, a mutiny immortalized in Sergei Eisenstein's classic movie *The Potemkin*. In October massive strikes paralyzed the country, leading to the **October Manifesto**, which granted civil rights and a popularly elected legislative branch, the **Duma**. While the czar backtracked when he issued the **Fundamental Laws** limiting the powers of the legislature, the reforms proved the impetus for **Peter Stolypin**, Chief Minister, to push through land reforms. These broke down collective village ownership of land and encouraged the most enterprising peasants to produce for the market. Thus, on the eve of World War I, Russia was partially modernized, with a conservative constitutional monarchy and a peasant-based but industrialized economy free of foreign political control.

The liberalism and industrialism of western Europe provided a mystique of power and success attractive to many countries. Japan, the Ottoman Empire, and Russia all followed different paths to modernization but the impetus for all was military strengthening and the process for all was from the top down. Unlike western Europe, individual freedoms were weakened and those of the state strengthened. In all cases, money for the capitalization of industry in Japan, the Ottoman Empire, and Russia came from abroad or from agriculture at the expense of the peasantry. In the Japanese case, industrialism occurred without liberalism or foreign control, but with ample nationalism. In the Russian case, industrialism proceeded with some liberalism and nationalism but heavy foreign borrowing. In the Ottoman Empire, heavy borrowing led to growing foreign control despite attempts to liberalize and modernize.

CULTURE AND SOCIETY

The New Class of Factory Owners and Workers

The Industrial Revolution brought two new classes to the fore—a strengthened middle class with factory owners and industrial capitalists added to the ranks of merchants and professional people, and a much larger group of factory workers. In terms of social structure based on wealth, there remained a great disparity between rich and poor, despite the fact that real wages for British workers between 1850 and 1906 doubled. In almost every advanced country around 1900, the richest 5 percent received one-third of the national income and the richest one-fifth received between 50 and 60 percent. The middle class was smaller than today, about 20 percent of the population.

The new class of factory owners came from a variety of backgrounds and exhibited great class mobility. Some were from merchant families; others were from religious minorities previously discriminated against; and still others, from the artisan and skilled worker ranks. Competition was fierce and profits uncertain. By the 1860s many more industrialists inherited their businesses. Advancement depended on education. While the middle class was diverse, their occupations required mental rather than physical skill. The upper middle class, composed of business families from banking and industry and large-scale commerce, aspired to an aristocratic lifestyle. They bought houses in the country, had servants and private carriages, and attempted favorable marriages with the upper classes. The middle class was composed of successful industrialists, merchants, and professionals. Shopkeepers, traders, and small manufacturers composed the lower middle class. Many other professions joined the middle class, including engineers, architects, chemists, accountants, white-collar office workers, teachers, and nurses. Although occupationally diverse, the middle classes could be united by a certain style of life. They were clothes-conscious and they rented, rather than owned, their own homes. Homes usually included tiny rooms for the servants under the eaves. Education was a growing expense. The middle classes observed a code of morality and behavior that stressed hard work, self-discipline, and personal achievement. People who fell into poverty were looked on as irresponsible. The largest part of the family budget and time was devoted to food. Middle-class families ate three substantial meals, spent lavishly on dinner parties, and employed an array of help to serve guests.

Did You Know?

The nineteenth century was the golden age of the middle class (bourgeoisie) because their culture and habits became the aspirations for many.

The Working Class

About four out of five people belonged to the **working classes** (proletariat), meaning people who depended on physical labor and did not employ domestic servants. Many were landowning peasants, especially in eastern Europe, though in England only 8 percent worked in agriculture. The rest worked in factories.

The condition of the working class has been controversial in history. Marx and Engels tended to portray them as exploited, and William Blake called early factories "satanic mills." Others saw improvement in the life of the masses because they were increasingly able to buy more of the necessities and a few luxuries. Statistics seem to show that during the years before 1850 prices rose faster than wages, but after that time there was considerable improvement. Generally speaking, food and clothing became cheaper and more plentiful, but housing worsened. The same sort of improvement occurred in working conditions. Cottage workers were used to working as a family, hard and long but at their own pace. They had difficulty getting used to the monotony and discipline of factory life.

Furthermore, the presence of the whole family in the factory kept the family together but meant that young children were working with dangerous equipment and parents did not have time to tend to their needs. Although large numbers of parents worked in factories, female working patterns did not change. Studies of the year 1851 in Britain and France indicate that 40 percent of the women working in Britain were employed as domestic servants, and in France, 40 percent worked in agriculture. The number of women factory workers in Britain was 20 percent and 10 percent in France. Gradually, however, a sexual division of labor occurred—men worked in the factory and women worked in homes and tended children. Kinship ties were important in getting jobs as manufacturers often used subcontractors to hire and fire.

Like the middle class, the working class had several levels. The highly skilled working classes were construction bosses, makers of scientific equipment, and highly skilled workers such as metalworkers and locomotive engineers. They comprised about 15 percent of the working classes and earned twice as much as the unskilled workers. They maintained puritanical behavior not unlike the middle class though they did not aspire to become middle class. They were the leaders of the working class. Below the skilled workers were the semiskilled or unskilled urban workers. This group worked as carpenters and bricklayers, factory workers, wagon drivers, and domestic servants, many of whom were young girls from the countryside. The favorite leisure activities of the working class were drinking, sports, and going to music halls. In fact, this was the era when mass leisure began. As factories turned out massive quantities of goods, they had to be mass advertised to be sold. Middle-class families flocked to buy bicycles, a fad of the 1880s. Popular newspapers and organized sports like soccer and baseball emerged. Religion, however, was still an important component in a family's values and traditions, though church attendance declined.

Women and the Family

The tremendous changes wrought by the Commercial and Industrial Revolutions are no more evident than in the family and life of women. One of the most startling changes was the emergence of adolescence as a distinct stage of life, a necessity for the middle classes because of the necessity of job training. With couples increasingly coming from different towns and being away from home, illegitimacy exploded between 1750 and 1850. By the end of the century, however, marriage and pregnancy went hand in hand, thus strengthening the urban family. Welfare services were limited before the twentieth century. Kinship ties remained strong and people depended on family in times of disaster, death, and crisis.

The biggest change for women in this era came from the strict division of labor. The ideal was the wife as mother and homemaker, the husband as provider. The result was that men were hostile to women in the workplace and in education. Women were subordinated to their husbands financially and legally. Thus began the struggle for women's rights. On the other hand, women had considerable power within the family, often controlling the purse strings and managing the home, providing emotional warmth and stability. One of the most important signs of change in middle-class family life was in child-rearing. Loving care was lavished on infants. A greater concern was given to adolescents, who entered the workplace at increasingly older ages. Declining birth rates contributed to the reduction of family size. Greater individual attention to and expenditures on children demonstrated a hope of improved economic and social status for them. Children became financial liabilities rather than assets. Despite an increasingly stable and redefined family and social life for many in the industrial world, for many others, it was a time of limited opportunity and great upheaval caused by mass migrations.

Population and Migration

Liberalism and industrialism gave rise to one of the great migrations in world history. People fled Europe in great numbers to find political freedom and economic opportunities in the Americas. It was part of the West's global expansion and growing power in which millions of people left their ancestral lands and planted stakes in a new land.

There were several reasons for the great migration, one of which was population pressures. The population of Europe, including European Russia, more than doubled between 1800 and 1900, from approximately 188 million to 432 million, not including the 60 million who left Europe. Since population grew more slowly in Africa and Asia than in Europe, people of European origin jumped from 22 percent of the world's total to about 38 percent. The reason was rising birth rates and declining death rates due to a better standard of living and improved medical care. In the twentieth century this same phenomenon led to rising population and migration on the part of Asiatic populations. Europeans migrated primarily to the United States (slightly less than half), Canada, Argentina, Brazil, Australia, and Asiatic Russia. Much of the movement was **migration** (moving from one place to another) rather than **immigration** (to become part of another country). One of three immigrants to the United States, one in two to Argentina, and seven out of eight emigrants from the Balkans returned to their homeland. At the other extreme, only one in 10 from Ireland and one in 20 of eastern European Jews returned. Other reasons for movement were the hope of land ownership, social mobility, and political freedom.

European Migrations

The sequence of migration was determined by the circumstances in the European countries. People left Britain and Ireland in large numbers from the 1840s on. In fact, fully one-third of all Europeans who migrated between 1840 and 1920 came from the British Isles because of rural poverty, the need for skilled industrial technicians in the new lands, and preferences shown to British migrants in the British Empire. In the case of Ireland, the **Great Potato Famine** was a major reason. Once potatoes were introduced into Ireland from the Americas, Irish peasants became dependent on them and population grew because of them. In 1846, 1848, and 1851 the potato crop failed as blight attacked the single strain plants. Widespread starvation and mass epidemic followed. One million emigrants fled between 1845 and 1851 and at least 1.5 million died. British relief, when it did come, was too late and hampered by a poor distributional infrastructure.

Another wave of emigrants left Europe after the 1848 revolutions for political reasons. In the 1880s a wave of five million Russian Jews left their homes due to the **pogroms** (organized persecutions or massacres) that began in 1881 under Czar Alexander II. Also in the 1880s, Italians began to migrate due to deteriorating agricultural conditions in Italy after the influx of cheap North American wheat and the lack of jobs. Many Italians went to the United States but more went to Argentina and Brazil.

Not all migration was to the Americas from Europe. At least three million Asians, primarily Chinese, Japanese, Indians, and Filipinos (as opposed to 60 million Europeans, a situation reversed in the twentieth century) moved abroad before 1920. Most were indentured laborers used on plantations and in gold fields to supplant African labor in Latin America, California, Hawaii, and Australia. Between 1853 and 1873, 130,000 Chinese laborers went to Cuba. More Asians might have come except that Asian migrants competed with natives for jobs. Americans demanded a halt to Asian immigration. This was another reason why Europeans and peoples of European ancestry reaped the main benefits from migration and monopolized the best overseas opportunities.

After the American Revolution, the English colonized Australia with debtors and convicts from British prisons. Other English pioneers followed. When gold was discovered in 1851, prospectors flooded in from all over the world. New Zealand also attracted English settlers. Chinese moved into Southeast Asia in the 1870s, where unskilled workers were employed as plantation laborers and miners. There, educated Chinese became traders, money lenders, and commercial agents. By the time of World War II, 15 million Chinese had settled in Southeast Asia and Africa as laborers and merchants.

Thus, industrialism and liberalism significantly altered world culture and society. Industrialism created a larger middle class and a burgeoning laboring class. Both classes infiltrated liberal governments and developed legislation in their interests. The habits and values of the middle class—good food, leisure, family, hard work, social advancement—became the prototype for industrializing societies everywhere. As middle-class women's roles became more connected with the home, opportunities in the workplace declined. Rising standards of living caused a population explosion, a circumstance that served as the impetus for migration alongside a quest for economic opportunities, social mobility, and political freedom.

Unit Review

Cross-Regional Developments

This period in history is the beginning of world Westernization. European culture spread worldwide. Developments that crossed borders include the following:

- European liberal thought based on the Enlightenment ideas of liberty, rights, and equality ignited revolutions in the Americas and France and Napoleon's advance over Europe helped spread them further across Europe;

- a second agricultural revolution that began in the Low Countries spread to England, where it created the necessary environment for the Industrial Revolution;

- the development of machines, new energy sources, and transportation networks allowed Europeans to travel far and wide and improve their military capabilities;

- soon Europeans overwhelmed the native populations and created empires that delivered markets and resources;

- industrialism created tremendous social change, a new middle class of factory owners and professionals, and a lower class dominated by factory workers;

- conditions of industry became the basis for new ideologies, especially socialism, which advocated an end to laissez-faire policies and the active role of government in the economy;

- the revolutions of 1848 failed due to middle-class fears of the workers and their new agenda;

- middle-class values and culture set the style of life, including sexual division of labor, leisure, consumerism, self-discipline, hard work, a get-ahead mentality, and infatuation with the metropolis;

- industrialism caused a population explosion and migration of Europeans around the world, especially to the Americas;

- the attractiveness of modern ways caused other countries to attempt to industrialize from the top down;

- industrialism and liberalism fed the flames of national pride and power, causing new countries like Germany and Italy to coalesce;

- nations became highly competitive, especially in contests over empire.

Legacies

Many of the legacies of this period endure and cast their brilliance and shadow over today's world. These include

- Enlightenment thought;

- bourgeois revolutions in North America and France;

- political fragmentation and independence but not social revolution in Latin America;

- the balance of power concept for Europe;

- failed liberalism in eastern Europe;

- romantic art, literature, and music;

- the machine, energy, and transportation revolutions;

- modern cities and architecture;

- socialist thought;

- European empires in Africa and Asia;

- adaptations to the Western model of modernization;

- middle-class culture and the rise of the worker;

- European mass migration; and

- sexual division of labor and women's rights movements.

Quiz

Unscramble:

Arrange the following in chronological order.

1. Haitian Revolution, Reign of Terror, European Liberal Revolutions, Latin American Revolt, French Revolution, Waterloo, American Revolution

2. Boxer Rebellion, Enclosure Acts, Suez Canal, Opium War, Sepoy Rebellion, Taiping Rebellion, First Locomotive, Boxers

3. Emancipation of U.S. Slaves, Emancipation of Russian Serfs, Russo–Japanese War, Crimean War, Meiji Restoration

Matching:

1. Inductive method	A. Groups controlling governments after revolutions
2. Deductive method	B. Observation, measurement, experiment, hypothesis, verification
3. Juntas	
4. "Natural rights"	C. A mathematical approach beginning with self-evident truths and advancing to more complex truths.
5. Socialism	
6. Great Trek	D. Government-sponsored violence against Jewish communities in Russia
7. Pogroms	
8. Zaibatsus	E. Life, liberty, and property
	F. Government should organize the economy, the poor should be protected, wealth should be more equally distributed
	G. The Dutch migration into the interior of South Africa
	H. Japanese industrial combines

Questions:

1. The site of the liberal revolution led by Toussaint L'Ouverture was

    (A) Paris.
    (B) Moscow.
    (C) Colombia.
    (D) Haiti.
    (E) Venezuela.

2. In which of the following choices are events arranged in the correct chronological order?

    (A) Napoleonic Era, Latin American Revolutions, American Revolution, French Revolution, Reign of Terror
    (B) Latin American Revolutions, Napoleonic Era, American Revolution, French Revolution, Reign of Terror
    (C) American Revolution, Napoleonic Era, Latin American Revolutions, French Revolution, Reign of Terror
    (D) American Revolution, French Revolution, Reign of Terror, Napoleonic Era, Latin American Revolutions
    (E) American Revolution, Reign of Terror, Napoleonic Era, French Revolution, Latin American Revolutions

3. What was the Ottoman response to growing European imperialism in the nineteenth century?

    (A) zaibatsus
    (B) the Crimean War
    (C) Ulama
    (D) the Sepoy Rebellion
    (E) the Tanzimat Reforms (Reorganization)

4. Enlightenment thought rejected the belief

    (A) that rulers govern only in accordance with God's will.
    (B) in progress.
    (C) that the discovery of the laws of nature and man will improve the human condition.
    (D) that there are rational laws that describe social behavior.
    (E) that all men have natural rights including life, liberty, and property.

5. During the French Revolution, July 14, 1789, marked the

    (A) call for a National Assembly.
    (B) fall of the Bastille.
    (C) execution of Louis XVI and Marie Antoinette.
    (D) acceptance of universal male suffrage.
    (E) presentation of the Declaration of the Rights of Man.

6. The only Napoleonic battlefield victory of those sites listed below was

    (A) Trafalgar.
    (B) Austerlitz.
    (C) Moscow.
    (D) Waterloo.
    (E) Tilsit.

7. Which of the following countries unified in the second half of the 19th century?

    (A) Austria
    (B) Germany
    (C) Greece
    (D) Russia
    (E) China

8. Those instrumental in Europeanizing life in Latin America were

   (A) the caudillos.
   (B) women who controlled the local markets.
   (C) mestizos.
   (D) Creoles.
   (E) church officials.

9. Of those listed below, who were the first to initiate a political campaign to abolish slavery?

   (A) French philosophers
   (B) the British navy
   (C) Quakers, Baptists, and Anglicans
   (D) Dutch merchants
   (E) Cubans

10. Between 1814 and 1850 revolutions occurred in all of the following countries EXCEPT

    (A) Greece.
    (B) France.
    (C) Russia.
    (D) Belgium.
    (E) Prussia.

11. The romantic hero of goodness and justice, Jean Valjean, in *Les Misérables*, was the creation of

    (A) Victor Hugo.
    (B) William Wordsworth.
    (C) Joseph Conrad.
    (D) Rudyard Kipling.
    (E) Feodor Dostoevsky.

12. In his *Essay on Liberty*, which of the following men argued that voting rights should be extended to protect the rights of individuals and minorities?

    (A) Robert Owen
    (B) Adam Smith
    (C) John Stuart Mill
    (D) Jeremy Bentham
    (E) Karl Marx

13. An early romantic composer, and one who inspired patriotic sentiments, was

    (A) Bach.
    (B) Mozart.
    (C) Beethoven.
    (D) Tchaikovsky.
    (E) Berlioz.

14. The Industrial Revolution had its beginnings in

    (A) France.
    (B) Spain.
    (C) England.
    (D) the United States.
    (E) Germany.

15. Which was least likely to benefit the English economy in the nineteenth century?

    (A) a stable government.
    (B) a central bank.
    (C) a strong domestic market supplied by navigable rivers.
    (D) an expanding colonial market.
    (E) corvee labor

16. Which of the following inventors developed the steam engine, the source of power for the Industrial Revolution?

    (A) George Stephenson
    (B) Richard Arkwright
    (C) James Hargreaves
    (D) James Watt
    (E) Jethro Tull

17. Which of the following men is incorrectly linked with his work?

    (A) Adam Smith—*Inquiry into the Nature and Causes of the Wealth of Nations*
    (B) Pierre Joseph Proudhon—*What Is Property?*
    (C) David Ricardo—*Essay on Liberty*
    (D) Karl Marx and Frederick Engels—*Communist Manifesto*
    (E) Charles Darwin—*On the Origin of Species by Means of Natural Selection*

18. Motivation for empire among industrialized nations included

    (A) a desire for overseas commodities and raw materials.
    (B) the opportunity for a rapidly expanding population to emigrate.
    (C) profit from the rapid transport of people and products from remote corners of the world.
    (D) a focus for national adventure and missionary zeal.
    (E) all of the above

19. Classical liberals believed government should

    (A) be the watchdog over environmental problems.
    (B) protect private property.
    (C) supervise and regulate public health.
    (D) establish a graduated income tax.
    (E) provide sewage disposal and street maintenance.

20. All of the following are connected with modernization movements ca. 1800 C.E.–1914 C.E. EXCEPT

    (A) Emperor Meiji
    (B) Mahmud II
    (C) Muhammad Ali
    (D) Thomas Malthus
    (E) Sergei Witte

21. Marx and Engels addressed their appeal to the

    (A) bourgeoisie.
    (B) proletariat.
    (C) peasants.
    (D) democrats.
    (E) rulers.

22. Based on the audience for whom the *Communist Manifesto* was written, Marx and Engels might have predicted a revolution in

    (A) England, France, and Germany.
    (B) Brazil, Mexico, and Egypt.
    (C) India.
    (D) Russia.
    (E) the United States.

23. Realist art reflected

    (A) the abstract expression of quantum physics.
    (B) scenery as the preferred subject matter.
    (C) a romantic approach.
    (D) national consciousness and increasing feelings of nationalism.
    (E) an interest in the life of workers and peasants.

24. What can be said about the position of women as a result of the revolutions in energy, industry, and transportation at the end of the nineteenth century?

    (A) Marx and Engels believed women were exploited under a capitalist bourgeois system.
    (B) *The Declaration of Rights of Woman* proposed that wealth should be communal between men and women and that activities should be joined.
    (C) Married women gained full property rights in England.
    (D) The principle of female subordination was encompassed in the Napoleonic Code.
    (E) *Vindication of the Rights of Women* by Mary Wollstonecraft was published in reponse to Marx and Engels.

25. The Russian sphere of influence ca. 1904 in East Asia was in

    (A) Formosa.
    (B) Mongolia.
    (C) Tibet.
    (D) Indochina.
    (E) Manchuria.

Answers

Unscramble:

1. American Revolution, French Revolution, Reign of Terror, Haitian Revolution, Waterloo, Latin American Revolutions, European Liberal Revolutions, Unification of Italy and Germany
2. Enclosure Acts, First Locomotive, Opium War, Sepoy Rebellion, Defeat of the Taiping Revolutionaries, Suez Canal, Boxer Rebellion
3. Crimean War, Emancipation of Russian Serfs, U.S. Emancipation of Slaves, Meiji Restoration, Suez Canal, Russo-Japanese War

Matching:

1. **(B)**		5. **(F)**	
2. **(C)**		6. **(G)**	
3. **(A)**		7. **(D)**	
4. **(E)**		8. **(H)**	

Questions:

1. **(D)**	10. **(C)**	19. **(B)**
2. **(D)**	11. **(A)**	20. **(D)**
3. **(E)**	12. **(C)**	21. **(B)**
4. **(A)**	13. **(C)**	22. **(A)**
5. **(B)**	14. **(C)**	23. **(E)**
6. **(B)**	15. **(E)**	24. **(C)**
7. **(B)**	16. **(D)**	25. **(E)**
8. **(D)**	17. **(C)**	
9. **(C)**	18. **(E)**	

STUDY TIP

- Review the framework of World History by rereading the introductions to each of the 8 units.
- Revisit the legacies and cross regional developments at the end of each unit.

  - Legacies remain from one historical period to the next. Many can be traced to the present day.
  - Cross regional developments are the significant changes during the era.

Subject matter has greater meaning within the context of a global framework.

The Twentieth–Century World

SCIENCE AND TECHNOLOGY IN WORLD HISTORY

One might be tempted to call the twentieth century the classical age of science and technology. The explanations for this near worship are not hard to find. Governments and people believe that science and technology produce practical benefits that result in a better quantitative and qualitative lifestyle. They believe that technologically advanced countries are wealthier, more modern, and more fun (cell phones, videos, and so on). They believe science and technology are "good." There is also the feeling that the twentieth century is unsurpassed in its scientific and technological breakthroughs, from automobiles to atomic and nuclear weapons and power, airplanes, penicillin, computers, and cell phones.

From an historical perspective, the "triumph" of science and technology and particularly the inseparability of the two is a new phenomenon. For most of the human record, **science** (the study of the natural world) constituted a scholastic endeavor that was commissioned by kings and recorded in scientific publications. **Technology** (knowledge regarding fashioning of implements), on the other hand, was understood as the crafts practiced by unschooled artisans (craftsmen). In simple parlance, the scientists were the thinkers and the artisans the doers. Until the second half of the ninteenth century, few artisans or engineers received any schooling. Conversely, the science curriculum centered on pure mathematics and science, was literally the "philosophy of nature." Not only were science and technology separate for most of history, but technology often directed the development of science in contrast to the present assumption that science advances technology. In the twentieth century, however, science and technology became intricately intertwined.

Technology in the form of stone tools went hand in hand with the evolution of humankind (*Homo habilis*, the "handyman"). Only toward the end of the prehistoric era did humans begin to observe the natural world in a way that is considered scientific. Only when city-based societies emerged about 10,000 years ago did political leaders begin to value abstract learning for its possible application in the management of complex societies (as in irrigation systems that required sophisticated measurements and natural observations). These sorts of endeavors seemed to have developed in indigenous traditions in Hellenic Greece, China, India, and Central and South America. In many of these societies, the scientists were linked to the priesthood, signifying a link between the natural world, the world of the spirits, and the institutions of statecraft that were aimed at control over people by means of control of nature. Beginning in the fifteenth century, Europeans began to master critical technologies like firearms and oceangoing ships, thus establishing an important place for technology in society. Only in the sixteenth and seventeenth centuries did modern science unfold in a "Scientific Revolution" that from the beginning was tied to crucial practical questions like knowing the shape of the earth so that monarchs could direct ships to sail west in search of "India" or fashioning the technology of the sextant so that mariners could accurately calculate location. In the eighteenth century, industrialization began to demonstrate what reason and experiment could accomplish, and in the ninteenth and twentieth centuries what thinkers and tool-makers could forge together. The new sciences—electricity, industrial chemistry, molecular biology, and aerodynamics, to name a few—are really a merger of the the-oretical and craft traditions.

The belief in the benefits of science and technology has elevated them to two of the creeds of modern times (along with beliefs in freedom, equality, and secular-ism). Modern culture is heavily influenced by them—cars reflect style, cell phones reflect being connected, and computer technology reflects hopes of instant wealth and reinforces the entrepreneurial spirit. Modern science and technology also reflect and influence our perceptions and understandings of the world we experi-ence. For instance, Enlightenment thinkers of the eighteenth century envisioned a Newtonian world that worked like a clock—predictably and according to certain rules of nature that need only be discovered to be conquered. Political ideas like balance of power proceeded from that. Scientists of the twentieth century, how-ever, have "discovered" other rules of nature. These rules are randomness, inter-connectedness, chaos, and choice in the universe. These rules are reflected in the arts and even in world history. In art, "modern" reflects the twentieth century sci-entific notions of chaos, unpredictability, and uncertainty by means of abstract symbolism and random color. World history describes the rise of western Europe beginning in the fifteenth century as a process of human interconnection and ran-dom circumstances rather than as a process of linear certainties based on the nature of European society.

In the twenty-first century, many predict that the next great human story will be humans in space. If this is so, science and technology will be one of the bases for that adventure.

Europe and the World

(ca. 1900 C.E.–1970 C.E.)

TIMELINE	
1911 C.E.	End of the Manchu Dynasty China
1914 C.E.–1918 C.E.	World War I
1919 C.E.	Government of India Act
1929 C.E.–1942 C.E.	Great Depression
1935 C.E.	Nuremburg Laws
1939 C.E.–1945 C.E.	World War II
1945 C.E.	Dropping of the atomic bomb and United Nations Charter
1945 C.E.–1989 C.E.	Cold War
1957 C.E.	Sputnik
1969 C.E.	Man on the Moon

TWENTIETH-CENTURY WARFARE

In 1900 a person riding in a horse-drawn buggy to visit with friends and relatives a few miles distant would be astounded at life at the end of the twentieth century. During this period the world changed from typewriter to computer, from telegraph to e-mail, from Western industrialization to a global market, from travel within countries to travel between countries and into outer space, and from local foods and handmade clothes to those of international design and manufacture. Ironically, world wars are partially responsible for this dramatic shift. War produced new technologies and inventions, and troop movements on a global scale introduced people to different cultures. As in all world history, times of great interaction stimulate new ways of doing things and new habits of thought.

During the first half of the twentieth century, explosive intra-European conflict ended Europe's global political hegemony. Decolonization, national liberation movements, communist revolutions, and alternative routes to modernization followed. The West's decline is exhibited by the decline in its population as a percentage of the world's total, the end of European empire and monopoly over advanced weapons systems, and the end to its unchallenged preeminent position as the world's leading trader and manufacturer. Yet, not unlike Greek and Islamic history, the end of global political power did not mean the end of global influence. Western culture and especially American culture continued to set world trends.

Industrialism and its technology led to new weapons and methods of warfare. Nationalism caused whole nations and peoples to be involved, leading to total war and the blurring of lines between civilian and military. The Crimean War in Europe and the Civil War in the United States were two of the last wars to be fought in the style developed during the preceding centuries. In these wars, armies lined up on the open fields with cavalry and artillery and engaged in man-to-man combat. Increasingly in the twentieth century, war became mechanized combat, mobilized by national political systems that greatly expanded the powers of government.

Weaponry

Twentieth-century weaponry completely changed the face of war, from a war of men to a war of weapons. Nations that were modern and wealthy won in this contest because they could support the research, development, innovation, and application of technology necessary to gain the edge. When World War I began, countries with the telegraph and railroad had an advantage in the strategic organization for war. The only defense against the machine gun and powerful artillery was the trench. From 1914 to 1917, trench warfare led to a stalemate, which was ended, in large part, by the introduction of new military technology. The tremendous power of artillery ended the role of cavalry, though animals were still used in transport. The stalemate that occurred on World War I battlefields led to a technological change that ended the war in 1918. In 1916 tanks, airplanes, poison gas, and submarines were all introduced.

Aviation history actually began in 1783 when hot air balloons were used during the Napoleonic Wars to drop propaganda leaflets. In 1914 all the belligerents together only had 500 aircraft, used mainly for reconnaissance. By 1918, 300,000 British officers were engaged in aviation and there were 50,000 flying machines. On the seas, the great advance was the iron-clad steamship and then the battleship, fueled by petroleum rather than coal. This greatly extended the range and flexibility of naval warfare. The submarine was actually invented in the 1890s by John Holland. It used the mechanisms of two machines, one for above water and one below. When put to use at sea in 1916, there was no defense against it.

All the weapons introduced in World War I were perfected in the interwar period and put to battle in a swift, systematic barrage, or **blitzkrieg**, in World War II. In a typical blitzkrieg, airplanes moved forward first to establish air superiority, followed by parachutists, ground force movement, and then armored divisions. On sea, war was a contest of carrier and submarine. In fact, pilots dropped tremendous payloads and never saw their victims and submarines sank ships they never saw. This added to war's impersonality. Defenses against this were few, but acoustic sonar and radar made dramatic differences in defense capabilities against the blitz. As with many inventions, radar was developed in the private sector and taken over by the military, which had vast resources to develop it. By the end of World War II, the sentiment prevailed that "weapons, if only the right ones can be found, constitute ninety-nine percent of victory."

THE HORRORS OF TRENCH WARFARE

After a few hours we are finished with the barbed wire. But there is still some time before the trucks return for us. Most of us lie down to sleep. . . .

Then it begins in earnest. Bombardment. . . . Green rockets shoot up the sky line. Barrage. The mud flies high, fragments whizz past. . . .

Not a moment too soon. The dark goes mad. The flames of the explosions light up the graveyard. There is no escape anywhere. . . .

The earth bursts before us. It rains clods. My sleeve is torn away by a splinter. Now a crack on the skull. . . .

I open my eyes. My fingers grasp a sleeve, an arm. A wounded man? I yell to him—no answer. A dead man. Now I remember that we are lying in a graveyard. But the shelling is stronger than any other thought so I merely crawl deeper into the coffin. It should protect me. . . .

Cautiously, I breathe through the gas mask. The gas still creeps over the ground and sinks into the hollows. . . .

In 1929 a former German soldier, Erich Maria Remarque, wrote a novel titled All Quiet on the Western Front. *This book remains the classic description of the horrors of trench warfare on the Western Front during World War I. Written through the eyes of a young German soldier, it has become the story of all soldiers in an age of total war.*

After 1945 atomic and nuclear weapons, cruise missiles, drones, and automation in the form of computers, transformed the battlefield once again. In 1945 the Americans had a monopoly on atomic weapons, but by 1949 the Soviet Union, by efficient espionage, had caught up. The U.S. and U.S.S.R. both engaged in nuclear research development, producing an even more fearsome collection of weapons—hydrogen bombs in the 1950s, intercontinental ballistic missiles (ICBMs) and nuclear powered and armed Polaris submarines in the 1960s, neutron bombs and a prolific range of intermediate and short-range ballistic missiles (Cruise and Trident) in the 1970s. By 1985 there were some 20,000 thermonuclear weapons in existence. Ninety percent were in two countries. The effect of these nuclear devices was to deter war rather than to contribute to it because of the fear of MAD, "**mutually assured destruction**." Paradoxically, the sheer expense of it all ensured that nuclear weaponry would be confined to countries with large economies. Consequently, wars of traditional and guerrilla nature, often supplied from the post-World War II stockpiles of large nations, continued around the world among those who did not possess such advanced weapons capability. By the 1990s, however, nuclear proliferation spread to other countries like India, Pakistan, Israel, and China. This had a destabilizing effect on world power politics.

Economy

Modern warfare had traumatic effects on the economies of countries. The cost of World War II alone was four trillion dollars, counting lost employment, consumption of resources, and destruction. Britain spent four billion pounds more on post-World War II weapons than on education and two billion pounds more than on social expenditures. The Soviet Union devoted almost a fifth of its resources to Cold War weaponry and the United States almost one-tenth to it. Perhaps a third of American industry depended on defense contracts. With little to show for this, the Soviet Union and the United States embarked on a complicated space exploration program. In 1957 the Russians put the first satellite into space, *Sputnik I*, and in 1961 they put the first man, **Yuri Gagarin**, in space. The United States then devoted more to space research and won the "Space Race" by putting **Neil Armstrong** on the moon in 1969.

To meet the cost of these vast spending programs, economies were completely revamped. All economies—capitalist and socialist alike—came under greater government control. Organization for war included not only massive, compulsory recruitment, the draft, but also government control of the economy via obligatory planning, rationing, altered management policy, controlled labor relations, and personal consumption patterns. One example of total planning in World War I was the German economy developed by Walter Rathenau. Under his direction, every conceivable raw material was inventoried, rationed, and distributed. Moreover, attempts to produce substitutes, like synthetic rubber, were started. In England, 90 percent of all imports were bought and allocated by the state. In most countries during World War II, gas, women's stockings, liquor, tobacco, and rubber were all rationed.

THE CAUSES AND RESULTS OF WORLD WAR I

The wars that occurred from 1914–1918 and from 1939–1945 were called "world wars" for a number of reasons.

- First, theaters of warfare occurred not just in Europe, but in many places around the world.

- Second, the wars were fought for world imperial holdings as much as for land and power in Europe.

- Third, soldiers and economic resources from all over the world became part of the war effort.

- Fourth, the conflicts drew many non-European countries into them in pursuit of their own nationalistic war aims. During World War I, for instance, Japan hoped to gain power in East Asia by joining the Allies.

The long-range causes of World War I are nationalism, imperialism, militarism, and the alliance system. There were several ways nationalism became a factor. First, minorities like the Bosnians began to assert themselves in the Austro-Hungarian Empire; encouraged by outside powers like the Russians, they maneuvered to declare their independence. Second, the formation of the new nations of Italy and Germany in the late 1800s threatened the existing European balance of power so carefully negotiated at the Congress of Vienna in 1815. European states participated in imperialist contests around the world that damaged European relationships. Russia and Austria-Hungary sparred in the **Balkans**, Germany's plans for a Berlin to Baghdad railroad threatened British control of the Suez Canal, and Germany and France competed for territory in North Africa. Militarism also played a part. Industrial power led to a great buildup of weapons and elaborate plans for their use. This was particularly true of Germany, which built up an army of 95 divisions, twice the size of the French army, and a navy, with 20 modern battleships, large enough to rival Britain's. Countries began formulating carefully worked-out mobilization and attack plans that dictated irrevocable courses of action should war become imminent. Finally, by 1914, two opposing alliances developed. The growing power of Germany on land threatened France and Russia, and at sea, Britain. France, Russia, and Britain became allies in the **Triple Entente**. To Germany this seemed like encirclement, causing her to draw closer to Austria and Italy in the **Triple Alliance**.

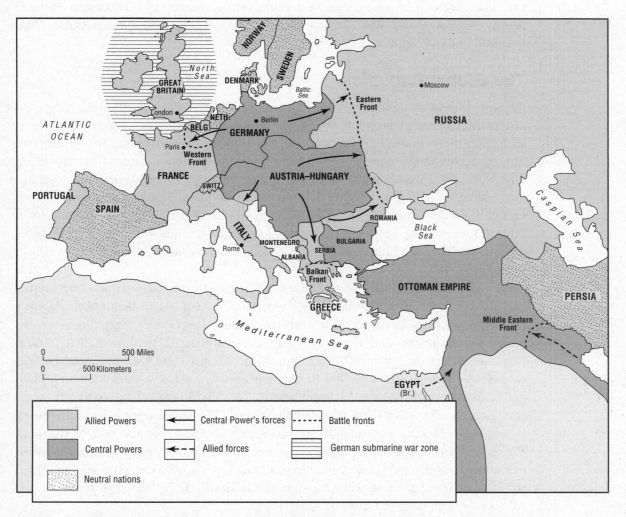

Europe in 1914 C.E. The basic framework of World War I was put in place in the first year of the war. Europe was divided into two camps and two fronts. This situation remained until 1917 when new weapons, revolution in Russia, and the entrance of the United States ended the stalemate.

The Balkans

The chief bone of contention among the European powers was in their own back-yard, the Balkans, the **Powder Keg** of Europe. During the 1800s Greece (1830), Bulgaria, Serbia, Montenegro, and Romania (1878) had secured their independence. The Ottomans, Austria, and Russia all desired to extend their influence in the area. In 1908, for example, Austria annexed the Turkish provinces of Bosnia and Herzegovina, and then, in 1911–1913, the Balkan states fought against Turkey and then among themselves, resulting in gains for Austria's enemy, Serbia. When Austrian **Archduke Franz Ferdinand** was assassinated on June 28, 1914, by Serbian-backed terrorists, Austria soon got revenge. Austria, which had received a "blank check," or free hand, from Germany, sent an ultimatum to Serbia and, when it was rejected, declared war on Serbia. Russia mobilized, causing Germany to call up its forces and then to declare war on Russia. Instead of invading Russia, however, Germany moved west against France, according to the **Schlieffin Plan** that advocated a swift knock-out blow against France before turning on Russia. On August 3 Germany declared war on France and the next day invaded Belgium. Then the alliances came into play. Britain declared war on Germany, and Austria declared war on Russia. World War I began with enthusiasm and the high expectation that it would "be over by Christmas."

The Global Battlefield

Because European countries were fighting for their empires, battlefields stretched across the globe and involved peoples of numerous ethnicities, races, and cultures, including their resources. The results of the wars were more global than European too, especially in the context of the creation of independent states in its aftermath. The world wars were a completely different experience abroad than in Europe but they were part of a greater struggle than for the lands of Europe. In World War I, French colonies supplied 500,000 soldiers to fight in European trenches and over 200,000 workers to keep war industries running. One million soldiers from India fought for Britain in France and the Middle East in World War II, 60,000 of whom were killed.

In Europe at the **Battle of the Marne**, German troops were stopped by French and British forces. For the rest of the year, outflanking maneuvers failed. Along a 400-mile western front, **trench warfare** began. Losses were appalling due to artillery, poison gas, and the horrors of the trenches. At Verdun, half a million Frenchmen were killed in 1916. At Ypres, the Menin Gate war memorial records the names of no less than 70,000 British officers and men who died with no known grave. As war poet Siegfried Sassoon wrote, "Who will remember, passing through this gate, the unheroic dead who fed the guns?" The stalemate in the west caused Germany to launch a campaign against Russia in 1915. By the end of the year, Russia had lost two million men and most of Poland, a blow Russia never recovered from. Meanwhile, the Turks, who entered on Germany's side, repulsed an Allied attempt to invade via the Dardanelles at **Gallipoli**. Italy, which entered on the Allied side, was bogged down in Austria.

The stalemate ended in 1917 when Germany initiated two new lines of attack. The first was equipping a submarine fleet to destroy shipping to the Allies, and the second was a new offensive against Russia. Unrestricted **U-boat** (submarine) activity succeeded in destroying 25 percent of all shipping leaving British ports, but it brought the United States into the war (April 1917). On the eastern front, the Russian revolution began even before German troops arrived. Russia left the war in early 1918 by the **Peace of Brest-Litovsk**. Russia lost much of its industrial and resource capacity in western Russia. Germany then launched an all-out attack in the west. On March 21, 1918, the British stood "with their backs to the wall." The Germans were within 40 miles of Paris. By then, however, the Americans had arrived, over one million by November. In August 1918, the Germans fell back; in September Bulgaria and Turkey surrendered, and in October Austria gave in. Emperor William abdicated on November 9 and the **Weimar Republic**, which replaced him, authorized a cease-fire.

War's End

At war's end, there were 30 million casualties and 8 million dead. The land was ravaged. The spirit of liberalism and faith in progress were shattered. Pessimism replaced optimism and existentialism proclaimed God is dead. The classic statement of disillusionment with war was German author **Erich Maria Remarque**'s *All Quiet on the Western Front*, a novel that documented life in the trenches for young Germans. At the other end of the spectrum was the giddiness of the Roaring Twenties in the United States and the revival of Christianity.

The peace treaties the belligerents signed were influenced by American President **Wilson's Fourteen Points** and by the interests of the victors. In redrawing the map of Europe, the principle of "**national self-determination**," allowing historic peoples and ethnic groups to form their own nation-states, was applied. Out of the former German, Austrian, and Russian Empires, new nation-states like Czechoslovakia, Poland, Austria, Hungary, Latvia, Lithuania, Estonia, and Yugoslavia were created. This principle of national self-determination was not applied to European colonies as politicians determined that these areas were inhabited "by peoples not yet able to stand by themselves under the strenuous conditions of the modern world." Instead, the former colonies of the defeated powers in Africa and Southwest Asia were transferred under the **mandate system** (theoretically, "nations on the road to independence") to the "tutelage" or supervision of one of the victors. Out of the former Ottoman Empire, Lebanon and Syria went to France, and Palestine and Mesopotamia (present day Iraq) to Britain. Kurdish and Armenian demands were ignored. Most former German colonies were transferred to Australia, New Zealand, and Britain. The mandate system was administered by the **League of Nations**, the first worldwide association of governments in world history dedicated to the resolution of disputes by peaceful means, or, as President Wilson asserted, "to make the world safe for democracy," as well as to improve general social and economic conditions the world over.

World realities did not match the expectations of the World War I victors. The United States never joined the League of Nations. The U.S. intervened in the Mexican Revolution (1910–1920), and then withdrew into political isolationism when it came to European affairs. Russia became communist, isolated, xenophobic, and adversarial in world affairs. Economic and political instability in Italy led to the fascist regime of Mussolini. Bulgaria (1923), Poland (1926), Greece (1926), and Yugoslavia (1929) fell to military coups. Meanwhile, China and Germany struggled

Did You Know?

The Treaty of Versailles was negotiated by 30 sovereign states and blamed Germany for the war. Reparations and demilitarization of Germany resulted.

to make new democratic republics work while India made strides toward self-rule. World stability might have returned had it not been for the **Great Depression**, which started in the United States in 1929 and spread throughout the world in the early 1930s. In its wake came extremist governments in Japan, Germany, Italy, and Russia, and in the West, pacifism, isolationism, and **appeasement**.

Economic and Social Consequences of World War I

At the end of World War I, the withdrawal of government involvement was a severe shock to the economy and, in some measure, led to the Great Depression. Economic theories were postulated, like those by **John Maynard Keynes** that stressed the importance of government spending to compensate for loss of purchasing power during the Depression.

War also added to the growth of the **welfare state**. Wartime planning in Britain had pointed to the need for new programs to reduce the impact of economic inequality and to reward the lower classes for their loyalty. The welfare state elaborated a host of social insurance measures from medical care to housing, retirement insurance, and child care. In dictatorial states like Germany and Russia, government control was even greater. After World War II, the Western and communist countries remained highly militarized, thereby avoiding the post-war economic shock experienced after World War I.

Total war also affected the social aspects of life. Both in democracies and dictatorships it included unprecedented control of the media through censorship, jailing

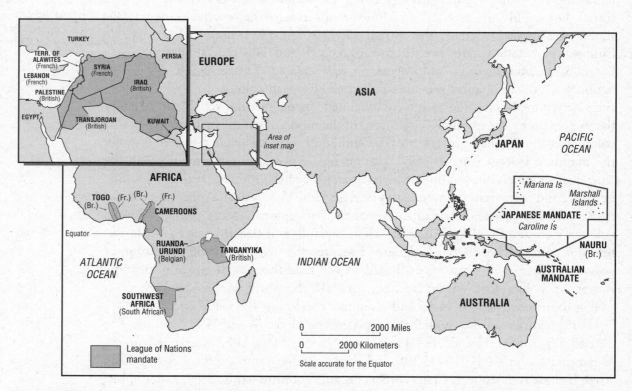

League of Nations Mandates 1920 C.E. In treaties that ended World War I, imperial territory of the defeated powers was taken and handed over to the League of Nations, which then mandated that winning states oversee them until independence. The mandates in Southwest Asia became the most contentious, primarily because of wartime promises to Jews and Arabs alike.

dissidents, and distribution of powerful propaganda to incite passionate support for war and all-out commitment to the national cause. Vivid posters, movies, and flaming speeches combined in the mobilization effort. Direct bombings of civilian populations, internment, forced labor, and poison gas caused great suffering. The position of women drastically changed as a result of war. With so many men at the front, women increasingly joined the workforce. By 1916, 1.6 million women were working, half in engineering plants. As they did so, women gained the right to vote (the 1920s), began to smoke and drink in public, enjoy leisure activities, and be active in politics. The importance of workers also gave greater power and prestige to labor unions. All in all, total mechanized warfare transformed governments, economies, and societies into war machines where personal liberties and individual actions mattered little.

ECONOMIC AND POLITICAL CHANGE IN THE 1920s

France and England

All participants of World War I suffered severe dislocation at war's end, but most recovered to some extent by the late 1920s. In France, communists and socialists battled for support of the workers, and the franc fell to 10 percent of its prewar value, but under the careful leadership of Raymond Poincaré, democratic government and financial stability returned by 1930. Britain faced severe unemployment (two million were unemployed in 1920) because it had lost its best markets during the war. Labour Party government responded with creation of a welfare state. This led to a strengthened Labour Party, which was able to elect its leader, Ramsay MacDonald, to the prime ministership in the 1924 and 1929 elections.

Italy and Germany

In Italy there was chaos. Communist insurrections led to numerous right-wing groups that broke up strikes and protected capital assets. **Benito Mussolini** and his party, the **Fascists** (after the *fasces* used as a symbol of authority in the Roman Republic), seized power in 1922 and ruled Italy thereafter as a one-party state. The Fascist program was both antidemocratic and anticommunist. Fascists advocated nationalism, authoritarianism, totalitarianism, militarism, and idealism. Fascist rhetoric and hyperbole viewed liberty as a "putrefying corpse," strife as ennobling, internationalism as a gross perversion of human progress, the state as effecting the highest loyalty, and the Mediterranean as an Italian lake.

A similar seesaw between leftist and rightist groups occurred in Germany after the war. In 1918 Karl Liebnekcht announced the creation of a Soviet state, but it was soon suppressed by the army. In 1923 **Adolf Hitler** and his fascist **National Socialist** or **Nazi party** attempted a takeover in Munich. By 1924, the German mark was virtually worthless, 1.5 trillion to the dollar.

China

In China, meanwhile, the fragile new national republic established by **Sun Yat-sen** after the fall of the Manchu Dynasty in 1911 began its existence on the defensive. At war's end the Allies had signed the **Twenty-One Demands**, giving Japan control of Shantung and southern **Manchuria**. This resulted in the **May Fourth Movement** in 1919. Chinese students protested betrayal by both the Allies and the republican government. In the face of civil disorder, Sun allied his Nationalist party, or **Kuomintang**, with the communists. For the Russian communists, this was the first of many "national liberation fronts," but for Sun, it was a helpful blueprint for party reorganization. He initiated a campaign against the warlords who threatened Chinese republican unification. In his **Three Principles of the People**—nationalism, democracy, and people's livelihood, nationalism remained of prime importance. When Sun died in 1925, the task of uniting China fell to **Chiang Kai-shek** (1887–1975). Fearful of communist subversion, Chiang purged the communists in 1927. This led the communists, under their leader **Mao Zedong (Mao Tse-tung)**, to shift the focus of their activities to the countryside.

India

In India, the 1920s saw the beginnings of independence. During World War I, 1.2 million Indian soldiers and laborers volunteered for duty in Europe, Africa, and Southwest Asia. In return, Indians pressed for self-governing status as a British dominion, especially after the **Lucknow Pact** in 1916 in which Muslims and Hindus joined to work for this goal. The British capitulated to the extent that, in 1919, the **Government of India Act** established dual administration, part Indian and elected, part British and authoritarian. Bipartisan rule was rolled back, however, in 1919 and the repressive **Rowlatt Acts** indefinitely extended "wartime emergency measures." Protest erupted at a Hindu religious festival leading to the **Amritsar Massacre** in which 379 Indians were killed and another 1137 Indians were wounded by British troops. India was on the verge of violence when national liberation took a different path under the leadership of **Mohandas Gandhi** (1869–1948). Gandhi's vision of nonviolent protest, or **Satyagraha** (*satya*—"spiritual truth," *agraha*—"strength"), was formed during his early years as a lawyer with dark skin in South Africa, where he was treated as a second-class citizen. In 1915 Gandhi returned to India and in 1920 he launched a national campaign of nonviolent resistance to British rule. Throughout the 1920s radical nationalists led by **Jawaharlal Nehru** called for outright independence. Gandhi tempered this and for the first time involved the general population. Reminiscent of the American colonists dumping the tea in Boston Harbor, Gandhi defied British rule. He led 50,000 people in a spectacular march to the sea to make salt rather than pay the British salt tax. For this he was jailed. He was released in 1931 during the Depression. In 1935 the British negotiated a new constitution, a virtual blueprint of independence.

The Great Depression

The quest for economic and political stability and colonial independence that took place in the 1920s was severely undermined by the Great Depression. World War I reparations and war debt set the stage for the Depression. According to the **Dawes Plan** worked out in 1924, German reparations to Britain and France would pass on to the United States in repayment of war debt. This led to a massive imbalance in the international economy as more and more resources of Europe were diverted to debt payment, thereby reducing the market for American industrial goods.

When American banks called in their foreign loans, the effects of the Wall Street Crash reverberated around the world. In 1931 the largest Austrian bank declared bankruptcy, followed by many others. International trade decreased 60 percent. World industrial production (except in the Soviet Union) fell 40 percent, leading to unemployment everywhere. In democracies like the United States, Britain, and France, governments spent massively on welfare and public works projects.

In weak democracies like Germany, Italy, and Japan, dictatorships came to power that put people back to work with military spending. In the 1930 German elections, the Nazis polled 18 percent of the vote, but by 1932 they gained 37 percent, enough to bring Adolf Hitler to power in 1933. In 1933 the **Enabling Act** abolished the Reichstag, or parliament. Hitler immediately began a program of Nazification. Trade unions, news media, and schools were brought under Nazi control. Military and economic affairs were closely regulated and public works like the autobahn system and military spending brought people back to work.

Japan, meanwhile, suffered a drastic decline in trade as a result of the Depression. Between 1929 and 1931 Japanese foreign trade halved. Besides that, there were natural disasters—an earthquake in 1923 that destroyed three-quarters of Tokyo—and population increases of .1.5 percent per year. Empire, particularly in Manchuria, seemed a solution to Japanese economic problems. In 1931, just as the nationalists under Chiang Kai-shek were poised to reunite China, Japan invaded Manchuria and took control of the province with its rich industrial resources. Chinese protests to the League of Nations failed to mobilize international action. In 1933 Japan annexed Manchuria, after which Chiang Kai-shek made a final desperate effort to rid China of the communists. He chased Mao and his followers, on what became the legendary "**Long March**," from their southern bases in Kiangsi and Hunan to a new base in the northwest. There, a truce based primarily on fears of Japan was forged between the communists and nationalists.

In 1937, Japan launched a full-scale invasion of northern China. For China, World War II had begun. The other powers, uncertain of which way Japan would next move, began to secure their positions. Russia initiated hostilities along the Manchurian border to deter the Japanese in the summer of 1939. The United States, fearing an attack to the south on the Philippines, restricted iron and steel exports to Japan, threatened to cut off oil supplies, froze Japanese credit in America, and stepped up aid to Chiang Kai-shek. On April 13, 1941, the Japanese signed a nonaggression pact with the Soviet government, saving Russia but paving the way for the Japanese move southward.

WORLD WAR II

German-Italian Aggression

Meanwhile, in Europe, both Italy and Germany embarked on unimpeded paths of aggression because Britain and France followed policies of appeasement (giving in for the sake of peace). Hitler's domestic and foreign policy goals, which he quickly began to realize, were outlined in his book **Mein Kampf** (*My Struggle*). Domestically, Hitler began to enforce his idea of German racial superiority by instituting the **Nuremberg Laws** of 1935, which deprived Jews of their civil and commercial rights. By 1941 the Nazi state proceeded to what became known as the "**Final Solution**" of the Jewish problem, the deliberate extermination of Jewish communities throughout Europe. Many of the estimated six million killed were transported by rail to concentration camps like **Dachau** and **Auschwitz** where they were systematically gassed. Germany turned into a police state run by the **Gestapo** (secret police) and SS, Hitler's private army.

THE LAW FOR PROTECTION OF GERMAN BLOOD AND GERMAN HONOR

Clearly realizing that the purity of the German blood is the prerequisite for perpetuating the German people, and inspired by an inflexible determination to secure the existence of the German nation for all time to come, the Reichstag has unanimously passed the following law. . . .

1. Marriages between Jews and citizens of German or kindred stock are prohibited. . . .
3. Jews shall not employ in their household female citizens of German or kindred stock under 45 years of age.
4. Jews shall not hoist the Reich or national flag nor display the Reich colors.

Issued September 15, 1935, this law was the beginning of Jewish genocide at the hands of the Nazis. Based on Hitler's theory of a superior Aryan (German) race, put into practice, it led to discrimination, then confiscation of property, exploitation of Jewish labor, and finally execution as the "final solution" to the so-called "Jewish Problem."

On the foreign front, Hitler began by rearming Germany in defiance of the Versailles Treaty. In 1938 he annexed Austria (**Anschluss**) and large areas of Czechoslovakia, a move sanctioned by Great Britain and France in the **Munich Agreements**.

Meanwhile, Italy attacked Ethiopia and both Germany and Italy aided the fascist leader General **Francisco Franco** during the Spanish Civil War, a war whose horrific cruelties for civilian populations were immortalized in artist **Pablo Picasso**'s *Guernica*. The painting commemorates the bombing of an ancient Spanish town by fascist planes, an attack that took the lives of one of every eight inhabitants in a single night of terror.

By March 1939, Hitler proceeded to occupy the rest of Czechoslovakia and seized the port of Memel from Lithuania. In April, Mussolini overran Albania. On August 23 Germany and Russia signed a **Non-Aggression Pact** that allowed Hitler to attack Poland on September 1 from the west while **Joseph Stalin** ordered Soviet troops to invade Poland from the east. At this point, Great Britain and France ended their appeasement and declared war.

The Course of the War

Hitler's shadow spread quickly over Europe. In April 1940, his forces overran Denmark and Norway. On May 10 he initiated successful attacks on Holland, Belgium, and France. France surrendered on June 22. The northern half of France was occupied by Germans; the southern half was ruled from **Vichy** by a puppet government. Now Britain stood virtually alone. Under the dogged leadership of **Winston Churchill**, England withstood massive German bombings without capitulating. This caused Hitler to turn in the other direction against Russia. In 1941 the brilliant German general **Erwin Rommel** advanced across North Africa toward the Suez Canal.

THE BATTLE OF BRITAIN

What General Weygand called the "Battle of France" is over. I expect that the battle of Britain is about to begin. Upon this battle depends the survival of Christian civilization. Upon it depends our own British life and the long continuity of our institutions and our Empire. The whole fury and might of the enemy must very soon be turned on us. Hitler knows that he will have to break us in this island or lose the war. If we can stand up to him all Europe may be free, and the life of the world may move forward into broad, sunlit uplands; but if we fail then the whole world, including the United States, and all that we have known and cared for, will sink into the abyss of a new dark age made more sinister, and perhaps more prolonged, by the lights of perverted science. Let us therefore brace ourselves to our duty and so bear ourselves that if the British Commonwealth and Empire lasts for a thousand years men will say, "This was their finest hour."

Winston Churchill became the prime minister of Great Britain in May 1940. At this time, Soviet Russia was allied with Hitler, France was about to fall to German invaders, and the United States was not in the war. Britain stood alone against fascist tyranny, which looked like it might sweep Europe and the world. Churchill's eloquent language and steadfastness helped Britain survive. Britain provided the necessary European bastion of defense prior to United States' entry into the war. After the Battle of Britain was won, Churchill gave another memorable speech in which he saluted the British airmen. He said, "Never in the field of human conflict was so much owed by so many to so few."

Meanwhile, the Japanese, certain now that they had nothing to fear from Russia, attacked **Pearl Harbor** on December 7, 1941, bringing the United States into the war. Shortly thereafter, Japan took the Philippines, Malaya, Singapore, and Hong Kong.

At this moment, at the height of fascist power, the tide turned. Gradually, the Axis powers were stopped. The Germans suffered two crucial defeats in 1942—one in North Africa at **El Alamein** and one in Russia at **Stalingrad**. Stalingrad became the turning point of the war. In addition, the United States began to supply huge amounts of weapons and war materiel to Britain and Russia through the **Lend-Lease** program and became the "**Arsenal of Democracy**." Slowly Germany and Italy were beaten back and defeated. In 1943 the Allies invaded Italy. Rome fell in June 1944, the same month Operation Overlord (the **D-Day** landings) across the English Channel started. On June 6 the largest amphibious operation in history began, involving 100,000 assault troops, 5000 ships, and 14,000 aircraft. In the spring of 1945 Allied strategic bombing against German industrial cities culminated in the destruction of Dresden, the counterpart of the German bombardment of London. On May 7, 1945, the Nazi leadership finally surrendered.

By this time, in the Pacific, only Burma and the Philippines had been recovered. There were one million undefeated Japanese troops in China and another half million in Malaya, Thailand, Indonesia, and Indochina. The American strategy of island hopping or gaining control of strategic Pacific Ocean islands important to launch an attack on Japan itself proved costly. The aerial bombardment of Japanese cities failed to make the Japanese surrender. In hopes of ending the war without invading Japan, President **Harry Truman** ordered atomic bombs dropped on **Hiroshima** on August 6 and Nagasaki on August 9. On August 8 Russia declared war on Japan, and on August 14 Japanese emperor **Hirohito** accepted the terms for Japan's surrender.

TRUMAN ANNOUNCES THE BOMBING OF HIROSHIMA

Sixteen hours ago an American airplane dropped one bomb on Hiroshima, an important Japanese Army base. That bomb had more power than 20,000 tons of T.N.T. It had more than two thousand times the blast power of the British "Grand Slam" which is the largest bomb ever yet used in the history of warfare. . . .

It is an atomic bomb. It is a harnessing of the power of the universe. The force from which the sun draws its power has been loosed against those who brought war to the Far East. . . .

Let there be no mistake; we shall completely destroy Japan's power to make war.

It was to spare the Japanese people from utter destruction that the ultimatum of July 26 was issued at Potsdam. Their leaders promptly rejected that ultimatum. If they do not now accept our terms, they may expect a rain of ruin from the air . . .

The fact that we can release atomic energy ushers in a new era in man's understanding of nature's forces. Atomic energy may in the future supplement the power that now comes from coal, oil, and falling water . . .

I shall recommend that the Congress of the United States consider promptly the establishment of an appropriate commission to control the production and use of atomic power within the United States. I shall give further consideration and make further recommendations to the Congress as to how atomic power can become a powerful and forceful influence towards the maintenance of world peace.

On August 6, 1945, the United States dropped an atomic bomb on Hiroshima, obliterating the city and killing over 78,000 civilians. Russia declared war on August 8 and swept into Manchuria. The next day, a second bomb was dropped on Nagasaki. On August 15 Emperor Hirohito announced Japanese surrender. Hiroshima ushered in the Atomic Age and the Cold War. It has been controversial ever since. Some equate it with German atrocities against the Jews; others defend it on the basis that it saved lives by ending the war quickly. Truman seemed well aware of its awesome power if not the historical ramifications.

Results

The world lay in ruins. Europe's hegemony had ended. The Pacific Rim was a political vacuum. While Russia lay exhausted, it survived as a power ready to take advantage of its position as the sole Eurasian power. Only the United States, whose borders had seen no direct action, emerged with any sort of power position. Americans, however, were weary of war and its costs. The surrender and the mushroom cloud set the stage for a new age in world history.

At war's end, all who had been involved were appalled at the death and destruction. As after World War I, the answers to establishing a new and peaceful world seemed to lie in punishment of the perpetrators of war and founding of representative world organizations to keep the peace. Fascist regimes were blamed for the war; Nazis were put on trial for "crimes against humanity" at the **Nuremberg** tribunals. All the defeated were made to establish democratic governments with civil liberties ensured.

The League of Nations was dissolved. In its place the **United Nations** was chartered in June 1945, with 50 nations. The main power in the United Nations rested with the Security Council, whose permanent members—the United States, Soviet Union, Britain, France, and China—could veto any decisions. Subsidiary agencies like the World Health Organization and Food and Agricultural Organization made important contributions to combating disease and starvation, and to promoting social and cultural understanding. The United Nations became involved in many political disputes worldwide, but was often hampered by Cold War power politics. The real mechanism of peace was fear of the atomic bomb.

THE COLD WAR

Origins

The paradoxical effect of atomic weapons was to promote peace. After the dawn of the Atomic Age the two countries that possessed atomic, and then nuclear, capability—the United States and the Soviet Union—faced off in a "Balance of Terror." Enemies politically, economically, and ideologically, these two combatants carried on a war of words, a contest for allies, and a policy of expansionism—all just short of outright war. Both feared unforeseen consequences if the new weapons were used. The Cold War was a face-off between the United States and its allies and the Soviet Union and its allies. It had many aspects—an expansive arms buildup of colossal and frightening proportions, support for small wars as in Korea, Southwest Asia, Africa, and Southeast Asia, and the quest for the minds and hearts of people through propaganda, political infiltration, and cultural exchanges.

The origins of the Cold War can be found in World War II wartime aims and agreements. During the war, despite differing aims, the United States and Soviet Union made victory over Germany the highest priority. Lurking beneath this shared goal were differences. Stalin's territorial gains in Poland ran counter to the "**Atlantic Charter**" of August 1941, an expression of war aims by Great Britain and the United States. It called for peace without territorial expansion or secret agreements, and for free elections and self-determination for liberated nations. By an agreement at **Tehran** in 1943, Soviet troops could liberate eastern Europe. In February 1945 at **Yalta**, the Red Army was already in eastern Europe but Britain and France had yet to cross the Rhine into Germany. Meanwhile the United States was fighting alone against Japan in the Pacific. Therefore, U.S. President **Franklin Roosevelt** agreed to divide Germany, pay reparations to the Soviet Union in the form of agricultural and industrial goods confiscated in the occupied areas, and welcomed Soviet help in the war against Japan. After Roosevelt's death in 1945, President Truman demanded free elections in eastern Europe at a meeting in **Potsdam**. Stalin refused. Instead, elections were held under the aegis of the Communist party and the Soviets delivered power to communist officials.

Containment

This was the beginning of the Cold War. The American response to Soviet occupation and the co-opting of elections was to "get tough." In May 1945, Truman cut off all aid to Russia, and in October he declared the United States would never recognize any government formed against the will of the people. In March 1946, Winston Churchill informed an American audience that an "**Iron Curtain**" had fallen across the continent, dividing Europe into two camps. Only Yugoslavia in eastern Europe remained outside the Soviet sphere, mainly because communist leader **Tito (Josip Broz)** had his own army and had not been dependent on Soviet troops to liberate Yugoslavia from the Nazis.

THE IRON CURTAIN

From Stettin in the Baltic to Trieste in the Adriatic, an iron curtain has descended across the continent. Behind that line lie all the capitals of the ancient states of Central and Eastern Europe. Warsaw, Berlin, Prague, Vienna, Budapest, Belgrade, Bucharest, and Sophia. All these famous cities and the populations around them lie in the Soviet sphere, and all are subject, in one form or another, not only to Soviet influence but to a very high and, in many cases, increasing measure of control from Moscow. . . .

Whatever conclusions may be drawn from these facts—and facts they are—this is certainly not the Liberated Europe we fought to build up. Nor is it one which contains the essentials of permanent peace. . . .

Last time I saw it all coming, and cried aloud to my fellow countrymen and to the world, but no one paid any attention. . . .

We surely must not let that happen again.

While on a visit to the United States in 1946, Winston Churchill warned the world of coming dictatorship and war. Unlike before World War II, when he was ignored, this time the world listened. Immediately the West set in place a number of measures to prevent more nations from becoming communist by setting up a bulwark of containment. Thus began the Cold War.

The foreign policy that guided the United States through the Cold War was "**containment**," that is, taking action where necessary to stop the spread of Soviet and communist influence. The policy the Soviet Union followed was expansionism under the banner "the ideological struggle against capitalist imperialism." When the

Soviet Union put pressure on Iran and Turkey, and civil war raged in Greece and China between communists and loyalists, the United States announced the **Truman Doctrine**. "I believe it must be the policy of the United States to support free people who are resisting attempted subjugation by armed minorities or by outside pressure." Truman asked for military aid for Greece and Turkey. On behalf of America, Secretary of State George Marshall offered economic aid to rebuild Europe. This **Marshall Plan** was a huge success. A similar plan was undertaken in Japan after Japan was occupied by the United States under the direction of General **Douglas MacArthur**. The Japanese military establishment was dismantled, a democratic constitution adopted, and large amounts of American aid restored the economy. Thus, former enemy nations like West Germany and Japan became allies. The Soviet Union, meanwhile, supplied aid to communist parties in China amd eastern Europe. China became a communist state in 1949. The eastern European countries of Bulgaria, Hungary, Poland, Czechoslovakia, and Romania also installed communist governments.

Cold War Alliances

The Cold War manifested itself in a series of alliances and wars. The United States formed a European defensive alliance called **NATO**, the North Atlantic Treaty Organization. This was countered by the **Warsaw Pact**, a military alliance between the Soviet Union and eastern European allies. The western European economic union, the **European Economic Community** (EEC), was opposed in eastern Europe by **COMECON**, a trade union between the Soviet Union and its allies. In Asia, the United States signed **SEATO**, the Southeast Asia Treaty Organization, countered by Russia with the **Sino-Soviet Alliance**.

Soon the alliances were tested. The Soviet Union closed the highway in July 1948 from West Germany to West Berlin. The United States responded with a massive airlift for over a year, supplying West Berliners with everything needed from coal to food. In May 1949, the Soviets backed down. Massive desertions from East Germany to the West resulted, until August 1961, when the Soviets built the **Berlin Wall**, sealing off East Berlin from West Berlin.

The next confrontation was in Korea. From 1910 to 1945 Korea had been a colony of Japan. Stalin's troops entered North Korea two days before the atomic bomb was dropped on Hiroshima. By the war's end, the U.S.S.R. had driven to the 38th parallel. The Soviet Union occupied the north and the United States the south. Elections in 1948 in the south established a republic under **Syngman Rhee**. In the north the communists set up a Democratic Peoples Republic led by Moscow-trained **Kim Il Sung**. In June 1950, North Korea, heavily armed by the Russians, invaded the south. This began the **Korean War**, which lasted from 1950 until an armistice was signed at Panmunjom in 1953. The United States and South Korea, with the support of the United Nations troops, drove the North Koreans to the Yalu River at the border of China. The Chinese, with massive troop reinforcements, pushed U.N. forces back to the 38th parallel. There the division has remained to this day.

There were other confrontations as well. In 1962 the Soviet Union placed missiles in Cuba. The **Cuban Missile Crisis** began when the United States issued an ultimatum to end further shipments and demanded that the missiles be dismantled. The Soviets backed down.

Did You Know?

North Korea is separated from South Korea at the 38th parallel.

Cold War Europe 1955–1957 C.E. After World War II, Europe once again became divided, this time between communist and non-communist blocs led by the Soviet Union and United States, respectively. The dividing line became known as the Iron Curtain, a line that roughly coincided with the area occupied by Soviet troops when the war ended.

Peaceful Coexistence and Détente

By 1965, outright hostilities between the United States and Soviet Union began to subside. This period is known as **peaceful coexistence**, a time when both countries accepted the existence of an antagonistic relationship between the superpowers but began to work together where possible. An example of peaceful coexistence occurred when the United States and Soviet Union joined the United Nations in an effort to end the Suez Crisis in 1956. During this crisis, Russian-backed Egyptian President **Gamal Abdel Nasser** seized the Suez Canal from Great Britain, bringing Egypt to the brink of war with Great Britain and France. Since such a war might have expanded into a superpower war, both the United States and the Soviet Union worked to end the crisis. Another example of peaceful coexistence was the **Test Ban Treaty** signed between the two superpowers in 1962. This treaty prohibited nuclear tests in the atmosphere, outer space, and underwater.

Between 1965 and 1975, the Cold War relationship went a step further in its softening, entering a period of **détente**, or a relaxation of tensions. Reasons for more amicable relations have to do with the fragmenting of Cold War blocs and nuclear proliferation (the spread of nuclear capability). In 1963, the largest of Russia's allies, China, left the Soviet bloc after a number of disputes over Soviet aid to India and differing interpretations of communism. The United States, meanwhile, struggled with the war in Vietnam and disturbances in its own hemisphere. Both the United States and the Soviet Union lost monopolies over nuclear technology. India gained the capability to produce nuclear weapons and several other countries, such as Iraq, Iran, Pakistan, Turkey, South Africa, Brazil, and Israel were thought to be capable of making nuclear weapons. Because of these developments, neither the United States nor the Soviet Union could count on a secure satellite system of support or control over their allies. This situation prompted attempts to reach an understanding between the two Cold War contestants.

End of the Cold War

By the 1980s, the Cold War was all but over. It was no longer a bipolar political world. Other countries had obtained a nuclear capability, like France and China, and the world had other economic superpowers, like Japan and Germany. While the Cold War between the United States and the Soviet Union never resulted in outright confrontation, military conflict between their proxies did occur. Decolonization and revolutions in the Third World countries were peripheral aspects of the Cold War because they were often engineered and orchestrated by the superpowers in their quest for allies. Both the United States and the Soviet Union tried to woo countries to their side with economic aid, ideological propaganda, and military materiel. This fanned the flames of decolonization and nationalist wars.

Revolution, Decolonization, and Wars of National Liberation

CHAPTER 24

(ca. 1917 C.E.–2000 C.E.)

TIMELINE	
1917 C.E.	Russian Communist Revolution and Mexican Revolution
1947 C.E.	Partition of India
1947 C.E.–1962 C.E.	African decolonization
1948 C.E.	Arab-Israeli War
1949 C.E.	Chinese Communist Revolution
1954 C.E.–1975 C.E.	Vietnam War
1958 C.E.	Sino-Soviet Split
1965 C.E.	Chinese Cultural Revolution
1967 C.E.	Six-Day War
1978 C.E.	Iranian Revolution of Ayatollah Khomeini
1980 C.E.–1988 C.E.	Iran-Iraq War
1989 C.E.	Tiananmen Square Protest

THE RUSSIAN REVOLUTION

Within the context of this chapter, **revolution** refers to a complete change in the political, economic, and social system within a country. Examples of this would be Russia in 1917 and China in 1949. Both countries replaced quasi-republican states with communist states. **Decolonization** refers to the process by which colonial powers gradually turned over power and gave independence to former colonies. An example would be India. In 1947, Britain granted independence to India (and Pakistan). **Wars of national liberation** refers to wars of independence fought by former colonies against former colonial powers. Often wars of national liberation used communist anti-imperialist rhetoric and envisioned the creation of a communist state when liberation was obtained. An example of a war of liberation is the war in Vietnam 1954–1975. This was fought for independence first from the French and later from U.S. domination. The ultimate result was a communist Vietnam. Many countries in the twentieth century experienced one or more of these changes.

The Russian Revolution was the first successful communist revolution of the twentieth century. It provided a blueprint with variations for all subsequent communist revolutions of the century. It provided a mechanism for revolt (the Communist party) and a vision of a new government and economy (state ownership and state economic planning). The vision was diffused widely from China to Cuba and to many countries in Africa. Its failure as a system that provided freedom, rights, and prosperity formed the basis for its world collapse in 1989.

Marxism in Russia

Marxism was the ideological foundation for the formation of the Russian Social Democratic party, founded in 1898. In 1903 the party split into two factions, the **Mensheviks**, who argued that Russia was not yet ready for a Marxist revolution because it was not industrialized, and the **Bolsheviks**, who believed in the inevitability of the proletarian revolution in Russia. Bolsheviks like **Vladimir Lenin** were disappointed by the bourgeois nature of the **1905 Russian Revolution** because it resulted in the beginning of a liberal government on the Western model instead of a Marxist government. During the 1905 Revolution, Social Democrats refused to have anything to do with the Duma, or Parliament. Instead they formed a **soviet**, or workers' council. When the czar restored order, many like Lenin were forced to go abroad. In England and Switzerland Lenin worked out the necessary adaptations to Marxism to make it fit the Russian situation (Marxism-Leninism).

Noting that in Russia 80 to 90 percent of the population were peasants, Lenin called for a revolution of workers (symbolized by the hammer) and peasants (symbolized by the sickle). This was the beginning of the ironic situation wherein Marxist revolutions have tended to be successful only in nonindustrialized nations instead of in industrialized nations as envisioned by Marx. In view of the failure of the 1905 Revolution, Lenin also disregarded the spontaneous nature of revolution. Instead he called for a planned and directed revolution that would end in the "**dictatorship of the proletariat**," instead of in communism (a utopia of abundance on the withering away of the state).

The third adaptation Lenin made to classical Marxism was to link capitalism with imperialism. In classical Marxism, the capitalist was the enemy of the worker. In Marxism-Leninism, capitalists are by nature imperialists, broadening the enemy to include colonial powers. Stalin added the last tenet to Marxism-Leninism. He reinserted the nation, in this case Russia, as the vanguard of the revolution worldwide. Thus, the **Communist International (Comintern)** exported the Soviet brand of communism to other places in the world. These tenets—a revolution of worker and peasant, a planned revolution ending in dictatorship of one class over another, imperialists as well as capitalists as the enemy, and the power of the state to carry out socialism—became known as **Marxism-Leninism**, or what is generally thought of today as **communism**.

The February-March Revolution, 1917

Lenin and Bolshevism were of little threat to Russia until Russian war losses, terrible conditions in the cities, and finally the toppling of the czar left Russia vulnerable to a new ideology and strong leadership. During the war, workers became highly politicized due to close working conditions and public subscription to government bonds. On March 8, 1917, in protest against military defeats at the front and lack of fuel and food in the cities, workers in St. Petersburg called for a general strike. The streets filled with demonstrators. Unlike in 1905, the troops were sympathetic and refused to fire on the workers. In fact, the army's rank and file joined the workers. The czar, **Nicolas II**, was away at the front. When he started back to St. Petersburg to personally direct the repression, his train was held up by striking railway workers. With the government in collapse, the Duma asked for the czar's abdication on March 15.

Power now fell to two groups—the Duma, which called itself the **Provisional Government**, and the Soviet of Workers' and Soldiers' Deputies. The Duma knew how to run the machinery of state. The **soviets** (worker-soldier committees) controlled the streets. Disregarding the Duma, the Soviet issued Order No. 1 (dated March 14, 1917), depriving all officers of authority and placing military affairs under the control of the street committees elected by officers and men. Immediately, the situation at the front became chaotic, with desertions and fraternizations across enemy lines. Seizing the opportunity to end Russian involvement in World War I, Germany sent Lenin in a sealed train back to Russia to foment a Marxist revolution. The hope was that it would lead to Russian withdrawal from the war as called for in Marxist doctrine. Lenin arrived in Russia on April 17 with radical aims—"All power to the Soviets" and "Land, Peace, and Bread." This extreme position did not immediately find any support, but the failure of the July 1917 offensive at the front discredited the Provisional Government.

The Duma became more radical. Moderate socialist **Alexander Kerensky** was appointed prime minister. To restore order, he exiled Lenin once again, this time to Finland. From there, Lenin orchestrated the Bolshevik takeover of the St. Petersburg and Moscow soldiers' and workers' soviets.

The October-November Revolution, 1917

Lenin returned to Russia on November 7. The Bolsheviks seized strategic points in St. Petersburg, arrested the Provisional Government, and assumed power. The next day, Lenin issued a Land Decree that ordered immediate redistribution of all large landed estates among the peasants, nationalization of banks, worker control of the factories (but they lost the power to strike), the repudiation of the national debt, and confiscation of church property. The timing of Lenin's move was determined by his control of the soviets and the coming constituent elections, the first all-Russian elections to elect delegates to a constitutional convention. Lenin feared if he did not control the elections, the vote would go against him. He was right. The vote was taken and the greatest number of votes (approximately 40 percent) went to the Socialist Revolutionaries who represented the peasants not the workers' party of Lenin. Lenin immediately dispersed the Constituent Assembly and took control of the country. In 1919 the Comintern, or Communist International, was formed to export communism abroad.

Civil War, 1918–1921

Immediately, Lenin demanded an end to Russia's participation in World War I. His reasoning was both ideological and practical. Ideologically, socialists opposed participation in what they considered a capitalist war. More important, however, was the disintegration of Russia. Scarcely a month after the Bolshevik revolution, many groups mobilized against the Bolsheviks. The Don Cossacks organized separatist movements in Ukraine, Azerbaijan, Armenia, and the Baltic provinces, and started rebellions in eastern Siberia and Byelorussia. The Civil War (1918–1921) pitted separatists, former officers, and Provisional Government proponents (**Whites**), against the **Reds,** or communists. Japanese, Polish, and Western armies assisted the Whites, some because they opposed communism and others in order to take advantage of Russian weakness. At this point, Lenin appointed a brilliant Bolshevik orator and strategist, **Leon Trotsky**, to organize a Red Army. The Bolsheviks controlled the central part of Russia and the railroads. They had superb organization and ruthless fanaticism. The Reds were able to pick off one White enemy after another and they assassinated the czar. By 1921 the Bolsheviks were victorious, but the cost was enormous. Russia was in shambles and a remnant of its old self. Lenin went out immediately to meet the situation. He instituted the **New Economic Policy** (NEP), which injected some capitalism at the consumer level, but Lenin kept control of finance and industry. The wheels of the economy slowly began to move again. By the time of Lenin's death in 1924, Russia had reorganized as the **Union of Soviet Socialist Republics** (U.S.S.R.). Lenin had reintegrated Ukraine, Byelorussia, and Transcaucasia into the new state.

Lenin's successor, Joseph Stalin, had assumed power in 1928. In order to fully implement communism, he embarked on a program of forced industrialization and **collectivization**. A class of small peasant landowners, the **kulaks**, was purged and political famine ensued in which an estimated 7 million died (**The Great Famine**). As the threat from Nazi Germany increased in 1936–1937, Stalin purged the military ranks as well in a series of show trials. In addition to purges a system of labor camps or **Gulags** was developed to which actual or potential opponents of Stalin were sent. It is estimated that 18 million Russians passed through these camps between 1929 and 1953. In 1936 the Stalin constitution outlined a democratic framework for government but gave all power to the Communist party. The signing of the Nazi-Soviet Non-Aggression Pact in 1939 could be interpreted as a sign of weakness on Stalin's part or an attempt to turn the war west. Whatever the case, the Russian effort during World War II held Hitler at bay in Leningrad, Moscow, and Stalingrad. Russia emerged from World War II weakened internally but enlarged territorially. The Russian model of revolution, creation of the state-directed economy, and military strength became a model for many Third World countries in their quest for national liberation, modernization, and an end to poverty.

REVOLUTION AND DECOLONIZATION IN MEXICO, INDIA, AND SOUTHWEST ASIA (THE MIDDLE EAST)

Nationalism was a potent and popular force in the twentieth century despite its tragic manifestations in World War I and World War II. People outside Europe often equated it with liberty, civil rights, and economic empowerment. As the imperial hold of Western countries weakened after World War I, and completely

---

Did You Know?

By the time of Lenin's death in 1924, Russia was reorganized as the Union of Soviet Socialist Republics (U.S.S.R.).

collapsed after World War II, national independence movements gained strength. In Mexico, India, and Southwest Asia, Western powers tried to manage and oversee decolonization efforts. They hoped to steer former colonies in the direction of liberal democracies and establish a world order favorable to the democratic countries of the world. This became particularly important during the Cold War as a strategy for keeping these countries from falling into communist hands.

The Third World

Attempts at independence and liberal democracy did not always meet with initial success. This was because Western ideas often ran counter to local traditions and because these experiments were being attempted in **Third World** countries. Third World countries as a whole lacked the literacy, national cohesiveness, strong middle class, and business economy necessary to make liberal democracies work. Many, as a result, ended with nations that were free of colonial dictate but ruled by dictators of the right or left.

Mexico

Mexico was one of the first Third World countries in the twentieth century to engage in decolonialist struggles. Although Mexico was never a colony of the U.S., it was within the economic and political sphere of the United States. The Mexican struggle was also a revolution that attempted to complete the social and political revolution begun by independence movements in the 1820s. Mexico was ruled by a dictator, **Porfirio Diaz**, from 1881 to 1910. Despite his dictatorial regime, Mexican economic development made great strides. Railroad mileage increased more than fortyfold, but the price was heavy U.S. investment. By 1910 U.S. companies controlled three-fourths of Mexico's mines and almost three-fifths of its oil production. Mexico became a powder keg of political, social, and antiforeign discontent. From 1910 on, rival politicians produced a decade of violent revolution. By 1920 two Mexican presidents had been murdered and about one of every eight Mexicans had died.

In 1917 a radical constitution was written that guaranteed universal suffrage, gave Mexican workers the right to organize and strike, authorized eight-hour work days, and called for the redistribution of land to peasants. Rival claimants to power, including **Pancho Villa** and **Emiliano Zapata**, challenged the "constitutionalist" politicians. In 1920 the Institutional Revolutionary party (**PRI**) was organized and claimed to represent all factions of Mexican politics, but politicians in Mexico City gained the upper hand. By 1923 President **Alvaro Obregon** had reneged on most of the constitutional promises. American companies continued to control Mexico's oil. Little land changed hands.

Thus Mexico remained a dictatorship and in a semi-colonial position, becoming a producer of foodstuffs and raw materials, exporter to Europe and the United States. This had devastating effects during the Depression of the 1930s when the Mexican export market collapsed. The Mexican response was to gain control over industry by means of huge tariffs and to expropriate foreign-owned oil properties. During World War II, Mexican prosperity increased though much of it went into the hands of the upper classes. The rest was wiped out by population increases.

Other floundering Latin American economies and the Cold War fears of the growth of leftist governments like that in Cuba caused the United States to pledge $10 billion in economic assistance through the **Alliance for Progress** (1961). Unfortunately, the aid often propped up dictatorships at the expense of democratic social reforms. Independence has not led to prosperity or equality. This is no more evident than in the propensity of Mexicans to flow across the border into the United States.

During the last decade of the twentieth century, two events helped Mexico move toward a more democratic government and a stronger economy. In 1992, the **North American Free Trade Agreement** (NAFTA) took effect in the United States, Mexico, and Canada. This agreement decreases tariffs and customs among the three countries and breaks down barriers to the free flow of money, investment, and goods and services. NAFTA has had the effect of helping to modernize the Mexican economy as U.S. production know-how moves south across the border. Second, in 2000, **Vicente Fox** was elected president of Mexico in what is regarded as a free and democratic election. President Fox is credited with implementing reforms like guaranteeing freedom of the press and stabilizing the economy that saw single digit inflation for the first time in 30 years, maintaining a solid value of the peso, implementing national health insurance, and ushering in credible voting procedures. However, he is criticized for failing to stem the migrations of Mexicans across the border into the United States. Statistics from the Mexican government state that over the period 2000–2006 an average of about one-half million people left Mexico. Migrants are primarily from rural areas indicating a familiar pattern in economic modernization whereby industrialization pushes people off the land. Barred from running for a second term, the 2006 election saw **Felipe Calderón** of the right-center National Action Party (PAN) elected. Bedeviled by drug violence, Calderón's party fell in the 2012 election. The Institutional Revolutionary Party (PRI) led by Peña Nieto, who ran on a platform of peace and prosperity, won in a close election.

India

Decolonization and then national independence in India was closely connected with the religious traditions of Hinduism and Islam. By the 1930s, the populist nationalist movement, which had coalesced around Gandhi and Hindu nonviolence, began to disturb the Muslim minority. The leaders of the Muslim League began calling for a Muslim nation, a "**Pakistan**" or "land of the pure." These conflicting nationalisms were to lead to tragedy. By 1937 Gandhi's movement had matured into the **Congress Party**. In the face of this, the British gave in to limited self-rule, but when Britain declared war on Germany on India's behalf without consultation, Gandhi called on Britain to "**Quit India.**" He and other Congress Party rulers were quickly arrested and remained jailed for the rest of the war. This allowed the rival Muslim League led by English-educated **Muhammad Ali Jinnah** (1876–1948) to assert the right of Muslims to separate independence areas.

Gandhi was appalled at the notion of a two-nation India, but murderous clashes between Hindus and Muslims after World War II led to the partition of India in 1947 into India and Pakistan. Since most Muslims lived in the western and eastern parts of northern India, the new Muslim nation was split into West and East Pakistan (today Pakistan and Bangladesh, respectively). It proved to be only the beginning of tragedy. An estimated 100,000 Hindus and Muslims were slaughtered and about five million refugees fled in opposite directions. Gandhi himself was gunned down by a Hindu fanatic in 1948.

India, meanwhile, was ruled for a generation by **Jawaharlal Nehru** and the Congress Party, which introduced a string of reforms—abolition of the untouchable caste, legal and social rights for women, economic advancement under democratic socialism, and a neutral stance in the Cold War. But population growth of 2.4 percent per year inhibited India's ability to progress. This strained the fragile democracy. Nehru's daughter, **Indira Gandhi** (her deceased husband was no relation to Mahatma Gandhi) in 1975 subverted parliamentary democracy in order to attack corruption and carry on a campaign of mass sterilization. Despite the unpopularity of her campaign, both she and democracy survived.

Other political problems rooted in ethnic diversity and religion became the next challenge to Indian democracy. **Sikhs**, with their own religion, which is a blend of Islam and Hinduism, and a military culture marked by wearing coiled turbans, had long been a dominant force in the **Punjab** (a border region between India and Pakistan). In 1984 militant Sikhs occupied the Golden Temple of Amritsar, sacred to all Sikhs, and used it as a base for armed attacks against the anti-Sikh government. In June 1984 the Indian army, in the process of occupying the temple, killed hundreds of militants. In response, Indira Gandhi was assassinated and hundreds of Sikhs were killed in revenge. As her son Rajiv campaigned for office, he also was assassinated by a Tamil militant from an ethnic minority in the south. Despite violence, population pressures, ethnic and religious diversity, and corruption, India remains dedicated to elected representative government based on the English model. It is the world's largest democracy. During the 1990s, India's middle class increased in part due to participation in the world computer industry.

Persia/Iran and Afghanistan

In Iran and Afghanistan religious tradition also played a crucial role in establishing a national framework for independence. Russia and Britain struggled to maintain imperial control over Persia. In 1906 a nationalist coalition of merchants, religious leaders, and intellectuals revolted against the puppet **shah** (the Persian word for "king"), forcing a constitution and national assembly, the **Majlis**. This was crushed by Britain and Russia, who divided the country into spheres. After World War I and the Bolshevik revolution, Great Britain in 1919 negotiated a treaty installing British "advisers" in every government department, a move that aroused deep nationalist sentiment.

Following the Turkish example, in 1921 a strong military dictator, **Reza Shah Pahlavi** (1877–1944) came to power, ousting the British. He reigned until 1941 and tried, as in Turkey, to build a modern secular nation. However, his increasingly brutal rule and support of Nazi Germany during World War II led to his overthrow and the installation of his son, Muhammad Reza Pahlavi (r. 1941–1979). He also angered Iranian nationalists by courting Western powers and Western oil companies. With oil revenues, the shah undermined large landowners and religious leaders in order to carry out his modernization program of land reform, secular education, and centralized government. The result was violent revolution in 1978. The spellbinding religious leader **Ayatollah Khomeini** seized power and forced the shah to flee abroad. In order to establish national independence, the Ayatollah set up a radical Shi'ite Muslim government isolating Iran from the West and irritating neighbors, mostly Sunni Muslim states. In 1980 Iran and Iraq fought a bloody war with both Soviet and American weapons. The economic consequences of that war and the drive for power by Iraq's leader, **Saddam Hussein**, led to the Iraqi invasion of Kuwait in 1990 (the Persian Gulf War). Swift action on the part of the United States and other Arab states foiled the invasion. At the dawn of the 21st century, political power in Iran remained largely in the hands of Shi'a (Shi'ite) Islamic institutions but was ruled outwardly by a president. Lack of foreign investment weakened Iran's oil production, putting strains on the economy. Iran remains in the world spotlight primarily due to its continued research and production of the ingredients that make nuclear weaponry, in defiance of the United Nations.

Afghanistan followed a similar route to national independence. Under a religious banner of anti-British sentiment, Amir Amanullah (1892–1960) declared a holy war on Britain. In 1919, Afghanistan won complete independence. Like the shah, his radical attempts at modernization led to religious revolt, tribal civil war, and retreat from reform. This weakness led to external intervention on the part of the Soviets (1979) and a protracted war. Sovietization and communist changes in the political, economic, social, and cultural life of Afghanistan led to a revolt by the conservative Islamic rebels known as the **mujahidin** ("holy warriors"). The Soviets began to retreat only during the restructuring under Mikhail Gorbachev in the mid-1980s. In the case of Iran and Afghanistan, the Islamic religion formed the basis of national sentiment and the nexus around which decolonization occurred. However, religious sentiment also stymied secular modernization efforts in these countries and served to divide the new nations. By the late 1990s, one group, the **Taliban** ("students") took leadership control. Taliban leadership has instituted strict Islamic rules and spends large sums of money on fighting internal opposition rather than on economic development. Taliban affiliation with international Islamic terrorism led to the September 2001 invasion of Afghanistan by the United States. Currently Afghanistan has a fledgling democracy under the leadership of **Hamid Karzai**.

Independence from the Ottoman Empire

The course of Arab independence in the former Ottoman Empire was colored by religion but also by wartime agreements, primarily involving the Jews. During World War I, Arabs, led by Hussein Ibn-Ali (1856–1931), a direct descendant of Muhammad, allied with the British against the Ottoman Turks with the vague promise of independence after the war. However, in the secret **Sykes-Picot treaties** of 1916, Britain and France agreed that France would receive modern-day **Syria** and Lebanon after the war and Britain would receive Palestine, Jordan, and Iraq. A related source of irritation was the British **Balfour Declaration** of November 2, 1917, which said, "His Majesty views with favor the establishment in Palestine of a National Home for the Jewish People . . . ."

IRAQ, EGYPT, SYRIA, LEBANON, AND SAUDI ARABIA

After World War I, the establishment of British (Palestine, Jordan, and Iraq) and French (Syria and Lebanon) mandates forced Arab nationalists to seek independence gradually. In 1930 Iraq gained independence in exchange for a long-term military alliance with Britain. Egypt followed a similar course. A protectorate since 1914, it gained independence in 1922. Saudi Arabia was granted independence from Britain in 1932. The French held on longer, playing ethnic and religious groups against each other in Syria. In 1936 Syria became independent in return for a treaty of friendship. The French carved out a second mandate, **Lebanon**, which became a republic dominated by Christians, a situation that never found favor among the Muslim minority, resulting in civil war and the collapse of the state in 1990. A civil war followed (1989–1991), ending with a return to a quasi-democracy that has been plagued with sectarian tensions, Syrian occupation, Israeli and Palestinian influence, and various terrorist militias like **Fatah** (Palestinian), **Hezbollah** (Shi'a Islamic), and **Hamas** (Palestine Liberation Organization or PLO).

THE BALFOUR DECLARATION

His Majesty's Government views with favor the establishment in Palestine of a National Home for the Jewish People, and will use their best endeavors to facilitate the achievement of this object, it being clearly understood that nothing shall be done which may prejudice the civil and religious rights of existing non-Jewish communities in Palestine, or the rights and political status enjoyed by Jews in any other country.

In November 1917, the British foreign secretary issued the Balfour Declaration stating Britain's intention to provide a homeland for the Jews in Palestine after World War I. As a secret wartime agreement, it was intended to rally as many countries as possible to the Allied side. A careful reading of the document reveals contradictory promises to both Jews and Palestinians. It has been the subject of passionate debate and many wars ever since. Only in 1995 did Jews and Palestinians come to some agreement about rule of this area of the world.

ISRAEL

Meanwhile, the Jewish population in Palestine leaped from 10 percent to 30 percent in the interwar period. The reasons were twofold. First, the United States limited Jewish immigration from Europe in the 1930s. Second, the increasing persecution of Jews in Germany and Poland made them flee to Palestine. Resentment between Jews and Arabs grew, especially over land. By 1939 Britain proposed an independent Palestine and a limit on Jewish immigrants. Technically, sovereignty had been attained in the Middle East, but these former mandates were still under the economic and political influence of the West. This was especially true as World War II approached.

During World War II, the Western nations maintained their influence in the Middle East despite German efforts to capture the Suez Canal. After the war, Arab nationalism intensified. One strand of sentiment envisioned Pan Arab nations united under the banner of Islam and in alliances like the Arab League (in opposition to Jewish immigration) and **OPEC** (Organization of Petroleum Exporting Countries). The other strand concentrated on the growth of nationalism within countries. National independence proved greater than Arab solidarity, fragmenting the nations of the Middle East. Divisions occurred along ethnic lines (Persians and Arabs), religious lines (Sunni and Shi'ite Muslims), and economic lines (oil-producing and non-oil-producing states). Only the overriding problem of the Jewish question united them. Jews demanded that all survivors of Hitler's death camps be allowed to settle

Did You Know?

The Arab League is made up of Egypt, Iraq, Jordan, Lebanon, Saudi Arabia, Syria, and Yemen.

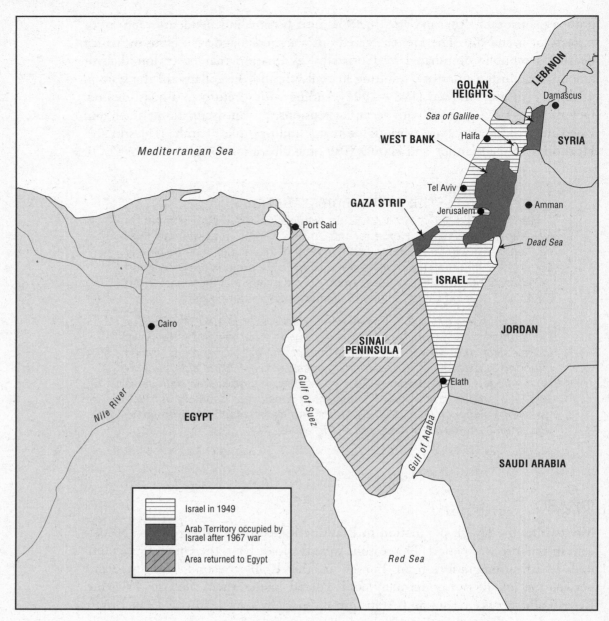

Arab-Israeli Conflict 1949–1973 C.E. The struggle for Israeli national existence in the face of Arab resistance led to several wars favorable to the Israelis. Complicating the situation was the Cold War, during which both the Soviets and Americans kept the situation volatile by supplying weapons and support.

in Palestine, but Palestine and the **Arab League** were opposed. The issue became explosive. The question went to the United Nations, which partitioned Palestine between Jews and Arabs. When the British mandate in Palestine ended in 1948, the Jews created the Jewish state of **Israel** out of the former Palestine.

PALESTINE

The Arab countries united in attack, but the Israelis defeated them decisively with modern weaponry they had acquired with U.S. help. Almost one million Arabs fled Palestine. This 1948 **Arab-Israeli War** left a bitter legacy between Israel and its political allies, the United States and Great Britain on the one hand, and the Arab states and their growing ties with the Soviet Union on the other. It also gave rise to a virulent Palestinian independence organization called the **Palestine Liberation Organization** (PLO). This organization remained the nerve center for anti-Israeli and pro-Palestinian nationalism. Terrorism became the major Palestinian weapon of retaliation. After persistent Palestinian raids, Israel invaded the Egyptian Sinai in 1956, and in 1967, the "**Six-Day War**" between Israel and the Arab states resulted in Israeli occupation of Gaza, Sinai, Old Jerusalem, the Golan Heights, and the West Bank. This expansion at the expense of Egypt, Jordan, Syria, and Lebanon made the Middle East a tinderbox. In the Yom Kippur War of 1973 Egyptian forces under **Anwar el-Sadat** demonstrated new fighting ability against the Israelis, led by the surprised coalition government of **Golda Meir**. As the war ground to a halt, U.S. secretary of state **Henry Kissinger** began efforts to find a diplomatic solution. In 1982, bowing to economic pressures, Egypt broke ranks with the Arab countries and recognized Israel in return for the Sinai. This historic agreement between Egyptian president Anwar Sadat and Israeli prime minister **Menachem Begin** frustrated the PLO. Its flamboyant leader **Yasser Arafat** then moved into Lebanon and instigated its dismemberment. Not until the Cold War ended did the United States and the Soviet Union come together to sanctify a settlement in the area. Gradually during the 1990s more Arabs accepted Israel's right to exist and more Israelis accepted the principle of a homeland and independence for the Palestinians.

In 1993, Israel and the PLO reached an agreement calling for Palestinian autonomy (self-government) in return for recognition of the Israeli state. Talks have continued to the present regarding the implementation of the agreement and the issue of control of Jerusalem but violence has continued to flare.

REVOLUTION AND NATIONAL LIBERATION IN CHINA, SOUTHEAST ASIA, AFRICA, AND LATIN AMERICA

In China, Southeast Asia, Africa, and Latin America, independence movements took another path. In these areas, decolonization led initially to new liberal nations, but for one reason or another, they failed. A period of **neocolonialism** (economic or political dependence) followed. This was the context within which wars of national liberation occurred. Wars of national liberation freed countries from Western imperialism using communist slogans and help from communist states like China and Russia. The net result of national liberation and decolonization for world history has been an explosion of fragile new nations susceptible to dictatorships of all types, the dilution of Western and communist influence, the rise of fledging democracies and of religious fundamentalism, and modernization programs. The rise of the developing nations changed the economic and political balance of the twentieth-century world.

China

The Chinese Communist war of national liberation began in the 1920s and culminated in the **Chinese Communist Revolution** of 1949. As in Russia, when the Chinese imperial system fell (1911), two strands of thought competed for the new government. One attempted to follow Western-style liberal democracy as represented by the Chinese nationalists (Kuomintang) led by Sun Yat-sen and then

Chiang Kai-shek, and the other followed the Marxist-style communist model led by **Mao Zedong**. As in Russia, the first phase of change was dominated by Western liberalism. In the 1920s Nationalists attempted to set up a Western-style government and to modernize along capitalist lines. Throughout this period, however, the nationalists struggled with the communists.

THE SAYINGS OF MAO TSE-TUNG

It is up to us to organize the people. As for the reactionaries in China, it is up to us to organize the people to overthrow them. . . .

Just as there is not a single thing in the world without a dual nature (this is the law of the unity of opposites), so imperialism and all reactionaries have a dual nature—they are real tigers and paper tigers at the same time. . . . On the one hand, they were real tigers; they devoured people, devoured people by the millions and tens of millions. . . before the victory in 1949. Look! Were these not tigers, dead tigers, iron tigers, real tigers? But in the end they changed into paper tigers, dead tigers, bean-curd tigers. . . .

Without a people's army the people have nothing. . . .

We should be modest and prudent, guard against arrogance and rashness, and serve the Chinese people heart and soul. . .

With the increasing bankruptcy of the rural economy in recent years, the basis for men's domination over women has already been undermined. With the rise of the peasant movement, the women in many places have now begun to organize rural women's associations; the opportunity has come for them to lift up their heads, and the authority of the husband is getting shakier every day. In a word, the whole feudal-patriarchal ideology and system is tottering with the growth of the peasants' power. . .

Since the key cities have long been occupied by the powerful imperialists and their reactionary Chinese allies, it is imperative for the revolutionary ranks to turn the backward villages into advanced consolidated base areas, . . . bastions of the revolution from which to fight their vicious enemies.

The leader of the Chinese Communist Revolution in 1949 was Mao Zedong (Tse-tung) (1893–1976). In his plans for a new China, he used Marxist-Leninst ideas of class struggle, but he adapted them to fit the Chinese situation. For instance, he placed the revolution in the countryside rather than the city, he talked in Chinese terms emphasizing Chinese complementary dualism and proper conduct. At the same time, he envisioned a new world and liberal changes for women. His sayings have been collected in a little handbook widely read in the 1960s and 1970s, The Little Red Book.

Mao converted to Marxian socialism in 1918 but his lack of success in leading the country to communism led him to make major changes in the doctrine. After the Long March pushed Mao and his followers to northwest China, Mao mapped out a new course for his Chinese revolution. While Marx had envisioned the workers as the engine of revolution and Lenin, the workers and peasants, Mao envisioned the peasants as the engine of change. This was because they were the majority of the population and because they were the most oppressed, now not by the old regime, but by the nationalist Kuomintang. Mao also shifted the locus of the revolution from the city to the countryside. In a campaign among peasants, his communist cadres preached communist doctrines. Warfare in the countryside demanded a different kind of war, **guerrilla warfare**. Mao went back to the ancient Chinese martial expert, Sun Tzu, to find inspiration. "The enemy advances, we retreat; the enemy halts, we harass; the enemy slackens, we attack; the enemy retreats, we pursue." Finally, Mao defined the enemy as the imperialist rather than the capitalist. A peasant revolution carried on in the countryside with guerrilla tactics against imperialists instead of capitalists became the model for Third World peasant revolution.

Like Lenin, Mao used war and its tragic effects to bring his vision of revolution to reality. In fact, as one historian has noted, "Japanese aggression was. . . the most important single factor in Mao's rise to power." When Japanese armies advanced rapidly into China in 1938, the nationalist government of Chiang Kai-shek was forced to form a "united front" with Mao's communists in order to avoid having to fight the Japanese and the communists at the same time. This alliance allowed Mao to build up strength in guerrilla bases in the countryside behind Japanese lines where his forces avoided pitched battles and concentrated on winning peasant support. The communists began to appear in peasant eyes as genuine nationalists and true patriots, especially because they promised radical land redistribution. Meanwhile, the nationalists took the brunt of the fighting. A staggering three million Chinese were killed. Chinese deficits and runaway inflation discredited the nationalist government. When the Japanese collapsed in 1945, both communists and nationalists rushed to seize evacuated territory. Civil war began in which the United States aided the nationalists and the Soviet Union the communists. By 1948 the nationalist forces were in disarray and demoralized. The following year, Chiang Kai-shek and a million mainland Chinese fled to **Taiwan**. In October 1949, Mao proclaimed the **People's Republic of China** and laid claim to a new Mandate of Heaven.

Immediately, Mao liquidated over 800,000 "class enemies" and carried on a relentless campaign of "reeducation." In the mid-1950s, China followed the Soviet Union closely and seemed to be firmly in the Marxist-Leninist mold. By 1958, however, China began to go its own way both politically and economically. When Russian leader Nikita Khrushchev criticized Chinese policy, Mao condemned the Russians as "modern revisionists." Competing national and international interests led to the Sino-Soviet split in the early 1960s.

THE CULTURAL REVOLUTION

Apprehensive that China was becoming bureaucratic, capitalistic, and "revisionist," Mao launched the **Great Proletarian Cultural Revolution**. Its object was to purge the party of time-serving bureaucrats and recapture the revolutionary fervor. To do this, he dispatched the "**Red Guards**," young people who denounced their teachers and parents. Party officials, professors, and intellectuals were exiled to remote villages to "purify" themselves with heavy peasant labor.

CHINESE LIBERALIZATION

The chaos and persecutions of the Cultural Revolution caused a counterattack. This liberal shift in China, coupled with actual fighting between China and the Soviet

Union on the northern border in 1969, led to reconciliation with the United States in 1972. The moderates were led by **Deng Xiaoping**. After Mao's death in 1976, Deng and his supporters began to free the economy from socialism. Economic liberalization, however, led to demands for political liberalization. Deng, witnessing how such a program had gotten out of hand in Russia under Gorbachev, quickly crushed the liberal student revolt in **Tiananmen Square** on May 17, 1989, the year the Berlin Wall fell in Europe.

Southeast Asia

The Chinese revolution based on the Marxist and Soviet model became the guide for the wars of national liberation in Southeast Asia. The national liberation struggles in Southeast Asia were first against the French, then against the United States. **Indochina**, including **Vietnam**, **Laos**, and **Cambodia**, had been a French colony since the 1880s scramble for empire. The French had been interested in the area as early as the seventeenth century when Christian missionaries successfully entered the region and won converts. As in China, the failure of Vietnam's Confucian government to repel outside invasion discredited it and made French colonization easier. The French were more reluctant than the British to decolonize after the war because French civilization was more universalist, claiming that all natives were entitled to be considered French, and because Indochina was a much valued colony with its plantations and rubber. French presence completely disrupted indigenous systems of local agriculture and impoverished many peasants.

As in the history of other revolutions of this era, the new Western-educated middle-class children of the former elite became the backbone of the nationalist revolutions. While the French were embroiled in World War I, they lost control of the clandestine Nationalist party, but in 1929 they were still strong enough to repress and severely weaken a nationalist uprising. The demise of the Nationalist party, however, only served to empower the nascent Communist party, which had been formed in the 1920s by **Ho Chi Minh**, a converted Marxist who had studied in France and Russia during World War I. In the 1930s, Ho followed Mao's lead and switched the emphasis of revolution from worker to peasant.

LIBERATION FROM FRANCE

When the French were weakened by the Japanese invasion of Indochina in 1941, the communists used France's setback to advance their struggle for national liberation. Calling themselves **Viet Minh**, they established bases in south China and from there, by 1945, they advanced into the Red River delta as the Japanese withdrew. The Vietnamese communists reached Hanoi in August 1945. Along the way, they had gained support of peasants in rural regions much as Mao had, by a system of reeducation, building programs, and assistance, particularly during the famine of 1944–1945. After World War II, the French, with British aid, regained control of territory in the south, reoccupying Saigon and attempting to regain the rest of Vietnam. For almost ten years, the communist Vietnamese carried on a guerrilla war against them. In 1954 the Viet Minh decisively defeated the French at **Dien Bien Phu** despite American aid, which was part of the Cold War effort to contain the spread of communism. Their victory at Dien Bien Phu won for the Viet Minh control of the north at an international conference at Geneva.

THE VIETNAM DECLARATION OF INDEPENDENCE

"All men are created equal.". . . This immortal statement was made in the Declaration of Independence of the United States of America in 1776. . . . The Declaration of the French Revolution made in 1791 on the Rights of Man and the Citizen also states: "All men are born free and with equal rights, . . . "

Nevertheless, for more than eighty years, the French imperialists, abusing the standard of Libery, Equality, and Fraternity, have violated our Fatherland and oppressed our fellow-citizens. They have acted contrary to the ideals of humanity and justice.

In the field of politics, they have deprived our people of every democratic liberty. . . .

In the autumn of 1940 when the Japanese Fascists violated Indochina's territory to establish new bases in their fight against the Allies, the French imperialists went down on their bended knees and handed over our country to them.

Thus, from that date, our people were subjected to the double yoke of the French and Japanese. . . .

For these reasons, we, members of the Provisional Government of the Democratic Republic of Vietnam, solemnly declare to the world that Vietnam has the right to be a free and independent country—and in fact is so already. The entire Vietnamese people are determined to mobilize all their physical and mental strength, to sacrifice their lives and property in order to safeguard their independence and liberty.

One of the many results of World War II was the stirring of independence movements in former colonies. The words and aspirations of nationalist leaders echo those of the other great liberal revolutions of modern times. On September 2, 1945, Ho Chi Minh, leader of the Viet Minh, or Vietnamese Army, issued this declaration of independence. While a trained communist, his words seem more familiar to the world of democracy than to that of communism.

VIETNAM, CAMBODIA, THAILAND, AND MYANMAR (BURMA)

The second phase of national liberation came with U.S. involvement. Despite cooperation between the Viet Minh and the United States during the war against Japan, the anticommunist sentiment of the Cold War turned the Viet Minh into enemies. The United States feared that if one country fell in Southeast Asia others would fall in a "**domino effect**." The United States began to back **Ngo Dinh Diem** as leader of South Vietnam. To counter U.S.-supported Diem, the Viet Minh began supplying weapons to communists in the south, the **Viet Cong**. When Diem proved unable to stem the tide of communism in the south, the U.S. approved a military coup to overthrow him. Then the United States stepped up military intervention so that by 1968 there were 500,000 Americans in Vietnam. Their very presence served to add to the popularity of the national liberation sentiment. Meanwhile, popular sentiment in the United States against involvement mounted. The new president, **Richard Nixon**, withdrew U.S. troops (1973). In 1975 the South Vietnamese state was overrun by the communists. Within a few years, many who supported the South were in prison camps and another substantial proportion fled by sea in leaky boats, many coming eventually to the United States in a "**boat people**" migration.

The American fear of the domino effect was partly realized when Laos and Cambodia also fell to the communists. Cambodia became a "killing field." First Chinese-backed communists, the Khmer Rouge, led by **Pol Pot** ravaged the country and then the Vietnamese communists invaded. The beleaguered nation has yet to awaken from the consequences of a holocaust in which over one-third of the population was killed or died. During the 1990s both Vietnam and Cambodia liberalized their politics and opened their economies to world trade. Vietnam, in particular, has made great strides in modernizing the country and encouraging companies like Nike to invest and set up plants in the country despite communist rule.

Two other Southeast Asian countries, **Thailand** and **Myanmar (Burma)**, have taken unique journeys on the road to nationhood. In both countries, the Thais in Thailand and the Burmans in Myanmar (Burma), are the majority ethnic groups as well as being Theravada Buddhist. Both ethnic groups have asserted authority over the variety of ethnic groups within their borders including various hill tribes, Muslim peoples, and immigrant trading communities primarily of Chinese and Indian origin. Here, perhaps, the similarity ends. Thailand (once known as Siam) was the only Southeast Asian country to avoid colonization. As a result, Thailand built a national culture based on a reverence for Buddhism and the monarchy. This led to a stable environment that invited world trade, investment, and tourism. However, the Cold War and decolonization problems nearby have spilled over into Thailand. Various Muslim and communist insurgent factions caused political problems that led to increasing authoritarian and corrupt rule. A military coup in 2006 threatened the stability of Thailand and its economic prosperity.

Myanmar (Burma), a former British colony and the largest of the Southeast Asian countries, remains shrouded in isolationism. Unlike Thailand, it was occupied and devastated by the Japanese during World War II. After the war, the British negotiated independence for Burma under the nationalist leader, **Aung San**. After Aung San's assassination, a Buddhist idealist and supporter of democracy, **U Nu**, ruled, but in 1962 the army deposed him. After that, Myanmar was closed, and the many tribal communities were suppressed. Military leaders, who renamed Burma Myanmar, quashed dissenters like the popular **Aung San Siu Kyi** who had been under house arrest for years. In 2012, however, a new president, Thein Sein, opened the country to foreign investment and incorporated opposition leaders like Aung San Siu Kyi into a more progressive government.

Malaysia and Indonesia

The national independence movements in **Malaysia** and **Indonesia** illustrate that many newly emerging nations wished to maintain independence and neutrality in the Cold War in order to avoid becoming the Cold War battleground that Vietnam, Cambodia, and Laos had become.

In 1950 the Dutch East Indies was united as the Republic of Indonesia under the leadership of President **Ahmed Sukarno**. He feared American and European neo-colonialist efforts to exploit Indonesian natural resources. To address this challenge, Sukarno sponsored the **Bandung Conference** in 1955, which represented 29 Asian and African countries and nearly one and a half billion people. The Bandung Conference called on these newly independent states to form a Neutral Bloc in the Cold War. Prime Minister **Nehru** of India became the leading spokesman for the "neutralists." However, the threat of old-style colonialism was soon overshadowed by the new threat of communism. Communist China occupied Tibet in 1959 and later invaded the northern borders of India. Nehru turned to the United States and Britain for assistance. Meanwhile, Sukarno, who had moved closer to communist China and had become more dictatorial, was toppled in a government coup led by General **Thojib Suharto**. Suharto then began to court Western capital to develop Indonesia's great natural resources. Malaysia, meanwhile, continued a steady course of neutrality and economic development, also relying on the West.

Africa

Between 1947 and 1962, almost every African country was decolonized and gained formal independence. The first phase of the African national independence movement was

> **Did You Know?**
>
> Many African countries found in communism a program for fast economic development, a legitimization for dictatorship, and a banner under which they could become economically and politically independent.

dominated by relationships with Europe, the second with the United States and Soviet Union. The African road to national independence began with political decolonization, but most African countries remained economically dependent on the West. Democracy and constitutionalism occupied a fragile position in African countries, which had neither the political experience nor the national identity and unity to make a liberal political government work. This became the context within which Marxist ideas of the Soviet and Chinese brand began to take hold. In this search for national independence and stability, first on the liberal model and then on the Marxist, the Cold War played its part. The Soviet Union and China supported Marxist governments, and the United States supported the opposite.

GHANA

In many newly independent African states, the seeds of leadership had been planted after World War I by educated Africans who studied in Western countries and became acquainted with both Marxist and liberal thought. The Senegalese poet and political leader Leopol Senghor is an excellent example. In the 1920s and 1930s he and other black and white intellectuals formulated the idea of **negritude**, or blackness, meaning racial pride, self-confidence, and black creativity. When the Depression hit, many of these intellectuals lost their jobs to whites, while the masses suffered also as their labors depended on foreign markets for raw materials that also deteriorated. This radicalized them into calling for outright independence. World War II both interrupted and strengthened the movement. African mines and plantations burgeoned with wartime production. New African leaders were of humbler origin—former schoolteachers, union leaders, and government clerks. These leaders accepted the existing boundaries that Europeans had drawn to avoid border disputes and focused instead on solidifying their own power positions much as Lenin had. A good example of this was **Kwame Nkrumah** (1909–1972), who led Ghana (former British mandate of Togoland/Gold Coast) to independence. Nkrumah built a mass party, injecting it with a religious revival sentiment and indigenous historical forms. They staged strikes and riots. In 1957, under Nkrumah's influence, Ghana became the first African state to emerge from colonial rule. Nkrumah soon fell under the spell of Marxism. In 1964, he set up a one-party socialist state, claimed dictatorial powers, and went heavily into debt. In 1966 he was overthrown by a police-army coup. Political instability continued in the 1970s. In 1993, a new constitution (Fourth Republic) was written. Under the leadership of Jerry John Rawlins and his successors, Ghana has become more democratic, economically prosperous, and socially progressive.

BLACK POWER

The demand for Africanization is made by the black people and means a replacement by them of those of different origin. Despite the wider meaning than the term African has acquired today, the Blacks are still at the bottom of every ladder and identify themselves completely and practically with the struggle for change. To ask the indigenous Africans to forget the agony of their past is to ask them to ignore the lesson that their experience has taught them. Asians and Europeans are crying in Tanganyika today for non-racial parties, but just how practical is this? Those non-racial parties which have been formed in Tanganyika (present day Tanzania) have never succeeded, for they never aimed at emancipating the African, but only at deluding him into satisfaction with the lowest rung. It is the experience of the present that will constitute African reaction in the future; and the place that the Asian and the European will build for themselves in Africa will be governed by the degree of sacrifice they are prepared to make in the cause of a life in joint advancement and dedication with and amongst the Africans.

The aspirations of African blacks to direct their own destiny were eloquently stated in 1960 by Rashidi Mfaume Kawawa. He succeeded Julius Nyerere as prime minister of Tanganyika. Independence in Africa was intimately tied to race, which became an identifiable banner around which liberation could occur. Once independent, these countries had to find new ideologies of rule. In this case, race proved inadequate as a vision of progress.

NIGERIA

The same sequence of events was played out in other African countries like **Nigeria** (former British protectorate). Nigeria encompassed an ethnic mix of Yorubas in the west, who had strong military traditions, and Ibos in the east, who had a tradition of business and independent villages. There was also a religious mix—Islam in the north and Christian and indigenous religions in the south. In response, Nigeria adopted a federal system after independence. By 1965 ethnic rivalries caused law and order to break down. An Ibo-led army group seized power. When a countergroup overtook them, Ibos were massacred. In ensuing years, military dictatorships dominated the political, social, and economic landscape of the country. The result has been corruption, ethnic violence, and squandered oil wealth.

ZAIRE/DEMOCRATIC REPUBLIC OF THE CONGO

The Congo, Kenya, and South Africa illustrate the same kinds of problems in their struggles for national independence. Belgian rule in the Congo had been so dictatorial that, when the Belgians retreated, there were few African college graduates in

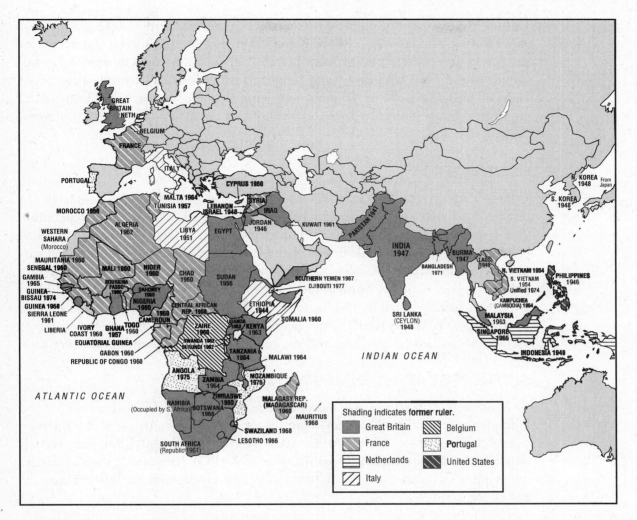

Political Independence in Africa and Asia 1945–1985 C.E. After World War II, countries in Africa and Asia gained independence either by a process of decolonization, or wars of liberation, or both. The predisposition to form new states based on national-liberal principles was a major world political characteristic of the twentieth century.

the country. No organized national movements and no mechanisms for rule existed. When independence came to the Belgian Congo in 1960, a series of rulers came to power, one after another. In 1964 leftist rebels set up a People's Republic causing U.S. paratroopers to rescue thousands of whites and hostages. In 1971 the "republic" of Zaire was formed by General **Joseph Mobuto**, who created a military rule from 1971–1997. In 1997 Laurent-Desire Kabila ousted Mobutu after which the name of the country reverted to the Democratic Republic of the Congo.

KENYA

In Kenya, the independence movement was led by **Jomo Kenyatta**. In 1956 the British crushed the rebel movement, called **Mau Mau**, but by 1963 a multiracial Kenya had won independence from Britain under Kenyatta's leadership. Kenyatta sought the broad support of both blacks and whites. He encouraged Europeans and Asians to remain in Kenya as long as they accepted African rule. However, Kenyatta's leadership became increasingly repressive and autocratic. His successor

Daniel Moi maintained political power from 1978–2002. From 2002–2007 under Moi's former vice-president, **Mwai Kibaki**, Kenya witnessed spectacular economic prosperity but it was not evenly distributed. Political unrest and ethnic violence followed. In the 2013 elections, Jomo Kenyatta's son, **Uhuru Kenyatta**, won a tight election pledging to bring regional and ethnic conflict to an end. He is 2013's youngest African political leader and symbolic of the new group of African leaders that are to come.

SOUTH AFRICA

In South Africa, the Afrikans (Dutch) won control from the British in 1948. To cement their rule, they instituted a policy of **apartheid**, or legal racial separation. The legislature gave certain tribes "homelands" (much like the American Indian reservations) but reserved the best jobs and lands for whites and made political participation impossible for blacks. Key nationalist leaders like **Nelson Mandela** were jailed. In general, Soviet arms went to the blacks and U.S. arms to whites. Only after the Berlin Wall fell in 1989, ending the Cold War, did the white president of South Africa, **F. W. de Klerk**, begin discussions with Nelson Mandela. This paved the way for an end to apartheid and the beginning of rule based on racial equality.

SOUTHWEST AFRICA/NAMIBIA

In Southwest Africa, national independence also became wrapped up with Cold War ideologies and involvement. **Namibia**, or Southwest Africa, was a German colony mandated to South Africa after World War I. In 1966 the Marxist **Southwest Africa People's Organization (SWAPO)** launched guerrilla warfare involving both superpowers. Namibia finally gained independence in 1990 after the end of the Cold War.

The Cold War and Nationalist Struggles in Cuba, Chile, and Nicaragua

The story of African national liberation movements illustrates how European withdrawal led to struggles for power in African states. This power struggle became intertwined with Cold War politics. The U.S. gave aid to one side and the Soviet Union or China to the other. This was true also in Latin America, particularly in Cuba, Chile, and Nicaragua. Under agreements in 1903 and 1934, the United States leased a naval base at **Guantanamo Bay** and gained a dominant role in the Cuban economy. In 1952 **Fulgencio Batista** assumed dictatorial control. Subsequently, guerrillas, led by communist-trained **Fidel Castro**, who was backed by the Soviet Union, led a successful overthrow of Batista and instituted a communist government in Cuba. From then on, Cuba became a Soviet satellite and a threat to the U.S. In Chile, Marxist **Salvador Allende** took over in 1970 and nationalized the country's economy on the Soviet model. By 1973 there was a backlash against this regime and a military junta took over, vowing to "exterminate Marxism." Repression followed and only in 1989 did Chile rid itself of military dictatorship. In Nicaragua, Marxist **Sandinista** guerrillas battled the U.S.-backed "elected" president General **Anastasio Somoza**. In 1979 Somoza fled, leading to increased U.S.

intervention to prevent Marxist control of the country. Only in 1989 did national elections lead to the democratic election of Violeta Chamorro.

The end of European world hegemony occasioned by World Wars I and II led to national independence movements worldwide. Begun in World War I and completed after World War II, these movements took two forms. Decolonization movements were aimed at removing European rule and setting up independent states based on Western models. National wars of liberation were aimed at removing European and U.S. rule and economic domination and setting up states more on the Marxist model. Both movements became intertwined with Cold War politics and indigenous social, religious, and political revolutions. In many cases, they failed to establish stable sovereign states or to fulfill revolutionary social and political aims.

The results of decolonization and wars of national liberation for world history have been an explosion of new nations, the dilution of Western and communist influence, the rise of religious fundamentalism, and economic power blocs to challenge Western and communist political and economic hegemony. One of the quests of all new nations has been economic modernization because it is equated with power, wealth, and inclusion in the world system on an independent rather than dependent basis. Modernization took many forms in the twentieth century, some more successful than others in terms of economic prosperity and social and political justice.

The Diffusion of Modern Systems

(ca. 1945 C.E.–Present)

TIMELINE	
1947 C.E.	Invention of the transistor
1958 C.E.	Invention of the silicon chip
1989 C.E.–1991 C.E.	Collapse of the Soviet Union
1991 C.E.	Maastricht Treaty
1992 C.E.–1995 C.E.	Bosnian War
1994 C.E.	Rwanda Genocide
1994 C.E.	Nelson Mandela becomes president of South Africa
2001 C.E.	Al Qaeda attacks on the World Trade Center
2003 C.E.	U.S. Invasion of Iraq
2004 C.E.	Expansion of EU to include East European countries

TWENTIETH-CENTURY MODERNIZATION OUTSIDE OF EUROPE

An important characteristic of the twentieth century was world modernization. Not only has industrialism spread throughout the world, second and third industrial revolutions—the communications and computer revolutions—have completely transformed world political, economic, social, and cultural life. Modernization has challenged the earth's people to deal with problems like population pressures, resource depletion, and environmental disequilibrium. The tempo of change, scientific discoveries, and uncertainties of a nuclear age have led to angst and protest as well as optimism and opportunity.

Before the twentieth century, modernization was closely linked with the European concepts of secularism, industrialism, and liberalism. For many of the world's nations, however, this model, which had taken centuries, seemed impossible, if not too slow, to follow. Increasingly, the road to modernization encompassed other models including the socialist, communist, and variants in between. Until recently, the drive to modernize ignored the costs. The nineteenth-century costs seemed mostly to be social in nature, like poor living and working conditions. Increasingly important in the twentieth century are the ecological costs like resource depletion and pollution, particularly as more and more countries joined the ranks of industrialized nations. In the twentieth century, secularism sometimes has appeared to lead to base materialism, and liberalism to unchecked behavior. By the end of the century, therefore, there has been a resurgence of religious fundamentalism and a call for moral responsibility as well as rights. For some, the answers to the modernization dilemma can be found in the very science and technology that had given birth to industrialism. For others, the answers are in conservation, preservation, and deindustrialization. Despite the problems, modernization made the twentieth-century world wealthier, more highly educated, and more culturally integrated.

One model of modernization was capitalistic. However, many countries entering the industrial age had neither the political structures, commercial infrastructure, or capital for such a revolution. In fact, 80 percent of the world's population lives in **less developed countries (LDCs)**. These LDCs are characterized by subsistence agriculture, shortage of capital, poor infrastructure, poor technology, an illiterate workforce, and dependence on primary products (mining, raw materials, and so on). To remedy this situation, many LDCs began to imitate Western political structures while borrowing heavily from abroad. The result was, in many cases, problematic, as has been seen in the histories of Iran and others where modernization turned into reactionary revolution. In addition, huge debts were incurred, destabilizing the monetary systems of both industrialized and nonindustrialized countries alike. These obstacles caused many countries to look for another modernization model—a socialist or collective model in which the state owned the property and the capital earned from the agricultural sector became the capital used for industrialization. Often, in this model, the commercial stage of development was bypassed. This caused distribution and cost problems for socialist and communist systems that had no market mechanism to establish price and profitability.

The method of industrialization also became a question of philosophy and morality. Collective structures put the group ahead of the individual, while the Western model continued to rely on individual participation and motive. The U.S.S.R. and China provide good examples of the communist/socialist model, and Germany and Japan of the capitalist model. The attempts by the LDCs illustrates the difficulty of either the socialist or capitalist model to provide universal successful blueprints for modernization.

Soviet Modernization

In 1927, when Stalin came to power, he abandoned the **NEP** (New Economic Policy), which, in the consumer sectors, had allowed private trade and property. Unlike the czarist government that had borrowed heavily from abroad, racking up debts to build railroads and factories, debts that were later repudiated by the Bolsheviks, Stalin pressed for rapid industrialization in 1931 without Western aid, which was, in any case, impossible, due to the Depression. He structured development on **Five-Year Plans**, in which all parts of the economy were owned, planned, and controlled by the state and communist bureaucrats. Food rationing was introduced, production of consumer goods curtailed, and all private enterprise abolished. Heavy industry like steel and hydroelectric power took precedence. Beginning in 1929 Stalin **collectivized** agriculture in order to earn capital for industrialization. Farms were gathered into huge collectives in which peasants used their own implements and seed, but were provided with state tractors. Each collective was required to meet production quotas, and the profits after the state took its share were divided among peasants in the collective. At first, the peasants resisted, slaughtering their animals and burning their crops, creating a man-made famine of epic proportions. Grain output from 1928 to 1938 was identical to that in 1913. Instead of agricultural profit, the state had to invest heavily in agriculture. Collectivization was an economic failure but a political success as it created a subservient peasant class and assured grain for urban workers.

The industrial side of the planned economy was more successful. Soviet industry produced four times as much in 1937 as in 1928. The great industrial drive did not lead to a better living standard, however, because over one-third of the net income went to investment, bureaucracy, and the military. The communist model of modernization used state ownership and a planned economy. To this was added the idea of social paternalism—improved free education, health care, and pensions. On the other hand, poor housing (in 1926 there were 2.7 per room and in 1940, 4.04 per room), a lack of motivation, and a climate of fear and terror accompanied the communist/socialist model. In order to make industrial gains, Russian women went to work, giving them opportunities, especially for education, but adding to their home responsibilities that men refused to share.

During World War II, all the trends put in place in the 1930s continued. In 1956, however, after Stalin's death, Nikita Khrushchev (1894–1974) at the Twentieth Party Congress denounced Stalin and promised liberalization or "de-Stalinization." He pressed for increased agricultural output by opening up vast areas in Central Asia for cotton ("white gold") production, but the failure of vast irrigation projects meant that only three out of five crops were productive. Meanwhile, the consumer sector, despite increased production, failed due to an underdeveloped distribution system.

Chinese Modernization

China followed the same pattern as the U.S.S.R. except that, in the initial stages of modernization on the communist model, emphasis was on agricultural rather than industrial development. Chinese leaders realized that in a country of one billion people, the failure of agriculture would mean the failure of the state. Thus, all land in China was collectivized and then "**communized**," meaning farms worked like factories. Peasants became agricultural workers who received wages. State farms in which peasants worked in state fields and lived in barrack conditions were common in the 1950s. Family ties were destroyed. Some 20 million Chinese died between 1959 and 1962. This so-called economic utopia turned out to be not only a social disaster but an economic disaster. Only efficient rationing prevented starvation. To mitigate agricultural failures, Mao in 1958 launched a program of industrialization called the **Great Leap Forward**. This program emphasized development of heavy industry, but on a small-scale model rather than in the Russian-style big factories. Iron, for instance, was produced in backyard furnaces. As in Russia, the five-year-plan system of development displayed spectacular statistical gains, mostly because, as in the U.S.S.R., the country had been so destroyed by the war that any gain was a leap forward. As in the U.S.S.R., heavy industry made spectacular gains at the expense of the consumer economy and was built on agricultural profits. Per capita consumption in the 1950s was only slightly higher than in 1937.

By the time **Deng Xiaoping** came to power in 1976, the clamor for a better standard of living forced him to liberalize the consumer economy. Deng and his supporters initiated a series of new policies embodied in a campaign called the "**Four Modernizations**"—agriculture, industry, science and technology, and national defense. Not unlike NEP in the U.S.S.R., Deng introduced capitalism into the consumer and agricultural economies. Peasants were encouraged to produce and dare to be rich. The results were spectacular. Food production increased 50 percent between 1978 and 1982. Because the Chinese had historically had a strong commercial expertise and tradition, the Chinese economy grew at an annual rate of 10 percent between 1978 and 1987, and the per capita income doubled in those years. Still, only 3 percent of the urban workforce was employed by private enterprise in 1986 and industry remained largely state owned. As in the U.S.S.R., the people's economy basically ran on the black market. In both examples, military expenditures are a heavy drain on the ability of the socialist model to make gains, and the concept of a planned economy has fallen short of the ideal as an efficient way to allocate resources and produce efficiently. The 1990s saw China struggle to improve economic performance by instituting some market reforms and free enterprise without unleashing political demands for democracy.

The 1990s, however, saw a dramatic shift toward a consumer economy under the continued aegis of the Chinese Communist Party. The party sought popular support by offering consumer goods rather than political reforms. In 1989 the party offered the "three bigs"—bicycles, wrist watches, and sewing machines. Today televisions, computers, and washing machines are the "bigs." The result has been that in 2005 the Chinese economy ranked ahead of Germany and was in the number three position in the world economy as industries like textiles can produce goods more cheaply due to lower labor costs and energy consumption that avoids heavy investment in pollution technology. China also has become a mecca for intermediate stages of production like automobiles. Industry has helped China face the enormous task it has in providing employment for its large population, 60 percent of whom still live in the countryside. Many live poorly off the land and supplement their income by becoming a migrant workforce in urban areas. Mechanization of agriculture is a conundrum for China as urban areas are not able to accommodate the accompanying movement off the land to cities.

Did You Know?

Exports have played a big part in Chinese growth.

Growing economic dynamism has produced other challenges. China has become the number two producer of greenhouse gases in the world although its output is about one-eighth of the world total. There also is a growing gap between rich and poor. By 2004, some 236,000 Chinese were millionaires and the Chinese talk about the "Five Colors" or the purest road to riches: Communist Party connections, prostitution, smuggling, illegal drug trading, and criminal gangs. Health care has declined and about 1.5 million Chinese have HIV or AIDS. The Chinese continue to live under the one-child policy, which has produced an imbalance between sexes as boys are preferred. Meanwhile, Western popular culture has spread into China. Every city has discos, Internet cafes, and Western stores. More than 100 million Chinese are Internet users (out of a population of about 1.3 billion). Religious believers practice at their own peril, and the government continues to crack down on missionary sects like *Falun Gong*.

China today is enjoying tremendous influence in the global economy but has faced roadblocks as a global power. It has uncertain relations with its neighbors like Taiwan and Southeast Asian nations that fear Chinese economic and political power. China's tremendous size, population, natural resources, military strength (the largest military in the world), national confidence, and sense of history have placed it in the unusual position of being a global economic power with a lower standard of living and isolated political position. However, tremendous exports to countries like the United States have resulted in China becoming a world bank of sorts for foreign currency. It has also resulted in heavy Chinese investment and resource ownership in countries around the world.

Japanese Modernization

While the communist/socialist model made spectacular industrial gains and provided a safety net for old age, health, and educational services, it floundered in both the agricultural and consumer sectors, it failed to provide investment capital, and it created a police state. By contrast, Japan and West Germany rebuilt their economies on the capitalist model, paying attention to the consumer sector, building a commercial infrastructure of banks, law, and highways to facilitate it, allowing private property and profit, and obtaining investment capital from abroad. After Japan's surrender in 1945, American occupation forces under General Douglas MacArthur introduced political reforms including democratization and demilitarization. With this in gear, American antitrust laws were introduced (later rescinded) to break up the zaibatsu firms, and Japan carved out perhaps the most successful agricultural development program in twentieth-century history. The Japanese Diet bought up the land of absentee landlords who were generally well-educated elite. The elite were then forced to become managers of new factories. In this way, industrial production utilized a highly educated managerial workforce. Meanwhile, instead of redistributing land to peasants, the land was sold on generous terms, creating a new class of entrepreneurial peasant farmers. The United States provided investment capital both in the form of grants and loans and by the creation of a stock market enticing private world investment.

The Japanese, meanwhile, blended their own traditions like family and state direction with American-style capitalism. State policymakers and factory enterprises worked together. In 1952 U.S. occupation ended and between 1950 and 1970 real growth averaged 10 percent a year. The measures that aided the recovery in Japan were the same as in Europe—cheap labor, a freer international market, investment capital, an alliance between government and business, a respect for education, a disciplined family, and the loyalty of workers to factories because of job security, pensions, and so on. Women did not advance under these changes.

In the 1970s and 1980s the Japanese economy was one of the strongest in the world but utilized a hybrid capitalist system that wedded government and industry and produced high inflation rates. In 1989 the Japanese economy went into a tailspin. Many investors went bankrupt, and 1 million workers were laid off. For the next 10 years, the economy lagged, but in early 2000, Japanese leaders began to reorder the loose relationship between government and business (known as "**Japan Inc.**") by slashing salaries and benefits and instituting policies that foster higher growth rates. Japanese companies sought cheaper labor costs by setting up shop in Southeast Asia. Despite being a powerful economic force in the world, Japan continues to be reluctant to assert political and military power. The growing power of China, however, has raised new challenges in this regard.

West German Modernization

West Germany's economic miracle was not unlike Japan's. Under the Marshall Plan, investment capital by the United States helped rebuild factories. Under Minister of Economy Ludwig Erhard, West Germany bet on the free market while maintaining the welfare network of Nazi Germany. West Germany also reformed its currency, became part of the international investment and consumer economy, and participated in the European Free Market. West Germany was soon supplying automobiles and electronics to the West, and its prosperity compared with the communist East German economy was one of the major reasons why the Berlin Wall fell in 1989. Since 1989 Germany has successfully integrated the East German economy, but it has been challenged by an economic system that lacks flexibility in hiring and firing and promises welfare benefits like long vacations and life-time employment.

Modernization in Third World Countries

Most Third World leaders saw rapid industrialization and "modernization" as the answer to their triple challenges of poverty, malnutrition, and disease, as well as a reason for their rule. At first they chose the communist model of the "plan" as their approach in order to avoid dependence on the West for capital and markets, and to avoid the class conflict that capitalism seemed to engender. Socialism also seemed more compatible with village culture and historical conditions that emphasized communal sharing and equality. Following the communist model, land was taken from large landowners and divided among the peasantry, but the peasantry continued to farm it the old way and divided it among their families. Increasingly smaller plots producing smaller amounts of food kept agriculture at subsistence levels with little left for investment. Poverty was the result, not because they consumed too much but because they produced too little. Industry fared little better under the socialist model. Master Plans floundered because of inadequate statistics on which to base the plans and scarcity of knowledgeable personnel to implement them.

The failures of socialist experiments have caused many **LDCs** to either return to capitalism or move to rigorous Marxism-Leninism or "**Afro-Marxism**." Each approach has had problems. The Western model encouraged borrowing investment capital from private sources, the **World Bank** (a U.N. agency whose purpose is to provide economic and technical assistance for development), or the **International Monetary Fund** (an international bank funded by industrialized countries to make money available to countries having difficulty securing loans). This floundered too because sometimes as little as five cents of every dollar was used for development, the rest being eaten up by government bureaucracies, military spending, and corruption. The other problem was massive foreign debt that reached crisis proportions after the OPEC oil cartel in 1973–1974 reduced supply, causing prices to soar. In 1982 Mexico, Brazil, and Argentina owed foreign banks and governments $600 billion and could not make the interest payments. Debt repudiation was avoided only when industrialized countries rewrote the debt. The other problem for Third World countries following the capitalist model was the rise of the **multinational corporation**. While American, European, and Japanese corporations invested in Third World countries, their profits flowed back to Europe, Japan, and the United States. Their products cornered the local markets and they employed local people at low wages. In this way, local development was stunted. Soon LDCs were again tied to the international market only by the production of raw materials.

TANZANIA

Tanzania under the leadership of **Julius Nyerere** provides an excellent example of the experience of LDCs with economic socialism. Tanzania began independence with a "mixed economy," part socialist, part capitalist; there was, for instance, an important private sector. By the mid-1970s, however, the state controlled 80 percent of medium and large-scale economic activity. In addition, the government sought to relocate by persuasion or coercion a scattered peasantry into **compact villages** (*ujaamas*) to which modern services could be more readily provided. While there have been some impressive results, the socio-economic results have been dismal. By 1985 the country had a literacy rate of 85 percent (up from 15 percent at independence in 1961) and health care improved. On the other hand, inefficiency, corruption, and lack of a commercial infrastructure created many unprofitable enterprises, some of which were returned to private ownership. In the countryside, peasants resisted the experiment in rural socialism because it disrupted traditional economic patterns that were rooted in family farms rather than communal enterprises. In the decade of 1974–1984 the country suffered a negative rate of per capita GNP growth. A recent assessment of experiments in African socialism by historian John Iliffe is as follows: "African governments have shown that they can prevent capitalism; they have not yet shown that they can replace it with anything else that will release their people's energies."

MOZAMBIQUE

The Afro-Marxist experiments fared little better. In **Mozambique** (part of former Portuguese East African territories), for instance, the government created a series of large state farms from abandoned Portuguese estates, and gave priority to the purchase of machinery for them. The result was the disruption of millions of family farms and the lack of incentives to produce for the market because there were few goods available for consumption, like sugar, salt, soap, cloth, and bicycles. Thus, production for export and the ability to import ceased. Mozambique, like Cuba, became hostage to economic subsidization and political control of communists. Since the end of the Cold War, Mozambique has made adjustments to its plan, like courting Western investment, including a contract with Exxon for oil exploration, and signing a security pact with South Africa in order to regain valuable economic connections with its wealthy neighbor.

Rich and Poor Nations

Less developed countries continue to search for an effective method of modernization. The failures of both socialist and capitalist models to date have led many to the conclusion that there are "rich" countries and "poor" countries in the world and that they are divided geographically between "North and South." According to this theory, the rich industrialized countries of the United States, Europe, and Japan, all located in the Northern Hemisphere, gobble up most of the world's resources and produce most of the pollution, while the Third World countries suffer increasing poverty and famine, as in Ethiopia. In turn, this has led to the rise of drug trafficking, as drugs are one of the few ways LDCs can create capital. Others contend that this is a simplistic view and that, in fact, there are many different levels of modernization going on in the world. Countries like Brazil and South Africa, both in the Southern Hemisphere, are economic dynamos that have found their own paths to successful modernization. Another division between rich and poor is based on resources. Having oil and precious metals has made some populations spectacularly rich like Saudi Arabia and the UAE.

Two out of three of the world's desperately poor are women; women's banks, now in 50 countries, make small loans to women starting businesses. Scrap paper collectors, embroiderers, and sheep raisers borrow as little as $10 with 10 percent collateral. These banks are copied after the **Grameen Bank**, which has lent small sums to three million women in the villages of Bangladesh. Half of the Grameen loan recipients are now out of poverty.

Newly Industrializing Countries

In between the "less developed countries" and the industrialized countries are a group of states called **newly industrializing countries**. These are countries like **Taiwan**, **South Korea**, **Singapore**, and now **Vietnam** which have made spectacular industrial gains by integrating their own traditions with aspects of both the communist and capitalist models. Newly industrializing countries are distinguished by their emphasis on education and their cohesive social and political structures. Education is regarded as a must, an important capital investment ensuring the modernization process success. South Korea's literacy rate (99 percent) is the highest in the world. After the Korean War, huge industrial firms were created by a combination of government and active entrepreneurship. Exports were encouraged and the capital earned from these was fed into technology, technical training, and worker housing. Workers, as at Hyundai, responded in kind, putting in six-day work weeks and participating in almost worshipful ceremonies when a fleet of cars is shipped abroad. Taiwan has followed a similar course—rapid industrialization and high capital investment. Singapore, meanwhile, has become not just a production center, but a center of merchant and individual capital for Southeast Asia. While Singapore has been ruled by a strong political leader, South Korea and Taiwan are also "newly democratizing countries" with nascent political parties and open elections. Vietnam has become the most recent economic dynamo in the area, welcoming foreign investment, upgrading the educational system, and fostering industries that are competitive in the global market place while under a quasi-communist political system.

Latin America

Latin American politics, economics, and culture are a kaleidoscope. Beginning in the 1980s some Latin American nations adopted **neoliberalism**, an economic model encouraged by the United States that promoted free markets, Western investment, and privatization. The neoliberal path produced some growth but was weakened by government and judicial corruption, continuation of rich elites, and dependence on foreign loans. Argentina, for instance, adopted the neoliberal model but saw its economy collapse in 1998. Since then, the economy has recovered under the guidance of a more state-oriented, paternalistic style of government led by President Nestor Kirchner, a **Peronist** (a term used in Argentina to describe supporters of Juan Peron and his wife Eva who ruled Argentina as "autocratic reformers," 1946–1955). In oil-rich Venezuela, left-wing **Hugo Chavez** was elected president in 2005 and has been attempting to export his brand of Castroism to other countries. In Brazil in 2002 leftist candidates gained 80 percent of the vote and elected as President **Luis Ignacio da Silva**. However, in Chile General Agusto Pinochet, who gained power in a military coup in 1973 and subsequently carried out a reign of terror, abruptly shifted Chile to a free enterprise economy. In 1989, Chile restored democracy and has been chipping away at poverty and unemployment. In Brazil, which had become the economic miracle of Latin America in the 1970s and 1980s due to its exploitation of resources in the Amazon Basin under authoritarian governments, turned to a leftist candidate in the 2002 elections. Brazil has become the first nation in the world to be oil independent, relying entirely on its own production of ethanol.

Did You Know?

Brazil has become the first nation in the world to be oil independent, relying entirely on its own production of ethanol.

Privatization

In general, in the last quarter of the twentieth century, world economic policies veered away from state welfare programs and planned economies, and toward **privatization**. Privatization means relying less on government to meet people's needs and more on private institutions like the marketplace, family, and voluntary organizations. Privatization can take many forms, from "denationalization" (when a government divests itself of a company it owns) to delegation of some functions by contracting them out to private companies. While privatization is not new in world history (in 1492 Queen Isabella and King Ferdinand hired a private contractor to seek an alternative route to India!), it has exploded in the present era because of disillusionment with the inefficiences and economic and ecological costs associated with socialist economies and big government, and the renewed popularity of liberalism and freedom as enshrined in the concept of private property and ownership. In 1974 an unlikely leader, General **Augusto Pinochet** of Chile, launched privatization when he unilaterally freed prices, gutted labor laws, and auctioned off hundreds of companies. Then, in 1979 Margaret Thatcher, prime minister of England, privatized the British aviation and telecommunications industries. France, Japan, and New Zealand followed with their own large-scale privatization programs. When the Berlin Wall fell in 1989, an avalanche of privatization rolled across eastern Europe and the former Soviet Union. Even in the United States, the growth, inefficiencies, and inequities of state entitlement programs like social security and medicare as a proportion of state income had led to calls for privatization of the health care and pensions systems.

All in all, the twentieth century saw an increasing drive on the part of all countries on the globe to modernize, largely because modernization equals a higher living standard and greater world power. A patchwork of approaches has emerged, and for many parts of the globe, has resulted in increasing prosperity rather than poverty. The greatest testament to this is the rise in world population. The drive to modernize, however, has put great stress on planet Earth in terms of resource utilization, environmental balance, and waste disposal.

COLLAPSE OF THE SOVIET UNION

Gorbachev's Reforms

In the face of economic collapse from decades of heavy defense spending and an inefficient consumer economy, Russian leader **Mikhail Gorbachev** in 1985 launched a series of reforms. By his program of "**glasnost**," or openness, he attempted to gain new political allies among the intellectual class and to explore new solutions to Soviet problems. By his program of "**perestroika**," or economic restructuring, he encouraged private investment and growth of the consumer economy. In his program of democratization, he hoped to revitalize the Congress of People's Deputies by electing a group of progressive representatives to replace the old class of privileged communist deputies who were resistant to change. In foreign affairs Gorbachev brought "new political thinking" to the field. He withdrew Soviet troops from Afghanistan, encouraged reform movements in Poland and Hungary, and sought to reduce East-West tensions. He denounced the **Brezhnev Doctrine**, which had proclaimed the right of the Soviet Union and its allies to intervene at will in eastern Europe.

The End of the Soviet Union

Gorbachev's reform program soon got out of hand. Openness gave way to free speech and expression, restructuring gave way to free enterprise, and democratization to calls for greater national autonomy on the part of the republics that made up the U.S.S.R. In 1990 Russian politicians in the newly elected Parliament, joined by a strong Russian environmental movement, independence-minded republics, and the communist old guard, challenged Gorbachev. At the Communist party congress in July 1990, a group of desperate hardliners tried to seize control, but Gorbachev was rescued by the progressives. Now beholden to them, he watched while an anticommunist and nationalist revolution swept Russia. The Soviet Union was dissolved and independence of all republics proclaimed, and East European states become independent of Moscow.

Gorbachev's failure to renounce communism and to follow rather than to lead the revolution led to his downfall and his replacement by **Boris Yeltsin**. Boris Yeltsin faced problems including the transformation of the economy from socialist to free market and the political system from communist to republican swiftly and dramatically. This produced more consumer goods, a growing middle class, and freedoms, but the newly privatized companies often fell into the hands of former party officials who became **oligarchs** (well-placed former communists who amassed enough property, prosperity, and wealth to control major segments of the Russian economy). Yeltsin also faced secession movements within Russia such as that from the oil-rich Chechnya, declining health care, inflation, and poverty of pensioners. In 2000 Yeltsin resigned and was replaced by **Vladimir Putin**. Under Putin, liberalism has faded. He has taken under state control much of the media and privatized companies especially in resource industries like oil. The contrast between the rich and the poor has become stark. Seventy percent of the Russian economy flows through Moscow and its oligarchs.

PERESTROIKA

We have come to the conclusion that unless we activate the human factor, that is, unless we take into consideration the diverse interests of people, work collectives, public bodies, and various social groups, unless we rely on them, and draw them into active, constructive endeavor, it will be impossible for us to accomplish any of the tasks set, or to change the situation of the country. . .

Perestroika is a word with many meanings. But if we are to choose from its many possible synonyms the key one which expresses its essence most accurately, then we can say thus: perestroika is a revolution. A decisive acceleration of the socioeconomic and cultural development of Soviet society which involves radical changes on the way to a qualitatively new state is undoubtedly a revolutionary task. . . .

In accordance with our theory, revolution means construction, but it also always implies demolition. Revolution requires the demolition of all that is obsolete, stagnant and hinders fast progress. . . . Perestroika also means a resolute and radical elimination of obstacles hindering social and economic development, of outdated methods of managing the economy and of dogmatic stereotype mentality. . . .

And like revolution, our day-to-day activities must be unparalleled, revolutionary. Perestroika requires Party leaders who are very close to Lenin's ideal of a revolutionary Bolshevik. Officialdom, red tape, patronizing attitudes, and careerism are incompatible with this ideal. . . .

In April 1985, party secretary and president of the Soviet Union Mikhail Gorbachev announced a policy of far-reaching reform. As the reading suggests, he had no intention of abandoning either communism or the party. He was simply attempting to breathe life into the bureaucracy that typically builds up within communist systems. This phenomenon was first noted by Yugoslav writer Milovan Djilas in The New Class. *Mao Tse-Tung attempted to deal with it by means of a cultural revolution; this attempt did not bring down the communist state. The "restructuring" that Gorbachev set in motion, however, went on to become a revolution of such proportion that communism was repudiated and the Soviet empire collapsed.*

Eastern Europe

In a world of instant communication, events in Russia reverberated worldwide. In 1989 in eastern Europe, liberal revolutions overturned existing communist regimes and led to the formation of new states dedicated to democratic elections, human rights, and national rejuvenation. **Solidarity**, the Polish democratic movement that represented the workers, Catholicism, and nationalists, led the way. Profiting from Gorbachev's lenient attitude, Solidarity pressed for free elections, and in 1989 it

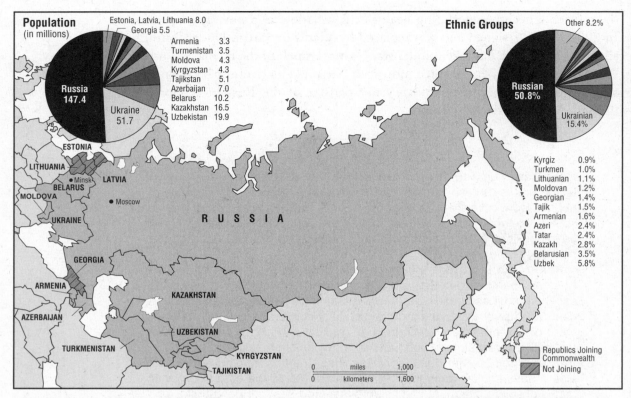

Population
(in millions)

Estonia, Latvia, Lithuania 8.0
Georgia 5.5

Armenia	3.3
Turmenistan	3.5
Moldova	4.3
Kyrgyzstan	4.3
Tajikistan	5.1
Azerbaijan	7.0
Belarus	10.2
Kazakhstan	16.5
Uzbekistan	19.9

Russia 147.4

Ukraine 51.7

Ethnic Groups

Other 8.2%

Russian 50.8%

Ukrainian 15.4%

Kyrgiz	0.9%
Turkmen	1.0%
Lithuanian	1.1%
Moldovan	1.2%
Georgian	1.4%
Tajik	1.5%
Armenian	1.6%
Azeri	2.4%
Tatar	2.4%
Kazakh	2.8%
Belarusian	3.5%
Uzbek	5.8%

Republics Joining Commonwealth

Not Joining

The Dissolution of the Soviet Union and Rise of the Commonwealth of Independent States 1989–Present. In 1989 the Berlin Wall fell and with it came the end of the Soviet empire and communism. New independent national states emerged, some of which rejoined Russia in a commonwealth grouping of economically interdependent states.

won every single contested seat. Hungary followed Poland. In 1989 the Communist party renounced one-party rule, scheduled free elections, began welcoming Western investment, and moved toward multiparty democracy. Hungarians gleefully opened the Iron Curtain separating Hungary from Austria and East Germany. East German refugees flowed in on the way to prosperous West Germany. Huge candlelight demonstrations brought revolution in East Berlin. People danced for joy on the Berlin Wall as it came tumbling down. In July 1990, German Chancellor Helmut Kohl and Gorbachev removed the last obstacles to German reunification. Communism died in Czechoslovakia in December 1989, when, in ten short days, **Václav Havel** was elected president after massive demonstrations forced communist leaders to resign in the so-called **Velvet Revolution**. In Romania, the revolution was violent and bloody. Communist dictator **Nicolae Ceausescu** ordered ruthless extermination of the political opposition, but his forces were defeated and a coalition government emerged. With the triumph of liberalism in Eastern Europe and Russia, the Cold War ended.

During the 1990s democratic and semidemocratic governments were installed in most Eastern European countries. More consumer goods and freedoms have been the result. However, rapid changes have also led to destabilizing ethnic rivalries. The Slovaks, for instance, seceded from Czechoslovakia. The greatest instability came to Yugoslavia where secessions and wars led to the breakup of the country and the creation of new states including Serbia, Slovenia, Croatia, Bosnia-Herzegovina, Montenegro, and Macedonia. The breakup became bloody in the **Bosnian War** (1992–1995). Bosnia became the nexus of conflict because it was peopled by

Did You Know?

In August 1989, Solidarity's leader, Lech Walesa, was sworn in as the first non-communist leader in Eastern Europe.

Muslims, Serbs, and Croats. At one point, Serbia invaded Bosnia and is accused by Bosnian Muslims of genocide. The war was brought to an end in 1995 under the Dayton Accords. Research places the number of military and civilians killed at 100,000–110,000 and 1.8 million displaced. Today NATO is overseeing the continuing peace process.

SCIENCE AND TECHNOLOGY

Since the Renaissance, the West, and then the world, has tended to equate advancement with the world of science. The liberal view was that the patterns of nature could be discovered, and that their balance and symmetry, once discovered, could be applied to all sorts of human problems, from politics to social order. This view of scientific predictability was shattered in the twentieth century by the new science, primarily chaos theories of the universe and quantum physics. The optimism of the eighteenth and nineteenth centuries gave way to skepticism and pessimism in the twentieth century.

Quantum Physics

To Newton, the world was a billiard ball with everything determined by the initial forces of the universe. These were, in turn, determined by discernible rules of behavior. God was the supreme clockmaker and man ticked right along with the rest of creation. The first challenge to this notion came with the work in radiation of German physicist **Max Planck** (1858–1947). He showed that subatomic energy is emitted in uneven little spurts called "quanta" and not in a steady stream. His discovery called into question the old sharp distinction between matter and energy and the notion that atoms are stable basic building blocks of nature. **Albert Einstein** went a step further, taking Newtonian laws and explaining what happened to them at the speed of light. This led to the idea of **relativity**, the notion that time and space are not absolute. The 1920s opened the "heroic age of physics," a phrase coined by **Ernest Rutherford** (1871–1937), who showed that the atom could be split. Subsequently, physicist **Niels Bohr** held that, within the atom, properties are "massless" and that particles within this world of **quantum physics** (*quantum* meaning quantity or discrete amount with the connotation of smaller, rather than subatomic, particles—hence the metaphor, quantum leap, meaning sudden jump from one level to another without the usual process of climbing through the steps) move randomly rather than predictably. There is no quantum world, he wrote, only "an abstract quantum description. . . ." According to this theory, the world changes just by looking at it and the Big Bang was a random event. Besides physics, there have been significant discoveries in the world of biology, the most important being in the field of genetics. In 1953 **James Watson** and **F. H. C. Crick** developed a model for the DNA molecule that carries genetic heritage. Since then, DNA has been used to track diseases, manipulate plant biology, and find remedies for genetically inherited disease.

These scientific theories have spilled over into other aspects of life, giving the modern world a sense of uncertainty and lack of objective reality. Moral certainties have vanished, and in their place is cultural relativity. Historians think about complex systems rather than isolated nations. The theory of evolution appears less linear and more random. Chaos is accepted as the order of things. Randomness, thinglessness, and interconnectedness have become realities. The twenty-first century generation accepts the possibility of many jobs, the uncertainty of employment, and a state of constant change. The psychology of flux has become permanent and the business of reeducation constant. The new science has led to new technologies that have transformed global communication.

New Technologies

Two of the most important technologies of the twentieth century were probably the rocket and the computer. Rocket technology was developed by the Germans during World War II, and in 1957 the Russians put the first satellite in space, *Sputnik I.* In 1961 they put the first man in space. The United States then initiated a crash program devoted to space research, putting the first man on the moon in 1969. While this lacked tangible benefits, it caused breakthroughs in photography and communications. Satellites have become an everyday occurrence, used for everything from cellular phones to navigation. Unmanned crafts have been increasingly used to explore the solar system and beyond. In 2005 a probe landed on Saturn's large and cloud-covered moon, Titan. More exciting, perhaps, have been the Mars landings for their potential in terms of future human habitation and resource development. In 2004 **NASA** (National Aeronautics and Space Administration) successfully landed twin Mars Exploration Rovers *Spirit* and *Opportunity.* Among the significant scientific returns was the conclusive evidence that liquid water existed at some time in the past. Since August 6, 2012, there have been two rovers on the surface of Mars with the capability of drilling into the planet's core and three orbiters surveying the planet.

The **Hubble Space Telescope** has been one of the most important of the new astronomical and physics technologies. It is a large, space-based observatory which has revolutionized astronomy and human understanding of the Universe by providing unprecedented deep and clear views of space out of the way of earth's atmosphere. Its view extends from our own solar system to extremely remote, fledgling galaxies formed not long after the Big Bang 13.7 billion years ago. Hubble is a project for the astronomical community world-wide as any astronomer can request time on the telescope as long as results are published and shared with the entire scientific and world community.

The **computer** is undoubtedly the greatest technological advance of the twentieth century. The computational needs of the military in World War II led to the construction of the first successful general-purpose computer, "Mark I," in 1944. Subsequently used to guide space travel and keep records, it is the equivalent of the writing revolution of the first millennium B.C.E. and the printing revolution of the first millennium C.E. As an extension of memory and a machine of numeracy, computers have transformed business, education, medicine, electronics, record keeping, vehicle operation, travel, and communications. The technology behind the computer and later Internet includes the microchip that can store and manipulate vast amounts of information and fiber optic cable that can transmit information at lightning speed.

Did You Know?

In 2012 there were over 6 billion cell phones in use, influencing the way people interact socially, economically, and culturally.

The **Internet** was originally developed for U.S. defense research purposes in the 1960s to link academic, government, and business computer networks. With the proliferation of computers in the 1980s, the technology of linkage moved to the public sector largely due to the work of **Tim Berners-Lee** who is credited with creating the web's technical underpinnings such as HTML and HTTP, the protocols used to encode web pages and transmit them across the Internet. In 2005 the number of Internet users reached 1 billion, enabling users to exchange jokes, articles, music, and films worldwide. Seventy percent of users were in North America, while just 11 percent were in Asia and 4 percent in Africa. Today the Internet is increasingly accessed through cell phone technology. In the future the Web 2.0 or the "semantic web" will allow individuals in online communities to provide data in the form of links and allow for more complex and syndicated information. One offshoot of this technology is that English has become the linking language of the world.

THE COMPUTER AND THE FUTURE

The spread of cheap, universal computer power will result in a gradual loosening of restraints on the movement of information within society. . . . Characteristically this favors the kind of open society which most of us in the Western world enjoy today, and has just the opposite effect on autocracies—both right and left—who like to make sure that all information is handed very firmly downward. . . .

Another dramatic effect of the Computer Revolution may be to put an end to war. . . . Today, when the same statistics are fed into the computer's unemotional, apolitical interior, what comes out is as true and objective an appraisal as can be made from the facts. Furthermore, whenever the data involves confrontation between nuclear powers, the unequivocal message that spills out—to both sides—is: you will lose!. . .

. . . the increased affluence of the computerized world will inevitably spill over into the less developed quarters. . . .The third factor promoting the rise of the underdeveloped world concerns the way in which computer power can be brought directly to bear on its problems.

. . . One of the most intriguing features of the 1990's will be the way in which the new, freely communicating societies will control their own destinies.

Christopher Evans, in his book The Micro Millennium, *argues that the computer will have a positive effect on society by preventing war, helping developing countries progress, and nourishing freedom. Certainly the information age had a dramatic effect on the events in the former Soviet Union and eastern Europe. News of the changes outpaced the ability of the institutions themselves to maintain control of the revolution set in motion. Around the world, newsviewers saw the Berlin Wall come down before the leadership in these countries could act.*

SOCIETY AND CULTURE

Race, Ethnicity, and Gender

In the twentieth century, global mobility and communication led to a great mixing of races, ethnic groups, and genders. Living, working, and traveling side by side, people have not only become more aware of the differences that separate them, but have had the means at their disposal to unite under a common banner or cause.

The twentieth century has witnessed the increasing power of ethnic groups to promote their rights within nation-states and in many cases to destroy nation-states.

The multiplicity of ethnic groups in Yugoslavia, the former Soviet Union, and in various nations in Africa led to bloody wars as in Bosnia, Georgia (in the former Soviet Union), and South Africa. The more homogenized world culture has become, the more virulent has become ethnicity as a means of identity and a safeguard of minority rights.

More than any other event, the twentieth-century wars elevated the position of women, especially in the workplace. As more women took the place of men in the factories, they began asserting their rights. Birth control also played a part as women could gain control over their position as mothers and employees. Educational levels for women in many parts of the world have risen as has the appearance of women in political and leadership positions. A simulation study by the World Bank of 72 countries in 1995 showed that, if all factors were held constant, doubling female secondary school enrollments in 1975 would have reduced average fertility rates in 1988 from 5.3 to 3.9 children and lowered births by almost 30 percent. At the **Fourth World Conference on Women** held in 1995 in Beijing, 45,000 women participants from 189 countries made clear gains by reaching a consensus platform that stated that women's rights are human rights. The quest for women's rights continues. In 2005 **Mukhataran Bibi**, an illiterate woman from an impoverished Pakistan village who resisted conservative Muslim practices against women, gained worldwide sympathy for her support of women's rights, equality, and justice. Publicized through the Internet, donations flowed to fund her travels in the name of education and justice for women. Women's rights increasingly is intertwined with cultural differences between the old and the young, modern urban areas that support more gender equality and rural areas that cling to old gender norms, and religious affiliations. It is estimated that 10 percent of the population of France is Muslim and since 1989 there has been conflict over the rights of Muslim girls to wear the **hijab** or veil in secular public schools.

Mass Media, Culture, Education, and Metropolis

The radio, movies, and television, all inventions of the twentieth century, have made it possible for people around the globe to interact on a world scale. Radio became possible with the transatlantic "wireless" communication of **Guglielmo Marconi** (1874–1937) in 1901 and the development of the vacuum tube in 1904. Only after 1920 did every major Western country establish national broadcasting networks. By the late 1930s, more than three out of every four households in both democratic Great Britain and dictatorial Germany had at least one radio. Roosevelt's "Fireside Chats" and Hitler's speeches informed the masses who sat huddled around them. The transistor radio has penetrated the most isolated hamlets of the Third World and today no automobile is without it. The continued development of the radio in the form of "Walkmans" makes radio listening a worldwide phenomenon.

The second communications revolution—the visual one—in the form of movies and television has penetrated the deepest corners of the earth. The camera was invented in the mid-nineteenth century and the movie camera in the early twentieth century. **Sergei Eisenstein** in Russia was the first to use the camera as a device to tell a story rather than record events. His epic film *The Battleship Potemkin* gave all future filmmakers the techniques necessary to turn the camera into an art form. **Leni Riefenstahl**, in her documentary *The Triumph of the Will* used the camera as an instrument of Nazi propaganda.

Did You Know?

Television was invented during World War II.

Movies remain one of the great instruments of mass media. Today, a movie made in any country of the world is apt to be seen around the world.

The radio, movies, television, travel, and a world market have created a world culture. The popularity of Western fads, from blue jeans to Reeboks and popular music, has created a culture, especially among the younger generation, that is generic. It is possible to travel to most of the world's cities today and buy a McDonald's hamburger or stay in a Hilton Hotel. One of the most important aspects of this culture has been education. The importance of "human capital" and faith in "book learning" has spread rapidly to the world's masses, for whom education principally means jobs. Increasingly, knowing English has been the key to economic and social improvement. Students from developing countries studying in the United States are apt to pursue professions like engineering and medicine, giving them skills directly applicable to improving the standard of living in their home countries.

Megalopolis

Modernization has led to mass movement to cities where job opportunities, education, and social safety networks attract many disadvantaged. The cities of the Third World expanded at an astonishing pace after World War II. Many doubled and some even tripled in size in a single decade. In 1920 three out of every four of the world's urban inhabitants lived in Europe and North America. By 1990, 60 percent of the planet's city dwellers lived in the cities of the Third World. Gigantic "super cities" of two to ten million people arose. Mexico City, for example, grew from 3 million in 1950 to 12 million in 1975 and to a staggering 31 million in 2000. More than half of all urban growth has been due to rural migration, and more than half of all industrial jobs in Mexico have been concentrated in Mexico City. The attraction of cities has not only been for jobs, but for educational opportunities, medical care, amenities like a ready water supply (rural women spend much of their time carrying water and grinding grain), and modern cultural amusements. In many cases, men migrated to cities first, leaving women to become unprecedentedly self-reliant and independent. Surging urban population has created overcrowding, shantytowns, crime, unemployment, drug trafficking, and pollution. However bad this life may be, the rush to the cities has continued unabated. In today's world the cultural differences between urban and rural dwellers are greater than between people of different countries. Today's world resembles Hellenistic times when the mixing of cultures in urban settings has produced a world culture.

Art, Protest, and Counterculture

Rapid change, insecurities, the unseen world of the atom, and cross-cultural pollination have been reflected in twentieth-century art. Modernism in art, architecture, and music has been marked by rejection of old forms, and constant experimentation and a search for new kinds of expression.

ARCHITECTURE

Modern architecture has revolved around the principle of "functionalism." Believing that buildings, like industrial products, should be useful, designers have used less ornamentation and found beauty and esthetics in simple lines and new materials. Steel and concrete allowed for the development of the skyscraper, which was invented by **Louis Sullivan** and his school of architects. His student, **Frank Lloyd Wright**, built a series of truly modern houses featuring low lines and attentiveness to the surrounding environment. During the 1920s an interdisciplinary group called the **Bauhaus** worked to merge the schools of fine and applied arts with architecture. Their work culminated in buildings using steel frame and glass walls.

VISUAL ART

In painting, the realism and social commentary of late nineteenth-century art gave way to impressionism. **Claude Monet**, **Pierre-Auguste Renoir**, and **Camille Pissarro** tried to capture the momentary overall feeling, or impression, in their work. Modern art grew out of a revolt against this. The "Postimpressionists" or "Expressionists" experimented with styles that allowed them to depict worlds other than the visible world of fact. **Vincent van Gogh** in *The Starry Night,* for instance, painted the vision of his mind's eye—flaming cypress trees, exploding stars, and a comet-like Milky Way—a great cosmic vision. Fascination with form also was part of the Expressionist experiment. **Paul Cézanne** told a young painter, "You must see in nature the cylinder, the sphere, and the cone." Expressionism in the hands of painters like **Henri Matisse** became increasingly abstract and nonrepresentational. In the hands of **Pablo Picasso**, **Marc Chagall**, and **Salvador Dali**, expressionism turned into surrealism, in which painters depicted the fantastic world of wild dreams and complex symbols where watches melted and giant metronomes beat time in alien landscapes.

MUSIC

The same kind of experimentation also occurred in ballet and music. Led by Viennese composer **Arnold Schoenberg**, traditional harmony and tonality was abandoned in favor of abstract mathematical patterns, or "tone rows." The influence of African music turned the music and format of ballet into pulsating rhythmic movement. African music also inspired popular music forms like jazz and rock.

LITERATURE

The homogenization, Westernization, and mechanization of twentieth-century culture repulsed many and led to protest and countercultures. In the Third World, for instance, writers like **Frantz Fanon** in *The Wretched of the Earth,* and **Chinua Achebe** in *Things Fall Apart* argued that real independence would come only with a total rejection of Western values. The "wretched," according to Fanon, were the colonized who must purge themselves not only of the colonizers but of the local collaborators, the "white men with black faces." Achebe's message was that African people must rediscover their own culture, its depth, volume, and beauty. In communist areas of the world, protest literature often went underground to escape totalitarian authorities. In the Soviet Union, for instance, writers like **Alexander Solzhenitsyn** opened up the secrets of the slave labor camps and psychological torture in books like *One Day in the Life of Ivan Denisovich* and *Cancer Ward.* Yugoslav writer **Milovan Djilas** in *The New Class* unmasked the ideological failures of communism like the growth of new bureaucracies and party corruption. Environmental protest also emerged, as in **Rachel Carson**'s *The Silent Spring.* Among the world's youth, protest against violence, war, and dogmatism of all types is reflected in the 1960s counterculture characterized by long hair, drugs, casual and unkempt dress styles, and music, as in that of the Beatles.

GLOBAL CHANGE AND CHALLENGES

The Green Revolution

National elites in Third World countries had neglected agriculture in the 1950s and 1960s for a variety of reasons—their desire to industrialize, the need to squeeze agriculture to provide investment for industry, neglect by absentee landlords, ignorance and reluctance by peasants to change ways of farming, the food surplus of the United States, that allowed importation of cheap grain, and the political volatility of land reform. Population increase and famine, however, led to alarm and the **Green Revolution** (higher yields and more land in cultivation). In the United States and Europe, scientists developed new strains of corn and rice that enabled farmers to double their yields. The positive effects were most evident in China and Mexico. The negative effects were that the new strains needed more water and fertilizers, putting increased pressure on resources and the environment. Also, the new strains failed to be adopted in countries where there were large numbers of landless peasants and tenant farmers, as in the Philippines and Latin America. Furthermore, the increased population due to the new strains has meant demand for land. The result is the chopping down of rain forests and the move into virgin lands by farmers. In Africa, the strain is evident in the constant pressure exerted by the population to limit game park land.

Deforestation, Pollution, and Global Warming

Likewise, industrialism has produced unprecedented amounts and dangerous kinds of pollution and resource depletion. In rural areas, **deforestation** has become a major problem. Both Haiti and India were all but denuded of trees. Industrialism, with its huge urban landscape, has created mountains of garbage and waste material. Landfills have run out of space. There are threats of nuclear pollution, as evidenced in the 1980s when the nuclear reactor at **Chernobyl** in the Ukraine experienced a meltdown and devastated immediate regions with radiation. In the Persian Gulf War in 1991, massive oil spills and oil fires blackened the atmosphere, and in 1989 a series of spills in Alaska, notably the running aground of the *Exxon Valdez,* severely damaged the shoreline and marine life. In Russia, diversion of tributaries to the Aral Sea to irrigate cotton fields has caused the drying up of the sea. In its wake is salt and mineral pollution. Increasing use of hydrocarbons has damaged the ozone layer, exposing planet Earth to dangerous levels of sunrays. World fossil fuel usage may one day lead to oil and gas scarcity.

To address such problems, the **Earth Summit**, or the U.N. Conference on Environment and Development, was held in **Rio de Janeiro**. There, 178 nations reached accords on "**sustainable development**," reconciling economic needs with environmental responsibility. In addition, the capitalist, industrialized world has begun to see resource depletion and pollution as a cost factor of doing business. The lumber business in the United States, for instance, is dominated by "tree farms," in which forests are replanted as they are depleted. For many, science and technology have been the perpetrator of the very assault on planet Earth. For others, science and technology provide the keys for solving environmental and ecological problems.

Human activity has altered environments since prehistory sometimes with catastrophic results. The appetite for energy resulting from industrialization and modernization the world over has threatened twenty-first century economic and political stability and sustainable environments. On every continent, growing utilization of gas, coal, and oil by automobiles, factories, power plants, aircraft, and large farming organizations has produced large amounts of pollutants, and some think it has led to the rising average temperature of the earth or **global warming**. Some scientists attribute this phenomenon to such gases as carbon dioxide, chlorofluorocarbons, and methane that accumulate in the atmosphere and destroy the shield that blocks sunlight. Other scientists dispute this and argue that global warming is a phenomenon connected with the ending of the last Ice Age. Still others dispute that there is global warming as a phenomenon given growing ice sheets accumulating in some areas. Especially disturbing to some is the threat posed by the industrialization of China with its 1.6 billion people and of India with its 1.3 billion people, increasing the world competition for energy sources and spewing more pollutants into the atmosphere. To address these challenges, many nations in 1997 signed the **Kyoto Protocol**, pledging to begin reducing harmful gases that contribute to global warming. Many countries are seeking alternative energy sources and encouraging recycling programs. Another growing environmental threat is trash. Heaps of computers contain poisonous substances that are difficult to contain.

Fundamentalism

The reaction to industrialism, consumerism, and moral relativism has spawned a religious revival. Christian evangelism and the extensive travels of Pope John Paul II exemplify this in the Christian world. Islamic fundamentalism in the form of strict adherence to Koranic custom and "Islamic Republics," as in Iran, have tried to turn back the clock. Along with religious revivalism has come the search for the mystical experience. The popularity of figures like the Dalai Lama and of Eastern religions like Hindusim and Buddhism have replaced faith in endless progress and secularism. By 2000 the world contained 2 billion Christians, 1.3 billion Muslims, 800 million Hindus, 350 million Buddhists, and 900 million who practice a local faith such as Daoism, Shamanism, or agnosticism. The easy spread of ideas in the globalized world has facilitated increased evangelical movements, but it has also led to religion as the basis of political and ethnic hostilities. Catholics and Protestants opposed each other in Ireland and Uganda, while Sunni and Shi'ite Muslims have fought each other in Pakistan and most recently in Iraq. Religious militancy has grown among some Muslim believers who have turned to the old notion of *jihad* or "struggle" against **infidels** (nonbelievers) to strengthen the faith and use physical combat in God's name. Such movements have found favor especially among the young, poor, and unemployed who are embittered toward their own government or the West.

Terrorism

Terrorism (small-scale but violent attacks aimed at undermining a government or demoralizing a population) is an old story in world history. The Mongols practiced such tactics with great success. Russian terrorists in the late 1800s carried on a long campaign against the czarist regime. Terrorism in Ireland continued throughout most of the last half of the twentieth century. At the nexus of the terror was the **Irish Republican Army (IRA)** and its party Sinn Fein. This group wanted the independence of Ireland from Britain. The six provinces in Northern Ireland that were Protestant wanted to remain with Britain. Thus, war between Protestants and Catholics, Northern Ireland and the rest of Ireland, and Ireland and Britain were all parts of this long war of resistance. Financing and weaponry were sourced worldwide, and tactics such as bank robberies, extortion, smuggling, counterfeiting, and killing were all in the IRA arsenal.

While terrorism has remained local in scope, an increasingly interconnected world has spurred terrorist organizations to operate on a global scale. Such a phenomenon is reflected in Muslim terrorist groups like **Al Qaeda** ("The Base"), which has been involved in terrorist operations in Afghanistan, Saudi Arabia, the Persian Gulf, U.S. embassies in Kenya and Tanzania, and attacks on the World Trade Center in New York on September 11, 2001. At that time Al Qaeda's leader, **Osama bin Laden**, cleverly used cable news networks, web sites, e-mail, and satellite phones to further his cause. Bin Laden argued that "to kill the Americans and their allies is an individual duty of Muslims who can do it in any country in which it is possible to do so." Terrorist groups are not confined to large networks but possibly get inspiration from them.

There are a number of possible reasons why terrorism has emerged as such a big part of modern history.

1. First, in conventional wars, smaller powers and interest groups have no chance against the sophisticated military of powerful nations and, thus, must use terror tactics.
2. Second, since the fall of the Soviet Union, there is no longer a world controlled by two superpowers that could hold at bay such insurgency movements in their proxy states.
3. Third, much of the terrorism occurring in the world is a result of restlessness and frustration on the part of many for change.
4. Finally, world communication links promote and popularize the world of terrorism.

Population

For many, the most disturbing trend in contemporary world history is the dramatic increase in world population. While population growth has slowed markedly or even topped out in the industrialized world, it has exploded in the Third World. This is due to better health care, nutrition, foreign aid, and the unpopularity and inaccessibility of birth control programs. In 1985 Africa led the world with a population growth of 3.2 percent per year, enough to double the continent's numbers in only 22 years. The world's population in 1900 was 1.6 billion; in 1987 it was 5 billion, and it is not expected to stabilize until the mid-twenty-first century, when it will have reached 10 to 12 billion. While this puts tremendous stress on the world's resources, it is instructive to realize that, even at 11 billion, the earth would not be as populated as Europe is today. Mandated population control programs have been controversial and, in many cases, failures. Opposition to Indira Gandhi's compulsory sterilization and the objection to the one-child family in China illustrate both cultural and religious resistance to forced family planning. The most promising aspect of population control is the statistical evidence that suggests that industrialization and modernization slow population growth. They also open up educational, economic, and political opportunities for women.

Migration and Refugees

Population pressures, poverty, lack of economic opportunity, and political turmoil caused major migration movements in the twentieth century. Many of these migrants were refugees or people seeking sanctuary abroad from wars and civil strife. The number of refugees has grown from 2.5 million in 1970 to 7.5 million in 1980 and 15 million in 1990 and 20 million today. In the Horn of Africa there are more than 2 million refugees as a result of regional conflicts involving Ethiopia, Sudan, and Somalia. After the Vietnam War in 1973, over 1.5 million people fled to the West. The violence in Bosnia in 1992–1995 killed 200,000 and generated 4 million refugees. In addition to people, disease has traveled across borders, most principally **AIDS**, which has now spread from Africa to many other parts of the world.

Besides disease, violence, and political turmoil, economics plays a crucial role in migration. By the late twentieth century the world contained some 100 million voluntary migrants to foreign countries, some prosperous and some impoverished, but all seeking a better economic situation. Millions of Asians and Africans have moved to Southwest Asia seeking work. Migrants pour over the border into the United States mostly from rural areas in Mexico and Central America where prospects for work are meager. In 2000 there were 19 million immigrants in Europe. As of 2004, 5 percent or 20 million of the European Union's population identify themselves as Muslim. The fear among many is that this large corps of Muslims will become disillusioned and join the world terrorist movement. The story of Begsjon, Sweden, reflects this concern. Begsjon was built between 1967 and 1972 to house workers at the giant SKF ball bearing plants. Seventy percent of the residents were foreign-born immigrants including Somalis, Turks, Syrians, and Iraqis. Now the plant is closed, the settlement ghettoized, and the second generation is without jobs. Sweden itself faces the problem of a seventh of the working population being foreign and the challenges of a multiethnic, multicultural, and multiracial country.

Genocide

Another aspect of migration is the twentieth-century phenomenon of **genocide**. The word *genocide* first appeared in a 1944 book by Phael Lemkin, a Polish-born law professor and Jew who lost 49 family members in the Holocaust. He defined genocide as any effort to destroy a national, ethnic, racial, or religious group. Psychologists have found the reason for genocide in the turmoil, change, and uncertainty of the twentieth century. These insecurities and frustrations, they say, have led to the impulse to blame or find scapegoats. Others explain genocide in terms of the quest for fulfillment of political and nationalist aspirations. The early twentieth century witnessed a number of genocides, from the Turkish disposal of 1.5 million Armenians in 1915 to Stalin's purges in the 1930s. In 1948 the United Nations approved Lemkin's Genocide Convention, a treaty that has been signed by 120 countries. Still, genocide goes on, from China's Cultural Revolution (1966–1976,

1.5 million), Cambodia's killing fields (1975–1979, 1.7 million), Guatemala (1980–1984, 100,000), Iraq's gassing of the Kurds (1987–1988, 100,000), the Serb "ethnic cleansing" in Yugoslavia (1992, 1 million Bosnians), and the Rwandan massacres (1994, 500,000). In Sudan, the Arab-Muslim government imposed its will on rebellious African Christians and animists resulting in 2 million deaths. In 2005 when the government faced further rebellion in **Darfur**, primarily between African Muslim farmers and Arab pastoralists, further genocide was carried out. Such genocide has sent millions of people fleeing their countries in migrations of epic proportions.

Famine

Another challenge for the modern world is **famine**, a catastrophic drop in food supplies causing widespread death and the diseases of malnutrition. Famines occur as a result of commercial changes, or are politically motivated. India, particularly dependent on monsoon rains, has been particularly prone to such natural calamities. Commercial famines occur when the distribution system collapses. In 1974 a catastrophic flood covered half of Bangladesh, and the government was unprepared to distribute stocks of rice, while merchants bought what they could and exported it to India. Political famines are induced by governments to achieve political ends. The most famous politically induced famine was by Stalin in Russia (1932–1933) when he collectivized agriculture. Even worse took place in China during the Great Leap forward (1958–1961). Requisitioning of food by the state left farmers between one-fifth and one-half of their usual subsistence diet. An estimated 20 million to 30 million Chinese starved. In the twenty-first century political famine is evident in the Darfur region of Africa.

Globalizing Economics

In the decades after 1945 the world economy has become increasingly characterized by **globalization**, a pattern in which economic, political, and cultural processes reach beyond political boundaries. Globalization has transformed the world through worldwide commercial markets, finance, and telecommunication exchanges. The production of many consumer goods like cars takes place in a number of countries before its final delivery. Rising or falling prices on the Tokyo and New York stock exchanges quickly reverberate around the world.

Various institutions have shaped and spurred the international economy. The World Bank funds development projects like dams in countries that could otherwise not afford to do so. The International Monetary Fund (IMF) regulates and facilitates currency dealings between countries. Trading blocs like the North American Free Trade Agreement (NAFTA), the Association of Southeast Asian Nations (ASEAN), the Central American Free Trade Association (CAFTA), and the Latin American Free Trade Association (LAFTA) reduce national and border barriers to trade. In 1947 twenty-three nations established the **General Agreement on Trade and Tariffs (GATT)**, an organization that evolved into the **World Trade Organization (WTO)**. The WTO was comprised of 124 nations and by the twenty-first century the organization included former communist nations with market economies, like China and Vietnam. The **Doha** trade talks were initiated to integrate the developing countries in GATT but the talks have become stalled.

According to many, the **European Union (EU)** is the most recognized example of a trading bloc economic union that facilitates cross border trade by lowering tariffs and systematizing regulations. In 2007, European leaders gathered in Berlin to celebrate the fiftieth anniversary of this union that has grown from a six-member trade group to a twenty-seven-member political organization and the world's largest economic entity. Most EU citizens can travel and work in member states with few restrictions. The European Commission estimates that the single market has created 2.5 million new jobs. In 1991, the **Maastricht Treaty** recognized for Europe a single currency, the **euro**, a central bank, and the goal of achieving an economic and monetary union. By 2002, eleven of the fifteen signers had adopted the euro. The example of the euro prompted discussions to create a unified currency in West Africa (the eco) and in the Persian Gulf states. Challenges remain for this union, among them the continuation of rigid labor rules and high payroll taxes in individual countries, an aging work force, the influx of workers from Eastern Europe to Western countries, fiscal instability, and enlargement fatigue that have stalled negotiations for entry for Croatia, Turkey, and Macedonia. However, economic disparities, and political and foreign policy integration remains a challenge. Until 1997 the EU did not have a foreign policy mission and has made little headway on a proposed rapid-action force of 60,000 soldiers, though the EU has overseen numerous peacekeeping operations as in the Balkans and Congo since 2003. One of the great challenges for the global economy is the continuing progress of these global trade organizations and the generation of wealth worldwide that they can produce.

Shifting Trade Systems and Power

Since 2000 the Asian economies, especially China's, have grown disporportionately to the rest of the world. With the largest and growing population of the world at 1.3 billion, China has used a state capitalist/communist model to industralize and modernize from the top down. Because of an excess of labor and low labor cost, China has become competitive in the manufacture and production of consumer goods. This large outflow of product and a government-controlled currency have led to a growing global trade imbalance reflected in huge currency capital flows into China. The scale of the Chinese economy and the perpetuation of its growth are dependent on the import of primary commodities from elsewhere in the world. China's increasing capital spending is on the import of food and raw materials that it lacks. China has invested worldwide—food from the United States, oil seed from Brazil, copper from Zambia, timber from Southeast Asia, oil from Angola, and so on. Eight hundred Chinese companies are now operating in 49 African countries using both Chinese and local labor. Many of the trade and real estate agreements between China and African nations have been government to government with little transparency and open to corruption and wealth generation at the top.

Along with Chinese economic penetration is growing political involvement in African, Latin American, and Southeast Asian countries—a twenty-first-century version of twentieth-century European global power. According to Chinese sources China seeks to foster "a security environment conducive to China's peaceful development." As a nuclear power China has gained inclusion in the small group of the world's nations that possess such power and is increasingly involved in participating in the United Nations and other forums where it can protect its own human rights sensitivities. The Chinese continue to consider Taiwan part of China. The concept of nationality particularly of the Han Chinese and its history is portrayed in the large number of parades, building projects, and events like the Olympics that can demonstrate Chinese power and prestige. Tight control of ethnic minorities like the Uighurs, suppression in Tibet, and hegemony in Vietnam reflect the present policy of **Sinicization** (becoming Chinese). Despite growing economic, political, and military involvement on the world stage, China remains an underdeveloped country with about half its population still small farmers and living as if centuries ago. Wealth is tightly controlled within the Communist Party ranks. Rising awareness of China has led some to predict that the twenty-first century will be a "Global-Asian Era" (GAE) in world history.

Twentieth-century society/culture has been noted for its international character, its rapid tempo of change and propensity for experimentation, and its mass movements of people and communications technologies. Tremendous cultural and social mixing reminds us of other ages in world history, like the Hellenistic or age of expanding empires, when cultural blending rather than construction of classical forms provided the major historical narrative. Historians have reflected this in their attention to world history and to its propensity to concentrate on cross-cultural encounter, trade, and world themes.

Unit Review

Cross-Regional Developments

Almost all developments in the twentieth century have been cross-regional. These include

- a communications revolution that has made what happens in one area instantly knowable in all other areas of the globe;

- the development of a global economy, monetary system, trade, and regional economic zones;

- migrations that have flowed from one country to another, one region to another, one continent to another, and one hemisphere to another;

- concern about environmental problems, from pollution to disappearance of rain forests, that have become global concerns;

- rapid scientific and technological change, from weaponry and nuclear proliferation to television and computers that leapfrog across borders and regions;

- the emergence of a global culture in which McDonald's hamburgers are as common in China as Chinese food is in America;

- the spread of ideologies like communism and the wholesale quest for modernization;

- the rising power of women and youth to unprecedented heights as illustrated by the 1995 International Conference on Women;

- decolonization and wars of national liberation that occurred over large parts of the globe after World War II;

- the establishment of many new nations and the welcoming of nation-states in the face of multinational corporations, international organizations, regional economic groupings, and racial and ethnic mixing.

Legacies

The legacies of the twentieth century are for many living history and part of a living experience. They include

- a half-century or more of world war, which led to the development of fearsome new weapons like the airplane, submarine, atomic and nuclear bombs, poison gas, and guided missiles, to wars of weapons rather than men, and to economies over which governments gained increasing control and spent enormous sums;

- a Cold War between ideological and political adversaries that led to a paralyzing arms buildup and support of small conflicts worldwide;

- experiments with totalitarian government, which led to a legacy of terror and human holocaust;

- world economic depression, which led to the accommodation of capitalism with welfare state socialism;

- the end of European colonialism and the rise of a myriad of new nations in Africa and Asia;

- a quest for modernization that has largely disregarded the environment and human spiritual yearnings;

- the triumph of liberalism over communism;

- population increases that have strained planetary resources and environmental health, and created a world of megalopolises;

- homogenization of world culture despite ethnic and national yearnings;

- amazing scientific and technological advances like DNA, space travel, and the computer, which have redefined geographical, social, and intellectual frontiers;

- modern art, architecture, and literature reflective of experimentation and the unseen world of math and science; and

- a world of instant global communication and interaction.

The twentieth century has completed one of the human narratives addressed in Chapter 1—The Emergence of Early Human Communities and the Peopling of the Earth. The twenty-first century may well see the peopling of the galaxy.

Quiz

Unscramble:

Arrange the following in chronological order.

Great Depression; Cuban Missile Crisis; World War II; Chinese Communist Revolution; Vietnam War; Fall of the Berlin Wall

Matching:

1. Welfare state
2. Containment
3. Détente
4. Soviet
5. Deforestation
6. Guerrilla warfare
7. Apartheid
8. LDCs
9. Genocide
10. Multinational corporations

A. A period when political tensions between the U.S. and U.S.S.R. relaxed
B. Racial separation
C. Fighting in small organized bands, resistance to larger forces
D. Government programs to reduce the impact of economic inequality
E. Taking action to stop the spread of communism
F. Worldwide business organizations
G. Any effort to destroy a national, ethnic, racial, or religious group
H. Workers' councils
I. Lesser developed countries
J. Cutting whole forests

Questions:

1. The first man in space was

   (A) Yuri Gagarin.
   (B) Neil Armstrong.
   (C) James Watson.
   (D) F. H. C. Crick.
   (E) John Holland.

2. The economist who advocated government spending during the 1930s to compensate for the loss of purchasing power was

   (A) Walter Rathenau.
   (B) John Maynard Keynes.
   (C) Adam Smith.
   (D) Margaret Thatcher.
   (E) Frederick Engels.

3. Indicators of the decline of the West include

   (A) a decline in population as a percentage of the world's total population.
   (B) the end of European empires.
   (C) the end of the West's advanced weapons monopoly.
   (D) a challenge to the West's manufacturing and trading positions in the world market.
   (E) all of the above.

4. The immediate cause of World War I was the

   (A) assassination of Archduke Franz Ferdinand.
   (B) German invasion of Belgium.
   (C) Austrian declaration of war on Russia.
   (D) Serbian rejection of Austria's ultimatum.
   (E) German and French competition for North African territory.

5. In August of 1939 Hitler signed a nonaggression pact with

(A) Spain.
(B) Poland.
(C) Lithuania.
(D) Italy.
(E) the Soviet Union.

6. The turning point of World War II was

(A) Gallipoli.
(B) El Alamein.
(C) D-Day.
(D) Stalingrad.
(E) the Philippines.

7. After both World War I and World War II

(A) the World Health Organization continued its work.
(B) the U.N. Food and Agricultural Organization delivered food to the needy.
(C) world organizations were established to keep the peace.
(D) less developed countries became protectorates.
(E) a ban on new weapons development was instituted by the victors.

8. The agreement that designated the Red Army to liberate Eastern Europe was

(A) the Atlantic charter.
(B) Yalta.
(C) Tehran.
(D) Potsdam.
(E) the Treaty of Versailles.

9. Which of the following conflicts was a United Nations peace-keeping operation?

(A) the Six-Day War
(B) the Korean War
(C) Vietnam
(D) the Cuban Missile Crisis
(E) Angola

10. Which of the following Cold War alliances was between the United States and its allies in Asia?

(A) NATO
(B) the Warsaw Pact
(C) COMECON
(D) SEATO
(E) EEC

11. Which of the following is arranged in correct chronological order?

(A) World War II, the Depression, United Nations Charter
(B) World War II, Cuban Missile Crisis, Korean War
(C) World War II, Berlin Wall, Cuban Missile Crisis
(D) United Nations Charter, Korean War, the Depression
(E) Berlin Wall, Korean War, World War II

12. Which technologies were developed with twentieth century government funding?

I. microscope
II. Hubble space telescope
III. computer
IV. Internet
V. camera

(A) I, II, III, and IV
(B) II, III, IV, and V
(C) II, III, and IV
(D) I, II, and IV
(E) all of the above

13. Which of the following countries escaped wars related to decolonization?

(A) Algeria
(B) Pakistan
(C) Bangladesh
(D) Iran
(E) Thailand

14. Decolonization in Mexico failed to result in

    (A) challenges to the established, "constitutionalist" government by revolutionaries like Pancho Villa and Emiliano Zapata from 1910 to 1920.

    (B) the organization of the PRI or Institutional Revolutionary party to represent all factions of Mexican politics.

    (C) U.S. control of the Mexican oil industry until 1938.

    (D) economic and social reform through the use of tariffs and nationalization of foreign-owned properties.

    (E) a constitution advocating an eight-hour workday and redistribution of land, and guaranteeing universal suffrage and the right of workers to organize.

15. Bangladesh is a society in which the majority of the people are

    (A) Hindus.
    (B) Muslims.
    (C) Sikhs.
    (D) Christian.
    (E) Buddhist.

16. The Balfour Declaration

    (A) promised the Arabs independence following World War I.

    (B) pledged Syria and Lebanon as French mandates.

    (C) pledged Palestine would remain under British control.

    (D) guaranteed Palestine as a Jewish homeland.

    (E) guaranteed Palestine independence.

17. The national wars of liberation in Southeast Asia were first waged against the

    (A) British.
    (B) French.
    (C) Germans.
    (D) Americans.
    (E) Chinese.

18. The South African leader who opposed apartheid in South Africa was

    (A) Jomo Kenyatta.
    (B) Kwame Nkrumah.
    (C) Nelson Mandela.
    (D) Daniel arap Moi.
    (E) Jonas Savimbi.

19. Which of the following artists was not an impressionist?

    (A) Claude Monet
    (B) Pierre-Auguste Renoir
    (C) Edgar Degas
    (D) Camille Pissarro
    (E) Salvador Dali

20. Which statement is probably NOT accurate given the documentary evidence?

    (A) Truman had no idea of the consequences of using the atomic bomb.

    (B) Discrimination against Jews was legal in Germany after 1935.

    (C) Churchill warned against the increasing threat of communism after World War II, much as he had warned against the increasing threat of Nazism in the 1930s.

    (D) Following decolonization, Africans believed that nonracial political parties would exclude blacks.

    (E) The spread of cheap computers resulted in a gradual loosening of restraints on the movement of information between societies.

21. By World War I, Britain had formed the Triple Entente with France and

    (A) Germany.
    (B) Russia.
    (C) Italy.
    (D) Austria.
    (E) Turkey.

22. The leader of the Red Army in the civil war that lasted from 1918 to 1921 was

    (A) V. I. Lenin.
    (B) Karl Marx.
    (C) Leon Trotsky.
    (D) Alexander Kerensky.
    (E) Joseph Stalin.

23. Once Lenin seized power, he opposed

    (A) participation in World War I.
    (B) nationalization of the banks.
    (C) redistribution of large landed estates among peasants.
    (D) worker control of factories.
    (E) confiscation of church properties.

24. The leader of the Muslim League and founding father of Pakistan was

    (A) Indira Gandhi.
    (B) Jawaharlal Nehru.
    (C) Muhammad ali Jinnah.
    (D) Rajiv Gandhi.
    (E) Mahatma Gandhi.

25. Which treaty recognized a single currency (the euro) for Europe?

    (A) European Union (EU)
    (B) General Agreement on Trade and Tariffs (GATT)
    (C) Maastricht
    (D) Yalta
    (E) The Atlantic Charter

26. Which of the following countries declared war on Japan one week before Japan surrendered in 1945?

    (A) England
    (B) France
    (C) China
    (D) Soviet Union
    (E) India

27. What was the reason Belgium became important to the outbreak of World War I?

    (A) It was part of the Triple Alliance.
    (B) Its mountainous terrain prevented implementation of the Schlieffin Plan.
    (C) Belgium had a defense alliance with France.
    (D) Belgium was Germany's highway into France.
    (E) Russia had an alliance with Belgium.

28. Which of the following were adaptations Lenin made to Marxism?

    I. The revolution was to be led by workers and peasants.
    II. The revolution would be planned and directed.
    III. The new government was to be a "Dictatorship of the Proletariat."
    IV. Capitalists were identified as imperialists and the enemy of all who experienced colonialism.

    (A) I, II, and III
    (B) II, III, and IV
    (C) I, III, and IV
    (D) I, II, and IV
    (E) all of the above

29. What can be said about the contemporary challenge of terrorism?

    (A) It is intensified and facilitated by the Internet.
    (B) It is a form of genocide.
    (C) It is a completely new phenomenon in world history.
    (D) It is primarily sponsored by Russia.
    (E) The success of the IRA provided a prototype for such underground war.

30. The Bosnian War (1991–1995) was caused by

    (A) the large movements of Croatian refugees into Bosnia.
    (B) an assassination in Sarajevo.
    (C) the death of Tito.
    (D) the collapse of the Soviet Union.
    (E) the invasion of Bosnia by Serbia.

31. The Gaza Strip borders

    (A) Egypt
    (B) Saudi Arabia
    (C) Jordan
    (D) Syria
    (E) Lebanon

32. Mao Zedon (Tse-Tung) envisioned a Communist revolution of

    (A) labor unions
    (B) peasants
    (C) university students
    (D) red guards
    (E) ethnic minorities

Answers

Unscramble:

Great Depression; World War II; Chinese Communist Revolution; Vietnam War; Cuban Missile Crisis; Fall of the Berlin Wall

Matching:

1. **(D)**	6. **(C)**
2. **(E)**	7. **(B)**
3. **(A)**	8. **(I)**
4. **(H)**	9. **(G)**
5. **(J)**	10. **(F)**

Questions:

1. **(A)**	11. **(C)**	21. **(B)**	31. **(A)**
2. **(B)**	12. **(C)**	22. **(C)**	32. **(B)**
3. **(E)**	13. **(E)**	23. **(A)**	
4. **(A)**	14. **(D)**	24. **(C)**	
5. **(E)**	15. **(B)**	25. **(C)**	
6. **(D)**	16. **(D)**	26. **(D)**	
7. **(C)**	17. **(B)**	27. **(D)**	
8. **(C)**	18. **(C)**	28. **(E)**	
9. **(B)**	19. **(E)**	29. **(A)**	
10. **(D)**	20. **(A)**	30. **(E)**	

FINAL STUDY TIP

- Review your notes and flash cards one more time.
- Reread the section on major world religions and belief systems, pages 131–134.
- Consider the test taking suggestions on page 7.

MODEL TESTS

Model Test 1

Directions: Below each question or incomplete sentence are five answer choices. Select the best answer or completion for each question and fill in the appropriate circle on the corresponding answer sheet.

1. "L'etat c'est moi!" (I Am the State) is a quote by Louis XIV which best illustrates

    (A) lay investiture.
    (B) constitutional monarchy.
    (C) divine right of kings.
    (D) absolutism.
    (E) socialism.

2. Mary Leakey's discovery of *Zinjanthropus* is important not just because it was evidence of a species called *Australopithecus boisei* but because it was found *in situ*, which means that

    (A) bone fragments represented a complete skeleton.
    (B) fragments could be matched chronologically with specie fragments.
    (C) fragments were found in their original place along with other remains including indications of lifestyle.
    (D) surrounding fragments had been washed away.
    (E) fragments, discovered along a river bed, offered evidence of the surrounding geologic formations.

3. According to recent DNA research,

    (A) humans with similar DNA characteristics share similar skin color.
    (B) each of the modern races probably descended from a single ancestral type.
    (C) individuals with darker skin tones are of a single race.
    (D) some black-skinned peoples share closer DNA to people outside their race than within it.
    (E) racial characteristics and skin tones were well established as hominid types evolved.

4. In an effort to strengthen his power against the pope, Philip IV of France organized the Estates General of

    (A) Protestant dissenters.
    (B) nobles and clergymen.
    (C) university faculties of law, medicine, and the arts.
    (D) clergy, nobility, and commoners.
    (E) bankers, merchants, and guilds.

5. Early human migrations out of Africa may have been because of

    (A) climate change.
    (B) plagues.
    (C) changes in social organization.
    (D) improved technological development.
    (E) warfare between Cro-Magnon and Neanderthal.

6. The least important reason for European emigration in the second half of the nineteenth century was

    (A) pogroms in eastern Europe and Russia.
    (B) the Irish potato famine.
    (C) rapid increases in population.
    (D) demand for skilled technicans.
    (E) access to easy credit.

7. Early Christians were persecuted by Romans because they

    (A) refused to pay taxes.
    (B) supported the rebellion led by Spartacus.
    (C) refused to serve in the Roman legions.
    (D) refused to offer sacrifices to the Roman emperor.
    (E) instigated the assassination of Julius Caesar.

8. One principle of Hammurabi's Code that would probably not be considered "just" today is

    (A) less punishment for the first offense.
    (B) the less important the social status, the more severe the punishment.
    (C) the more important the social status, the more severe the punishment.
    (D) the punishment equals the crime.
    (E) all of the above

9. The majority of slaves in the Atlantic Slave Trade ended up in

    (A) the United States
    (B) Mexico
    (C) Tangier
    (D) Brazil
    (E) Ecuador

10. Within the United Nations, who has the power to veto any decision made by the organization?

    (A) permanent members of the United Nations Security Council
    (B) the World Court
    (C) a majority of the membership of participating nations
    (D) the secretary general of the United Nations
    (E) the fifty-one original members of the United Nations

11. A polytheistic religion is characterized by belief in

    (A) a patron deity for each person.
    (B) the conflict between good and evil.
    (C) the immortality of the human spirit.
    (D) many deities.
    (E) spiritual power that resides with the life-giving sun god.

12. The Black Plague of the 1300s spread

    (A) from Europe to China across the Silk Road.
    (B) faster by land than by sea.
    (C) by the Mongols across Asia.
    (D) mostly among poor people.
    (E) along the international trade routes.

13. Which of the following is arranged in the correct chronological order?

    (A) Aztec Empire, Mississippian culture, Pueblo peoples, Inca Empire, Mesa Verde
    (B) Indus civilization, Siddhartha Gautama is born, Alexander the Great's conquests, Mauryan Empire, Gupta Empire
    (C) Ming Dynasty Voyages, Bartholomew Dias rounds the Cape of Good Hope, Vasco Da Gama reaches India, Columbus discovers the West Indies, Pedro Alvares Cabral discovers Brazil
    (D) Conquests of Genghis Khan, Crusades, Mongol invasion of Japan, Ottoman conquest of Constantinople, the Black Plague spreads to Europe
    (E) Olmec civilization, Egyptian civilization, Chavin civilization, Mesopotamian civilization, Greek civilization

14. Which of the following statements is untrue of the Chinese dynastic rule?

    (A) The belief in the mandate from heaven
    (B) The belief that new dynasties restore order and establish peace
    (C) The right of the oldest child to rule
    (D) The right of people to revolt if the ruler has lost the mandate of heaven
    (E) The belief that floods or famine indicate the ruler's loss of the mandate of heaven

15. Which nation's recent history displays the most successful top-down change without revolt?

    (A) France
    (B) United States
    (C) China
    (D) Japan
    (E) Russia

16. The consequence of the Balfour Declaration was

    (A) the independence of Syria, Lebanon, and Iraq
    (B) the right of ethnic groups to establish their own nation-states
    (C) the agreement that Kurdish and Armenian territories would become part of Iraq
    (D) that Germany would be deprived of its colonies and the Ottoman rule ended in Turkey
    (E) Palestine would become the Jewish homeland.

17. The immediate consequence of the diffusion of iron technology developed by the Hittites was

    (A) the development of new agricultural tools.
    (B) increased trade.
    (C) exploration of new territory in search of iron deposits.
    (D) a wave of barbarian invasions.
    (E) rule by aristocratic warriors.

18. "Blessed are the poor in spirit: for theirs is the kingdom of heaven."

    This excerpt from the Christian "Sermon on the Mount" is closest to the orientation of what other world belief system?

    (A) Confucianism
    (B) Daoism
    (C) Buddhism
    (D) Hinduism
    (E) Zoroastrianism

19. The man who argued that population could be controlled by wages was

    (A) Thomas Hobbes.
    (B) David Ricardo.
    (C) Thomas Malthus.
    (D) John Stuart Mill.
    (E) John Maynard Keynes.

20. Kush, Meroe, Egypt, and Carthage were all located in

    (A) the Mediterranean Basin.
    (B) the Indian Ocean Basin.
    (C) Europe.
    (D) Southwest Asia.
    (E) Africa.

21. After Mao Tse-tung's (Mao Zedong) death, what happened in China?

    (A) Population declined.
    (B) The Cultural Revolution spread.
    (C) The Sino-Soviet split intensified.
    (D) The economy was liberalized.
    (E) Per capita income decreased.

22. The concept of zero was developed independently by both Hindus and

    (A) Egyptians.
    (B) Greeks.
    (C) Chinese.
    (D) Romans.
    (E) Mayans.

23. Americans born in the New World of African and European parents were known in Brazil as

    (A) Mestizos.
    (B) Mulattos.
    (C) Zambos.
    (D) Peninsulares.
    (E) Creoles.

24. The founder of psychoanalysis, who theorized that much of human behavior was motivated by unconscious emotional needs, was

   (A) Charles Darwin.
   (B) Herbert Spenser.
   (C) Charles Fourier.
   (D) Sigmund Freud.
   (E) Joseph Lister.

25. Greek classical styles were adapted by Central Asian Buddhists as a result of

   (A) the expulsion of early Christians and Jews from the Roman Empire.
   (B) Alexander's conquests in Central Asia.
   (C) the introduction of Greek art by Roman silk merchants.
   (D) the increased presence of Central Asian Buddhists in Athens and Sparta.
   (E) none of the above

26.

Relative Shares of World Manufacturing Output 1750–1900

	1750	1800	1830	1860	1880	1900
(Europe as a whole)	23.2	28.1	34.2	53.2	61.3	62.0
United Kingdom	1.9	4.3	9.5	19.9	22.9	18.5
Habsburg Empire	2.9	3.2	3.2	4.2	4.4	4.7
France	4.0	4.2	5.2	7.9	7.8	6.8
German States/ Germany	2.9	3.5	3.5	4.9	8.5	13.2
Italian States/ Italy	2.4	2.5	2.3	2.5	2.5	2.5
Russia	5.0	5.6	5.6	7.0	7.6	8.8
United States	0.1	0.8	2.4	7.2	14.7	23.6
Japan	3.8	3.5	2.8	2.6	2.4	2.4
Third World	73.0	67.7	60.5	36.6	20.9	11.0
China	32.8	33.3	29.8	19.7	12.5	6.2
India/Pakistan	24.5	19.7	17.6	8.6	2.8	1.7

What conclusion can be drawn from the chart of relative shares of world manufacturing output between 1750 and 1900?

   (A) Asians increased their share.
   (B) Europeans decreased their share.
   (C) European countries industrialized.
   (D) Literacy rates increased in Asia.
   (E) The Chinese developed superior technology.

27. The Crusades failed to

   (A) permanently free the Holy Land from Muslim control.
   (B) increase the sale of feudal rights to the peasants and towns.
   (C) introduce Europe to ideas from Muslim universities
   (D) increase royal authority at the expense of the popes.
   (E) promote the wealth and influence of commercial towns like Venice.

28. The principles of nonviolence and asceticism taught by Mahavira are central to

   (A) Hinduism.
   (B) Jainism.
   (C) Theravada Buddhism.
   (D) Mahayana Buddhism.
   (E) Zoroastrianism.

29. Rising population in Third World countries in the twentieth century can best be linked to

   (A) government incentives for large families.
   (B) growth of poverty.
   (C) decline in death rates.
   (D) industrialization.
   (E) the Columbian exchange of foods.

30. Which plant is correctly matched with its place of origin?

   (A) yam—Southwest Asia
   (B) millet—China
   (C) maize—Southeast Asia
   (D) wheat—Mexico
   (E) sugar—Nile Valley

31. The idea that time and space are not absolute, but relative, was the result of research by

   (A) Max Planck.
   (B) Niels Bohr.
   (C) Albert Einstein.
   (D) James Watson.
   (E) F.H.C. Crick.

32. The Portuguese profited from their exploration of the west coast of Africa through the trade of

(A) lumber and fish.
(B) slaves and gold.
(C) tobacco and salt.
(D) wool.
(E) cattle.

33. Which of the following is an example of cultural diffusion resulting from Silk Road trade and exchange, ca. 300 B.C.E.?

(A) Buddhism in China
(B) paper in Rome
(C) pagoda architecture in Ceylon (Sri Lanka)
(D) civil service examinations in Greece
(E) poured iron tools in Jerusalem

The Granger Collection, New York

34. Which of the following statements about the above painting is accurate?

(A) This is an example of twentieth-century abstract expressionism.
(B) This painting is an example of romanticism.
(C) This painting is an example of nonrepresentational abstract art.
(D) This painting is a forerunner of impressionsim.
(E) This painting is a forerunner of realism.

35. Which of the following evolutions in European warfare occurred last?

(A) the invention of gunpowder
(B) fortress construction with low walls, vast moats, and outworks
(C) ships with side-mounted guns
(D) field armies of 100,000 men
(E) the development of gunpowder weaponry

36. In which sentence is the historical term incorrectly used?

(A) A *synthesis* of Chinese and Indian cultures occurred with the introduction of Buddhism to China.
(B) An example of *cultural diffusion* is the use of Indian numerals, first by Arab traders and then by others around the globe.
(C) Polynesian maritime *migrations*, facilitated by the outrigger canoe, spread over a 20,000-mile area of the Pacific Ocean.
(D) The gradual *Sinification* of Arabic peoples began two centuries before the birth of Christ and continued into the 1400s.
(E) Kaifeng, capital of China during the Song (Sung) dynasty, became the eastern *entrepot* for both locally manufactured and long-distance trade items on the Yellow River.

37. Which country was not occupied by the Soviet Army following World War II?

(A) Romania
(B) Yugoslavia
(C) Bulgaria
(D) Czechoslovakia
(E) Poland

©2000 The Art Institute
of Chicago

The Granger Collection,
New York

38. Compare the Turkish mug on the left,
produced in Ottoman Turkey at a royal kiln
south of Istanbul, with the example on the
right of Chinese porcelain design, popular
in China from the tenth through the
thirteenth centuries. What principle in
world history do the similarities in design
appear to illustrate?

   I. Cross-Cultural Exchange
  II. Cultural Diffusion
 III. Competition
 IV. Syncretism
  V. Synthesis of designs

(A) I, II, and III
(B) I, II, IV, and V
(C) I, III, IV, and V
(D) All of these
(E) None of these

39. During the Han-Roman Period, which state
was least interested in purchasing products
abroad?

(A) Rome
(B) China
(C) Parthia (Persia)
(D) India
(E) Kushan

40. Because of the work of the Byzantine
missionaries, all of the following became
societies where the Orthodox faith
predominated EXCEPT

(A) Greece.
(B) Russia.
(C) Romania.
(D) Poland.
(E) Serbia.

41. All but one of the following were
characteristic of both Song China and the
Umayyad Caliphate. Which is the
exception?

(A) Agricultural surplus, which was the
foundation of economic security.
(B) Manufactured products developed a
solid base for taxation.
(C) The development of the concept of
religious salvation.
(D) Loss of status for women.
(E) New urban centers of wealth and
prosperity.

42. Which of the following was not
characteristic of feudal societies?

(A) The state was decentralized.
(B) Small trade towns and/or agrarian states
reorganized.
(C) Warriors and nobles predominated in
the ruling class.
(D) Religion played a central role in
preserving and identifying the culture.
(E) village schools for the peasantry

43. "The history of all hitherto existing societies
is the history of class struggles . . . The
proletarians have nothing to lose but their
chains. They have a world to win.
WORKING MEN OF ALL COUNTRIES
UNITE!"

The probable author of this passage was

(A) Vladimir Lenin.
(B) Karl Marx.
(C) Mao Tse-tung (Mao Zedong).
(D) Ho Chi Minh.
(E) Fidel Castro.

44. Characteristics of pastoral nomads include

(A) their displacement of hunter-gatherers
across Eurasia.
(B) a symbiotic relationship with settled
societies.
(C) acting as carriers of overland, long-
distance trade.
(D) herding reindeer in the north, camels in
Arabia, llama in the Andes, and cattle in
South Africa.
(E) all of the above

45. All of the following are true of Christianity, Buddhism, and Islam. However, Christianity and Buddhism

    (A) sought religious converts.
    (B) encouraged pilgrimages to holy sites.
    (C) ceased to be important in the land of their origin.
    (D) profited from the support of merchants.
    (E) developed a concept of immortality.

46. The nation-state differed from earlier traditional political entities in that it was based on

    (A) monarchy.
    (B) dictatorial rule.
    (C) religious bonds through a state religion.
    (D) the rule of law.
    (E) sovereignty of the people.

47. Demographically, the history of the Americas since 1492 was shaped by

    I. Europeans.
    II. Africans.
    III. Asians.
    IV. Amerindians.

    (A) I, II, III, and IV
    (B) I and III
    (C) I and II
    (D) I, II, and III
    (E) I, II, and IV

48. The Great Depression affected western Europe in all of the following ways EXCEPT

    (A) welfare programs.
    (B) appeasement.
    (C) creation of the IMF.
    (D) increase in protectionism.
    (E) increasing involvement of government in the economy.

The Granger Collection, New York

49. This figure constructed of bronze using the lost wax process is representative of the art of

    (A) Benin.
    (B) Nok.
    (C) Ethiopia.
    (D) Ife.
    (E) Yoruba.

50. Name the European power that established hegemony over the Asian trade in the sixteenth century.

    (A) Dutch
    (B) English
    (C) Spanish
    (D) Portuguese
    (E) French

51. By the eighteenth century, both the French and the Portuguese had lost their bid for controlling trade in India for which of the following reasons?

    I. The Mughal Emperor Jahangir granted trading concessions to the British in 1619.
    II. The British had built the Suez Canal.
    III. The British established 28 trading ports, or factories, along the Indian coast including Madras, Bombay, and Calcutta.
    IV. Substantial profits were made by both Indian and English merchants.
    V. English seapower prevented reinforcements.

    (A) I and II
    (B) I, III, IV, and V
    (C) I, IV, and V
    (D) IV only
    (E) all of the above

52. Which of the following was unknown to people of the preindustrial period?

    (A) knowledge that the earth is round.
    (B) understanding of the heliocentric theory.
    (C) the knowledge that there were two types of nerves, motor and sensory.
    (D) the technology to produce paper and plastic.
    (E) knowledge that the blood circulated through veins and arteries.

53. In a SOCIAL sense the American, French, and Latin American revolutions can all be regarded as wars that

    (A) protested against taxes.
    (B) established religious freedom.
    (C) implemented governments that would foster commercial expansion.
    (D) protected the populace from growing foreign dominance.
    (E) reflected the growing power and culture of the bourgeoisie.

54. Humanism, the mortar of Greek culture, permeated religion, politics, philosophy, and the arts. Which of the following does not reflect the Greek concept of humanism?

    (A) anthropomorphic examples of Greek gods
    (B) Greek tragedies in which fate was shaped by decisions of the hero
    (C) rationalism, or the belief that reason is the source of knowledge
    (D) the Sophist belief that humans were the proper subject of study
    (E) the belief that humans seek release from a cycle of rebirths

55. France's financial crisis of the 1780s was due to the

    (A) loss of agricultural markets to India.
    (B) suppression of the popular revolt in Haiti.
    (C) Napoleonic wars in Europe.
    (D) French Empire abroad.
    (E) support for the American Revolution against Britain.

56. Which of the following provides an accurate account of the worldwide exchange that developed after Columbian discovery?

    (A) Europeans to the Americas, American foods to Africa, and Asians to Europe
    (B) Europeans to the Americas, Africans to Asia, European grains to America
    (C) Europeans to America, American silver to Asia, Africans to the Americas
    (D) European grains to America, Africans to Australia, American foods to Europe
    (E) none of the above

57. Napoleon's greatest achievement as dictator of France was the institution of the Civil Code in 1804. Which of the following was least likely to be part of the Civil Code?

    (A) equality of all citizens before the law.
    (B) protection of private property.
    (C) guaranteed freedom of the press.
    (D) the recognition of men as heads of the household.
    (E) voting rights for women.

58. A factor that precipitated the Industrial Revolution was the

(A) development of intensive agriculture.
(B) liberal political revolution in France.
(C) widespread use of serfs and sharecroppers.
(D) demand for luxury goods.
(E) none of the above

59. The man who established the Tokugawa Shogunate was

(A) Ieyasu.
(B) Yoritomo.
(C) Hideyoshi.
(D) Nobunaga.
(E) Ashikaga.

60. "If, therefore, we take from the social compact everything that is not essential to it, we shall find it reduced to the following terms: 'We, the contracting parties, do jointly and severally submit our persons and abilities, to the supreme direction of the general will of all, and, in a collective body, receive each member into that body, as an indivisible part of the whole.'"

The author of this passage was probably

(A) Jean-Jacques Rousseau.
(B) Baron de Montesquieu.
(C) Adolf Hitler.
(D) Voltaire.
(E) John Locke.

61. "It is true that reason ought to be the torch which lights the conduct of both princes and their states. It is also true that there is nothing in nature less compatible with reason than emotion."

This was most likely written by a political leader in

(A) sixteenth-century Italy.
(B) seventeenth-century France.
(C) eighteenth-century America.
(D) nineteenth-century Japan.
(E) twentieth-century Africa.

62. Where did European colonies become independent in the ninteenth century?

(A) Latin America
(B) sub-Saharan Africa
(C) Southeast Asia
(D) Southwest Asia
(E) North Africa

63. Dar-al-Islam is best described as

(A) a new type of Muslim faith that spread to the Spice Islands.
(B) a Eurasian sea and land system 200 C.E. to 1500 C.E.
(C) maritime trade routes that reached from the Middle East to the Far East.
(D) a type of mercantile jihad.
(E) the "abode of Islam."

64. Which of the following ninteenth-century groups believed the proletariat would conquer the bourgeoisie in revolution?

(A) Chartists
(B) Communists
(C) Social Revolutionaries
(D) Democrats
(E) Anarchists

65. Although the consequences of the Agricultural Revolution were dramatic, they do not include

(A) disappearance of hunting and gathering societies.
(B) growth of permanent villages and towns.
(C) peasant farming becoming the occupation of most people in settled societies.
(D) alterations to the environment.
(E) development of new technologies such as the wheel and timekeeping.

66. The Russian emancipation of the serfs was a consequence of

(A) Franco-Prussian War.
(B) Napoleonic Wars.
(C) Russian Revolution of 1904.
(D) Crimean War.
(E) Seven Weeks' War.

Courtesy of Wright Water Engineers, Inc.

67. Which great American civilization left these ruins?

   (A) the Aztecs of Mexico
   (B) the Olmec of Mesoamerica
   (C) the Maya of the Yucatan
   (D) the Moche of Peru
   (E) the Inca of Peru

68. Which of the following tactics did Europeans use to colonize Africa?

   I. Christian conversion
   II. Western education of the elite
   III. Economic self-sufficiency
   IV. Construction of transcontinental roads and canals
   V. Undermining tribal loyalties

   (A) I, II, and III
   (B) II, III, and IV
   (C) I, II, and V
   (D) III, IV, and V
   (E) I, II, and IV

LAS CASAS AND THE BLACK LEGEND

This infinite multitude of people (the Indians) was . . . without fraud, without subtlety or malice. . . toward the Spaniards whom they serve, patient, meek and peaceful. . .

   To these quiet Lambs . . . came the Spaniards like most cruel Tygres, Wolves and Lions, enrag'd with a sharp and tedious hunger; for these forty years past, minding nothing else but the slaughter of these unfortunate wretches, whom with divers kinds of torments neither seen nor heard of before, they have so cruelly and inhumanely butchered, that three millions of people which Hispaniola itself did contain, there are left remaining alive scarce three hundred persons. . .

69. Spanish settlers in the Americas might refute Bartolome de las Casas' report above with all of the following points EXCEPT

   (A) the principal cause of the high number of Indian deaths was diseases.
   (B) the report represents Indians as being without fraud, subtlety, or malice. They are not.
   (C) the Spanish mistreatment of the Indians was exaggerated.
   (D) the report characterizes all Indians as patient, meek, and peaceful. They are not.
   (E) the duty of the Church and government is to ensure fair treatment for the Indians.

> ## MATTEO RICCI
>
> The Chinese are the most industrious people, and most of the mechanical arts flourish among them. They have all sorts of raw material and they are endowed by nature with a talent for trading, both of which are potent factors in bringing about a high development of the mechanical arts. . . Their skill in the manufacture of fireworks is really extraordinary and there is scarcely anything which they cannot cleverly imitate with them. . . . Their method of making printing books is quite ingenious. . . . The simplicity of Chinese printing is what accounts for the exceedingly large number of books in circulation here and the ridiculously low prices at which they are sold. Such facts as these would scarcely be believed by anyone who has not witnessed them.

70. Based on Matteo Ricci's description of China, one can conclude that in 1583

    (A) the number of inexpensive books in China was less than the number in Europe.
    (B) the Chinese lagged behind the Europeans technologically.
    (C) the Chinese were disinterested in trade.
    (D) the availability of raw materials and a natural ability for trading stimulated Chinese technology.
    (E) the Chinese economy was in disrepair, with increasing unemployment, famine, and inflation.

71. In India, the British imperial policy in the second half of the nineteenth century encouraged

    (A) railroad construction.
    (B) industrialization.
    (C) Asian immigration.
    (D) land reform.
    (E) universal suffrage.

72. Which of the following italicized terms is used INCORRECTLY?

    (A) The growing *bourgeois* influence led to a National Assembly of lawyers, government officials, and merchants.
    (B) *Balance of power* was used by Klemens von Metternich at the Congress of Vienna to preserve the freedom and independence of the great powers.
    (C) Liberty, political equality, and representative government are hallmarks of eighteenth- and nineteenth-century *liberalism.*
    (D) The *romantic* movement defended the power of the nobility, aristocratic privilege, and the monarchy.
    (E) The *proletariat* developed as a new class of urban workers in the 1800s with industrialization and urbanization.

73. Russia was reunited under the rulers of Moscow following Mongol rule because

    (A) Russian rulers assumed the title of Czar and claimed descent from Rurik.
    (B) Moscow repelled an assult by the Mongols in 1408.
    (C) the Russian Orthodox Church with its patriarch recognized the Prince of Moscow as the Autocrat of Russia, responding to the weakening Mongol rule.
    (D) Ivan III declared independence.
    (E) all of the above

74. Which of the following statements incorrectly describes twentieth-century warfare?

    (A) The increased efficiency of the artillery by the time of World War I led to trench warfare.
    (B) Battleships using petroleum rather than coal extended their fighting range and their flexibility during World War I.
    (C) The blitzkrieg of World War II depended on aircraft carriers and submarines.
    (D) Acoustic sonar and radar served as defenses against the rapid deployment of military forces in the 1940s.
    (E) Intercontinental Ballistic Missiles (ICBMs) and nuclear-powered Polaris submarines of the 1950s and 1960s increased the ability of nations to accurately target nuclear weapons.

75. Both Machiavelli's *The Prince* and Kautilya's *Arthashastra* contain advice to rulers on statecraft. Both writers share the opinion that

    (A) taxes must be collected from peasants and landlords during the harvest and merchants should be taxed in the markets.
    (B) just rulers, who appeal to the nobility of their subjects' spirits, will be loved and will be supported in times of crisis.
    (C) spies should be sent throughout the state to report on the honesty of officials.
    (D) a ruler is wise to support his friends and depend on their friendship in times of trouble.
    (E) the science of government is punishment and it is safer for a ruler to be feared than admired.

76. Which was untrue of the mandate system instituted after World War I?

    (A) Most of Germany's former colonies were transferred to Australia, New Zealand, or Britain.
    (B) The principle of "national self-determination," or the joining of historic peoples and ethnic groups, was to be applied to all areas subject to the mandate system.
    (C) Non-European peoples lacked the preparation to become independent and were assigned to World War I victors for "tutelage."
    (D) The mandate system was administered by the League of Nations.
    (E) Britain received Palestine from the former Ottoman Empire.

77. Legalism with its adherents Han Fei Zi (Tzu) and Li Si (Li Ssu) considered that humans were by nature evil. Which of the following is a clear consequence of that system?

    (A) History was interpreted as a dynastic cycle.
    (B) The role of a leader is to provide discipline and maintain order.
    (C) Chinese society worked best when all citizens understood their places and duties within the system.
    (D) Immoral leaders lacked the mandate from heaven.
    (E) The best ruler was the one who governed least.

78. In 1935 Hitler instituted the Nuremberg Laws that

    (A) began the rearmament of Germany.
    (B) organized the Gestapo, the secret police.
    (C) provided employment on public works projects like the autobahns.
    (D) denied Jews civil and commercial rights.
    (E) declared the Treaty of Versailles null and void.

79. From the Islamic World, western Europe received

    (A) glass lenses for magnification.
    (B) identification of diseases and their causes in the *Canon of Medicine* by Ibn Sina (Avicenna).
    (C) the Chinese inventions of the compass, gunpowder, and paper.
    (D) Greek and Roman classics.
    (E) all of the above

80. The term *Green Revolution* refers to

    (A) reforestation of the Third World.
    (B) deforestation of the Third World.
    (C) expanded irrigation farming due to water-diversion projects.
    (D) the assault on the rain forests.
    (E) increased agricultural output using fertilizers and seed breeding.

81. Reasons for a successful communist revolution in Russia included all EXCEPT

    (A) Russian losses during World War I.
    (B) working conditions in cities.
    (C) army support for the czar.
    (D) politicized workers' unions.
    (E) the czar's abdication.

82. Which of the following statements concerning economic agreements is not correct?

    (A) North American Free Trade Agreement in 1994 established a partnership involving the U.S., Canada, and Mexico.
    (B) OPEC created an oil cartel among oil-producing countries to set the price of oil.
    (C) The Marshall Plan provided economic aid for the rebuilding of western Europe following World War II.
    (D) The European Economic Community was founded in response to the pressures of the Cold War.
    (E) The International Monetary Fund was organized to provide small loans to the desperately poor (particularly women) in developing countries.

THE MAGNA CARTA

John, by the grace of God king of England, Lord of Ireland, duke of Normandy and Aquitaine, count of Anjou: to the archbishops, bishops, abbots, earls, barons, justices, foresters, sheriffs, provosts, serving men, and to all his bailiffs and faithful subjects, greeting . . .

1. First of all . . . the English church shall be free and shall have its rights intact and its liberties uninfringed upon . . .

8. No widow shall be forced to marry when she prefers to live without a husband . . .

12. No scutage or aid shall be imposed in our realm unless by the common counsel of our realm. . .

14. And, in order to have the common counsel of the realm in the matter of assessing an aid . . . we shall cause, under seal through our letters, the archbishops, bishops, abbots, earls and great barons to be summoned for a fixed day—for a term, namely, at least forty days distant, —and for a fixed place. . .

39. No freeman shall be taken, or imprisoned, or disseized, or outlawed, or exiled, or in any way harmed—nor will we go upon or send upon him— save by the lawful judgment of his peers or by the law of the land . . .

. . . Given through our hand, in the plain called Runnimede, between Windsor and Stanes, on the fifteenth day of June, in the seventeenth year of our reign.

83. Which of the following rights is incorrectly linked with agreements approved in the Magna Carta?

    (A) The King must convene Parliament in a timely manner to approve or diapprove tax proposals—No. 14
    (B) No person can be imprisoned without trial before a jury of peers—No. 39
    (C) No taxation without representation—No. 12
    (D) Women who inherited property from their husbands were entitled to the same rights as men—No. 8
    (E) Separation of the English church from the political interests of the court—No. 1

84. Which twentieth-century leader led the way in industrialization by means of top-down, agriculturally capitalized modernization?

    (A) Castro
    (B) Stalin
    (C) Lenin
    (D) Mussolini
    (E) Hitler

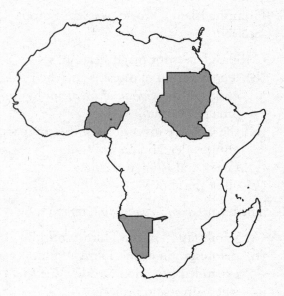

> "Take up the White Man's burden—
>   Send forth the best ye breed—
> Go bind your sons to exile
>   To serve your captives' need;
> To wait in heavy harness,
>   On fluttered folk and wild—
> Your new-caught, sullen peoples,
>   Half-devil and half-child."

85. The above passage from Rudyard Kipling's "The White Man's Burden" refers to which European motivation for the imperialization of Africa?

    (A) the desire to convert African peoples to Christianity
    (B) the quest for natural resources
    (C) the quest for land and power
    (D) the duty to spread the benefits of civilization to native peoples
    (E) the desire to give disinherited sons access to land

86. On this map of Africa, the modern states shown are

    (A) Kenya, Ethiopia, and South Africa.
    (B) Ghana, Egypt, and Tanzania.
    (C) Namibia, Nigeria, and Sudan.
    (D) Angola, Ivory Coast, and Mali.
    (E) South Africa, Angola, and Zimbabwe.

87. The U.S. occupation of Japan after World War II resulted in which of the following?

    (A) demilitarization
    (B) industrialization
    (C) rapprochement with China
    (D) collectivization of agriculture
    (E) U.S. control of industry

88. Hellenistic society represented a diffusion and merging of cultural traditions. All of the following are examples of this cultural amalgamation EXCEPT

    (A) India's construction of monuments carved and decorated with stone.
    (B) use of Ionic, Doric, and Corinthian columns.
    (C) Bactrian Greek art.
    (D) the development of the trade language of Koine.
    (E) dependence on the phalanx in land-based warfare.

89. As a result of the Truman Doctrine, military aid was offered to

   (A) Greece and Turkey.
   (B) Italy and Germany.
   (C) Britain and France.
   (D) the Soviet Union.
   (E) Iran.

90. Fighting between Hindus and Muslims continued following the partition of the subcontinent, with both Pakistan and India claiming the disputed area of

   (A) Punjab.
   (B) Bengal.
   (C) South India.
   (D) Kashmir.
   (E) Ceylon

91. Under the leadership of the Ayatollah Khomeini, Iran became a

   (A) modern secular state with a one-party system.
   (B) fundamentalist Sunni nation.
   (C) radical Shi'ite government isolated from its neighbors.
   (D) military dictatorship.
   (E) liberal, Westernized republic.

92. Leaders who implemented the Great Proletarian Cultural Revolution were the

   (A) party officials.
   (B) professors and intellectuals.
   (C) Red Guards.
   (D) peasants.
   (E) Russian advisers.

93. Which is a legacy of the twentieth century?

   (A) the Enlightenment ideas of liberty, rights, and equality.
   (B) the Industrial Revolution.
   (C) the expansion of the plantation system.
   (D) the rise of nation states.
   (E) the emergence of global culture

94. Which of the following is most closely linked to the Roman concept of universal law?

   (A) canon law
   (B) jus civile
   (C) jus gentium
   (D) jus naturale
   (E) Justinian's Code

95. "By preferring the support of domestic to that of foreign industry, he intends only his own security; and by directing that industry in such a manner as its produce may be of the greatest value, he intends only his own gain, and he is in this, as in many other cases, led by an invisible hand to promote an end which was no part of his intention."

   The "invisible hand" in this passage by Adam Smith refers to the

   (A) integrated European market.
   (B) government's mercantilist policies.
   (C) accumulation of profit.
   (D) free market laws of supply and demand.
   (E) human propensity toward greed.

96. In the development of hominids, which is in the correct chronological order?
   (A) *Australopithecus afarensis, Homo habilis, Homo erectus, Ardipithecus ramidus*
   (B) "Ardi," "Lucy," "Handy Man," "Turkana Boy," Neanderthal
   (C) *Ardipithecus ramidus, Homo erectus, Homo habilis, Australopithecus afarensis*
   (D) *Ardipithecus afarensis, Homo habilis, Homo erectus, Australopithecus ramidus*
   (E) *Homo habilis, Homo erectus, Australopithecus afarensis,* Neanderthal, Cro-Magnon

Answer Key
MODEL TEST 1

1. D	21. D	41. C	61. B	81. C
2. C	22. E	42. E	62. A	82. E
3. D	23. B	43. B	63. E	83. D
4. D	24. D	44. E	64. B	84. B
5. A	25. B	45. C	65. A	85. D
6. E	26. C	46. E	66. D	86. C
7. D	27. A	47. A	67. E	87. A
8. B	28. B	48. C	68. C	88. E
9. D	29. C	49. A	69. E	89. A
10. A	30. B	50. D	70. D	90. D
11. D	31. C	51. B	71. A	91. C
12. E	32. B	52. D	72. D	92. C
13. B	33. A	53. E	73. E	93. E
14. C	34. A	54. E	74. C	94. D
15. D	35. D	55. E	75. E	95. D
16. E	36. D	56. C	76. B	96. B
17. D	37. B	57. E	77. B	
18. C	38. B	58. A	78. D	
19. B	39. B	59. D	79. E	
20. E	40. D	60. A	80. E	

Model Test 1

Answers

The study of history is based on questions, research, and conclusions. It is not memorization. The model test questions are selected to help you review critical changes in world history. Although the answers are provided, good review involves understanding historical information in context rather than simple memorization.

1. **(D)** In absolutist states authority is embodied in rulers who often claimed to rule by divine right, responsible to God alone.

2. **(C)** Discoveries found *in situ* among tools and remains of animals can help scientists understand how early humans lived.

3. **(D)** DNA research has begun to shed light on theories of race. Some black skinned peoples have been found to share closer DNA characteristics with people outside their race than within it.

4. **(D)** Philip IV "Fair" challenged the power of the Chruch and called the Estates General of clergy, nobility, and commoners from towns.

5. **(A)** During the climate changes between two million and 11,000 years ago called the Ice Age or Pleistocene period, ice covered large portions of the Northern Hemisphere and receded. Cro-Magnon survived with better shelter and better clothes.

6. **(E)** Reasons for emigration included Eastern European progroms, the Irish potato famine, population increases, and demands for skilled workers.

7. **(D)** Romans thought Christians were traitors because they refused to offer sacrifices to the emperor.

8. **(B)** Under the Hammurabi Code, slaves received more severe punishments than a free man.

9. **(D)** The majority of slaves in the Atlantic Slave Trade ended up in the West Indies and Brazil.

10. **(A)** Permanent members of the Security Council, originally Britain, China (Taiwan), France, the Soviet Union, and the United States, had the power to veto UN decisions.

11. **(D)** Polytheism refers to religions with beliefs in many powerful, immortal gods.

12. **(E)** The plague's passage replicates the paths of "international trade."

13. **(B)** The correct chronological order is Indus civilization, Siddhartha Gautama is born, Alexander the Great's conquests, Mauryan Empire, Gupta empire.

14. **(C)** Chinese dynastic rule excluded the right of females to rule.

15. **(D)** Japan's Meiji modernization avoided revolutionary pressures while maintaining rule from above.

16. **(E)** The Balfour Declaration established Palestine as the Jewish homeland.

17. **(D)** The first major consequence of iron was that it set off another wave of barbarian invasions.

18. **(C)** Buddhism like Christianity placed emphasis on love, the life of spirit, and an attainable Heaven.

19. **(B)** David Ricardo, in his *Iron Law of Wages*, argued that population could be controlled by wage rates. If wages rose, families would have more children; if wages were just high enough to keep people from starving, population growth would equal the supply of food.

20. **(E)** Kush, Meroe, Egypt, and Carthage were all located in Africa.

21. **(D)** After Mao Tse-tung's death in 1976, Deng Xiaoping and his supporters began to liberalize the economy.

22. **(E)** Both Hindu and Maya societies developed the concept of zero.

23. **(B)** The scarcity of European women in Brazil led to a mixing of the three major ethnic groups—mestizo (European-Indian), mulatto (African-European), and zambo (Indian-African).

24. **(D)** Sigmund Freud was the founder of psychoanalysis.

25. **(B)** Gandaran art used Greek styles to portray Buddhist subjects; while Buddhist art influenced the West. The use of halos in Western art is reminiscent of earlier Buddhist work. The diffusion was the result of Alexander's conquests.

26. **(C)** European shares of world manufacturing output increased from 23.2% in 1750 to 62.0% in 1900. European industrialization led to the remarkable increase in European production.

27. **(A)** The Crusades failed to free the Holy Land from Muslim control though they did lead to new wealth for the Italian city states and Muslim traders, royal authority increased as the Pope's influence declined, peasants and towns ended feudal practices, and European warfare changed.

28. **(B)** Central to Jainism are Mahavira's principles of nonviolence and asceticism.

29. **(C)** The decline in death rates in the 20th century led to rising populations in the Third World countries.

30. **(B)** The plant and its place of origin which is correctly linked is millet and China.

31. **(C)** The theory of relativity is the result of Albert Einstein's work.

32. **(B)** The Portuguese developed a profitable trade in slaves and gold as they explored the west coast of Africa.

33. **(A)** Buddhism was disseminated in China by merchants and missionaries following the fall of the Han Empire, a time marked by economic distress and political instability.

34. **(A)** The style of Picasso's *Guernica* is twentieth-century abstract expressionism.

35. **(D)** Field armies of 100,000 men developed after the invention of gunpowder and gunpowder weaponry.

36. **(D)** The term Sinification refers to the process of becoming part of Chinese culture.

37. **(B)** Yugoslavia remained independent of Soviet occupation mainly because Communist leader Tito had his own army and had not been dependent on Soviet troops to liberate Yugoslavia from the Nazis.

38. **(B)** The two examples of porcelain illustrate the cross-cultural exchange across the vast network of Silk Roads spanning the Eurasian continent, cultural diffusion of products along the trade route, syncretism or combining a design idea with others from different sources, and synthesizing or using a combination of ideas to create something new. Since the two pieces were created at different periods of time, in different societies, it is doubtful that the markets for these two pieces were competitive.

39. **(B)** Even as early as the Roman-Han period, the Chinese were confident of their civilization and had little need of the products of other cultures.

40. **(D)** While Greece, Russia, Romania, and Serbia became Eastern Orthodox Christian states, Poland became Roman Catholic.

41. **(C)** The concept of religious salvation existed in the Muslim world of the Umayyad Caliphate but not among the Song Chinese who followed Confucian and Dao teachings. By the Song period, Buddhism had been discredited.

42. **(E)** Political decentralization, small trading towns and agrarians states developed, warriors and nobles predominated in the ruling class, and religion played a central role in preserving culture. Village schools for the peasantry were not characteristic of feudal societies.

43. **(B)** Karl Marx is the probable author of "Working men of all countries unite!"

44. **(E)** Pastoral nomads herded reindeer in the north. Displaced hunter-gatherers participated in a symbotic relationship with settled societies, and acted as long-distance carriers of overland trade.

45. **(C)** Buddhism and Christianity ceased to be important in the land of their origin.

46. **(E)** The strength of a nation-state differed from previous states as it is a sovereignty of people rather than leadership.

47. **(A)** The history of the Americas since 1492 was shaped by Europeans, Africans, Asians, and Amerindians.

48. **(C)** The International Monetary Fund was created in 1944 as an international bank funded by industrialized countries to make money available to countries have difficulty securing loans.

49. **(A)** Benin was a large African state ruled by the Oba whose authority was the theme of artistic works in ivory and caste bronze.

50. **(D)** Resulting from the explorations started by Prince Henry the Navigator, the Portuguese discovered an all-water route around Africa to the Indian Ocean and established hegemony over the Asian trade in the sixteenth century.

51. **(B)** 1869 was the year the Suez Canal opened.

52. **(D)** Plastic was unknown in the preindustrial era.

53. **(E)** The revolutions of the United States, France, and Latin America, inspired by the Enlightenment, reflected the growing power of the middle-class and the culture of the bourgeoisie.

54. **(E)** Anthropomorphic examples of Greek gods, rationalism, Greek drama, and the separation of natural science from philosophy with humans the subject of study are all examples of humanism. Buddhists and Hindus believe in cycles of rebirths.

55. **(E)** French support of the American Revolution led to a financial crisis in the 1780's. The monarchy's attempt to raise taxes from new sources led to the French Revolution.

56. **(C)** A world system was initiated with the Columbian discovery, establishing the Atlantic trade between Europe, Africa, and the Americas, and was completed with the Manila galleons, which tied the Pacific to the Indian and Atlantic Ocean shipping.

57. **(E)** The Napoleonic Code did not establish voting rights for women; women remained dependent.

58. **(A)** Intensive agriculture precipitated the Industrial Revolution. A surplus of food freed agricultural laborers for industry.

59. **(D)** Nobunaga established the Tokugawa Shogunate in 1560.

60. **(A)** Jean-Jacques Rousseau argued in the *Social Contract* that sovereign power is vested in the people and that social and legal relationships are based on equality and rule of the majority.

61. **(B)** This quote is more than likely an expression of the Enlightenment.

62. **(A)** Spanish-speaking colonies in Latin America became independent republics in the nineteenth century.

63. **(E)** Dar-al-Islam or "abode of Islam" refers to the economic and cultural system that linked the Muslim world together from 1000 C.E to 1500 C.E. across Eurasia and its seas.

64. **(B)** Marx and Engels described history as a class struggle which would lead to the victory of the proletariat or working class and produce a utopian communism.

65. **(A)** Hunting and Gathering societies did not completely disappear as a result of the Agricultural Revolution. Elise Boulding, a twentieth-century scholar, researched agricultural practices among the Kung bushman of South Africa.

66. **(D)** Russia lost the Crimean War to France and England in 1854. To avoid revolt and free serfs for industrial labor, serfs were emancipated in 1861.

67. **(E)** The Inca Empire existed for less than a century for some 2000 miles along the Andes. These ruins are of Machu Picchu, an Incan City 7,000 feet above sea level.

68. **(C)** Europeans did not encourage economic self-sufficiency. Among others, J.A. Hobson, a 19th-20th century economist, argued that imperialism was an outgrowth of capitalism's need for labor, raw materials, and markets.

69. **(E)** de las Casas argued that the Spanish treatment of the Americn Indians was not worthy of a Christian monarch.

70. **(D)** Ricci observed that the Chinese "have all sorts of raw material and they are endowed by nature with a talent for trading, both of which are potent factors in bringing about a high development of the mechanical arts."

71. **(A)** In the second half of the nineteenth century, the British encouraged Indian railroad construction for military purposes and to develop markets.

72. **(D)** The Romantic movement was artistic and cultural, not political.

73. **(E)** Russia reunited under the leadership of Moscow following Mongol rule because of Moscow's military power, the role of the Orthodox Church, and the claim to independence and the sovereignty of the czar.

74. **(C)** The German blitzkrieg of World War II was a swift systematic land-based assault strategy.

75. **(E)** Both Niccolo Machiavelli (1469–1527), a Florentine who wrote *The Prince* for his Medici ruler during the Renaissance, and Kautilya, who advised the Indian ruler Chandragupta (322 B.C.E.) in matters of statecraft, shared the belief that it is safer for a ruler to be feared than admired.

76. **(B)** The mandate system established a system of tutelage for nations on the road to independence.

77. **(B)** The ideal legalist state was authoritarian because human nature was evil. Laws should replace morality.

78. **(D)** Hitler instituted the Nuremburg Laws that marked the beginning of the Nazi genocide of the Jews, the final solution to the so-called "Jewish Problem."

79. **(E)** Europe was an inheritor of numerous Muslim accomplishments of the Golden Age of Islam including Indian numerals, medical advances, glass lenses for magnification, dissemination of the Greek and Roman classics, as well as Eastern inventions like the magnetic compass, gunpowder, and paper.

80. **(E)** The Green Revolution, scientific advancements which resulted in higher crop yields and more land in cultivation, was the result of population increases and famine in the Third World.

81. **(C)** On March 8, 1917, workers in St. Petersburg called for a general strike to protest military defeats and the lack of fuel and food. The troops were sympathetic and refused to fire on the workers.

82. **(E)** The Grameen Bank was organized to provide small loans to the desperately poor (particularly women) in developing countries.

83. **(D)** Women who inherited property were not entitled to equal rights. Basic liberties were granted to the Church, nobles, and the city of London.

84. **(B)** Stalin developed a state-directed plan for modernization by forced industrialization and collectivization.

85. **(D)** Rudyard Kipling refers to the duty of civilized peoples of industrialized Western societies to spread the benefits of civilization to native peoples, populations with dark skins.

86. **(C)** The modern states shown are Namibia, Nigeria, and Sudan.

87. **(A)** American occupation forces under General Douglas MacArthur introduced political reforms including democratization and demilitarization.

88. **(E)** The Hellenic style of warfare, the use of the phalanx, was replaced by the Greco-Macedonian style of warfare.

89. **(A)** In response to a civil war in Greece and Turkey between communists and loyalists, the United States announced the Truman Doctrine, a policy to support free people resisting armed minorities or outside pressure. Truman asked for military aid for Greece and Turkey.

90. **(D)** Both India and Pakistan claimed the disputed area of Kashmir. Fighting between the two countries, both armed with nuclear weapons, continues to this day.

91. **(C)** Iran became a radical Shi'ite theocracy under the leadership of the Ayatollah Khomeini in 1978.

92. **(C)** Mao launched the Great Proletarian Cultural Revolution to purge the party and recapture the fervor of the Chinese Communist Revolution. The Red Guard were young people who denounced teachers and parents, party officials, professors, artists, and intellectuals and forced them to publically confess to crimes against the state. Many lost their lives while others were sent to the country to purify themselves with heavy peasant labor.

93. **(E)** Twentieth century culture is noted for its international character. The communications revolution has made what happens in one area instantly knowable in all other areas of the globe resulting in the emergence of a global culture.

94. **(D)** The Roman concept of universal law or *jus naturale* was the result of special courts established to deal with the differences between Roman law and the laws of other societies. The judge made decisions that seemed fair, thus promoting the idea of justice over the laws of a particular country.

95. **(D)** Adam Smith, the father of economics, outlined the characteristics of a free capitalist economy as (1) private property, (2) profit, and (3) a free market. The invisible hand refers to economic decisions made by the public that influence supply and demand.

96. **(B)** The chronological order from oldest is *Ardipithecus ramidus* "Ardi," *Australopithecus afarensis* "Lucy," *Homo habilis* "Handy Man," *Homo erectus* "Turkana Boy," *Homo sapiens* "Neanderthal," *Homo sapiens sapiens*, "Cro-Magnon."

Answer Sheet
MODEL TEST 2

1 Ⓐ Ⓑ Ⓒ Ⓓ Ⓔ	33 Ⓐ Ⓑ Ⓒ Ⓓ Ⓔ	65 Ⓐ Ⓑ Ⓒ Ⓓ Ⓔ
2 Ⓐ Ⓑ Ⓒ Ⓓ Ⓔ	34 Ⓐ Ⓑ Ⓒ Ⓓ Ⓔ	66 Ⓐ Ⓑ Ⓒ Ⓓ Ⓔ
3 Ⓐ Ⓑ Ⓒ Ⓓ Ⓔ	35 Ⓐ Ⓑ Ⓒ Ⓓ Ⓔ	67 Ⓐ Ⓑ Ⓒ Ⓓ Ⓔ
4 Ⓐ Ⓑ Ⓒ Ⓓ Ⓔ	36 Ⓐ Ⓑ Ⓒ Ⓓ Ⓔ	68 Ⓐ Ⓑ Ⓒ Ⓓ Ⓔ
5 Ⓐ Ⓑ Ⓒ Ⓓ Ⓔ	37 Ⓐ Ⓑ Ⓒ Ⓓ Ⓔ	69 Ⓐ Ⓑ Ⓒ Ⓓ Ⓔ
6 Ⓐ Ⓑ Ⓒ Ⓓ Ⓔ	38 Ⓐ Ⓑ Ⓒ Ⓓ Ⓔ	70 Ⓐ Ⓑ Ⓒ Ⓓ Ⓔ
7 Ⓐ Ⓑ Ⓒ Ⓓ Ⓔ	39 Ⓐ Ⓑ Ⓒ Ⓓ Ⓔ	71 Ⓐ Ⓑ Ⓒ Ⓓ Ⓔ
8 Ⓐ Ⓑ Ⓒ Ⓓ Ⓔ	40 Ⓐ Ⓑ Ⓒ Ⓓ Ⓔ	72 Ⓐ Ⓑ Ⓒ Ⓓ Ⓔ
9 Ⓐ Ⓑ Ⓒ Ⓓ Ⓔ	41 Ⓐ Ⓑ Ⓒ Ⓓ Ⓔ	73 Ⓐ Ⓑ Ⓒ Ⓓ Ⓔ
10 Ⓐ Ⓑ Ⓒ Ⓓ Ⓔ	42 Ⓐ Ⓑ Ⓒ Ⓓ Ⓔ	74 Ⓐ Ⓑ Ⓒ Ⓓ Ⓔ
11 Ⓐ Ⓑ Ⓒ Ⓓ Ⓔ	43 Ⓐ Ⓑ Ⓒ Ⓓ Ⓔ	75 Ⓐ Ⓑ Ⓒ Ⓓ Ⓔ
12 Ⓐ Ⓑ Ⓒ Ⓓ Ⓔ	44 Ⓐ Ⓑ Ⓒ Ⓓ Ⓔ	76 Ⓐ Ⓑ Ⓒ Ⓓ Ⓔ
13 Ⓐ Ⓑ Ⓒ Ⓓ Ⓔ	45 Ⓐ Ⓑ Ⓒ Ⓓ Ⓔ	77 Ⓐ Ⓑ Ⓒ Ⓓ Ⓔ
14 Ⓐ Ⓑ Ⓒ Ⓓ Ⓔ	46 Ⓐ Ⓑ Ⓒ Ⓓ Ⓔ	78 Ⓐ Ⓑ Ⓒ Ⓓ Ⓔ
15 Ⓐ Ⓑ Ⓒ Ⓓ Ⓔ	47 Ⓐ Ⓑ Ⓒ Ⓓ Ⓔ	79 Ⓐ Ⓑ Ⓒ Ⓓ Ⓔ
16 Ⓐ Ⓑ Ⓒ Ⓓ Ⓔ	48 Ⓐ Ⓑ Ⓒ Ⓓ Ⓔ	80 Ⓐ Ⓑ Ⓒ Ⓓ Ⓔ
17 Ⓐ Ⓑ Ⓒ Ⓓ Ⓔ	49 Ⓐ Ⓑ Ⓒ Ⓓ Ⓔ	81 Ⓐ Ⓑ Ⓒ Ⓓ Ⓔ
18 Ⓐ Ⓑ Ⓒ Ⓓ Ⓔ	50 Ⓐ Ⓑ Ⓒ Ⓓ Ⓔ	82 Ⓐ Ⓑ Ⓒ Ⓓ Ⓔ
19 Ⓐ Ⓑ Ⓒ Ⓓ Ⓔ	51 Ⓐ Ⓑ Ⓒ Ⓓ Ⓔ	83 Ⓐ Ⓑ Ⓒ Ⓓ Ⓔ
20 Ⓐ Ⓑ Ⓒ Ⓓ Ⓔ	52 Ⓐ Ⓑ Ⓒ Ⓓ Ⓔ	84 Ⓐ Ⓑ Ⓒ Ⓓ Ⓔ
21 Ⓐ Ⓑ Ⓒ Ⓓ Ⓔ	53 Ⓐ Ⓑ Ⓒ Ⓓ Ⓔ	85 Ⓐ Ⓑ Ⓒ Ⓓ Ⓔ
22 Ⓐ Ⓑ Ⓒ Ⓓ Ⓔ	54 Ⓐ Ⓑ Ⓒ Ⓓ Ⓔ	86 Ⓐ Ⓑ Ⓒ Ⓓ Ⓔ
23 Ⓐ Ⓑ Ⓒ Ⓓ Ⓔ	55 Ⓐ Ⓑ Ⓒ Ⓓ Ⓔ	87 Ⓐ Ⓑ Ⓒ Ⓓ Ⓔ
24 Ⓐ Ⓑ Ⓒ Ⓓ Ⓔ	56 Ⓐ Ⓑ Ⓒ Ⓓ Ⓔ	88 Ⓐ Ⓑ Ⓒ Ⓓ Ⓔ
25 Ⓐ Ⓑ Ⓒ Ⓓ Ⓔ	57 Ⓐ Ⓑ Ⓒ Ⓓ Ⓔ	89 Ⓐ Ⓑ Ⓒ Ⓓ Ⓔ
26 Ⓐ Ⓑ Ⓒ Ⓓ Ⓔ	58 Ⓐ Ⓑ Ⓒ Ⓓ Ⓔ	90 Ⓐ Ⓑ Ⓒ Ⓓ Ⓔ
27 Ⓐ Ⓑ Ⓒ Ⓓ Ⓔ	59 Ⓐ Ⓑ Ⓒ Ⓓ Ⓔ	91 Ⓐ Ⓑ Ⓒ Ⓓ Ⓔ
28 Ⓐ Ⓑ Ⓒ Ⓓ Ⓔ	60 Ⓐ Ⓑ Ⓒ Ⓓ Ⓔ	92 Ⓐ Ⓑ Ⓒ Ⓓ Ⓔ
29 Ⓐ Ⓑ Ⓒ Ⓓ Ⓔ	61 Ⓐ Ⓑ Ⓒ Ⓓ Ⓔ	93 Ⓐ Ⓑ Ⓒ Ⓓ Ⓔ
30 Ⓐ Ⓑ Ⓒ Ⓓ Ⓔ	62 Ⓐ Ⓑ Ⓒ Ⓓ Ⓔ	94 Ⓐ Ⓑ Ⓒ Ⓓ Ⓔ
31 Ⓐ Ⓑ Ⓒ Ⓓ Ⓔ	63 Ⓐ Ⓑ Ⓒ Ⓓ Ⓔ	95 Ⓐ Ⓑ Ⓒ Ⓓ Ⓔ
32 Ⓐ Ⓑ Ⓒ Ⓓ Ⓔ	64 Ⓐ Ⓑ Ⓒ Ⓓ Ⓔ	96 Ⓐ Ⓑ Ⓒ Ⓓ Ⓔ

Answer Sheet

Model Test 2

Directions: Below each question or incomplete sentence are five answer choices. Select the best answer or completion for each question and fill in the appropriate circle on the corresponding answer sheet.

1. Which of the following statements concerning the aftermath of World War I is false?

   (A) The Fascists, both antidemocratic and anticommunist, seized power in Italy under Benito Mussolini.
   (B) Germany's National Socialist party, led by Adolf Hitler, gained a majority in the election of 1933.
   (C) Mohandas Gandhi launched a non-violent protest against British rule following the Amritsar Massacre in India.
   (D) To support President Wilson's 14 Points, the United States became a leader in the League of Nations to make the world safe for democracy.
   (E) Mao Tse-tung and his communist army fled the nationalist Chinese army of Chiang Kai-shek in their Long March to a new stronghold in northern China.

2. Which INCORRECTLY links the technology with the people of the fifteenth century?

   (A) Germans and Koreans—printing press with moveable type
   (B) Indians—vertical loom, block printing, and spinning wheel
   (C) Chinese—compass and ocean-going ships with water-tight compartments
   (D) Arabs—dhows and lateen sails
   (E) English—steam engine and spinning jenny

3. Between 1880 and 1900 the only European country which did not establish an empire in Africa was

   (A) Britain.
   (B) France.
   (C) Germany.
   (D) Italy.
   (E) Austro-Hungarian Empire.

4. What was the immediate cause of the French Revolution?

   (A) rising power of the middle class
   (B) inspiration of the American Revolution
   (C) threat of national bankruptcy
   (D) feudal dues paid by the peasants
   (E) nationalizing church property

5. "It is true that we are called a democracy. . . For we are lovers of the beautiful, yet with economy . . ."

   This probably describes the people of which classical city?

   (A) Athens
   (B) Sparta
   (C) Rome
   (D) Pataliputra
   (E) Changan

6. Which nation remained outside the Soviet satellite system after World War II?

   (A) Poland
   (B) Czechoslovakia
   (C) Hungary
   (D) Yugoslavia
   (E) Bulgaria

7. Maritime shipping in the Indian Ocean before the arrival of Vasco da Gama was

   (A) dominated by the Chinese, who demanded tribute trade in exchange for safe passage.
   (B) equipped with more advanced Arab sailing technology that included the lateen sail, two or three masted ships, and water-tight compartments.
   (C) defended by teakwood dhows of Indian design armed with brass cannon.
   (D) multiethnic, peaceful, and dependent on the monsoon winds.
   (E) an exchange of African gold and slaves, Indian cotton and calicos, Arabian pepper and cinnamon, and Chinese silks and tea.

8. In Marco Polo's account of the use of paper money in China, which of the following were reasons Chinese accepted "paper" in payment for goods and services is FALSE?

   (A) paper money was authenticated with much form and ceremony.
   (B) the designs of Chinese money made the work of counterfeiters difficult.
   (C) paper money was circulated to every part of the empire in large quantities.
   (D) no person dared to refuse to accept paper money on pain of death.
   (E) paper money was used to purchase gold, silver, pearls, or any other article.

9. Which of the following philosophers and philosophies is mismatched?

   (A) Locke—All people have the right to life, liberty, and property.
   (B) Hobbes—People gave up their freedom to a ruler who established order.
   (C) Montesquieu—The state should be divided so that no one person or one group has unlimited power.
   (D) Voltaire—People are rarely fit to govern themselves and should, without reservation, submit themselves to the rule of an enlightened monarch.
   (E) Rousseau—People are born free but everywhere are in chains.

10. Leaders of the Taiping Rebellion favored

    I. rapid economic development.
    II. defense of the Amur basin and Manchuria against Russian encroachment.
    III. redistribution of land.
    IV. equality between men and women.
    V. reduction in taxes.

    (A) I, II, and III
    (B) I, III, and V
    (C) II, III, and V
    (D) III, IV, and V
    (E) I, II, and IV

11. According to Bernardino de Sahagun in his *General History of the Things of New Spain*, the principal reason Montezuma was "terror struck" was because the Spanish

    (A) possessed guns.
    (B) ate strange food.
    (C) were thought to be strange gods.
    (D) represented an unknown threat.
    (E) were accompanied by huge dogs and large "deer" that they rode.

12. In Persia, the new Safavid Dynasty (1501–1736) established a state religion that was

    (A) Sunni Islam.
    (B) Shi'ite Islam.
    (C) Eastern Orthodox Christianity.
    (D) Hinduism.
    (E) Zoroastrianism

13. James Watt's steam engine was powered by

    (A) electricity
    (B) petroleum
    (C) wind
    (D) coal
    (E) natural gas

14. Who was responsible for nationalizing the Suez Canal?

    (A) Anwar Sadat
    (B) Menachem Begin
    (C) Gamal Abdel Nasser
    (D) Queen Victoria
    (E) Lawrence of Arabia

15. Common to both the Aztec and Inca Empires was

    (A) control of conquered peoples through able administration, peace, and financial rewards for loyalty.
    (B) conquest of new lands to support rulers in their afterlife through systematic collection of tribute.
    (C) a slave system in which slaves could own property, purchase their freedom, and own their own slaves.
    (D) a complex system of agriculture and a state religion that included human sacrifice.
    (E) the development of an extensive system of paved roads, bridges, and tunnels.

16. A school of navigation to explore and map the west African coastline was founded by

    (A) Zheng He, the Muslim admiral for the Ming Court.
    (B) Tamil traders from the Chola state.
    (C) Prince Henry.
    (D) Baltic and Italian merchants.
    (E) Malaysian spice traders.

17. The only two countries in Africa to escape European colonization in the "Scramble for Africa" were

    (A) Egypt and South Africa.
    (B) Liberia and Ethiopia.
    (C) Kenya and Madagascar.
    (D) Morocco and Libya.
    (E) Nigeria and Congo.

18. European influence did not penetrate the interior of Africa until the

    (A) nineteeth century.
    (B) eighteenth century.
    (C) seventeenth century.
    (D) sixteenth century.
    (E) fifteenth century.

19. The most likely explanation for this is

    (A) the lack of adequate maps.
    (B) the ineffectiveness of European military technology in the interior.
    (C) malaria.
    (D) rain forests.
    (E) all of the above

Model Test 2

©UNESCO/G. Boccardi

20. The picture above shows

    (A) Winter Palace at St. Petersburg.
    (B) Forbidden City in Beijing.
    (C) El Escorial in Madrid.
    (D) Versailles outside of Paris.
    (E) White Heron Castle in Japan.

21. Which battle is INCORRECTLY linked with its consequence?

    (A) Battle of Manzikert—The Seljuk Turks defeated the Byzantines and claimed land from Palestine to Turkey.
    (B) Battle of Talas River—The Muslims with their Central Asian allies learned the technology for producing paper after defeating the Chinese and their Central Asian allies.
    (C) Battle of Tours—The Muslim advance into eastern Europe ended with this battle.
    (D) The fall of Constantinople—The victory of the Ottoman Turks and the end of the Byzantine Empire.
    (E) The fall of Kiev—The founding of Moscow and new city-states in the northeast by the Russians.

22. The Boer War (1899–1902) was fought between

    (A) Britain and Afrikaners for control of South Africa.
    (B) France and Britain over the Sudan.
    (C) Germany and Britain for control of East Africa.
    (D) Afrikaners and Zulu for the Orange Free State.
    (E) Germany and France for Morocco.

23. All of the following illustrate the ideas of Descartes and Bacon EXCEPT

    (A) reason is the foundation of knowledge.
    (B) reason could be used to interpret the results of experimentation and observation.
    (C) inductive and deductive thought are the basis of reason.
    (D) rationalism is the basis of science.
    (E) natural law can be applied to society.

24. Which of the following geographical advantages was shared by Egypt and Mesopotamia?

    (A) Gradual rise of flood waters with yearly deposits of silt
    (B) Borders protected by natural geographic barriers
    (C) Large deposits of stone
    (D) Access to timber and copper
    (E) Access to water for irrigation

25. In 1453 the Ottoman Turks gained control of

    (A) the Balkans.
    (B) Constantinople.
    (C) the Adriatic Sea.
    (D) Syria, Palestine, and Egypt.
    (E) Vienna.

26. Chinampas were

    (A) subordinate provinces within the Aztec state.
    (B) marketplaces within the city of Tenochtitlan.
    (C) neighboring states that paid tribute to the Aztecs.
    (D) artificial gardens that supplied the Aztecs with food.
    (E) pyramids built by the Aztecs to honor their gods.

27. Israel occupied Old Jerusalem and the Golan Heights

    (A) with the end of the British Mandate in 1948.
    (B) during World War II.
    (C) as a consequence of the Arab Israeli War.
    (D) during the Six-Day War.
    (E) at the conclusion of the Yom Kippur War.

28. Corvee labor was labor

    (A) required of peasants as a service to the state.
    (B) expected of a slave.
    (C) required of soldiers to build forts, walls, and moats.
    (D) required of anyone who refused to pay taxes.
    (E) expected of prisoners in exchange for food.

29. Athenian democracy differed from modern American democracy in that

    (A) only citizens voted.
    (B) public buildings and the arts were open to all.
    (C) government was a direct democracy.
    (D) juries were chosen by lot.
    (E) the executive branch included the commander-in-chief.

30. Which of the following statements defines stateless societies?

    (A) indigenous peoples related by bloodlines
    (B) agricultural colonists supported by an organized state
    (C) caravans of Muslim traders who moved from market to market
    (D) culturally and ethnically homogeneous societies with local governments
    (E) feudal societies lacking a central government

31. What was the international significance of Italy's invasion of Ethiopia and Japan's invasion of Manchuria?

    (A) the failure of appeasement
    (B) the weakness of the United Nations
    (C) the injustice of the Treaty of Versailles
    (D) the ineffectiveness of the League of Nations
    (E) the formation of the Rome-Berlin-Tokyo axis

32. Characteristic of both Hindu and Buddhist thought is a belief in

    (A) the caste system.
    (B) Nirvana.
    (C) the Eightfold Path.
    (D) reincarnation.
    (E) enlightenment.

33. Which was a nineteenth century art form?

    (A) abstractionism
    (B) expressionism
    (C) romanticism
    (D) socialist realism
    (E) Bauhaus design

34. The "mother" civilization of South America was

    (A) Mohenjo-Daro.
    (B) Maya.
    (C) Olmec.
    (D) Chavin de Huantar.
    (E) Altiplano.

35. Which of the policies advocated by Robert Owen directly resulted in reform legislation?

    (A) Healthy people are better workers.
    (B) Profits should be shared through philanthropy.
    (C) There should be improved wages for all laborers.
    (D) There should be better working conditions for women and children.
    (E) The community should be the focus of manufacturers.

36. Which of the following countries remained independent of European colonial rule during the nineteenth century?

    (A) India, China, Iraq
    (B) Japan, Thailand, Ethopia
    (C) Liberia, Egypt, South Africa
    (D) Algeria, Myanmar (Burma), Philippines
    (E) Korea, Vietnam, Sudan

Model Test 2

37. All of the following are reactions to the development of nuclear weapons EXCEPT

    (A) fear of MAD, "mutually assured destruction," which led to the suspension of nuclear war.
    (B) the decline in the number of guerrilla wars with their dependence on traditional weapons.
    (C) the proliferation of modern military technology.
    (D) the space exploration programs of the Soviet Union and the United States, which included a consideration of the use of weapons technology.
    (E) the proliferation of nuclear weapons.

38. "If a man has put out the eye of a free man, they shall put out his eye.
    If he breaks the one of a free man, they shall break his bone . . . .
    If he puts out the eye of a free man's slave or breaks the bone of a free man's slave, he shall pay half his price."

    The source of this quote is most likely

    (A) the New Testament
    (B) Draco's Code of Law
    (C) Hammurabi's Code
    (D) Justinian's Code
    (E) Laws of Manu

39. "*Red-haired* is a general term for the barbarians of the western islands. Amongst them are the Dutch, French, Spaniards, Portuguese, English, and Yu-su-la (Muslims?), all of which nations are horribly fierce. Wherever they go, they spy around with a view to seize other people's territories."

    H. A. Giles

    This passage was probably written by

    (A) a Chinese official in the sixth century C.E.
    (B) an Aztec official in the sixteenth century C.E.
    (C) a Chinese official in the eighteenth century C.E.
    (D) a Japanese official in the nineteenth century C.E.
    (E) a Korean official in the twentieth century C.E.

40. Human migrations to remote areas of the world were facilitated during the Paleolithic period by

    (A) development of the wheel.
    (B) exploration and development of overland trails.
    (C) land masses that were closer together because ocean levels were lower.
    (D) domestication of the horse.
    (E) better tools produced by grinding and polishing.

41. What is classicism?

    (A) culture developed at urban centers by an agricultural-based society
    (B) cultural trends evolving from the cross-cultural exchange of art and ideas
    (C) cultural expression that is copied or imitated by another society
    (D) an idea within a complex urban society that remains popular over a long period of time
    (E) a distinctive and long-lasting civilizational pattern shaped by a belief system

42. The Solidarity movement in Poland, which ultimately toppled the communist regime, was helped by what other Polish institution?

    (A) the Polish army
    (B) the Catholic Church
    (C) the Polish parliament
    (D) the peasantry
    (E) the dissident Communist party members

43. The last site to develop agriculture was

    (A) Nile Valley in present day Egypt.
    (B) Huang Ho (Yellow) River valley in present day China.
    (C) Rhine River valley in present day Germany.
    (D) Western slopes of the Zagros Mountains in present day Iran.
    (E) Tigris and Euphrates river valleys in present day Iraq.

44. What was behind the ten-year Mexican Revolution and the Civil War?

    (A) revenge for the U.S. acquisition of Texas
    (B) unification of Mexico and Central America
    (C) return to indigenous Indian rule
    (D) return to classical liberalism
    (E) demand for land reform, voting rights, and the right to organize and strike

45. Central to the beliefs of Zoroastrianism was a new concept of divinity and human life. That concept was

    (A) monotheism.
    (B) polytheistic gods representing elements of nature.
    (C) establishment of a theistic state.
    (D) a god with anthropomorphic characteristics.
    (E) dualistic beliefs in good and evil.

46. The historical interpretation of the French Revolution as a liberal revolt by the bourgeoisie is challenged by the evidence that

    (A) only 8 percent of France's population was middle class.
    (B) the middle and upper classes were disunited in their objectives.
    (C) the French were governed by a dictator.
    (D) France eventually returned to a partial monarchy.
    (E) all of the above

47. Which of the following is an example of a primary source?

    (A) the Romance of the Three Kingdoms
    (B) History of the Peloponnesian War
    (C) the Decline and Fall of the Roman Empire
    (D) Pericles' funeral oration
    (E) A Study of History

48. Who launched a series of Soviet reforms known as glasnost (political openness) and perestroika (economic restructuring)?

    (A) Mikhail Gorbachev
    (B) Helmut Kohl
    (C) Boris Yeltsin
    (D) Lech Walesa
    (E) Nikita Khrushchev

49. The least likely consequences of industrialization during the 1800s was

    (A) increasing importance of education.
    (B) beginning of the age of mass consumption and culture.
    (C) increasing migration of workers from cities to the countryside.
    (D) gradual improvement in urban living conditions.
    (E) a new class of urban workers, the proletariat.

50. The first African state to gain independence after Word War II was

    (A) Algeria
    (B) Nigeria
    (C) Kenya
    (D) Sudan
    (E) Ghana

51. Karl Marx believed that the Industrial Revolution would lead to all of the following EXCEPT

    (A) a world revolution of the working class.
    (B) the overthrow of the bourgeoisie.
    (C) the triumph of communism.
    (D) the state withering away.
    (E) a universal religion based on Christianity

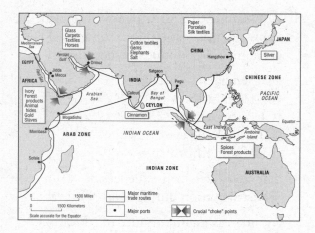

52. On the map above, three areas are indicated as "choke" points or strategic shipping lanes between land masses similar to the strategic modern shipping lane from the Atlantic to the Mediterranean. Which of the following is not a "choke" point or strategic shipping lane between land masses?

    (A) Suez Canal
    (B) Panama Canal
    (C) Straits of Gibraltar
    (D) English Channel
    (E) Black Sea

The Granger Collection, New York

53. What architectural features are unique to Gothic architecture?

    (A) flying buttresses and stained glass windows
    (B) domes and steeples
    (C) cross-vaulting and barrel arches
    (D) minarets and calligraphy
    (E) icons and gargoyles

54. The most likely reason that people's republics were established in Central and East Europe after World War II is the

    (A) presence of Soviet troops.
    (B) presence of Tito's troops.
    (C) preference of East and Central European countries for communism.
    (D) preference in Central and East Europe for republicanism.
    (E) treaties signed at Yalta and Teheran.

55. The world population increased dramatically following the Agricultural and Industrial Revolutions. Why?

    (A) increased food supply
    (B) new technology reduced labor demands
    (C) changes in lifestyle and family structure
    (D) climatic change
    (E) a period of rapid economic development marked by peace and prosperity

56. Which of the following is arranged in CORRECT chronological order?

    (A) Cuban Missile Crisis, Korean War, World War II
    (B) United Nations Charter, Wall Street Crash, construction of the Berlin Wall
    (C) Korean War, Cuban Missile Crisis, construction of the Berlin Wall
    (D) Korean War, construction of the Berlin Wall, Cuban Missile Crisis
    (E) World War I, United Nations Charter, World War II

57. Which country today speaks Portuguese as a result of the Treaty of Tordesillas in 1494?

    (A) Colombia
    (B) Argentina
    (C) Cuba
    (D) Brazil
    (E) Haiti

58. Based on linguistic and physical evidence, all of the following were sites of Polynesian migrations EXCEPT

    (A) Hawaii.
    (B) Australia.
    (C) New Zealand.
    (D) Madagascar.
    (E) Fiji.

59. The medieval Roman Catholic Church often was in conflict with secular rulers over the issue of

    (A) selection of the pope.
    (B) excommunication.
    (C) punishment of heretics.
    (D) lay investiture.
    (E) all of the above

60. Which cultural and linguistic group during the classical period of Africa dominated the Sudan?

    (A) Bantu
    (B) Nok
    (C) Mande
    (D) Griots
    (E) Phoenician

61. World War II began for the Chinese in

    (A) 1910 when the Japanese annexed Korea.
    (B) 1931 when the Japanese invaded Manchuria.
    (C) 1937 when the Japanese invaded China.
    (D) 1941 when the Japanese invaded Singapore.
    (E) 1941 when the Japanese attacked Pearl Harbor.

62. The success of the Mongol army was for all of the following reasons EXCEPT

    (A) The army unified Central Asian tribes, loyal to one leader.
    (B) The army ruled all conquered peoples under one law, one language, and one religion.
    (C) The army used intimidation and deception to demoralize the enemy.
    (D) The army surpressed uprisings in conquered territory.
    (E) The army established a chain of command with commanders at each level responsible for discipline and training.

63. The first society to undergo early industralization was

    (A) England.
    (B) France.
    (C) the United States.
    (D) China.
    (E) India.

64. Which of the following men is CORRECTLY linked with the subject of his achievements?

    (A) Euripedes—science
    (B) Pythagoras—algebra
    (C) Hippocrates—medicine
    (D) Phideas—drama
    (E) Pericles—history

65. The Byzantine Empire and its capital, Constantinople, were previously part of

    (A) Persia
    (B) the Mauryan Empire
    (C) Palestine
    (D) Alexander the Great's kingdom
    (E) Rome

66. Which of the following statements is inaccurate?

    (A) Times of great interaction stimulate new ways of doing things and new habits of thought.
    (B) Total wars of the twentieth century required nations to field large, professional armies, which were separate in their training and deployment from the civilian population.
    (C) With modernization have come population pressures, resource depletion, and environmental disequilibrium.
    (D) Wars of the twentieth century resulted in new technologies and inventions and introduced people to new ways of doing things.
    (E) Western culture has continued to set worldwide trends.

67. Cultural achievements of the Indian society from 300 B.C.E. to 500 C.E. included all of the following EXCEPT

    (A) rust-free iron.
    (B) plastic surgery.
    (C) cotton textiles.
    (D) civil service examinations.
    (E) decimal system.

68. Which of the following argued that population tends to expand faster than the supply of food?

    (A) Adam Smith
    (B) Thomas Malthus
    (C) David Ricardo
    (D) George Hegel
    (E) Frederick Engels

69. Which of the following architectural masterpieces is incorrectly linked with the society that constructed it?

    (A) Forbidden City—Ming China
    (B) Taj Mahal—Mughal India
    (C) Tenochtitlan—Aztec
    (D) Machu Picchu—Inca
    (E) Hagia Sophia—Ottoman Turkey

70. Unlike the Russians, the Chinese communists under Mao

    (A) depended on foreign aid from the Allies following World War II.
    (B) envisioned a revolution of peasant guerrilla fighters.
    (C) centered their efforts in cities, organizing through labor unions.
    (D) took the brunt of the fighting against the Japanese invaders.
    (E) were discredited among the peasants and workers at the end of World War II because of inflation and corruption.

71. While the development of writing led to many advantages for a more complex society, writing failed to

    (A) centralize rule and enforcement of government regulations.
    (B) empower peasant villages.
    (C) increase the body of knowledge passed from one generation to another.
    (D) centralize records of tax payments, land ownership, and contracts.
    (E) create an educated bureaucratic class.

72. The mostly likely explanation for the economic miracles that occurred in Taiwan and South Korea during the 1970s was

    (A) loans from the World Bank.
    (B) education and industrialization.
    (C) democratic governments.
    (D) large amounts of raw materials.
    (E) adequate land.

73. Famines in India in the late 1880s were the likely result of

    (A) the Sepoy Rebellion.
    (B) the doctrine of lapse.
    (C) British policy to encourage the production of cotton rather than food.
    (D) policies of the Indian National Congress.
    (E) sporadic peasant revolts.

74. Examples of expanding diffusion of technology and cultural expressions include all of the following EXCEPT

    (A) Chinese block printing in England.
    (B) Indian cotton crops in China.
    (C) Chinese gunpowder in Ottoman Turkey.
    (D) Japanese adoption of Chinese Buddhism.
    (E) Indian sugar cane in Southwest Asia.

75. All can be said of the slave trade that occurred across the Atlantic Ocean from Africa to the Americas ca. 1500–1800 EXCEPT

    (A) more males than females went across the Atlantic.
    (B) the slave trade gave rise to new kingdoms and empires in Africa.
    (C) European slavers went into the African interior to capture slaves.
    (D) European slave trading companies and governments founded "factories" along the western coast of Africa to collect slaves.
    (E) the voyage across the Atlantic from Africa to the Americas is often called the Middle Passage.

76. The most immediate consequence of the Russian defeat in the Crimean War was

    (A) Western investment in Russian manufacturing.
    (B) construction of a network of railroads.
    (C) implementation of high tariffs to protect Russian industry.
    (D) banking reform.
    (E) the emancipation of serfs.

77. Which group of population centers is INCORRECTLY linked with the historical period?

    (A) Harapa and Mohenjo Daro, San Lorenzo, and Ur—Iron Age
    (B) Crete, Troy, Nineveh, and Jerusalem—Bronze Age
    (C) Dunhang, Carthage, Pataliputria, and Persepolis—Classical Period
    (D) Changan, Nara, Borobadur, Timbuktu, and Mogadishu—Post-Classical Period
    (E) Manila, Mexico City, Madrid, Amsterdam, and London—Early Modern Period

78. The term *diaspora* is exemplified by the history of

    (A) Lydians
    (B) Jews
    (C) Phoenicians
    (D) Minoans
    (E) Olmecs

79. Which organizations are centered around economic rather than political activities?

      I. OPEC
     II. NATO
    III. SEATO
     IV. SWAPO
      V. NAFTA

    (A) I and II
    (B) I and V
    (C) III and IV
    (D) II and IV
    (E) IV and V

80. The Magna Carta was significant in English history because it established

    (A) Norman rule as the treaty following the Battle of Hastings in 1066.
    (B) the royal court system with trial by a jury of 12 peers and made English law the common law for all Englishmen.
    (C) the principle of the rule of law and promised that no tax would be imposed without approval by the common council of the kingdom.
    (D) the process the king would use to appoint the archbishop.
    (E) Parliament as a permanent institution with two assemblies, the House of Lords and the House of Commons.

Model Test 2

81. Which organization was not associated with twentieth-century independence movements?

    (A) Sans Culottes
    (B) African National Congress
    (C) Kuomintang
    (D) Viet Minh
    (E) Muslim League

82. Which of the following East Asian philosophies is INCORRECTLY paired with its characteristics?

    (A) Confucianism—filial piety and proper family relationships
    (B) Taoism—harmony of opposing forces
    (C) Legalism—rule by laws and the use of discipline to maintain order
    (D) I Ching—folk rituals to establish communications with the gods
    (E) Neo-Confucianism—political thought that supported the ending of the dynastic system

83. Increases in the Irish population up to 1840 were because of

    (A) better public health.
    (B) industrialization and better job opportunities.
    (C) introduction of the potato as a staple for peasants.
    (D) improved education.
    (E) improved economic conditions in the eighteenth and nineteeth centuries.

84. All were reasons for the rapid extension of the Inca Empire EXCEPT

    (A) equal rights for common peasants.
    (B) Quechua, a shared common language.
    (C) an elaborate system of roads, bridges, and tunnels.
    (D) a state religion headed by the Inca.
    (E) a highly trained bureaucracy.

85. All reflect the part that Indian Ocean monsoon winds played in history EXCEPT

    (A) they provided wind power for shipping from India to the East African coast.
    (B) they facilitated ocean trade across the Arabian Sea.
    (C) they provided the necessary rain for rice paddy farming in China and India.
    (D) they stimulated the construction of a complex irrigation system with three crops a year in Southeast Asia.
    (E) they kept China out of the Indian Ocean trade system.

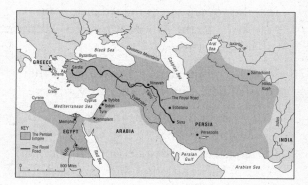

86. The map on this page illustrates

    (A) the Byzantine Empire in 565 C.E.
    (B) the Roman Empire in 117 C.E.
    (C) Alexander the Great's Empire in 323 B.C.E.
    (D) the spread of agriculture in Europe.
    (E) Cyrus the Great's Empire in 486 B.C.E.

87. All of the following were characteristic of both the Persian and Roman Empires EXCEPT

    (A) a system of roads to link the administration within the empire.
    (B) a policy of toleration toward differing peoples and religions.
    (C) a state religion and a civil code of law.
    (D) division of imperial lands into small regional units for administration.
    (E) a measure of local self-rule within the imperial borders.

88. What is the most likely explanation for the fact that China maintained its independence in the nineteenth century when other Asian societies were colonized?

    (A) The geography of China offered natural protective barriers.
    (B) The Treaty of Paris prohibited such imperialization.
    (C) The Russian presence was very powerful.
    (D) Europeans, Americans, and Japanese all claimed spheres of influence which kept China from being conquered by any one power.
    (E) The Chinese, like the Japanese, closed their borders to foreigners.

89. Of the following forms of political organizations, which is the most prevalent state structure in the modern era?

    (A) city-state
    (B) dynasty
    (C) empire
    (D) theocracy
    (E) nation

90. Southeast Asian cultures represent a synthesis of cultural expression introduced from all of the following societies EXCEPT

    (A) Korean monks.
    (B) Polynesian sailors.
    (C) Muslim traders.
    (D) Indian Brahmans.
    (E) Chinese merchants.

91. Which of the following issued the Balfour Declaration in 1917 with its contradictory assurances to Jews and Palestinians?

    (A) League of Nations
    (B) United Nations
    (C) the Allies
    (D) Great Britain
    (E) Ottoman Turkey

The Granger Collection, New York

92. This Diego Rivera mural emphasizes which aspect of the Mexican Revolution?

    (A) anti-U.S. imperialism
    (B) communist insurgency
    (C) Pancho Villa's insurgency
    (D) machismo
    (E) the peasant insistance on land reform

93. Which nomadic group is incorrectly paired with the geographic region of their migrations?

    (A) Aryans—Northern India
    (B) Slavs—Eastern Europe
    (C) Bantus—Sub-Saharan Africa
    (D) Hsiung-nu/Huns—Southeast Asia
    (E) Aztecs—Central Mexico

THE WEALTH OF NATIONS

The annual revenue of every society is always precisely equal to the exchangeable value of the whole annual produce of its industry, or rather is precisely the same thing with that exchangeable value. As every individual, therefore, endeavours as much as he can both to employ his capital in the support of domestic industry, and so to direct that industry that its produce may be of the greatest value; every individual necessarily labours to render the annual revenue of the society as great as he can. He generally, indeed, neither intends to promote the public interest, nor knows how much he is promoting it. By preferring the support of domestic to that of foreign industry, he intends only his own security; and by directing that industry in such a manner as its produce may be of the greatest value, he intends only his own gain, and he is in this, as in many other cases, led by an invisible hand to promote an end which was no part of his intention. Nor is it always the worse for the society that it was no part of it. By pursuing his own interest he frequently promotes that of society more effectually than when he really intends to promote it. I have never known much good done by those who affected to trade for the public good.

The Granger Collection, New York

94. In the excerpt from the *Wealth of Nations*, Adam Smith is an advocate of

(A) individuals guided by God to promote good works for the society.
(B) societies regulating their economies to promote the common good.
(C) individuals who successfully pursue their own welfare and benefit society.
(D) individuals who invest in businesses with international interests.
(E) aid to individuals who are unable to support themselves.

95. Using scenes of daily life, Japanese wood block prints, or ukiyo-e, like this one by Hokusai, was produced as one of many copies for

(A) peasants.
(B) laborers.
(C) samurai.
(D) the imperial court.
(E) merchants.

96. What geologic and climatic features in the earth's history are closely aligned with the spread of *Homo erectus* over large portions of the earth?

(A) the Great Rift Valley
(B) the breaking up of Pangaea
(C) plate tectonics
(D) forming of the Himalayas
(E) the most current ice age

Answer Key
MODEL TEST 2

1. D	21. C	41. E	61. C	81. A
2. E	22. A	42. B	62. B	82. E
3. E	23. E	43. C	63. A	83. C
4. C	24. E	44. E	64. C	84. A
5. A	25. B	45. E	65. E	85. E
6. D	26. D	46. E	66. B	86. E
7. D	27. D	47. D	67. D	87. C
8. B	28. A	48. A	68. B	88. D
9. D	29. C	49. C	69. E	89. E
10. D	30. A	50. E	70. B	90. A
11. A	31. D	51. E	71. B	91. D
12. B	32. D	52. E	72. B	92. E
13. D	33. C	53. A	73. C	93. D
14. C	34. D	54. A	74. A	94. C
15. D	35. D	55. A	75. C	95. E
16. C	36. B	56. D	76. E	96. E
17. B	37. B	57. D	77. A	
18. A	38. C	58. B	78. B	
19. E	39. C	59. E	79. B	
20. E	40. C	60. C	80. C	

Model Test 2

Answers

The study of history is based on questions, research, and conclusions. It is not memorization. The model test questions are selected to help you review critical changes in world history. Although the answers are provided, good review involves understanding historical information in context rather than simple memorization.

1. **(D)** The United States never joined the League of Nations despite President Wilson's support for the concept.

2. **(E)** The steam engine and spinning jenny were developed in the eighteenth century, not the fifteenth century.

3. **(E)** The Austro-Hungarian Empire attempted expansion in the Balkans, not Africa.

4. **(C)** The most IMMEDIATE cause of the French Revolution was the threat of bankruptcy. To meet the crisis, Louis XVI imposed a general tax which then ignited calls for broadened representation in the parliament and revolt by the lower classes due to inflation and food shortages.

5. **(A)** None of the other choices include the element of democracy.

6. **(D)** Yugoslavia, though communist, never became a Soviet satellite because its leader, Tito, had not been dependent on Soviet troops to liberate Yugoslavia from the Nazis.

7. **(D)** Indian Ocean maritime shipping prior to Vasco da Gama was not dominated by the Chinese, unilaterally dependent on Arab ship design, or armed. Pepper and cinnamon came from Indonesia, not Arabia.

8. **(B)** There is no indication in Marco Polo's account of the use of paper money during the Yuan Dynasty that Chinese design prevented counterfeiting.

9. **(D)** Voltaire did not believe that people should submit themselves to monarchical rule WITHOUT RESERVATION. Rather, he supported the idea of a good monarch but with reservations like equality before the law and civil rights.

10. **(D)** The Taiping Rebellion was partly the result of expansion into the world silver and opium market (A). The Taiping leaders focused on internal misery not external affairs like the Amur basin and Manchuria (B).

11. **(A)** Montezuma was amazed at Spanish food, iron gear, and the animals the Spanish rode, but what made him "faint away" was the "great Lombard gun."

12. **(B)** The Safavids proclaimed Shi'ite Islam as the official and compulsory religion of their empire.

13. **(D)** James Watt's steam engine was powered by coal.

14. **(C)** Anwar Sadat and Menachim Begin are known for an historical agreement in 1982 in which Egypt recognized Israel as a state. The nationalization of the Suez Canal by Nasser occurred in 1956. The reign of Queen Victoria occurred

from 1837–1901, while the activities of Lawrence of Arabia took place during World War I.

15. **(D)** Control of conquered territory by able administration and conquest tribute to support rulers in the afterlife was typical of the Inca but not the Aztec (A and B). Slaves in Aztec society could possess goods, buy land, have slaves of their own and buy freedom. Peasant workers in Inca society were generally not slaves (C). The development of roads and bridges was a great Inca but not Aztec achievement (E). Both Inca and Aztec societies had systems of agriculture (chinampas and terracing, respectively), state religions and human sacrifice.

16. **(C)** Zheng He, Tamil traders, and Malaysian spice traders explored in the Indian, Arabian, and South China Seas, while the Baltic and Italian traders explored in the North and Mediterranean Seas, respectively.

17. **(B)** See the map. Liberia probably remained independent because Dutch, English, French, and German trading merchants competed in the area. Then in 1817 American resettlement of Black Americans in Liberia further complicated the situation. In Ethiopia, a strong king (Menelik), lack of access to the sea, meager resources and British-Italian competition may have contributed to Ethiopia's continued independence.

18. **(A)** Disease, lack of transportation infrastructure, and European politics kept European powers out of the interior of Africa until the nineteenth century. Industrialization and competition among European powers for empire stimulated a scramble to obtain land, not just trading rights. The development of anti-malarial drugs and railroads furthered interior exploration and settlement.

19. **(E)** See the explanation above.

20. **(E)** Japanese gunpowder castles, like the White Heron Castle, offered protection from firearms and cannons.

21. **(C)** The Battle of Tours stopped the advancement of Islam into France, not East Europe.

22. **(A)** The British first pushed the Dutch (Afrikaners or Boers) into the interior of South Africa in 1835 and then conquered them 1899–1902.

23. **(E)** Descartes and Bacon are famous for the ideas and promotion of reason and rationalism. They influenced the "philosophes" who then applied their laws of nature to society.

24. **(E)** The gradual rise of flood waters with silt and borders that offered protection was characteristic of Egypt but not of Mesopotamia (A and B). On the other hand, Mesopotamia has deposits of stone, copper, and forests (C and D). Both Egypt and Mesopotamia had access to water for irrigation through the Nile (Egypt), and Tigris and Euphrates rivers (Mesopotamia).

25. **(B)** The Ottoman victory in 1453 over the Byzantines and occupation of Constantinople put an end to the thousand-year Byzantine rule of the Eastern Roman Empire. The victory was followed subsequently by Islamic infiltration and conversion in Eastern Europe.

26. **(D)** Chinampas were a critical part of the agricultural system that led to the rising agricultural population.

27. **(D)** Israel occupied Old Jerusalem and the Golan Heights during the Six-Day War.

28. **(A)** Corvee labor was labor required of peasants who could not pay their taxes in money or goods as a service to the state.

29. **(C)** Modern American democracy is a representative not a direct democracy.

30. **(A)** Stateless societies vary in terms of size and location but have been used to describe African societies where ethnic and blood ties (kinship groups) order political relationships that are not established governments per se.

31. **(D)** The invasions of Manchuria and Ethiopia illustrate the ineffectiveness of the League of Nations to solve crises of international significance. Later appeasement policies were based on the knowledge that the League of Nations had no power to stop aggressive behavior by states like Italy and Japan.

32. **(D)** The caste system and Nirvana are Hindu concepts while the Eightfold Path and enlightenment are Buddhist concepts. Both Buddhism and Hinduism believe in another life after death.

33. **(C)** Romanticism was a nineteenth century art form.

34. **(D)** Mohenjo Daro is one of the great cities of the Indus Valley civilization. The Maya were the classical peoples of Mesoamerica. Chavin de Huantar is a ceremonial center in the Altiplano or highlands of Peru.

35. **(D)** Robert Owen noted poor working conditions in factories for women and children. This led to the Factory Act of 1833 that limited the workday for children.

36. **(B)** China, Japan, Thailand, Ethiopia, and Liberia remained independent. All the remaining countries in Africa and Asia experienced colonial rule during the 19th century.

37. **(B)** Guerrilla wars have increased because it is often the only way that small nations and groups lacking sophisticated weaponry and nuclear power can protest.

38. **(C)** See the document "Hammurabi's Code."

39. **(C)** The Chinese tended to see peoples beyond their borders as barbarians. When the Europeans began arriving in the eighteenth century, the term "red-haired" was often applied to them.

40. **(C)** The development of the wheel and domestication of the horse came after the Paleolithic era. Better tools for grinding and polishing suggests Neolithic times when agriculture began to develop. Migrations were generally along unestablished routes. Land masses were closer together during the Paleolithic Era because ocean levels were lower. This encouraged movement of peoples.

41. **(E)** While answers A–D may be characteristic of classical societies, answer E most closely defines and explains what classicism is.

42. **(B)** Dock workers and factory labor, the Catholic Church and nationalists supported Solidarity, but not the Polish Army or parliament that were under the control of the Soviets, Polish communist officials or dissident communist party

members who had a lot to lose by the overthrow of the Polish communist regime. The peasantry was also against communist rule but it is a group of people, not an institution.

43. **(C)** Early agriculture developed in the Nile Valley in Egypt, along the Huang Ho (Yellow) River in China, in the Tehuacan Valley in Mexico, by the Tigris and Euphrates rivers, and along the rain-watered land in the Zagros Mountains. Agriculture along the Rhine River developed much later.

44. **(E)** The revolution and civil war that rocked Mexico from 1910–1920 was caused primarily by antiforeign discontent on the part of the Mexicans due to foreign control of economic assets, and internal economic conditions, primarily low wages, lack of land for the peasant farmers, and political corruption and dictatorship.

45. **(E)** Zoroastrianism was not monotheistic. Instead it believed in a pantheon of gods with anthropomorphic characteristics (human and elements of nature), and chief gods that represented good and evil. Zoroastrianism provided the basis for co-religious and state rule (a theistic state).

46. **(E)** The fact that the French Revolution was led by a small minority, resulting in a dictator (Robespierre and then Napoleon) and then a partial monarchy (Louis XVIII), challenges the theory that the Revolution was for political liberty and civil rights.

47. **(D)** Pericles' funeral oration is a primary source.

48. **(A)** Mikhail Gorbachev initiated a series of reforms that ultimately resulted in the end of Soviet communist rule in the Soviet satellite states of Eastern Europe in 1989 and then in Russia itself.

49. **(C)** Migration was from the countryside to the cities, not the other way around.

50. **(E)** Ghana was the first African state to emerge from colonial rule. The year was 1957.

51. **(E)** Marx dismissed religion as the "opium of the masses."

52. **(E)** The Bosporus and Dardanelles provide a narrow access from the Mediterranean Sea to the Black Sea, but since the Black Sea is land-locked, it is not a strategic shipping lane.

53. **(A)** Domes and cross-vaulting were typical of Romanesque architecture, steeples were typical of Protestant church architecture, and minarets and calligraphy were typical of Islamic architecture. Icons and gargoyles are decorative pieces.

54. **(A)** There is no evidence that Eastern European states preferred either communism or republicanism after World War II. Tito's troops were in Yugoslavia only. The treaties at Yalta and Teheran spoke to the idea of Soviet liberation of Eastern Europe from Germany but not of occupation. The presence of Soviet troops in Eastern Europe at the end of the war gave Russia power to impose new communist leadership favorable to the Soviets.

55. **(A)** Reduced labor demands, changes in lifestyle, and climate change may have obliquely caused an increase in world population, but an increase in world food supply caused by improved agricultural techniques and industrial technology

prevented famines and improved health. Peace and prosperity did not coincide with rapid economic development.

56. **(D)** World War I (1914–1918). Wall Street Crash (1929). World War II (1939–1945). United Nations Charter (1945). Korean War (1950–1953). Construction of the Berlin Wall (1961). Cuban Missile Crisis (1962).

57. **(D)** The Pope negotiated the Treaty of Tordesillas in 1494 between Spain and Portugal, which gave Portugal trading rights in India, China, the East Indies, and Brazil. The Spanish reserved the rights to the Americas.

58. **(B)** Hawaii, New Zealand, Madagascar, and Fiji were all peopled by migrating Austronesians. Australia and New Guinea were peopled earlier, and were of another language group, though Austronesians migrated there also.

59. **(E)** The struggle for power in Western Europe between church and state led to conflict over all of the issues listed.

60. **(C)** The Bantu peoples spread from their original homeland in eastern Nigeria to Central, East, and South Africa. The Nok peoples settled in present-day Nigeria. Griots are historians and musicians. The Mande peoples (Soninke, Mandinka, Malinka, and Babmara) reflect Sudanic classical culture. The Phoenicians settled the east coast of the Mediterranean which is now Lebanon.

61. **(C)** The Japanese annexation of Korea in 1910 was relevant to World War I, not World War II. In 1941 the Japanese invasion of Singapore and attack on Pearl Harbor occurred after World War II began. China protested the Japanese invasion of Manchuria in 1931 and its annexation in 1933. China referred the aggression to the League of Nations but it did not act to roll back the invasion despite its mandate to do so. The start of World War II for China was the invasion of China proper by the Japanese in 1937.

62. **(B)** The Mongols' conquests never resulted in Mongolization of the conquered peoples. On the contrary, while the Mongols sometimes affected cultures as in Russia and Persia, they often were absorbed into more advanced cultures as in China.

63. **(A)** England was the first society to undergo industralization, followed by France and the United States. Industralization in China and India occurred in the twentieth century.

64. **(C)** Hippocrates is correctly lined with medicine. Pericles is known for his leadership of Athens. Herodotus is known for history; Euripedes, drama; Pythagoras, geometry; and Phideas, architecture.

65. **(E)** The Byzantine Empire, ca. 500 C.E.–1453 C.E., was formerly part of the Eastern Roman Empire ca. 500 B.C.E.–500 C.E.

66. **(B)** In the total wars of the twentieth century, military and civilian activities comingled.

67. **(D)** Civil service examinations were an important achievement of China, not India.

68. **(B)** Adam Smith is known for his description of the capitalist system. David Ricardo is known for the idea that population could be controlled by wages.

George Hegel developed a theory of societal change and Frederick Engels of class struggle.

69. **(E)** The Hagia Sophia was a masterpiece of the Byzantine Empire.

70. **(B)** The Chinese communists under Mao did not depend on foreign aid, centered their efforts in the countryside, and let Chiang Kai-shek and the Nationalists bear the brunt of fighting against Japan. (E) describes the Chinese Nationalists at the end of World War II.

71. **(B)** The peasants rarely learned to write and so did not reap the benefits of its development.

72. **(B)** Neither Taiwan nor South Korea took significant loans from the World Bank, or possessed large amounts of raw material or adequate land. They had quasi-democratic governments. It was education and industrialization that made the difference.

73. **(C)** The British policy of encouraging the production of cotton took land for food out of cultivation.

74. **(A)** Chinese block printing did not appear in England. Rather, printing techniques like moveable type came from Europe, particularly from Johann Gutenberg around 1450 C.E. The Koreans had used moveable type prior to this time.

75. **(C)** Slavery was practiced within Africa so slaves were delivered to the coast for European slavers to pick up. Slaves were often exchanged for guns which facilitated the growth of African kingdoms.

76. **(E)** The Russian defeat in the Crimean War signaled to the Russian monarchy that Russia had fallen behind in terms of economic and military development. This prompted actions like (A) through (D). However, before industrialization could occur, a free labor force was needed. This was obtained by emancipating the peasant serfs from bondage to the land on which they worked.

77. **(A)** Harappa and Mohenjo-Daro, San Lorenzo, and Ur were connected with the agricultural revolution and rise of civilization.

78. **(B)** Romans expelled the Jews from Judaea in 135 C.E. Jewish communities were established in Europe, North Africa, and as far away as Ethiopia, India, and China.

79. **(B)** The Organization of Petroleum Exporting Countries (OPEC) and the North American Free Trade Association (NAFTA) are both organizations that concentrate on economic matters.

80. **(C)** The Magna Carta was signed in 1215. Norman rule was established before that time. Henry II established the royal court system in 1166. Later, under kings Henry III and Edward I, Parliament was established. Henry VIII took control of the English church.

81. **(A)** Sans Culottes is connected with the French Revolution of 1789, not the twentieth century.

82. **(E)** Neo-Confucianism emphasized self-perfection that supported the dynastic system in power.

83. **(C)** Once the nutritious potato was introduced into Ireland from the Americas, Irish peasants depended on them. Population grew until a blight caused crop failures in 1846, 1848, and 1851.

84. **(A)** Inca society was not equal. Common people were denied choice and were regimented by the state.

85. **(E)** China became active in the Indian Ocean especially during the Ming Dynasty when expeditions led by Zheng He crossed the Indian Ocean to Ceylon, the Persian coast, and the east coast of Africa.

86. **(E)** Alexander the Great's Empire extended also into Europe while Cyrus the Great's Empire did not.

87. **(C)** Rome developed a civil code of law while Persia developed a state religion.

88. **(D)** China is a huge country but has been easily invaded especially along the northern border. The Treaty of Paris (1763) established colonial rule between England and France in various parts of the world but not China. The Russian presence in China during the last part of the nineteenth century and early twentieth century was along the Amur River primarily. The Chinese, unlike the Japanese, opened their borders. Multiple spheres of interest and competition among European countries for trade no doubt saved China from colonization.

89. **(E)** Political boundaries in the modern world are based on national identity, coherence, and sovereignty.

90. **(A)** Korea had little influence in Southeast Asia.

91. **(D)** The Sykes-Picot treaties between France and England during World War I promised respective spheres in the Middle East once the war was over and Ottoman imperial rule there destroyed. In 1917, hoping to get as many allies on its side in order to end the war, Britain in the Balfour Declaration promised both Palestinians and Jews a homeland in the same area.

92. **(E)** Land reform was the most pressing need and cause of the Mexican Revolution.

93. **(D)** The Hsiung-nu or Huns migrated across Asia to Europe.

94. **(C)** Adam Smith explained how individuals working in their own best interests in an economic environment free of government control would also benefit society.

95. **(A)** Japanese wood block prints like those by Hokusai were produced during the Tokugawa Shogunate. The Tokugawa brought peace to Japan and protected Japan from Western imperialism. Internal commerce unified the country and led to the return of prosperity. The arts were supported by an expanding merchant class living in urban areas.

96. **(E)** The current ice age began c. 2.58 million years ago and provided land bridges and increased food supplies in warming climates.

Index

m = map